# Süssen Is Now Free of Jews

WORLD WAR II: THE GLOBAL, HUMAN, AND ETHICAL DIMENSION

*G. Kurt Piehler, series editor*

Süssen

# Süssen Is Now Free of Jews

## World War II, The Holocaust, and Rural Judaism

Gilya Gerda Schmidt

Fordham University Press | New York 2012

Frontispiece:
1911 Süssen postcard with Lang house in the very front right-hand corner. (Courtesy of
Süssen City Archive.)

Library of Congress Cataloging-in-Publication Data

Schmidt, Gilya Gerda.
    Süssen is now free of Jews : World War II, the Holocaust, and rural Judaism / Gilya
Gerda Schmidt ; foreword by Werner Runschke.
        p. cm. — (World War II: the global, human, and ethical dimension)
    Includes bibliographical references and index.
    ISBN 978-0-8232-4329-7 (cloth : alk. paper)
    1. Jews—Germany—Süssen—History—20th century.    2. Lang family.    3. Jews—
Persecutions—Germany—Süssen.    4. Holocaust, Jewish (1939–1945)—Germany—
Süssen.    5. Holocaust, Jewish (1939–1945)—Germany—Süssen—Reparations.
6. Süssen (Germany)—Ethnic relations.    7. Jebenhausen (Göppingen, Germany)—
Ethnic relations.    8. Kirchheim unter Teck (Germany)—Ethnic relations.    I. Title.
    DS134.36.S87S36 2012
    940.53′18092243471—dc23

                                                                    2012006284

Printed in the United States of America
14 13 12    5 4 3 2 1
First edition

# Contents

To the memory of Leopold and Eva Lang, Louis and Fanny Lang, Alfred and Hermine Baer, Hans Baer, Siegfried Baer, Werner Baer, Alfred and Eugenie Metzger, Rudolf Metzger, Walter Zeimann, Falk Sahm, and Luise Ottenheimer. I would also like to remember the two or three unnamed Christian euthanasia victims in Süssen who were murdered by the Nazis. Erwin Tänzer, Poldi Guggenheim, and Werner Ottenheimer died while I was writing this book. May the memory of all above-mentioned individuals be for a blessing. In honor of any surviving members of the Ottenheimer and Lang families, and with much gratitude to Hugo and Inge Lang and their family, Ruth Tänzer, Lilo Guggenheim, and Mel Levine.

# Foreword:
## *Siezzon*—Not Always a Good Grazing Land

### The History of the Jews of Süssen

During the persecution of the Jews in the Nazi period, dark spots also formed on the clean vest of Süssen, a small village in the center of southern Germany. At the bottom of a list of names of the sixteen deported Jews, to whom an additional name has to be added, we read in perfect Sütterlin handwriting the cynical sentence, "Süssen is now free of Jews!" In contrast to other places where violence or even physical attacks on Jewish fellow citizens occurred, this did not happen in Süssen. Rather, when the need of the local Jews was greatest, they were secretly supported by a number of Süssen citizens, through groceries that were secretly left on their doorstep, for example. Most of the repressive measures against the Jews were brought into the village from outside. Non-Jewish citizens, too, understood the meaning of deportation. After a Jewish neighbor said goodbye, the son of a couple overheard his father saying to the mother, "They will not return."

Until the beginning of the twentieth century, the village had no Jewish history whatsoever. To be sure, the names *Judengasse* and *Judenzoller* are mentioned in old accounts and maps. These hints refer merely to a street for Jewish travelers, for whose use they had to pay a fee.

The history of Jews in former Gross-Süssen began in 1902 and ended with their deportation on November 28, 1941, with a brief continuation when three of the sixteen who had been deported, and who survived the hell of the labor and concentration camps, returned in 1945. As was the case in many other villages and towns, the memory of the former Jewish fellow citizens was repressed. Nevertheless, a few Süssen citizens maintained contact with former Jewish residents, especially with Hugo Lang, who was the last to succeed in emigrating to the United States.

The passage of time allowed for a more open conversation of the events from the Nazi period. Hence, in 1989, then Mayor Martin Bauch extended an invitation from the city council to the surviving members of the Jewish families to visit Süssen. This invitation had a ripple effect that continues to this day.

A second impetus arose from the visit of an American professor. Mrs. Gilya Gerda Schmidt teaches Judaic Studies at the University of Tennessee, with a focus on the Holocaust. She was born Gerda Dauner in Stuttgart-Bad Cannstatt and grew up in Süssen. She remembered from her mother's stories that Jews also lived in Süssen. In the summer of 1998, she received an invitation to give a lecture at the Evangelische Akademie in Bad Boll near Süssen; she took this opportunity to establish first contacts with the town. Since that time the Jews of Süssen have had their historian.

In the intervening years, Professor Schmidt has been in Süssen again and again, for many weeks, and tirelessly researched the fate of the Süssen Jews. She likewise explored the fate of the members of the Ottenheimer family. Although the Ottenheimers lived in the nearby district capital of Göppingen, they owned a factory in Süssen that was Aryanized in 1938. For this research she traveled all the way to Cuba, which was not easy for an American citizen.

Professor Schmidt's kindness and human warmth, along with a consistent single-mindedness and diligence, earned her respect, appreciation, and affection from those who came in contact with her.

I hope that the book will help to send racism and nationalism where they belong—to the rubbish heap of history.

Werner Runschke
Süssen Stadtarchivar

# Acknowledgments

In spite of our reliance on technology, a project of any kind takes people to succeed, and a project that deals with the fate of human beings and requires a detailed understanding of how a particular local system functions, even more so. Most important for the success of this kind of project are those people who have intimate knowledge of the sources—people who direct and work in archives and libraries in a variety of lands. They are the true heroes of studies such as this, for without their cooperation and help there would be no project. While it is true that research often takes place in isolation, the work prior to sitting in a cubicle with a bunch of dusty folders or newspapers is not the researcher's, but the expert's, who first locates the sources. And as this project has taught me, eyewitnesses are also indispensable. They, too, are heroes, though of a different kind from archivists and librarians—adding a voice of humanity. Eyewitnesses are the clothes that dress the skeleton of documents that are so essential, yet not sufficient.

Nearly fifty years ago I emigrated to the United States, much as a number of Süssen citizens had done since the nineteenth century, some of whom attained success. The credit for maintaining contact for nearly half a century belongs to my classmate from elementary school Gerda Schwenger, née Stahl, who doggedly wrote and called many times over the years. Another classmate and good childhood friend, Beate Lehle, née Ziegler, also sent signs of life periodically. In this way, contact was not entirely broken even after my parents died in 1977 and 1978.

Although I envisioned this study about thirty-five years ago, it began in earnest with a find in a used bookstore in Knoxville, Tennessee, in the spring of 1993. While in Knoxville, interviewing for the newly created Endowed Chair of Judaic Studies in the Department of Religious Studies at the University of Tennessee, one of my future colleagues, Dr. Rosalind Gwynne, took me to McKay's, a used bookstore, to show me their *Judaica* collection. Among the books I found a volume in English with a blue cover that bore a gold *chai* (Hebrew letters *yud* and *chet,* meaning *life* as well as the number 18) on the front that dealt with the Jews of Württemberg.[1] In it I found confirmation for the seeming mirage I had carried in my head since my childhood in Süssen, Germany, that there had been Jews living in Süssen until the Holocaust. I recall my mother's telling me so when I was a child. When, after living in the United States for fifteen years, I returned to Süssen for a visit, my mother showed me a historical study of Süssen, published on the occasion of the 900th anniversary of the town in 1971. Alas, there was no sign of any Jewish presence in it. Nor was I able to elicit any clear answers from anyone on anything related to Jews in Süssen. Today I understand that it would not have been possible in 1971 to publish information on the Jewish citizens of Süssen, it was barely possible in most of Germany to speak about things connected with the Holocaust. The teaching of the Holocaust in German schools did not begin until the 1970s. As my mother died after my visit, finding this book in Knoxville was the first evidence I had that I had not been hallucinating. Now, for the first time, I had a few names, though not yet any faces to put with the vague memory of whispers about the Jewish families and the euthanasia victims who had lived in Süssen. It nevertheless took five more years and the completion of several other projects before I could seriously look into the reality behind this lingering mystery. Much to my surprise, I was neither the first nor the only person interested in the subject.

The village of Süssen, now under the leadership of an enlightened mayor who was born after the Holocaust, had taken the initiative in 1983 to create an exhibition and accompanying *Dokumentation* for the citizens to revisit the fifty years since Süssen was unified in 1933. Assembled by the Volkshochschule (adult education institute), a section of these documents was recycled and expanded in 1989, when Mayor Bauch invited the surviving former Jewish citizens to a reunion, much in the manner of similar official reunions all over Germany.[2] The bottom line was not a pretty picture—twelve members of one family, the Lang family, as well as three other Jews not on the Nazis' official list, were deported for the purpose of ethnic cleansing.[3] The triumphant bottom line of the Nazi-era municipal secretary's list of deported Jews reads, "Süssen is now free of Jews [*judenfrei*]."[4]

I was most interested to learn what this statement meant for the victims. I was also curious to learn how Jewish life could have existed at all in a village that had no Jewish community, no synagogue, no rabbi, and no cemetery. What would it have been like to move to a town with clear divisions along religious lines, where Catholics and Lutherans were strictly segregated not into two parts of town, but literally into two separate towns? Where in this pattern would two Jewish families fit? And how could they survive as Jews with the closest Jewish community ten kilometers away, at a time before the automobile was a common mode of transportation?

Professionally and personally, I was fortunate to meet some truly exceptional people who, from the very beginning, showed an interest in my project and offered their unconditional support. First among these are Bärbel and Werner Runschke, who not only once, but repeatedly, have shared their beautiful and comfortable home in Süssen with me for extended periods, and have become not only valued colleagues, but cherished friends. It is fortunate for me that Werner is also interested in *altem Glomp* (old stuff), though in his case this refers to actual local artifacts such as tools and pottery as well as documents and pictures that tell how it once was. He is a scholar in his own right. Werner sees it as his mission to make sure that Süssen's local history is preserved.[5] I am happy to say that, since we began working on this project together, teaching about the Jews of Süssen has become a regular part of his local history lessons to school classes and visitors. In his capacity since 1993 as *Stadtarchivar* (director of the newly relocated and reopened City Archive in Süssen at the time I began this research), Werner became an invaluable colleague, facilitator, source of information, and friend. He introduced me to officials and colleagues who were able to lend support in various ways. He became my wheels to out-of-the-way places and trusted comrade-in-arms for photographic and technical adventures. His generous, diligent, and painstaking efforts in helping me locate needed materials, explaining technical terms, and deciphering the Sütterlin handwriting make this book also his book. Together with his wife, Bärbel, they constituted my research team. Bärbel and I enjoyed long hikes and interesting conversations in the beautiful countryside, and she graciously gave of her time to help me decipher tombstone inscriptions and track down buildings. We all benefited from and enjoyed Werner's excellent cooking and Bärbel's delicious baking. In a place where most meals contain pork, Werner creatively resorted to delicious vegetarian meals for my benefit. Thank you so much, Bärbel and Werner, for all your support. Any existing shortcomings are mine alone.

On November 24, 2006, the municipality of Süssen recognized Werner Runschke's achievements in educating the local population on their history and customs, when Mayor Lützner awarded him the *Johann-Georg-*

*Fischer-Bürgermedaille mit Bürgerbrief,* the highest honor the city can bestow on its citizens and a rarely awarded distinction for truly deserving residents of Süssen.[6]

Walter Ziegler, director of the Göppingen District Archive, is another valuable colleague. Years of experience with local matters have molded him into a real power. Born in Süssen, Mr. Ziegler served his apprenticeship in the City Hall of Süssen and thus has decades of knowledge about local and regional documentation. I owe him thanks not only for access to all the materials in the Göppingen District Archive, but also for valuable hints regarding sources and materials in other collections and for access to his personal collection. The archive is located in the castle of Filseck, which is a grand historical location in beautiful surroundings.

Walter Lang (no relation to the Lang family in this study) was district archaeologist for Göppingen when I started this research. He had already been an interested party in Holocaust research and published several pieces of his own, including some on Kristallnacht in Göppingen. He was one of Hugo and Inge Lang's hosts during their visits to Süssen in 1989 and 1991 and became the keeper of materials and pictures that Hugo left for the Süssen City Archive.

An individual who has truly distinguished himself not only in historical scholarship but also in Jewish scholarship is Dr. Karl-Heinz Ruess, director of the Göppingen City Archive. Dr. Ruess has single-handedly revived a lost community. Göppingen had a vibrant Jewish community that was completely destroyed by the Nazis. Today only one Jewish man who returned from Israel in the 1970s lives in the city. The Jews of Süssen belonged to the Göppingen Jewish community with its brilliant rabbi of thirty years, Aron Tänzer. Dr. Ruess was instrumental in the creation of the Göppingen Jewish Museum, located in the old Lutheran church in Jebenhausen.[7] The church houses the benches and the chandelier from the Jebenhausen synagogue, which was torn down in 1905 after the community was disbanded.

Much of the postwar information for both the Lang and the Ottenheimer families came from the Ludwigsburg State Archive. This study would not be nearly as complete without the help of Mrs. Michaela Mingoia and her colleagues, who cheerfully responded to the many queries over the past decade. Mrs. Mingoia was a tremendous help in locating information not only in Ludwigsburg but throughout Germany.

Thanks are also due to Mayor Marc Kersting, who took on the leadership of the city in 2010, and to the City of Süssen for their hospitality during my research stays. Thanks also go to former Mayor Wolfgang Lütz-ner and to the employees at the city hall for their kindness in supplying me with technical support during the 2002 stay. I would like to extend a special thank you to former Mayor Rolf Karrer for his personal interest, initial encouragement and endorsement of this project in 1999. Not until 2007 did I meet yet another former mayor, Martin Bauch. I am grateful to Mr. Bauch for reaching out to the Langs when the opportunity arose; otherwise, I might never have found Hugo Lang.

Hugo Lang is the only surviving descendant of his family with whom I established extensive contact, because he was the only Lang family member accessible to me; his sister Ruth died at the very beginning of this research, in 2000. Hugo and his wife, Inge, an Auschwitz survivor from Berlin, have become wonderful friends and have given me tremendous support and help. They have allowed me to photograph the entire family album and shared with me stories, letters, documents, and memories. After we met in 2000, my colleague in the History Department at the University of Tennessee, Dr. Kurt Piehler, who hails from the same town as Hugo and Inge in New Jersey, interviewed Hugo for his oral history project. I would like to thank Kurt for sharing his materials with me.[8] Inge also wrote down her powerful and sad story to include in this book. The Langs have been gracious hosts during a number of visits to their home for a series of interviews, the most recent in 2010.

A few years ago I also had the opportunity to meet a son of Rabbi Tänzer's, Erwin Tänzer, who was around ninety and, with his wife, Ruth, lived in Pennsylvania. Sadly, Erwin Tänzer died on May 19, 2007. May his memory be for a blessing. A very emotional moment occurred for me in May 2007, after the *Stuttgarter Zeitung* published a story about this research. Through the generosity of a German tourist who knew Werner Ottenheimer, a phone call while in Germany connected me with ninety-one-year-old Werner Ottenheimer in Havana, Cuba. Finally, there was a living witness to the Ottenheimer story. In December 2007, I traveled to Cuba to talk with Mr. Ottenheimer about his childhood in Göppingen. Unfortunately, Werner Ottenheimer has also died since our visit, on December 19, 2008. And yet another connection was established as a result of the newspaper article. A German friend of Liese Lotte (Lilo) Guggenheim Levine's, formerly from Göppingen, told Lilo about this research. On August 5, 2007, I visited Lilo and her husband, Mel, in Saranac Lake, New York, where we were joined by one of Lilo's childhood friends, Isolde Lilli Netter Vandermeulen, and her daughter Debbie. And then, in 2008, Rivka

Ribak from Haifa came to Knoxville with her family and, upon their return, her husband Yair made the connection for me with Shavei Zion in Israel which led to a surprising meeting with Alisa Klafter, born in Rexingen, Germany, and a cousin-by-marriage to Hugo Lang. These are rare and special moments that will remain with me forever.

A thank you is also due to my classmates from elementary school in Süssen, first and foremost to Inge Honold, née Vetter, who arranged a class reunion in 1999, after I had been in contact with only Gerda Stahl Schwenger and Beate Ziegler Lehle for nearly forty years. It was a memorable experience and rekindled childhood friendships.

Over the years, I have benefited from reading papers and giving lectures on issues related to this project at professional conferences and in academic settings. These include, in 2000, "The Recovery of Small-Town German Jewish Life: An Example," Association for Jewish Studies; in 2001, "From Cattle-Dealing to Riga: A German Jewish Family Before and During the Holocaust," Southeast Conference for the Study of Religion; in 2006, "Recovering Lost Jewish Communities," East Tennessee History Center, Knoxville; in 2007, "Das Schicksal der Süssener Juden," Jewish Museum, Jebenhausen, Germany; "Can Grand Larceny and Good Neighboring Exist Side by Side?" "The Case of Two Jewish Families in Rural Swabia during the Nazi Era," and "Requisitions-Restitution-Reparations: The Story of the 'Judenhaus' in Süssen," all at the University of Tennessee; in 2009 "Süssen is Now Free of Jews," International Humanities and Arts Conference; "Return to the Black Forest," Association of Writers and Writing Programs; "Friend or Foe: A Tale of One Family's Journey into the Holocaust," Southeast Commission for the Study of Religion; "The 'Other' Victims: In a German Village, Perpetrators and Survivors Battle Over Their Victimhood," Association for Jewish Studies; in 2010 "Suezza—No Grazing Land for Jews," International Association for the History of Religions, and in 2011 "Stolpersteine—The Mark of Cain or Redemption?" International Humanities and Arts Conference. My thanks to all the colleagues who commented on my work and made valuable suggestions for improvement and expansion.

During the past six years I have derived great benefit and encouragement from my colleagues in the German Research Seminar here at the University of Tennessee, funded by the Humanities Initiative of the College of Arts and Sciences. Professors Daniel Magilow, David Lee, Vejas Liulevicius, David Thompkins, Stepfanie Ohnesorg, Maria Stehle, and Denise Phillips not only afforded me the opportunity to present my work for their comments but connected me with scholars they know who work in German Studies. Thank you for this most stimulating experience. I owe a special thank you to Professors Magilow and Lee, who read and commented on the entire manuscript. Professor Andrew Bergerson, from Missouri State University–Kansas City, as well as Stephanie and Eric Bank likewise gave the manuscript a thorough reading that resulted in many excellent queries and comments. In the fall of 2007 and 2010, I used the manuscript as one of the texts for my RS/JS 385 class on German Jewry. We read and discussed the completed sections, and the students' comments were invigorating and their questions profound. My thanks to all of the students for participating in these discussions and also for catching some of my mistakes! R. Michael Booker was my 2006–10 teaching assistant and helped with the details and revisions of this project, as did Krystyn Linville, Jenny Salata, and Erika Magnuson, our work study students.

Many thanks to Fordham University Press for including this study in its World War II series: Professor Kurt Piehler, series editor; Fred Nachbaur, director of the Press; and Wil Cerbone, editorial associate. My thanks also to the two anonymous readers for their excellent and timely comments and suggestions. A very special thank-you to Michael Koch, outside editor of this book, for his interest, care, and tremendous help in making this a much more readable book, and to Eric Newman.

Last, but certainly not least, I would like to thank my employer for the past eighteen years, the University of Tennessee, including former Dean Bruce E. Bursten and the College of Arts and Sciences, and former colleagues, Professors James Fitzgerald and Charles Reynolds in the Department of Religious Studies, and Professor J. P. Dessel in the Department of History for their encouragement and support. Jim and J. P. made considerable sacrifices by taking on the leadership of the Department of Religious Studies and the Judaic Studies Program so that I could have a research leave that allowed me to advance this project. Invaluable to getting us through the day were our two departmental specialists, Debbie Binder and Joan Riedl, now also retired, who supported my work since my very first book in 1995. Many thanks to all of you!

As I make final revisions at the beginning of 2011, I am beholden to a new set of colleagues. The new head of the Department of Religious Studies is Professor Rosalind I. J. Hackett; our new department wizard is Karen Windham, and our interim dean is Dr. Hap McSween. My gratitude to all for your continued support of my work. The final big thank you goes to my current graduate assistant, Ashley Combest from the English

Department, who is a scholar in her own right. Her comments and counsel have been very insightful and helpful, her technical skills superb, and her dedication to helping me get this manuscript to press in a timely manner is exemplary. Thank you so much, Ashley!

Financial support for research in Germany in 1999, 2002, 2006, 2007, and 2010 was provided by the Fern and Manfred Steinfeld Chair Endowment in Judaic Studies, the Judaic Studies Support Fund, the College of Arts and Sciences, the Graduate School, and the Department of Religious Studies at the University of Tennessee.

The title, *Süssen Is Now Free of Jews,* is taken from the page in the Süssen *Gemeindechronik,* which lists the thirteen Jews who were deported from Süssen on November 28, 1941. This list is reprinted in the Süssen Lang *Dokumentation,* 1989, p. 97. All translations of German sources are my own unless otherwise noted.

# Introduction

*Hohenstaufen*
*I saw it from afar,*
*It resembled a coffin;*
*I approached it,*
*There was dead silence all around;*
*I climbed it,*
*Two spirits flapped their wings*
*Descending the mountain,*
*A death's head moth,*
*A shroud.*
   —J. G. Fischer, *Dichtungen,* 1841.[1]

Geographical entities often gain recognition for some unique feature. The district of Göppingen, located in the middle of Baden-Württemberg in the southwestern part of Germany, is known for its connection to the distant past. Hardly a week goes by without a report or article about a new archaeological find, be it dinosaur remains, Ice Age fossils, Stone Age artifacts, or Roman relics.[2] The geological makeup of the area dates to the Jurassic period, 290 million years ago.[3] Deep inside the earth, gneiss and granite still connect this region with the Black Forest in the west and the Bavarian Forest in the east. A massive ocean, followed by a Mars-like atmosphere, gradual decay of the Jura, and tectonic plate movement formed the land with its variation of hills and mountains. Surviving reefs to this day form a "crown" of mighty rocks along the foothills known as the Schwäbische Alb (Swabian Jura).[4] Twenty-six million years ago volcanic activity led to higher earth temperatures, generating many thermal springs, and creating carbonic acid which is of great importance to this region, for it, in turn, produces mineral water, which is abundant here.[5] Originally used for its therapeutic value in regional spas only, the mineral water from this region is sold worldwide today.[6] Minerals also used to play a role in the industry of the area, especially iron. Because of foreign competition, the last iron ore mine, located in Geislingen, closed in 1963. Pebbles, sand, stone, and loam for cement and roof tiles are also big business in the entire region.[7]

The landscape as it is today evolved during the past 1.8 million years. Warm periods alternated with cold periods, creating *Karst*, an impressive array of mountains with outcroppings and formations, much like the much larger and world-famous Stone Forest in Shilin, outside of Kunming, in Yunan Province, China.[8] The entire region is full of caves, some of considerable size, and it is still possible to find a variety of fossils among the rocks.

Archaeological evidence of human life in this region dates back to before 10000 BCE. In some of the caves an archaeologist discovered in 1930 flint tools and blades, as well as fireplaces with bones from a variety of animals. Following the end of the last Ice Age about 10000 BCE food sources and ways to procure food changed. So, as a result, did the tools. Microlithes, small geometrical flint artifacts, became the primary hunting tools.[9] A great many were located in this area. During the Neolithic period, 4500–2000 BCE, people domesticated animals and planted crops. This necessitated a more sedentary way of life than had been customary until then. With it came technical expertise in construction and handicrafts, requiring new types of tools.[10] A stone axe for forestry was found in the district, as were many other tools of the period.

The climate of today evolved about 10,000 years ago and, according to archaeologists, the area under discussion was settled about 5,000 years ago (in about 3000 BCE),[11] preceding the biblical Abraham by more than a thousand years. Until the Middle Ages, a tribe in the area known as Schwaben (Swabia) enjoyed living in small communities. In the Middle Ages, castles were established as fortified villages and, over time, mostly walled towns, such as Göppingen in 1098, took the place of castles.[12] All the while, village life outside of these walled towns continued unabated, as was the case with the farming villages of Jebenhausen and Süssen (then known as Siezun).

According to an 1844 description, the Oberamt (administrative district) of Göppingen reaches from Kirchheim and Esslingen in the west to Schorndorf and Welzheim in the north to Gmünd and Geislingen in the east to Geislingen and Kirchheim in the south. The circumference totals thirty-six to thirty-eight walking hours (or some 112 miles) because of the winding boundary line.[13] It is a picturesque, hilly part of Germany, with diversified forests and numerous buttes—often dotted with charming castles or their remains, vast fruit orchards, and rich fields. Elevations range from about 1,000 to 1,400 feet above sea level, temperatures average about 48 degrees Fahrenheit, and rainfall is ample at 29.5 inches annually.[14] The main river flowing through the valley is the Fils, with the Lauter being a sizeable tributary, especially during the spring snowmelt. The Fils eventually confluences into the Neckar near Plochingen, east of Stuttgart and west of Göppingen. The climate and rich soil are suitable to agriculture and fruit production.

Jews have lived in Swabia as far back as the Middle Ages. Swabian cities such as Göppingen, Geislingen, Esslingen, Heilbronn, Reutlingen, Ulm, Augsburg, and others show a Jewish presence that ebbs and flows over time.[15] Rural Jewish communities developed primarily when Jews were expelled from cities and settled in nearby villages, thus creating the phenomenon known as *Dorfjuden* (village Jews).[16]

Life for Jews in Württemberg was at best unstable over time, and at worst intolerable. Their most powerful enemies were not noblemen, but the guilds of artisans established in the Middle Ages who would not tolerate Jews sharing the same living space with them. "Until 1806 the statutes of the Württemberg guilds arose from two leading thoughts . . . a) the attempted expulsion of the Jews from the *Land*, and b) the effort to restrict and complicate Jewish trade and life as much as possible, especially through tributes and taxes."[17] This basically meant that the only professions open to village Jews outside the Jewish community were money lending and the much despised peddling. The cattle trade was just barely more respectable than peddling, an important distinction because it was not outlawed in 1828, unlike peddling. Initially Jews were not allowed to deal in new wares; they had to restrict their business dealings to second-hand commodities. Peddlers traveled from Sunday till Friday, loaded down like pack horses with wares, sometimes accompanied by a helper, and they covered a large territory each week. The permanent exhibition catalog in Buttenhausen states, "Peddling is one of the most painstaking ways to make a living, the peddling Jew has to be on the road in all kinds of weather. . . . What he doesn't have to suffer in the inns! He has terrible worries. Out of prejudice, his [Christian] compatriot, who isn't wealthy, hardly ever buys from a Jew, he takes his cash to a Christian dealer. When his wallet is empty, then he goes to the Jewish dealer, and why? Because a Christian person won't lend him any money."[18] Likewise, the director of the Göppingen City Archive, Karl-Heinz Ruess, writes in *Spuren schreiben Vergangenheit*, "When the Jews did not deal with cattle, they peddled." They traveled with a carrier or "with a burlap sack on their back through the surrounding villages and towns, went from house to house and offered to farmers and *Bürger* (citizens) fine cloth, cotton and linen materials, ribbons and borders, leather, skins, bed stuffs, watches, and all kinds of second-hand goods."[19] The ethnographer and philosopher Friedrich Georg Friedmann reports, "One of my great-grandfathers traveled from fair to fair with a heavy sack on his back. Someone told me how the children made fun of him because he was a Jew."[20] As many farms were quite isolated, the weekly visits from the peddler not only served to provide needed goods for the housewife but they also doubled as a news source for the family.

During the years of the Black Death pandemic (1348–49), illness and persecution further reduced the Jewish presence in Swabia. In their book, *Jüdisches Leben im Wandel der Zeit*, Paul Sauer and Sonja Hosseinzadeh note that "already in the first half of the fourteenth century there was a small Jewish community in Stuttgart, which suffered terribly during the gruesome plague, the Black Death, in 1348/49, but was apparently not totally destroyed."[21] Karl-Heinz Burmeister notes that the available lists of Württemberg residences show that at the time of the plague "all Jewish communities across Württemberg were affected," that the area was "blanketed" with pogroms against the Jews living in Württemberg.[22] The Deutzer *Memorbuch* (book of remembrance; Deutz is a place near Cologne) contains a long litany of *kehillot*, or Jewish communities, that bewail the death of members, including fifty such communities in Medinat Schwaben, among them also Göppingen and Geislingen.[23] Other city names in this book that will reappear in the twentieth century are Ulm, Esslingen, Heilbronn, Stuttgart, Bad Cannstatt (today a suburb of Stuttgart), and Reutlingen.[24] Helmut Walser Smith argues that much of German behavior during and after the Holocaust was not new but recurring behavior that dates back to the Middle Ages. Upon their expulsion, Jewish property was appropriated and transformed for German religious and secular use.[25] Life in the countryside became a viable alternative to city life, especially in light of the fact that expulsion from cities could and did happen at any time. Arguably, from the time of the Black Death in 1348 on, Altwürttemberg was even less hospitable to Jews than it had been before.[26]

Until 1360, all Jews who lived in the Grafschaft Wirtemberg were *Kammerknechte* (pages) of the emperor, whose property they were to keep, sell, or gift.[27] "On September 15, 1360, Kaiser Karl IV bestowed on the two coregents Count Eberhard II (der Greiner) and Ulrich IV among other privileges also the right to engage *Schutzjuden*."[28] From the information transmitted, Jews settled in Stuttgart in 1434, 1441, 1443, 1459, and in Göppingen in 1462.[29] They had rights and privileges and were allowed to live wherever they wanted. Sauer and Hosseinzadeh write, "Between 1393 and 1488 Jews again lived in Stuttgart under favorable conditions. The center of the small *kehillah* with synagogue and *mikvah* was in the Brennerstrasse, also called Judengasse."[30] This state of bliss did not last, however. During his rule, Eberhard I (1445–96)—also known as Eberhard im Bart (Eberhard the Bearded)—added a clause to his will that Jews should be expelled from his territory.[31] This statute, while taking effect upon his death on February 24, 1496, did not seem to have been strictly enforced because Jews continued to do business in the region, even if they could not live there.[32] Besides, not all subsequent rulers felt the same way about Jews as the anti-Jewish Eberhard; some aristocrats were eager to take advantage of Jewish expertise in business matters. Historians Sauer and Hosseinzadeh note that the dukes of Württemberg could not manage without Jewish financiers and merchants.[33]

A Jewish presence was restored to parts of the region at the time of the Thirty Years' War (1618–48) when Jewish money was needed either to arm for battle or to recover from battle. But these relaxations of statutes continued to be uneven, as in 1621, when a Württemberg statute declared that "Jews are allowed to buy and sell only at fairs and only for cash."[34] It was thus understood (by some) that Jews were not to settle in Württemberg but would merely pass through on their way to some other destination. "Jews must buy safe passage at the border from the first mayor or official [they encounter], either in the form of a letter [of safe passage] or in the form of *Leibzoll* [body tax], depending on their wealth."[35]

In 1710 Duke Eberhard Ludwig of Württemberg allowed the first *Hoffaktor* (court Jew) to settle in Stuttgart, adding four more by 1712; by 1721 seven Jews were living at the court in Stuttgart.[36] "The citizenry of Stuttgart treated the privileged court Jews with hostility. The merchant guild especially saw them as life-threatening competition. This upset the duke. He threatened those who harangued, insulted, or even physically attacked the Jews who enjoyed his special protection with severe punishment."[37] The most famous of these early privileged Jews at the court of Württemberg was Süss Oppenheimer, or Jud Süss as he was known, whose ascendancy as Carl Alexander's court Jew caused such envy that the Stuttgart citizenry hanged him for all the misdeeds of his lord upon the latter's sudden death. His body was left hanging in a gibbet suspended in midair, where the birds tore off his flesh bit by bit.[38] These continuing tensions led to another law, passed in April 1739, that expelled within six months all Jews who had been permitted to settle in villages or towns that were incorporated into the Duchy of Württemberg—and thus did not belong to the *Reich* (empire).[39] Those in power must have been torn between their dislike of Jews and their greed to benefit from the Jewish presence. Jews were subject to a variety of taxes that they had to pay to the local lord as well as to the emperor. There was a body tax, a head tax, a tax for birth, a tax for death, a tax for pursuing a profession or trade, a tax for passing from one territory to another (different for Jews travelling on foot than for Jews travelling on horseback), a tax on livestock, and a tax to maintain wells and paths and bridges.[40] In 1753 a Jew paid a fee of three kreuzer to travel two *meilen* (about nine miles), for a longer stretch it cost thirty kreuzer. For the transport of a body the fee was a hefty two florin.[41] In 1764 there were some Jews living in Württemberg territory whose *Schutzgeld* (protective tariff) was doubled.[42] In 1768 it was necessary for a Jew to possess at least five hundred to six hundred florin in order to qualify for protection.[43] Taxes also came in the form of tributes. In Freudental, Jewish residents were expected to deliver livestock, feathers, and "a sugar cone for the *Gnädige Frau* (lady of the lord) for New Year's . . . made of the finest Canari sugar,"[44] no less, and, of course, the customary holiday geese to the dignitaries of a town for Martini, or Martinmas, on November 11—in the case of Ichenhausen the tribute was twenty-four geese per family.[45] Geese were also the tribute in Rexingen and in Baisingen.[46]

Starting in the second half of the eighteenth century, Jewish families were welcome in two types of habitations in Swabia: those under the direct rule of the emperor and those owned by imperial knights.[47] Imperial or "free" cities were *reichsunmittelbar*, meaning directly under the jurisdiction of the emperor or his representative, the *Reichsritter* (imperial knights, local nobility).[48] While any walled habitation was automatically a city, not all cities were under the jurisdiction of the emperor. *Reichsritter* lived in *Schlösser* (castles) that were not necessarily in walled cities. A case in point is Baron of Liebenstein who lived in a castle in Jebenhausen. When the danger of war lurked—which was often—the baron and his family moved to safety within the city walls of neighboring Göppingen. But Göppingen, in spite of its proximity to Mount Hohenstaufen (former home of Emperor Barbarossa in the Middle Ages), was no longer an imperial city; it now belonged to Württemberg. Hence no Jews were allowed to live in Göppingen until 1806, but they were allowed to live in the neighboring village of Jebenhausen, only two kilometers to the south. In 1777 the Liebensteins granted *Schutz* (protection) to twenty Jewish families. In this time period, Jewish communities were similarly established in Buttenhausen (1787 with twenty-five families), Laupheim, Rexingen, Haigerloch, Hechingen, and other places. These habitations often had rural character, and Jews lived and worked side by side with local Christian artisans, merchants, storekeepers, and farmers—though never as farmers, since they were not allowed to own farmland.

Up to 1806, the conditions of *Schutzjuden* varied drastically depending on the perception of a given lord concerning the function of Jews in his territory. Still governed by medieval statutes, the number of Jews receiving protection was usually limited. As a rule, only one son per family was allowed to remain, get married, and establish a household in a particular community. The other children of a family had to move away. Where did they go? Members from any given family could be found far distances from home, though usually within the territory of Schwaben or among the extended territories settled by the tribe—unless they emigrated to faraway lands, mostly the United States. Albert Einstein's family may serve as just one example. The family originated in Bad Buchau am Federsee, one of the great rural Jewish communities of the nineteenth century. His great-great-grandfather lived and is buried in Laupheim, his maternal grandparents, Julius Koch and wife, lived in Jebenhausen, about sixty miles west of Buchau, where his mother, Pauline Koch, was also born. Einstein, however, was born in Ulm, twenty-two miles east of Jebenhausen, and lived the latter part of his life in the United States. His father later moved to Munich in Bavaria and from there to Italy, where he died. Each of these localities has evidence of an Einstein presence, either in the form of real estate or tombstones.

Although there were no *shtetls* in southern Germany patterned on those in Eastern Europe, this did not mean that Jews were allowed to live wherever they wanted to. They could only settle in certain locations in a village or town, often in a section entirely separate from Christian residents. These areas were known as the *Judengasse, Judenviertel, Judenhof*, or by some other name identifying the residents as Jews (examples are Jebenhausen, Ichenhausen, Laupheim, Schwäbisch Gmünd). In Ichenhausen, for example, Jews were not allowed "to live within the three gates of the town square."[49] Jews usually were not allowed to buy houses from Christians (see Buttenhausen in 1788) either, but were assigned to houses that were specifically built for them by their benefactor (for example, Freudental, Ichenhausen, Laupheim, Baisingen). If a Christian house came into Jewish possession as part of a business deal, the house had to be resold to a Christian buyer within a certain period of time. Still, in 1797 Duke Friedrich II had to retract a promise he made to his court Jew, Jakob Raphael Kaulla of Hechingen. That year the duke had granted banker Kaulla and his family the right to reside in Stuttgart. But the citizens of Stuttgart complained bitterly, forcing the duke to reconsider. He changed his mind a few months later, although he was convinced of the "total invalidity and nullity of the raised objections." He voiced his regret at losing the benefits of "considerable financial transactions," which would have come from the far-flung business ventures of Madame Kaille Kaula, the banker's sister, and one of the most powerful Jewish women ever,[50] an equal to the famous Glückel of Hameln in the seventeenth century. Madame Kaula, though doing the duke's bidding, preferred to retain her residence in her Prussian home city of Hechingen, where she is buried.

When the Holy Roman Empire, which had been in existence since 800 CE, came to a formal end in 1806, the territory of Schwaben was divided between the duchies of Bavaria and Württemberg. Both duchies were also elevated to kingdoms by Napoleon, in gratitude for their services to the emperor. In 1800 only 534 Jews were recorded as living in the territory of Altwürttemberg.[51] In 1801, 58 of these lived in Stuttgart,[52] mostly as tenants. The Peace of Pressburg in 1805 expanded Württemberg's territories, so that by 1810 the total population of what was now known as Neuwürttemberg had jumped from 650,000 in the dukedom to 1,400,000 in the kingdom.[53] This brought the Jews in the western area of Swabia (stretching from Ulm to Breisach in the Black Forest[54]), who had formerly been under the protection of the *Reich* or local nobility, under the jurisdiction of the King of Württemberg, making them *Landesunterthanen* (subjects).[55] The new structure also permitted Jewish immigration to all parts of the kingdom, albeit only to existing Jewish communities. Jews also endeavored to become *Bürger*, or citizens, of a given village, small town, or city. Acquiring *Beisitzerrecht* (resident status) or *Bürgerrecht* (citizen status) was crucial for carrying on business or taking part in the civic life of a town. Since there was no unified Germany until 1871, this did not yet mean that Jews were German citizens. But since the *Reichsritterschaft* (imperial nobility) had also come to an end, it did mean that they ceased to be *Schutzjuden*.

Although merely *Untertanen* (tolerated subjects) and as such constrained by many rules and regulations in the Kingdom of Württemberg, some relief from restrictions and oppressive taxation began in 1806 with Elector Friedrich II's abolition of the guilds as an antiquated institution. This ruling also abolished the *Ausschliessungsgesetz der Juden* (exclusionary law for Jews) without, however, providing an alternative legal basis for citizenship. As their *Schutzbriefe* became invalid, the new conditions still had to be worked out.[56] The elector lost no time in doing so, and on June 4, 1808, the Oberlandesregierung (main provincial government) presented a draft of a new statute, *Ordnung für die Juden in den Königlichen Staaten* (Ordinance for Jews in the Royal States), which was, however, not acceptable to the king.[57] Between 1806 and 1828, a number of individual statutes were established in Württemberg, even though no uniform law for Jewish residents was produced.[58] For instance, in 1807 the *Leibzoll* (body tax) and *Geleitgeld* (tax for safe passage) for Jews at the borders to and from Württemberg were abolished. Jews were allowed to acquire land for agriculture,[59] and in 1809 the guilds that didn't give up easily relaxed their restrictions and allowed Jews to participate in some professions that had until then been restricted for Jews.[60] In 1811 Jewish integration was advanced even further, as they were allowed to acquire real estate.[61] Special tariffs and gifts to lords were abolished in 1812 and privileges connected to the right of residence were bestowed along with the residency tax.[62] In 1815 the *Schutzgeld* for Jebenhausen Jews, for example, was reduced from twelve to four florin.[63]

The king passed a series of statutes for the cultural amelioration and integration of Jews into the existing society. A further push for a uniform *Judengesetz* came with the coronation of King Wilhelm I on October 30, 1816, following the Congress of Vienna (1815).[64] However, one step forward often meant two steps backwards. While the abolition of taxes and work-related restrictions after 1806 were a welcome step forward, not all was well. On September 25, 1819, Württemberg received a new constitution and became a constitutional monarchy.[65] This system of governance gave the Jews religious freedom, but not civil rights. Only those citizens belonging to the three recognized Christian denominations—Lutheran, Reformed, and Roman Catholic—had full civil rights. However, this law did give Jews the right to attend university.[66] Simultaneously, demands could be heard from the population that Jews should be isolated from the general population in special colonies or reservations, an idea reminiscent of the medieval ghettoization in Frankfurt and other cities and the later ghettoization connected to the Final Solution.[67] Statutes in 1825 such as obligatory school attendance for Jewish children foreshadowed things to come,[68] as both Jewish trade permits were restricted to a particular district and peddling licenses were painstakingly monitored.[69] These restrictions cast a long shadow and were turned into law by the fateful *Israelitengesetz*

(Jewish law), also called the *Erziehungsgesetz* (education law), of April 25, 1928, which regulated the ways in which Jews were permitted to make a living.[70] In spite of these drawbacks, for Jews these statutes were mostly steps in the right direction. As Jacob Katz writes in *Out of the Ghetto*, "In Germany the struggle for emancipation was focused first on the legislative bodies of the respective states—the *Landtage* and senates of the independent towns. Important improvement in their legal status was achieved by the Jews of . . . Württemberg in . . . 1828. . . . Free choice of occupation and right of residence were obtained."[71] Given the documented difficulty for Jews to eke out a living during the nineteenth century in places like Jebenhausen, it seems ironic that Württemberg is held up as an example. It does, however, speak well for the enterprising spirit and the persistence of the Jewish community there.

At the height of rural Jewish life between 1806 and 1864, Württemberg was saturated with rural Jewish communities, a result of immigration as well as territorial expansion. In 1828 a total of 9,991 Jews lived in eighty towns and villages.[72] Sixty-nine of the communities[73] had a *kehillah* that functioned according to age-old tried-and-true methods of autonomous administration. Rabbi Aron Tänzer of Göppingen wrote, "In these 69 communities one could find 57 synagogues, 51 rabbis, 67 cantors, 22 teachers, 23 cemeteries, 20,407 florin in endowments and 24,145 florin in communal debt."[74] Stefan Rohrbacher puts the figure in 1832 at 93 percent of Jews living in approximately sixty rural villages.[75]

The *Israelitengesetz* not only gave new opportunities to Württemberg Jews, it also took away existing opportunities. It forbade Jews to peddle on danger of losing their *Bürgerrecht* (status as citizens). Thus the government restricted the issuance of licenses and the sphere of trade, strictly supervising all business transactions, and imposing legal disabilities on trade with Christians.[76] Jews were to learn a "*bürgerlich* [bourgeois] occupation."[77] But Christian guilds, despite their abolition in 1806, continued to make it difficult for Jews to enter the professions. Apprenticing an observant Jew to a Christian master was also a problem because of the dietary laws and Sabbath observance, so that the new law was a curse. With few alternative employment opportunities available, the law caused untold hardships for families and encouraged large-scale emigration to the United States before 1848 and to German cities in the second half of the nineteenth century. Professions that were needed in the Jewish community, such as butcher, baker, tailor, and shoemaker, had of course not been subject to Christian guilds all along. But the government did not count these individuals in their statistics, as these bourgeois professions were not newly adopted, hence did not reflect "a change of heart." Since Jews had never been allowed to own farmland, agrarian professions such as farming were brand-new. Cattle dealing was the major profession among rural Jews and as such was not prohibited. However, *Viehverstellen*, or boarding of cattle with a farmer for a period of time to fatten them up, was prohibited, even though it went hand in hand with cattle dealing. Likewise, foreign Jews were a thorn in the side of the watchdogs, because they not only came to cattle fairs but also did business at other times. This practice was considered peddling, forbidden from 1828 on.[78] Jews were also obligated to adopt surnames, as had become the norm among Germans.[79] Although Rabbi Tänzer wrote that there was much good in the new law, the new regulations also seem to have complicated Jewish life, even while setting it on the road to emancipation. Emancipation in German lands occurred gradually from the time of Napoleon, in fits and starts, beginning in 1806 in Northern Germany and concluding in Württemberg on August 13, 1864, Bavaria in 1869, and in all of Germany in 1871.

Internal changes occurred alongside the external ones. Rabbi Tänzer considered the formation of a "Jewish Synod" of Württemberg as one of the most valuable and empowering outcomes of the Law of 1828.[80] As part of the new status of Jews as religious "equals" to Christians, the structure for Jews as members of a religious body was modeled on that of the other publicly recognized confessions. On January 5, 1832,[81] this umbrella organization, known as the Israelitische Oberkirchenbehörde (Jewish Religious Authority) became the spokes organ for all Jewish communities in relation to the state, and thereby disempowered individual communities at the state level.[82] The choice of name for the umbrella organization was not an entirely fortunate one. The authorities might have found a more neutral term, as the word *Kirche* (church) is identified with Christianity. This is especially true since the organization dealt with matters of civic administration as well as religious matters.[83] In order to become a real part of the state bureaucracy, the Jewish community of Württemberg established the Israelitische Zentralkirchenkasse (Central Treasury of the Jewish Religious Authority) to which Württemberg Jews paid a church tax, six florin for a self-supporting male and three florin for a self-supporting widow.[84] The tax was unpopular and was discontinued in 1873,[85] to be replaced by the similarly unpopular, but commonly accepted, system of tithing.[86]

In 1832 Jewish communities were reorganized according to economic viability. They were also provided with an organizational structure. The new system called for *Kirchengemeinden* (religious communities) and *Rabbinate* (Rabbinic districts).[87] After reorganization, instead of sixty-nine communities there were now forty-one, which were assigned to thirteen Rabbinic districts.[88] Tänzer stresses that the purpose of the religious communities was the common worship of God and that these communities were religious congregations with no separate corporate standing (such as the old Jewish communities had).[89] All Jews in Württemberg were compelled to belong to a Jewish community. In this context, modernization of religious practice and Jewish education was instituted by the state as well.

One of the most important tasks of the *Israelitengesetz* was the *Hebung* (cultural elevation) of Württemberg Jews. This affected every walk of life, from rabbis and cantors to peddlers, farmers, artisans, and merchants. Starting in 1834 the Jewish Religious Authority was obliged by the state to ensure that all rabbis, cantors and teachers, who were now state employees,[90] took two civil service examinations. The rabbis were also to prove that they were citizens or residents of the town in which they lived. It appears from Rabbi Tänzer's account that only six of the previous rabbis were retained, implying that forty-five (of the fifty-one) old-time rabbis were deposed. Apparently none of the cantors made the cut, which created an additional employment problem—what to do with rabbis and cantors who could no longer earn their keep? The Jewish community collectively was responsible for servicing the indigent, so these poor souls, who were often older, became a burden on the community. The government recognized this and gave the Central Treasury of the Jewish Religious Authority an annual state subvention of 1,500 florin for 1836–39, "for the support of the old rabbis and cantors who lost their livelihood due to no fault of their own."[91]

The government also regulated synagogue worship. A synagogue order of service was instituted for the purpose of decorum, a prayer for the monarch became obligatory, and sermons in German, an organ, and a mixed choir in progressive synagogues, as well as other innovations were instituted. A prayer book, composed and compiled by Rabbi Maier of Stuttgart and published in 1836, became mandatory for all Jewish worship services in the Kingdom of Württemberg, but did not prove popular.[92] Rabbis also had to wear a robe similar to that of Christian clergy.[93]

"Israelite" schools seem to have been particularly well positioned to make the transition to the reorganization with minor difficulties, which of course speaks well for the Jewish system of education. As David Sorkin writes in *The Transformation of German Jewry 1780–1840*, in 1829 all eleven of these schools transitioned to state-funded elementary schools without any difficulty whatsoever.[94] From 1836 on, Jewish *Volksschulen* (elementary schools) with more than sixty families were funded by the local municipality and no longer by the Jewish community.[95] These schools were located in Aufhausen, Buchau, Buttenhausen, Crailsheim, Freudental, Jebenhausen, Mühringen, Nordstetten, Oberdorf, and Rexingen.[96] Rabbi Tänzer lists the subjects taught in Jebenhausen. The German teacher was responsible for biblical history, German reading and language, mental and written arithmetic, German spelling and calligraphy, and German singing.[97] The Jewish teacher was in charge of Hebrew language, religion, and Hebrew calligraphy.[98] Other educational opportunities for Jewish children were the voluntary Jewish religious schools, whose only difference from the Jewish elementary schools was that their establishment did not require a minimum of sixty families and was funded by the Jewish community, similar to the Jewish day schools in the United States today.[99] The curriculum was identical to that in public schools. If there was neither a Jewish elementary school nor a voluntary Jewish Religious school, Jewish pupils had to attend the *allgemeine Ortsschule* (local elementary school) with Jewish religious instruction paralleling that of their Christian classmates. Although they had to attend school on the Sabbath, accommodations were made for pupils not to take tests or write on that day and to attend worship services if possible.[100] The administration of the Jewish pupils was the responsibility of the Oberschulbehörde (Christian State School Board), not the Jewish Religious Authority. A local pastor or priest was charged with the immediate supervision of any instruction of Jewish children.

Did the *Israelitengesetz* of 1828 make a difference? According to government statistics, in 1828, out of 3,041 Jewish males over the age of fourteen, 2,600 were peddlers, none were scholars or artists (by German standards; they were of course by Jewish standards), 32 were farmers or helpers, and 409 were artisans or apprentices. Twenty-four years later, the picture looked quite different. Out of 3,930 Jewish males over fourteen, only 695 were peddlers, a drop of 75 percent; 214 were scholars and artists (acceptable by German standards), 405 were farmers, and the biggest jump was among the artisans and merchants, namely 2,526, a six-fold increase.[101]

Although some Jewish traditions were regrettably lost during this period of reorganization, the danger of drastic change was greater in cities than in rural communities. Jewish village life as a rule was more conservative and traditional. Older community members enjoined their children to adhere closely to tradition. One father, in his ethical will, admonished his sons "never to shave with a razor blade."[102] For the most part, while the children of this generation remained in the village they obeyed the religious laws, but when they moved or were forced to move either to cities or abroad, they often adjusted their ways to those of the new environment. Since these rural communities were farther removed from the watchful eyes of the authorities, local leaders sometimes ignored the orders for change and kept to the old ways. Nachum Gidal writes, "While in the 18th and 19th centuries Jewish society in the large cities was riven by the differences between the orthodox, liberals, and extreme reformists, and also by the gulf between rich and poor, the communities in villages and small towns remained homogeneous."[103]

Being Jewish in German lands had been a challenge since the Middle Ages. After Emancipation in 1871, however, there was much optimism and hope for a better future. Then, some sixty years later, the perpetrators of the Holocaust came to power. One would think that none of the survivors would ever want to return to a place where friends and neighbors caused them so much pain. However, as this study demonstrates, one should never underestimate the pull of home, even if, as historians Jack Kugelmass and Jonathan Boyarin as well as Omer Bartov document, the beautiful gardens of the survivors' youth continue to exist only in their memories.[104]

Chapter 1 tells the remarkable tale of a mayor, Martin Bauch, reaching out to a survivor, Hugo Lang, in an attempt to reconcile victims and perpetrators in 1989. Chapter 2 focuses on the village of Süssen, which was home to two Jewish families from 1902 until they were expelled by the Nazis. The chapter also touches on some of Süssen's history—including its military history and the presence of Napoleon, the devastation from war, the suffering caused by famine, and the ravages of epidemics such as the plague—in an attempt to illuminate some of the town's collective past. Chapter 3 introduces the Ottenheimer family who in 1902 branched out from their hometown of Göppingen and were welcomed in Klein-Süssen. The chapter discusses the family's contributions to village life, their business successes and challenges, and their eventual loss of property due to Aryanization as well as the resultant personal tragedy of the Ottenheimer families. Chapter 4 introduces Jakob Lang, the patriarch of a successful extended family in Süssen, and tells the story of his half-brothers, Louis and Leopold, and their families until the time when the Nazi laws began to impinge on their daily lives in 1937. Chapter 5 documents the grisly details of the Nazis' ever tightening noose around the Langs' necks—the loss of their livelihood, their arrest and imprisonment in the Dachau concentration camp, and the loss of their home and property in 1939. Chapter 6 covers Hugo Lang's departure from Süssen, only three months before the rest of his family was deported "to the East," and his adventures and new life in the United States. Chapter 7 describes the tragedy of the Lang family's deportation. Chapter 8 grapples with the Lang cousins' liberation and return from the concentration camps and their struggle to reclaim their belongings, illuminating the continuous wrangling among the German authorities over the financial responsibility for compensation of the victims. Chapter 9 delves into the bewildering maze of bureaucratic hassles that surrounded the Langs' reparations proceedings—a messy tale of compensation for real estate and other losses, such as liberty, education, and good will. Chapter 10 focuses on the history of the Jewish communities in Jebenhausen and Göppingen, to which the two principal Jewish families discussed in this book belonged. Chapter 11 summarizes the history of the little known satellite Jewish community in Kirchheim unter Teck for those who do not have access to the German publications. Chapter 12 describes some of the darker history of picturesque Geislingen, including its concentration camp and the local Finanzamt (tax office) to which Süssen paid its taxes.

This book is an essential chapter in the history of the town of Süssen. It is also a chapter in the history of the city of Göppingen, because the Süssen Jews belonged to the Göppingen Jewish community. It is furthermore a contribution to our understanding of World War II, Holocaust studies, and the scholarship of *Landjudentum* (rural Jewry), a category of scholarship that has taken root primarily in Germany, and primarily as a consequence of the Holocaust, in an effort to document some of the hundreds of rural Jewish communities that have been lost forever.[105] This book is also an important chapter in the personal history of two Jewish families—the Langs and the Ottenheimers—who lived and worked in Süssen for nearly forty years. Laura Levitt, in her book, *American Jewish Loss After the Holocaust*, pleads for our appreciation of "ordinary legacies" of ordinary Jewish families.[106] The Langs once led such ordinary lives, as Hugo Lang's family photo album shows.

Last but hardly least, this study concludes a chapter in my own life, for once upon a time Süssen was my hometown as well. But that story will have to wait for another time.

# 1 Post-Nazi Süssen: An Attempt at Reconciliation

*We mourn, but we live in hope of reconciliation among the people and peoples of the world and in hope of peace.*
—Mayor Martin Bauch, SPD, *Volkstrauertag*, November 13, 1988

In 1981 the picturesque town of Süssen, located within view of the famous butte that once was the home of Emperor Friedrich Barbarossa (1123–90) and the Hohenstaufen monarchy, began dealing with its past by unveiling a bronze fountain in the market square that depicts fifteen highlights from the town's history—from its first mention in 1071 to 1981.[1] The fountain was designed by Black Forest artist Jo Homolka (born in Stuttgart in 1925) and cast in bronze by the local firm of Strassacker, the same company that in 1938 had cast a giant wreath with a swastika for the *Parteitag* in Nuremberg. One of the scenes on the historical fountain depicts the deportation of the Jews of Süssen.[2] In 1983, on the occasion of the fiftieth anniversary of the unification—under Nazi pressure—of then Gross-Süssen (Greater Süssen) and Klein-Süssen (Smaller Süssen) into one settlement, the local Volkshochschule researched and published its first attempt at local Nazi history, entitled, *50 Years of Süssen*.[3] Somewhat flawed—with omissions and errors because the town's history had not yet been thoroughly researched—the publication presented a sanitized version of historical events, but nevertheless contained the first evidence of the Nazi-inspired persecution of the Jews of Süssen, including the deportation records. In a special feature, "50 Jahre Gemeinde Süssen," the regional newspaper, the *Neue Württembergische Zeitung*, also reported on the fate of the Jews.[4] However, it was not until 1988 that the town's officials were ready to engage with the survivors of the Nazi atrocities.

In 1988 Ruth Lang Lemberger wrote to the city hall in Süssen in an attempt to obtain a birth certificate. She was then sixty-three years old and was probably getting ready to apply for Social Security in the United States which requires applicants to provide a birth certificate. On October 31, 1988, then Mayor Martin Bauch responded to Ruth in an effort to establish contact "similar to that already underway in other cities and communities of the Federal Republic in order to prepare a meeting in Süssen." He noted that in 1983 Süssen had opened its archives so that the citizens could learn about the events of the Holocaust, adding an official apology for the wrongs perpetrated on Ruth and her family and informing her of the naming of a lane in memory of the Lang family who used to call Süssen their home. He also requested the addresses of other members of the extended Lang family who were deported in 1941. Ruth must not have responded to his request, because on November 18, 1988, Mayor Bauch wrote to Ruth again, asking her to share her story with him. "We younger people have to rely on eye witnesses and victims to help us with remembering and to serve as a warning." This was clearly an appeal to her on the grounds that he was too young to have been a Nazi. To my knowledge, Ruth did not share her story with the mayor. Mayor Bauch also sent her a program from the *Volkstrauertag* (National Memorial Day) on November 13, 1988, and a transcript of his speech for the occasion.[5] In his speech, Mayor Bauch minced no words: "Auschwitz remains unique. It was carried out by Germans in the name of Germany. This truth is irrevocable. And we will not forget."[6] He then mentioned Louis and Leopold Lang, who had served and had been decorated for their service in World War I. "That the gratitude of the fatherland drove those who returned into exile, deported them, and subjected all too many of them to the National Socialist concentration camps, will forever be one of the most shameful and depressing chapters of German history."[7]

On May 12, 1989, Mayor Bauch sent a letter to the former Jewish citizens of Süssen inviting them to a weeklong visit in the town they had to leave "during the years of persecution." Based on the responses, invitations were extended to Hugo Lang and Ruth Lemberger, and their cousins Siegfried, Kurt, and Henny Lang. The letter stressed that "the town of Süssen has changed considerably in recent decades; some of the things that used to be familiar no longer exist or have been redesigned." The town also offered the visitors kosher meals if desired. They also were allowed to bring a significant other to the all-expenses paid reunion. A registration form was enclosed.[8]

On May 30, 1989, Ruth's brother, Hugo Lang, former Jewish citizen of Süssen, and his wife of forty-one years, Inge, living in New Jersey, replied to the invitation. "We both accept the invitation and will leave from JFK in New York on October 1."[9]

On the morning of October 2, Hugo and Inge arrived in Süssen, accompanied by their daughter Evelyn and her husband Anthony Donofrio as well as Hugo and Inge's son, Ken, and his wife, Maria, and two grandchildren, Victoria, age five, and Kendra, one and a half years old. Manfred Lang's widow, Rose, and her son from her (Rose's) first marriage, Michael Fabian, also joined them. The city arranged for them to stay at the Hotel Löwen. The official program commenced that afternoon with a welcoming session in the city hall to which all city council members were invited. All of the painful memories were temporarily suppressed when Hugo Lang thanked the city for the invitation, including his old friend, "former Deputy Mayor Häfele,"[10] and stating that he was proud to be able to show his wife and children his "old home in Württemberg." He noted that "forty-eight years have passed since I left my homeland in 1941, had to leave. . . . Unfortunately, my parents, aunt, uncle, grandparents, sister, and cousins remained behind. None of them could get a visa at the time. You know what happened to my parents, grandparents, aunts and uncles—I won't speak about it. Those who do not know only have to read the memorial plaque in the cemetery. This plaque clearly describes their terrible fate." Hugo expressed his thanks to the town for erecting "the memorial plaque" in the cemetery and for not allowing the family names of "Lang and Oppenheimer [sic! Ottenheimer]" to be forgotten. "We also appreciate the memorial on the historical fountain, and will not forget these things."

The plaque in the cemetery Hugo was referring to was the war memorial for World War II soldiers, affixed next to the World War I war memorial on the outside wall of the chapel in the Süssen cemetery, Stiegelwiesen. For years I have puzzled over how the names of Holocaust victims could have gotten on the same plaque with their perpetrators. In organizing the Süssen files in the District Archive in Göppingen, a colleague found an alphabetical listing of "fallen and missing soldiers of the *Gemeinde* [municipality] Süssen," which included police officer Josef Holl, who accompanied and guarded the Jews of Süssen to the collection camp in Stuttgart, on the same page with his victim, Rudolf Metzger. For Holl it says "missing in action in Poland in January 1945," and he was subsequently declared dead; for Rudolf Metzger the listing says *umgekommen* (died), not *verstorben* (deceased) as for a prisoner-of-war on the same list. In other words, those compiling the list knew the semantic difference between the two terms. Alfred and Hermine Baer, Eva and Leopold Lang, Louis and Fanny Lang, and Alfred and Eugenie Metzger are also on this list.[11] Though he did not let on in his public speech during his visit to Süssen, Hugo told me that he was horrified that his loved ones were intermingled with the dead who had served Hitler and the Nazi state.

In his speech, Hugo also noted, "Honestly, all Lang family members were very happy to live in Süssen at that time. My father often said, 'We will never leave our hometown voluntarily.' But unfortunately things turned out quite different than my parents had planned." He then gave those present an update on the relatives who also live in the United States and were not able to be present. "My brother Manfred did very nicely for himself. He had a good job and a beautiful house. Two years ago [1987] he died of cancer." He also acknowledged that Fred's widow Rose and her son Michael came to Süssen with them. He continued, "My sister Ruth also would have liked to join us on this trip, but that wasn't possible this year. She and her husband have a [kosher] butcher shop that they couldn't close. Maybe in a few years when she is retired." He then added, "My sister Ruth met her husband in the concentration camp. At that time they promised that if they survived they would keep kosher. This they did. They keep *milchig* [dairy] and *fleischig* [meat] separate. They became observant. They survived the camps and promised to go the whole way, not only half."[12] Hugo continued, "My cousin Siegfried lives in Florida. His health is not good. He always had problems with his hip. He was born with one leg shorter than the other. Already then he wore a brace. He was operated on four times, but it didn't get any better. So he couldn't come with us."[13] And Hugo's "cousin Kurt lost his twenty-six-year-old son three months ago, so he couldn't come for that reason."[14] About his other cousin, Inge Lang, he said that she had died of cancer in 1973. "She was the oldest of the Louis Lang family. And my cousin Henny lives in Florida. She moved there from New York a few years ago. She isn't well. That's why she couldn't come."[15] Hugo then thanked the town for the invitation, and wished everyone continued good fortune "under the excellent leadership of Mayor Bauch."[16]

The visitors and the town's people had to feel each other out. When asked about his first contact with the citizens of Süssen, Hugo responded, "The first meeting was a little difficult for us, because we didn't know what might be discussed, what might happen. But that is no longer the case, we now know that the town and the city council, and especially Mayor Bauch, had put a lot of effort into the research. We are convinced that this community will remember the Lang name."[17]

On Tuesday, October 3, a reception was held in the city hall, followed by an all-day tour of the town, including their former home. As a boy, Hugo had to help store the produce for the winter in the cellar. He obviously had fond memories for, after visiting his house, Hugo commented, "The cellar is still the way it was fifty years ago. The stone plates, the steps are the same. I am happy to have seen the cellar again."[18] In the evening there was a get-together with acquaintances from the neighborhood and former classmates of Hugo's in the *Mostkeller* (a room named for a cellar where cider is stored) of the Gasthof Löwen. When asked what it felt like to be in the presence of former classmates, Hugo responded, "Honestly, I was a little bit nervous to see people with whom I went to school and whom I no longer recognized. But I had the courage to shake their hand and greet them. Meanwhile we have become more familiar. Many said that they had to join the war effort. They had to join in like all others, I understand that."[19] He was also given a list of classmates who had died during the war or were missing in action. There were thirteen of them—the same number of dead from a whole school class as from one family, the Langs.[20]

To the question whether this gathering brought back any special memories, Hugo responded, "Yes. Hermann Fischer, a classmate, fought in the same battle in the Ardennes where I was captured. He was a German soldier, I was an American GI. We both were in the same town at the same time, on the same day—December 18, 1944. That was quite a coincidence. That was the high point of the meeting for me. We talked for an hour and parted again as friends."[21]

There were no scheduled activities for Wednesday morning, October 4. The afternoon plans included a bus trip to Stuttgart for a meeting with Rabbi Joel Berger, chief rabbi of the state of Baden-Württemberg, and a visit to the Stuttgart synagogue. Rabbi Berger was somewhat anxious about the timing, as the visit coincided with the High Holy Days that year, September 29 to October 9.[22] Mr. Kurt Eifert, a retired school principal, served as the Langs' escort. The evening concluded with a dinner at the kosher Restaurant Shalom in Stuttgart.

On Thursday, October 5, the group visited Göppingen, which used to be home to the Jewish community to which the Langs belonged. They visited the site of the destroyed synagogue and the Jewish section of the Göppingen municipal cemetery. Their escorts were Walter Lang (no relation), teacher and district archaeologist, who had to be excused from teaching so he could conduct a tour of Göppingen for the guests.[23] Mr. Kurt Eifert also joined them again. The afternoon was set aside for a stroll through Göppingen, and the day concluded with dinner with Mayor Bauch as well as a consultation on the remainder of the stay.

No activites were scheduled for Friday, October 6.

On Saturday, October 7, the group traveled to Ulm, 19 miles east of Süssen, for a city excursion and visit to the Ulmer Münster, a beautiful cathedral with its famous "Hebrew" window. Ulm had special meaning for Hugo who had apprenticed as a waiter in the Jewish Restaurant Moos at Weinhof, in the vicinity of the cathedral, before Kristallnacht in 1938. He also has a good and lifelong friend in the United States, Walter Gundel, whom he knows from their Ulm days. The day concluded with a dinner in Süssen, hosted by the municipality, again in the *Mostkeller* of the Gasthof Löwen, and attended by the mayor and members of the city council as well as Mr. Eifert and wife.

Sunday, October 8, was reserved for any desired farewell visits—farewells that were quite different from those of Louis, Leopold, and their relatives in 1941.

Some time during the visit, two cookbooks from the Lang kitchen were also returned to Hugo and family.[24] Asked how he felt when he received the two cookbooks from Frau R. H., the woman who had held on to them all these years, Hugo responded, "I would have never believed that they still existed. Especially since they were my mother's, may her memory be for a blessing. I was very pleasantly surprised and would like to thank the woman personally." According to archival records, Frau H. is the daughter of a couple who acquired the Lang's kitchen cupboard (presumably at auction after deportation). The cookbooks, which dated back to the time of the kaiser, were inside.[25] The mayor noted that the "old kitchen cupboard" was handed down to Frau H.'s daughter and has been refurbished so that it serves as the centerpiece in their household.[26] I asked Hugo if he had the cookbooks. Hugo replied that he gave them to his sister, Ruth.[27]

The visitors departed on Monday, October 9. The town's October 15 bulletin featured the meeting in the city hall on the front page with the headline, "A group of former Jewish citizens and their families spent last week in Süssen. During the Third Reich some of them were assisted with emigration and were thus spared the horrors of the persecution against the Jews."[28] Those assisted were Fred and Hugo, and their cousins Henny and Inge.

Before leaving Hugo offered the town a gift of DM 10,000 for a proper memorial for his murdered family. The town, while declining his money, promised to erect a separate memorial plaque for the victims of the Holocaust. They kept their promise. Less than two years later, Hugo and Inge received an enthusiastic letter from Rolf Karrer, SPD member,[29] informing them that he was elected mayor on November 26, 1990, and was ready to tackle the memorial plaque the city had promised.[30] He also sent them a proposal for the inscription for the memorial plaque, to which Hugo immediately responded by telephone. From this letter it becomes apparent that the city did not know for sure the names of the Lang family members who were murdered.[31] According to a letter of July 22, 1991, the city council decided in March to approve the memorial in the cemetery Stiegelwiesen. Mayor Karrer then invited Hugo and Inge to a dedication of the handsome bronze memorial on Tuesday, July 30, 1991, at 5 P.M. in the cemetery Stiegelwiesen, with dinner to follow.[32]

The plaque, which is placed in front of the burial hall, but at a 45-degree angle to the memorial plaque for the war dead, has all the correct information and reads,

> In memory of our fellow Jews who were deported and murdered during the Nazi reign, as a daily reminder for us, and as an obligation not to tolerate racial hatred and intolerance. 1933–1945–1991.

Those listed are Leopold Lang; Eva Lang, née Liffmann; Louis Lang; Fanny Lang, née Landau; Alfred Baer; Hermine Baer, née Lang; Hans Kurt Baer; Siegfried Baer; Werner Baer; Alfred Metzger; Eugenie Metzger, née Baer; Rudolf Metzger; Falk Sahm, and Walter Zeimann.

During this visit, Hugo and Inge's guide was again District Archaeologist Walter Lang. According to a letter to Hugo and Inge dated September 17, 1991, Mr. Lang at that time also conducted research on the Jews of Göppingen, authoring a publication on Kristallnacht which he sent to the Langs in 1992 along with Inge Auerbacher's book, *I am a Star*.[33] He was also at that time involved with the Jewish Museum in Jebenhausen, and became the keeper of pictures and mementos that Hugo gave to the town of Süssen.

An article on the front page of the *Süssener Mitteilungen* of August 15, 1991, pointed out that the unveiling of the memorial took place "a few days after the anniversary of the attempt on Hitler's life [by Count von Stauffenberg on July 20, 1944] in the presence of members of the Jewish family Hugo Lang." Acting Mayor Karl Müller noted in his remarks that "at that time in Süssen very few people were willing to help the victims, there practically was no resistance." He, too, noticed the irony of the entry in the city council minutes of 1941 "in the most elegant Sütterlin script" that Süssen was now free of Jews.[34]

In spite of hopes to visit Süssen in 1992, the occasion of the unveiling of the memorial plaque was Hugo and Inge's last visit to Süssen, although they regularly have visitors from Süssen in their New Jersey home.[35] Both Mr. Bauch and Mr. Karrer stayed in touch with Hugo and Inge. On July 4, 1995, Mayor Karrer wrote to Hugo and Inge informing them that he had met Hilde Schmalz, née Meissnest, a good friend of Hugo's since childhood, who was about to visit the Langs for six weeks. He was going to send along a booklet that the town had put together in its application for cityhood, asking them for their opinion.[36] Two local industrialists likewise visit Hugo and Inge regularly when on a business trip to the United States. Hugo routinely receives the Süssen information bulletin, a gift initiated by Mayor Karrer in 1991,[37] which he reads with great interest and sometimes sends on to Knoxville for further perusal.

To my knowledge, no such official visit to Süssen has taken place by survivors of the other Jewish family that is part of this study, the Ottenheimers. Since the Ottenheimers were considered primary residents of Göppingen, an invitation may have been extended from the city of Göppingen, which has hosted a number of visiting Holocaust survivors over the years.

# 2        A Village Called Süssen

*I wish to rush from my home*
*For it is no longer such!*
*Alien and oppressed I feel here*
*Never again will I return.*
—Johann Georg Fischer, *Dichtungen*, 1841.[1]

An erstwhile resident of Süssen who reads Johann Georg Fischer's poem, no matter the reason for his or her leaving, will recognize the sentiment. Although Hugo Lang, who was forced to leave, and I, who chose to leave, have been graciously welcomed back upon our return, the sentiment expressed in Fischer's poem resonates. For me researching the story of two Jewish families in the first half of the twentieth century on location was at once satisfying and disturbing. As it happens, both of these Jewish families established contact with their respective parts of Süssen in the same year, 1902. Jakob Lang moved to Gross-Süssen from Göppingen, and Alfred Ottenheimer, also from Göppingen, bought land for a factory in Klein-Süssen. Although a good bit of the history of these two families points to cordial relations with their municipalities, there is also evidence of betrayal.

The village of Süssen, with its historic buildings and breathtaking gardens and window boxes, is located in the center of the district of Göppingen, along the old road from Stuttgart (31 miles to the west) to Ulm (24.8 miles to the east), surrounded by spacious fields and lush orchards. Until 1933, Süssen was split into two parts—Gross-Süssen (Greater Süssen), which was Lutheran, and Klein-Süssen (Smaller Süssen), which was Catholic. The two villages were separated by the river Fils, which flows through the center of town and gives the entire twelve-mile-long valley from Göppingen to Geislingen its name—the Filstal. The valley is framed on both sides by gently rolling hills, which are dotted with picturesque medieval castles such as Staufeneck and Ramsberg in the north. Dominantly rising in the northwest is the Hohenstaufen, one of three Staufer mountains, erstwhile home of the medieval Emperor Barbarossa.[2] At the eastern end, above Geislingen, protrude the ruins of Castle Helfenstein and the Ödenturm. In tax matters, Geislingen remained the center for Süssen even after its rezoning and annexation to the district of Göppingen in 1938.

The name *Süssen* is a modern version of a word that predates the existence of the settlement. Derived from an Old High German word, it means "wooded grazing land" or "wooded grazing land for cattle." Several formulations of the word are known, including *Siezun* and the earlier *siaza* or *sioza*.[3]

Walking through this town today, one is struck by the multicultural makeup of the population. A larger percentage of Süssen residents are Muslim than ever were Jewish, and Muslim women live out their religiosity in public by wearing headscarves, though no burkas are in evidence.[4] Süssen also has a Muslim Community Center. However, at the concert celebrating Süssen's tenth anniversary of obtaining the title of town, which was held in the Lutheran church on July 7, 2006, there was no observable Muslim presence. Even so, the city has made tremendous progress. When I was a child, there was little diversity. Back then, the locals received the World War II refugees—Germans from eastern Europe, such as Silesia, Sudeten Territory, Estonia, Czechoslovakia, and Hungary (Hungarian nationals with German roots called *Donauschwaben*)—only grudgingly and with resentment because of their material needs at a time when native Süssen citizens themselves experienced a severe shortage of food and jobs.[5] Hungarian women back then also wore headscarves, something the local population got accustomed to because the women did not acquiesce to the cultural pressure to assimilate. It nevertheless took a long time for the refugees to be accepted and integrated. Only in 2000 did the town of Süssen formalize its long-time partnership with Törökbalint, a sister city in Hungary.

And then there were the *Gastarbeiter* (guest workers) from Italy, Turkey, Yugoslavia, and Spain, who had been invited by the German government to pick up the shortfall in labor following the economic recovery in the 1950s. They did well, and helped the population of small towns like Süssen, and Germany in general, to regain and maintain their high standard of living. But what about the quality of the foreign workers' cultural lives? Many started families, and their offspring born in Germany were considered German citizens. Yet the parents were not nor, under German law, could they ever become citizens. Had Germany really changed that much in regards to how it treated foreign-born residents since the Holocaust? The question whether Germany is an *Einwanderungsland* (immigration country) has been hotly debated for more than thirty years. In spite of all the visible diversity, even in a small town like Süssen, the country continues to fight immigrants instead of embracing them. In 2006 the state of Württemberg introduced a *Gesinnungstest*, also known as the *Muslimtest*, to determine whether immigrants are sincere about wanting to integrate into German society.[6] This is reminiscent of the *Israelitengesetz* of 1828 whose purpose it was to integrate Jews into the German artisan class, a move that deprived many of them of their traditional livelihood, yet did not open up new opportunities for them. It seems that every generation has to fight the battle of belonging all over again.

## A History of Conflicts

The discovery of Merowingian burial grounds near Süssen's railrod station suggests that people may have settled in the area as early as the seventh or eighth century CE.[7] The first written evidence of a settlement dates from 1071[8] in a document of the cloister of Lorsch at Bergstrasse,[9] located geographically far from the farm they owned in Süssen. Lorsch was founded in 763 CE,[10] well before the start of Charlemagne's reign in 800 CE. The farm in Süssen was a gift to Lorsch along with other bequests that stretched from the North Sea to Graubünden, Switzerland. A historian of the cloister reported that "members of the Lorsch Abbey could travel from one end of the Holy Roman Empire of the German Nation to the other without sleeping on foreign soil even for one night!"[11] Although Süssen, at first, had only one farm to offer, that was important, for it helped to feed the monks of Kloster Altenmünster, a monastery near Lorsch.[12]

From the ninth century on the population of the region was Christian and relied for religious guidance on the cloister in Adelberg—established in 1178 by Ritter Folknand von Staufen.[13] In 1267 Count Ludwig of Spitzenberg-Helfenstein and his son, Eberhard, whose castle was perched on a mountain of the same name above the village of Kuchen, three miles east of Süssen, gifted the church in Süssen with all rights to the Cloister Adelberg "as an indulgence for their and their forebears' eternal salvation."[14] With the death of Konradin (the last of the famous and powerful Staufen clan) in 1268, their possessions were appropriated and administered primarily by lesser nobility, such as the counts of Spitzenberg, Helfenstein, and Rechberg. In the thirteenth century Süssen seems to have had some nobility of its own, probably officials of the Count of Spitzenberg. In his book, *Von Siezun bis Süssen*, Walter Ziegler mentions Gottefrido de Siezon in 1241, Sigfrid in 1290 and 1291, and Knight Eberhard von Süssen, and his son Johann, in 1321, 1331, and 1332.[15] It is not known where in the village these noblemen resided; they disappeared from history after 1332. Johann von Süssen's emblem was the emblem of Gross-Süssen until 1933. The Süssen emblem since 1933 incorporates parts of the former Gross- and Klein-Süssen emblems.[16]

Personal status in the Middle Ages was all about possessions, of both land and people. Everyone—the emperor, the king, the Church, the Pope, and all the dukes and other lesser nobility—vied for bigger and better land holdings. Properties were won, lost, bought, sold, gifted, inherited, and swapped among the nobility, including the residents of these territories. Communities were split up among several different overlords.[17] Süssen was no exception and over time became a place of many masters. In 1270 two farms and a farm on loan to the current "owner" were sold by one nobleman to another—actually to a noblewoman.[18] Ten years later two more farms were sold to someone else and in 1290 yet another property was sold. The respective properties went to politically competitive owners, the first two to the counts of Helfenstein (and in 1396 to the *Reichsstadt*, or Imperial City, of Ulm), and the second and third properties to the Spital zum Heiligen Geist, a Church-owned hospital, in the Imperial City of Schwäbisch Gmünd. In 1290 the resulting separate ownership of large tracts of property in Süssen split the village in two. For the next 640 years the two settlements developed relatively independently of each other. The part north of the river Fils became known as Minnern Siessen or Klein-Süssen, while the part south of the Fils was known as Gross-Süssen.[19] What they shared, however, is a wild and unstable history due to robber barons, traveling soldiers to and from military battlefields, fires, natural disasters, religious wars, witch trials, and political upheavals. Two incidents shall serve as an example. Süssen is located on the main thoroughfare from the Rhineland to Bavaria. In 1441, despite the paid armed guard detail that escorted and protected their caravan, a group of merchants returning from a fair in Frankfurt was ambushed and robbed of 40 horses and 5,000 florin (gulden),[20] not to mention the loss of 8 or 9 lives.[21] On September 6, 1449, both parts of Süssen and neighboring towns were burned to the ground during the Schwäbische Städtekrieg (Swabian Cities War), a war between the Duchy of Württemberg and the Imperial City of Ulm. Recovery from this devastation was slow, and the peace did not last. The region suffered at least one major war every one hundred years, often more frequently than that.

If politics were complicated, so was religion, and the consequences cast a long shadow. In 1493 religious rivalry put Klein-Süssen on the map of the Vatican when their priest decreed that the local church, the Marien-kirche, could celebrate high mass and therewith collect the taxes previously due to the neighboring district of Hürbelsbach.[22] Klein-Süssen remained Catholic until after World War II. Two years after Martin Luther's posting of the Ninety-Five Theses on the doors of Wittenberg University in 1517, Lutheran Count Ulrich of Württemberg was ousted and exiled by the Catholic Kaiser. The residents of Gross-Süssen were reformed in 1531 along with all of the subjects of the district of Ulm.[23] Yet until 1535, their shepherd was a Catholic priest provided by the Cloister Adelberg. The cloister became one of the casualties of the Reformation, closing its doors in 1535. Many of the indentured servants in Gross-Süssen were former subjects of the monastery who did not necessarily gain their freedom at the time. During the continuing hostilities in the region, the suffering brought on by the indenture of the men affected primarily their wives and children, because the troops destroyed their property and the men weren't present to defend it. In 1552 this prompted the wives in several villages, among them also Gross-Süssen, to band together and petition Duke Christoph of Württemberg for protection of their property.[24] Gross-Süssen remained Lutheran until after World War II. Count Ulrich's exile was not easily forgotten. Nearly thirty years later, in 1546, the incident led to another religious war, the Schmalkaldische Krieg (Schmalkaldic War).[25]

Gross-Süssen was initially spared from the hostilities of the Thirty Years' War,[26] which raged in German lands from 1618–48, because the Schwäbische Reichskreis (Swabian Imperial District), which included the imperial city of Ulm and its territories, declared its neutrality. Because of its location on the main thoroughfare from east to west, however, every time there was a military campaign in the region, both parts of Süssen received a large number of military boarders whom they had to supply with the needed provisions. Crucial for the destructive turn of events of the Thirty Years' War in this region was the Battle of Nördlingen on September 6, 1634.[27] Although the Filstal had been housing Swedish troops from April 1634 on, following the Battle of Nördlingen, the Austrian Emperor's soldiers invaded and devastated many of the towns in the valley, including

Gross-Süssen. According to the death register, 180 people died in 1634, and 31 died in 1635 while fleeing for their lives.[28] 1634 also brought a drought to the area, so that the crops matured prematurely, requiring an early and therefore reduced harvest.[29] The residents of the valley suffered on two fronts during this tragic period in their history: devastation from war and from disease. The effects of the war and hunger were exacerbated by repeated outbreaks of the plague, which had periodically killed thousands since its initial horrific outbreak in the fourteenth century that gave rise to all kinds of ugly rumors, including rumors about the Jews.[30] When the last foreign troops finally left the area in 1649, the population was so ravaged and decimated that they failed to plant crops, causing a severe food shortage.[31] Walter Ziegler writes that peace could at last be welcomed in the territory of Ulm on August 25, 1650.[32]

By 1688, however, the region faced the possibility of an invasion by the Ottoman Turks which was averted, just in time, by the Austrian emperor's conquest of Belgrade. This led to military muscle-flexing between Austrian and French forces, during which Klein-Süssen was the recipient of 1,100 musketeers for lodging. The damage was considerable and the suffering citizens of Klein-Süssen lamented that the total damage of 3,000 florin[33] amounted to a hefty 37.5 florin per person—the value of one horse—turning the population, in their own words, into "totally useless poor people."[34] Gross-Süssen fared somewhat better, as "only" 400 French soldiers were housed in this village, and the residents had to contribute 800 reichstaler to cover damages from robberies and arson. No reports of extensive damage exist. Nevertheless, these extra burdens impoverished the people, so that they could hardly keep up with their own obligations. On December 17, 1688, the altercation ended and life in Ulm and its territories returned to normal.[35]

Events far from home had a way of expanding beyond anyone's wildest imagination, even as far as the Swabian Imperial District and therewith Süssen. The War of Spanish Succession (1701–14), of no consequence to Süssen whatsoever, nevertheless managed to involve the entire valley in costly and painful military entanglements. Because of disagreements between France and Austria over succession rights to the throne following the death of King Karl II of Spain, a "great [military] alliance" was formed between England, Holland, Portugal, Prussia, Hannover, and Austria against Louis XIV of France. The Swabian Imperial District decided to join this alliance; thus Gross-Süssen by association went to war again.[36]

The electoral prince of Bavaria, on the other hand, allied himself with France. The Imperial District of Ulm was between Bavaria and Württemberg. Hence the Kurfürst's first order of business was the conquest of Ulm, which involved the emperor and the imperial troops in the hostilities. After much maneuvering, Margrave Ludwig Wilhelm of Baden, nicknamed "Türkenlouis" for his victories over the Turks,[37] took up position in Gross-Süssen with his 16,000-man army.[38] Fortunately the decisive battle of the Spanish War of Succession on August 13, 1701, was waged far from Süssen, near Höchstadt on the Swabian Alb, so that the village "merely" suffered the ravages of occupation, not of actual war in its territory.[39] In 1704 the French lost, and the War of Spanish Succession came to an end. Ulm and its territories were once more freed from French-Bavarian occupation.

Only three years later, however, French soldiers twice ravaged the unlucky village of Gross-Süssen, on June 17 and July 16, 1707. According to an eyewitness,

> They marched to Gross-Süssen, also setting fire to that beautiful village, so that one third of that poor village burned to the ground, including the beautiful church, parsonage, school and administrative buildings. But that wasn't enough for those ruffians, rather they decapitated and killed a man who had begged them on his knees to spare his little house; they cut off another man's arm who ran to save his burning house so that he died the same day. When a widow here, who lived next to the inn Goldener Stern saw that these evildoers wanted to set fire to her house, she stepped outside with her seven children and sank to her knees before the officer. This moved him to such a degree that he commanded his people to stop and desist from further damage. In general they treated women badly and caused them such pain that words cannot adequately express it.[40]

After the second attack, the official report stated that "all but 20 buildings in Süssen were burned down, including the beautiful temple [church]."[41] Others, including houses "in the *Judengasse*," were saved.[42] When the overall damage was assessed, 82 of 140 buildings, or 59 percent of the village, had been destroyed.[43]

In spite of all of these difficulties, in 1789, at the time of the French Revolution, a visitor to the area observed,

> [Gross]-Süssen is a fabulous place and is located in a paradise-like region; one can see the most luscious orchards, fields, stately woods, three castles

towards the north, and a number of fertile fields, some of which still carry ample produce. The local residents grow much hemp and flax and in addition they carry on significant trade with fruit and cattle. The valley is a blessed land and a true treasure chest for Ulm. Too bad that the residents have to pay so much tribute. This is probably the reason that I did not see many happy and cheerful faces; they seem to have lost all zest for life.[44]

Territory changed hands quickly in the early nineteenth century. While Süssen had been part of the Imperial District of Swabia from the fifteenth century on, in 1802 this district was divided between Württemberg and Bavaria. Ulm was incorporated into Bavaria, as was its possession, Gross-Süssen. Following the Peace of Pressburg on December 26, 1805, the imperial nobility was abolished. At the time Klein-Süssen likewise became Bavarian. After the successful Battle at Austerlitz,[45] Napoleon planned to return from Vienna to Paris via Stuttgart. The duke, Kurfürst Friedrich of Württemberg, had been Napoleon's ally during the warring years. He now ordered the construction of three *arcs de triomphe* for the emperor's passage. One was erected at the Württemberg-Bavaria border (which had been the Württemberg-Ulm border until 1802), directly west of Süssen, in the Schweinsbach area. This arc, whose dimensions were fifty-two by twenty-six feet, cost 2,466 gulden to construct. Out of gratitude for the duke's loyalty, Napoleon promoted the duke of Württemberg to king, and the duchy of Württemberg became a kingdom.[46] On January 18, 1806, Napoleon and his empress arrived at the *arc de triomphe* at the Württemberg-Bavaria border and were welcomed by two counts in the name of the king of Württemberg.[47] In 1810, both parts of Süssen were integrated into the kingdom of Württemberg.

**Beyond Wars and Religion**

Although military and religious affairs played an important role in the history of Süssen, the town has much more to offer than hostilities. An 1842 description of Gross-Süssen by the regional administration, the *Oberamt* (administrative district) Geislingen, noted that "Gross-Süssen is two hours' [walking] distance northwest of the Oberamt [Geislingen]," about 5.6 miles. "The place has a clean and friendly appearance. There are 264 major buildings. The residents are diligent and frugal and mostly well-to-do; their main line of work is agriculture . . . their fields and grazing lands are fertile. They grow excellent hemp and flax and for their large herds of cattle they grow a large amount of feed. In addition, the population conducts considerable trade with fruit, flax, linen, hay, cattle, and so forth. . . . Residents try to combat the shortage of fire wood by planting quick-growing types of trees [such as poplars]."[48]

Of Klein-Süssen the same source notes that the settlement "is located two and a half [walking] hours northwest [of the Oberamt of Geislingen] in the friendly valley of the Fils, and is separated from Gross-Süssen merely by a bridge that spans the river Fils. . . . There are fifty-two buildings with twenty-seven apartments. The residents belong to the lower bourgeoisie and make their living from farming. The municipality has neither debts nor assets."[49]

Perhaps because of all the military activity, both parts of Süssen were well endowed with inns for the thirsty residents and visitors. Citizens of Süssen developed a reputation as *Moschtköpf* or "hard cider heads," attesting to the consumption of pungent cider produced from local apples and the local population's delight in frequenting their inns.[50] Hard cider is a potent drink, yet inexpensive for the agrarian population, as apples are ample in the region. Today the production and consumption of *Most* (hard cider) has decreased considerably in favor of beer and wine. Some inns, such as the Gasthaus Krone in Klein-Süssen, date back to the Thirty Years' War, the Rote Ochsen and the Rössle were documented in the middle of the eighteenth century.[51] The Pelikan and Restauration Frick round out the early sources of libation. In 1848, a year after the completion of the railroad, a mail service was established in Klein-Süssen, and the village became the central location from and to several different destinations.[52] The local citizens used this trump card when they were hoping to get permission to establish yet another inn, but to no avail. The former *Zollhaus* (customs house), another eatery, also was technically located in Klein-Süssen, although by jurisdiction it belonged to Gross-Süssen.[53] Gross-Süssen did not lag behind, also documenting six or seven inns, among them the inn Lamm at 42 Hauptstrasse in 1672.[54] Others included the Löwen, Stern, Schwanen, and Adler. The most prominent was the Schwarze Adler, dating back to the sixteenth century.[55] Not only did it provide food and drink, and a bed to sleep for the visitors, but feed and shelter for their animals as well. This was the most coveted location in the village, because it was located on the thoroughfare from north to south and west. In 1826 the municipality of Gross-Süssen bought the property and turned it into a school and later the city hall, which it still is today.[56]

In spite of their humble beginnings, some of the native sons nevertheless became famous through peaceful activities. Johann Georg Fischer

(1816–97), a native of Gross-Süssen, along with Stuttgart poet Ludwig Uh-
land, to whom Fischer sent his first poems, and Geislingen poet Eduard
Mörike, with whom Fischer was friends, was one of the best-known poets
of this region. He was one of ten children. Walter Ziegler relates the moving story, told by Fischer's son Hermann, that the poet's father, a carpenter,
on his deathbed told his then ten-year-old son to "learn to be different."[57]
He obeyed, and left Süssen forever, to make something of himself as a poet
and teacher. He first attended the teacher seminary in Esslingen, and then
the University of Tübingen, where he found kindred spirits who shared his
love for literature.[58] An enthusiastic devotee of the poet Friedrich Schiller
(1759–1818), Fischer was a popular speaker for the Stuttgart choir "Lieder-
kranz" on the occasion of their annual Schiller celebration. On Schiller's
100th birthday in 1859, Fischer was chosen to give the keynote address for
the ceremony in which Schiller's birth house in Marbach was dedicated
as a monument. In 1883, the city of Marbach (Schiller's city of birth) bestowed honorary citizenship on Fischer because of his efforts to create a
monument for the great poet,[59] and in 1894 Süssen (Fischer's village of
birth) likewise accorded the poet honorary citizenship; Fischer died three
years later.[60] Unfortunately, Fischer's quaint but inconveniently located
birth house in Süssen has been razed to help improve the traffic in the
Bachstrasse.

Other Süssen citizens have done as Fischer did, leaving the limited opportunities for greener pastures. Some, like Fischer, remained in German
lands, others emigrated in droves to America. This was long before the
immigration quotas of 1924, at a time when access to the United States
was wide open. Among those trying their luck overseas was Johann Jakob
Bausch (1830–1926), a poor farmer's son with six siblings, whose mother
died in childbirth when he was seven. He learned the production of eye-
glasses from his brother. Because eking out an existence was a constant
struggle, he decided in 1849 to immigrate to the United States. Here, too,
he was not successful at opening a lens business and tried several other
types of work, including woodwork, which he had learned back home;
this experience cost him two of his fingers. In 1853 he married a fellow
Süssen émigré, Barbara Zimmermann, and started a lens business in New
York. His partner was Henry Lomb, also an immigrant, from Hesse. After a tremendous struggle the two founded Bausch & Lomb in Rochester,
New York. The Bausch & Lomb website is modest in its praise of their
founders:

One of the oldest continually operating companies in the U.S. today, Bausch & Lomb traces its roots to 1853, when John Jacob Bausch, a German immigrant, set up a tiny optical goods shop in Rochester, New York. When he needed more money to keep the business going, Bausch borrowed $60 from his good friend, Henry Lomb. Bausch promised that if the business grew, Lomb would be made a full partner. The business did grow and the partnership was formed. In the early years, Bausch & Lomb manufactured revolutionary rubber eyeglass frames as well as a variety of optical products that required a high degree of manufacturing precision.[61]

In 1895 Bausch and Lomb employed five hundred workers, as many as the German company of Carl Zeiss in Jena, with whom Bausch had forged a partnership in 1892. Bausch was sometimes dubbed the "American Zeiss."[62] He also cooperated with George Eastman of Eastman Kodak fame.[63] "By 1903, the firm had been issued patents for microscopes, binoculars, and even a camera shutter based on the eye's reaction to light."[64] Bausch remained attached to Süssen and visited several times. After his death, the family donated 100,000 marks to the Lutheran Church in Süssen, which the congregation used to build a community center and kindergarten,[65] later remodeled and now used as a *Bürgerhaus*. Bausch's son and wife visited Süssen for a family reunion in 1930 and even after the Nazis had already come to power, in 1933 and 1934.[66]

### The Beginnings of Industrialization

Long before the construction of the railroad in the mid-nineteenth century, Gross-Süssen benefited from the river Fils that flowed through the village. The earliest industrial enterprises seem to have been mills of all kinds—around 1500 there was a mill for grinding grain, a saw mill in the seventeenth century, and in 1780 an oil and plaster mill.[67] In 1789 visitor Michael Dietrich reported that there was a *Gipsmühle* (gypsum mill) in Süssen "which is powered by an arm of the river Fils."[68] This "arm" probably refers to a canal that has been running the length of the settlement from east to west since at least the sixteenth century. A number of businesses that harnessed water for energy successfully settled along the canal as early as 1830,[69] thus facilitating the industrial development of this land of farmers. An 1842 description reveals that the businesses included a linen weaving business, silk production, a ribbon factory, and a spinning mill for wool as well as for cotton, a dyeing factory, a yarn factory, a straw production facility, a paper factory, a construction firm, a carpenter business, and a rope factory as well as a creamery facility which "annually uses up 5,000 florins' worth of milk."[70] In 1894 one such businessman, Konrad Kayser from Geislingen, bought one of the factories that had gone bankrupt for his business of ivory carvings and horn products.[71] The municipality allowed him to build a special kind of water wheel for energy production, which is today a historic landmark. The industry did not create any competition for the farmers, as there was plenty of land for cultivation and grazing. In fact, some of the farmers, such as the *Kirchenbauer* and others, were quite well-to-do, with large properties.[72]

The location also benefited Klein-Süssen, because better connections between Stuttgart and Ulm were highly valued for expanding business in the region. Already before the creation of the Second German Empire in 1871, railroad tracks were constructed from Stuttgart to Plochingen. In 1847 these tracks were expanded from Plochingen to Süssen, and two years later from Süssen to Geislingen.[73] Then, in 1901, a line that started in Süssen was developed through the Lautertal to the mountainous town of Weissenstein.[74] With the ability to lay tracks directly to the factory to get their goods to market, two businesses simultaneously established factories in Klein-Süssen, one being the Firma Kuntze, an industrial complex that had already built a factory in Klein-Süssen in 1889, and to this day manufactures giant pipes, oxygen tanks, and other construction items. It is thanks to the Kuntze firm that both parts of Süssen received electricity in 1901,[75] thus liberating both the economy and private households from the need of water for energy production.[76] Telephone service also was established in Süssen in the same year. The second company in Klein-Süssen was owned by the Ottenheimer family, who had already established a weaving business in Göppingen in 1862 and before that in Jebenhausen in 1854. "The two firms gave solid financial support to the Klein-Süssen municipality through World War I and provided an opportunity for many workers in Süssen to find gainful employment."[77]

Besides transportation, Klein-Süssen had ample land for construction along the railroad tracks.[78] Other businesses followed after World War I. They included a foundry, Ernst Strassacker (1919), producer of bronze art that has endured through the different political climates. During the Nazi period, the company created a bronze eagle for the University of Heidelberg, another eagle for the Erich-Koch-Plaza in Königsberg, and a huge swastika inside a laurel wreath for the central stage of the Zeppelinwiese at the *Parteitag* in Nuremberg in 1938.[79] Other businesses in Klein-Süssen following World War I included a spindle factory (1921) with 32 employees, a construction company (Keller Bau-KG, 1919), a masonry business (Natur- und Kunststeinwerke, 1921) with 100 employees, as well as a steel factory (Stahlbau Süssen GmbH).[80] Friedrich Bader relocated from Gingen in 1916 with 30 workers, and Kammgarnspinnerei Süssen with 150 employees was established in 1925.[81]

Although industrialization helped the economic base of both small villages, industrialization also introduced new problems, such as long work days of fifteen hours or more, back-breaking and underpaid labor for women, child labor, lack of health insurance, lack of workmen's compensation, and no organized system to fight back against abuse. Likewise, more work places attracted outsiders who were looking for work, creating an additional need for housing, social services, health care, schooling for children, and other resources.

Both parts of the village were politically conservative, yet when the Socialists organized a political party in 1896, they were able to enlist a respectable number of members. At the turn of the century, communism rose in cities around Süssen, like Geislingen and Göppingen, places that had many and large factories; Geislingen even had an iron ore mine. By the 1920s, communism had found its way to Süssen as well, largely as a result of the German defeat in World War I and the resultant political unrest and economic depression.

Although political parties such as the SPD were able to influence the social situation for the benefit of workers—an eight-hour workday, cessation of child labor, and health insurance—other social ills not connected to industrialization continued. Süssen's sewage ran into open waters that traversed the unpaved streets of the village, causing concern for local citizens. "Next to the Reichsstrasse [Imperial Highway] 10 Stuttgart-Ulm, and the immediate connective cross street that is planned as a Landstrasse [main road] of the first order, Süssen-Heidenheim (Bachstrasse), there runs a deep, open rill which is a constant source of danger for automobiles and others who use this street."[82] There also was a shortage of doctors and nurses. By the end of World War I, some of these ills had been redressed, and in 1919 women in all of Germany received the vote. But the advances achieved did not offset the ills for long. During the Weimar Republic, the citizens of Süssen suffered the same economic setbacks as did other industrialized regions. The rampant inflation, loss of work, lack of food, and lack of housing led to labor strikes wherever factories existed and to social discontent among the population, perhaps paving the way for the enthusiastic embrace of Nazism.

## United under the Swastika

When the Nazis came to power in 1933, the very first act of the new regime was to install a loyal party member as mayor of Gross-Süssen with the goal of uniting the two municipalities of Gross-Süssen and Klein-Süssen into one administrative unit known henceforth as Süssen.[83] The then mayors of the municipalities, Mayor Theodor Zwick (Klein-Süssen), who had been mayor for ten years, and Mayor Max Ehmann (Gross-Süssen), in office only since 1929, were dismissed. The newly appointed mayor was *Parteimitglied* (party member) Fritz Saalmüller (1904–94), who served until 1945. Saalmüller was drafted in 1939 and did not return until the end of the war, when he was arrested, convicted, and sentenced to life in Landsberg prison for a war crime he committed in 1944.

The unification proposal for the two municipalities was presented to the city council on June 9, 1933, before the first public meeting of the local Nazi chapter on July 8, 1933. The cleansing of the city council in Gross-Süssen had already taken place. Now it was time for the Nazi mayor to divest himself of any members of the Klein-Süssen city council who might prove a liability. Besides the mayor and the secretary that did not seem to be much of a problem. "The personnel issue, often a major issue in the unification of communities, is easily taken care of here, as most of the officials of the Klein-Süssen municipality can remain in their jobs."[84] That would be because they were all party members, not a good thing for the Ottenheimer brothers and the Lang brothers who suddenly became real outsiders in Süssen. The newly appointed mayor managed after a three-hour discussion to get a 5-to-1 vote for unification, with city council member Mühleisen the lone dissenting vote.[85] An article in the Nazi newspaper *Hohenstaufen* of September 15, 1933, stated that unification had occurred.[86] Thereafter the Gemeindepfleger (municipal treasurer) of twenty-five years, Georg Fischer, was retired. "The unification of the two communities Klein- and Gross-Süssen made it necessary to put an expert in charge of the good and welfare of the community. As is known, Karl Häfele got the job, he was born in Süssen and has up to now been working in Faurndau [a neighboring town]."[87] Häfele was a participant in and witness to all of the events that affected the Lang and the Ottenheimer families thereafter. On December 23, 1933, the *Geislinger Zeitung* reported that Mayor Saalmüller was confirmed in office. "The current acting head of the municipality Süssen, Mayor Saalmüller, has now been confirmed in office. We congratulate Mayor Saalmüller and wish him continued success in his work in Süssen. We would also like to congratulate the united village of

Süssen. Mayor Saalmüller's firm leadership ensures the development and progress of the community."[88]

From press reports it is evident that "nazification" and a show of strength by the various Nazi groups in the village of 3,500 were of primary importance during the early years of the totalitarian regime, to bring the population in line.[89] For this purpose there were frequent parades, including goose-stepping, brass bands, and the hoisting of flags. Great was the joy when the *Turnerjugend*, the youth who belonged to the local sports club, and the Evangelische Jungschar (Lutheran Youth) integrated into the Hitler Youth. An article in the *Geislinger Zeitung* of March 9, 1934, commented that it was only a pity that the Catholic Youth had not yet joined them.[90] Solidarity and enthusiasm for the cause were stressed in all of the events, and public speakers were not shy to coerce their audience. Peer pressure was applied liberally. The election results of August 20, 1934, show the Nazis firmly in the saddle with 2,169 or 89 percent of the vote in favor. Voter turnout was 97.9 percent, only 10 percent of those who voted opposed the Nazis.[91]

All types of occasions were used to show that Süssen citizens were coming on board. One wonders what the Langs and the Ottenheimers thought of these rallies and demonstrations. They dominated life visibly, and the newspapers were full of propaganda articles. There were sports events and "feel good" evenings, Nazified Christmas celebrations, winter solstice celebrations, a rally in support of the Saarland, whose citizens had voted to rejoin Germany, and charity drives for the poor. Indoctrination and arm-twisting was part of all of them. It is no overstatement to say that politics consumed a large part of every citizen's life.

The party members also took advantage of propaganda opportunities connected to communal issues such as the need for housing, a new swimming pool, support for families with large numbers of children, a separate home for the Hitler Youth, a sewage system for the local streets, the investiture of a new pastor (Holl), the shortage of fat, the opening of a new local museum, and the First State Prize for the communal bull, "Hanno 2060."

# 3 Klein-Süssen: The Ottenheimer Family

*A few steps from [Gross] Süssen is the Catholic village of Kleinsüssen, which be-
longs to the Freiherr of Bubenhofen, Geheime Rat in Würzburg: here [the Imperial City of] Ulm collects a tax for the bridge that crosses the river Fils, and they
have their own tax collector in the village. For this reason it is the responsibility
of Ulm to keep the bridge across the river Fils in good repair.*
—Michael Dietrich, 1789, in *Von Siezun bis Süssen,* 1971[1]

December 23, 2007. As the charter plane from Miami touched down in
Havana, Cuba, I was wondering what my visit with ninety-one-year-old
Werner Ottenheimer would bring. It was a slightly overcast day, with
temperatures in the eighties, and I had to go through a very elaborate
customs inspection. Because of the American economic boycott, Castro's
retaliation, and the resultant travel boycott for US citizens, most Americans are restricted to communicate with Cubans citizens using telephones
or email—which, in turn, presumes Cubans have access to a telephone
or the financial means to afford a computer and an Internet connection.
Mr. Ottenheimer does have a telephone, but no computer. American scholars, however, are exempt from the travel embargo and can enter Cuba
under a general license. Cuban authorities approve the visit upon arrival
in Cuba: US travelers return the permit upon leaving Cuba. I had chosen
a hotel that appeared to be located close to Mr. Ottenheimer's flat, but in
the end wasn't; and finding the stairs to the second floor at the back of a
government-owned row house in which he lived was a challenge.

Cubans are poor. Everyone is subject to food rationing and substandard government housing. For an American this is a jarring awakening,
yet the Cuban people are fairly resigned to their lot and take every day
in stride. The poverty certainly does not dampen their enthusiasm and
friendliness. Perhaps the temperate Caribbean climate with its dazzling
sunshine compensates for their harsh living conditions. If only there
weren't mosquitoes!

Mr. Werner Ottenheimer was kind enough to receive me on Christmas Eve 2007. Energetic and clear-minded, but somewhat monosyllabic, he was willing to return for brief intervals to his privileged childhood in Göppingen and his family's weaving business in Göppingen and Klein-Süssen. He noted that it was all far away, but it was evident that he had not forgiven the thugs who murdered his mother, Luise, and broke his father Alfred's heart. He was also somewhat bitter about having had to leave behind his lifestyle in Europe and the turn of political events between the United States and Cuba. His son, also named Werner, his daughter-in-law, and grandchildren now live in the United States, while he lives with his daughter Isabel and granddaughter Erika in their very small apartment in Havana.[2]

Born at Bethesda Hospital in Stuttgart on March 30, 1916, Werner Ottenheimer grew up in Göppingen where he attended the local Evangelische Knabenschule (Lutheran boys school), and then the *Realschule* (nonacademic track secondary school). He remembers a happy childhood with his older brother Richard. Every year around Christmas the family assembled their Märklin toy railroad, with which the boys enjoyed playing. Werner played accordion and belonged to the local sports club. The family took day trips to the surrounding countryside. Although not religious, the family participated in traditional Jewish community events. After his bar mitzvah in 1929 he asked his father's permission to abstain from attending services. In explanation he noted that he always had a leftist bent. In 1936, after considering the universities in Stuttgart and Munich, he decided to attend university in Zurich, Switzerland, instead. This decision may well have saved his life. He studied textile engineering, a profession that would have served him well if he had returned to Germany and the family's textile business. Due to the worsening political situation for Jews, however, his father Alfred decided to sell the family business in Süssen at the end of 1937—just in time to get out of Germany, one would think. However, this decision served neither parent. Alfred died in 1938 after a short illness. Both Werner and his mother were able to obtain visas to Cuba, but the Nazis would not permit his mother to leave Germany. Instead, after being moved to Stuttgart, Luise was deported and murdered. Since Werner was in Switzerland, he was able to use his visa and emigrate to Cuba in 1940. Most Jews who had valid visas to Cuba—many of the visas were fake and therefore worthless—did not choose to stay in Cuba, but used the country as a stepping stone to the United States. Werner Ottenheimer had no such ambitions. He found work in a textile factory in Cuba, some of it at the supervisory level, and remained, even when most of Cuba's Jews left in

1959. One of the pictures he showed me was from a trade mission to China during the era of Chiang Kai-shek (1948–75). Mr. Ottenheimer was part of a Cuban delegation that negotiated a trade agreement with the Republic of China. Even in Cuba, he was never part of the Jewish community. In 1940 he married a beautiful local woman, Isabel Garcia Garbalena, now deceased, with whom he had two children.

Surely it was painful for Mr. Ottenheimer to return in his mind to the happy days of his childhood and youth—no doubt emphasizing the contrast to his current life—and I am deeply grateful to him for the time we spent together and for the information and pictures he shared with the author.

### Mechanische Weberei Gebrüder Ottenheimer, Jebenhausen and Göppingen

From early in their residence in Jebenhausen under the name *Mechanische Weberei Gebrüder Ottenheimer,* the Ottenheimer family was focused on the production of textiles, which was not controlled by the guilds. I constructed a lengthy family tree that shows, very much like the Lang family tree, that families stuck to the line of work with which they had begun, even when they changed location.

Isai and Zettlin Ottenheimer from Mühringen were among the original families admitted to Jebenhausen with a Schutzbrief dated July 7, 1777. Their great-grandson was Salomon Ottenheimer, born May 12, 1830 and died November 18, 1906, who was married to Sara née Ottenheimer (June 9, 1837–September 17, 1897), daughter of Maier. The other great-grandson and brother of Salomon was Josef Ottenheimer, born January 2, 1842 and died November 9, 1918, who was married to Helene Strauss (1849–1913). Salomon and Josef were the sons of Jesaiah Israel (1800–June 13, 1874) and his wife Babette Brändel née Raff (June 15, 1802–December 23, 1868). Jesaiah Israel was the son of Maier Salomon Ottenheimer (1768–1846) and his wife Madel née Dreifuss from Hechingen, born May 20, 1766, in Mühringen and died February 17, 1824, who was the son of Salomo Ottenheimer (1724–91), and his wife Jettle (1735–?). Salomo Ottenheimer was the son of Isai (no additional information) and Zettlin Ottenheimer, the patriarch and matriarch of the family.[3] Five generations of Ottenheimers lived in Jebenhausen. Who says Jews didn't like to stay in the same place? They did when they were allowed to, and happily so.

According to his tombstone, Salomon Ottenheimer was *"ein vornehmer Mann, er ging auf dem geraden Weg* [a man of noble character who walked the straight and the narrow]." Rabbi Aron Tänzer of Göppingen also praised him for his "outstanding business sense and unusual energy."[4] In 1854 he had, in his grandson Max's words, founded "a small manual weaving business" in Jebenhausen.[5] In 1862 he invited his brother Josef, one of the first graduates of the Reutlinger Webschule, a weaving institute in Reutlingen, to become a partner. By 1863 the company employed approximately five hundred manual weavers, who resided primarily in the surrounding hills of the Swabian Jura.[6] The Ottenheimer firm was one of the first companies who relocated from Jebenhausen to Göppingen in 1865 after the railroad expanded service from Plochingen to Göppingen in 1847, and from Göppingen to Geislingen in 1849. There they continued a manual weaving business for nearly forty years, until 1904, in which they employed the *Verlagssystem*. According to Max Ottenheimer, son of Josef, the *Verlagssystem* is a process in which

> only the *Zettel*[7] [warp] was manufactured in the factory. The *Zettel* were then distributed to the manual weavers near and far, along with the *Schuss-material* [necessary yarn]. The weavers then completed the weaving process, creating the fabric in their own homes. Upon completion, they took the product back to Göppingen where it was sold by Ottenheimer representatives. During the height of the *Verlagssystem* the Ottenheimer firm employed more than forty *Zettler,* who made the warps in the factory and created work for six to eight hundred manual weavers in the rural areas.[8]

The Göppingen address book of 1912 lists founder Salomon and his wife Sara Ottenheimer as residing at 40 Marstallstrasse. His brother Josef lived at 7 Uhlandstrasse. Josef's son Alfred, who was Werner's father, lived originally at 29 Freihofstrasse (1912); by 1930 he had moved to 29 Gartenstrasse—Milton Rohrbacher, another giant in the Jewish community, lived at 31/33 Gartenstrasse—then, in 1934, Alfred moved to 14 Wilhelmstrasse. This is the address Werner remembers. In 1937 they moved to a new home at 14 Schumannstrasse which they had to sell in 1938 under pressure of Aryanization. According to Werner Ottenheimer, his father Alfred was *"ein biederer Göppinger Schwabe* [a steadfast Swabian man from Göppingen]" who served as a soldier in World War I; he also was cofounder of the *Schwimmverein* (swim club) in Göppingen.[9] Werner told me that the family was *lokaltreu,* that is to say, their loyalty was with their immediate communities of Göppingen and Süssen, Jewish and non-Jewish. I had not seen any pictures of Alfred Ottenheimer until 2007. Thanks to his son Werner, we now know that Alfred was a tall, slender man with a serious face. By the mid-thirties, his hair had turned white. He dressed conservatively in shirt and tie, suit, and coat. Werner told me that his father drove to the factory in Süssen by car. Werner's mother Luise née Kaufmann seems to have been the studious type. The picture Werner has of her shows a comely woman, somewhat plump, with an almost melancholy expression on her face, perusing a book while sitting in an armchair.

Alfred's brother Max, born October 6, 1873, became a partner in the firm on February 1, 1902, after Salomon, the founder, had retired.[10] According to Werner Ottenheimer and an elderly lady from Süssen, Max took the train to work. She described Max as a man of medium build, wearing horn-rimmed glasses. She said he always wore an overcoat and a Homburg hat. Max had begun his career as an apprentice in 1888. Reportedly a frugal man, in 1912 Max lived at 14 Burgstrasse and subsequently, until 1937, at 14 Wolfstrasse,[11] the new suburb of the upper class. Max was married to Hedwig Heimann. They had two children, Erich (in 1915) and Alice Berta (in 1907). In 1927 Alice married Arthur Rothschild, born September 8, 1896, and they had two children, Ruth (in 1931) and Gert (later Gary Eric) (in 1929). They changed their name to Rodgers.

The Ottenheimers were generous benefactors of the Jewish community in Göppingen, financially as well as organizationally. All the men were engaged in community activities. Rabbi Tänzer called them "men of noble character and unending diligence, who led the company they founded to a great reputation through their wisdom and energy."[12] He likewise noted the excellent contribution they made "through the honorary offices they held in the Jewish community of Göppingen."[13] Salomon Ottenheimer Sr., the patriarch, led by example. He served first as chairman of the Jebenhausen community and then of the Göppingen community for thirty-five years (1871–1906).[14] From 1914 on, Salomon Ottenheimer Jr. (not the founder of the firm, but another relative) held the position of chairman of the Jewish community in Göppingen, while his wife Sana (Sara) served on the board of directors of the Israelitischer Frauenverein.[15] Josef Ottenheimer, "Opa 'Lade' [*Schokolade*]," as Werner Ottenheimer called him because he satisfied his grandson's sweet tooth for chocolate, was membership chairman from 1872–92, and from 1886–92 he was the treasurer of the Israelitischer Wohltätigkeitsverein.[16] From 1910 to 1927 Alfred Ottenheimer was a member of the board of directors of Merkuria, an organization for junior Jewish businessmen.[17] In 1931 Alfred Ottenheimer served as treasurer of the Israelitischer Unterstützungsverein Göppingen.[18] And Max Ottenheimer served as the president of the local chapter of the Centralverein deutscher Staatsbürger jüdischen Glaubens from 1922 to 1935.[19]

## Mechanische Weberei Süssen, Gebrüder Ottenheimer, Göppingen and Süssen

After adding a new rail connection to Weissenstein, Klein-Süssen had become an attractive location for a business. Land was ample and cheap. In the negotiations for lot 189, the price was set at five marks per are,[20] also the price assigned in the reparations documents. Beginning in 1902, the Ottenheimers bought lots of land in Klein-Süssen along the railroad, with the intention of opening a branch of the business, and constructing a factory as well as workers' residences. Max explained that since moving from Jebenhausen to Göppingen, the company had become a leader in the textile field.[21] Because the "quality and beauty" of the products created by mechanical production had conquered the market, the Ottenheimer firm felt it was the right time "to build this factory [in Süssen] in 1904."[22] Plans to build a factory as well as living quarters for overseer Oberascher and his family—Werner Ottenheimer called him the *Betriebsfaktotum* (the soul of the company)—were approved on April 12, 1904. In 1905 the company *Mechanische Weberei Süssen, Gebrüder Ottenheimer, Göppingen and Süssen* was established on lot nos. 88, 88/1, 88/2, 88/3, 88/4, and 298/1—a total of 131 are, a territory the size of a large football field.[23] According to the *Handelsregister* (trade registry) this establishment now became the headquarters and the Göppingen business became a branch. Alfred Ottenheimer in Göppingen was the *Prokurist* (business manager), while Josef and Max Ottenheimer were partners and involved in the day-to-day operations of the Süssen business. This structure was approved on May 31, 1905.[24]

The Ottenheimer families kept their permanent residence in Göppingen, no doubt because the family was an important part of the Jewish community, and because they needed the Jewish school and the secondary schools for their children. Surely there were many occasions for portraits or group pictures of a family as prominent as the Ottenheimers, but no pictures of the adult Ottenheimers—Salomon, Josef, Max, or their wives—have surfaced. Thus, with one exception, we do not know what they looked like or how they dressed. Only the somewhat dry words transmitted through Rabbi Tänzer's notations to posterity tell us that they were upstanding and successful.

We do have several school pictures of the Ottenheimer children with their Göppingen classmates from the 1920s and 1930s. A 1924 picture taken in front of the Evangelische Knabenschule with the synagogue in the background shows Erich, son of Max and Hedwig as a handsome lad of nine and his then eight-year-old cousin Werner, son of Alfred and Luise— they do not look particularly thrilled to have their picture taken. Like the other boys in the group, they are standing straight, with their hands at their side, and with neatly folded-out shirt collars. Not to be missed in this picture is Poldi Guggenheim, Lilo Guggenheim's half-brother and a good friend of Werner Ottenheimer and Erich Ottenheimer. Two more pictures show Lore Ottenheimer, a daughter of Salomon and Sana, in grades one and four of the Evangelische Mädchenschule. Lore, with short dark hair and modest long-sleeved dress in a picture from 1927/28, seems somewhat shy, while a smile plays across her face in a picture from 1931/32. Two other Jewish classmates were Beate Bernheimer and Eva Fleischer.[25]

According to a recent company history by the current owners, Josef Ottenheimer was accorded honorary citizenship in Süssen in 1904.[26] A company letterhead dated August 2, 1906, shows a stately factory with a belching chimney as the impressive foreground to the majestic mountain scenery of the Filstal and Lautertal. At the very left one can see the water tower erected by the company and on the far right the art deco house which Betriebsfaktotum Oberascher and family occupied. The stationery also shows awards won by the company at fairs in Paris (1867), Vienna (1878), and Chile (1875).[27]

Relations with the village administration were mostly cordial, although there was a disagreement right at the beginning. It appears that an initial assessment of the property and business value, which the Ottenheimers had set at 16,000 marks, was reassessed by the Grundbuchamt (real estate registry office) at a hefty 220,000 marks, and taxed accordingly. The company protested this tax assessment on June 2, 1905, asking the municipality to adjust the amount. This request was denied on July 3, 1905, as unfounded.[28] No additional correspondence exists on this matter.

In 1909 Josef Ottenheimer's second son, Alfred (born January 7, 1879) also became a partner in the company. He had been an employee in the business since 1905. He was accorded *Bürgerrecht* or citizenship in Klein-Süssen as of October 16, 1910,[29] having already achieved that status in Göppingen as of April 1907.

In 1905 the company had fifty *Webstühle* (mechanical looms) running in the Süssen factory. On December 1, 1908, the business employed seventy-seven workers.[30] The Mechanische Weberei Gebrüder Ottenheimer was the first large factory to move to the impoverished Klein-Süssen. This

was of great importance to the economic development of this backwa-
ter village. Almost concurrently, other businesses such as the Kuntze pipe
works also established themselves in Klein-Süssen, thus raising the tax
base of the village significantly. In spite of a strong socialist trend, Klein-
Süssen was no worker's haven. The life of a laborer was hard and meager.
In November 1908 a worker earned an average of 2.80 marks per day, or
84 marks a month. In 1912 a technical employee working for the Kuntze pipe company earned 130 marks a month.[31] During two consecutive
pay periods in 1915, the pay of a female laborer, Luise Weber, who did
piece work, averaged 3.35 marks per day or 100.50 marks a month, and
3.20 marks a day, which amounted to 96 marks a month, respectively.[32]
The family of a factory worker could afford only simple, inexpensive
meals. At the rate of nearly 2 marks per kilogram (about 2 pounds) of meat
in 1912, and daily wages that were less than twice that much, the family
of a laborer could not afford to eat meat on a regular basis. During World
War I, between 1914 and 1916, meat rose from 90 pfennig per pound to
1.35 marks, and increased drastically from then until 1923, when inflation
devalued the currency.[33]

Construction of the new factory and technical innovations, such as the
mechanization of the manual looms, as well as fiscal constraints brought
on by World War I, compelled the city council and the industrial sector to
cooperate to the fullest. Hardly a year passed in which the Mechanische
Weberei Gebrüder Ottenheimer did not submit a petition to the city council for consideration. The *Gewerbeverzeichnis* (trade registry) of October 1
and December 31, 1911, noted that "the Mechanische Weberei Gebrüder
Ottenheimer moved into the new building [an addition to original factory]
in which there are twenty new looms." They reported further that another
forty will be added "during the course of this year [probably 1912]."[34] On
December 4, 1913, connections from the water main line to the workers'
houses and the requisite *Anerkennungszinsen* (user fee) of two marks are
discussed.[35]

Sometime before 1914, Max Ottenheimer was also accorded the honor
of "honorary citizen" of Klein-Süssen, as he then was elected as one of four
members of the citizens' council with fifty-nine votes.[36] On January 10,
1917, the citizens' council decided to delegate one of their four members
to the *Amtsversammlung*, a body of representatives from various official
organizations. The term of those previously in office had ended on December 31, 1916. Since this was wartime, the municipality thought it safer to

choose two delegates, presumably in the event that one would be drafted. One of these alternates was Max Ottenheimer, with five votes.[37]

Josef Ottenheimer, brother of Salomon and father of Max and Alfred, died on November 9, 1918; he is burial in Stuttgart. During the city council meeting of December 18, 1918, two citizens were honored posthumously, one of them being Josef Ottenheimer. The *Ortsvorsteher* (administrator) warmly eulogized "Herrn Josef Ottenheimer, Fabrikant in Göppingen, partner of the Gebrüder Ottenheimer Company here," who died "since the previous meeting," recognizing his achievements "in strengthening the industrial sector, as well as strongly supporting the good and welfare of our community." The administrator requested that the members of the council should rise for a moment of silence "as an expression of thanks and *in memoriam.*" This motion was carried out unanimously. Now the company consisted of two partners, the brothers Alfred and Max, who donated "500 marks to the village of Klein-Süssen in memory of their father." This money, the administrator announced, was to be used "for needy residents of Klein-Süssen," and there were many of those after World War I.[38]

During the same meeting the members were reminded that they had approved a resolution on August 14, 1917, to create an *Eisernes Buch,* or honor roll which would serve as a memorial book of World War I, a history honoring those from the community who served during the war and those who died as a result. According to the city council minutes, the book was completed and delivered to the village at a cost of 342.50 marks. The expenses incurred were underwritten jointly by the companies of Kuntze and Ottenheimer. The dedication reads, "This book is donated with deepest thanks to all those who helped to save our dear Fatherland and our precious homeland: Firma Gustav Kuntze, Dampfziegelei, Röhrenwerk u. Galvanische Kunstanstalt Süssen; Firma Gebrüder Ottenheimer, Mechanische Weberei Süssen." Citizen signatories are Obmann (chairman) Joh. Fetzer, Joseph Saur, Anton Koch, Franz Bundschuh, Franz Staudenmaier, Albert Hillenbrand, and Max Ottenheimer.

There were apparently no improvements or additions to the Ottenheimer establishment during most of World War I. Only towards the end, on July 25, 1918, did the company submit a petition for an industrial railroad track from the factory to the main line. The city council moved "not to object to the planned industrial track and to approve it, provided that there will be no obstruction of traffic, that the paths [along the track] will not be damaged or narrowed, and that all costs that will arise as a result of the track installation, the adjustment of the path and such will be borne by the petitioner without exception."[39] Toward the end of 1918 the *Gewerbeverzeichnis* noted that the Mechanische Weberei Gebrüder Ottenheimer "installed a rail connection operational since the beginning of October 1918 at a cost of 20,000 marks."[40] On March 15, 1921, a petition for a steam boiler was submitted. After consideration of the plans and review of the files, the city council decided "not to object to the construction and operation of a steam boiler plant."[41]

During the "roaring twenties" the economic situation was bad in Klein-Süssen. Many labor strikes as well as short workweeks occurred. These measures hurt employees as well as employers. The poverty of individual families paralleled the poverty of the community, which, along with many other problems, also experienced a severe housing shortage.

In 1921 the Ottenheimer firm built two two-family dwellings on Lot no. 286 that were not intended primarily as homes for Ottenheimer laborers, but also for the general population. On June 23, 1921, the company applied for the connection of these two new structures, located at Donzdorfer Strasse, to the main water pipeline. This was approved "on condition that the cost incurred by the municipality for the installation of pipes and other things for the connection" would be reimbursed by the Ottenheimer firm.[42] The State Interior Ministry of Württemberg issued a directive concerning loans in support of the construction projects of the Ottenheimer company. This measure was discussed by the city council on November 2, 1921. Following notification, the Gebrüder Ottenheimer firm agreed to "submit completely to the rules of the *Reichsrat* [council] on the granting of loans from state funds for the creation of new loans." The city council agreed that the company "had already shown this to be the case in September of this year when they rented four apartments," since it "assigned the apartments to local residents in closest consultation with the city. Only one of the four families who moved into the apartments in these new buildings on October 1 actually worked for the firm. Yet the rental agreement of this one head of household was hardly seen as related to his work for the company. Thus, 'it is crystal clear' that the apartments should not be considered workers' housing and are, in fact, not used in that way." The city council members voted, "1) To approve payment of 10,000 marks, or one-sixth of the state loan of 60,000 marks, from the communal treasury, to the Ottenheimer firm, and to pay this amount immediately. A further request for reduction of the communal share from the ministry was not approved. 2) To once more urgently request from the ministry that they disperse the loan as soon as possible, as the four apartments had already been occupied since October 1 of that year. 3) To further petition the ministry to sell the construction materials [wood] to the Ottenheimer company for the lowest possible price and further reduce the already established price, as the Ottenheimer firm built the apartments to alleviate the housing shortage for the general public amidst great sacrifices and for the admirable benefit of the weak and small community [Klein-Süssen]."[43]

On November 17, 1921, the company applied for the purchase of lot no. 189, a 26 are 39 square meter (about 3,110 square yard) field, known as *die langen Morgen,* as "two two-family houses for the general community" have already been built on lot no. 286, a 22 are 48 square meter (about 2,630 square yard) field, called *die Falbenäcker,* and they intended to build a third two-family house on it, thereby saturating construction on this plot.[44] The city council conceded that "construction of these houses for local residents really alleviated the worst cases of housing shortage here [in Klein-Süssen]." The municipality further "acknowledges with gratitude that the applicant in exemplary fashion contributed something good to the small and weak community and for those seeking housing." Partner Max Ottenheimer, who was present at the meeting, stated that "construction of a third two-family house [on lot 286] would begin soon." However, he could not make any promises concerning construction of a fourth two-family house because of the uncertain [economic] times. The company nevertheless had every intention of building "a fourth and even fifth house on lot no. 286."[45] It was further emphasized that the alleviation of the housing shortage could not be achieved without considerable sacrifices by the town, but that "it is still cheaper for the community to provide lots and loans" than to have to build themselves.[46] The resolution reflected as much, approving the sale of the property, lot no. 189, to the Ottenheimer firm for 5 marks per square meter, or a total of 13,195 marks.[47]

In 1922 the company submitted plans for an extension of the factory. However, economic conditions had begun to deteriorate. The branch in Göppingen was dissolved that same year[48] and Max Ottenheimer reported that they felt compelled to transform the company into a publicly traded corporation "because of the uncertain situation."[49] Grundbuch Heft 164 contains an entry of December 4, 1922, which states,

We are establishing a corporation under the name, "Firma Mechanische Weberei Süssen Gebrüder Ottenheimer Aktiengesellschaft," located in Klein-Süssen, Oberamt Geislingen. The base capital of the corporation consists of 2 million marks and is divided into 2,000 fully vested shares of 1,000 marks each; 1,400 of these shares are *Stammaktien* [ordinary shares] and 600 *Vorzugsaktien* [preference shares], some of the latter having more than one vote. The following shareholders of the company own shares:

| | | |
|---|---|---|
| 1. Max Ottenheimer | 300 *Vorzugsaktien* | à 1,000 Mark = 300,000 Mark |
| | 692 *Stammaktien* | à 1,000 Mark = 692,000 Mark |
| 2. Alfred Ottenheimer | 300 *Vorzugsaktien* | à 1,000 Mark = 300,000 Mark |
| | 692 *Stammaktien* | à 1,000 Mark = 692,000 Mark |
| 3. Moritz Wolf | 4 *Stammaktien* | à 1,000 Mark = 4,000 Mark |
| 4. Isidor Reis | 4 *Stammaktien* | à 1,000 Mark = 4,000 Mark |
| 5. Theodor Spiegelthal | 4 *Stammaktien* | à 1,000 Mark = 4,000 Mark |
| 6. Dr. Ludwig Ottenheimer | 4 *Stammaktien* | à 1,000 Mark = 4,000 Mark |

2,000 shares of 1,000 marks each amounts to 2 million marks.[50]

The agreement for the corporation of December 4, 1922, was registered with the Oberamt in Geislingen on January 9, 1923. According to these documents, it was the purpose of this enterprise, "1) to continue the business hitherto operated as Firma Mechanische Weberei Süssen Gebrüder Ottenheimer whose operation consists of the following: a) manufacture of woven fabrics and their production into clothing, b) installation of equipment to dye fabric, c) trade in woven fabrics; 2) participation in the weaving trade and other aspects of the textile industry. The establishment of branches of this company or a special firm will be permitted. Base capital 2 million marks. . . . Directors will be 1. Max Ottenheimer, 2. Alfred Ottenheimer, both business men in Göppingen." The following entry can be found in the registry for businesses (1906–23) of January 7, 1923: ". . . 5. Mechanische Weberei has ceased operations due to the transformation of the company." And further, "6. Mechanische Weberei has been transformed into a corporation, *Gemeinde Kataster* [municipal land registry] no. 75."[51]

Because of the economic situation, the company had to break its promise to the town to build a third house.[52] A letter of June 26, 1922, notified the town that the firm was forced "to delay the construction of the third two-family house because of the early and lengthy winter on the one hand and the rise in cost of several hundred percent, as well as the necessity to expand the factory."[53] The city council, "in recognition of the achievements of the Ottenheimer company towards the alleviation of the housing shortage and fully accepting the stated reasons," agreed to the delay of the third two-family home.[54]

Inflation was so great in 1923 that the Ottenheimer company printed emergency money. Although we do not know how extensively it was used and for what purpose, one specimen came to light some time ago. The bill was submitted to the stock exchange in Weinstadt and carried the serial number 24. A 1999 article by Jürgen Klotz in the journal *Der Geldschein Sammler* stated that "we unfortunately do not know anything about the quantity, its use, or whether it existed in denominations other than this one at a value of 100,000 marks, dated August 15, 1923. The bill is printed in black on one side and has a facsimile signature of Alfred Ottenheimer. Also on the front there is a diagonal red stamp with the name of the firm. The bill, series A, no. 24, lets one assume that the printing was rather small. On the back there is a handwritten note, 'Caritasverband Dr. J. Sträubinger,'"[55] presumably the creditor.

The difficult economic situation of 1924 also affected the village of Klein-Süssen. In December 1923 the Ottenheimers applied for one of many reductions of city taxes. They specifically requested that the town "refigure their corporate tax for the factory," as "the firm had to curtail production considerably because of the critical situation. Since February 1923 the company was able to carry out production only on four days, and mostly only on three days a week, a considerable number of looms were idle, and the company furthermore was transformed into a corporation."[56] The city council decided for the months of December 1923 and January and February 1924 to base the business tax on only two thirds of the property value. Two letters from the company, dated May 9 and 14, 1924, again brought the issue of tax reduction and due date extension of the corporate tax before the city council.[57] The deliberations of the city council showed that the base for the corporate tax for 1922 was 4,477,450 marks. Sixty percent of this served as the base for taxation and for payments to the Housing Loan Office. The city council determined that the productivity of the company did not justify the burden of these taxes as well as the installment to the Housing Loan Office in addition to the continual corporate tax estimate payments, and that an extension should be granted. On June 25 the issue was once more presented. However, the city council did not come to a decision, as the various ministries had not yet weighed in on the decision of May 23, 1924.[58]

On August 26, 1926, the company again requested a reduction in corporate tax for 1925 because of "reduced work time, idleness of some machines, and a deficit in December 1925."[59] On December 20, 1927, the weaving business requested an extension for 20 percent of the 1927 corporate tax.[60] In 1927 the company had ninety-seven employees, only twenty more than in 1908, a less than 25 percent increase.

The economic situation of Klein-Süssen worsened in the late twenties. Müller writes, "In 1929 Gross- and Klein-Süssen [together] had about 3,500 residents. . . . While there were still 695 jobs in 1929, in 1931 there were only 548."[61] This is a drop of 21 percent of job opportunities within a two-year period. Not only did businesses shorten their workday, but many also had to lay off employees. Important businesses reduced production sharply, so, for example, the Kuntze pipe factory cut 51 employees, or 40 percent of their entire work force, while the municipal construction company Keller Bau laid off 29 of their employees, or 35 percent.[62] These laid-off workers often became the responsibility of the municipality. In 1927 the workers of the Kuntze firm went on strike, as the company was among those with the lowest wages in all of Württemberg.[63] Fortunately the workers of the Ottenheimer firm did not strike, which did not necessarily mean that there were no issues. Already before World War I, an article in the *Geislinger Zeitung* of May 11, 1912, noted that the Social Democrats had previously complained about conditions in the company in this section of the paper, but that matters concerning labor relations "have not improved with the *Obermeister* [supervisor]." The author continued, "The wages of the weavers, male and female, have also not been raised; on the contrary, we get more and more complaints. We blame mostly the *Obermeister*. He knows how to attract weavers from elsewhere. For one or two pay periods they make good money doing piece work. But then business drops off and the workers leave. Those who live here are left with poor quality material." The author of this article urged the workers to check the Ottenheimers' references before accepting work there. They further urged the regular workers to organize, to join the Deutsche Textilarbeiterverband (German Textile Workers Union), so that their situation could be improved.[64] In 1929, both the employees and the employers suffered greatly from the poor economy.

Shortly before the 1929 stock market crash there were difficulties in the municipality of Klein-Süssen because of the corporate tax collection, and not only with the Ottenheimers. In a discussion of July 23, 1929, the city council decided "to grant an extension for the disputed [tax] amounts," but to charge 5 percent interest from the first day.[65] On July 24, 1930, when the debate was resolved, the Ottenheimer company owed the municipality 151,180 reichsmarks (RM) in interest. The company refused to pay the interest.[66] On September 9, 1931, two new requests for tax extensions were submitted to the city council, one of them by the Ottenheimer firm,[67] and on October 23 as well as December 30, 1931, the city council received business tax extension requests.[68] Apparently a ruling from the *Finanzamt* (tax office) based on earnings reports for 1927–30, and dated September 8, 1931, adjusted the taxable income. On that basis, the Ottenheimers, who were in arrears with their taxes, were ordered to pay corporate tax of 3,321.50 marks to the state and municipal tax of 10,343.80 marks immediately, as well as an additional 500 marks every quarter to reduce the tax in arrears. This hit the company hard, although the city council, in an effort to lessen the financial impact on the firm, voted against one of its members and in support of the Ottenheimers, "because of the great relationship between the Firma Mechanische Weberei Süssen Gebrüder Ottenheimer A.G. [and the municipality]."[69]

On November 30, 1929, the company celebrated the seventy-fifth anniversary of its founding in 1854. An article in the *Geislinger Zeitung* reported that "In the company dining room a celebration took place on that occasion in which the owner, the *Angestellten* [white collar workers], and the factory workers participated." The company then employed "more than one hundred workers."[70] In his address to the celebrants, Max Ottenheimer pointed out the "difficult economic situation [inflation and stock market crash] and the seriousness of the times [due to political changes]," and explained that "the company therefore decided not to stage a lavish celebration." Instead they gave every employee "a small gift of money . . . leaving it up to the individual how to best use it in celebration of this event."[71] On December 3, 1929, the mayor of Klein-Süssen, Mr. Zwick, sent a letter of congratulations in which he wrote,

> For the 75th anniversary of your company and the 25th anniversary of your establishment in Süssen we send you hearty congratulations. The Ottenheimer brothers managed through hard work and great determination to advance the company to success and esteem and we are happy to acknowledge that the economic progress as well as the general development of the community are due primarily to the celebrated and esteemed company, especially our deceased honorary citizen, Mr. Josef Ottenheimer, and the current directors, Messrs. Max and Alfred Ottenheimer. May the company continue to thrive for the company's sake as well as that of the community.[72]

The economic slowdown and recession following the stock market collapse of 1929 had a long-term effect on the well-being of the Ottenheimer business as well as the economy in general. On October 17, 1958, in connection with reparations, the Landratsamt für die Wiedergutmachung (State Office for Reparations) in Stuttgart sent an inquiry to the municipality of Süssen concerning taxation of the firm. *Gemeindeamtmann* Häfele (the reinvented Gemeindepfleger or municipal treasurer from the Nazi years) responded on October 24, 1958, providing a record of the corporate tax which the Ottenheimers paid from 1930–37, in other words, until Aryanization of the company. Based on this information, it wasn't until 1935 that the company again showed a gross income of RM 69,610, and a taxable income of RM 33,830 at 17 percent, netting the municipality RM 5,751.10.[73]

Environmental issues as well as financial ones preoccupied the Ottenheimer company.[74] They proposed to install a sewage treatment plant at Landstrasse no. 17 to treat factory sewage flowing into the river Lauter.[75] On February 21, 1925, Ignaz Heinzmann, a farmer, spoke against the sewage treatment plant, but the city council permitted the installation.[76] Similarly, a debate took place in 1925 concerning sewage from flush toilets also flowing into the river Lauter. A questionnaire reveals that in March 1925 there was one flush toilet and one latrine, neither shared a common waste depository with the factory and office building. Ten people worked in the office. "The sewage is treated in the treatment plant . . . and then flows into the Lauter. Permitted by the river police on February 10, 1925."[77] A report of the Oberamt Geislingen to the mayor's office in Klein-Süssen, dated March 25, 1930, states that on November 8, 1929, the sewage system of the Ottenheimer A.G. passed inspection. The report adds that "the toilet sewage should also pass through the treatment plant, in order to allow for a more thorough decay of the factory sewage." Correspondence between the company and the Oberamt on this issue is extant. There is renewed communication by the Ministry Division for District and Corporate Administration to the Oberamt Geislingen on account of the sewage from the second cesspool. Changes are suggested, and on October 5, 1933, the Oberamt reports that "the sewage from the second cesspool is now running into the sewage entrance for industrial waste."[78]

On January 29, 1926, the city council members revisited the Ottenheimer promise to build a third two-family house, and possibly a fourth and fifth. In the minutes of July 12, 1926, the city council noted that the Ottenheimer firm built the apartments at Donzdorfer Strasse with considerable support (in the form of loans) from the municipality and thus had the responsibility to help alleviate the local housing shortage by building a total of four to five two-family homes as apartments.[79]

Since the Ottenheimer firm was also a landlord, the question of rent came up repeatedly in the city council despite the fact that the Ottenheimers had paid back the municipality's loan. On August 6, 1926, the city council returned to the topic of rent from the July 12 meeting and decided to have the municipal rental office regulate the rents for the Ottenheimer apartments,[80] further distancing the houses from the firm.

In 1928 the topic of water preoccupied the dealings with the municipality. On January 13 a house line of 90 mm (3.6 inches) in diameter extending from Donzdorferstrasse to the Ottenheimer factory was requested. On October 24, as well as on December 21, 1928, the company petitioned for a reduction in the water rate for 1928 because other mass users of the group were paying a lower rate.[81] On December 21 it was decided "to charge users who used more than 1,000 cbm [cubic meters] water during 1928 12 pfennig instead of 15 pfennig for every additional cbm," and to introduce a staggered rate from 1929 on.[82] Water rates (a big issue for a company that processes yarn in varying stages) were once more debated in 1931,[83] dragging on from September 4, 1931, to May 18, 1934. In 1934, the company paid only 6.5 pfennig per cbm for the use of 30,000 cbm of water.[84] The final transaction between the firm and the municipality before Aryanization also dealt with water. At that time the Nazi-appointed Mayor Saalmüller notified the Mechanische Weberei Gebrüder Ottenheimer that it would no longer be granted a special water rate.[85]

On May 27, 1930, the *Ortsbaulinie* (borderline) for the area in which municipal construction was permitted, and which ran through the Ottenheimer property, was eliminated, as the property now belonged to the Ottenheimers for future development.[86] Interestingly, only recently did some businesses build in this area, and still today there is a large patch of undeveloped land between the factory and the railroad bridge that connects the two sections of Süssen on both sides of the tracks.

### Firma Mechanische Weberei Süssen Gebrüder Ottenheimer under the Nazis

In 1933 the Gebrüder Ottenheimer firm employed 133 workers. On September 15, 1933, the two parts of Süssen were united according to the Nazi plan. On September 16, 1933, a special edition of the local newspaper showcased Süssen industry, including the Mechanische Weberei Süssen, though "Gebrüder Ottenheimer" was not used in the heading. The text reads,

> Mechanische Weberei Süssen. Josef Ottenheimer, father of the current own-
> ers Max and Alfred Ottenheimer, in 1862 became a partner with his brother,
> who founded the firm in 1854. Josef Ottenheimer was one of the first stu-
> dents of the Reutlinger Webschule, which was able to celebrate its 75th an-
> niversary a few years ago. The factory, which is located right next to the
> railroad tracks and which is *modern and spacious,* produces cotton fabric.
> The company has its own bleaching operation, dye works, and equipment.
> They currently employ about 120 workers. Their main territory for distribu-
> tion is within Germany. They have enough business to run the machines
> at full capacity. In the past few years, employment in the textile industry
> has been bad; for the past few months there seems to be something of an
> improvement. Sound management by the owners avoided layoffs, even in
> times of economic depression, a fact that is commendable. It should also be
> noted that the company actively contributed to relieve the shortage in hous-
> ing through the construction of a number of small apartments.[87]

In 1947 a local writer noted, "Following World War I, the weaving business added a bleach operation, a dye operation, and a department for manufacturing finished goods. In 1936 115 workers processed 250 tons of cotton yarn using 180 of *the most modern looms.*"[88] This was a slight decrease in employees from 1933.

The company had a few more dealings with the municipality. In 1935 they requested permission to be connected to the main electricity supply line. A letter from the Neckarwerke Aktien-Gesellschaft in Esslingen am Neckar of January 24, 1935, shows that the company contacted the Bür-germeisteramt (mayor's office) in Süssen about connecting them to their *10KV Netz.* "The plan is to lay a high voltage cable from the transformer building no. 88/3 to the transformer station of the above firm. This station will be newly constructed at the factory. The cable will be 80 cm below the surface and will be cased in sand and brick."[89] Another letter from the Württembergische Wirtschaftsministerium (State Interior Office) to the Oberamt Geislingen dated June 13, 1935, stated that this process had been completed.[90]

That the political direction had changed was publicly discernible. Al-ready on November 10, 1934, the joint and Nazi-approved city council voted to delete Heinestrasse and Ottenheimerstrasse from the street name index, "since they are merely rural paths," and decided "henceforth to use only their numerical designations." Not until 1938, after the Ottenheimer business had been Aryanized and the family had left Süssen, did the town gather the courage to be honest about the reason for the name change. On July 8, 1938, the former Heine and Ottenheimer streets received new names. The Ottenheimerstrasse was now called Fabrikstrasse and Heinestrasse was renamed Scharnhorststrasse, "because the eternalization of a Jewish name is no longer justifiable."[91] Not even in the 1980s, when Süssen decided to name two alleys for the Langs and the Ottenheimers, did they reverse the Nazi decision. Fabrikstrasse continues to run by the prominently visible former Ottenheimer complex while neighborhood side streets in the vicinity are named for the Ottenheimers and the Langs.

An entry in the Handelsregister Abteilung Gesellschaftsfirmen (Trade Register, Section for Corporations) for Firma Gebrüder Ottenheimer A.G. in Süssen, dated July 16, 1935, has to do with the *Gesetz über Umwandlung von Kapitalgesellschaften* (law for the transformation of capital corporations) of July 5, 1934, a Nazi measure that affected the Ottenheimer firm as well as many others. The entry reads, "During a regular annual meeting on May 10, 1935, the base capital of RM 400,000 was reduced to RM 150,000. The devaluation occurred in that ordinary shares of the corporation with a face value of RM 250,000 that were owned and in possession of the corporation were collected and destroyed. . . . The base capital of RM 150,000 is divided into 750 fully vested ordinary shares issued to the owner with a face value of RM 200 each [totaling RM 150,000]. Each share is worth one vote."[92]

In 1937, the 1934 Law for the Transformation of Capital Corporations further affected the Ottenheimer business. An entry in the *Handelsregister* of the Amtsgericht (lower court) Geislingen/Steige of December 2, 1937, reveals that the company had convened a shareholders meeting on November 22, 1937. At this meeting it was decided to transform the *Aktiengesellschaft* (corporation) into an *offene Handelsgesellschaft* (*O.H.G.*, or privately held firm) with the new name, Firma Mechanische Weberei Süssen Gebrüder Ottenheimer, headquartered in Süssen, so that the corporation could be dissolved.[93] From here it was only a matter of time before the Ottenheimers would be completely excluded from the German economy.

The Firma Mechanische Weberei Süssen Gebrüder Ottenheimer was Aryanized on December 31, 1937. The *Geislinger Zeitung* wrote on August 12, 1950, that the company had been sold "long before World War II,"[94] but in reality, it was sold in 1937 because of Nazi pressure. Although the

Ottenheimers were not directly forced to sell their property, as the Langs were, Alfred Ottenheimer and his brother Max understood the signs of the times and acted accordingly. This preemptive move on their part benefited Max and family somewhat, less so Alfred and his family. Max and family lived past 1945 and carried on vigorous reparations negotiations after World War II, while Alfred died and Luise was murdered by the Nazis.

The new owners were Johannes Abt, *Güterbeförderung* (transport company), Süssen, and Eugen Weidmann, *Kaufmann* (businessman), effective January 1, 1938. According to the Grundbuch volume 1105, section 1, "the non-Aryan company, Firma Mechanische Weberei Süssen Gebrüder Ottenheimer" sold, "on January 3, 1938, their business for 720,000 RM."[95] The property consisted of "lot no. 295, vegetable garden behind the house (no. 87); lot no. 296, vegetable garden in front of the house (no. 87); lot no. 87 house, yard adjacent to street to Donzdorf; lot no. 138, house, yard adjacent to street to Donzdorf; lot no. 297, empty land, rail connection at Kreuz; lot no. 299, vegetable garden at Kreuz adjacent to street to Donzdorf; lot no. 286, field 'die Falbenäcker'; no. 187, house; no. 188, house; no. 189, western yard; lot no. 298/2, orchard and commercial track area; lot no. 266, orchard; lot no. 185/2, grassy meadow, valued at RM 250,000." In addition, the Ottenheimers also sold the machines and other items valued at RM 150,000 (for a total of RM 400,000). This was not the total value of the business, only the tangible assets.

Paragraph 5 of the *Kaufvertrag* stated, "The transfer of the property and all other items sold, including rights, takes place on January 3, 1938." The sales contract further stipulated that the seller was to deposit RM 1,000 each into accounts for workers Thomas Henn, *Webermeister* Süssen, and Georg Kessler, *Weber* in Süssen, for construction of a house with the Bausparkasse Leonberg.

Paragraph 17 detailed that the two partners of the Firma Mechanische Weberei Süssen Gebrüder Ottenheimer must desist from opening or operating a business that will in any way compete with this business for five years after the transfer of the business. Other conditions of interest included paragraph 14, which describes the inclusion of a patent, and paragraph 23, which discusses the transfer of "any company secrets" to the new owners. The seller is further bound in paragraph 19 "to send a letter together with the buyer to all customers, suppliers and other businesses in their field, informing them of the sale."

It was certainly in the interest of the Ottenheimers to conclude this transaction as quickly as possible. The Lang situation is instructive as to the way things went later. The total sale price was RM 720,000.[96] Presumably the buyers did not have RM 720,000 in cash on hand. The seller, the Firma Mechanische Weberei Süssen Gebrüder Ottenheimer, thus advanced to the buyers RM 175,000 by mortgaging the property.

On January 3, 1938, the notary in Donzdorf sent a notice to the Landesfinanzamt Steueraussenstelle Stuttgart, the state revenue office, stating,

> The non-Aryan business Firma Mechanische Weberei Gebrüder Ottenheimer in Süssen sold on December 6, 1937, the company with the above name to the Firma Mechanische Weberei Süssen Weidmann & Co. in Süssen for RM 720,000. In order to be able to pay the purchase price on the due date, January 1, 1938, the buyer had to take out a loan. . . . In order not to delay the approval of the loan, the partners who are the sellers agreed to debit the property with RM 175,000 payable to the Württembergische Bank. . . . [P]ersonally liable [for the debt] is the Firma Mechanische Weberei Süssen Weidmann & Co. in Süssen.[97]

This debt was paid off in 1940. A further Grundbuch entry of May 20, 1938, notes that the "first purchase option" for the Ottenheimer property no. 266, meadow *in der langen Halde,* has been nullified "as it is no longer relevant."[98] Aryanization superseded all else.

The final document in the reparations concerning the Süssen business was dated May 19, 1950, following the court's *Schlussbericht* (closing report) of May 17, 1950. The Firma Mechanische Weberei Süssen, Weidmann & Co., Süssen, committed to a payment of DM 650,000 in return for the cessation of any future claims on the business by the Ottenheimer family.[99]

A number of Ottenheimer family members were able to emigrate. Reparations documents from 1948 show Sana Ottenheimer (her husband Salomon had died in 1933) and both of their daughters, Lore Kadden, born in Göppingen on June 12, 1920, and Bianca Auguste Simon, born July 18, 1905, also in Göppingen, living in New York. Lore has one child, and Bianca has a son, Walter, born in Stuttgart in 1936.[100]

Until April 2007 I was not aware of any other correspondence involving the Ottenheimers. During a visit to Jerusalem I searched the Yad Vashem database and discovered that seventy-nine pages of Ottenheimer reparations documents were located in the State Archive in Ludwigsburg. When

I requested these files in Ludwigsburg a month later, the archive director pointed out that there were a number of other reparations files for the Ottenheimers as well as some for the Langs.[101] These documents have helped considerably in filling in the Ottenheimer story.

The Ludwigsburg documents also disclose the drama of the loss of Alfred and Luise's house in Göppingen and reveal the shabby way in which the Ottenheimers were treated. The initial sales contract for the Alfred Ottenheimer house at 14 Schumannstrasse in Göppingen was drawn up on March 5, 1938, long before Kristallnacht. The contract stipulated that "the seller promises to vacate the sold property no later than January 2, 1939, but may move out earlier, provided he notifies the buyer four weeks in advance."[102] However, Alfred Ottenheimer was ill. In May 1938, he moved from Göppingen to the spa town of Baden-Baden, where he died on June 14.[103] He is buried in the Jewish section of the Göppingen municipal cemetery (no. 92a). His wife, Luise née Kaufmann, born February 16, 1889 in Kirchheim/Bolanden, Palatine, was moved—Werner Ottenheimer says "*sie wurde gegangen*"—to Stuttgart. There are two dates given in different records for the move. The first is January 12, 1938, which would have been before Aryanization of their home and, if correct, while her husband Alfred was still living in Göppingen. The other date given is October 12, 1938.[104] This date would make more sense than the January date.

The reparations documents add details to this story.

The persecuted couple Alfred and Luise Ottenheimer had the one-family house [at 14 Schumannstrasse in Göppingen] built by architect Hohlbauch in Göppingen just a few years before the confiscation. . . . The house was in perfect shape. The sales contract was signed by Alfred and Luise Ottenheimer on March 5, 1938. The transfer and entry into the Grundbuch [real estate registry] happened only after the death of the persecuted Alfred Ottenheimer [on January 29, 1940]. . . . Since they were *Volljuden* [full-blooded Jews], the couple Ottenheimer belonged to the *israelitische Religionsgemeinschaft* in Göppingen. They belonged to the group of persons who were directly subjected to persecution by the German Nazi regime due to their race and religion. I do not know on what basis the sales price was negotiated. The agreed-upon price was RM 49,000. It is certain that the Ottenheimers only agreed to sell the house for this price due to the pressure of the time, namely the *Preisstoppverordnung* [capping of house prices], as it cost much more than that [to build] just a few years earlier. The buyer unfairly reduced the price after the conclusion of the sale to RM 45,000.[105]

That would have been on August 18, 1939,[106] when Luise is shown as living at 51 Auenbergstrasse in Stuttgart.[107] In another document Luise's address is given as 33 Breitlingstrasse in Stuttgart.[108] Werner Ottenheimer told me that his mother was shuttled from Jewish family to Jewish family in Stuttgart until her deportation "east" in 1941. "The sales contract was authorized by order of the Württembergische Wirtschaftsminister dated April 4, 1939, on condition that the sales price was reduced to RM 45,000." Even this amount was further reduced to RM 44,000. "We are adjusting the sales contract of March 5, 1938, to RM 44,000."[109] Luise did not get the money, as it was deposited into a *Sperrkonto* (restricted account) like that of Max and Hedwig and that of the Langs in Süssen.[110] Luise died during her trials, but the circumstances are not known. The attorney for her son Werner stated, "Frau Luise Ottenheimer was deported to Riga by the Nazis in late fall of 1941 and, according to a private source, murdered shortly thereafter by the Nazis with the other Jews from the transport. No later information about her is available."[111] Luise was declared dead as of March 1942. Her name was added to her husband's tombstone in Göppingen (no. 92b).[112]

### Post-Holocaust Matters: Ottenheimer Reparations

On December 10, 1948, Ludwig Ottenheimer, Werner's uncle, applied for restitution to the Zentralanmeldeamt (central registration office) Bad Nauheim, American Zone of Germany, as Werner's representative.[113] It appears, according to the final report of August 10, 1950, that the reparations efforts did not have a positive outcome for Werner, though no reason is given.[114]

Sometime after the end of World War II, Alfred and Luise's son Richard, Werner's older brother, tried to make some sense of all that had happened. Richard had emigrated to the United States in 1937, worked for the firm of Herward-Ranger Inc., in Walpole, Massachusetts, and was an American GI.[115] There is an affidavit from a US soldier, dated December 9, 1949, that discusses Richard Ottenheimer's presence in Göppingen. Richard, who had changed his last name to Otten, requested permission of this officer to live with his detachment "for about ten or fifteen days in order that he might make an investigation concerning his mother who had previously lived in Göppingen." Richard apparently made contact with the current owner of their house, who convinced him not only that he had helped Luise "to find a home in Stuttgart," but also that Mrs. Ottenheimer's death had occurred from natural causes and that "the sale of the house . . .

was perfectly normal transaction freely and voluntarily accepted by his mother."[116] May her memory be for a blessing.

Alfred's brother, Max, and his wife, Hedwig Irma née Heimann (born September 13, 1887 in Göppingen), and one of their children, Erich Adolf (born December 29, 1915, in Stuttgart), lost their citizenship. The document for Max is extant.[117] In October 1938, before Kristallnacht, Grandma Hedwig with grandchildren Ruth and Gert emigrated, though their initial destination is not disclosed; Max and his son Erich Adolf emigrated to England on June 26, 1939, from where Erich continued to Caracas.[118] Max and Hedwig both made it to Los Angeles. Their daughter Alice Berta Rodgers also emigrated to Los Angeles.[119]

Some of the Ottenheimers vigorously pursued reparations in the late 1940s and 1950s, with considerable success. Documents from 1948 reveal that in 1930 Max bought the house at 14 Wolfstrasse from Professor Kolb for RM 33,000. After some improvements and renovations, which amounted to RM 15,000 to 18,000, the property was valued at approximately RM 48,000 to 50,000. Max lived in the house together with his wife Hedwig and their son Erich. Architect Hohlbauch, who built Alfred's house, estimated the value at RM 45,000. Max recalls that the racial and religious persecutions forced him to sell his business in early 1938. Furthermore, "After the events of November 9, 1938, there was no doubt that life for Jews in Germany was dangerous." He thus made arrangements to emigrate and succeeded in leaving for England at the end of June, 1939. He asked the Dresdner Bank to find a suitable buyer and sold his house on June 12, 1939. The amount of the sale was RM 40,000. "According to the contract, the sales price was deposited into my *Sperrkonto* with Dresdner Bank, Göppingen branch."[120] After World War II the buyer, who claimed not to have been a Nazi Party member, argued that he had spent much money on renovations and offered Max Ottenheimer a settlement of DM 20,000.[121] The final settlement of August 22, 1949, seems to have been DM 30,000.[122]

Under the category "Other," Max stated, "The authorities know in what destitute condition we had to leave the country in 1939. Everything was stolen from me; after I had already lost my citizenship in 1940, I was then also robbed of my *Liftvan* (crate) of household goods and furnishings."[123] He did not hesitate to try for restitution of these goods, and on December 6, 1948, filed a claim with the Zentralmeldeamt Bad-Nauheim, in the American Zone of Germany. The claim is sizeable. If totaled, it would have amounted to RM 300,000. Without giving an exhaustive listing, some of the losses included his bank account with the Dresdner Bank upon loss of citizenship in 1940; monies deposited with the moving company Barr, Moering & Co.; monies deposited with the travel agency Rominger in Stuttgart; and Hedwig Ottenheimer's life insurance policy with the Victoria Insurance Company in Berlin. In connection with the contents of his crate, valued at 5,000 RM, he noted, "It was auctioned off on orders of the *Oberfinanzpräsidenten* (president of the state revenue office) in Hamburg on behalf of the Gestapo."[124] Historian Götz Aly, in his book, *Hitler's Beneficiaries,* also discusses that "the practice of confiscating emigrants' belongings stuck in transit was typical throughout Germany."[125] In addition, Max Ottenheimer recorded 7 pieces of jewelry and other items of precious metal, among them 403 silver items, 26 gold items, such as table settings, dishes, decorative items, and pocket watches. The seven pieces of jewelry belonged to Hedwig.

In these documents, we also get a sense of the heavy punitive taxes levied against Jews purely as a means to harass them. Max listed six different "taxes" that were directly withdrawn from his bank account, among them the *Judenvermögensabgabe* or Jewish assets tax, also called levy on Jewish wealth, totaling RM 90,250;[126] mandatory payment to the *Reichsvereinigung der Juden* (National Organization of Jews) in Stuttgart of RM 15,750; payment to Reichswirtschaftsministerium for releasing his crate RM 1,230; extortion by the Deutsche Arbeitsfront (German Labor Service) in Stuttgart RM 20,000; and *Reichsfluchtsteuer* (emigration tax) in the amount of RM 50,514.[127] All of these levies are substantiated in detail by the Rhein-Main-Bank in Stuttgart, the successor to the Dresdner Bank, as well as by Reisebüro Rominger, moving company Barr, Moering & Co., and Victoria insurance company in Berlin.[128] This shows that not all wartime records were lost, something many German offices were very quick to claim.

Max Ottenheimer, former citizen of Göppingen, and former honorary citizen of Süssen, stripped unceremoniously of his German citizenship, died on American soil on August 2, 1953. Hedwig carried on the reparations battle, even stronger than before. Her brother-in-law, Ludwig, a practicing attorney, previously in Stuttgart, now in the United States, planned to visit Stuttgart to take up the matter of reparations for Hedwig.[129] He provided a detailed sketch and description of Hedwig's jewelry, which had been prepared by Max, in connection with their insurance policy with Lloyds of London. Coverage by Lloyds ceased with the involuntary surrender of the jewelry to the Städtische Pfandleihanstalt (municipal pawn shop) Stuttgart on June 8, 1939. Among the items detailed were a pearl necklace of 111 pearls, a diamond pin, a diamond ring with onyx, a diamond ring with 2 diamonds and 10 smaller stones, a pearl ring with 12 pearls, a diamond ring that was an heirloom from her mother, another diamond ring from her mother, a diamond necklace with 4 large diamonds, a small gold Swiss watch, a gold watch with gold band, a gold watch from her mother, 2 diamond buttons, 2 gold and pearl cuff links, a gold men's watch, a gold watch chain, 2 gold necklaces, a necklace, a golden bracelet, 2 gold armbands, a brooch with amethysts, and a gold wedding band. The total value was 17,060 marks.[130] A court date was set for November 30, 1955. A report from the proceedings states that Hedwig Ottenheimer was awarded DM 14,000 in restitution for her jewelry.[131] When all was said and done, the final report from the German court, dated December 23, 1955, awarded Hedwig DM 18,500 ($4,625) for gold, silver, jewelry, stocks and bonds which in 1930s currency had amounted to RM 94,170.[132]

In 1971, on the occasion of the 900th anniversary of the first mention of Süssen in the records, the owners of Weberei Süssen, Weidmann & Co. wrote a short and sanitized summary of their business for the program.

Our company was founded in 1904 by Mr. Josef Ottenheimer from Göppingen. The *Gemeinde* Kleinsüssen at that time bestowed on him honorary citizenship. In 1938 Mr. Eugen Weidmann, previously co-owner of the Kammgarnspinnerei Süssen, bought the company and within a few years completely modernized the previously fairly outmoded collection of machines.

In 1951 a new building was erected for dyeing fabric pieces and in 1961 we installed a fully air-conditioned factory area for our looms, with adjacent bright offices. It was our goal, in addition to a modern workspace, to create dignified apartments for our workers. At this time we are building a house at the Donzdorfer Strasse with nine apartments. This house will be ready for occupancy this year. Our production is divided into weaving, dyeing, manufacture of finished goods, and manufacture via home production. We produce

1. High-quality fillings for bedding, upholstery and pillows
2. Materials for the upholstery industry
3. Synthetic materials that are used primarily for filters

We complement our collection by buying materials from other weaving businesses whose production is beyond our production capacity. We dye and improve these fabrics, or immediately turn them into articles. In this way we can manufacture these items during times when the business is slow and thereby guarantee full employment for our workers.[133]

And so life goes on, without missing a beat, even better than before. The details of the successes and the suffering of the Gebrüder Ottenheimer between 1904 and 1938 never come up.[134]

# 4     Gross-Süssen: The Lang Families, 1902–37

*Just how difficult life was in the middle of the previous [nineteenth] century can be seen from the many who emigrated to "the promised land" of America in the hope to be able to start a better life there. . . . Much was lacking during this time: poor education of the lower classes, child labor in Süssen and environment, no unemployment insurance, low wages, hence work by women and children in their home.*

        —Karl Müller Jr., *1896–1996 Sozialdemokraten in Süssen*[1]

Although Rabbi Tänzer in his history of Göppingen cites from earlier sources that there had been a Jewish community in Göppingen and Geislingen at the time of the Black Death, there is no such paper trail for Süssen.[2] This in spite of the fact that a 1926 source discusses the presence of Jews in Gross-Eislingen in 1526, just 4.97 miles west of Süssen, and 1.24 miles east of Göppingen.[3] However, it is highly likely that Jews regularly traveled to and through Gross-Süssen in pursuit of their trade, but highly improbable that any of them actually lived in Süssen. The 1735 Saalbuch contains a reference to the *Beybuch Folio* of 1704, which is based on the 1506 Saalbuch.[4] The reference states that "Joseph Vetter, tailor and *Judenzoller* (collector of Jewish taxes) built a house in the Juden Gass." Two more properties were located near the Juden Gass: those of "Antoni Joseph Gairing, Kübler, Hofraiten" and "Hannss Fezer jung, Herrschaftlich gemeinschaftlicher Soeld," both of whom were employed by the government of Württemberg. Tailor Vetter's house, and therefore the Juden Gass, were located between these two properties (Gairing and Fezer).[5] What the reference to the *Judenzoller* means is not clear. Was the tax collector (Vetter) Jewish or did he collect taxes from Jews for Württemberg? The exact location of the Juden Gass is also unclear. It is highly likely that it was at or near the main street by the Schweinsbach (a creek), at the western end of town, which marked the border between the Imperial City of Ulm and Württemberg, as is signified by two historical corner or border stones.[6] Historical sources reveal that tailor Vetter's house sported the emblem of

Württemberg, the "Hochfürstlich Württembergische Wappen," with the notice "Here the guard detail of the count of Württemberg begins and ends."[7] Until 1810, the guard detail for a party traveling from point A to point B was crucial to a safe journey. A source from 1770 tells us about the following procedures for merchants traveling to and from the Frankfurt fair twice a year. "Prior to the Easter and fall fairs, the imperial cities of Ulm and Augsburg requested from the Count of Württemberg safe passage for their merchants."[8] Augsburg had one of the oldest Jewish communities in Swabia, and based on our knowledge of Glückel of Hameln's extensive travels in the seventeenth century, one may assume that some of these merchants passing through Gross-Süssen were Jews.[9]

> Upon receiving their orders, the guard detail of the Imperial City of Ulm assembled at a certain time in their place. The Geislingen guard detail [Ulm] accompanied the merchants from Geislingen to Süssen where they were met by the Württemberg guard detail at the Schweinsbach border. The Württemberg guardsman who lived in Süssen watched for them. At last both groups arrived and paraded. Following a festive ceremony, the merchants were passed on to the protection of the Württemberg detail. They, in turn, continued with their wards to Göppingen, where they were issued a letter of safe conduct for their journey through Württemberg. On the way back from the fair the merchants were handed over to the Ulm guard detail with the same ceremony.[10]

Gross-Süssen always was a farming village. Until about thirty years ago, nearly every house in the village had a stable with a few cows or goats for milk and the proverbial dung heap in front of the house. Farm animals were a necessity. For this reason Süssen would have been an excellent district for cattle dealers. However, there were no cattle dealers in Süssen until Jakob Lang arrived in town in 1902. Farmers did things the way they always had. If they had cash they did business, if they did not, they abstained. Credit was an unfamiliar concept. The Langs were the only cattle dealers until their deportation. Neighbors across the street went into the business only after there were no more Jews in town.[11]

The village of Ernsbach, in the Öhringen district, was the home of the Lang family. It is located several mountain ranges beyond Süssen. Even today it takes about two hours to drive from one town to the other via the winding country roads, over hills with breathtaking views and through picturesque villages. Nestled among luscious vineyards, Ernsbach is located "three walking hours" or nine miles from the district capital of Öhringen. It had a Jewish presence beginning in 1680, when the local *Schirmherr* (lord), Count Wolfgang Julius von Hohenlohe, allowed as many as twelve Jewish families to settle in the village.[12] Yet in 1702 there were only three families left. The number must have increased again, for by 1721 Jews were no longer allowed to buy additional houses, thereby curbing the influx of Jews into the village.[13] In 1828, a time when the Kingdom of Württemberg actively tried to assimilate the Jews in their territories, the Jews of Ernsbach, among them the Lang forebears, took on family names.[14] In 1834 the Jewish community of Ernsbach built a new school building.[15] The Jewish population increased to 224 in 1843[16] (233 in 1844 in Rauser),[17] about 30 percent of the population. In 1865 Ernsbach had a synagogue and a cantor and a religious school with 34 pupils.[18] Thereafter the Jews of Ernsbach also left this rural area for life in the city, and their numbers steadily decreased to 40 in 1910 and to 2 by 1933.[19]Although the Jewish community was not dissolved officially until 1925, local residents told my associates and me on May 28, 2002, that the synagogue was no longer in use after 1920 but had been used as a fire station.[20] Since the end of the Holocaust, the building has been used for special events.

The men in the Lang family were mostly businessmen. The Langs have a long family history in Ernsbach, with about five generations documented in the Jewish cemetery of the region. The patriarch of the clan was Isak Feis, whose Hebrew name was Eljakim bar Uri Schraga, a peddler from Ernsbach, who married Bela, and sired one son who lived to adulthood. Although I was not able to locate dates for Isak Feis, his son, Falk (Felkle) Feis (Lang), was born to Isak's wife on April 17, 1777. Falk also made his living as a peddler and served as a Beysass.[21] His marriage to Madel Krautheim, "a hard-working woman, Matel," produced three sons, Isak Falk Lang, born in 1771; Abraham Falk, who died in 1835; and Feis Falk Morgenroth, born in 1768; as well as a daughter, Bela, born in 1803, who died in 1833 without having ever been married. Professions listed for them range from peddler to salesman to real estate salesman. All three sons married and had children of their own. "A perfect and honest man, Isak Falk Lang [Itzik bar Eljakum]," who married "a brave woman," Frummet Isak, in addition to being a peddler, also served as Beysass to the community. It was "honorable" Löb Lang, born in 1801, "a perfect and honest man," son of "the honorable" Isak Falk Lang, "of blessed memory," and his wife Zipora Bauer, "a noble woman, a beloved mother, Zirle," who died in 1871, and were the parents to Samuel Lang, the patriarch of the Süssen branch of the family.

Samuel (Shmuel) who was one of five children, was born in Ernsbach on September 19, 1845, and died in Süssen on April 18, 1925. He was a tallish and stout man who dressed modestly. His profession is listed as *Handelsmann* (business man); he successively had three wives. Adelheid Victor, born on January 12 1847, was "an honest and cultured woman," who "died with a good name" on June 20, 1887. She bore or carried nine children, one of whom was Jakob, who moved to Süssen in 1902. Samuel's second wife, Fanny Hirsch, was born on April 16, 1858, and died on March 8, 1891. She bore Samuel two children and died in childbirth. Veile, as she was known, "from the holy community of Ernsbach, died . . . with a good name." Both children also seem to have died at or soon after birth. In 1892 Samuel married a third time. His bride was Regine or Rachele Heilbronner from Fellheim, born June 10, 1859.

Regine is lauded as being "a brave woman, crown of her home . . . with a good name." She is the mother of Lazarus Louis, born February 2, 1893 in Ernsbach and deported in 1941 to Riga Kaiserswald, where he died, and Leopold, born November 2, 1895, in Ernsbach and deported in 1941 to Latvia; he was declared dead on May 6, 1951. Louis and Leopold are two of the main figures in this study.[22]

In the early twentieth century, Jakob, who was born in Ernsbach on November 23, 1873, and died in Stuttgart on May 4, 1918, left his hometown and migrated southeast, to Göppingen, which at that time had a sizeable Jewish community. Jakob appears to have been slight of build, but handsome. One source describes him as often sickly, hence his death at age 45 was perhaps not a surprise. We know nothing about Jacob's life in Göppingen. In 1902 he moved 6.2 miles further east, to Gross-Süssen, where he became engaged to Fanny Pressburger, daughter of cattle dealer Samuel Sigmund Pressburger in Rexingen. Fanny was eight years his senior and the sister of his brother-in-law Sigmund, who was married to Jakob's sister, Frieda Lang. His address on the engagement announcement in the *Göppinger Zeitung* is listed as Süssen/Göppingen.[23] When he married Fanny on August 18, 1902, the wedding announcement listed his residence only as Süssen.[24] Their first street address in Gross-Süssen is not known.

The death of Jakob Mühlich, Hauptstrasse 45 (property no. 15 on lot no. 15), provided the desired opportunity to acquire a spacious property at a choice location. In 1905 Jakob and Fanny bought a house on the main thoroughfare between Göppingen and Geislingen. On June 16, 1905, Mühlich's widow, "Anna Barbara, née Fischer, and the other heirs sold property no.15: a two-story home and courtyard; no.15a: a barn; and no.15b:

a *Hinterhaus* [another two-story house] with a stable and shed; and with it also the use of properties nos. 224/1, 224/2, and 1580; as well as the use of property 1690/7 so long as building no.15 stands, to Jakob and Fanny, née Pressburger, 50 percent each for 19,000 marks."[25] Fanny was a full partner in the purchase. During the Nazi period, this house became known in the vernacular as the *Judenhaus*, a type of shorthand among locals that needed no further explanation.[26] We do not have a picture of the complete Lang property, but we do have the plans. The main house (no. 15) is still standing. Characterized as a *Fachwerkhaus* (wooden beam house) in one document,[27] all of the pictures extant show it painted. One picture shows a footbridge from the front door across the ditch that ran the length of the street from east to west. The garden in front of the house has given way to the widening of the Hauptstrasse, and the front door and steps have been removed and replaced by one window. The barn (no. 15a), which was indeed a *Fachwerkhaus*, has been torn down. The garage had not yet been built in 1905; it was constructed in 1932.

Few details are known about Jakob and his family during their life in Gross-Süssen. He had many siblings and stepsiblings. His father, Samuel, lived in Ernsbach until 1925. Fanny and Jakob had three children—Alma, born June 11, 1903, Adolf, called Otto, born July 12, 1904, and Lina, born December 23, 1908. In a family portrait of uncertain date, perhaps shortly before Jakob's death in 1918, the slight but handsome Jakob, dressed in suit and bow tie, is surrounded by his loving family. He casually drapes his right arm over the back of Fanny's chair. Fanny, pretty in face and elegantly dressed, sits upright, almost regally, facing the camera, with her dark hair parted in the middle and pulled back in a bun. Alma, on the far right, and Lina next to her, are dressed in demure, matching long-sleeved flowered dresses. Perhaps age fourteen and nine (or thirteen and eight), they have dark braided hair. Adolf, called Otto, a slender, good-looking young man in a suit and tie, stands between his father and sisters, at perhaps bar mitzvah age, thirteen or twelve.[28]

Jakob is first listed in the municipal records of Gross-Süssen in 1906. On August 6 and 9, respectively, Mr. Bühler, a butcher and the owner of the Hirsch inn, and Jakob Lang were notified of an official ordinance concerning the record-keeping of purchases and sales that was of importance to horse and cattle dealers.[29] The first recorded business transaction took place on March 8, 1906, when Otto Eisele, a farmer, recorded the purchase of a *Kalbel* from Jakob Lang, cattle dealer in Süssen, for 350 marks.[30] Eisele noted in his business ledger that he paid 100 marks down and would pay the rest "whenever I can afford to," that is, whenever he would take in the necessary cash, up to a year. Jakob Lang confirmed receipt of the 100 marks down payment in farmer Eisele's notebook.[31] There is no lack of trust here! This kind of arrangement was almost as good as a handshake. By 1910 Jakob had a telephone (his number was 17) and he regularly publicized his "French horses" in the regional newspaper, the *Göppinger Zeitung*.[32] There also was a regional horse dealers insurance company, the Bezirks-Pferde-Versicherungs-Verein, in Geislingen which was open for membership to horse owners in the district. It was an insurance company that compensated owners for the loss of their animals and provided other types of support.[33]

Several times during the years 1908 and 1912,[34] and again in 1913 and 1917,[35] there is a notation in the Gross-Süssen Gemeinderats-Protokoll (minutes of the city council meeting) that Jakob had violated some unspecified statute for which he was cited and had to pay a small fine. The infraction could not have been too serious and was probably connected to permits of some kind or rules to do with cattle dealing. On November 10, 1908, the minutes reflect that "Jakob Lang installed two heating stoves without permit. There are no objections."[36]

On December 6, 1912, the city council minutes reflect that "Jakob Lang, cattle dealer, born November 23, 1873, in Ernsbach, requested to be granted citizenship" in Gross-Süssen. There were no obstacles or objections, and the city council granted Jakob Lang the right of *Bürger* (citizen) "in this community."[37] This was not only an honor and a privilege but a necessity for full participation in the business and civic life of the town. Sharing in the responsibilities of the village by serving in office or contributing to the welfare of the community in other ways went a long way towards success in business.

By the first decade of the twentieth century, various efforts of the Socialists who had organized in Süssen in 1896 bore fruit, and several of the grievances they had pointed out had been redressed. Workers now enjoyed an eight-hour workday, higher wages and health insurance, raising the morale of the workers. The district now had a number of political, cultural, and social welfare organizations, including two district health insurance organizations, the Bezirkskrankenpflegeversicherung (District Health Care) and, from 1910 on, the Bezirkskrankenkasse (District Health Insurance). Both list Jakob Lang as an employer. For most of the years for which we have records, between eight and eleven employees are listed for the Lang business. For 1914, 1915, and 1916 there are registers of employees who worked for Jakob Lang, insured by the Allgemeine Ortskrankenkasse (General Local Health Insurance Company) Geislingen an der Steige.[38] Most of them seem to have been short-term employees or day laborers, either for the household, the children, or the business.

Another document, the *Verzeichnis der Dienstboten, Lehrlinge, Gehilfen und Arbeiter von Gross-Süssen* (registry of service personnel, including apprentices, farm hands and laborers in Gross-Süssen) from 1913–30, lists a total of 132 employees of the Lang families. These records indicate that Jakob, Louis, and Leopold were each separate employers, something borne out in the reparations documents. Most of the employees were temporary man- or maidservants who helped with housework, cattle and horse care, and farm work. An indication of how hardworking a family the Langs were is that Leopold, Jakob's younger half brother, already worked for Jakob as a *Handelsgehilfe* (clerk) in 1913, at age eighteen.[39] Child labor was still common before World War I, but the records do not indicate that Jakob employed anyone of such tender age.[40]

A *Kundenliste* (index of customers) for the various businesses in Gross-Süssen from 1918 lists Jakob Lang, self-employed, as customer no. 257, in a population of less than three thousand. He bought his groceries from Mr. Grupp, the green grocer. According to the information, he fed six people, five of them older than six years, and one younger than six.[41] Who this young child may have been has not been previously established, although post-Holocaust correspondence gives us a clue. The archives contain a letter from Mayor Eisele about Hans Baer, stating that he was born illegitimately to Hilda (Hermine) Lang, Jakob's sister, on December 4, 1917.[42] In those days out-of-wedlock pregnancies were severely frowned upon, no matter the ethnic or religious group. Hermine married Pauline Baer's brother, Alfred, on July 2, 1920, and the mayor surmises that Alfred might have adopted Hans at that time.[43] It is therefore possible that Herminchen, as her niece calls her later, came to Süssen to escape from the inquisitive eyes and ears of her Ernsbach family and friends. The deportation list in the *Gemeindechronik* (municipal chronicle) claims that Hans's place of birth was Pforzheim, not Süssen. If Hans was born in Pforzheim, it is conceivable that Hermine came to Süssen for a while with her baby and returned to Ernsbach after some time. The six people living in Jakob's family in 1918—and I assume that that would have been before Jakob's death on

May 4—could have been Jakob, Fanny, Alma, Lina, Hilda, and baby Hans. Perhaps Otto, at age thirteen, had gone to live with relatives as Lina later does. Conversely, if the *Kundenliste* is from after Jakob's death, Hans and Hilda and all the Lang children may have been staying with Fanny. Louis, Jakob's half-brother, married Pauline Baer on July 6, 1920, just four days after Hermine and Alfred's marriage.

Jakob's half-brother Louis's birth was preceded by the birth of twelve half-siblings, not all of whom lived. Little is known about Louis's childhood in Ernsbach, or that of his younger brother Leopold. In a picture of Louis after World War I, when he was already middle-aged, he is tall and slender, a dapper, elegantly attired man with a walking stick and a pocket watch. Leopold seems to have been in many ways quite different from Louis. When World War I broke out, both Louis and Leopold joined the 1,674 other Jews[44] from Württemberg and Hohenzollern who served their country in battle. Louis was a grenadier, serving with Grenadier Regiment No. 119. He was wounded and received the Iron Cross Second Class as well as the Württemberg Silberne Militär-Verdienstmedaille (Silver Military Service Medal).[45] Leopold served as a Pioneer in Pionier Battalion No. 13. He, too, received the Iron Cross Second Class as well as the Württemberg Silberne Militär-Verdienstmedaille.[46] Both also received an Austrian decoration, the Österreichische Verdienst Medaille für Frontkämpfer III. Klasse (Austrian Service Medal for Front Soldiers Third Class), which is not listed in the booklet honoring Jewish World War I soldiers from Württemberg and Hohenzollern.[47] A precious picture of Louis and Leopold as soldiers in World War I exists, with their plain uniforms, high boots, and caps.[48] The picture is captioned, "An Unexpected Reunion on the Battle Field in the World War 1914–1918." It was addressed to Fräulein Sophie Ottenheimer in Rexingen, where their half-sister Frieda was married, and dated September 18, 1918. Jakob had already died at that point, and World War I would end on November 11, 1918. The message says, "To all Loved Ones, best wishes from a completely healthy Louis." Another picture shows a group picture of wounded soldiers, among them Leopold. And finally, a proud Leopold displays the imperial uniform and the pointed steel helmet of the Grenadiers. Hugo recollected in 2002, "My father and uncle fought in the battle of Tannenberg with Hindenburg. That was one of the larger battles; after that they were sent to France."[49] The Battle of Tannenberg certainly was one of the major battles of World War I within the first month of the Great War.[50] In John Keegan's words, "[it] became for the Germans their outstanding victory of the conflict."[51] If Germany's fortunes had continued in that direction, they might have won the war. Fortunately both of the Lang brothers returned from active duty.

Much later, in 1938, Louis and Leopold were included in the book of World War I war heroes from Gross-Süssen, the *Eiserne Buch* (honor roll).[52] This occurred after they had already lost their license to trade in cattle and their livelihood and were in the process of losing their home to the Nazis as well. The reason the book came about at this late date is that towns were being pressured by the *Reichs- und Preussische Minister*, Dr. Frick, to demonstrate their patriotism either by publishing their version of an *Eisernes Buch*, or by keeping a town *Chronik* (history). The Gemeinderats-Protokoll of December 14, 1937, reflects that "during his tenure [in 1918] the mayor of the former *Gemeinde* of Klein-Süssen, Mayor [August] Storr,[53] accepted an *Eisernes Buch* from two local firms in which the names of the soldiers on active duty and those killed in action are recorded." One of the local firms sponsoring the publication were the Ottenheimer brothers, discussed in the previous chapter. "This book of honor is meant as a manifest sign of thanks to all those who helped to save our dear fatherland and to preserve our precious homeland. The former village of Gross-Süssen also owns such a book, but it has not been completed. Therefore the question arises whether it wouldn't be better to catch up on missed opportunities as quickly as possible."[54]

Perhaps the town that didn't have such a treasure was not seen as being sufficiently patriotic. Representatives of publishing houses, such as G. Hirth Publishers in Munich and Karl Höhn in Ulm, helped several other towns in this region to produce such a World War I honor roll by collecting, evaluating, and inscribing the desirable honorees in the book. The cost would depend on the number of participants, who in turn would be determined according to the chosen parameters.[55] The parameters must have been drawn fairly broadly, for Louis and Leopold, who did not live in Süssen in 1914 (although Leopold worked there) and served for their hometown Ernsbach,[56] not for Süssen, were nevertheless included. The regional newspaper carried the city council minutes verbatim. "The city council members admire the creation of the honor roll of [World War I] soldiers that G. Hirth Publishers in Munich produced for the municipality of Süssen. All who served during the Great War 1914–18 have been entered in this book. It is already now an informative source of reference for the younger generation, and will be even more so in years to come. The cost of RM 456 is being paid by the municipality."[57] The schizophrenia of the time is reflected in the fact that the book was completed and presented to the municipality during the same meeting of the city council in which the name Ottenheimerstrasse was changed to Fabrikstrasse because the "eternalization of a Jewish name can no longer be justified."[58]

On May 4, 1918,[59] while Louis and Leopold were at the front, their half-brother, Jakob, a civilian twenty years their senior, died in Stuttgart, leaving behind a widow with minor children and a business. Though there was a mention of illness, the death was apparently unexpected and the cause is not known. Jakob is buried in the Jewish section of the Göppingen municipal cemetery (no. 21). In a eulogy in the form of a poem, Louis and Leopold both lamented their brother's death, "at home immersed in his duties" rather than "in the noise of battle," as they were, where they were constantly in harm's way. They were keenly aware that his family had "lost their provider" and that "his loved ones are now abandoned."

### Eulogy

For our brother, Jakob Lang, Süssen,
Who died on May 4 of this year [1918]

We certainly are in danger
Here, deep in enemy territory.
We lay down our lives,
That is God's Will.

However, the pain of death did not strike us,
But our dear brother.
His family is now deserted,
He went to his eternal rest.

He did not die in battle,
But at home carrying out his duties;
Hence the news hit us twice as hard,
Us two brothers [in the war].

From your life's peak period
Death snatched you,
From that time [in your life] when nothing was too far away
And no work was too much for you.

Now your loved ones stand by your grave
And cry [over the loss] of their breadwinner,

And we are only able to send our love
As a great and noble consolation.

The task of the war
Which demands more from us all,
Brought you the sting of death;
That was God's Will.

In spite of your illness
You were in charge of all your affairs;
"I bet we'll find a way,"
You used to say.

You always served as an example
As a model in your family,
Even if the skies were dark and dreary,
You always managed to cheer things up.

But the test which God sends us all
Did not spare you;
Illness, this terrible word,
Befell you.

It tore you irrevocably
From your path of happiness.
Only too early and too young,
Your stay [on this earth] was a short one.

May God comfort your loved ones
Who were devoted to you.
Only God can bring them consolation
In the valley [of death].

Human consolation which is small and weak
Seldom suffices.
Only God's comfort will last,
Human comfort is transient.

Rest now peacefully in your grave
At which we sadly stand.
We hope that it will not happen to us for a long time,
But eventually we will also have to die.

We will be called from this world
Of toil and of sorrow.
All the money in the world will not help us
If our turn comes tomorrow.

Wait, therefore, in your tomb
Until we meet again,
Until God calls us to His side
And we embark on our final journey.

Don't cry, don't suffer,
We all expect
That God will take every good human being
To His Kingdom.
    Dedicated by his brothers Leopold
    and Louis who are at the front.[60]

What should Fanny do now? A hundred years ago, it was still very difficult for a woman alone, and a widow at that, to run a large business with many employees. Father Samuel was already seventy-three years old and probably too advanced in age to move to Süssen and run Jakob's business. Although Fanny acted on her own behalf in legal matters, it is quite likely that Jakob's death led first Louis, and a few years later his brother Leopold, to Süssen to help the family out and further their late half brother's horse and cattle business.

The year of Jakob's death, Fanny Lang bought a piece of land that consisted of two fields, nos. 1639/1 and 1639/2 somewhat outside of town, in a place called Sieben Jauchert, from a farmer, Ernst Renftle, as an investment for 5,000 marks.[61] After the Nazis came to power, on June 7, 1933, Fanny transferred the property of nearly 72 are (about 8,600 square yard) to her oldest daughter, Alma, who at that time worked in Saulgau, Germany. Fanny gave as her reason that "Alma has for years supported me from her income and has been largely responsible for my being able to live according to my social status."[62] The transfer was "to compensate Alma for her support and services."[63] On August 31, 1935, Max Liffmann, Eva's brother and Alma's uncle, who at that time still lived in Düsseldorf, sought a judgment against Alma in which he claimed that she owed him money, referring to the Süssen property as collateral. On May 20, 1941, under duress from the Württembergische Wirtschaftsministerium Alma sold both fields to a local farmer (Emil Keller) for RM 1,750 through trustee Paul Guhl in Horb am Neckar.[64] "Alma Lang is a Jewess and was ordered by decree from the Württembergische Wirtschaftsministerium in Stuttgart to sell her property."[65] On July 10, 1941, Gemeindepfleger Häfele notified the Finanzamt in Geislingen that the trustee sold properties nos. 1639/1 and 2 *Acker in den Sieben Jauchert* on May 20, 1941, for RM 1,750 on behalf of "Jüdin Alma Lang in Amerika."[66] Another document mentions the sale of this property by Alma to Keller for RM 910.[67] Later it underwent the same restitution process as the Louis Lang property. The Amt für Vermögenskontrolle (Office for Property Control) instructed the Grundbuchamt in Süssen "to consider the transaction [the sale of the property to Keller] as not having taken place because it occurred on the basis of *Entziehung* [seizure]." Karl Schlecht, the trustee for Louis's and Leopold's heirs, was also Alma's representative. On March 29, 1955, the property was once more sold to the farmer Emil Keller for DM 2,800. Whether Alma actually received this amount is not known.[68]

Louis and Leopold's mother, Regine née Heilbronner, died on April 25, 1920. She is buried in the Berlichingen Verbandsfriedhof (no. 1066), a cemetery owned by several Jewish communities together. Both sons nevertheless married in 1920. This was most unusual, as Jewish custom generally calls for a one-year betrothal period as well as a prohibition on weddings during the eleven-month mourning period. Louis, who became engaged in March 1920,[69] had moved to Süssen before his engagement, as the announcement of his engagement lists his place of residence as Süssen rather than Ernsbach. That he already lived in Süssen before his marriage is also documented in the Süssen *Pferde-Zählung* (horse census) of March 1919, where Louis is listed among twenty-two horse owners with one horse, a *Fuchs* (brown horse), age five or older.[70] Louis and his bride, Pauline Baer, born December 25,1885, in Odenkirchen and died November 22, 1935, in Tübingen, were married on July 6, 1920, three months after the death of his mother. All four of Louis and Pauline's children were born in Süssen or Göppingen—Regine Ingeborg "Teddy" in 1921, Henriette "Henny" in 1922, Josef Kurt on July 7, 1924, and Siegfried "Siegi" on July 10, 1925. We do not have a picture of the family together, only pictures of the children. In contrast to their cousins Fred and Hugo, Josef Kurt and Siegi were dark-haired, and like Ruth, Ingeborg "Teddy" and Henny also had short dark hair. Pauline, like Leopold's wife Eva, gave the appearance of comfort and calm and of being good-natured.

Three years later, on August 4, 1923, Louis bought at auction the property of Juliane Schuster, née Geiger, widow of Jakob Schuster. The property, located at 31 Heidenheimer Strasse (formerly building no. 89), consisted of a house, barn, barn annex, additional section added to the house, stable building, and courtyard. As this was the time of tremendous inflation in the Weimar Republic, Louis paid 800 million (inflation) marks for the property.[71] In front of the house was a vegetable garden as well as a lawn, rows of berry bushes and fruit trees (9 are 34 square meters, about 1117 square yard), and another piece of land (property no. 61, 7 are 46 square meters, about 892 square yard). Louis—and this would be very important for a cattle dealer—also had grazing rights for a pasture of 20 are 40 square meters (property no. 2485, about 2,439 square yard).[72] On October 2, 1923, Louis applied for and received a building permit to renovate the home and to add to building no. 89 a one-story coach house as well as a one-and-a-half story stable.[73] According to the records of February 16, 1925, the renovation of the home was not carried out.[74] On May 3, 1924, Louis applied for a permit to lay a pipe of about 8 inches in diameter below the local *Ortsweg*, something less than a street or road, so that the rainwater would not accumulate in his yard but would run off into the mill canal.[75] The poor sanitation in both parts of Süssen was legendary.

There were other reasons why this was a most fortunate purchase for Louis. The property was located at the main road from Göppingen or even Stuttgart to Heidenheim, hence the name of the street. Heidenheim was a town in the same direction as, but even further north than, Weissenstein which had been made accessible by the railroad in 1901. In addition, across the street was located the inn Der Schwarze Adler, which could provide rooms for Louis's customers and stables for their horses and carriages, so that the property was in an ideal location for someone in the business of selling and trading livestock.

Probably stretched financially, Louis, on November 7, 1923, sold half of this property to Rudolf Rothschild, a cattle dealer in Göppingen, for 400 million inflation marks.[76] Rothschild also owned property in Schwäbisch Gmünd in the 1920s, so he was widely connected in the region through his business. On October 8, 1925, after inflation had been brought under control, Rothschild sold his part of the Heidenheimer Strasse property back to Louis for RM 7,500.[77] On January 31, 1924, Louis and Pauline drew up a last will and testament, according to which each owned 50 percent of all their possessions.[78] Yet only in a 1936 court document, after her death, do we learn that Pauline had brought a substantial dowry of 40,000 marks into the marriage.[79]

That the Langs and the municipality were mutually cooperative can be seen from Louis's offer, on July 11, 1924, of an even exchange for the municipal bull, which was being housed by Mr. Heinzmann. If there were a difference in weight, he, Louis, would pay the municipality for the difference. The city council decided to accept Louis Lang's offer of a bull. It was a good deal, as Louis was fully liable if anything went wrong with his bull, while the city offered no such guarantee for their bull.[80]

On July 24, 1928, Louis applied for a permit from the police department to construct a chicken coop and gasoline storage room on property no. 61 for about 300 marks. He requested permission to store approximately 100 kilograms gasoline "for [his] automobile." The family had acquired a car of the Adler make. In the late 1920s, one could not simply drive up to a gas station and fill up. Apparently the specifications were "mistakenly set too low"; instead of requesting to store 100 kilograms, he needed to request permission for two times 150 kilograms, for a total of 300 kilograms. Louis made the required changes to his plans and resubmitted them on August 22, 1928. On September 12, 1928, he received a permit "to store 300 kilograms of mineral oil, Hazardous Substance Classification I (gasoline), on property no. 61," along with detailed safety instructions. On December 12, 1928, the Württembergische Oberamt Geislingen, the district office, inquired whether *Viehhändler* (cattle dealer) Lang had built the approved gasoline storage room. The answer must have been in the affirmative, for there was an inspection on January 10, 1929, during which it was noted that the sign, "Attention, Fire Hazard," had not yet been affixed to the entrance door of the storage room. This was corrected on January 21, 1929, when a sign, "*Vorsicht, feuergefährlich*," was affixed to the door. However, on January 23, 1929, the mayor's office was reprimanded because the warning sign affixed was not adequate. The case was closed when, on February 8, 1929, Louis affixed a second sign to the door to the storage room which read, "Smoking Prohibited."[81]

Building ordinances and trading regulations were only part of the family's worries—the fear of hoof and mouth disease was ever-present. On August 14, 1929, this dreaded disease broke out in the neighboring village of Grünbach near Donzdorf. To determine its origin, the Oberamt Geislingen launched an investigation in which Louis Lang was mentioned. "The investigations of an outbreak of hoof and mouth disease in Grünbach by the district veterinarian showed the possibility that the disease may have been introduced by cattle bought from cattle dealer Louis Lang. Since we were not able to determine where Louis Lang recently bought cattle, because of Lang's current absence from Gross-Süssen, we are asking the Mayor's office in Süssen to find out whether anyone there bought cattle from cattle dealer Lang since July 27. This might be done most effectively through a public announcement [by the town crier]."[82] One person apparently did buy cattle from Louis, and on August 16, 1929, the municipality of Süssen reported to the Oberamt, "A local farmer, Johannes Clement, locksmith, bought a cow from cattle dealer Lang. It has already been examined by the district vet."[83] And given a clean bill of health, one assumes. It therefore sounds as if all was well with Louis's cattle and his cattle was not the cause of the outbreak in Grünbach. Had it been, a public announcement such as this might have been detrimental to the Langs' reputation and therefore business.

Louis's brother, Leopold Lang (Arje ben Shmuel), married even before Louis, on June 15, 1920, only two months after the death of their mother, in Rodalben, near Pirmasens, in the Saar Territory. His bride was Eva Liffmann, born November 11, 1896, in Odenkirchen, deported November 28, 1941, and declared dead May 6, 1945. An undated picture of Leopold and Eva shows a handsome Leopold and a dark beauty with velvety eyes in an elegant blouse and scarf. Eva played the piano and was cultured. One can tell here where Ruth got her dark eyes. The text on the back of the picture is revealing, for it states, "There is nothing so terrible on earth / That something good can't come of it. / The facing picture shows us / The only good thing that the war has created."[84] Indeed it had. Leopold and Eva remained in Ernsbach with father Samuel and his business. Their first two children, Manfred "Fred" and Hugo, were born in Ernsbach on August 26, 1921,[85] and April 27, 1923, respectively.[86] A picture of September 1923 shows a proud Leopold, a strong and strapping man, who is not yet as obese as he later became, and a sweet-faced, pretty and elegant Eva, with her right arm around Fred, who was two, and the newborn Hugo, not yet six months old, on her lap.[87] On March 5, 1925, the year the Ernsbach Jewish community was dissolved,[88] Leopold, a pregnant Eva, Manfred, Hugo, and patriarch Samuel, who was now eighty, moved to Süssen. Unfortunately Samuel died less than a month later, on April 18, 1925. He, too, is buried in the Jewish section of the Göppingen municipal cemetery (no. 51). A third child, Ruth Regina, was born to Leopold and Eva in Gross-Süssen on July 27, 1925.[89]

Hugo provided a rich storehouse of delightful family pictures, and one has no difficulty at all envisioning the family's life in Süssen.[90] Truly a cultured farmer, an oxymoron to be sure, Leopold, in a family portrait from 1930, sits in the grass behind his two boys, Hugo and Fred. He is a big man, and though dressed in a white shirt, there is no doubt that he is a rural resident, with work pants and boots. He is smiling and in his hand he holds a cigar. Eva sits next to him, holding five-year-old Ruth with her dolly in her lap. Eva has a sweet face, with smiling eyes and curly hair that is pulled back (in a bun?). Her slim figure is clothed in a checkered, short-sleeved dress. Ruth isn't so sure about this picture-taking, clamping her mouth shut. Wearing a white dress, she has short-cropped dark hair. Fred, the oldest, dressed in a sailor suit—a popular German way to dress boys—frowns, perhaps at the camera, and Hugo on the right seems to be lost in thought. While a smile plays around Eva's and Leopold's lips, the children are somber.[91]

Even before Leopold and family, as well as father Samuel, moved to Gross-Süssen in 1925, Louis had appealed to the town to grant Leopold permission to live with "Frau Witwe Lang," Jacob's widow. In exchange, Louis apparently promised to lend the town 1,000 marks without charging interest for the duration of one yeare. While Leopold had taken up residence on March 5, by December the town had not yet received the 1,000 marks. "Already in May of this year he was asked to pay up, but he couldn't raise the money."[92] On December 10, 1925, the city council decided by a vote of 7–4, "to take out a loan of 1,000 marks, to lend Louis Lang 1,000 marks from the municipal treasury at 15 percent interest for one year, so that Louis can lend the promised 1,000 marks to the community."[93] As there always was a housing shortage, the 1,000 marks would be used to build additional housing. The previous confirms Hugo Lang's recollection that his family, from the beginning, lived with Jakob's widow, Fanny, at Hauptstrasse. Until 1929 Louis and family lived on the property at Heidenheimer Strasse.

From June 1925 on, the Allgemeine Ortskrankenkasse in Geislingen / St. lists Louis and Leopold Lang as employers. Leopold had sixteen employees (see Table 2) and Louis had twenty-four employees as shown in Table 1.[94]

Falk Sahm, not a short-term employee, but for eight years Leopold Lang's permanent farmhand, is also listed. Sahm, born on May 6, 1870, to Salmann Löb and Nannette Sahm in Braunsbach, district Öhringen, just a short distance from Ernsbach, was single, and was also Jewish.[95] It is likely that his family knew the Lang family in Ernsbach. He worked for Leopold from April 21, 1929, until his forced relocation to the Jewish old-age home in Heilbronn-Sontheim on July 1, 1937,[96] just a short time before the

## Table 1. Louis's Employees

| Name, Residence | DOB | Occupation | Period |
|---|---|---|---|
| 1. Weckherle, Hedwig, Kuchen | Feb. 31, 1904 | Dienstmädchen (servant) | June 15, 1924– Aug. 2, 1926 and Sept. 8, 1927– Oct. 15, 1927 |
| 2. Eckert, Joh., Laichingen | May 25,1906 | Dienstknecht (servant) | February 2, 1925– August 10, 1925 |
| 3. Bauer, Klara, Spraitbach | August 11, 1901 | Maid servant | June 1, 1925– July 7, 1925 |
| 4. Pack, Johann, Fürth | September 11, 1900 | Servant | August 15, 1925– Sept. 19, 1925 |
| 5. Waibel, Erna, Gmünd | June 24, 1906 | Maid servant | October 8, 1925– Nov. 29, 1925 |
| 6. Stark, Josef, Schrobenhausen | February 15, 1895 | Servant | October 1, 1925– Nov. 15, 1925 |
| 7. Hausch, Lydia, Gross-Eislingen | June 17, 1905 | Pflegerin (nurse) | December 8, 1925–May 1, 1926 |
| 8. Lausinger, Karl, Langenau | Sept. 15, 1902 | Servant | December 8, 1925–Nov. 1, 1926 |
| 9. Röcker, Anne, Machtolsheim | January 30, 1898 | | February 25, 1926– August 1, 1926 |
| 10. Röder, Elisabeth, Gross-Süssen | March 4, 1910 | Kindermädchen (nanny) | May 1, 1926– July 15, 1926 |
| 11. Preissing, Luise, Owen T[eck] | March 20, 1907 | Nanny | July 15, 1926– Sept. 1, 1926 |
| 12. Rampf, Hedwig. Mühlhausen | Sept. 16, 1909 | Maid servant | August 1, 1926– March 31, 1927 |
| 13. Bosch, Amalie, Untersullmertingen | November 16, 1907 | Maid servant | Sept. 1, 1926– August 15, 1927 |
| 14. Thumm, Hermann, Nehrbach | May 6, 1905 | Servant | November 5, 1926– April 9, 1927 |
| 15. Rumpelmaier, Franz, Weingarten | October 25, 1896 | Servant | April 11, 1927– April 18, 1927 |
| 16. Keinat, Emma, Jebenhausen | Sept. 25, 1901 | Nanny | April 15, 1927– May 30, 1927 |
| 17. Süringer, Ignaz, Birkland | Sept. 6, 1905 | Servant | May 15, 1927– June 15, 1927 |
| 18. Schad, Hedwig, Böttingen | April 8, 1902 | Nanny | August 15, 1927– October 1, 1927 |
| 19. Walter, Josef, Weilerstoffel | September 16, 1910 | Servant | August 15, 1927– February 21, 1928 |
| 20. Helferich, Margarete, Nenningen | June 21, 1903 | Maid servant | November 1, 1927– February 1, 1928 |
| 21. Käsbeck, Fanny, Weissenhorn (Ulm) | November 4, 1901 | Nanny | November 15, 1927–? |
| 22. Erhard, Anna. Gross-Eislingen | June 23, 1903 | Maid servant | February 15, 1928– February 26, 1928 |
| 23. Högg, Saberstein (?), Hörenhausen | December 10, 1901 | Servant | March 1, 1928–? |
| 24. Reichert, Gretel, Süssen | February 12, 1910 | Maid servant | April 15, 1928–? |

**Table 2. Leopold's employees**

| Name, Residence | DOB | Occupation | Period |
|---|---|---|---|
| 1. Mayer, Luise, Basel | Apr. 16, 1908 | Servant | Mar. 25, 1925–Jan. 1, 1926 |
| 2. Racher, Max, Gundelfingen | Dec. 2, 1903 | Servant | May 10, 1925–Jun. 8, 1925 |
| 3. Roth, Friedrich, Mess-stetten | Nov. 15, 1897 | Servant | Aug. 6, 1925–Jun. 15, 1925 [info not correct, entry correct] |
| 4. Räpple, Hermann, Diefenbach | Dec. 21, 1901 | Servant | Jun. 15, 1925–Aug. 10, 1925 |
| 5. Lippert, Erhardt (*Rufname*), Sulb | Aug. 26, 1897 | Servant | Aug. 11, 1925–Sept. 6, 1925 |
| 6. Müller, Karl, Kleebronn | Jun. 23, 1887 | Servant | Sept. 16, 1925–Sept. 30, 1925 |
| 7. Eckert, Joh., Laichingen | May 25, 1906 | Servant | Sept. 30, 1925–Sept. 12, 1926 |
| 8. Kölle, Maria, Aufhausen | Jan. 30, 1908 | Servant | Jan. 8, 1926–Mar. 15, 1926 |
| 9. Röcker, Angelika, Hemmenhausen | May 15, 1900 | | Mar. 15, 1926–May 30, 1926 |
| 10. Helferich, Katharina, Radelstetten | Mar. 16, 1908 | Maid servant | Jun. 15, 1926–Dec. 31, 1927 |
| 11. Weidenbacher, Friedrich, Oberböhringen | Jul. 12, 1899 | | Oct. 1, 1926–Dec. 18, 1926 |
| 12. Eckert, Joh., Laichingen | May 25, 1896 | | Dec. 15, 1926–Apr. 9, 1927 |
| 13. Thumm, Hermann, Urbach | May 6, 1905 | Servant | Apr. 11, 1927–May 7, 1927 |
| 14. Fauth, Willy, Göppingen | Oct. 13, 1905 | Servant | May 15, 1927–? |
| 15. Reutter, Magd(alene), Scharenstetten | Sept. 11, 1897 | Maid servant | Feb. 7, 1928–Mar. 5, 1928 |
| 16. Pöllath, Johanna, Frankfurt am Main | Jul. 21, 1913 | Maid servant | Mar. 6, 1928–? |

widow of Rabbi Aron Tänzer, Berta Tänzer, moved there as well. Hugo remembers that he was a short man who ate with them in the house. Only a month earlier, on May 28, 1937, the city council had authorized a monthly increase of RM 13.10 in Sahm's disability payments.[97]

Because it was a Jewish family tradition that the oldest son would take responsibility for all of the family, Leopold worked in silent partnership with his brother Louis, contributing his services and his funds to the business without any written documentation. This, too, was normal in Jewish families, though not in the German bureaucracy. After the Holocaust, this undocumented business arrangement was to the detriment of Leopold's surviving heirs, as none of the property from before the Holocaust was in his name and his heirs therefore were not able to put in any claims for their losses of real estate.

The Lang business seems to have flourished in the 1920s. Hugo recalls, "My father sold to all the farmers in the area, in the district, and they made a nice living. My uncle, his brother, worked with him. The two brothers owned the business."[98] The two primary regional newspapers, the *Göppinger Zeitung* and the *Geislinger Zeitung*, carried many of Louis's advertisements for "pregnant *Kalbeln*—both *Simmentaler* and *Allgäuer*" [brands] and beautiful "*Einstellvieh* [boarding cattle]."[99] Leopold, whose name is absent in the ads, took great pride in his cows. In 1930 he won first prize for one of his cows at a cattle fair in nearby Esslingen.[100] Leopold's second love was cigars. Hugo remembers, "He smoked thirteen cigars a day! My father put a toothpick in the end of the cigar and smoked it until he practically burned his lips. Then he lit another one from the tiny stump."[101] Only in a letter dated October 6, 1941, just a few weeks before deportation, do we learn that "Father has stopped smoking almost completely."[102]

After his father Samuel's death, Louis began to consolidate the family holdings. In 1929 Louis made overtures to sell the house in the center of town at Heidenheimer Strasse, probably in anticipation of buying out Jakob's widow. He offered "his property at Heidenheimer Strasse to the town for RM 30,000" possibly for a religious school for the Lutheran church.[103] The municipality did not take him up on the offer, choosing another property for the school instead.

In spite of the obvious financial risk in the year of the New York Stock Market crash, Louis went ahead with the purchase of Fanny's property. On February 27, 1929, "Fanny Lang née Pressburger, widow of cattle dealer [Jakob] Lang in Gross-Süssen who died in Stuttgart on May 4, 1918, and acting on behalf of her minor daughter Lina Lang, single, office worker in Gross-Süssen, and through power of attorney dated February 26, 1929, on behalf of her daughter Alma Lang, single, office manager in Ludwigsburg, and Adolf, known as Otto, Lang, of New York, single, electrical engineer, currently residing in Gross-Süssen," sold to "Lazarus, known as Louis, Lang, cattle dealer in Gross-Süssen and his wife Pauline née Baer, who live in a legally recognized union of 50 percent coownership of all property," the property at Hauptstrasse for 25,000 goldmarks effective March 1, 1929.[104]

The conditions were as follows: Five thousand goldmarks were to be paid in cash, 15,000 goldmarks in three annual rates of 5,000 goldmarks each, due on March 1, beginning in 1930, and the remaining 5,000 goldmarks after an optional three-month mutual cancellation clause had expired. The mortgage of 20,000 goldmarks was payable to Fanny Lang.[105] Fanny also had the right to free residence in the house until April 15, 1929. On that date, Jakob's widow returned to her hometown of Rexingen, where she lived until 1937 when she emigrated to the United States.[106]

Louis made several necessary changes to the property. He had a number of dealings with the municipality concerning building matters. On June 21, 1932, the mayor's office ordered the inspection of a newly constructed chimney which Louis had built to replace the old one.[107] As noted earlier, already in 1928 Louis had built a gasoline storage room at Heidenheimer Strasse property,[108] and the 1935 inventory also lists an automobile of the type Adler. On August 11, 1932, Louis received permission to construct an automobile garage for RM 400 on lot no. 224/2 on the street *in der Türkei*.[109] The final application for a permit dates from October 1932 and is for a gasoline storage shed, also for lot no. 224/2. This was authorized on November 2, 1932.[110]

There is no mention of why Louis was interested in selling his house in the center of town (Heidenheimer Strasse), but on April 5, 1932, Louis succeeded in selling the house to a local businessman, Carl Stahl, *Seilermeister*.[111] The sales price was RM 18,000, of which Mr. Stahl paid RM 10,000 down and took out a mortgage for the remaining RM 8,000. The sale was approved on April 6, 1932. The mortgage for this amount, converted into goldmarks, was transferred to Fanny Lang by Louis on July 22, 1932. On April 1, 1933—the day of the Nazi boycott of Jewish stores—Fanny in turn transferred the mortgage to her son Adolf Otto in the United States.[112] When the family received final payment from Mr. Stahl in 1937, well after the Nazis came to power, Louis was able to settle accounts with Fanny, enabling her (though not him or most members of his family) to emigrate to the United States to live with or near her children. She died in New York in 1953.

Knowledge of Jakob Lang's descendants continues to be sparse. Most of the information comes from sales contracts and other legal documents. In 1929, Alma, the oldest of the children, was twenty-six years old, single and an office manager in Ludwigsburg. In 1933 she worked in Saulgau (see earlier entry), and in 1935, when Max Liffmann sued her, she was living in Zurich, Switzerland. She can be traced to Italy in 1937,[113] and from there to the United States, where she married Fred Friesner and lived in Teaneck, New Jersey.[114] They had a daughter Beatrice and have three grandchildren.

Otto, the second child of Jakob and Fanny, was twenty-six years old when Fanny sold the house to Louis and had already emigrated to and settled in New York. He, too, was single, an electrical engineer—whatever that required in the 1920s—and he returned to New York after the transaction was completed.[115]

The baby was Lina, also single in 1929 and still a minor by ten months. According to their statement in *The Jews of Württemberg*, she attended the *Realschule* in Göppingen. This was a nonacademic track secondary school, and one usually graduated from it by age sixteen. From Lina we learn that members of her family were active in the Göppingen Jewish Community. There is visual evidence that all of the Jewish children in the district participated in the programs of the Jewish community, such as Hanukkah celebrations. A picture celebrating Hanukkah 5682, taken at the Hotel Dettelbacher in 1922/23, was donated to the Göppingen City Archive by Sig Rosental, formerly of Göppingen. Portrayed are a group of girls about fourteen years old, so of "confirmation" age. The picture shows Lina, the youngest daughter of Fanny Lang and the deceased Jakob, among her friends. The girls are dressed up in country dresses with white aprons, scarves and hats.[116] About her youth, Lina also recalls, "as a young teenager I lived with my guardians Sigmund and Millie Victor [maternal grandparents] in Heilbronn and continued to attend school there. Later I worked for two years in the Seidenpapierfabrik Eislingen [crepe paper factory owned by Fleischer where Fred later also worked] and in 1929 visited the United States. Circumstances convinced me to stay. [First] I worked as a secretary at New York University, thereafter I worked for two businesses."[117] In 1938 Lina married Selly (Sally) Pressburger from Rexingen. According to Hugo Lang, they adopted one son, Mark, and have grandchildren.[118] Selly, born in 1909, was the son of Max and Pauline Pressburger; his father died in Rexingen in 1938, and his mother was deported to Theresienstadt where she perished.[119] There were seven children, most of whom emigrated to the United States. Selly states that he went to school in Rexingen, worked as a shoe salesman, and in 1930 briefly made a living as a cattle dealer. He visited Palestine in 1935, hoping to settle there, but got malaria and returned to Germany for health reasons. Selly emigrated to the United States in 1937, became a (kosher) butcher, and was drafted into the US Army in 1943. After being discharged, he opened his own retail store, and three years later he founded and managed Bergen Whole-sale Meats in Hackensack, New Jersey. Lina retired when her husband was discharged from the military and dedicated herself to being a mother, grandmother, and homemaker. Both of them were religious and active in Jewish organizations.[120]

Leopold and his family lived in the *Judenhaus* from the time of their arrival in Süssen in 1925. It is likely that Louis and family joined them there in 1932, when Louis sold his other house at Heidenheimer Strasse. From then until deportation in 1941, they lived together in the house at 45 Hauptstrasse. When visiting Süssen in 1989 Hugo remembered, "When we lived here there was one large room, the living room. The entire floor was one apartment and downstairs as well. The kitchen was next to it and the bedrooms on the other side. It was laid out the same upstairs and downstairs. Only the living room had heat. We did not have any heat in the bedrooms. We had a *Kachelofen* [tile stove] in the living room, that was it. There was an old stove in the kitchen, wood and coal. Nothing else, no gas and no electricity, not yet."[121] He knew that his uncle owned the house, "we rented from him."[122] He continued, "My parents and us two brothers and our sister lived on the ground floor. My uncle, his wife and their children, there were four of them—Ingeborg, Kurt, Henny, and Siegfried—lived on the first floor."[123]

The Lang property did not lack anything that a self-sufficient family needed. "Next to the house there were three beautiful gardens. One of them was a large orchard that produced a lot of fruit every year. We had apples, pears, plums, and two cherry trees. We also had a quince tree and a walnut tree. The fruit was handpicked and placed on a bed of straw in the cellar. We also had two more gardens. One was in front of the house, the other next to the shed. My parents bought different vegetable seeds from green grocer Eugen Mayer at Heidenheimer Strasse each year. We tilled the soil and mixed in much cow dung, and at the end we added the seeds. We had a lot of vegetables, including black radishes and potatoes [here Hugo uses the Swabian word *Krumbieren*]. My mother made hard cider. Then we sometimes enjoyed some hard cider with Limburger cheese and homemade dark bread. That was great! In the garden next to the house we grew gooseberries, raspberries, and red and black currants. My mother always canned a lot of the vegetables and fruit. In winter we periodically ate currant or gooseberry cake. Ruth [Hugo's sister] helped a lot in the kitchen. That's how she learned Swabian cooking. We often ate lentils and *Spätzle* [a Swabian homemade type of pasta] with bits of smoked meat."[124]

Hugo continues, "All of us children—Manfred and Teddy [1921], Henny [1922], I [1923], Kurt [1924], and Ruth and Siegi [1925]—went to the local Lutheran elementary school" named for the local poet Johann Georg Fischer.[125]

> When the three of us—Manfred, Hugo, and Ruth—came home from school, we had to help with housework. I had to fetch eggs from the chicken coop, coal from the shed, and split firewood. In our living room stood a large tile stove; in winter we dried apples on top of it. The living room was the only room that was heated in winter. Our beds were warmed with copper hot water bottles. We loved that. Fred and I also had to clean the horse stable and provide the two cattle barns with fresh straw. We had four workhorses and about one hundred cows. We bought the cows and then sold them again [in contrast to a farmer who bought cows for milk and for breeding]. We also had chickens, ducks, and geese as well as a dog, a cat, and a peacock. Every evening Ruth had to clean our shoes, close the shutters, and stack newspapers and wood in the kitchen stove for the next morning. In winter we enjoyed sleigh riding at Sarenwang [a local hill close to their house] and skiing. In summer I had to take our horses to the local canal, the Mühlbach, to wash them. Of course we also went swimming in the canal. Each of us had a bicycle, and we had to clean and oil it every Saturday [on the Jewish Sabbath!]. We also had outdoor swings and many toys. After we were done with our homework in the afternoon, we spent many pleasant hours in our garden, in the yard, and with the animals. Of course we also spent time with our friends, and we had many of them.[126]

A picture in the orchard in 1933 shows a growing Fred—trim, with dark hair and wearing knickers. He sits on a bench next to his sister Ruth, already a young lady, with pretty dark hair, cut short, a white dress, white socks, and black shoes, holding what must have been her favorite kitten of the moment. On the right is Hugo, in long-sleeved shirt and corduroy shorts, all of them watching the kitten with smiles on their faces.[127] All of the pictures speak of the rural idyll that the family lived—from the pictures in the orchard with the animals to Eva and the boys in deepest winter skiing and sleigh riding on a local hill.[128] Another picture of the three children, approximately from the late twenties, shows a reflective Hugo, whose blondish-brown hair has been trimmed, and a considerably more dark-haired Fred, both wearing matching sweaters. Their sister Ruth, in the middle, is wearing a dressy little jacket with a big bow. She has short hair, almost black, and piercing dark eyes. One sees why she is wearing glasses in some pictures, as she is cross-eyed.[129]

Manfred and Hugo did well in school. We have report cards for both of them from 1936 and 1937, respectively, by which time the formerly Lutheran elementary school which they attended was already aligned with Nazi ideology and staffed with aligned teachers. As of June 4, 1936, it was called the *Deutsche Schule* (German School),[130] and was a school for boys and girls of "all" confessions—Lutheran and Catholic as well as the Langs until 1937—in the united town of Süssen. Interestingly, the classes continued to be separated by gender.

By 1936 Manfred had attended all eight grades of elementary school, starting on April 1, 1928. His eighth-grade report card, dated May 26, 1936, shows a grade of *"gut"* (good or roughly B) for all subjects. The traditional categories of "behavior, effort, attention, and intelligence" had been replaced by the Nazi values of "physical strength, character, and intellectual effort and overall effort." The headmaster of the school, *Rektor* (principal) Wilhelm Schnitzler, wrote that Manfred was physically strong and participated in class, but was sometimes uneven in his work habits and was easily distracted. His overall achievement was good.[131]

Hugo also has an eighth-grade report card dated February 15, 1937. His teacher, Mr. Ferdinand Reick, wrote that he was "physically healthy, strong and active; his work pace in class is even, he is quiet and consistent; his behavior decent, he is orderly, diligent, attentive, and willing to learn." Not quite a top student in "free" drawing, Hugo's "overall achievement is good."[132] A class picture from 1936, when Hugo was in seventh grade, shows a strapping young man who is in no way different from the other boys in the picture except that he doesn't wear Lederhosen as some of the other boys do.[133] In accordance with the family's middle-class way of life, Hugo also took piano lessons and played the harmonica. In 1937 he had to give up the piano lessons as the teacher, Mayer, was no longer allowed to instruct him.[134]

All the Lang children participated in gymnastics, including swimming, and the boys participated in wrestling. They all belonged to the TSV (Turn- und Sportverein) Süssen, the local sports club. A picture from August 1933 shows a proud Eva, with glasses; a mischievous Hugo, a proud Fred; and Ruth, also with glasses now, in their gym suits.[135] Several of Manfred's certificates of achievement have survived. On September 20, 1931—age ten—he participated in the *Vierkampf* (tetrathlon) competition at the *Gau-*

*jugendtreffen*, a regional youth meet in Reichenbach near Donzdorf. On September 3, 1932, he participated in the *Reichsjugendwettkämpfe* (youth competition) in Süssen, a national meet for youth, and on May 29, 1932, he again participated in the regional meet for the youth of the Province Hohenstaufen. On August 19 and 20, 1933, eight months after the Nazis came to power, he won twelfth place in Class B at the fortieth anniversary of the Süssen Turn- und Sportverein e.V. (local sports club). In 1934 one notices a shift in participation from the German to the Jewish realm. Being excluded from competition with non-Jewish Germans, in that year Manfred participated in the *Leichtathletische Meisterschaften* (track and field championships) of the Göppingen sports group, Reichsbund jüdischer Frontsoldaten e.V. (Organization of Jewish Veterans), where, on September 23, 1934, he won second place in broad jump class I with 3.30 meters (about 10.8 feet). This is the organization to which both Louis and Leopold belonged as Jewish veterans of World War I.[136] Yet the Langs continued to participate in events of the German sports organizations to some extent. In 1936 there is a picture of an outing that the TSV Süssen took to Wasserberg, a popular tourist spot to this day. The picture shows Hugo and Fred, their cousins Inge, Kurt, and Henny, as well as Werner and Hans Baer, the cousins from Rodalben, who must have been visiting.[137]

Hugo also experienced discrimination. He was especially enthusiastic about his participation in the Süssen *Turnverein*. The first signs of the deteriorating situation occurred for Hugo in 1937 at the age of fourteen. He remembers, "We had a great teacher. His name was Richard Meissnest. He was a good, decent person—there were only a few of them in those years. In 1937 we played soccer or handball twice a week in the afternoon. Once in a while I scored a goal. A few of my former teammates then went to the coach and insisted that Jewish goals don't count. The coach disagreed and told them that they do indeed count. He was very nice."[138] Upon completion of eight grades of elementary school,[139] on April 1, 1937, his parents sent Hugo to the city of Ulm to absolve an apprenticeship as a waiter at the Restaurant Weinhof,[140] managed by Mr. Max Moos for the Jüdische Kulturbund (Jewish Cultural Club). The restaurant was located next to the synagogue which was destroyed during Kristallnacht. It was closed in January 1939.

When asked to comment on the family's Jewishness by Professor Kurt Piehler, Hugo noted, "Our family was reformed.[141] Friday night we celebrated the traditional rituals, we lit Shabbat candles. My mother al-

ways kept *milchig* and *fleischig* separate, she also had separate dish towels for *milchig* and *fleischig*. We went to synagogue two to three times
a year,"[142] which would be Rosh Hashanah and Yom Kippur, but as is
evident from surviving pictures, the children clearly participated in the
communal celebration of Purim and Hanukkah. On December 6, 1929,
Hugo, Manfred, Inge, and Henny participated along with other children,
among them some of the Ottenheimer children, in a Hanukkah play,
called "Princes[s] Forget-me-not,"[143] at the Hotel Dettelbacher. This celebration is discussed at length in chapter 10, "Jews in Jebenhausen and
Göppingen."

When I asked the surviving sons of the Tänzer, Ottenheimer, and Lang
families about each other, they did not seem to know each other well.
Erwin Tänzer, son of Rabbi Aron and Berta Tänzer of Göppingen, commented that he had little recollection of the Langs from childhood. He
did, however, have a very specific memory of Hugo after emigration to the
United States that he shared in a letter to Walter Lang in 1990.

> In February 1943 I was drafted into the American Army. For the first two
> weeks I was at Ft. Dix, New Jersey, where it was decided at which camp the
> recruits were to receive their basic training. We were housed in tents. It was
> cold and we had snow. I was there two or three days when someone came
> into our tent with a flashlight and called my name. To my surprise, it was
> one of the Lang brothers, whom I knew of course. He informed me that I
> was to report to the kitchen for duty. KP means "kitchen police" [*sic*] which
> includes such chores as sweeping the floor, setting tables, peeling potatoes,
> etc. I forgot the first name of the messenger. I think it was Hugo Lang.
> I haven't seen him since, but I still remember this encounter, forty-seven
> years ago.[144]

One of the reasons that they had little to do with each other may have been
the special arrangements made for the Lang children, as well as the Kirchheim children, because they lived "in the diaspora," that is, outside of Göppingen. Hugo explains, "There were seven children in our house, in my
family and my uncle's. Once a month the teacher, Cantor [Berthold] Levi,
came to us for religious instruction, we didn't have to go to Göppingen
[to the religious school at the synagogue]."[145] Two of the boys became bar
mitzvah, Hugo on September 2, 1936, and Kurt on June 19, 1937. There is
no information on Fred and Siegfried.

On November 22, 1935, Pauline, wife of Louis, and mother of Teddy, Henny, Kurt, and Siegi, died of bladder problems in a Tübingen hospital. According to a former neighbor, the funeral was attended by many people, including Nazi spies. Pauline is also buried in the Jewish section of the Göppingen municipal cemetery (no. 130). Pauline's will of January 31, 1924,[146] was presented to the Nachlassgericht (inheritance court) on November 26, 1935; there it was opened by Bezirksnotar (district notary) Walzer in the presence of Louis on December 5, 1935.[147] According to Pauline's will, her legal heir was Louis, to whom she had been married on July 6, 1920. As they had no prenuptial agreement, Louis was entitled to one fourth of the inheritance; the four children to the remaining three quarters or each to three-sixteenth of the total. On that date, the chairman of the Nachlassgericht ordered the compilation of an official inventory of all household goods and personal items.[148] This inventory was taken by an inventory committee that consisted of three individuals—city council member Josef Staudenmaier, Zweiter Beigeordnete Hermann Wiedenmann, and Georg Fischer, farmer. The result was presented to Louis on December 14, 1935. This list provides a good sense of the Langs' middle-class status and way of life. The total value of the movable property amounted to RM 4,976.70, of which RM 2,069.80 was credited to Pauline and RM 2,906.90 to Louis. Later, after deportation, when their property was auctioned off, the witnesses claimed that the total receipts, including furniture, at auction came to only RM 3,000 for Louis's and Leopold's belongings together.[149] Household goods included china and silver for a large family. In addition the Louis Langs owned thirty silver spoons, twelve knives and forks with silver handles, three rings (RM 250), pendants and brooches (RM 100), two gold pocket watches (RM 100), and one gold watch chain (RM 50). Pauline owned six better dresses (RM 100) and four hats or caps. They further possessed a radio, an electric iron (RM 3), a sewing machine (RM 30), a washing machine (RM 40), a Waschschleuder (laundry wringer) (RM 30), a grandfather's clock (RM 60), and a car (RM 150) of the model Adler. All of these possessions, including the car, were later stolen from the Langs by the Nazis.

On February 28, 1936, Louis once more appeared before the court, this time the guardian court, to regulate the share of the estate to which his children were entitled. Documents reveal Pauline's sizeable dowry of RM 40,000, as well as their respective life insurance policies in the amount of RM 10,000 each. In this document Louis asserts that he paid for their property from his own money, thus debiting his late wife's account with 50 percent of the real estate value. The total inheritance sum for the four children was RM 8,683.60; split into four parts this amounted to RM 2,145.90, half of which is what Louis owed each child (RM 1,072.95). He increased this amount to RM 1,300 for each of them.[150] The children most likely never received their inheritance from their mother, as their father not only lost his property, but his life in the Holocaust.

# 5         Süssen under the Nazis: The Lang Families, 1937–41

*That our actions concerning the property confiscation of the Jews were not the
right thing to do we knew too; but these decrees were official business handed
down to us from above whose execution we could not refuse at the time.*
      —Paul Mayer, tax assistant, Finanzamt Geislingen[1]

*She [Anna Kölle] says that the Jews in Süssen were really nice people. One
woman already had a washing machine at that time and washed their neighbors' laundry for them, she was such a good person. A cattle dealer who had
been very rich had to work in a factory. They were really nice people, and they
were happy to work. "The [barn] was torn down. I don't know what happened
to the people."*
      —Paraphrasing Anna Kölle, in *Begegnungen*[2]

Dealing in livestock was big business in the rural areas of southern Germany. Cattle dealers were a breed all of their own, with a friendly personality, a keen sense of business, and a close network of associates.[3] During
a 2006 conference in Rexingen survivor families described some of the
details of the prewar cattle trade to their audience.[4] Dr. Fredy Kahn, son
of a long line of cattle dealers from Baisingen, and long-time friend of the
Langs, noted that "the cattle trade observed its own particular conventions.
Business was conducted with a handshake, expressing trust between Jews
and Christians. Networks of subdealers and informants were cultivated in
villages. Of special interest was the presentation of cattle in the barn. The
floor was strewn with light-colored sawdust and tiled more beautifully
than many a bathroom." He also noted that the floor was at a slight angle
for a better presentation of the cattle.[5] The government required licenses
and fees, necessitating painstaking record keeping of sales and trades, not
least because of the feared hoof and mouth disease, a scourge that was as
feared by earlier generations as mad cow disease is today. The region under discussion, Gross-Süssen included, experienced repeated outbreaks of
the disease. In 1938 the town's senior bull had to be slaughtered for that
reason.[6]

**The Cattle Trade**

Most important for every business dealing in livestock was the *Kontroll-buch* (ledger), but apparently there was plenty of room for improvement in keeping the book. A directive of May 28, 1925, from the Interior Ministry to State Police Headquarters in Stuttgart, as well as to all of the Oberämter in the state noted the problem.

> We received information from official sources that the keeping of *Kontroll-bücher* by cattle dealers is not always carried out conscientiously. A fairly large number of horse dealers keep no *Kontrollbücher* at all; dealers in other livestock also often do not have a *Kontrollbuch* or a *Handelsverzeichnis* [transaction ledger]. When these books are kept, the entries are often poor; many transactions, especially those that involve barter, are not recorded at all. The entries in the *Kontrollbuch* and *Handelsverzeichnis* often do not match. Several cattle dealers have recently . . . and against the directives of the Interior Ministry, given their transport supervisors an excerpt from the *Vieh-Kontrollbuch* instead of the book itself. A number of dealers declared to have lost their books; others claimed to have destroyed them already before the end of the year in which the final entry was made.

Thus, "the Oberämter are instructed to remind those concerned of these regulations and to have the *Landjäger* [gendarme] check thoroughly that these rules are followed and to report any defiance without leniency."[7]

A directive of September 19, 1929, from the Interior Ministry to the Oberamt Stuttgart declared, "According to Article 31 . . . cattle dealers must keep a *Hauptkontrollbuch* at the location of their business in which all livestock is recorded that goes through their hands. This book must remain permanently at the site of this business. Thus, every business location of a cattle dealer [main office and any branches] must have a *Kontrollbuch* at all times that is accessible for inspection by police and the veterinarian on duty."[8]

In contrast to cattle dealer and farmer, the level of trust between authorities and businessmen was not very high, as a directive from the Interior Ministry in Berlin of August 30, 1926, concerning *Viehkontrollbücher* shows (received at Oberamt Göppingen on September 2, 1926). "A *Haupt-kontrollbuch* can only be started after the local police of the town in which the business is located has notarized the total number of pages on the first page."[9] The implication is that otherwise one could tear out a page with an entry before an impending inspection.

Officials made every effort to regulate trade, in large part for the protection of the consumer. In all instances, any individual dealing in foodstuffs needed a *Gewerbelegitimationskarte* (business permit). This permit was valid only for business dealings within a restricted area, such as a municipality. If individuals wanted to do business beyond this area, they also needed a *Wandergewerbeschein* (peddler's license).

A 1925 directive dated December 2, 1925, provides insight into the issues at hand. Based on directive no. b. 5475 of December 4, 1924, those intending to pursue such a business in 1925 had to provide an affidavit that they did not have "infectious or horrible diseases [such as leprosy] and are not suspected of having such a disease." Furthermore, "a special permit was required for trade with cattle and meat." Both of these were now no longer necessary. However, "the prohibition to deal with '*Gegenstände des täglichen Bedarfs*' [daily necessities such as milk and eggs perhaps] continues to be in force because of 'unreliability' [of the products, that is, they could be contaminated]." In general, "further expansion of the *Wandergewerbe* [peddling] cannot be currently justified in the interest of the general public nor in the interest of those pursuing this line of work. It should therefore be limited as much as possible."[10]

The peddler's license was not unproblematic. While it made the business dealings of an individual legal, it could not regulate the ethical behavior of the officials. Paragraph 7 addressed complaints that the Labor Ministry received repeatedly from "those in possession of *Wandergewerbescheine* . . . who paid the appropriate fee but were often denied the necessary permit by the local police department, so that they paid the fee for expansion [of territory] in vain." The Oberämter are asked to inform applicants for the *Wandergewerbeschein* that a local police permit is required and to perhaps designate one particular municipal office in the district as the permit office. Paragraph 8 states that "there seems to be a worrisome increase in the number of applications for *Wandergewerbescheine* by persons younger than twenty-five. This is especially true of the so-called peddler communities. Since there is societal interest in encouraging our youth to take on a more settled occupation, the permits in these cases . . . are to be more limited."[11] This is of course exactly what the *Israelitengesetz* or *Erziehungsgesetz* of 1828 tried to achieve in the Kingdom of Württemberg, with disastrous consequences for the primarily targeted population—Jews. Excluded until 1864 to a large extent from professions because of religion and from the practice of agriculture because of status, one of the few ways of making a living—peddling—was also taken from them without a viable alternative. While the laws in the 1920s were in no way discriminatory against Jews, one can easily see how they could be manipulated by the Nazis to become punitive.

## Cattle Fairs

Participation in cattle fairs was an intrinsic part of the cattle business. The Gross-Süssen farmers and cattle dealers were no exception. "From 1864 on every animal was assessed a two kreuzer fee for the community treasury. The fair took place on the *Wasen* [grassy area] along the Heidenheimer Strasse. Today the J. G. Fischer [Elementary] School and the Lutheran community center are located there."[12] However, the right to hold fairs could not be taken for granted. Walter Ziegler writes, "Süssen did not have an ancient claim to a fair. Rather, two government decrees of January 21, 1873, established the cattle and retail fairs on Easter Monday and September 29. Two years later the latter fair was moved to the holiday of St. Thomas [December 21]."[13] This fair consisted of entertainment, produce, and other goods, as well as livestock and horses. Pigs were not added until the 1930s. In 1915 the location was changed to Marktstrasse and Kirchstrasse, behind the Lutheran church in Gross-Süssen, and the cattle were tied up on wooden bars near the church.[14] However, the cold December weather kept attendance down. Thus, the municipality, on January 22, 1929, discussed moving the fair to the Monday of the *Kirchweih* weekend, "the third Monday in October."[15] For this change they needed the permission of the Württembergische Landesgewerbeamt (Chamber of Commerce). Before a decision was made, the application was circulated to communities in the vicinity who also held fairs on the Monday of *Kirchweih* weekend. And since these communities feared that a competing event would detract visitors from attending their fairs, the request was denied. In a letter of April 22, 1929, the Württembergische Landesgewerbeamt notified the Oberamt Geislingen, the administrative superior for Süssen, that "We cannot tolerate that one community in the vicinity moves its fair to the Monday of *Kirchweih* [weekend] and thereby harms the fairs of the other communities."[16] They recommended finding a better date that would not threaten the interests of other communities. When the city council was notified, they refused to accept the rejection and tried once more, unsuccessfully.[17] The community then decided to move the "cattle and retail fair of December 21 (holiday of St. Thomas) to the Saturday before *Kirchweih* [weekend]" in October of every year and to request permission from the Württembergische Landesgewerbeamt to do so.[18] On August 2, 1929, the Württembergische Landesgewerbeamt notified the municipality that they would receive permission to move the fair to October for a trial period from September 1, 1929, to August 31, 1932, for a fee of RM 20.[19] At the conclusion of this trial period, the municipality debated whether they should once more request the Monday of *Kirchweih*, but decided to apply for a permanent move of the fair to the already temporarily approved Saturday before *Kirchweih* Sunday.[20] The Württembergische Landesgewerbeamt granted an extension of the trial period to August 31, 1935, but then the municipality had to reapply (on February 2, 1932). Also, the permit was now not only for cattle, but also for pigs. The municipality was charged a fee of RM 45—which they protested as out of line with the proceeds from the fair. The fee was then reduced to RM 15 (on March 3, 1932) by the Württemberg Landesgewerbeamt payable to the Oberamt Geislingen.[21]

### Jewish Cattle Dealers and the Nazis

There were few mentions of fair activities in the local press until 1933. Apparently fair attendance had been less than satisfactory in the intervening years. The community may even have considered abandoning the fair. That all changed when the Nazis came to power. The Nazis were particularly zealous to give the cattle fair a nationalistic character and to exclude Jews from the cattle trade. Thus, there now was more interest in reporting on activities at cattle fairs in the press. All three regional newspapers carried notices of the "Krämer- und Viehmarkt" to be held on Easter Monday in 1934.[22] Afterwards the Nazi newspaper *Der Hohenstaufen* reported, "The Easter fair, which was held yesterday, as is the tradition, enjoyed again this year an extremely lively attendance. . . . Unfortunately the sales for both the cattle fair in the morning and the retail fair were not exactly outstanding."[23] The Nazi newspaper, *Die Nationale Rundschau*, reported on April 4, 1934, "Early in the morning, when the merchants set up their booths, there was already lively activity at the cattle fair. The farmers from near and far eyed the cattle knowingly. Here and there a deal was in the making, and right away a small group of experts assembled to give their opinion on the transaction."[24]

In 1934 the city council noted that attendance at the October goods, cattle, and swine fair had improved and that they would continue to hold the fair, on the *Kirchweih* weekend, not on the *Thomasfeier* (December 21).[25] For this to happen, they had to request again an extension of the permit, and decided to do so for six more years.[26] But the Württemberg Landesgewerbeamt kept a close eye on this fair, noting on January 15, 1935, "Over the past three years, supply as well as demand for the October cattle fair in Gross-Süssen have diminished. Thus, in October 1933 two animals were sold at the fair, and in October 1934, none. There is no need for a future cattle fair in October." On January 21, 1935, this communication to the Oberamt Geislingen was sent on to the mayor's office in Süssen with the query, "whether under the current circumstances the Süssen application for a fair permit dated December 5, 1934, shall be continued." The municipality turned to their expert, cattle dealer Louis Lang, for an answer. The municipality asked police officer Holl—who later allegedly carried out the deportation order on Louis—to consult Louis on the matter. Holl reported to Mayor Saalmüller on February 1, 1935, "I consulted cattle dealer Louis Lang concerning the application. He answered, 'I do not consider the October fair important for my business and wouldn't mind if that fair was to be discontinued. Even though we were not able to attract much cattle, we had expenses related to the fair, but no sales. If it would pay at all, I would be the first who would advocate continuation [of the October fair].'" On February 2, 1935, the mayor wrote at the bottom of the report, "For the time being I forego the privilege of holding an October fair."[27] The mayor then informed the city council, "The inquiry shows that the interested parties [Louis Lang and the municipality] no longer care to hold this fair."[28] The city council voted to abolish the October cattle fair, but to continue the *Krämermarkt* (flea market) and move it to Saturday before the *Kirchweihfest* for its duration.[29]

But criticism of the cattle fairs continued. Concerning the Easter Monday market, the *Geislinger Zeitung* concluded that "Our Easter fair on Easter Monday has the same significance for Süssen and environs as the *Maientag* fair has for Göppingen and environs." However, not all parts of the fair were satisfactory. "In the morning there was a cattle fair. The newly created plaza for the cattle fair is very advantageous. The cattle can be presented to the visitors without disturbing the traffic at the J. G. Fischer Strasse. Nevertheless, sales were not on a par with the number of visitors."[30] In a May 7, 1936, article, the author deemed the Easter Monday fair a great success, but criticized the cattle fair and claimed it was no longer relevant. The *Hohenstaufen*, reported on April 14, 1936, that "the morning cattle fair was dull."[31] The *Geislinger Zeitung* of April 15, 1936, steering clear of sales figures, put a positive spin on matters. "Since we had real April weather with a snow storm on Easter Sunday, many a businessman may have worried about the Easter Fair on Monday. But there was no need to worry! . . . The cattle fair in the morning enjoyed numerous attendees;

especially noticeable was the large number of visitors from neighboring communities."[32] It is not immediately obvious that these criticisms of the cattle fairs are of a polemical nature. However, when the chairman of the Süssen city council, in a proposal to "expand the cattle fair," noted that in order to do that, it would be necessary to keep "*Kitsch* [junk] and Jews" from participating,[33] the underlying motivation becomes clear. Local farmers warmly welcomed the proposal for expansion, because they thought they would benefit if their Jewish fellow Germans, who were the middlemen, were excluded.

There was also an effort to generate interest in the cattle business regionally, as the *Geislinger Zeitung* of April 28, 1936, carried an article that announced the resumption of an event which hadn't been held in Geislingen (5.6 miles east of Süssen and seat of the Oberamt) in the past two years, namely a *Jungviehprämierung*—a competition of young cattle with prizes awarded for the best.[34] The reason for the hiatus had been an outbreak of the dreaded hoof-and-mouth disease. On January 7, 1937, the city council of Süssen also debated holding a *Viehprämierung*. Two city council members supported such a proposal.[35] The regional newspaper aggressively marketed the idea. The results were good. In April 1937 the *Geislinger Zeitung* reported, "Due to an extensive spread and advertising campaign, our Easter fair has evolved during the past few years into a *Volksfest*-like enterprise.[36] The main attraction for the farmers from near and far was the public judging of livestock and the awarding of prizes in conjunction with the cattle and pig fair. . . . The livestock judging event which will occur annually shall be an inspiration for every local peasant and farmer and give them valuable practical advice. This event shall also give the peasants and farmers clear insight into the achievements of the local cattle industry and stimulate the exclusion of the Jewish middleman and therewith promote the cattle trade between farmer and farmer."[37] However, an outbreak of the hoof-and-mouth disease in 1938 caused the cattle fair to be cancelled.[38] On April 13, 1939, the *Geislinger Zeitung* reported that "The spring fair reached an all-time high in visitors in spite of the fact that the cattle fair could not take place."[39] The *Hohenstaufen* of April 11 also headlined the "Record Number of Visitors at the Spring Fair in Süssen," noting that the beautiful weather had something to do with the large number of visitors which would have been even larger if the cattle fair could have been held.[40] On December 14, 1937, six months before Louis Lang would lose his cattle trading license, putting the only cattle dealer in town out of business, the city council even debated expanding the number of annual cattle fairs, especially "since it is only a question of time until the *Handelsjuden* have been completely *verdrängt* [eliminated] from fairs."[41] A cost of RM 2,000 for constructing a *Viehmarktplatz* (cattle fair plaza) was also budgeted[42]—for a fair that would take place without any Jewish participation.

From 1933 on, Nazi publications constantly agitated against Jewish cattle dealers and harassed them in their dealings.[43] The Nazi newspaper *Flammenzeichen* (Sign of Flames) was full of invectives against Jews, including the Langs. The September 1936 issue showed pictures of Leopold Lang, one in which he is carrying a whip and another in which he is holding a cigar. The caption derogatorily calls him "the model of a cattle Jew."[44] As cattle dealers were strictly licensed, the first restrictions, in 1937, were in the form of harassment when the dealers applied for their licenses to do business.

A slew of correspondence and notes at the Göppingen District Archive in Schloss Filseck testifies to the initially clumsy efforts by the Nazis to also draw cattle dealers into their surveillance network, and to the meaning of the new direction for Jews who were cattle dealers. This hyperactivity on the part of the Landratsamt in Göppingen was related to a new statute that was passed on January 25, 1937, the *Viehhandelsverordnung* (cattle trade ordinance). The issues raised are already familiar ones: Do cattle dealers keep *Kontrollbücher* (ledgers)? Is there an inspection of *Kontrollbücher*? Could individual customers verify that a given cattle dealer preordered the cattle and that the cattle dealer did not just "drive up to the customer without a previous order and offer the animals?" If cattle did not go directly from seller's stable to buyer's, did the cattle dealer have a peddler's license and not just a business permit, and were the cattle examined by a veterinarian (unless they were delivered directly to a butcher)? What were the chances of disease?

Now, however, the rules were no longer applied for the good of the general public, but to intimidate those cattle dealers who were Jewish and put them out of business. A particularly repugnant example is the harassment of Sally Sommer, a Göppingen cattle dealer and father of Margot. An article in the newspaper entitled "A Dangerous Swindler" reported that "Sally Sommer is a notorious captor of farmers." It is alleged that "Previously, he cheated farmers in Gunzenhausen in Bavaria, now he does business in Göppingen. He not only deals in cattle, but also in property, houses, and is responsible for the demise of innumerable farmers." After detailing Sally Sommer's "crimes," the writer expressed the hope that "he has lost his permit for the cattle business by now for," the writer assumes, "he must have surely committed new infractions."[45]

Some Christian cattle dealers also objected to the stringent measures and controls, and one went so far as to say he wished to trade places with the Jews. This brought a sharp rebuke from the Nazi official to whom he complained, and who threatened to impose a fine on him if there were any such future outbursts.[46]

In March 1937 the authorities in Stuttgart checked the *Kontrollbücher* of cattle dealers who possessed a business permit but not a peddler's license. "I did not find any significant irregularities. Since most of the cattle dealers have only *Gewerbelegitimationskarten* and are therefore not authorized as peddlers of cattle, I request the responsible officials to check the cattle dealers periodically. They should also check whether the *Nebenkontrollbücher* [subregisters] or the *Kontrollblöcke* [block registers] are kept properly."[47]

The next step in the process of delegitimization occurred with the segregation of "Jewish" cattle from "Aryan" cattle, which made anyone doing business with a Jew at fairs quite conspicuous. The *Göppinger Zeitung* of May 15, 1937, showed pictures from the local fair under the heading, "A Chapter in the Jewish Question—Jews Participate in the Göppingen Fair—Is That Necessary?" The captions to the pictures, which show the Langs, among others, were preceded by the question, "When will they be gone?" The article explains that although recently a number of local businesses were Aryanized, "we are still sufficiently blessed with the chosen people. Yesterday there also was a cattle fair here . . . in which approximately ten Jews participated." The article closed with the observation of "how important it is . . . to separate Jewish and 'Aryan' fairs so that it will be obvious who deals with Jews and who only watches out of curiosity. Even more desirable is the decision of most Württemberg cities to exclude Jews from fairs altogether."[48]

### The Case of the Langs

On July 1, 1938, Louis Lang's cattle dealing license was revoked by the Süssen municipality, putting Louis and Leopold out of business.[49] Hugo Lang's classmate Walter Sauter remembers, "Since the Langs were Jews, they were banned from being cattle dealers. The *Ortsbauernführer*, Emil Keller, was supposed to tell them. The *Ortsgruppenleiter* ordered him to go to the Langs and tell them to give up their business. Keller said, 'I am not going to do that. I was in the trenches with Louis [in World War I], I won't do it.' He refused. The mayor also refused to inform the Langs. The *Orts-gruppenleiter* had to do it himself."[50] The records thereafter show Louis as a *Privatmann*, an independently wealthy person. While this may have been true in good times, when the business was valued at RM 210,000,[51] he was now without any way to support the members of his immediate family. Within a short while, an additional eight relatives would take refuge with Louis prior to World War II because they were "evacuated" from the area of the western front. Hugo remembers that they now lived on savings. "We had enough money in the bank, but then the SS [*sic*] took that as well,"[52] during Kristallnacht, that is. The Langs were also still able to afford a cleaning woman, U. S. Ö., from Unterböhringen. She testified after the Holocaust, "In the years 1937–41 I worked as a cleaning woman for the Jewish family Louis Lang in Süssen. Because of this work I knew the entire house; I knew both families, Louis and Leopold Lang, and knew their familial circumstances very well. I myself enjoyed the trust of the Jews, especially since I lived in their immediate neighborhood [Haupt-strasse]. I can honestly say the families Lang [and later] Baer and Metzger did quite nicely in Süssen."[53] Municipal treasurer and Nazi Karl Häfele, installed in his post in 1933,[54] testified after the war that Louis was allowed to sell cattle unofficially until 1941 and that "Leopold Lang continued a commercial *Viehmästerei* [cattle fattening business] on the property [Hindenburgstrasse 45] that the *Gemeinde* had bought in 1938, and until 1941 also a cattle business, although such a business was generally forbidden to Jews from 1938 on. Even the *Öhmd* [hay] for Leopold Lang was secretly provided by the *Ortsbauernschaft* [local farmers organization] for this purpose."[55] This is corroborated in several sources, such as an inspection of the Lang property by Häfele in 1939 in connection with the possible rental of some of the property, as well as letters from Leopold and Eva to Fred and Hugo in the United States between August and November 1941, the month they were deported.

Because of being squeezed out of the economy, and because of the ever-worsening situation for Jews, the Lang families considered emigration. But, as historian Martin Dean points out, "Many attempts at emigration and capital transfer failed."[56] Already on August 29, 1938, nearly two months after losing their livelihood and more than two months before Kristallnacht, every family member applied for a visa to the United States. On September 22, 1938, the president of the *Viehhandelsverein* (Cattle Dealers Association) of Württemberg wrote to the head of the district administration in Göppingen that he had been ordered to conduct a survey of the number of

Jews in the cattle business in Württemberg. The Landrat (district administrator) gave the names of Julius and Heinrich Dörzbacher, Sally Sommer, and Berthold Wertheimer, all from Göppingen. He concluded his report with the comment that "no other Jewish cattle dealers in the district are known to me."[57] The Langs had been effectively excluded from making a living.

The event that changed the persecution of German Jews from personal, social, and legal harassment to physical attack occurred on November 9–10, 1938. Kristallnacht was a nationwide attack on German and Austrian Jews.[58] Although there are no reports of physical destruction in Süssen, Louis and Leopold Lang were arrested and sent to Concentration Camp Dachau, where they spent one month, from November 12 to December 12, 1938.[59] Leopold's concentration camp number was 25128.[60] Curiously, the arrests are not recorded in the town's Standesamt (register office), which ordinarily recorded every single movement to or fro. Although the arrests are noted in a government questionnaire used by a special office created after the war to document the individual fates of Jews during the Holocaust, the information is inadequate. A better record is available from the International Red Cross.[61] According to such postwar information, the Nazis at this time stole a sizeable amount of cash that Louis had in the home safe. Pertaining to this confiscation and in connection with the reparations process, Hugo and Fred wrote a statement on January 6, 1946, in which they stated, "As our father was taken to the Dachau concentration camp in the year 1938, the Stuttgart Gestapo confiscated the amount of RM 183,000 from our home safe."[62] This was money that Louis had hoped to use for the family (including Leopold's) to emigrate. "The intention was to exchange this money and transfer it to the United States. Our father was in touch with the Stuttgart Foreign Currency Exchange office about this matter but evidently he did not complete the transaction."[63] Nor could they recover from the loss, as their business had already been terminated. When his father and uncle were released from Dachau and sent home by train, Hugo was still working in Ulm. He found out on which train they would arrive and recalls, "I went to the railroad station [in Ulm] and we gave them everything we had. *Würstchen* (hot dogs), anything, until they got home."[64] Hugo told me that he bought from the vendor at the station whatever he had to sell.

Apparently Kristallnacht wreaked havoc on the Germans' pedantic tracking system of individuals. A directive from the Stuttgart Gestapo dated November 22, 1938, notified all police and district offices of the necessity to collect monthly statistics on the number of Jews in a given community.

"It has become necessary to update the statistics gathered on October 1, 1938, in Württemberg and Hohenzollern on *Volljuden* [also referred to as *Rassejuden*] on a monthly basis. I request that you report the additions and deletions, giving the new total, by the twentieth of the month, starting with November 30 (use statistics from November 1, 1938). Jews who are detained in other places are to be included in the numbers for their place of permanent residence, noting how many are in protective custody."[65] The first report from the District of Göppingen, dated November 30, 1938, noted, "The number of Jews in the District of Göppingen on November 1, 1938, was 237, one of them in protective custody." The breakdown listed 11 Jews for Süssen.[66]

In January 1939 the Nazis closed the Restaurant/Club Moos at Weinhof in Ulm where Hugo worked.[67] Hugo returned to Süssen, which was duly noted and transmitted to the Landratsamt by the mayor's office. "On January 23, 1939, Hugo Israel Lang, single, waiter's apprentice, returned to Süssen from Ulm. The total number of Jews in Süssen: 11."[68] All males in the *Judenhaus* now were conscripted as forced laborers for the Friedrich Bader lumber company, and Hugo Lang and Rudolf Metzger worked in its Eislingen branch (perhaps also other members of the extended family). Hugo remembers about 1939, "The next day, on order of the district leader, I had to report to the Eislingen branch of the Friedrich Bader lumber company.[69] I worked at a large wood cutting machine as a day laborer" until July 1941. "I could get there only with my bike, as we were no longer allowed to travel by train. My uncles and cousins also came along in the morning; all of us together rode there on our bikes."[70] In 1941 Leopold commented in a letter to Fred and Hugo that Ruth also works in the factory.[71]

There was a perception among the population that the relationship between the Langs and the local population was good. Mr. Schlecht testified that "the population of Süssen was on the whole well-disposed towards the Jews. The Langs never complained that the mayor's office or someone else caused them any difficulties."[72] The Langs' cleaning woman, U. S. Ö., testified, "Although other towns badmouthed the Jews and there were altercations, this never happened in Süssen. As I could hear for myself from what the Jews said, they liked Süssen."[73] This, even though the men had been reduced to forced laborers in the local industry. "Louis once told me that he didn't mind going to work in the factory if only he didn't have to leave Süssen. At that time, the Jews worked as day laborers in the Bader lumber business. The relationship between the Jews and the mayor's office was good."[74] Apparently she did not see anything wrong with Süssen citizens being deprived of their livelihood and performing forced labor? How could the relations between the oppressed and segregated Jewish citizens and the municipality be "good"? The municipality did not do anything to stop the abuse the Langs were experiencing nor prevent their deportation.

However, some individuals did help the Langs. Karl Schlecht, who was the trustee of the Lang property after the Holocaust, testified on October 2, 1948, "Many years before World War II, I got to know the Jew Louis Lang in Süssen. Since 1928 I was friends with Louis and with his family. Due to the unfortunate persecutions during the Third Reich I supported this family with whatever they needed and helped them in whatever way I could. During this time, until 1941, I visited the Jew Lang often and knew their personal circumstances intimately."[75] This seems to be largely true, as Kurt, after he returned from the camps, remarked what a good person Karl Schlecht was and how he had tried to help the family before deportation.[76]

In his interview with Professor Piehler, Hugo remembers that in "1938, 1939, 1940 . . . the neighbors came after dark and brought us eggs, or flour, or sugar, because we were no longer allowed to buy these groceries in the store; that's why the neighbors helped us. They came in the middle of the night, didn't even ring the bell, just left the groceries on our doorstep; they helped us. Sometimes there was a small note, but most of the time nothing. But we knew who brought the groceries. Nevertheless, there also were Nazis in town."[77] There certainly were. Marion Kaplan speaks of the ambiguity of German neighbors who performed "small kindnesses on the one hand" and exhibited "meanness on the other."[78] In a letter to Fred and Hugo after returning from the concentration camp, Kurt Lang lists the former Süssen Nazis and their fate.

The Lang families were not only deprived of their way of life, but of their property as well. On November 25, 1938, a strongly worded directive from the Gauamt für Kommunalpolitik (Province Office for Communal Politics) directed mayors "to buy suitable Jewish property immediately" because Jews were selling off their property as quickly and cheaply as possible.

According to reliable information during the past few days, the Jews are making every effort to sell their property as quickly as possible (as a result of Kristallnacht). In order to find interested buyers quickly, the asking price in the majority of cases is much below the true market value. Since the Jews are in such a hurry, only those qualify as buyers who have the necessary cash in hand, and it will thus only be possible for a few financially well-off Germans to take advantage of these offers. However, the sale of Jewish property is supposed to benefit the general public. For this reason, suitable property should be acquired by municipalities. Naturally, only those buildings and properties should be considered which can somehow be used for communal purposes or later be exchanged. The necessary monies for the purchase of these properties should be available. The *Gemeindeaufsichtsbehörden* [communal supervisory board] will not object to acquisitions of this kind. Taking out a mortgage for such a purchase should be considered only in special cases and sparingly. . . . *The matter is strictly confidential* [emphasis added]. The *Kreisamtsleiter* [district administrators] will share their perceptions [with the *Gauleitung* [leadership of the province] during their next activities report.

The state therefore was neither in control of ownership nor of price and sought to correct these "wild" transactions, steering them into quasi-legal and bureaucratic channels.[79] On November 29, 1938, the circular was forwarded to the mayors of five villages or towns by the Landrat in Göppingen, among them Süssen. This directive was pursued most conscientiously.

In the town of Süssen, sales contracts contained a clause that the town had a first purchase option for any local property, thus making the process of confiscation even easier.[80] The proceedings do not make for a pretty picture and are morally repugnant. On December 13, 1938—one day after Louis returned from Dachau concentration camp—the municipality "encouraged" Louis Lang to sell his property, located at the renamed Hindenburgstrasse (previously Hauptstrasse), to the town.[81] Because of his earlier arrest and incarceration in Dachau concentration camp, Louis surely understood the "voluntary" nature of this "invitation." This order also became a topic for discussion at the December 13, 1938, city council meeting, because property was to be bought for use or exchange by the town and without incurring any debts.[82] The city council discussed how to finance this purchase. The Gemeinderats-Protokoll recorded the decision of the mayor. "In a special circular of the Gauamt für Kommunalpolitik, dated November 25, 1938, communities are urged to acquire Jewish property. In Süssen this means the property of cattle dealer Louis Lang." This was followed by details of the property as well as the gardens. The real estate tax value was listed at RM 24,900, fire insurance estimate at RM 27,480. The gardens were valued at RM 17,900.

The municipality justified its action on the following bases: "Expansion of the municipality's real estate [the municipality owns two adjoining buildings], the creation of access to the area known as *Auen* at the spot designated by the local zoning office, creation of a new subdivision, storage of equipment by the *Bauhof* [municipal lumber yard], creation of an apartment in the servants house, storage of equipment of the local bank and the local farmers organization, stable replacement in the event that the municipal bull pen would have to be moved." The minutes continue, "The reasons for the purchase make sense to everyone. The Jew Lang, with whom I negotiated in this matter today, is absolutely willing to sell his property to the municipality of Süssen for RM 30,000. As this matter is urgent and is, per instructions [from higher up], to be kept strictly secret, I consulted with the *Beigeordneten* and city council members individually."[83] In other words, the mayor lobbied them privately before the city council meeting took place. The report states that six city council members and the *Beigeordneten*,[84] Finckh and S. were in favor of the purchase. Three city council members were either absent or ill.[85] The mayor decided to "immediately acquire the above named Louis Lang property for RM 30,000 based on the conditions detailed in the special sales contract; request the necessary permission as soon as possible; and provide for the necessary monies as much as possible in the 1938 operating budget."

Just how much the mass sale of Jewish property jeopardized the stability of the German economy is underlined by a circular from Hermann Göring himself as the Nazi official who was responsible for the economic Four-Year Plan, dated December 14, 1938.[86] In it, Göring admonished, "To ensure the necessary uniformity in dealing with the Jewish question, which most seriously affects the entire economy, I ask you to send me all directives and other important orders which concern the Jewish question, before they are released, for my approval. I ask you to inform all of the offices that are under your jurisdiction to abstain from any independent dealings in matters concerning the Jewish question."

According to a note in the files, a local businessman was also interested in the Lang property, and had been for some time.[87] However, at this point in time the Lang property could only be sold to the state, not to a private individual, because all of the transactions concerning Jews were strictly confidential and, as will become evident, in Jewish matters all of the government agencies were in collusion. Mayor Saalmüller wrote, "*Fabrikant*

G. called me this afternoon because of the Lang property. I had known previously that he was interested, but could not inform him of the acquisition of the Lang property by the *Gemeinde* because the order from the province office of the NSDAP was marked 'secret' or 'strictly confidential.' Given my previous conversation with Mr. G. it may have appeared to a third party as if I purposely didn't tell him about my plan. That is not the case. I explained this to him in detail. He understands my position as the community representative. I stressed especially that the obligation of secrecy forced me not to tell him anything about the municipality's plans. He said that that is the same everywhere and that he wouldn't hold this against me. Why did he call? Only to ask me to let him know when the *Gemeinde* apportions the Lang property. I told him that nothing like that has yet been pursued because the property does not yet belong to the municipality. I promised to let him know when we will consider the sale or rental [of the property]. This answer satisfied him. I asked him to also make a note of this conversation. . . ."[88]

The transaction was carried out swiftly and in strict secrecy. Since Louis needed money for his as well as Leopold's family to emigrate, he was willing to sell his property for RM 30,000. The municipality issued the sales contract on December 15, 1938.[89] On that day, "Justizpraktikant [legal assistant] Stohrer, representative of the district notary (who later helped Kurt repossess the Lang furniture), and notary public Walzer, with offices located in Donzdorf," wrote, 'Before me . . . appeared today the following persons whom I know personally and who are *geschäftsfähig* (of sound mind):

1) Lazarus called Louis Lang (*Jude*), *Privatmann*, formerly *Viehändler* in Süssen, Hindenburgstrasse 45,
2) Leopold Lang (*Jude*), *Privatmann*, formerly *Viehhändler* here,
3) his wife Eva Lang, née Liffmann (*Jüdin*), here,
4) *Bürgermeister* Saalmüller in Süssen, who acts as the legal representative of the Süssen municipality.

Before hearing their testimony, "the representative of the notary encouraged the participants, based on Statute No. 1121/7/2 concerning the sale of property by Jews, dated November 21, 1938, to get in touch with the *Gauwirtschaftsberater* (the Nazi economic advisor for the province) of the NSDAP, telephone 24768 Stuttgart."[90] To this the legal representative of the Süssen municipality, Saalmüller, responded as follows: "I have been instructed by the Province Office for Communal Politics to acquire suitable Jewish property for the community. The province economic advisor told me today on the telephone that he has absolutely no objection to the impending transaction."[91]

Thereafter all participants agreed to the sale. "Sales Contract: Paragraph 1: Lazarus called Louis Lang, *Privatmann*, formerly *Viehhändler* in Süssen, sells to the *Gemeinde* Süssen, the property in Gross-Süssen recorded in the Grundbuch Heft 435a, Abt. I, No. 17 and 18."[92] A list detailing what is included and what is not was part of the contract.[93] Louis further stated to the legal representative of the Süssen municipality: "Besides the *Muttergutsschuld* [inheritance from their mother] to my children in the amount of RM 5,200 [1,300 each, see previously mentioned court document] my regular [monthly] responsibilities amount to at most RM 300."[94] This statement indicates that Louis in no way expected the extra penalties that were immediately levied against him and his brother for being Jews and which kept him permanently indebted to the state. The amount the municipality was allowed to offer for the property was also regulated by the *Reich*. To this end there is a one-line sentence in paragraph 2 of the sales contract: "The *Preisstoppverordnung* [ordinance capping real estate prices] has been pointed out to the participants [in this transaction]."[95]

On December 19, 1938, the *Bezirksnotariat* (district notary) Donzdorf sent a memo to "Herrn Gauwirtschaftsberater der NSDAP" in Stuttgart, which stated, "Enclosed please find a notarized copy of the sales agreement between Leopold and Eva Land and the Gemeinde Süssen, as well as the rental agreements contained therein. Mayor Saalmüller, who will deliver these documents to you, can tell you more. Additional copies were sent to the Interior Minister in Stuttgart, the Württemberg Commerce Minister in Stuttgart, the Foreign Currency Office in Stuttgart (afterwards crossed out), and the State Revenue Office Geislingen."[96] The Louis Lang property had been successfully Aryanized.[97]

On December 21, 1938—by return mail—the mayor of Süssen received a *Pfändungsverfügung* (an attachment order) from the collection department of the State Revenue Office in Geislingen to seize the sales amount from "Louis Lang, cattle dealer" (note that his cattle dealing license had already been revoked on July 1, 1938).[98] The order was signed by the tax collector Knut Karl Oswald von Petzold, and stated that Louis "for the time being" owed the Reich "an unspecified amount," including RM 14,369.40 as follows: RM 394 income tax prepayment for September 10 and December 10, 1938; second, third, and fourth installment of the *Judenvermö-gensabgabe* (levy on Jewish assets) in the amount of RM 1,750 each for a total of RM 5,250; *Grunderwerbsteuer* (real estate acquisitions tax) in the amount of RM 1,538.40; and a confiscated claim from Leopold Lang to Louis Lang in the amount of RM 7,187.[99] Therefore the amount which "you [municipality] owe to the *Vollstreckungsschuldner* [debtor, person owing money to the State Revenue Office], namely Louis Lang, from the sale of his property will be attached. You are no longer permitted to pay the above-mentioned debtor. . . . You are further directed to pay the amount you owe [to the debtor], if it is not higher than the above sums which the debtor owes to the *Reich*, to the Finanzkasse [bursar] of the Finanzamt listed below (checking account of Finanzkasse: No. 616, Postscheckamt Stuttgart, or *Giro* account of Finanzkasse at Kreissparkasse Geislingen, no. 99) when it is due."[100]

On December 30, 1938, Gemeindepfleger Häfele added a note to the file that, according to the sales contract, the municipality (not the seller) was obligated to pay the real estate acquisition tax listed above.[101] What he then added is most interesting and puzzling: "I see the attachment order merely as a security measure of the Finanzamt and for the time being recommend no action."[102] Because the legalization of the Nazi theft of Jewish property was developing swiftly, it is possible that this municipal employee was not "in the know" as to the general Nazi measures taken to swindle German Jews out of their assets or, in a less charitable assessment, that he was covering his own tracks and those of the municipality.

In spite of the haste of the municipal officials to consummate the Lang house sale, the deal advanced slowly. On January 4, 1939, the district notary in Donzdorf sent a notarized copy of the sales contract to the Foreign Currency Office of the president of the Württemberg Finanzamt in Stuttgart, informing officials simultaneously of the four other offices that had received copies of the sales contract. It appears, however, that the notary public in Donzdorf, the official agent for the state as well as for the property owner, was not copied on the approval by the Foreign Currency Office.[103] On April 12, 1939, the Oberfinanzpräsident Württembergische Devisenstelle responded to an apparent inquiry from the notary in Donzdorf about the approval of the sale, informing him that they communicated the approval directly to "Herrn Louis Israel Lang" on March 14, 1939.[104]

An official communication from the head of the district administration in Göppingen to the mayor's office in Süssen, dated January 13, 1939, requested a response on four points regarding the Lang-Süssen transaction:

1) Verification of the status of the Langs. Were the sellers Jews according to Paragraph 5 of the I. VO of the *Reichsbürgergesetz* of November 14, 1935 (RG 131. IS. 1333) (First Regulation to Reich Citizenship Law [Nuremberg Laws] of September 15, 1935).[105]
2) A request to fill out an enclosed questionnaire.
3) Submission of an estimate from the leader of the local farmers' group concerning the harvest and market value of the property, as well as the appropriateness of the amount, and the buyer's need for the land.
4) An explanation of why and for what purpose the town of Süssen was buying the property.[106]

On January 24 the municipal authority responded to the district office on all four points.

1) Yes, the sellers were Jews in accordance with the law of November 14, 1935.
2) The enclosed questionnaire stated clearly that the reason for the sale of the property lay in the "Aryanization of Jewish businesses, loss of cattle dealing license, and emigration to the United States."[107]
3) The property was not a farm but a cattle business.
4) The purpose of the acquisition was as detailed in the city council minutes of December 13, 1938.[108]

This plan for "distribution" of the Lang property among the good citizens of Süssen complied with the Nazi directive to use Jewish property for the public good. This documentation also provides evidence that major local institutions from the mayor's office to the farmer's organization to the financial authorities were in collusion to defraud Jews such as the Langs.

On January 27, 1939, Louis wrote a letter to the mayor reporting that he had made an appointment and traveled to the Interior Ministry in Stuttgart to inquire what delayed the sale.[109] There he was told that the sales contract had not yet arrived from the Landratsamt in Göppingen. Louis was greatly agitated and wrote, "I ask you to speed up the approval process, as I have no other assets besides these, have to pay the second installment of the 'Jew tax', have to cover a larger commitment to my brother and former partner Leopold Lang, and have no means of any kind for my livelihood for the month of February. It is not possible for me to borrow money, since I cannot offer any collateral."[110] Louis asked Mayor Fritz Saalmüller to check for him [with the Landratsamt in Göppingen] why it took so long. The mayor did so the following day. His note of January 28, 1939, to the Landratsamt Göppingen stated, "The Interior Ministry seems to have made a mistake concerning the information which Lang received. I would also encourage the quickest possible approval of the completed sales transaction. The information provided by [Louis] Lang is credible. He had to give up his cattle business as of July 1, 1938. As far as I know he lives with his family of six primarily from his assets.[111] In expediting this approval process, it might also be important to consider that Lang would like to emigrate as quickly as possible, but that his desire to emigrate has been delayed by the authorities in control until all of his inner-German obligations, also to the revenue office, have been met."[112] Given the conditions, this would mean never. Since they had no more livelihood, Louis and Leopold could never escape from the advance taxing system that the Nazi state had put in place to defraud German Jews, hence they would never get permission to leave Germany. Dean observes that "The Nazi expropriation of Jewish property could be conducted on a grand scale only through the deployment of a wide array of special taxes, punitive measures, and confiscatory decrees that purported to provide legal title to the *Reich* and other beneficiaries. . . . Without a legal guarantee from the state, the market for stolen Jewish property would have remained limited, as would the revenue to be realized."[113]

In 1939 the Langs still hoped to emigrate to the United States. On January 30, 1939, the police department in Süssen received a notice that the moving company of Barr, Moering & Co. "would pack up the belongings of Mr. Louis Lang on February 13, 1939, from 8 A.M. on, and that they should send an official who would verify that the belongings were used items and not new ones."[114] Leopold's belongings were also packed for shipment. On September 3, 1945, Kurt Lang, on behalf of his cousin Ruth, submitted a list of the Langs' belongings that were stored in a trunk with Barr, Moering & Co. in Stuttgart and were confiscated by the state. This trunk [said to have been manufactured by the same carpenter Z. who wanted to rent the Lang garden] had included Ruth's dowry, consisting of "twenty sets of bed sheets, five tablecloths, and ten sets of kitchen towels."[115] A statement dated April 12, 1946, by the Office of Reparations for the Nazi Terror summarizes the activity. "There were two crates of used household goods which together weighed 572 kg [over 1,000 pounds]. They were the property of Louis Lang and Leopold Lang in Süssen. On December 4, 1939, the two crates, sealed by Customs, were sent to Rotterdam by Barr, Moering & Co. GmbH. There they were confiscated by the Gestapo. They were returned to Stuttgart and transferred to the president of the State Revenue Office Württemberg. On October 29, 1942, this office confirmed receipt of the crates to Barr, Moering & Co."[116] Crate J A 10 was addressed to Isidor Lang, New York, a cousin to Louis; crate J A 11 to Ingeborg Lang, New York, Louis's daughter.[117] Once they were confiscated, the contents were most likely auctioned off for the benefit of the *Reich*. Aly notes that "The practice of confiscating emigrants' belongings stuck in transit was typical throughout Germany."[118]

Four days later, on February 17, 1939, Louis had to report the still not approved property sale to the state authority, the Württemberg Industrie- und Handels-Beratungs- und Vermittlungszentrale (Industry and Commerce Consultation and Referral Service). From this correspondence we learn that the added shed and automobile garage are valued at an additional RM 15,000 [to the original 25,000 goldmarks that Louis had paid Fanny for the property] so that the town got a really good deal, as they should have paid the Langs at least RM 40,000 fair market price and not 30,000 as negotiated.[119] In addition, on March 11, 1939, Louis sold all of his farm and business equipment separately to the municipality for RM 750.[120]

Finally, on March 4, 1939 the Landrat in Göppingen received notice from the Interior Minister of the State of Württemberg that the sale was approved.[121] Apparently so did Louis Lang. "Based on paragraph 8 of the Statute Concerning the Use of Jewish Property dated December 3, 1938, Reichsgesetzblatt I, page 1709, I approve the . . . sale."[122] The letter was forwarded on March 7 to Mayor Saalmüller who, in turn, forwarded the letter to the Grundbuchamt on March 9, 1939. Because this transaction was top secret, he added the comment, "I will be happy to explain the [circumstances] of the transfer of ownership at any time."[123]

On March 9, 1939, the mayor dutifully reported to the Finanzamt that the sale had been approved, referring to the existing confiscation order of December 21, 1938, and inquiring whether it was still in effect.[124] The response arrived within five days, on March 14, 1939, the same day that the Foreign Currency Exchange approved the sale. The collection office of the Finanzamt Geislingen/Steige sent the mayor's office a "corrected order for seizure" that detailed Louis Lazarus Lang's "debts" to the *Reich*, for a total of RM 6,583.35—RM 474 for 1937 income tax, RM 124 for 1938 income tax; second, third, and fourth installments of the "Jew asset tax" in the amount of RM 5,250, and the remainder of Leopold Israel Lang's "Jew asset tax" of RM 735.35. "Because of these 'debts' the outstanding amount of RM 30,000 which you owe to the above-mentioned debtor [the Finanzamt] for the sale of his property is confiscated." It should be noted that this was in contradistinction to the original order, which specified an amount owed and that Louis would receive anything above what was "owed." The mayor was instructed to "pay RM 2,348 of the owed RM 6,583.35 immediately to the Finanzkasse Geislingen and to deposit the remainder of RM 4,235.35 into an account with the banking firm Gebrüder Martin in Göppingen. This money can only be spent with the permission of the State Revenue Office Geislingen." The corrected or updated order for seizure was also signed by tax collector von Petzold.[125]

On March 17, 1939, Mayor Saalmüller appeared before the representative of the notary public in Donzdorf, notary public assistant Fröhlich, for the *Auflassung*, that is, the transfer of the property, from Louis Lang to the municipality. Louis was not present. The mayor represented both sides.[126] He stated that "the approval of the Württembergische Wirtschaftsminister [interior minister] according to paragraph 8 of the Statute on the Use of Jewish Property has now been received." Thereupon the property changed hands. The new owner was the "Gemeinde Süssen." On that very day, the mayor nevertheless instructed the municipal treasury to pay Louis Lang for his property. Again, everything is listed in painstaking detail, including the deposit of the remaining RM 23,144.55 which was also to be remitted to the Bankhaus Gebrüder Martin "for the free use of Louis Lang."[127] Following the mayor's instructions, the municipal treasury immediately contacted the bank informing them that, based on the sales contract of December 15, 1938, and the approval of March 17, 1939, the town of Süssen owed "Louis Lang in Süssen, 45 Hindenburgstrasse, a remainder of RM 27,379.90. This amount will be remitted to you today for Louis Lang's account. . . . On orders of the State Revenue Office Geislingen we ask you to deposit RM 4,235.35 into a special account which may only be accessed with permission from the State Revenue Office in Geislingen."[128] Louis did not receive a penny of this money. As documented by Kaplan, Aly, and Dean, all moneys paid to German Jews at this time were deposited into a *Festkonto*, also called a *Sperrkonto*, at the bank in question.[129] These frozen funds never reached their intended recipients either because the recipients had to leave them behind when they fled, or because they were deported, in which case all of their property "fell" to the German state. A handwritten note by Mayor Saalmüller on this very directive, dated January 24, 1939, stated that he bought the property of "the Jew Louis Lang for 30,000 marks."[130] Deputy mayor Finckh, in the 1948 testimony, stated, "Presumably in 1938 the house was bought by the

*Gemeinde* according to the measures against Jews at that time. As far as I remember, the sale amount of presumably RM 30,000 was deposited by the *Gemeinde* into a *Festkonto* of which *the owner*, however, was *not allowed to avail himself*."[131] Here it appears as if this municipal official did know.

The next city council meeting after the approval of the sale took place on March 30, 1939. At the beginning of the meeting previously recorded items of business "up to and including March 6, 1939," were read, including the acquisition of the Louis Lang property, which was approved on March 4 by the interior minister of Württemberg. On this point, one of the city council members commented that "at that time he was basically in agreement with the purchase of the Lang property by the *Gemeinde*, but not with the price paid for the property, that the town had paid too much." The person added that even today he still felt that the price had been too high. That was also why he right away reported the transaction to the *Kreisleitung* (of the NSDAP). To this the mayor responded that he agreed with the first part of the remarks, but that he had always considered the price to be acceptable. In response to a query, he then informed the city council members of what he had so far neglected to tell them, namely that the sale had been approved without any hesitation and that the transfer of the property had already taken place on March 17. Besides, he claimed, others also wanted the property and would have paid more. "It is not without interest that numerous interested buyers locally and from outside [Süssen] came forward, offering even more than the town. The *Gemeinde* would never have been able to buy the property if we wouldn't have at least offered RM 30,000."[132] The town would dispute this claim in 1945.

From here on the situation of the Lang family deteriorated to the point of desperation. Although the rental agreement was contained in the sales contract, on June 1, 1939, Louis and Leopold each signed separate rental agreements with the town which allowed them to remain in their home as tenants for RM 50 rent per month each until December 31, 1939.[133]

Lazarus Lang, called Louis, private citizen, formerly cattle dealer in Süssen, currently living in Süssen as a tenant, signed the following lease: Paragraph 1) Use of the first floor in the house, 45 Hindenburgstrasse, [*Vorderhaus*] with five rooms, one kitchen, one hallway, one bathroom, one cellar space west, one attic space west, barn in the *Hinterhaus*, one toilet in the western part of the ground floor. Renter is allowed to use the *Waschhaus* (wash house), and he receives two keys to the house (front and back door), five room keys, one attic key, and two cellar keys. The apartment is to be vacated at the same time as that of his brother Leopold.[134]

Leopold's lease, issued to "Leopold Lang, private citizen, and formerly cattle dealer, as well as his wife Eva, née Liffmann, in Süssen," was "for the use of the ground floor of 45 Hindenburgstrasse (*Vorderhaus*), consisting of three rooms, one small room (*Kammer*), one kitchen, one hallway, one bathroom, one cellar space east, one toilet at the eastern end of the ground floor, attic east, barn in *Hinterhaus* as well as together with Louis Lang the shed attached to the *Hinterhaus*. The renter may also use the wash house. He is given two keys for front and back doors, five room keys, one attic key, two cellar keys. The apartment is to be vacated at the same time as that of his brother Louis."[135]

One can imagine the absurdity of the situation. Here are two brothers and their families, renting the very apartments in the house they had owned since 1929 and that had been in the family before, being given keys to each part of the house. One can only say, "*Ordnung muss sein!* [There has to be order]." Under the heading, "News from Süssen City Hall," this arrangement was broadcast in the regional newspaper, the *Geislinger Zeitung*, of June 10, 1939, quoting the city council minutes, "The contents of the limited lease between the *Gemeinde* and former cattle dealer Louis Lang and his brother was presented [to the city council]."[136] At this time everyone knew that the Langs no longer owned their property. Villagers make it their business to know everything. Did people not wonder what was going on? Already on June 2, 1939, the day after signing the rental agreements, Louis asked Häfele to extend their lease beyond the time period agreed upon (until December 31, 1939), as the visa office of the American Consulate had notified them that their number would be deferred in favor of Jews from the *Ostmark* and *Sudetenland* who needed to emigrate first.[137] He thus requested that they be allowed to remain in their house as tenants until July 1, 1940.[138] However, the only visa ever to arrive was Hugo's.

Of the Jewish residents in Süssen in 1933, only four managed to emigrate in time to escape deportation—Teddy, Henny, Fred and Hugo. The plight of the various Langs is obvious from their desperate efforts to find a way out of their situation.

Louis and Pauline Lang's daughter Regine Ingeborg, "Teddy," first moved voluntarily to Duisburg on August 24, 1934, but returned to Süssen on April 1, 1935; she then moved to Kassel on April 27, 1935, and from there to Bopfingen. From Bopfingen she returned to Süssen on June 17, 1937. She then left for Esslingen on August 25, 1937, and from there to Stuttgart. On May 17, 1938, she returned from Stuttgart, and again left Süssen for Stuttgart, 112 Seestrasse, on November 15, 1938 (after Kristall-nacht), only to return yet again to Süssen on December 23, 1938. The town informed the Gestapo that now "the number of Jews in Süssen is ten."[139]

Ingeborg [Teddy] and her sister Henny, "daughters of Lazarus Lang, formerly cattle dealer in Süssen," managed to emigrate to New York on February 17, 1939, "reducing the number of Jews in Süssen to nine."[140] This the Mayor's Office duly reported to the Landratsamt in Göppingen on February 22, 1939. The restitution claims filed by Kurt Lang reveal that Teddy and Henny had with them a number of valuables that had been approved by the Foreign Currency Office for export to the United States. Listed for Teddy are one golden wristwatch that was an heirloom from their mother, as well as a travel typewriter of the Hermes Baby brand, one Leica camera, and one Hohner harmonica. Listed for Henny Lang are one Swiss wristwatch, one travel typewriter of the Mercedes brand, one Leica camera, one valuable stamp collection that was an heirloom from their father, and one electric record player. All of these items were confiscated by the Zollfahndungstelle (customs inspection office) in February 1939.[141] Teddy lived into her fifties and died childless and of cancer in July 1973. Henny married Eric Gutenstein. They had three children. When her husband Eric died, Henny, who had lived in Great Neck, Long Island, for most of her life, moved to Florida where she lived until her death in 2004.

Leopold's son "Manfred Israel [Fred], single, tool and die maker, born August 26, 1921, in Ernsbach, District Öhringen," followed on April 26 [his bio says 25], 1939.[142] Hugo remembers that Manfred "worked for a Jewish company, Papierfabrik Fleischer, in Eislingen [5 miles west of Süssen]." The company produced paper goods. "The owner had a branch of the business in England. He told my brother to leave Germany. That was at the end of 1938. 'You have to leave for England within a month.' He sent him there to save him. That's why he sent him there."[143]

The Ludwigsburg documents contained two biographical sketches that Manfred wrote for reparations purposes in October 1955 and April 1956, respectively. Fred tried to get compensated for loss of education and train-ing. The first biographical sketch from 1955 is brief. It reveals that he had hoped to become an engineer, but could not get training because of his Jewish heritage. He states, "For this reason I went abroad; since I had not been able to study at the Technische Hochschule in Germany, I also could not pursue my chosen profession abroad." As a result, he was working as a *Werkschlosser*, a tool and die maker, with a monthly income of $360.[144] The second affidavit is more detailed, adding that, during his apprenticeship as tool and die maker between March 1936 and March 1939 in the Papierfabrik Fleischer in Eislingen, he had to take classes at the Gewerbeschule (trade school) in Göppingen once a week.[145] He again reiterated that he planned to continue his education as an engineer, but that no university or other institute of higher learning would accept him because he was Jewish. He also accounted for the short time he worked as a tool and die maker for Swan Mill Paper Company in Woolwich. These documents reveal something previous records did not, namely that he was arrested when the war broke out because of his German nationality and interned on the Isle of Man.[146] Since he succeeded in getting a visa to the United States, he must have been imprisoned sometime between September 1, 1939, and October 18, 1940.

In 1940 Walter Fleischer, the proprietor of Papierfabrik Fleischer in Eislingen and General Manager of Swan Mill Paper Co. Ltd. in London, as well as Dr. H. O. Fleischer, General Manager of Swan Mill Paper Co. Ltd., wrote two glowing letters of recommendation for Manfred to use for his new life in America. The first, from Dr. H. O. Fleischer, General Manager, and dated April 2, 1940, gives Fred a glowing character reference.

> I have known Mr. Manfred Lang for the last four and a half years, and I have known his Father, Mother and family for more than twenty years. I can truly state that Mr. Lang comes of a very highly respected family of the best standing, and that he can be recommended as a young man of good ability and character.
>
> I have had the opportunity to see him through three years' apprenticeship in a large paper mill, and a period of employment as a trainee in England for the last year. Mr. Lang is a very willing young man who is eager to learn and will certainly, on account of his knowledge of mechanics and English, be able to stand on his own feet and look after himself.

The second letter, from Walter Fleischer, proprietor of Papierfabrik Fleischer and general manager of Swan Mill Paper Co. Ltd., dated July 30, 1940, is equally as glowing as the first.

> Mr. Manfred Lang has been in my employ in my works in Germany and England from the 15th of April 1936 until the 12th May 1940 when he im-

migrated [*sic*] for America. He had a complete apprenticeship of 3 years as a mechanic in Germany and afterwards worked as a machine minder and mechanic at the Swan Mill Paper Co. Ltd. London S.E.

He had a thorough education and has been trained in repair work of all kind. He is a good turner, welder and shaper, grinder and has special knowledge of paper and paper converting machinery.

I found Manfred Lang always a most hard working and reliable member of my staff and I can only recommend him wholeheartedly to any firm who is interested to have a most conscientious worker.[147]

Manfred met Miriam Grünebaum in England. He left England for the United States on October 18, 1940.[148] Miriam followed later. They married in the United States on June 3, 1945. Their son, Peter, was born in 1945, and another son, Thomas, was born on May 12, 1956. In a second marriage Fred was wed to Rose Greenberg on September 10, 1982. Rose had two children by a previous marriage, Michael Fabian and Judy Milstein, and there is a granddaughter, Susan Lang.[149]

Manfred worked for General Cable Co. in New Brunswick, New Jersey. In 1955 and 1956 he tried to collect some damages for loss of livelihood. He stated that his salary was $360 a month, and that the loss of a higher income could never be corrected.[150] Fred used the law firm of Ulmer, Bundschuh, Ganssmüller, Schmidt and Reissmüller in Stuttgart for his reparations claims. But the Landesamt für Wiedergutmachung (State Office for Reparations) was not helpful. On August 2, 1957, they wrote to the lawyers that Fred's claim about completing an apprenticeship as *Werkschlosser* and his intention to become an engineer could not be accepted, "For this the applicant is lacking the necessary preprofessional training, in 1932 [fifth grade] he did not transfer to a higher education track. We therefore cannot comprehend how the applicant has been damaged in his training." They did have the records for Fred's disability insurance, from April 19, 1936, to February 29, 1938, and his profession was listed as *Schlosserlehrling* (tool and die maker apprentice).[151] Fred's lawyers responded on October 11, 1957, stating, "It is correct that the applicant has completed his training as a tool and die maker. He planned from the beginning to attend a technical college in order to become an engineer. It is not necessary to have a degree in higher education in order to attend a technical college. Rather, the requirement is that a student at a technical college has completed an apprenticeship."[152] A formal decision of November 27, 1957, declined Fred's claim for "reparations for loss of professional training" with the following justification: "The applicant attended the elementary school in Süssen/Württemberg until spring 1936 and then began training as a tool and die maker. This training he completed in spring 1939; then he emigrated via Holland and Scotland to the United States. There he worked in his profession."[153] The reason he could not be compensated for racial persecution was that he (even if he had not been persecuted on the basis of race), would subsequently have lost his livelihood anyway. "If the applicant had not been persecuted, he would have been conscripted to the *Arbeitsdienst* (labor service) and later drafted. Only after the end of World War II would he have been able to attend a higher technical college. The asserted damage to his training would also have happened without persecution." The German authorities surely had an answer for everything! The authorities then suggested that Fred sue the Land Baden-Württemberg.[154]

Additional reparations activity on behalf of Fred by the law firm included *Schaden an Freiheit* (loss of liberty) and emigration expenses.[155] The law firm withdrew the first claim, and a decision from the Wiedergutmachungsamt (Reparations Office), dated July 18, 1962, declined reimbursement for emigration costs on the basis that only Fred's emigration to England was to escape the Nazis. The costs for this journey were less than RM 500, and therefore below the limit that was reimbursable. "Emigration usually means the relinquishing of a previous home or permanent address and the establishment of a new home or permanent residence in a country which the emigrant has chosen as a refuge. The question whether the expenses of the further migration of a persecuted individual are also to be reimbursed depends on the originally chosen destination for emigration. From the statement of the applicant it is obvious that he, from the beginning, chose England as his destination. This can be seen from the fact that he settled in England and took a job there. Only the outbreak of the war and his subsequent arrest [in England] caused the applicant to move to the United States. Thus, the emigration from Germany due to persecution ended in England."[156] The compassion of these officials was zero. Of course Fred chose England since he had a sponsor there. It was better to get out than to be deported.

Fred was not very lucky in obtaining redress for the pain and suffering of the Nazi chicanery. He retired in 1984 and died on February 18, 1987, in New Jersey.[157] The obituaries noted that "Fred Lang, 65, of Cranbury, who retired as an engineer, died in the St. Michael's Medical Center in Newark. Born in Germany, he lived in Hillside before moving to Cranbury four years ago." Fred was survived by his wife Rose, two sons, Peter and

Thomas, a stepdaughter, Mrs. Judy Milstein, a stepson, Michael Fabian, his sister Ruth and brother Hugo. The funeral was held on Wednesday, February 18, 1987, at 11:30 A.M. at the Bernheim-Apter-Goldsticker Suburban Funeral Chapel, 1600 Springfield Avenue in Maplewood, New Jersey.[158] May his memory be for a blessing.

Of the Jakob Lang family, Jakob's widow, Fanny, who had returned to her hometown of Rexingen in 1929, emigrated to the United States in 1937. There she was able to join all three of her children, Alma, Otto, and Lina.

On April 28, 1939, Fred's cousin, "Kurt Israel Lang, single, student, born July 7, 1924, in Gross-Süssen," moved to Frankfurt a. M., Weberstrasse 15. The number of Jews now stands at 7."[159] Kurt Lang returned from Frankfurt to Süssen on September 3, 1939, and did not leave again until deportation.

On May 1, 1940, Ruth Sara Lang moved to Rheydt-Odenkirchen, 80 Horst Wessel Strasse,[160] where her maternal grandparents Jakob and Sofie Liffmann lived. However, she returned to Süssen on May 22, 1940, and stayed there.[161]

On May 6, 1940, her cousin, "Israel Siegfried Lang [sic], single student, born in Gross-Süssen on July 10, 1925, son of Louis Lazarus Lang, moved from Süssen to Frankfurt, 13 Fischerfeld. The number of local Jews now stands at 13."[162] He returned to Süssen.

### The Extended Family Takes Refuge with the Langs

Although Louis and Leopold and families were in dire straights, relatives from other places started to come and seek shelter with them. The first one was Eleonore Sara Plaut, née Samuel, known as Nellie. Mrs. Plaut, born on March 21, 1894 in Rodalben/Pfalz, and Siegfried Plaut, born April 23, 1892, in Obervorschütz, were married on June 26, 1913, in Obervorschütz. They had two children, Manfred and Hannelore. Mr. Plaut died on December 13, 1937.[163] The whereabouts of the children are unknown. Mrs. Plaut moved to Süssen from Göppingen on June 1, 1939.[164] Although she was not a relative of the Baers, who would also move to Süssen right before World War II began, she probably knew Louis and Leopold and families through their relatives in Rodalben, the Baers and the Metzgers. Louis's wife Pauline was also a Baer. There is no further mention of Mrs. Plaut in any of the town records, and, according to the records, she was not deported from Süssen. Hugo Lang has a picture of himself and his uncle Louis on an outing to Killesberg in Stuttgart in 1939. There is an elegantly dressed woman in the picture as well. When I asked Hugo who she was, he said she was Louis's housekeeper, but mentioned no name. This may indeed be Mrs. Plaut, especially when one considers gossip that Elonora was sweet on Louis. However, Louis married someone else shortly before deportation in 1941.[165]

On August 27, 1939, Alfred Israel Baer, brother of Louis's late wife Pauline and their three children, Werner, Siegfried, and Hans, came to Süssen from Rodalben, district Pirmasens, in the Rheinpfalz. Hugo Lang remembers that Alfred was an American citizen and married to Hermine (Louis and Leopold's half-sister Hilda, born in 1894).[166] Why he would be deported as an American citizen has puzzled me for a long time, as the Nazis were generally careful not to deport foreign nationals because of the diplomatic repercussions. According to existing correspondence, an old man in Rodalben remembers Alfred Baer as a native of Rodalben. "He is supposed to have been very poor and made a living as a peddler."[167] This would solve part of the mystery, as Alfred Baer was then German-born and had emigrated to the United States. The question is when? Hans was born December 4, 1917, in Süssen or Pforzheim, and Alfred, who may or may not have been the father of Hans, married Hermine on July 2, 1920. Could he have left Germany after the marriage to make something of himself? And did he plan to send for his family eventually? If his family asked him to come back in the thirties he probably did not yet have American citizenship, which is why the Nazis lumped him together with the German Jews they wanted to get rid of.

According to information from the mayor's office in Süssen, Siegfried Baer voluntarily moved to Frankfurt from Süssen on December 8, 1940.[168] Werner Joseph Baer voluntarily moved from Süssen to Gross-Breesen, Silesia on January 2, 1940.[169] The reason for this eluded me for some time, but an old newspaper clipping in Hugo Lang's possession gave a hint, with the internet doing the rest. Before World War II the Nazis tried to get German Jews to emigrate. One of the destinations was Palestine. In 1936 the Centralverein deutscher Staatsbürger jüdischen Glaubens obtained a 567 acre farm in Gross-Breesen from a wealthy Polish Jew who fled Germany. They hired Dr. Curt Werner Bondy (1894–1972), a communal idealist, to establish a two-year farm-training program for Jewish teens.[170] This program was supposedly approved by the Gestapo. The young people chosen belonged to the Zionist youth organization Bund Deutsch-Jüdischer Jugend (BDJJ). It is possible that Werner Joseph was one of the trainees. The training farm existed from 1936 to 1941 and was reportedly dealt with horribly during Kristallnacht. Gross-Breesen is better known as a concentration camp. The estate, as so many others, "was turned into a labor camp to support the German Army with Polish prisoners for slave labor."[171] The later reputation has survived to today while the earlier, positive function, is remembered by only a few. Only Alfred's son Herbert Heinrich Baer was able to emigrate to the United States without ever moving to Süssen.[172] He was the only survivor of his family.

In addition to the Alfred Baer family, Alfred Israel Metzger, his wife Eugenie Rosa, née Baer, and their son Rudolf Julius also arrived from Rodalben/Rheinpfalz. The Metzger's home had in fact been turned into the Rodalben ghetto, from which deportation to a concentration camp was certain. Both families had been "evacuated" from places in the Rhineland that were close to the western front in 1939. However, they were not evacuated for their safety, but for the sake of the *Reich*, as they were seen as potential spies and thus a security risk.[173] A post-Holocaust letter from the lawyer of Henriette Mary Schloss, née Metzger (daughter of Alfred) in Israel to the Süssen mayor, Eisele, dated July 15, 1958, states that "these three persecuted persons were first arrested at their home in Rodalben, then forcibly resettled to Süssen, and from Süssen it is said they had departed for Riga."[174]

In a letter, dated November 14, 1939, Rodalben Mayor, Eugen Willenbacher, was trying to find the Metzgers.[175] He inquired of the Einwohnermeldeamt (Resident Registration Office) in Göppingen whether "Kaufmann Alfred Israel Metzger, formerly of Rodalben," lived there.[176] The Göppingen police department responded that he had never registered with the office in Göppingen. After seeing a notice concerning Baer and Metzger, on December 18, 1939, Bürgermeister Saalmüller wrote to the Ortspolizeibehörde (local police station) in Rodalben, inquiring what was new concerning the evacuation of Rodalben. "Diverse Jewish refugees from Rodalben moved here to live with their relatives. Since you reported two of them because of a transgression against the *Reichsmeldeordnung* (*Reich* registration ordinance), I would be interested to know what is new concerning the evacuation of Rodalben. Did your residents return, similar to the residents of many locales in District Rastatt? Please respond as soon as possible so that I can consult with the Landratsamt [Göppingen] and the district leadership." Part II asks whether it was correct that businessman Alfred Israel Baer was an American citizen.[177] Willenbacher responded on December 22, 1939, that "The two Jewish families Baer and Metzger left here, like all Jews living here, without being ordered to do so and without notifying the Vital Statistics Office. A return of the Jews to the green zone cannot be permitted because of suspicion of espionage, at least I cannot take the responsibility for it. The living quarters of the Jews have been reoccupied, so that their return is impossible." The latter most likely was the key reason why the Baers and Metzgers were not welcome back. Willenbacher further stated, "If the Jew Alfred Israel Baer claims to be an American citizen, this is a lie. It may be appropriate to censure the Jew Baer because of these false statements and to report him to the police."[178] Saalmüller sent the mayor's letter to a higher authority for a decision.[179]

Eugen Willenbacher was also the *Ortsgruppenleiter* of the NSDAP, a much more zealous party member than Mayor Saalmüller. On February 1, 1940, he wrote to the district leadership of the NSDAP in Pirmasens as a precautionary measure to get some support in the matter. He reported to them that

> During the night of August 26–27, 1939, the rest of the Jewish families who lived in Rodalben disappeared, among them the Jews Metzger, Alfred Israel and Baer, Alfred Israel.[180] They moved to Süssen, District Göppingen. . . . Their move was entirely voluntary and without duress. The Jews had not reported their intention to move, which is required according to the registration statutes of the *Reich*. I searched for them for some time, so that I could bring about their punishment for breaking the law, but without success. Eventually I learned that the two families had settled in Süssen. Six months later the mayor of Süssen tried to send the Jews under discussion back to Rodalben, because he assumes that they were forced to leave Rodalben due to the danger of war. I deny this request, as I am in no way obligated to grant such a request. It was completely clear to me that, in regard to espionage, enemies of the state have no business behind the *HK* [*Hauptkampflinie*, main battle line] and in a place which houses three batteries of heavy artillery and more.[181] This especially since moving to the green zone is prohibited as of October 5, 1939, by order of the Army headquarters in Wiesbaden (Paragraph 3). Hereupon the mayor of Süssen turned to the Landrat in Göppingen and to the Württemberg Interior Ministry in Wiesbaden [for help].

The response was not to the Rodalben mayor's liking, for the civilian administration in Wiesbaden stated on February 8 that they had "no objections" to the return of the Jewish families under consideration.[182] The Rodalben mayor retorted that "the property previously owned by the Jews has now been appropriated by the Grundstücksverwertungsgesellschaft für das jüdische Vermögen G.m.b.H. [the Association for the Disposal of Jewish Real Estate] in Neustadt on Weinstrasse and sold to German countrymen who have taken possession thereof. Thus, it is technically impossible to again find housing for the Jews. Even Germans who are politically above reproach are denied residency rights in Rodalben, and if they live here, they are sent away on short notice." This assertion makes it again likely that the Metzgers were telling the truth about being expelled after all. Willenbacher assumed that "this is even more the case with Jews. I therefore go on record in this matter and state that I will continue to refuse residency to the Jews under discussion during the war on the basis of security concerns. Heil Hitler!"[183]

The correspondence between Mayor Saalmüller and Mayor Willenbacher continued to heat up. On February 27, 1940, Mayor Saalmüller angrily accused the mayor of Rodalben of having a Jewish problem.

> Since the Jews who temporarily live here with their relatives continue to have their residence in Rodalben, it is your job, and not mine, to again find housing for your Jews there as quickly as possible, especially since you deprived them of their previous homes. In any case, your plan to [ethnically] cleanse your Jewishly polluted village at the expense of other municipalities, especially under the current circumstances, cannot be reconciled with decency and lawfulness. That cannot be nor will I tolerate it for understandable reasons, at least as far as my municipality is concerned. Finally, I want to caution you that you continue to be the responsible welfare organization for the well-being of these families in the event that evacuation family support cannot be claimed. In the event that they are not entitled to evacuation care, this case is classified as plain deportation, according to the *Reichsfürsorgeverordnung* [imperial welfare statute], unless you give me evidence to the contrary.

He wrote that he expected an answer within eight days—or else.[184] On February 29, 1940, the Rodalben mayor responded, not in kind, "A return is completely out of the question. You can keep your comment that my action is incompatible with decency to yourself. I know in any case on what basis I need to act."

Mayor Saalmüller in no way agreed with the Rodalben mayor's stand. But he had been called up to the military and could not further deal with this matter at this time, although he would have liked to. "As a precaution I can only tell you that your action is sharply criticized by all officials with whom I have spoken about this matter. I only temporarily refrain from an official complaint against you." But later Saalmüller would have his own troubles, and the mayor of Rodalben would get away with murder.[185]

In post–World War II testimony, Häfele and others also weighed in on the matter. Häfele testified, "In 1939 the municipal administration, without any question, allowed the two Jewish families, Baer and Metzger, to move into the community-owned apartments occupied by Lang and without demanding additional rent. The families Baer and Metzger were, at the beginning of the war, evacuated from their places of residence in Pirmasens [Rodalben] and brought here—just like that. Baer and Metzger liked it here and after completion of the campaign against France they did not return to their former place of residence."[186] He does not mention what the previous correspondence revealed, namely that they were no longer welcome because their apartments were otherwise occupied.

When asked how many Jewish families lived in Süssen at that time, Deputy Mayor Finckh stated that "there were four families—cattle dealer Lang with two families, one Baer family and one Metzger family. In spite of the general persecution against Jews and Jew baiting, the Jews who lived in Süssen were generally liked and respected by the general population."[187] No information to the contrary has come to light.

Karl Schlecht, the trustee of the Lang estate, testified, "Later, at the beginning of the campaign against France, the two Jewish families Baer and Metzger came to live with the Langs. I got to know them personally as well and can honestly say that they were without exception people with a good reputation and of class who, before their arrival in Süssen and also in the later deportation, lost all their belongings."[188] A November 7, 1988, article, "Stationen auf dem Weg zur Vernichtung jüdischer Mitbürger" (Stations Towards the Destruction of Jewish Fellow Citizens), in the newspaper *Rheinpfalz* on the occasion of the fiftieth anniversary of Kristallnacht shows the original Metzger/Baer property at Untere Hauptstrasse, a stately two-story building with an attic apartment. It is attached on either side in the manner of urban structures along main streets. The structure became the Rodalben ghetto, from which the residents were deported to the concentration camp of Gurs in France. Had they not escaped, this also would have been the Metzgers' and the Baers' fate. We learn that the Metzgers and Baers together had a textile business. Businesswoman Eugenie Metzger was defamed on April 24 and 26, 1933, in advertisements in the local newspapers, the *Gräfensteinbote* and the *Mitteilungen*. Under the headline, "Juden-Frechheit" (Jewish chutzpah), Eugenie Metzger is accused by an eyewitness of having spoken these words to a Chemnitz salesman,

"Von einem Christen kaufen wir nichts mehr!" (We no longer buy from someone who is Christian).[189] The ad in the *Gräfensteinbote*, placed by the local Nazi group, demands that Rodalben citizens no longer frequent the Kaufhaus Metzger or they will be exposed in public, the ad in the *Mitteilungen* supports the *Gräfensteinbote* ad and produces a witness who is willing to swear to the truth of this statement. Whom to believe? Rodalben Christians are pitted against their Jewish neighbors and challenged to believe the witness's statement because she is Christian.[190]

So that the dragnet would be without mercy, a Gestapo circular of October 24, 1939, ordered local authorities "to also include those Jews [in their monthly count] who are moving here from the evacuation areas in the west [such as the Baers and the Metzgers] with a corresponding supplement."[191]

With one exception, the Metzgers and the Baers remained in Süssen until deportation on November 28, 1941. On December 1, 1940, "Siegfried Israel Baer, single student, born October 4, 1930, in Rodalben . . . moved to Frankfurt an der Oder, Rückertstrasse 53, from Süssen. The number of local Jews now stands at 13."[192] An additional note for the files was written on December 9, 1940. One of the items dealt with "the departure of the Jewish student Baer," noting specifically that this move was reported to the Gestapo in Stuttgart on December 9, 1940.[193]

The beginning of World War II on September 1, 1939, found a number of Süssen's civil servants conscripted for the military. On September 22, 1939, August Eisele, municipal *Obersekretär* (chief clerk) and post-war mayor from 1948–75,[194] sent a postcard to Mayor Saalmüller, informing him that "a branch of the Süssen mayor's office might be opened in Badenweiler," where he was stationed, as were members of the surveyor's office in Geislingen—Messrs. Kurfürst, Sperrle, Hilderhof—as well as Pfarrer Pfleiderer (Süssen), notary public assistant Fröhlich, and Herr Pfleghaar, all of whom had been detailed to his regiment. His conclusion, "If it continues to be as quiet here as it is now, then the war isn't bad."[195] Not yet in Badenweiler, but the horror of another kind of war was heating up at home. *Pfarrer* Pfleiderer also sent a postcard to Mayor Saalmüller, dated September 18, 1939, with a picture that may be Badenweiler, "Greetings from near the front from your Martin Pfleiderer. Greetings to the entire family, also to the children." This friendship signals more than just friendliness among the village leadership, it spells alignment with Nazi ideas. One of the biggest obstacles to a grassroots resistance movement against the Nazi policies was the long engrained anti-Judaism fostered by the churches over centuries. Robert P. Ericksen and Susannah Heschel as well as Helmut Walser Smith have explored the ways in which centuries-old Jew hatred nurtured the alignment of the churches during the Nazi period.[196] It would not be long before Mayor Saalmüller himself was also drafted, and the hell of the Holocaust would come down with full force on the Langs.

Louis Lang, whose wife Pauline had died in 1935, married a second time on February 24, 1941.[197] His bride was Fanny Landau from Munich, a short, stocky, good-looking woman, who was born in Frankfurt am Main on February 2, 1893.[198] According to the municipal report to the district authorities on March 12, 1941, with Fanny the total number of Jews in Süssen stood at 14,[199] the highest it had ever been. This was perhaps not a marriage made in heaven, but rather one of convenience. The Langs' cleaning woman, U. S. Ö., who lived alongside the stables and had two sons who died in World War II, testified: "Shortly before the deportation of the Jews the cattle dealer [Louis] Lang married his second wife [Fanny Landau]. From then on I did not clean any more, as the Jews were short of money and did their own cleaning. For this reason I do not know any details of the later deportation of the Jews, except what people were saying."[200] A witness commented that "the second Frau Lang" was not friendly, so she stopped visiting the family.[201] No wonder, this was in 1941!

On October 17, 1941, the Landrat in Göppingen reported to the Gestapo that on October 1, ninety Jews lived in the district of Göppingen, of these thirteen in Süssen, six of whom were *Rückwanderer* (returnees).[202] This report was compiled after Hugo left Süssen and before the deportation of his family. However, if the two Baer boys were in Süssen, there should have been eight returnees, not six, for a total of fifteen. On December 17, 1941, after deportation, Süssen disappeared from the monthly statistical report.[203]

### Confiscation of Radios Owned by Jews

During the time that the Nazi regime was in power, more than four hundred statutes restricting Jewish liberty and livelihood were enacted. After World War II began, the Nazis completely excluded Jews from society, making their lives not only difficult but dangerous. On September 12, 1939, less than two weeks after the beginning of World War II and right before Rosh Hashanah, the Gestapo passed a statute that ordered an 8 P.M. curfew for Jews. It further decreed that Jews had to construct their own air raid shelters.[204]

On September 22, 1939, the holiest day in the Jewish calendar, an order of the Gestapo instructed all police headquarters and state offices to confiscate radios owned by Jews.

In expansion of the statute of September 1, 1939, the Jews in Germany are to be excluded from every independent radio reception (also German radio). All radios owned by Jews are to be confiscated so that they can be put to use for the German *Volk* in a different way. The guidelines below are to be followed:

1. On September 23, 1939, all radios owned by Jews are to be confiscated. Collection [for redistribution] will occur later.
2. If Jews are in the possession of radios they do not own, but which have been only lent to them by a third (non-Jewish) party, (rented, borrowed, installment plan), they are to cease their use and return the radios immediately to the owner.
3. The appropriate post offices of the Reichspost are to be instructed to revoke the Jews' permits to own and operate a radio.
4. If non-Jews live in a household with Jews, it is to be assumed that the radio belongs to the Jew. Should the non-Jew claim ownership, he/she needs to prove his rights, if possible through an affidavit. If such evidence [of ownership] is not available, the radio is to be confiscated. . . . [205]
6. Foreign Jews are not affected with the exception of Polish Jews.[206]

At 2:30 P.M. that very day, September 22, the mayor of Süssen received the following order: "On Saturday, September 23, 1939, all radios in possession of Jews are to be confiscated. Preparations are to be undertaken immediately."[207]

The Langs were not spared. Louis owned a Saba 521 WL AC/DC unit. Leopold owned a Saba 341 WL AC/DC unit. Their two radios were taken away from them.[208]

The police officer in Geislingen reported to the Landrat in Göppingen on September 26 that on Saturday, September 23, 1939, "by order of the Landratsamt in Göppingen I confiscated two radios in Süssen and one in Salach from Jews and delivered them to the respective city halls. The proper lists will follow with confirmation of the *Aktion*."[209] The two radios in Süssen belonged to Louis and Leopold Lang; the radio in Salach to Emil Neuburger, a local industrialist.[210] The Mechanische Weberei J. H. Neuburger, was owned by the only local Jewish family. The Neuburgers also

belonged to the Göppingen Jewish community. The company was Aryanized in 1938 (acquired by Firma Steiger & Deschler in Ulm-Söflingen),
the family was able to emigrate to the United States.[211] After World War
II the company was returned to the original owners via a legal settlement.
The business no longer exists.

On the same day, September 26, 1939, the Gestapo Stuttgart weighed
in as well. "I ask you to present immediately duplicate lists of the radios
confiscated from Jews."[212]

An eager-to-please *Gendarmeriemeister* Frank in Gingen/Fils, a town
just a couple of miles to the east of Süssen, wrote on September 27, 1939,
"Based on instructions from the police department in Geislingen, I marked
the two radios of the Jews Louis and Leopold Lang, which are being held
in the mayor's office in Süssen, according to the instructions. Every radio
was tagged and a list was left with the mayor in Süssen. I immediately
instructed the post office to revoke the permit of the two Jews for radio
reception. I disarmed the connection to the antenna and the grounding.
Enclosed are two copies of the list with details of the radios and their
whereabouts."[213] This man was later involved in the deportation of the
Jews in neighboring Weissenstein.

On October 10, 1939, the *Assessor* (assistant judge) of the Landrat Göppingen wrote to the Stuttgart Gestapo concerning Jewish-owned radios.
"Enclosed I send you in duplicate a list of the radios confiscated from
Jews in the district of Göppingen (not including the city of Göppingen).
The radios were confiscated on September 23, 1939, and taken to the city
halls of Salach and Süssen. The post offices in Salach and Süssen were
simultaneously instructed to revoke the permits of the Jews in question to
operate a radio."[214]

Letters dated November 7, 1939, from the assistant judge at the *Landratsamt* to the respective mayors of Süssen and Salach notified them that,
according to information from the Gestapo Stuttgart, these radios were
being assigned by the chief of the security police to the SS Ellwangen. The
SS Ellwangen would come to pick up the radios immediately. "I ask you to
hand over the radios and obtain a signature and to send me a duplicate of
such a receipt."[215] A week later, on November 14, 1939, the assistant judge
at the Landratsamt wrote to the mayor in Süssen immediately requesting
a receipt of the transfer. Mayor Saalmüller wrote in a note, "Carried out
with report dated November 11, 1939."[216] Exactly a year after Kristallnacht,
Jews had been totally excluded from German society.

There is a stack of documents just on the Langs' two radios alone. In 1939 there were still about 230,000 Jews living in Germany.[217] The amount of paper work and time expended on this process is mind-boggling and says something about the pathology of the Nazi mindset.

The municipality of Süssen scrupulously adhered to Nazi directives and regulations, but in everyday life behaved as if nothing was different. While the town had taken the first legal step and would take all subsequent legal steps to exclude the Langs from life in Süssen in complicity with the Nazis, they continued to accommodate the Langs in other ways until deportation. When Mayor Saalmüller served a life sentence in Landsberg Prison as a Nazi war criminal after it was all over, he was asked by town officials to help them make their case before the Court of Restitution against the Langs. In doing so, he noted that it was important to carefully amass a collection of evidence. He suggested that the following points be included:

a.  Decent humane treatment of the Jews in Süssen by the municipality as well as the Nazi Party, obtain testimony from the two clergy.
b.  Award of the Iron Cross to [Louis] Lang, inclusion in the honor roll for soldiers [from World War I].
c.  Approval of food stamps.
d.  Lang meeting with mayor concerning permits, approval by Häfele.
e.  Proceedings against a criminal . . . who bothered Frau Lang, penalty by the lower court. . . .
f.  Permission for the Rodalben families [Metzger and Baer] to move to Süssen; periodic cause of concern to mayor.
g.  Extension of lease, no limitation of any kind by the municipality in the house, cattle business, purchase of house, etc.
h.  No insults, let alone bodily injury, against the Langs.
i.  No kind of local limitation whatsoever. Reason: Old Mrs. Lang [Fanny, widow of Jakob] did much good, Louis and his brother grew up in Süssen and were on friendly terms with most of the city council members.
j.  [no entry]
k.  Need to collect testimony from senior citizens . . . who can confirm the overall situation at that time. All of these details are important.[218]

In connection with the above "justification," there is not an iota of contrition in Saalmüller's attitude towards the Langs' misfortune and later demise.

## Public Distribution of Lang Belongings

Even before the sale of the house was finalized in 1939, and although the Langs still lived in the house, the municipality received requests from local residents to rent parts of the Lang property.[219] The regional newspaper quoted the city council minutes from April 25, 1939: "The possibility already now exists, while the seller Lang still lives here, to lease a part of the barn, building no. 45a of the Hindenburgstrasse."[220] With the "advertisement" of the situation in the newspaper, the "secret" was well known.

Apparently the local citizens were not at all bothered by running into the Langs during their comings and goings on the Lang property. What did they say to their victims when they came face to face with them? From all the postwar testimony one could surmise that such meetings were cordial, if not downright friendly.

Already on February 7, 1939, E. K., a local businessman, inquired whether he could rent the automobile garage for the usual rate of RM 8 per month.[221] This was authorized on April 1, 1939,[222] and reported by the regional newspaper on June 10. The lease was dated May 30, 1939,[223] and ran for two years. It was cancelled on March 31, 1941.[224] A gloss in the margin from the long-time post–World War II mayor, August Eisele, at that time a city hall clerk, noted, "Was rented out only for a short period of time."[225] Hugo remembers his family's car, an Adler, still being in the garage during the time K. rented it. What happened to their car has never been clarified. On May 20, 1942, Häfele commented that from now on the garage would be used to house the fire engine.[226]

On April 21, 1939, the chairman of the local bank wrote to the mayor, inquiring about renting the stable and shed. "As you know from E. K., we urgently need suitable space to store feed and fertilizer as well as machines and ploughs. Such space is available on the former Lang property. We therefore request rental of the stable in the barn [45a] as well as the wash house in the rear building [45b] as well as the automobile garage [45c] at an appropriate annual rental rate."[227] The bank's request was reflected in the city council minutes of June 2, 1939, as well as the newspaper report of June 10. "Among those interested in leasing the property are the Spar- und Darlehenskassenverein [a bank] Süssen, who require space for storage of fertilizer and farm equipment."[228] Häfele and the chairman undertook an inspection of the Lang property. On June 2, 1939, he wrote a note for the files that "Leopold Israel Lang—in contradiction to the lease—put cattle in the eastern stable in front [of barn 15a], but is not using the stable stipulated in the lease. Furthermore, the shed which was promised to the Darlehensverein to store equipment is rented to Lazarus Lang in the lease, so that it cannot be used otherwise before December 31, 1939, without his consent. In this shed he stores sawdust and harnesses as well as his cattle wagon. It is important for Leopold to be able to use the entire barn as long as he has his cattle in the barn. I arranged a rent of RM 15 annually with him for the eastern barn portion, which is not included in the lease."[229] The bank's request to rent "space on the Jewish property," was approved on June 17, 1939, at a rate of RM 15 per month, and signed by Häfele.[230] However, the bank's board of directors objected to the high rate,[231] not to the fact that the Langs were still living there, and the president declined the offer on June 19, 1939, on the grounds that "The necessary space in the rear building to store machinery will probably not be available for another year, until after the departure of Leopold Lang. Also, the rent of RM 15 is too high."[232] Another note in the margin from Eisele comments, "Did not happen."[233]

On April 12, 1939, a neighbor of the Langs, K. Z., a *Zimmermeister* (carpenter), wanted to rent the Lang's orchard,[234] although Louis and Leopold and their families had use of the vegetable garden (but not of the orchard) as part of their lease. Z. wrote, "Since the municipality is now the owner of the Lang property, I petition the mayor's office to lease the Lang orchard to me. Since space is very tight in my carpentry shop and will be even more so with the impending sewer construction, I would be grateful to the municipality for helping me out in this way. I intend to use half of the garden for storage space and a work area, the other half for feed for my animals. I would suggest that the municipality sell the fruit from the trees to me based on the average market price they would get. Auctioning off the fruit to others would be awkward."[235] The request was denied.

On April 7, 1941, yet another Lang neighbor, G. B., requested four meters of the yard by the house as a run for his chickens.[236] Acting Mayor Adolf Finckh wrote to Louis Lazarus Lang on April 7, 1941, "Your neighbor G. B. would like to rent approximately four meters next to the house for a chicken run. I am inclined to give him that piece. But since the garden is currently still rented to you, I am notifying you. Possible objections [by you] are to be submitted in writing by April 15, 1941."[237] Could Louis really have objected? The B. request was not approved at this time.[238]

After the Langs were deported, on November 25, 1941, Z. once more inquired about usage of the garden as a storage space [for wood], "as the situation concerning the Jewish property has changed considerably."[239]

Both Z.'s current and B.'s earlier requests were presented to the city council on December 5, 1941. "Zimmermeister Z., Süssen, applied to lease the [Lang] orchard. He wants to use this space for storage and carpentry. Neighbor G. B. wishes to rent a four meter stretch on the eastern side of the house for a chicken run." Most of the city council members were opposed to the requests, "because of the aesthetic effect on the town; the view of the garden at the entrance to the town will be unsightly." Thus the B. and Z. petitions were denied.[240] This is reflected in the still negative answer from Acting Mayor Finckh, of January 6, 1942, to Z. concerning the use of the garden—"*aus ortsbildlichen Gründen* [for aesthetic reasons]."[241] However, Finckh amended his letter of January 6, 1942, granting Z. permission "to store wood and finished barracks walls as needed and for the duration of the war on the northern side adjacent to the B. garden. Entry is to be made via the courtyard."[242] Z. responded to Finckh's original letter on January 13, 1942, expressing regret at the city council decision "concerning the *Juden-garten* [Jew garden].[243] But Z. didn't give up. On March 16, 1942, he once again requested to lease the place."[244] In a note in the files, dated March 19, 1942, and titled "Pachtweise Überlassung des Judengartens [Lease of the Jew Garden]," Acting Mayor Finckh reiterated that "[On December 5, 1941,] The city council did not approve the rental of the Langs' orchard for a stor-age and work area for K. Z. However, Z. once again requested to lease the place for agricultural purposes. He said he would only occasionally store finished items on the north side." Acting Mayor Finckh finally approved the request at a rate of RM 30 per month. "You are to store the materials on the north side of the place so that it is not unsightly." And besides, "the fruit harvest belongs to the municipality." Should Z. damage any of the trees, he would have to compensate the municipality.[245]

B.'s request was once more presented to the city council in May 1942 and was approved.[246] The city council minutes of May 8, 1942, reflect these actions by Acting Mayor Finckh: "Zimmermeister Z. once again requested rental of the [Lang] garden. I am now allowing him to store wood on the north side and to use the garden for agricultural purposes at RM 30 per month. Neighbor B. also received a four-meter-wide strip for a chicken run. When the new road to the *Auen* area is built, he will lose considerable land behind his house, so that I made this strip available for the time being as a rental, to accommodate him. The rental price is RM 5." The above excerpt is signed by Häfele.[247]

From the previous accounts one may deduce that the town did not expect the Langs to come back, nor is it possible to claim that the town's people did not know what was going on. The defrauding of Jews in Ger-many which occurred publicly and by public officials in the public domain in every respect, has been thoroughly discussed by Marion Kaplan in *Between Dignity and Despair*, and more recently by Götz Aly in *Hitler's Beneficiaries: Plunder, Racial War, and the Nazi Welfare State* and Martin Dean in *Robbing the Jews*.

A newspaper article of June 10, 1939, reported, based on the city council minutes of April 25, 1939, that there are plans "to renovate the back part of the Lang property (*Hinterhaus* 45b) to include a three-room apartment."[248] The city council members approved and the mayor authorized architect J. S. to draw up the plans and cost estimates.[249] According to the city council, on March 12, 1940,[250]

> *Bauingenieur* S., who was charged with a renovation of the rear building 45b Hindenburg Strasse presented a plan and cost estimate. The plans are to build a sales room 5.3 x 4 meters on the ground floor facing Hindenburgstrasse for the Freibank[251] and to tile the room up to the ceiling (2.3 meters). The plan calls for a three-room apartment with a spacious kitchen on the first floor. The doors and windows as well as the floors in the house are to be replaced. Estimate is RM 5,000. For the renovated apartment we ought to be able to charge rent in the amount of RM 30, so that the renovation will be recouped. *Bauingenieur* S. has now been drafted into the military. The projects are to be assigned as quickly as possible, as we have urgent requests for living space.

The city council agreed. "We will provide the means in the regular 1940 budget. . . . *Baumeister* K. will be in charge of the project."[252] However, any plans for renovation and addition were not carried out. Yet, if it were not for a handwritten note by then city hall clerk Eisele in the margin of a city council minutes excerpt dated April 25, 1939, another matter might have never been cleared up either. Eisele wrote, "Kam nicht zur Ausführung. Ab August 1940 Kriegsgefangenenlager [prisoner-of-war camp]."[253] The note seems to have been written later, though not dated.

### The Prisoner-of-War Camp on the Lang Property

My initial reading of these documents gave the sense that part of the property may have been used as a "camp." However, there is no mention in any of the existing documents or literature that this is so. It turns out that there were a number of camps in Süssen. This is first documented in the SPD book, *1896–1996 Sozialdemokraten in Süssen*, in the chapter, "Fremdarbeiter in Süssen," (Foreign Laborers in Süssen): "In Süssen soon after the

Nazis' rise to power the appropriate companies converted their production systematically to war production. . . . After the onset of the war on September 1, 1939, many foreign forced laborers and prisoners of war came to Germany." In the small community of Süssen there were a number of "camps for foreigners." The author of *1896–1996 Sozialdemokraten in Süssen* asks, "Where did the people come from, where did they live, where were they imprisoned, were they a conscious factor in the communal life of Süssen, were they ignored, how were these people treated, were they really perceived or did the population create a safe distance?"[254] In the next paragraph he somewhat answers these questions, not because of any possible guilt, but because of the passage of time. "The oft spoken words, '. . . here things weren't so bad' can hardly be verified today. Fifty years after the end of the war we can only answer these questions tentatively."[255] The map in the book shows some of the buildings used as camps which are still familiar today, such as the *Turnhalle* (gym), and the Löwen and Pelikan inns."[256]

However, the camp on the Lang property is not mentioned in the SPD book. During a research trip in 2002, I was given documents that had surfaced in a cleanup of the final old Süssen files to be deposited in the Süssen City Archive. Among them was correspondence between the electric company and Häfele from March 1941. This is the first time ever that a *Gefangenenlager* (prisoner-of-war camp) is mentioned. Hugo Lang remembers more than twenty French prisoners of war who had to perform forced labor for the municipality and local farmers. He also remembers that there were no beds for them. After reading what I had written, he wrote back, "I know for sure that French prisoners of war were already in Süssen in July 1941. I was still there and fed them apples in the evening from our orchards. After the guard locked the door, I threw apples against the windows upstairs. All windows had iron bars in front of the glass. They reached for the apples through the bars and ate them."[257]

The correspondence about the camp on the Lang property is very sparse and very confusing. A letter dated March 5, 1941, signed by Häfele to the Neckarwerke A.G. Esslingen concerned the price for electricity that the municipality was to pay for the prisoner-of-war camp located at 45 Hindenburgstrasse. Häfele confirmed that the municipality would pay for the electricity for the camp and requested a retroactive 40 percent reduction in the rate. He requested a separate bill for this building which was to be presented to the municipal cashier for payment.

The problem with this picture is that the Langs, fifteen or sixteen of them, were at this time still living in their home at 45 Hindenburgstrasse in Süssen. Yet it is impossible that Häfele made a mistake, as he was clearly in the know on municipal matters. A query from the Neckarwerke to the municipality on March 13, 1941, requested the name of the previous consumer who lived at the address. Häfele made a handwritten notation that "this is Louis Lazarus Lang. He still lives in building 45; the rear building, 45 b [the washhouse], is used as a prisoner-of-war camp."[258]

The municipality wrote again to the Neckarwerke A.G. on May 3, 1941 requesting a response to the Neckarwerke letter of March 13 and the mayor's response of [April] 5. An additional note was sent to the municipality on May 13, 1941, notifying the village that they were investigating the matter and asking for the municipality's patience.[259]The desired reply from the Neckarwerke A.G. arrived on June 3, 1941. "We found out that the prisoner-of-war camp is located at 49 Hindenburgstrasse.[260] The electricity for this building was metered via a submeter of the Louis Lang business, customer no. 431. Ordinarily we do not issue separate bills for a submeter and will have to investigate how we can do this per your request."[261]

After a six-week hiatus, on July 30, 1941, the electric company Neckarwerke informed the municipality that they checked the situation of the prisoner-of-war camp via their Göppingen branch and found out that the camp electricity was measured through a city-owned submeter connected to Louis Lang, without the city having first notified the electric company. Thus, they could not grant the municipality the rate of 24 pfennig, or rather the new rate of 25 pfennig for which the municipality qualified, but only the basic monthly rate of 40 pfennig. The letter concluded with the comment that the municipality needed to work with Mr. Lang concerning the process of electricity usage at the prisoner-of-war camp.[262]

And then there were complications between the municipality and the Nazi in charge of the prisoner-of-war camp. A note from Häfele, dated August 28, 1942, states,

The controlling officer, policeman Walter from Göppingen, asked me yesterday . . . about making a washhouse in the garage. I explained to him that orders had been given that civilians would not be allowed into the wash house as long as the prisoners of war are present. He replied that he would not tolerate any longer and under any circumstances that the civilians, i.e., the renters in the main house, wash at the same time as the prisoners of war.

The camp is a prisoner-of-war camp and no one has any business in it, not even the contracting partners [the municipality?]. If the municipality will not cooperate he will inform the Stalag, then the camp will be dissolved. I told him to go ahead, that it isn't that easy today to install a washhouse and buy a washtub. I already spoke with the workmen who told me that the washtub had to be manufactured first . . . I told him it would take at least three to four weeks.

Häfele wrote at the bottom, "We now either have to partition the wash house with a divider or make a wash house in the garage."[263]

The city council minutes of September 4, 1942, paragraph 207, deal with the issue of "Installation of a wash house for the former *Judenhaus* in the garage," and state,

The controlling officer for the prisoner-of-war camp of the municipality in the *Hinterhaus* (45b) Hindenburgstrasse has complained about the joint use of the wash house on the ground floor [of the *Hinterhaus*] by the residents of the *Judenhaus* and the prisoners-of-war. He demands that we stop this and plans the installation of a wash house in the former horse stable. According to the plan, this is to be used later as a sales room for the *Freibank* [slaughtering facility]. It contains water pipes. Run-off is also good, so that no additional changes will be necessary. A chimney should be installed for the laundry tub, which needs to be purchased. If the workers could completely renovate the horse stable, it would be good to make the renovations in such a way that the room could be simultaneously used as a sales room for the planned *Freibank* and as a washhouse. The city council members are in agreement.

The resolution is passed to "1. Turn the former horse stable in the rear of building 45b Hindenburgstrasse into a wash house and, if possible, to make the renovations in such a way that the space can be used for the *Freibank*. 2. The company of E. Fetzer, *Kupferschmid*, will manufacture the *Waschkessel* [cauldron]."

The final notes concerning the matter of the washhouse for the former *Judenhaus* are from October 13, 1942, paragraph 211. "In consultation with the city council members on September 4, 1942, it was decided to install a wash house in the former horse stable. It turned out, however, that this would be very difficult. I now decided to install a washhouse in the garage which we have accomplished with the help of municipal workers. The city council members acknowledged this development without comment." This note is also signed by Häfele.[264] The question one needs to raise is whether and what kind of run-off there was from the garage. This may have some bearing on post-Holocaust wrangling over the condition of the Lang property.

The *Gemeindechronik* is silent on this topic, as are any postwar publications authorized by the city. Only the SPD book of 1996 shed light on the forced labor situation in Süssen, though not on the camp on the Lang property.

In spite of some uncertainty as to the actual address, one can nevertheless be relatively certain that the Lang *Hinterhaus* (wash house) was used as a camp for French or Belgian prisoners of war who labored in the local economy. Müller observes, "We know that the strangers had to do [forced] labor, and we know in which businesses. How they lived, how the citizens of Süssen perceived them, remains unknown."[265] With the exception of Hugo's memory and the miller's wife's reminiscence, it still is. The many forced laborers over the period of World War II who labored in Süssen as well as the two or three euthanasia victims remain publicly unrecognized. In spite of the local perception by some individuals that the residents have done enough to right the wrongs of the Nazi era, there is still work to be done.

# 6

Hugo Lang's Escape and Life
in the United States

*To be honest, the beginning was difficult. But when you're young and from Swabia, you can do it.*

—Hugo Lang, 1989 speech delivered in Süssen

After the departure of Henny, Inge, and Manfred, the only member of the Lang family who still succeeded in getting a visa was Hugo (Jehudo ben Arje), the second son of Leopold, even though all members of his family had applied for visas in August, 1938. His number on the waiting list of the American Consulate in Stuttgart was 17449.[1]

On April 25, 1941, Gemeindepfleger Häfele confirmed that "Hugo Israel Lang does not owe any municipal [advance] taxes and there are no tax barriers that would keep him from emigrating."[2] A second affidavit dated April 25, 1941, and signed by the very man who confiscated Hugo's parents' money from the house sale, von Petzold, also confirmed that, since he had never worked full-time, "Hugo Israel Lang has never paid sales, income, and property tax and thus was not assessed any tax. He thus does not owe the Reich any taxes."[3]

The surviving correspondence bears witness to the precariousness of Hugo's situation. At the time when Hugo received his visa, his Aunt Fanny (with her children Otto, Lina, Alma) and his uncle Max Liffmann (with his wife Alice and son Kenneth) already lived in the United States. Sponsored by Arthur Fleischer,[4] Manfred moved from England to the United States in 1940; he then tried to raise the money for Hugo's passage from there. Apparently Hugo could have left Süssen as early as June, but this didn't work out. On April 23, 1941, Hugo telegraphed his uncle Max Liffmann, now in Providence, Rhode Island, to pay "immediately 370 dollars to Bancolisboa azores Lissabon for Servizio Italo toward Hugo Lang passage ticket, and 50 dollars for Hugo Lang, as well as 42 dollars to the 'Joint' [AJJDC] in New York," then "June 17 departure will be assured. Please cable confirmation of transaction."[5] On May 12, 1941, Hugo once more cabled Max Liffman regarding the transmittal of the money for his passage, "otherwise [June] departure in jeopardy."[6] Hugo may not have realized that his uncle Max was in dire straights. Upon arrival in the United States, Max made a living selling brushes. Aunt Alice gave piano lessons to supplement their income. On May 30, 1941, Hugo telegraphed Manfred, "June reservation cannot be held as the necessary money for the ticket did not arrive. Cable immediately whether 450 dollars are ready for a new reservation before expiration of the visa. Inform Isidor [Lang and] Max Liffmann. If unsuccessful, take out a loan."[7] On June 24, 1941, obviously desperate, Hugo once more telegraphed Manfred to approach "[Rudolf] Rothschild," a family friend from Göppingen, "[and Max] Lippmann [sic, Liffmann]," for help. Hugo asked that available funds be paid directly to the "Joint" in New York and no longer to Lisbon. "Cable how much you paid."[8] He would try to gather the rest from the Hilfsverein der Juden in Deutschland, the Self-Help Organization of Jews in Germany. Hugo's last surviving telegram to Manfred was dated July 17. He wrote that, while he received Fred's letter of June 25, he still "has no confirmation from the 'Joint' concerning transmittal [of the money]. Cable your response." Departure was now urgent,[9] as Hugo's visa would expire on August 23.

Two receipts for $120 each, from Fred, dated July 28, and from Mrs. Beatrice Persky for Fred, dated August 14, exist. There is also a receipt of August 23 from the "Joint" to an anxious Fred, confirming receipt of the August 14 deposit for a total of $340 towards Hugo's passage.[10] Hugo's uncle Isidor Lang, a second cousin of his father's, who had a department store on Long Island, supplied an affidavit for him, dated January 29, 1940,[11] but only for him, not for the rest of his family. It was none too soon. Although World War II was well under way, with all of Western Europe under Nazi control and the invasion of the Soviet Union complete, the United States had not yet entered the war. That would happen with the Japanese attack on Pearl Harbor on December 7, 1941. Nevertheless, traveling across the Atlantic was already a perilous undertaking.

Finally, on August 3, 1941, Hugo bade his family in Süssen farewell and left for Lisbon, Portugal. He remembers, "I will never forget that day. My mother wept so bitterly, and she gave me many warm clothes to wear, on such a hot day, since I was only allowed to take a small suitcase."[12] Hugo traveled to Stuttgart, and then continued on to Berlin. "I arrived in Berlin on the same day and then we were gathered by a Jewish organization and were put on a train. The train was bolted, that is to say, sealed, so that no one could get in or out. The train went via Frankfurt to France, Spain, and then Lisbon. We arrived in Lisbon in two day's time and received shelter in a hotel. We stayed there for three weeks, when a ship was ready, that is to say a banana boat, a small freighter, which got us finally to the United States. We were afraid of submarines. The freighter criss-crossed the ocean, so as to avoid the submarines. It took more than two weeks to get to the United States."[13] The freighter was named *Mousinho*, and made several runs across the Atlantic in the service of the *Kindertransporte* (refugee children movements) from Europe to the United States.[14]

Hugo had a premonition that he wouldn't see his family again, and he was right. The worry about Hugo is visible from letters that Eva Liffmann Lang sent to Hugo and Fred. On August 14, 1941, Eva wrote to Hugo in Lisbon: "Your second card arrived before the first one because 'Süssen' was almost illegible [on the first—this is a time before ZIP codes], so take your time [when writing]. Things should quiet down for you. We are also at peace. Uncle Louis returned to work today, but whether he can last? Alfred Metzger now also has to work on Saturdays. Your grandparents [Liffmann] send their regards. . . . Did you get to see [Louis Lang's daughters] Henny or Inge yet?" Ruth added, "Father says hello, he is in the stable."[15]

Another letter of August 17, 1941, went from Eva Lang to her dear boys. "*Liebe Jungens.* Now already 8 days have passed since you, dear Hugo, left and we hope that when these lines arrive you will be happily united with Fred. Our thoughts were with you during the passage and we hope that you all arrived well. We hope that you received our letter to Lisbon. The money came back promptly, 130 marks and as instructed we sent 170 marks to Oberdorf. All else is well, nothing new is happening. Everyone is working. . . . Did you play on your Hohner [harmonica]?"

No, Hugo told me, the Hohner harmonica was packed in the suitcase. It would have been a difficult time to be happy, knowing that he could not help his loved ones escape as well. Eva continues the letter,

Now to you, dear Fred. I acknowledge your letter of July 28. It arrived 5 days after Hugo's departure; we had hoped to hear before [he left]. . . . Did you have to repay all the expenses or could Hugo travel at the expense of the Hilfsverein [der Juden in Deutschland]? Please answer this question. And he always cabled with the reply prepaid so that you should not have had any expenses. But the main thing is that it worked and you will make it together. Our best regards to the Rothschilds and many thanks for everything. Now to the other part of your letter, dear Fred. How you must have suffered because of the unfortunate circumstances with your sponsor. Something like that is terrible. . . . Does Uncle Max [Liffmann] know about it? He should have helped to defend you, and you should have immediately written the truth, then Hugo would not constantly have pestered you, and not known why he withdrew everything. The straight path is always the best, please take these words to heart. All beginnings are difficult. Mother.[16]

A postcard dated August 27, 1941, from his mother confirmed Hugo's card from Lisbon.

Our thoughts accompanied you on the journey. . . . Thank God we are all fine. Ruth is quite comfortable in your room and the alarm clock does the trick every day. The voyage must have been fun with so many friends. Did you play on your Hohner a lot?

Dear Fred, your ears must have been burning yesterday [August 26]. Did you celebrate your birthday? Was the wedding on that day [Fred's birthday]?[17]

I cooked a nice meal in your honor and can hardly believe that 20 years have passed since you were born. Now both of you are abroad. If we now can also finally join you, together with Ruth, then everything will be fine. . . . Mother.[18]

On August 31, 1941, Hugo's father, mother, and Ruth again wrote to their "*Jungens,*" having not yet received confirmation of Hugo's safe arrival in the United States. There could not as yet have been any confirmation because Hugo did not arrive in the United States until September 2, 1941. His mother wrote,

Since your departure, dear Hugo, this is the third time that I write to your old address, dear Manfred. I hope that you are receiving all of our mail. Daily we are waiting yearningly for a telegram that will let us know that you all arrived ok. We haven't heard anything since your last postcard from Lisbon and only hope that you are both well. . . . When this letter arrives, the High Holy Days will be close. My wish for you is that all your wishes for yourselves [for the new year] will come true [in 1941 Rosh Hashanah was on September 22 and Yom Kippur on October 1]. I hope that you will go to temple to hear the wonderful voice of Cantor Hohenemser![19] Please give him the enclosed note. Are you, dear Hugo, less anxious now, and how do you manage with the language? Can you take evening classes? Please write as often as you can, I can hardly wait for the mailman. Best wishes and kisses, your Mother.

Ruth added, "Best wishes for the *Feiertage* [High Holy Days], I hope we can soon celebrate together." Eva added, "Vater took your advice and stopped smoking almost entirely." Eva enclosed a letter to her brother Max and family in Providence.

Dear Family, Today I am writing for the third time to the boys since Hugo's departure and want to include a few lines for you. We hope that they reach you in good health. We have not yet received news of Hugo's safe arrival but hope to receive the desired telegram within a few days. Maybe you spoke with him in the meantime. Surely you'll be happy to get direct information. His departure came quickly, and for you quite unexpectedly, as we saw from your letter, dear Max.

Now our dear Ruth is the *Nestkönig* [nestling], or rather, she is a young queen of labor and we enjoy her very much. I would love to attend your concerts, dear Alice, and we are thrilled with your success. For the new year we wish you all the best and much success with your work.

Your dear grandma is alright. I sent her a few things for daily use.

Ruth inserts here: "Mother is talking about groceries." Eva continues, "We would have loved to have them join us for the holidays, but we'll have to be patient. Eva."[20]

On September 11, 1941, Eva wrote to Hugo, "When we received your telegram of September 3, we breathed a sigh of relief. . . . Father works in the hay and bought another cow." Greetings are added from Alfred and Hermine Baer.[21]

When visiting his hometown of Süssen at the invitation of the mayor in 1989, Hugo, in a speech to invited guests, told a bit more about his experiences after leaving Süssen. Hugo traveled to "France, Spain, and Portugal for a few weeks. In September 1941, I arrived in the United States."[22] His brother Manfred—who, on April 26, 1939, had been transferred by the Papierfabrik Fleischer in Eislingen to England—had continued to the United States in 1940.[23] In 1989 Hugo reported, "Eight months later he [Fred] met me at the ship. He didn't have enough money for gas. I had $4 on me, given to me by the Martin Brothers Bank in Göppingen.[24] I didn't get any German money, only $4. I gave my brother $2 for gas." Hugo continued, "To be honest, the beginning was difficult. But when you're young and from Swabia, you can do it." The time was shortly before the United States entered the war, and his brother was working for an aircraft factory. "Although I had not learned the trade, I also began to work in this factory. They placed me at the *Drehmaschine* (lathe) and showed me what to do. I did everything as told. I worked [the night shift] from 6 P.M. to 6 A.M. for two months. Then I was able to improve myself and work during the day."[25]

From here until deportation we have another ten letters or so from members of the family, and some information on their situation, though the language is extremely guarded. In addition to Mother and Ruth, Father and Uncle Louis added a few words here and there, even Louis's new wife, Fanny, wrote to her relatives, as did Kurt Lang and Alfred and Hermine Metzger. Mail from Fred and Hugo is awaited eagerly and greeted exuberantly.

In an undated letter, Ruth wrote to her brothers, "I am happy that I can write to the two of you. I hope [dear Hugo] that you survived your journey well and have already acclimatized. Were you the only musician? I shouldn't ask so much, I am sure that you will write us everything. Don't forget anything, I can't wait. I am sure you, dear Manfred, were very surprised when you received the telegram." Again, Ruth alludes to problems with Hugo's sponsor, though it is not clear of what kind. Ruth comments, "I can't believe the things you write about your sponsor, hopefully you don't need him anymore. Dear Hugo, you'll have to go see him." Hugo's father Leopold also hopes that Hugo has arrived safely. "I hope these words find you safely with Fred. What did he think of you after all these many months? Don't bother the sponsor and find your own way. Now you know why we held back. Are you able to visit Onkel Max? Please give our regards to everyone. And please write to Onkel Hugo and Tante Martha." Leopold reprimands Fred for not writing, but is glad that all is well. "The business with your sponsor is no small matter. . . . I hope we don't need them any more."[26]

On September 24, 1941, Eva wrote that they received Hugo's detailed letter.

It was the Second Day [of Rosh Hashanah] and we had time to each read your letter attentively. . . . Dear Fred, you succeeded with the big surprise [he bought a car]. During the short time of your stay in the U.S. you achieved a lot. Are you driving carefully? . . . Dear Hugo, I can't quite believe that you want to be a tool and die maker. . . . Please express our thanks to the Persky family for their loving hospitality, it feels good to know that you are in such good hands. . . . We are having a beautiful fall. Tomorrow *Vater* will pick up the winter potatoes from [farmer] Hoyler. Today all the young folk stored potatoes for their boss [Bader]. Next week they will again work in the branch [Eislingen].

Much has changed since you left, dear Hugo. Everything is very quiet. This gives me time to go for walks with Ruth more often. She works hard and everyone likes her. She sings beautifully, and especially likes the melody, "Es leuchten die Sterne"; the movie is precious. Did you hear Aunt Alice play? She is a perfect artist, if only Ruth could be her student soon.[27] I expect that you, dear Fred, will speak about it with her soon. . . . Today I sent your letter and telegram to your dear grandparents. We were so excited. It already arrived here on September 20. Thank you so much. It was a ray of sunshine for the High Holy Days [there was no longer a synagogue in Göppingen]. May God allow us to spend the next one together with you. We are all well. Say hello to everyone in Providence [Max and Alice Liffman, Eva's brother and sister-in-law] and to Uncle Hugo and Aunt Marta. Mother.

Leopold added, "Everyone is still at work and says hello."[28]

The next letter, on October 5, 1941, came from Kurt. He confirmed the illness of Onkel Arnold (Hugo does not know who this relative is). To Hugo he wrote, "I will give your regards to Hägele and Öchsle [local Christians who had worked with Hugo at the Bader lumber company]. They are always asking about you." About things in general he wrote, "Nothing much new here. For the past few weeks we worked in new construction. You know that kind of work, dear Hugo, it is probably similar to what you do. I learned a lot and know now how to run the machines. The 'Gatter' in Eislingen [branch of Bader company] received a new remote control, this is much easier. . . . All else is ok. We have only one wish, to be able to join you as soon as possible. I would do any kind of work. I am doubly happy for you, dear Hugo. You worked hard for it. Kurt."[29]

Five days later, on October 6, 1941, Eva wrote again,

My dear boys, . . . We are all well and have plenty of work. . . . Ruth is so proud to be able to help, she has to do a lot. . . . Dear Fred, aren't you taking on too much? You have already been in the States for a year. . . . I am glad all our friends are doing well. *Vater* and I often wonder whether we will make it to Rudolf's level [in the United States]. . . . Canning is now finished, after sauerkraut and potatoes we now have beets. Vater brought them home from the field with the bull! Does Frau Persky cook the way I do? . . . Yesterday Siegfried [Baer] came from Frankfurt for ten days on vacation. He has gotten big and strong, just now he cleaned and oiled the beet mill for *Vater* and did a few other things that you, dear Hugo, would usually have fixed. If you continue your efforts to get us to the States, we will, God willing, celebrate the next [High Holy Days] together with you again. That is our wish. Ruth also perks up at that thought. . . . I always send your mail to the dear grandparents [Sofie and Jakob Liffmann] and Amanda [Gabriel, from Frankfurt, mother of Alice Liffmann, who is married to Max Liffmann]. . . . since my feet are very swollen I do not get out of the house and here there is nothing new. Mother.

Whatever ailed Eva must have been a new health problem, as she was fine on September 24, just two weeks earlier.

Also on October 6, 1941, Onkel Louis and Tante Fanny wrote, "Your letters are all festivals for us. . . . Kurt already wrote you that we are well. Write often and say hello to my girls [Henny and Inge] and all other relatives. Onkel Louis." Leopold also added a few lines, "We are always thinking of you, and I hope that we, with God's help, will be able to be together again. Dear Ruth always goes to the factory and works very hard. I now have three cows in my stable and am always busy. Dear Hugo, I received 100 *Zentner* [hundredweight] hay and will be able to feed the cattle till Spring. Siegfried is home on vacation. He turned out fine and will someday join you in your business, dear Fred. Please say hello to Henny and Inge from me. Tell Rudolf [Rothschild] and Frau Rothschild to write to me. Father."[30]

Eva Lang wrote again on October 19, 1941.

*Meine lieben Jungens,* Papa says that Ruth is the most important one [to emigrate], for when three of you earn money it will be much easier. You know, dear Hugo, that she is not even 18 years old. This is very important. Please keep working at it. Please tell Onkel Max that Amanda [Alice's mother] and grandparents [Liffmann] are well and everything is ok. Here as well—thank God. Everyone leaves early in the morning and returns at night, tired. . . . It is fall-like here. We had a good harvest of fruit and beets.[31] I helped to unload. *Vater* had two loads in the field. . . . Please speak to Rudolf Rothschild about Ruth. Hopefully he knows someone who can help, don't give up. Our plan is to stay healthy and strong so that we will be together again soon. Mother.

Ruth added, "Here everything is as always, we all go to work. This week *Vater* got two loads of beets. Four of us unloaded one wagon—Father, Mother, Herminchen and I; then Father and I unloaded the other wagon. I stood on the wagon and handed one beet after the other to Father and he threw them through the feed door to the *hinteren Stall* [rear storage area]. Afterwards we went in and picked each one up again and made a big pile; that was some drudgery, no one helped."[32]

On November 16, 1941, twelve days before deportation, Hugo and Fred's mother wrote, "I'll write so that you know that we are all OK. . . . We received mail from Onkel Max and Hugo [in Providence], dated October 5. Their worry [about us] is visible."[33]

What may be the last postcard has no date, as someone was interested in the stamp and cut it out. However, on it Eva acknowledges a letter from Hugo dated October 15, 1941.

> I went to the *Beratungsstelle* (application office) for Ruth, now we have to wait. She works hard as do all the others. *Vater* takes care of four animals, three cows and a bull.[34] We got the gardens ready for the winter. Did you take out some of your warm clothes? It has already been cold here and we had some snow. Did you, dear Hugo, visit [your cousin] Inge? Mother.[35]

There are some letters, one from Uncle Max, Eva's brother, in Providence, expressing the hope that "you two [Fred and Hugo] will soon be able to provide an affidavit for your parents and for Ruth. I really hope that they will still make it as well."[36] And there also is a letter from Hugo Liffman in London, dated November 17, 1941, worrying about his parents and other loved ones and wanting to know whether Hugo and Fred have spoken with Inge and Henny and with Otto.[37] The letter reveals that Aunt Fanny [Lang, Jakob's widow] also lives in New York and that Kenneth in Providence [son of Max and Alice] had his bar mitzvah. Hugo Liffman and his wife Alice only came to the United States from England in 1945.

Another letter, dated November 25, 1943, is from Resi Gideon, widow of cousin Alfred in Rexingen, who lives in Shavei Zion, Palestine.[38] Many Rexingen Jews as a group made *aliyah* to Israel in 1938 and established a *moshav* (community) north of Haifa which they named Shavei Zion. In

2010 I was able to visit Shavei Zion and to make contact with Resi and Alfred Pressburger's daughter Alisa. Her given name was Frieda. Born in 1933, she was four years old when she moved to Palestine with her family, where her father Alfred died almost immediately. Her mother Resi Gideon remarried, Hans Schwarz from Emmendingen. Both lived out their lives in Shavei Zion and are buried there. Alisa married Aron Klapfer, born in 1930. They have two children, seven grandchildren, and two great-grandchildren. From Marta Liffmann's letter we learn that she, Eva's sister, and her husband, Onkel Gustav, made it to Haifa with cousins Judith and Tamara.

The helplessness of the correspondents concerning those left behind is palpable. The only avenue of communication open to "the East" is via the Red Cross, if the Langs are even able to find out to which camp their loved ones were sent. One undated notification from the World Jewish Congress lets them know that "we have found in our Theresienstadt lists: Jakob Liffmann, Sofie Behr Liffmann [Eva Lang's parents], Bertha Behr."[39] That's not good news. And then an eerie silence settled over the void that separated Hugo and Fred and Inge and Henny as well as all the other relatives from their loved ones in Nazi Europe.

In August 1942 Hugo left the aircraft company and briefly worked for the Manhattan Screw Co. Inc.[40] On October 12 the president of the company, Mr. B. Slater, wrote a recommendation for Hugo: "This is to certify that Mr. Hugo Lang of 178 Beacon Ave., Jersey City, N.J., was employed with us from August 20, 1942, to October 9, 1942, as foreman. Among his duties was setting up of our machines, supervising of the crew and all round machinist work. He left his position upon his own request. Although the time he spent with us was comparatively short, we had occasion to appreciate Mr. Lang's ability and can recommend him to any employer who is seeking for a decent and efficient man."

After leaving the Manhattan Screw Co. he joined Stuart Machine & Tool Co., where he worked until he was drafted on December 17, 1943.[41] Upon discharge from the military in 1946, he asked I. J. Gamerov, the General Manager, for a recommendation. Gamerov wrote, "This is to certify that Hugo Lang was in our employ from October 20, 1942, until December 17, 1943, at which time he left due to the fact that he was inducted into the Army. During the time that Hugo Lang was employed by us, we found him to be a capable and industrious worker. He operated the turret lathe, drill press, shaper and set up his own work."

There was little time to lose after being drafted. Hugo remembers,

In 1943 I was drafted into the army. I hardly spoke any English. They accepted me nevertheless. Three months later I completed my training. After this training we all assembled in a large hall—500 people. We had to raise our hand, and then I was an American citizen. I was sent to France as a soldier. We landed in France on June 6, 1944 [invasion of Normandy]. We traveled throughout France with the army and I was their interpreter. From France we continued to Holland, Belgium, and Luxemburg. In Luxemburg the great attack of St. Vith (Ardennes) took place. I and my entire division were captured in the Ardennes. I was taken to Bad Orb [the German prisoner-of-war camp Stalag IX-B] near Hanau. [In the Piehler interview Hugo says it was in December around Christmas].[42]

The significance of this matter-of-fact report by Hugo about his prisoner-of-war experience in the German POW camp Bad Orb was lost on me, although Hugo tried to tell me, multiple times, in what real danger he was. Since these conversations took place before any of the publicity surrounding the movie "Berga: Soldiers of Another War" (2003),[43] I had never heard of that concentration camp or of Stalag IX-B. Only when the Tennessee Holocaust Commission, on which I served, subsequently sponsored an outreach program for Tennessee teachers on Berga called "Forgotten Victims: American Soldiers in the Holocaust" (2003), did I finally pay serious attention to what Hugo had been trying to tell me. He was not exaggerating!

The PBS preview notes used by the THC in their teacher package contained a description of Stalag IX-B. "Stalag IX-B held French, Italian, Serbian, and Russian POWs in late December 1944, when 985 American soldiers captured during the first two days of the Battle of the Bulge were sent there."[44] The prisoner-of-war camp was located just outside the spa town of Bad Orb, "about 35 miles east of Frankfurt." Roger Cohen, author of an article, "The Lost Soldiers of Stalag IX-B," in the *New York Times Magazine* of February 27, 2005,[45] interviewed American GI survivors. "In the hills was a camp called Stalag IX-B, a collection of one-story barracks surrounded by barbed wire."[46] Hugo describes his experience.

In the beginning in Bad Orb we received only soup. Within six months I lost 40 pounds. The Germans ate the dead horses from the front and threw away the bones. We American soldiers collected these bones at night and cracked them open with a stone to eat the marrow. That was at least some nourishment for us. That's how we survived. We had lice and much more. . . .

Those were difficult times. It was winter and bitterly cold. We were glad to receive a piece of bread. Seven men shared one loaf of bread. We ate snow. That was our water.[47]

The THC material notes, "Stalag IX-B is often regarded as the worst of the camps that held American POWs. . . . By the end of the war, Bad Orb held 4,700 American POWs, far more than it was equipped to handle. The food was terrible and rationed in insufficient quantities—by the time allied forces reached the camp, its captives were too weak to greet their liberators. The prisoners were not issued soap or towels, and each 160-person barrack had only one water tap, which provided only cold water. There was a hole in the ground for a toilet, and the barracks were so overcrowded that the prisoners had to take turns sleeping because there was not enough room on the floor. There were no beds, per se, and even the mattresses in the hospital were made of lice-infested straw."[48] An unidentified newspaper clipping in Hugo's possession notes, "Don't mention the Geneva Convention to those who were imprisoned at Bad Orb. For them it's just a joke."[49]

If the substandard treatment was terrible, there were more terrible things in store for about 350 of these American GIs. Hugo remembers, "I threw away all personal items—my watch, my pictures, and my dog tags because they had Hebrew on them. I pretended to be deaf and dumb. I gave them a false name, otherwise I wouldn't be alive today. That helped."[50]

Why did Hugo and other Jewish soldiers have to hide their Jewish identity as American GIs? One of Cohen's interviewees, William J. Shapiro, confirms what Hugo remembers. "I heard someone say, 'If you're a Jewish GI, throw your dog tags away because there are SS troops here.'"[51] The 2003 PBS preview section on the film "Berga—Soldiers of Another War," explains, "A [German] military order commanded all [American] Jewish soldiers to identify themselves. After the Americans refused to comply, Nazi guards selected GIs they 'identified' as Jewish, thought 'looked Jewish,' had 'Jewish-sounding' last names or whom they classified as 'undesirables.' Fewer than one third of the American soldiers selected [on this basis] were, in fact, Jewish."[52]

What happened to these soldiers? The same preview explains that they "were selected to fulfill a quota and shipped off [to Berga], a satellite of the notorious concentration camp at Buchenwald, where they suffered harrowing atrocities as slave laborers."[53] Berga was located a three-day train ride from Bad Orb in East Germany, near Leipzig. Cohen wrote, "Berga, which was later absorbed into Soviet-dominated East Germany, was thoroughly investigated in May and June 1945 by an American war crimes team on the scene. But the resulting documents were long classified . . . "[54] and therefore buried. For sixty years no one knew about the horrors of Stalag IX-B at Bad Orb and at Berga.

Fortunately, Hugo remained at Bad Orb, escaping the horror of Berga. This was primarily due to his caution. He did not even write a postcard to his brother Fred under his own name, but gave a false name so he would not be found out to be a Jew.[55] He reveals one final, horrifying detail. "After liberation a German soldier—an older man—approached me and said, 'I knew exactly that you were from Germany and that your parents were Jews, but I didn't turn you in.' The man was from Donzdorf [a town about one mile northeast of Süssen]. He didn't turn me in, therefore I wasn't shot"—or sent to Berga to build an underground synthetic fuel plant. "After liberation [around April 22, 1945][56] it took three weeks until we were restored to good health." Hugo concludes, "Then I returned to the States [May 1945][57] and went back to my job. I can't complain. The main thing is I survived."[58] Hugo's survival was a near miracle. War alone would have been enough. Being taken prisoner of war reduced his chances even more. But being a Jewish American GI reduced his chances for survival to near zero at that moment in history.

Hugo's brother Manfred, who helped him with the money for passage, spent the war years at Fort Leonard Wood, Missouri, in basic training. Together they were able to bring their sister Ruth, who eventually returned from the Riga-Jungfernhof concentration camp, to the United States in 1946.

Both Ruth and Hugo married survivors. Ruth married Sol Lemberger from Rexingen, born in 1923, who spent four years in Riga-Jungfernhof.[59] Unfortunately, his father, Isidor, a cattle dealer born in Rexingen in 1892, was also deported to Riga-Jungfernhof in 1941 and perished in Auschwitz in 1943. His mother, Rosa Gideon, born in Rexingen in 1900, was also deported to Riga in 1941 and was murdered in Latvia in 1942, as were all three of his brothers—Sigwart, Lothar, and Erich. Sol was the only survivor of his immediate family. Sol and Ruth became Orthodox in the United States. They had two sons, Aryeh and Yitzchok, who married twin sisters. There are numerous grandchildren. Ruth Lemberger died on December 12, 2000—"On Shabbos day, eighth day of Chanukah, second day of Teves 5760"—in Baltimore, Maryland, where she is buried. The inscription on her tombstone not only bears the necessary personal information, but an *eshet chayil* (woman of valor) laudation as well.

Much she has done for the education of her sons

That they should walk in the proper way of life.

And this she did quietly, which was her Royal crown.

Constantly yearning to strive to greater heights to serve her creator

She was well liked by everyone,

Always looking to make others happy.

A valiant woman is the crown of her husband

Look oh look how good was her kindness

This should be for us to learn from

And with this the Almighty's name should become greater and sanctified.[60]

After leaving the military in 1945, Hugo asked two sources, who knew him for the entire time he had lived in the United States—four short years—to write him character references. They were Edna and Louis Persky, Polish Jews from whom Hugo's brother Fred had rented an apartment and into which Hugo also moved, and Arnold Silverman, a friend in Jersey City.

On December 31, 1945, Mr. and Mrs. Persky wrote,

> To Whom It May Concern:
>
> We became acquainted with Fred Lang in 1940. In 1941 he became a boarder in our home. When his brother Hugo Lang arrived in 1941, he came to our home immediately. We grew to know the boys very well and can safely vouch for their splendid character. In the years they spent with us they were never disorderly or intoxicated. They saved their money and bought war bonds to the best of their ability. We have never known them to be dishonest or not to keep their word. Both boys served in the United States Army; Hugo having been taken prisoner. We feel we can honestly give them an excellent character reference without fear of reprisal.
>
> Mr. Louis L. Persky, Mrs. Edna Persky.
>
> 10 Paulmier Place, Jersey City, New Jersey.[61]

Mr. Arnold Silverman, 2102 Hudson Boulevard, Union City, New Jersey, wrote on December 31, 1945,

> To Whom It May Concern,
>
> This is to state that I have known Messrs. Fred and Hugo Lang for the past 5 and 4 years respectively. Two better men I have never met. I met Fred Lang just a few months after he had landed from Europe in 1940. From the

time he arrived he worked very hard and conscientiously; never drank any alkoholic [sic] beverages and consistantly [sic] saved all his wages. His only desire was to bring his family to the United States. In 1941 he succeeded in bringing his brother Hugo here from Europe. From the day that Hugo arrived until the time that he went into the service of the United States, I have never seen any two boys work so hard, save so much, pray so much as these boys did in the hope that their family may still be alive and that they may bring them to the United States. Knowing all this because I have seen it with my own eyes, I can honestly say that they are both trustworthy, conscientious, and would never shirk any duty set before them. I would personally recommend Fred and Hugo Lang to anyone who may deem it necessary to have a character reference for them.

    Signed: Arnold E. Silverman.[62]

From August 4, 1947, to February 15, 1950, Hugo went to work for Charms Candy Co. When he left there, or was let go because of union problems, E. H. Karleen, Works Manager, wrote him an excellent reference.

There are few occasions that one has the privilege to recommend a fellow employee of Mr. Hugo Lang's ability and initiative, if it were not that we would encounter union difficulties, this employee would remain with our firm. A brief resume of his advancements with our firm will outline his ability to organize the production of automatic packaging machinery. Mr. Lang began his employment with us on August 4, 1947, as a tool and die machinist. Jigs and fixtures designed and built by him are still in use and are saving man-hours in the assembly line.

    Demonstrating his ability to organize systematically sequential operations in the production of these machines together with his ability to get along with the men, they in turn executing his suggestions, resulted in bettering the assembly, timing, and the run-in-time by 46 percent. His abilities are as follows: Tool and die maker; jix and fixture for production; production methods; supervision—foreman; labor relations; safety control. Mr. Lang will demonstrate that he is a 100 percent company employee coupled with the "on-the-Job" attitude at all times. His absenteeism record is nil. Mr. Lang's compensation for his services will be forwarded upon receipt of your request.[63]

In 1950 Hugo was hired as a tool and die maker by the company for whom he worked for the rest of his professional life, Bristol-Myers in New

Jersey. They also had a branch near Frankfurt. In 1952 Hugo was promoted from Machinist, Toolroom A to Foreman Class C.[64] On the occasion
of Hugo's thirty-fifth anniversary with Bristol-Myers in 1985, the manager
of the Products Division congratulated Hugo, "expressing appreciation for
your loyalty and dedication, and for your contribution to the Company's
growth and success."[65] Linda Bakalian, the personnel manager, added her
congratulations, noting that "it would be hard to imagine how some of
our goals could be attained were it not for your efforts."[66] An unidentified newspaper article featured Hugo for his thirty-fifth anniversary on
March 6, 1985. Noting that he had spent the greater part of his working
life at Bristol-Myers Products, he concluded, "My being here all these years
makes it obvious that Bristol-Myers has been good to me and a pleasant
place to work." The article gave Hugo's work history at Bristol-Myers.

> Starting out in 1950 as a machinist in the Hillside Manufacturing Divi-
> sion, Hugo worked his way up to Packaging Machine Shop foreperson in
> a short ten-year period. In 1966, he transferred to Engineering, where to-
> day he is a senior project engineer. His responsibilities currently include
> designing, developing, purchasing and testing of new equipment, as well
> as maintenance and repairing of older machinery for our manufacturing
> operations. Although he headquarters at Hillside, his job frequently takes
> him to Morrisville and St. Louis as well as other areas of the United States
> and overseas in his search for better machinery and the latest technological
> developments.[67]

In fact, one of the places Hugo used to visit to buy machinery was Laupheim, near Ulm, a town in Swabia that used to have a large Jewish community. Quite an accomplishment for a poor immigrant boy! In his autobiography, Hugo wrote, "I worked for this company for nearly forty years,
until I retired [in 1987]."[68]

On July 18, 1948, Hugo Lang married Inge Feldtmann, an Auschwitz
survivor from Berlin.[69] They have two children and two grandchildren.
Inge's parents were Wilhelm and Hertha née Leibholz Feldtmann. Her father was Christian; he died of a heart attack when Inge was ten years old.
In November 2000, Inge wrote down her family history for this book.

> I was born in Berlin, Germany. I was an only child. . . . When I was young,
> we lived in West Berlin near Charlottenburg and then moved to Steglitz, not
> far from the Wannsee. . . . My father owned a little clothing factory, in which

he had approximately forty employees. We lived pretty well in a lovely big apartment with a balcony overlooking a park and could afford a lot of nice things, including a cleaning lady who came in once a week. We took nice vacations to the Baltic Sea or the mountains. My parents had a season pass for the opera, which they both enjoyed. I went to movies, to the park, or to the Wannsee swimming with my girlfriends. I had a normal, carefree childhood. My grandparents, on my father's side, owned a farm near Schleswig Holstein at the North Sea, where I spent four weeks of my school vacation every year. Of course, I had a great time there. My grandparents had so many nice animals to play with on their farm. . . . Nothing in these first wonderful years, which I spent with my parents, relatives, their friends and mine, prepared me for the dreadful years to come.

Then came the years of 1937–38. The bad years had started. The school years of 1937–38 and the next few years were torture for me and other Jewish children. They became continuously worse since the new government had taken over. We as Jewish children were treated so badly. We were singled out as outcasts by being required to wear the Star of David patch on our clothes at all times. The Christian children, my former classmates, did not look at us anymore and did not play with us at recess. I still remember when we took day trips to some nice places, we as Jewish children were forbidden to go. For a child to be singled out because of their religion, when this was not an issue in the previous years, was very traumatic. I was only eleven or twelve years old, and was extremely hurt and frustrated. I used to go home crying frequently. Then I had to leave school all together when I was fourteen years old. I was not allowed to finish the higher classes. My mother put me then in a finishing school for one year. This way, I did not have to go into the munitions factory for forced labor at such a young age which, as Jews, we were then told to do by the new government.[70]

At age fifteen, Inge and her mother worked in a munitions factory in Berlin. In 1942 Inge's mother was deported. As a *Mischling*, Inge was to be sent to Theresienstadt while her mother was to be sent to Auschwitz.[71] Inge did not wish to be separated from her mother. Rather than leave her, she went with her mother to the death camp of Auschwitz.

I didn't know what the showers were. And my mother went to the showers. I stayed in Auschwitz with my hair cut off and so forth. I was there a little over half a year. If I would have had to stay longer, I would no longer be alive. I got nothing to eat. We lay in the dirt.

Then they needed workers for another concentration camp. That was only for young people [who were considered] *Mischlinge*. And I happened to be a *Mischling*. I was very fortunate that they accepted me.

I was nineteen then. I was in Auschwitz from October, 1942 to March, 1943.

Then I was sent to Theresienstadt in Czechoslovakia, 64 kilometers from Prague. There things weren't as bad as in Auschwitz. I was lucky to be working somewhere else every ten days. They called it *Kaderschaft* (cadre work). Of course, I wore a Sing-Sing [prison] uniform, and didn't have any shoes. In winter it was very cold. And in summer it was too hot. We were in a small room. Fifty people slept together in one room on beds of straw. We would rather have slept outside with the mosquitoes. Inside there always were fleas. We always had diarrhea, an illness we never got rid of. That was due to the bad food. We worked hard—in agriculture, in the bakery, we had to carry heavy loads of wood. Once, during an assignment on a farm, we didn't get anything to eat for two days. There were lots of apples, and they looked so good. I ate twelve apples, that was a mistake.

I was in Theresienstadt from March 18, 1943, to May, 1945. The Russians thought that we were Germans because we spoke German and they wanted to shoot us all. We had to lock ourselves in our rooms. One of us stepped forward and told them we were German Jews. He explained it to them. Then they gave us to eat and we could go outside. We were there for another six months. All was fine. We received money. Then I returned to Berlin. I hoped to perhaps find someone from my family. But there was no one there anymore. Most had died. Some emigrated to South America.

My parents had very good Christian friends. They were wonderful people. They had a big house and wanted to hide us in their cellar. They weren't afraid. But we were afraid for these people. If we would have been discovered they would have been shot. We didn't want to do it.[72]

But, being the good friends they were,

They kept a few suitcases in their cellar that contained a few valuables that we still had before everything was confiscated by the government. . . . When I was liberated from this camp [Theresienstadt] in 1945, I only weighed 85 lbs. They had to feed me very bland foods for a few weeks until I could absorb solid foods again. I then wrote to my parents' friends in Berlin that I had survived and where I was. They were so happy to hear I was alive.

When I went back home to Berlin they invited me to stay with them. I did so for one year and a half.[73]

Having spent her teenage years in captivity, Inge's life was forever changed. "I was then twenty years old. When I returned to Berlin, everything was destroyed. We lost most everything. I have only one picture of my mother, and none of my father."[74]

Although her friends did not want Inge to leave Berlin, she couldn't bear to stay in the ruined city without her loved ones.

> Well, my first good luck was that I met a beautiful girl my age whose name was Kay [Elkeles] at the American Consulate in Berlin. We both applied for a visa to go to America. . . . Kay and I arrived in New York in February 1947. We got a small room in an apartment building in Washington Heights. We both got a job in the Garment District near Canal Street doing piece-work in a clothing factory. . . . My girlfriend, Kay . . . met her husband first. Walter [Gundel] came to this country from Germany six years before we did. . . . Walter introduced his best friend, Hugo, to me in December 1947. Walter and Hugo's friendship went back to their days in [Ulm] Germany. That's how I met my wonderful husband.[75]

Hugo's personal attempt to enter the fray of compensation politics dates from February 22, 1954. At that time he wrote to the mayor of Süssen, asking, at their earliest convenience, for four applications for *Entschädigung* (reparations) for the victims of Nazi persecution, Federal Law BGBl. I S. 1387, dated September 18, 1953. He signed it, "Hugo Lang, son of the murdered Leopold Lang."[76] He received a response from Mayor Eisele on March 22, 1954, advising Hugo that he forwarded his request to the Public Defender for Reparations in Stuttgart, noting that the reparations had still not been publicly announced.[77] Hugo promptly received a communication from the Public Defender for Reparations' office informing him that he was to contact the appropriate representative of the Federal Republic responsible for his former place of residence, Süssen.[78]

On June 17, 1957, Hugo applied to the German government for loss of education/vocational training. He wrote an affidavit as follows,

> I, Hugo Lang, started my apprenticeship as a bartender apprentice in the Restaurant Moos [at Weinhof] in Ulm an der Donau. My apprenticeship was interrupted because of the pogroms against Jews on September 9, 1939 [*sic*,

November 9, 1938] for which only the Nazis were to blame. The restaurant was destroyed and closed in that night and later burned down. In September 1939 I had to do forced labor at Firma F. Bader in Süssen as a day laborer. I wanted to thoroughly learn how to be a bartender, but I was denied that opportunity since the restaurant was closed.

When I arrived here [in the United States], I found work as a day laborer in a factory until I could learn the language. My income was barely enough to subsist, hence I am applying for damages due to the interruption and denial of my training in a profession. I resumed my apprenticeship in June 1945 and concluded in September 1948. Enclosed please find two recommendations which show that my apprenticeship was interrupted.

I hope that the two enclosed affidavits and the affidavit from the Bader Company which I already sent you in October 1955 will finally be sufficient.

Sincerely, Hugo Lang[79]

Hugo has documentation for his retirement contributions by the Bader company from the period of September 1939 until July 8, 1941.[80] On September 13, 1964, he resumed correspondence concerning the loss of his occupational training, and lawyer Kurt Reissmüller responded on September 18 that the office of the public defender no longer existed, but that they would increase his claim from DM 5,000 to DM 10,000 as soon as the "final law" was passed.[81] Not until June 6, 1967, is there additional correspondence between the lawyer and Hugo. At that time Reissmüller notified Hugo that they were able to submit a claim for an additional $5,000 for him and that the money would be available in about four weeks.[82] And indeed, on July 14, 1967, Hugo was notified by Herr Reissmüller that DM 5,000 (not DM 10,000), minus the fees of DM 293.80, for a total of DM 4,706.20, were being transferred to him. The transfer from the Commerzbank in Stuttgart to the First State Bank of Union, New Jersey, took place on July 24, 1967, in the amount of $1,172.90.[83] Thus, this matter was settled, albeit in depreciated currency.

Twenty-three years after leaving Germany, on July 14, 1964, Hugo also applied for reimbursement of his emigration costs. His transportation costs from Süssen to Berlin are documented. The travel expenses from Berlin to Lisbon were documented with money order receipts. However, the documentation for the ship's passage on the *Mousinho* had not been provided. The Office for Restitution pointed out that in many cases Jewish emigrants without means were assisted by a Jewish relief organization. Hugo thus had to document that he financed the sea voyage from Lisbon to the United States himself.[84] Confirmation that the case was being worked on was sent by lawyer Reissmüller et al. on July 17, 1964.[85] Another letter from Hugo, dated July 23, was likewise acknowledged by the lawyer.[86] Apparently Hugo's documentation of his transatlantic voyage was sufficient, for on August 27 lawyer Schmidt from Reissmüller's office notified him that he had been awarded DM 1,674.17 for emigration costs. Objections had to be submitted by February 25, 1965.[87] There must have been none, for on September 9 Reissmüller acknowledged another letter of Hugo's from September 2, 1964. The amount would be transferred to Hugo's account as soon as available.[88] The compensation was available on November 30. After expenses, the net amount would be DM 1,478.45 (about to $369.60).[89] This amount was transferred to Hugo Lang's account with the First State Bank of Union, New Jersey, via the Commerzbank of Stuttgart on December 10, 1964.[90]

Hugo Lang is a mild-mannered and kind individual. Yet the deep hurt of what happened to him and his loved ones was still with him in 1966, when he wrote a short summary of the persecutions they experienced. It is stronger than the statements he made during his visit to Süssen in 1989 or even in his autobiography.

My murdered parents had a cattle business in Süssen, district of Göppingen. After 1933 the leaders of the district forbade the farmers to deal with Jews. Therefore my father had to close down his business a few months later [sic, 1938]. At the same time my parents, along with other Jewish citizens, had to deliver their jewelry, as well as gold and silver, to the Stuttgart Foreign Currency Office. At that time it was impossible for a Jew to see a doctor or lawyer. They [doctors and lawyers] were afraid of the SA or SS. After 1936 no Jewish child could attend the business college or university. In most districts Jewish pupils or students were kicked out of school by the authorities. SA and SS members tried to dissolve mixed marriages. If that wasn't successful, German Jews and non-Jews were sent to concentration camps. Businesses, stores, and factories were zwangsverkauft (Aryanized). One could work only where the party authorized it. I myself did forced labor for the Bader Company, which had a branch in Eislingen. Of course Jews always had to do the worst work. Those who were not sent to a concentration camp had to do forced labor. On November 9, 1938, all [sic, about 100] synagogues in Germany were burnt down and destroyed. That alone is an eternal shame which many Germans will never forget. The Volk of culture has forgotten what culture means. In 1940–41 all German Jews had to wear the Jewish star. Many German Jews left Germany with a few suitcases or less. Everything else was confiscated or left behind. After the war was over, some former [Jewish] citizens returned to their former homes from the concentration and death camps half dead and starving. My sister Ruth was among them. The German Volk can never undo that six million citizens and soldiers were murdered. After a few months my sister was able to come to the United States. Many German Jews had to learn different jobs abroad because of the language.

My father was the bearer of the Iron Cross during World War I; he was wounded three times while serving with Field Marshall von Hindenburg during the battle of Tannenberg in Russia. When the Germans wanted to forget, no one remembered the former [World War I] soldiers. I am writing this report after twenty-five years with a heavy heart, and if God allows me to live to be a hundred, I and millions of others will never forget the terrible times. One never forgets that humans can be worse than the worst animals.

The shame remains forever.[91]

Today Hugo and Inge Lang, both in their high eighties, live in northern New Jersey, next door to their daughter, Evelyn, and son-in-law, Tony.

# 7    Deportation of the Lang Families

*As a neighbor I grew up with the Judenkinder of the sister-in-law of the Jew Lang who now lives in the United States [Fanny], and thus always had a good neighborly relationship with them.*
—Karl Häfele, municipal treasurer[1]

*His [H. W. Holl's] wife, née Brell from Nenningen, whose father was also a cattle dealer, was formerly household help in the Judenhaus for the Louis Lang family. For this reason there was a good relationship between Holl and the Lang family.*
—Karl Häfele[2]

*I own a hardware store in Süssen and the local Jews bought my wares, so that there always was a good relationship between us.*
—Adolf Finckh, acting mayor[3]

The sordid details of deportation on Friday, November 28, 1941, are murky at best. There are no eyewitnesses who survived the war or who are willing to step forward and share what they know. Only one former neighbor of the Lang family told me in 1999 that Louis came to her father around midnight in order to say goodbye. She remembers that he was weeping. When her father said to him, "but we will see each other again," Louis responded that he didn't think so. The witness added that she kept suitcases with Louis's belongings in her attic. The next morning the Langs, according to this witness, took their personal belongings to the railroad station in a little pull cart.[4]

In the municipal archives, we find terse and sparse information on the drama that unfolded that day. A dry notation in the city council minutes of December 5, 1941, (one week after deportation) states matter-of-factly—under the heading "Dejudaization of Süssen" —that "the Jews who lived in the town's building no. 45 in the Hindenburgstrasse were relocated by order of the Stuttgart Gestapo, dated November 18, 1941, to the Reichskommissariat Ostland. On November 28, 1941, they left Süssen *mit Sack und*

*Pack* [with all of their belongings]. The furniture that they left behind has become the property of the *Reich* and will be auctioned off publicly in the near future."[5] The city council minutes continue, "With their [the Langs'] departure, the apartments and the barn became available for rent. Ten families applied for the apartments. When acquiring the house [from its Jewish owners] in 1938, the town intended to add a staircase and a toilet at the northern end of building no. 45 and to create two larger dwellings for civil servants. But since construction is so difficult at the moment and it is hard to get usable construction material, we have decided to wait with all of these renovations until after the war and to rent the house to three families."[6] This document, totally without emotion or concern of any kind for the fate of the Lang family, is clearly more interested in the distribution of the available housing to the local population, the hardships of the war on everyday life, and the distribution of the loot, namely the belongings that the Jewish families could not take with them—which was all of their household items, clothing and furniture—than with the victims. Not one word of concern for or even interest in the fate of the deported families is mentioned. Did the city council know so clearly what the fate of these families would be that it didn't need to spell it out? Or were they simply relieved to be rid of their "Jewish problem"?[7]

A second, chilling document, under the heading, "Deportation of the Jews to the Reichskommissariat Ostland," in the *Gemeindechronik* states that

On November 28, 1941, the following Jews "emigrated" to the Reichskommissariat Ostland:

Lang, Leopold, cattle helper, born February 11, 1895, in Ernsbach
Lang, Eva Sara, housewife, born November 11, 1896, in Odenkirchen
Lang, Ruth Sara, factory worker, born July 27, 1925, in Gross-Süssen
Lang, Lazarus [Louis], day laborer, born February 2, 1893, in Ernsbach
Lang, Fanny Sara, housewife, born April 21, 1894, in Frankfurt a. M.
Lang, Kurt Israel, day laborer, born July 7, 1924 in Gross-Süssen
Lang, Siegfried Israel, tool and die maker apprentice, born July 19, 1925, in Gross-Süssen
Baer, Alfred Israel, day laborer, born September 14, 1875, in Rodalben
Baer, Hermine Sara, housewife, born January 5, 1894, in Ernsbach
Baer, Hans [Kurt] Israel, day laborer, born April 12, 1917, in Pforzheim
Metzger, Alfred Israel, day laborer, born October 11, 1880, in Kirchheim Bolanden

Metzger, Eugenie Sara, housewife, born December 3, 1881, in Rodalben
Metzger, Rudolf Israel, day laborer, born April 29, 1922, in Rodalben.[8]

Of interest in this listing is the purposeful humiliation inflicted on these Jewish citizens for no good reason at all, but as an end in itself. Basically all Jewish men are reduced to *Hilfsarbeiter* (day laborers), while all Jewish women are housewives. Also interesting is the absence of the middle name Israel for Leopold and Lazarus [Louis], both of whom are reduced in status from *Viehhändler* (cattle dealer) to *Viehpfleger* (cattle helper) and *Hilfsarbeiter*, respectively, but are for some reason not subjected to the identifying label of Israel common to all Jewish men starting January 1, 1939. As if the above listings were not injury enough, the recorder of this information eagerly added at the bottom of the page that "Süssen is now free of Jews,"[9] which gave rise to the title for this book. On the lease that both Louis and Leopold signed with the town, the middle name Israel is also absent for both names.[10] However, when Leopold on January 3, 1939, went to the city hall to fill out a change of name document for his son Manfred, adding Israel to Manfred, he signed his own name on this form as Leopold Israel Lang as well.[11]

Absent from the above list of deportees from November 28, 1941, in the *Gemeindechronik* are Falk Sahm, Walter Zeimann, Werner Josef Baer, Siegfried Baer, Luise Ottenheimer, and the nameless euthanasia victims.

There is no evidence that Werner and Siegfried Baer were deported from Süssen, only that they died in the Holocaust. After the Holocaust, Gemeindepfleger Häfele testified under oath that "the Baer family asked their boys in Schlesien, Gross-Breesen, and in Frankfurt/Oder to come home . . . shortly before deportation."[12] There is no evidence that Werner did. Yet Eva Lang in a letter to Hugo and Fred on October 6 wrote that "yesterday Siegfried came home on vacation for ten days [from October 5–15]." According to this scenario, certainly Siegfried Baer could have been deported from Süssen. This is, however, not confirmed in the very meticulous municipal records. The two young men are neither listed in the *Gemeindechronik* nor in the city's vital records files. However, after the Holocaust, the city records reflect that Siegfried and Werner Baer were declared dead, so they definitely were deported and perished, the question is from where.

Falk Sahm and Walter Zeimann were deported earlier, though the term *deported* was not used. Leopold Lang's long-time farmhand Falk Sahm "moved" on July 1, 1937,[13] to the Jewish old-age home in Heilbronn-

Sontheim. In his book, *Das jüdische Altersheim Herrlingen und die Schicksale seiner Bewohner,* Ulrich Seemüller talks about the fate of those elderly Jews who were forcibly relocated to places that became collection points for deportation. Seemüller explains that Sahm had given his monthly disability check of RM 37 to the Jewish governing organization, the *Kultusvereinigung.*[14] After the dissolution of the Jewish old-age home in Heilbronn-Sontheim, he was sent from one old-age home to another until he was finally deported to Theresienstadt in August of 1942. From there he was deported to Maly Trostinec on August 25, 1942, where the Nazis murdered him in a most gruesome way, in a gas chamber on wheels.[15]

Walter Zeimann, who was born Jewish, but had left the Jewish community, was a merchant and moved to Süssen, to Haus Waldeck, from Frankfurt on May 2, 1936, with his non-Jewish wife Paula, née Frömbsdorf. According to her postwar lawyer, he was arrested after Kristallnacht, on November 10, 1938, and deported to Dachau.[16] His death is recorded as November 20, 1938, in Prittlbach near Dachau, perhaps a subcamp of Dachau.[17] Cause of death is listed as ulcers. According to the mayor's post-Holocaust reply to Mrs. Zeimann's lawyer, Paula Zeimann left Süssen on January 24, 1939, and returned to Frankfurt am Main, 24 Odenweg. The day of Walter Zeimann's arrest is not noted in the records, nor is that of Louis and Leopold Lang. Mrs. Zeimann remarried. Her lawyer's 1959 inquiry is in the name of "Paula Müller, widowed Zeimann."[18]

Although the Ottenheimer family sold their business under the pressure of Aryanization to a non-Jewish owner at the end of 1937 and, according to her son Werner, Luise Ottenheimer thereafter "was moved" from Göppingen to Stuttgart, she is tied to Süssen through her husband Alfred, who ran the Mechanische Weberei Süssen Gebrüder Ottenheimer until the sale of the business. Luise was caught in the fall 1941 roundup and deported to Riga where she perished. Her name has been added to her husband's tombstone in the Jewish section of the Göppingen municipal cemetery (no. 92b), but is not on the Süssen memorial plaque installed by the city, since they were primarily residents of Göppingen.

In addition to the above Jewish citizens of Süssen, there were also two or three "nameless" non-Jewish victims of euthanasia whose lives were ended by the Nazis in the 1940s. Their names are not officially honored and remembered anywhere in the town, making one wonder what the difference is between one type of victim and another.[19] Of course, the local townspeople know very well who these victims are, but officially silence is still golden.

There is yet another source for details on the deportation of the Lang family that was not available to me until 2002, when a colleague in Germany generously shared his discovery with me. In 1948 the surviving Nazis from Süssen and other places who were directly involved in the deportation proceedings of Jews in Süssen and Weissenstein gave depositions to the state under oath. Their testimony has survived in the Staatsarchiv (State Archive) in Ludwigsburg. According to the sworn testimony, a slightly more concrete account of the deportation proceedings can be constructed, although some of the witness testimony is unreliable.

The testimony by Karl Häfele and acting Mayor Adolf Finckh about the deportation orders gives the impression as if both were only marginally involved in the process. In fact, there is no separate entry for Häfele in the summary report by the commission; he is included under Finckh, meaning that the commission members saw him as Finckh's lackey, carrying out some of the acting mayor's duties. To read the report this way, however, is to underestimate the power and autonomy that Häfele had as a municipal employee and as a loyal party member. It is obvious from several notes that he was intimately familiar with everything that concerned the Langs and acted independently in many matters concerning their fate.

Finckh and Häfele have different views of how the deportation process started. The commission went easy on Finckh because of his age (71) and his testimony is not very helpful. "I don't remember too many details. I still remember that the local Jews were taken away. I knew nothing at all about this matter. I found out the day before [deportation], I don't remember from whom. . . . I can assure you that I do not remember a written directive from the Landrat, the police or the party [NSDAP] concerning this pogrom against the Jews in my capacity as mayor."[20]

Häfele's memory is also faulty. "During the month of November 1941 the Mayor's Office here received the deportation orders for the local Jews. I don't remember whether the order came via the Landratsamt or directly from the Landespolizeiamt in Stuttgart. In this [written] order the Jewish individuals were listed by name and, if I remember correctly, they were to be sent to Stuttgart to a collection camp and from there shipped to the Reichskommissariat Ostland. In addition it stated a specific amount of luggage that those concerned could take along. This order stated that the listed Jews were to be officially notified of the contents of this letter."[21]

When questioned as to who broke the bad news to the Langs, later Lang trustee Karl Schlecht's testimony gives a different picture from Häfele's. Häfele only meekly stated, "I don't remember now whether I myself notified the Jews at that time or whether *Polizeihauptwachtmeister* (police officer) Holl did."[22] Would one be able to forget such a monumental event? The Schlecht testimony is more detailed, though it is impossible to say whether more accurate. "In November '41 [the month of deportation] when I again visited the Langs, I found the entire family sitting around the table in their living room. When I asked how they were doing, Louis Lang showed me a letter from the Stuttgart Gestapo Leitstelle, Hotel Silber, which read something like this: 'Within 8 days you will be evacuated or deported to Riga. Your estate will remain in your house. You are no longer allowed to give away or sell anything. You are merely allowed to take a piece of luggage weighing 50 kg.' Then the individual items which they were allowed to take were listed, such as warm underwear, clothing, etc. The letter concluded with the comment that additional orders would follow."[23] Schlecht added, "As far as I know every head of household received such an order directly from the Gestapo by mail. In each letter the individual family members were listed."[24] This was easy to do, as every move by a Jewish citizen was reported by *Assessor* (assistant judge) Fauser to the Gestapo in Stuttgart. Schlecht continued, "Within these 8 days and until the time of departure of the Jews I went to visit the Lang family every evening *"um nach dem Rechten zu sehen* [to see what I could do for them]".[25]

Häfele testified that "before their departure on November 28 or 29 the Jews were still able to sell their cattle unofficially, which was generally no longer allowed at this time."[26] Yet Louis and Leopold were allowed to take only very little cash, some RM 10 per person, but Leopold had three or four cows and a bull in his stables.[27] What happened to the money from these sales is not entirely clear, although it is probable that Louis and Leopold gave the cash to Schlecht for safe-keeping or for services rendered. In post-Holocaust correspondence Schlecht makes reference to RM 9,000 which Louis and Leopold gave him before deportation,[28] and Kurt in a letter to Hugo and Fred in the United States notes that Herr Schlecht had been very helpful to the family prior to deportation.[29]

Häfele also knew a little about the Langs' other preparations for departure. "Already several days before their deportation the Jews came to the mayor's office and requested applications for shoes and woolen materials for winter clothing, which we granted them in spite of the *Judenhetze* (general Jew baiting) at that time."[30] Hugo in his 1946 affidavit also stated that his parents knew of the impending deportation in advance.

According to Finckh's and Häfele's testimonies, Holl was solely in charge of the deportation of the Langs.[31] Häfele testified, "Depending on who received the mail concerning Jewish matters, *Polizeihauptwachtmeister* Holl received his orders concerning execution either from the mayor or from me. He was then still a municipal employee."[32] Häfele remembers correctly that Holl "was [only] incorporated into the state *Gendarmerie* on April 1, 1942,"[33] thus becoming a state employee. Finckh stated, "The deportation of the Jews was purely the business of the police which at that time was state police."[34] He is wrong. At the time of the deportation of the Langs in November 1941 Holl was still in the employ of the municipality.

The trump card for Finckh and Häfele is of course that "Hauptpolizeiwachtmeister Holl . . . [who] alone was charged with the job [ of accompanying the Langs to Stuttgart] by the mayor's office . . . is missing in action since 1945."[35] In light of the fact that no witness has volunteered information about the events of November 28, 1941, we will probably never know whether he was responsible for, acted alone, or was involved at all in the actual deportation of the Lang families from Süssen. Ruth does not mention him in her post-Holocaust account of deportation.

The day before deportation must have been taken up with getting the larger luggage items shipped off. These probably consisted of bedding, even mattresses. Also, according to Häfele, Leopold was allowed to take a laundry cauldron. Häfele stated, "As far as I remember, the deportation order stated that the larger luggage items of the Jews would be sent directly to Riga presumably through a Stuttgart moving company. Thus I assume that the Jews also were sent to Riga."[36]

Word of the impending deportation must have gotten around, for Schlecht testified, "When the Jews later had to leave, many of the citizens of Süssen came to say goodbye to the Jews, some tearfully. Acting mayor Finckh was also among them."[37] The Langs' cleaning woman (U. S. O.), Finckh, the neighbors, and Karl Schlecht may have been the last locals who saw the Langs alive. Mrs. Ö., who lived next door to the Langs, testified, "On the evening prior to the departure I met Leopold Lang in the street where he wished me a tearful goodbye. I did not learn from the Jews why they were being deported. I only know that they did not leave here willingly."[38] Finckh, who claimed to only have found out about the deportation orders that day, also went to the Langs to say goodbye. "Still the same evening I went to the Lang family and said farewell."[39] And Schlecht stated, "On the evening of November 27, 1941, I said my final farewell."[40]

And then came "*der letzte Weg*," as it says in the partisan song, the final road. Although neither Häfele nor Finckh owned up to being present at the time of deportation, they made statements about the event.[41] Mayor Saalmüller really wasn't present, as he was drafted in 1940 and returned in 1945, only to be arrested as a war criminal. Häfele was as unsure of the date of deportation as he was of who told the Langs about the order. "Either on November 28 or 29, 1941, he [Holl] took the individuals to the railroad station for the regularly scheduled train at 7 A.M."[42] He remembered, "Hauptpolizeiwachtmeister Holl was charged with the transport of the Jews on the previously mentioned date and time. Shortly before departure on November 29 [sic, 28], 1941, around 6 A.M., the Jew Louis Lang gave me all of the keys to the Judenhaus."[43] Häfele continued, "He [Holl] accompanied them to Stuttgart where he delivered them to a camp in the Reichsgartenschaugelände [Killesberg].[44] The Jews were allowed to take considerable luggage so that there was the general impression that they would [indeed] be resettled in the East."[45] Finckh testified, "I myself was not present when the Jews were deported and know only that this was carried out by Hauptpolizeiwachtmeister Holl. . . . No one told me where the Jews were taken and what would happen to them. To be sure there were rumors that they were deported to Riga, but whether that is true I do not know."[46] Schlecht also did not have the courage to face his friends for their final walk though Süssen, let alone accompany them to the station. "Who took the Jews to the train the next day and took them away and what else happened, I do not know," he testified.[47] At least one of the good citizens of Süssen was sleeping when the Langs were marched to the station. The Langs' former cleaning woman testified, "I myself was still in bed on the morning when the Jews were shipped off. I therefore do not know who accompanied them and what happened."[48]

But not everyone was this cowardly. According to the sworn testimony of Häfele, "while the larger luggage items had already been taken the day before . . . the [hand] luggage of the Jews was taken to the railroad station by the late innkeeper of the restaurant Stern [as far as we could determine this was Sternenwirt J. G. Geyer] with his vehicle.[49] Hugo Lang, who did not have to experience these events as he had managed to emigrate before, supported Häfele's testimony through his sister Ruth's memories, which she shared with him upon her return from the concentration camp. "One of our neighbors had a horse and wagon/cart. . . . When the SS [sic] came and took them away, he came over with his wagon/cart. . . . The SS told him that he couldn't drive them [to the railroad station], 'otherwise we take you, too.' The man was an older man, more than seventy. He said, 'Put your things in my cart. I'll take you to the station.' They walked behind the

172 | Deportation of the Lang Families

cart, to the railroad station. All the neighbors . . . in our neighborhood . . . came out of their homes and bid them goodbye. That's how it was."[50] This touching farewell, almost an honor guard of sorts by the local folks, would be moving if it was not so incomprehensible.

What might this final walk have been like? The property of Louis and Leopold Lang was located on the easternmost edge of the village of Süssen. In order to reach the train station located completely on the other side of town, in the north, they had to walk for a few meters west along Hauptstrasse [then Hindenburgstrasse] with its open sewer on the north side of the street and then turn right into Bachstrasse, also with open water running along the western side of the dirt road facing the castle of Staufeneck, visible directly ahead of them. Then they passed a number of farm properties, the birth house of the poet J. G. Fischer, turning right towards the "ice house" of the Grau family on the right, passing the Gasthaus Hirsch that fed the POWs, and the home of a man who had been murdered as well because he was mentally challenged. This branch of Bachstrasse runs into Heidenheimerstrasse [renamed Hitlerstrasse] right at the spot where the once Lutheran school is located that Kurt, Siegi, and Ruth as well as those brothers and sisters who were able to emigrate attended. They then crossed the bridge over the river Fils and passed a number of businesses, among them on the western side the Turner bakery next to the Weiss textile store and the once important Post inn. The Beck stationery store and the Restaurant Rössle were on the opposite eastern side of the street, and the *Zollhaus* sat at the bend in the street that leads over the railroad bridge to the Ottenheimer factory. At that point they had to turn left, passing the Nagel bakery, to Bahnhofstrasse, with the post office on the left [south] and the railroad station on the right [north].

According to the sworn testimony of Häfele, police chief Holl was the guard detail of the Lang family to Stuttgart. This seems to indicate that the thirteen Süssen Jews were not grouped with the Göppingen Jews, who were their friends, though they probably met up with them in the transit camp at Killesberg in Stuttgart for the final journey east.

In his testimony, Häfele volunteered the information that he was uncomfortable with the deportations. He testified, "As far as I know Holl also did not agree with the deportation and was reluctant to carry out the orders concerning the Jews. I personally did not accompany the Jews to the railroad station and therefore am unable to testify in more detail about their deportation."[51]

Since policeman Holl is dead, we have no testimony from him about the train ride to Stuttgart. There is, however, testimony from two gendarmes who were involved with the deportation of the Jews from Weissenstein.

Gendarmeriekreisführer (District Police Chief) Gottlieb Rall, the highest-ranking policeman in the district of Göppingen, merely stated, "I remember that in Süssen there lived a Jew by the name of Lang at the Reichsstrasse [Hindenburgstrasse]. I only know his name. I don't know anything else. Officially I didn't have anything to do with the Jews in Süssen, and I don't know when they were deported. I assume that the local police force, which at that time still employed their own municipal policeman, was charged with the deportation of the Jews."[52] This would be correct.

Another policeman, Wachtmeister Andreas Moll, was a hostile witness, refusing to sign his statement. His testimony is problematic because the dates don't match with those on which the Langs were deported. "For the first time, approximately in April 1942, I received a letter from the Gendarmeriekreisführer, Hauptmann Rall, via the Gruppenpostenführer, Meister der Gendarmerie Frank [who confiscated the Langs' radios in 1939], which stated that I was to inform specific Jews, listed by name, that they were to begin their journey from Weissenstein to Stuttgart at a certain point in time."[53]

"Weissenstein" refers to a town to the north of Süssen where a Jewish old-age home or collection point was established in the Weissenstein Schloss for the purpose of concentrating regional Jews before deporting them to a camp. They were deported in several waves, primarily to Riga and Theresienstadt, which often led to Auschwitz. According to the research carried out by Dr. Karl-Heinz Ruess, "in late fall 1941, fifty-eight persons, mostly older women from the Stuttgart area, were moved into the Schloss. Their movements were strictly limited, they were merely allowed to move around the courtyard of the castle and walk on a small path outside the castle."[54] In spite of a false sense of security—they had been allowed to bring some of their own furniture—their fate was sealed. The first transport of seventeen or nineteen persons to Riga took place on November 27, 1941,[55] at the time the Langs were also deported. The others were deported in April (nine persons) and August (twenty-six persons) of 1942.[56] Only one woman, married to a non-Jew, survived in Weissenstein until November 1942. She was deported to Theresienstadt from Stuttgart in 1944.[57] Whether she survived is not known.

Policeman Moll continued his account, "On the day of departure I myself supervised the Jews of the first transport [in Weissenstein] as they walked from the Schloss [the detention center] to the railroad station in the morning. In Süssen the Jews living there—Lang, Metzger, and Baer—were deposited in the same coach by Hauptwachtmeister Holl."[58] If we take Moll's testimony at face value, this "first transport" from Weissenstein refers to November 28, 1941, the date when the Langs were deported. Since Moll claims that he was first instructed to notify the Jews in Weissenstein in April 1942, there is a clear discrepancy. The information only makes sense if he is wrong about the date and right about the "first transport."

Häfele testified that he asked police chief Holl upon his return from Stuttgart, "What happened to the Jews?" To this Holl only answered, "It is a pity what is happening to the Jews. One Jew spoke to those who were taken to the camp in Stuttgart: 'The Jewish people have suffered much throughout their history and will survive this as well.' Holl spoke merely of a large camp in Stuttgart, where the Jews are being collected. He did not say anything about their further destination nor the state's intent towards the Jews."[59] He reiterated this, as if still shocked by what had happened. "Concerning the future of the Jews, concerning the intent of the evacuation [deportation!] I did not learn anything at this time or later. I can state that I never saw a secret order or other directive that would have let me understand the true situation. This I only learned in 1945 as a French prisoner of war."[60] One almost wants to believe him, but why did he think the Langs were totally disowned for no reason at all except that they were Jews?

In his history of the Jewish community in Württemberg and Hohenzollern, historian Paul Sauer wrote, "The transport participants were brought to Stuttgart mostly under police supervision. Until deportation they were housed in a collection camp at Killesberg,"[61] in inhumane conditions. A survivor, Alfred Winter, remembered that "At Killesberg, no provisions had been made for the so-called 'evacuees' to sit or to sleep. All men, women, and children had to lie on the bare floor in the big hall."[62] Sauer continued, "On December 1, 1941, the first transport left Stuttgart in the direction of Riga."[63] According to Winter, "It took three days to reach the point of destination. On December 4, 1941, the train stopped at 'Skirotava.' Here the evacuees were . . . chased out of the train with sticks by the SS and quite a few people, regardless of sex and age, were beaten up by the SS. It was bitter cold and snowing. A cold which none of the evacuees had ever experienced before."[64] And here was Eva with her swollen feet, and Leopold who had given up his beloved cigars. And for what? And Louis with his new wife Fanny, and "comely" Ruth, by her own description. And Louis's sons, Kurt and Siegfried, and the Metzgers and the Baers. "Under beating by the SS they were formed into a column and had to march a treacherous snow-covered road to an unknown destiny."[65] Not so unknown after the fact. Sauer reports the grim statistics: "Of the approximately 1,000 deportees only about 30 lived to see the end of the war."[66] Three of them were from Süssen.

In 1935 Riga was a beautiful city of 300,000 inhabitants with a Jewish population of 43,000 (14 percent). The Soviet Union protected the city from the Germans until June 27, 1941, when they withdrew, making room for a Latvian police force that was virulently anti-Semitic. When the Germans arrived on July 1, the terror had already begun, but the dragnet quickly suffocated any Jewish life in Riga. In August 1941 a ghetto was formed in the Moscow section of Riga and closed off with barbed wire. A *Judenrat* and Jewish police force were put in place, and on October 15 the ghetto was sealed. All Jews from Riga and environs were sent to the ghetto by October 25, approximately 32,000. The ghetto was horribly overcrowded. On November 30, two days after the Süssen Jews and many other German Jews, especially in southern Germany, were taken from their homes, about half the ghetto population—those housed in the large ghetto—was removed. "20,000 Jews were shot and buried in the Rumbula Forest."[67] The large ghetto was now empty, ready to receive the transport from Stuttgart that also included the Langs from Süssen and many of the Göppingen and Kirchheim Jews. Of a total of 16,000 German Jews who were taken to the large ghetto, 14,000 were murdered.[68]

Concentration camp Riga had many subcamps, the most infamous being Jungfernhof, Kaiserwald, and Stutthof. According to the postwar records, Ruth was sent to concentration camp Bromberg, while Kurt and Siegfried were sent to concentration camp Stutthof.[69] According to Ruth's post-Holocaust letter to her Uncle Max, dated February 25, 1945, the Langs were initially taken to the camp near Riga from which they were relocated several times.[70]

On March 16, 1942, the leader of the Gestapo in Stuttgart sent a memorandum to the leading offices of the State of Württemberg informing them that he was "immediately for reasons of bureaucratic simplification" nullifying his order of November 22, 1938, no. II B2–1776/38 to report monthly on Jewish residents. This meant of course that there were very few Jews left in Württemberg and in Germany as such. He reminded those in charge "to remain informed on the status of Jews living in their districts" so that they could be reported if necessary. He further informed these officials that "over the course of the next few weeks a second deportation of Jews to the East can be expected," advising them not to take any measures on their own and to wait for appropriate instructions. This communication was confidential.[71] The second wave of deportations from Southern Germany occurred in April 1942, when more of the Jews from the old age home in Weissenstein were deported. There was a small and final roundup in August 1942. With the exception of those who were in hiding or passing as non-Jews, the Nazis had succeeded in their murderous ethnic cleansing campaign. When asked about files concerning these events, both Häfele and another former city hall employee testified that they were destroyed. Häfele testified, "When I returned from a prisoner-of-war camp in 1946, I was told that the directives concerning the expulsion of Jews were burned at the end of the war."[72] The other employee remembered a bundle of files with a yellow cover and the label *Judenakten*, which was constantly locked up in the mayor's safe, no one else had access to it. According to this employee, on April 19, 1945, Mayor Finckh gave the order to destroy all personnel and secret files (files on Communists and Jews), which they did by burning them in the main furnace of the heating system. They did, however, not destroy all of the records. Thankfully, documents and correspondence concerning the Nazi persecution of the Jews were recovered from other sources as well.

Approximately five months passed from deportation of the Lang families to the auction of their belongings. Finckh stated, "Since the auction occurred quite a bit after deportation, the apartments of the Jews were under the care of Häfele and sealed. The Jew Louis Lang formerly owned a house at the Hauptstrasse in which he lived until the end [deportation]."

How did the Finanzamt in Geislingen know what possessions Jews like the Langs had to leave behind and would be available for auction?

The kingpin of the auction scheme in Oberamt Geislingen was Knut Oswald von Petzold, who was the head tax collector, "from July 1, 1940 to September 25, 1945,"[73] with an army of officials eager to help. Not a friend of the Jews, during his sworn testimony he explained, "Prior to their deportation the Jews had filled out preprinted asset inventories. Based on the property lists which were, however, pretty incomplete, the confiscated belongings were confirmed and disposed of according to the instructions of the *Oberfinanzpräsident* in Stuttgart."[74]

Häfele filled in the local picture. "After the deportation of the Jews, the furniture and other items left behind were inventoried by an official from the Finanzamt in Geislingen. Some time later, these items were sold through the *Vollstreckungsbeamten* [enforcement officer] of the Finanzamt. I do not know the name of this official."[75] The auction probably took place under Georg Niess, who was second in command of state finances under von Petzold, and was the expert on Jewish financial matters for the district the way Eichmann was the expert for all Jewish matters in the *Reich*. Häfele continued, "The receipts from the auction went to the Finanzamt. The municipal administration was not involved. Only [policeman] H. W. Holl and the municipal cashier Sauer, Süssen, 1 Kurzestrasse, were present."[76]

Finckh also contributed some testimony. "At the time, the Finanzamt in Geislingen merely requested that I attend the subsequent auction of the '*Judengut*,' which I did. The furnishings and personal items of the local Jewish families were auctioned off. The auction was carried out by two officials of the Finanzamt in Geislingen whose names I do not know."[77] At least one of these was the official auctioneer, Rösch (and presumably tax assistant Mayer).

Niess testified, "Approximately in April 1942 I was charged together with tax assistant Mayer to confirm the movable belongings of the Lang family in Süssen. The real estate of Lang had already been bought by the *Gemeinde*; the building and inventory were locked up by them. After taking inventory and assessment, the sworn auctioneer Rösch from Geislingen undertook the auction of the household goods, following local customs for public notification. He carried out the offer, surcharge appropriation, and collection of receipts himself, and had to be accountable to the *Finanzkasse* on the next day. According to the instructions of the *Oberfinanzpräsident* [Stuttgart], the collected monies were deposited into a special account for Lang and then attached. What happened to the money later I do not know. The Lang family no longer lived in Süssen at the time of the auction."[78] Or worse, some were no longer alive. According to Götz Aly we do know what happened to the receipts from any of the sales of *Judengut*, including auctions. They were sent on to Stuttgart and from there to Berlin to help finance the war.[79]

Acting Mayor Finckh testified that, although he was present at the auction, "I do not know the amount of money raised during the auction; it was taken to the Finanzamt in Geislingen by the two officials. The *Gemeinde* itself bought a *Waschanlage* (washing machine) as well as presumably a *Badeofen* (stove for heating hot water for washing of persons and clothes)."[80] There was a good reason the village needed these, as they had the prisoner-of-war camp and the unhappy representative of the Stalag who wanted the two populations kept apart. Finckh concluded, "As the auction was advertised days earlier in the newspaper interested persons also came from other places."[81] Although I tried to find a specific advertisement for the auction in the local papers, I did not succeed, even though many other auctions of this kind were in fact advertised in the newspaper to the regional population. The reason has come to light. A flyer was printed for this auction and posted in the town. Although still extant at the trial, the flyer is now lost.[82] The auction was also announced by the town crier, so there probably was no newspaper notice. We do know from restitution files who acquired some of the Lang belongings.[83] Some of these families lived quite a distance from Süssen. This will be discussed further in the chapter on post-Holocaust proceedings in relation to the Lang family.

The auction of the Lang property took place in April 1942, around the time of (or perhaps at the same time as) the auction of the belongings of the Weissenstein Jews, who were deported either in November 1941 or in April 1942. Besides the acting mayor from Süssen, Finckh, and the local cashier, Sauer, the individuals from the Finanzamt in Geislingen who were directly involved in the Lang auction are Petzold, Niess, Rösch, and Mayer.

Petzold also does not have correct information and one cannot help but wonder what happened to the proverbial meticulous record keeping for which Germans are known. Petzold testified, "In spring 1942, if I remember right it was in April [sic], about fifteen Jews who lived in my district—in Süssen and especially in the Jewish old-age home in Weissenstein—were deported to the East."[84] This statement is incorrect. According to all available records, the Langs were deported in November 1941. Petzold continued,

> The belongings of these Jews were confiscated by the Gestapo in favor of the *Reich* and transferred to the *Oberfinanzpräsident* [OFP] Württemberg in Stuttgart for administration and distribution. In those days the OFP Württemberg delegated the order to the local Finanzamt. Thus the Finanzamt Geislingen received *Einziehungsverfügungen* [warrants for confiscation] from the Gestapo Leitstelle Stuttgart concerning the belongings of the Jews who had been deported to the East as well as detailed instructions on how the confiscated property was to be administered and distributed. The warrants of the Gestapo were, as far as I remember, signed by 'Musgay' [Muschgai][85] or something like that. The confiscation was based on the statute of the *Reich* president for the Protection of *Volk* and State of February 28, 1933.[86]

Petzold continued, "As far as I can remember the Jews who were deported in April 1942 no longer owned any real estate. The distribution of the confiscated belongings occurred through auction in Süssen and Weissenstein. According to instructions, I charged the publicly appointed inventory taker [Rösch] with the auction itself."[87]

He also gives us insight into additional procedures for enrichment of the Reich.[88] "The distribution of the confiscated stocks and bonds was carried out by the Preussische Seehandlung [Prussian State Bank] based on instructions from a specially created office of the Reichsfinanzministerium, the so-called 'Patzer' Office."[89] Martin Dean explains that "when the imposition of the punitive tax caused Jews to surrender large numbers of securities to the *Reich*, including many shares in payment, the government appointed the Preussische Seehandlung as the sole agent for receiving shares."[90] What happened to the Langs' money from the real estate sale? Petzold testifies, "Bank accounts were, as far as I remember, transmitted to the Finanzamt Geislingen by the banking institutions, and sent together with the auction receipts to the Oberfinanzkasse [State Treasury in Stuttgart]. Before acting, the banks required notarized copies of the order for confiscation."[91]

The Langs' former cleaning woman stated, "Sure I know that there was an auction of the Jews' estate, but I do not know any details concerning those involved and the circumstances."[92] When Ruth returned from the concentration camp, she had occasion to visit some of her neighbors' homes. "I have already been in some local people's homes and accidentally saw there some of our own family's knickknacks."[93] However, she didn't want them back because the memory was too painful. It is common knowledge among the local population that Louis Lang's grandfather clock, purchased during the auction, stood in a prominent place in the Süssen City Hall for years.[94]

After the auction, there also had to be order. Petzold testified, "According to the instructions we were given, an index card was created for every deported Jew on which we noted the amount that the auction had brought."[95] Reparations documents reveal that the auction brought a total of RM 3,000.[96] Dean notes that the sales amount was "on average . . . roughly one-third below" the value assessed.[97] The house was now ready for occupation by new tenants. Because housing for the population was an acute problem at this time due to the fact that there was "a total ban on construction," in addition to the prisoner-of-war camp in the *Hinterhaus*, the Lang's main house (no. 45) was rented to local laborers. On January 7, 1942, a miller rented the first floor and vegetable garden for RM 50 per month,[98] and the ground floor was divided into two apartments and rented to a day laborer (east-facing apartment),[99] and a *Schlepperführer* (tractor operator) (west-facing apartment) for RM 25 each on April 14, 1942.[100] The city council minutes of May 8, 1942, note, however, that the deal did not work out with the tractor operator and that a returning soldier, who had been drafted, would move in starting May 1, 1942. "During discussions on December 5, 1941, it was anticipated that the apartments in the *Judenhaus* would be rented to a miller, a tractor operator and a day laborer from Süssen. Rental to the tractor operator was tied to the condition that another local family would move into the apartment being vacated by him. This effort failed [. . .] I thus leased the apartment to a soldier, currently in the military [. . .] starting May 1, 1942."[101] Several things in the house had to be fixed (before the tenants could move in).

In 1945, when Kurt and Siegi and then Ruth Lang returned after the Holocaust, they found tenants in their house and were not immediately able to reclaim their home.[102]

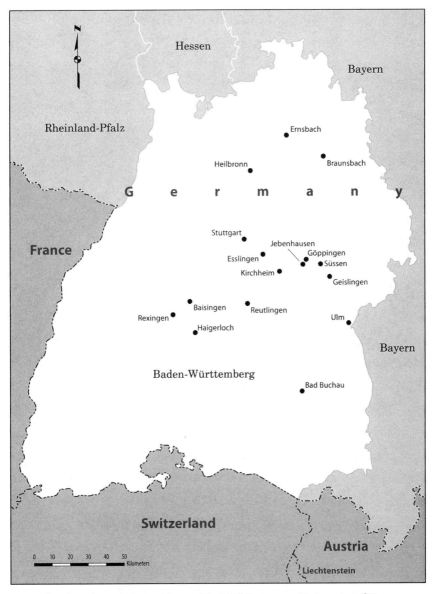

Map of Baden-Württemberg. (Created by Will Fontanez, University of Tennessee, 2011.)

Lang memorial in Süssen Stiegelwiesen cemetery.

Historical fountain in Süssen built by Jo Homolka in 1981.

Historical fountain in Süssen, closeup of deportation scene.

1911 Süssen postcard with Lang house in the very front right-hand corner. (Courtesy of Süssen City Archive.)

Ottenheimer factory in Süssen, 2002.

Ottenheimer foreman's house at Donzdorfer Strasse in Süssen.

Von dem Kgl.Württemb.Kameralamt Geislingen liegt bei uns eine Anfrage vom 2.ct. vor über den Arbeiter Romuald Gassner. Hierauf haben wir zu entgegnen,dass derselbe überhaupt nicht bei uns in Arbeit gewesen ist.

1906 Ottenheimer Süssen company letterhead. (Courtesy of Süssen City Archive.)

Two two-family houses at Donzdorfer Strasse in Süssen built by Ottenheimers as apartments.

Werner Ottenheimer (back row, 4th from left) with Cuban trade delegation visiting Chiang Kai-shek. (Courtesy of Werner Ottenheimer.)

Alfred Ottenheimer, father of Werner, no date. (Courtesy of Werner Ottenheimer.)

(*to left*)
Luise Ottenheimer,
mother of Werner,
no date. (Courtesy of
Werner Ottenheimer.)

(*below*)
Jakob and Fanny
Pressburger Lang,
with children Alma,
Lina, and Otto (Adolf).
Courtesy of Süssen
City Archive (in 1998
SPD-Kalender).

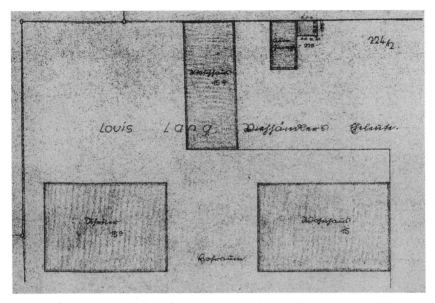

1932 Architectural rendering of Louis Lang property at Hauptstrasse in Süssen (excerpt). (Courtesy of Süssen City Archive.)

Lang house, popularly known as the "Judenhaus" at Hauptstrasse in Süssen.

Hugo and Inge Lang wedding on
July 8, 1948. Courtesy of Hugo Lang.

Lang grandfather clock.
(Courtesy of Werner
Runschke.)

Jakob Lang advertisement of French horses in *Göppinger Zeitung* of August 1911. (Courtesy of Göppingen District Archive.)

Grandfather Samuel Lang holding Kurt, with Inge (left) and Henny. (Courtesy of Hugo Lang.)

House at 31 Heidenheimer Strasse in Süssen owned by Louis Lang in the 1920s.

Leopold and Eva Lang with children Fred, Hugo, and Ruth, in Süssen. (Courtesy of Hugo Lang.)

(*above*)
Liffmann grand-
parents: Sofie and
Jakob. (Courtesy
of Hugo Lang.)

(*to left*)
Liffmann siblings.
*Front right*: Eva;
*left to right*: Max,
Hugo, and Marta.
(Courtesy of
Hugo Lang.)

Seven Lang cousins. *Back left to right*: Fred, Ingeborg, Hugo, Henny; *front left to right*: Siegfried, Ruth, and Kurt in Süssen (ca. 1929). (Courtesy of Hugo Lang.)

Four generations: Front: Frieda (Alisa) Pressburger; back: Sofie Schweizer Gideon (Alisa's grandmother), Resi Gideon Pressburger (Alisa's mother), and Dora Schweitzer (Alisa's great-grandmother), no date. (Courtesy of Alisa Klapfer.)

# Musterexemplar eines Viehjuden

Leopold Lang
depicted as "*Viehjud*"
in 1936 issue of
Nazi newspaper,
*Flammenzeichen.*
(Courtesy of
Göppingen District
Archive and Werner
Runschke.)

Ruth Lang and fellow inmate after release from concentration camp. (Courtesy of Hugo Lang.)

Ruth Lang and Sali Lemberger wedding on May 9, 1946. (Courtesy of Hugo Lang.)

PRINZES VERGISSMEINNICHTS HOCHZEIT v. LIESE ROHRBACHER

1929 picture of participants in Hanukkah play, "Prinzes[s] Vergissmeinnicht," at the Hotel Dettelbacher in Göppingen. *Back left to right*: Doris Fleischer, Erika Veidt, Erich Rosenthal, Erika Ries, Walter Böhm, Lore Ottenheimer, Elfriede Salinger, Helga Freudenberger, Beate Bernheimer, Manfred Rosenthal. *Front left to right*: Anne Bernheimer, Lilo Guggenheim, Kurt Oppenheimer, Inge Lang, Kurt Wassermann, Erich Banemann, Henny Lang, and lying on the floor, Hugo Lang. (Courtesy of Hugo Lang.)

Liselotte (Lilo) Guggenheim with doll carriage in Göppingen. (Courtesy of Lilo G. Levine.)

Rabbi Aron Tänzer with sons Fritz (left) and Paul during World War I. (Courtesy of Dr. Ruess and Göppingen City Archive.)

ROSA TÄNZER
GEBORENE HANDLER
GEB. 4. 5. 1875 - GEST. 12. 9. 1912
טו אלול תרע״ב
קמו בניה ויאשרוה בעלה ויהללה

DR. PHIL.
ARON TÄNZER
RABBINER IN HOHENEMS,
MERAN, GÖPPINGEN,
FELDRABBINER IM WELT-
KRIEGE 1915-1918, RITTER
HOHER ORDEN, VERFASSER
WISSENSCHAFTLICHER WERKE
GEB. 30. 1. 1871 - GEST. 26. 2. 1937
טו אדר תרצ״ו
ביתך בתבונה ובאהבה כוננת
צדקה וחסד בקהלתך בשרה

BERTA TÄNZER
GEB. 1876 ~ GEST. 1943 IM
LAGER THERESIENSTADT

Rabbi Aron Tänzer grave in Jewish section of Göppingen municipal cemetery.

Kirchheim unter Teck. Hulda and daughter Jeanne Bernstein *Stolpersteine* in front of former Jewish department store.

Geislingen memorial *"Geschundener Kopf"* for women forced laborers in
Heiligenäcker cemetery in Geislingen-Altenstadt.

Lilo Guggenheim Levine and Lilly Netter Vandermeulen in Saranac Lake, New
York, 2007.

Alisa (Frieda) Pressburger Klapfer, cousin-by-marriage to Hugo Lang, in Shavei Zion, Israel, 2010.

Hugo and Inge Lang in 2007.

Werner Ottenheimer in Cuba at age 91, 2007.

# 8

Lang Family Liberation,
Requisitions, and Restitution

*Yitgadal v'yitkadash sh'meh rabah,*
*B'almah di v'ra chiruteh,*
*V'yamlich malchuteh*
*B'chayechon uv'yomeychon*
*Uv'chaeh d'chal beit Yisrael,*
*Ba'agalah uviz'man kariv, v'imru amen.*
                                      —Mourner's Kaddish[1]

The sad balance of Nazi atrocities against one family in Süssen—twelve members of one family murdered for no reason other than that they were Jewish:

Lazarus Louis Israel Lang, 48, deported November 28, 1941.[2]

Fanny Sara Lang née Landau, (Louis's second wife), 47, deported November 28, 1941.

Leopold Israel Lang (Arje ben Shmuel, Louis's brother), 46, declared dead on May 6, 1951.[3]

Eva Sara Lang née Liffmann (Leopold's wife), 44, declared dead on May 6, 1951.[4]

Alfred Israel Baer (Louis and Leopold's brother-in-law), 66, declared dead on December 31, 1945.[5]

Hermine Sara Baer née Lang (Louis and Leopold's half-sister and Alfred's wife), 47, declared dead on December 31, 1945.[6]

Werner Joseph Baer (their son), 18, declared dead on December 31, 1945.[7]

Siegfried Baer (their son), 11, declared dead on December 31, 1945.[8]

Hans Kurt Baer (their son), 24, declared dead on December 31, 1945.[9]

Alfred Israel Metzger (Alfred Baer's brother-in-law), 61, declared dead on September 5, 1951.[10]

Eugenie Metzger née Baer (Alfred Metzger's wife and Alfred Baer's sister), 59, declared dead on September 4, 1951.[11]

Rudolf Israel Metzger (their son), 19, declared dead on September 4, 1951.[12] The explanation for the Metzgers states "the time of death was determined to be December 31, 1945, midnight."

Concentration camps and death camps in Eastern Europe were liberated by the Russian army more than half a year before the camps in the West, where World War II raged on for almost another year after the invasion of Normandy on June 6, 1944, and the subsequent Battle of the Bulge. Auschwitz was liberated on January 27, 1945, Treblinka and Sobibor even earlier than that, in the summer of 1944. By February 1945 the concentration camps associated with the city of Riga in Lithuania were also liberated. Ruth Lang, daughter of Leopold and Eva who perished, and sister of Hugo and Manfred, who had been able to emigrate in time and served in the US Army, was freed on January 24, 1945,[13] three days before the liberation of Auschwitz. She exuberantly, but wearily, wrote to her mother's brother, Max Liffmann, and his wife Alice, in Providence, Rhode Island. Her mother had written their address on a little piece of paper before being taken to her death, and Ruth had kept it in her comb case the entire time.[14] She was excited to be free and hoped to find her brothers Fred and Hugo.

Bromberg,[15] February 25, 1945

Dear Uncle Max and Aunt Alice, Fred and Hugo,

You will be surprised to get mail from me after three and a half years, but it's really me. I can hardly believe it myself, that I am allowed to again write a letter and be in touch with my loved ones. I have been liberated and am happy, I just can't allow myself to think [about things]. I am well. Currently I am still in Bromberg with many others [survivors], but I don't know whether we can stay. We will try to find work here and to get by until we see the possibility of emigration. In the last few days some members of the Warsaw Committee came to us and brought food and some money for us. I gave them your address. Perhaps you will be able to help me. Where are Fred and Hugo, my only solace and hope, for no one else is left. Are they working or are they soldiers?

I will not write to Fred as I am not sure that his old address is still valid: 178 Beacon Avenue, Jersey City. Unfortunately I cannot tell you where my dear parents are now. We were still together for six weeks in the camp near Riga, then I was sent to the ghetto in Riga and my dear parents were supposed to follow, as we were promised. Unofficially I had contact with them through Uncle Louis, who was assigned to a snow shoveling detail, one stop before Riga. I then also went with a group from the ghetto to that place, this way we were in contact for six weeks. On the estate [camp] there were 2,000 Jews from Stuttgart [and] 1,000 persons from Vienna and Berlin. Later there was a roundup and afterwards there were only 300 people left between the ages of 16–35 and a few older men, among them also Uncle Louis. And my dear father could also have stayed, but not my dear mother, and so they were both taken away together. Since then I have not heard anything [from them] and received no news and it is not possible for me to get any news [now], as this group was sent to the Beyond [death] as were so many others. Uncle Louis remained with his two sons, and after four months he joined me in the ghetto. There we stayed together until the ghetto was dissolved and we were sent to a camp. I was sent to a group of barracks and Uncle [Louis] with the sons went to work from the camp. I spoke with Uncle Louis a few more times. He became ill to the point where he could no longer get up. The doctors said that he had stomach cancer, and I still saw him from the window two days before he died, but he hardly recognized me. Siegfried and Kurt both were with him and they know where he is buried along with six other men. Siegfried and Kurt are still in a camp in Germany and I don't know anything about them. I don't know where my dear grandparents [Liffmann] are. I only know that they were sent from their home to Theresienstadt [Czechoslovakia] and nothing else. Uncle Max, Opa's brother with his wife, and Herta with husband and three children were in the ghetto and then disappeared. I am together with Grete Leven. She is from Beckrath. She is the niece of Herta's and Paula's husbands. She knows you. I could go on and on, but my heart overflows to the point where everything gets stuck in my throat.

If you would see me now you would be surprised how tall and slim I am. I have curves and am no longer plump, dear Fred. My hair is black and wavy, but still short, as the hair of all women was shorn. Haircut o—that means bald. We look like we escaped from an institution. My clothing and shoes are bad, I am waiting and hoping for help from and through the committee. I don't know where I will be until the end of the war. As we have no ID cards as yet, we cannot officially work and don't know what will happen yet . . . I know one thing: I will stay alive and hope to hear soon from and see my loved ones who have missed me. I would love to sit among you and tell you about everything and be happy when I look at you. The pictures which I saved I left in Riga and have some hope of getting them back.

Many greetings and a thousand kisses from your liberated Ruth.

184 | Liberation, Requisitions, and Restitution

If you write to me, please address the letter to: Grete Leven, Bygdoszez, ul. Gdan'ska 59/15 (Poland).[16]

Ruth added another page with names of friends who had survived, among them Inge Oppenheimer and Liesel Borg, "together we make up a three-leafed clover," asking her family to pass on the news to their loved ones. She noted that they could not write to everyone as they did not have any means to do so.[17] In a much later letter, dated September 13, 1945, Ruth wrote that she was working in an officer's mess, waiting tables, in Poland, and was able to regain some of the weight she had lost.[18]

World War II, and with it the Holocaust, ended on May 8, 1945. For the citizens of Süssen, it ended on April 20, 1945, at 8:00 A.M. when the Allies entered the town.[19] Written eyewitness reports from locals are hard to come by. Everyone is tight-lipped about the experience. In a 2005 article in the *Stuttgarter Zeitung*, Christopher Ziedler wrote about the end of the war in rural areas, using Süssen as an example. Entitled, in Swabian, "Ganget hoim zu eire Weiber [Go Home to Your Wives]," his article describes the final days of World War II in Süssen, including the *Volkssturm* when young teen-aged boys and old men banded together for a possible defense of their town against the approaching Allied soldiers. Ziedler tells how one man stole some abandoned *Wehrmacht* bread, then hid by the city hall to witness the official surrender of the village by the village cashier, Martin Sauer. "They [the Allies] put all Führer portraits and the sign 'Adolf-Hitler-Platz' beneath their tanks and drove back and forth [across the square] a few times. As there were no more shots fired, a few citizens appeared. The GIs gave them cigarettes and chewing gum." The Catholic Priest Johannes Holl wrote in his diary, "and thus we became American on the Führer's birthday [April 20]."[20] The collective human suffering and loss was staggering. Although the village of Süssen experienced only one isolated accidental incident of enemy bombardment, killing a child, there were horrific consequences to the local population because of its many war dead, wounded and missing. There also was a shortage of living space, of food and of firewood among the population, endangering especially the children. Because food was scarce, and many families did not have enough to eat, starting in 1947, an additional meal was apportioned to every child during school hours.[21]

The mayor of Süssen, Fritz Saalmüller, was a first lieutenant in the German Army. At the end of World War II he returned from the trenches to resume his civilian life but, on July 21, 1946, he was arrested and tried for a war crime he had committed while still a soldier in 1944. On December 18 he was sentenced to a life-long prison term and was subsequently imprisoned in War Criminal Prison 1 in Landsberg, Bavaria. At the time of the crime he was stationed in the Cherisy Caserne at Constance, near Wallmatingen, Germany. This information eluded me for more than a decade. Thanks to the excellent work of archival personnel in Ludwigsburg, Munich, Landsberg, and Konstanz, the trail led to the National Archives in College Park, Maryland, where documents connected to the case have been located and consulted. Lt. Saalmüller was charged with "violation of the laws of war." Although the original trial records were not among the papers, the particulars of the case are stated in a review document, dated November 19, 1947, namely, "In that Albert Heim, Fritz Saalmüller and Herbert Kunze, German nationals, did, on or about July 20, 1944, at or near Wollmatingen, Kreis Konstanz, Germany, willfully, deliberately and wrongfully encourage, aid, abet, and participate in the killing of three members of the US Army, who were then unarmed and surrendered prisoners of war in the custody of the then German Reich." The three fliers—Aron C. Slaughter, Ronald W. Cherington, and Strickland (no first name known)— had parachuted to safety after their airplane was hit by antiaircraft fire.[22] Saalmüller and the other two soldiers were tried in the so-called Dachau Trials, between December 16–18, 1946, before a United States General Military Government Court. The two codefendants were sentenced to death and executed by hanging on October 22, 1948, at 11:23 P.M.[23] Saalmüller was sentenced to life-long imprisonment.

Saalmüller began to serve his prison term on January 11, 1947.[24] A review took place on November 19, 1947, in which Saalmüller's sentence was upheld.[25] In 1948, pastor Martin Pfleiderer, in his annual report to the regional *Dekanat* (church office) in Geislingen, commented in chapter 4 on the mayor and other civilian colleagues. Pfleiderer wrote, "Until the very end Mayor Saalmüller was well disposed towards the church (currently he is imprisoned in Landsberg am Lech)." Next to the statement about the former mayor's life sentence, a notation in the margin (different handwriting) states, "So far no revision of this impossible sentence."[26] Several reviews took place over the next seven years. Finally successful in his efforts, Saalmüller was paroled on August 4, 1954, and released on October 1, 1957. The case was closed in 1961.[27]

An account from the local socialists notes that some of them—Fritz Sauter, Andreas Renftle, and Leonhard Deiss Jr. among them—met the very night of the surrender, and the next day went to see the Allies at city hall to suggest locals who would be eligible and qualified to help in the administration.[28] Friedrich Heinzmann became mayor of Süssen. Life resumed slowly and painfully for the local population. There was an almost immediate influx of 1,165 refugees from the East,[29] derogatorily and resentfully termed *Flüchtlinge* because they vied for the resources against the local "native" population. No doubt the postwar challenges to the local population were many, yet no single local family was as horrendously decimated as were the Langs. Of the thirteen Jewish residents who were deported "to the East" from Süssen on November 28, 1941—plus the two Metzger boys, so a total of fifteen—three returned from the hell of Riga: Joseph Kurt Lang and Siegfried "Siegi" Lang (Louis and Pauline's sons), and their cousin, Ruth Lang (Leopold and Eva's daughter). In his sworn testimony of October 2, 1948, Karl Schlecht erroneously claimed that "only two children, Ruth and Kurt Lang are still alive today and live in America."[30]

Siegfried Lang was the first to return to Süssen from Stutthof in June 1945. Thereafter his badge of shame, his middle name Israel, was stricken from the town's records. One of Hugo Lang's classmates, Walter Sauter, told a gathering in 1989 that "after the war, Siegfried Lang came home on foot. He stopped in front of my house and looked across the street to his house. He carried a little bundle that was tied to a stick with a rope. He was still wearing the clothes from the concentration camp."[31] Did Walter Sauter go out and greet Siegfried and ask him in? He doesn't say. Siegi had a difficult time adjusting. Ruth wrote to her brothers that he had suffered a lot and cried a lot.[32] He also had a hernia from carrying heavy motors in the camp[33] and would need to undergo a hernia operation, which was successful.[34] In a rare letter of September 22, 1945, to his relatives, still in the Sütterlin script favored during the Nazi period, Siegi wrote that he was in the hospital for five weeks and was recovering well.[35]

Siegfried's brother, Joseph Kurt Lang, returned from Stutthof on July 11, 1945. Although his letters mostly deal with what happened to the Nazis in town, in a letter of November 21, 1945, he broke the silence about his concentration camp experience. "Before liberation I worked sixteen-hour days in the submarine shipyard in Danzig, without warm clothing, hungry and cold, so that my hands froze to switches and cables. I was fortunate to be working as a welder during the coldest period. This way I could periodically apply the electrode and this provided an excellent source of heat."[36]

As previously noted, the first floor of the Lang house was rented to the miller, who expected to live there for a longer period of time, but had to move out when the Lang boys returned.[37] According to correspondence between the municipality and the tax authorities in Geislingen this occurred on July 31, 1945. However, comments in family letters reveal that the apartment was not fully furnished and functional until October 1945. Soon after their return Siegi and Kurt nevertheless moved into the very part of the house that they had occupied with their parents and sisters before deportation.

How does one resume life after such a nightmare and such physical, mental and emotional torment? The greatest need for those who survived was to find scraps of their past, to reassure themselves that there once had been a normal life with family and friends, and to find a place that they could call home. The reality was especially painful because the perpetrators fought the survivors every step of the way in their effort to take back the little of their previous life that still existed. If it weren't for pre-Nazi records and the help of the US Army, the Langs would have been excluded from the restitution process, as the town of Süssen twisted the truth to prevent the Langs from reclaiming their property.

After sifting through the correspondence from the Lang reparations process, one has to come to the conclusion that reparations were a struggle. One would have wished for painless and supportive interactions between those who suffered through the Nazi experience and their former neighbors. However, that was not the case. The requisitions process was arduous and shameful, the restitution process humiliating, and reparations in most cases unsatisfying, even useless.

### Requisitions for the *Geschwister* Lang

On July 30, 1945 the postwar mayor, Friedrich Heinzmann, wrote a straightforward confirmation of events.[38]

> The Louis Lang family, Jews, living in Süssen, 45 Hindenburgstrasse, were arrested in November 1941 and were sent to a concentration camp. The inventory was confiscated by the state and auctioned off by the Finanzamt Geislingen. The records are no longer extant at the financial institution. According to the testimony of many Süssen residents, one bedroom set can be found at the home of E. H., in Süssen, Hindenburgstrasse 30; the second one was supposedly acquired by police chief Holl[39] during the auction. In whose possessions the other pieces of furniture and belongings are could not yet be ascertained. Mr. Kurt Lang and his brother Siegfried, who currently reside

in Süssen, demand the recovery of their property. It is further confirmed that, in September 1939, two radios were confiscated from the Lang family. The radios were passed on by the police [to the police in Ellwangen].[40]

Upon his return, Kurt wasted no time in getting the wheels of requisitions turning. On July 31 and August 16, 1945, he wrote orders to the Landrat in Göppingen for furniture that he and his brother Siegfried required for living, such as a living room set with couch, their family's two bedroom sets as well as the bedding, a kitchen set, curtains, lamps, and a radio. He added, "I would like these items to be of the same first-rate quality as those that were stolen from us by the state in 1941."[41] A supplement requested additional items, such as office equipment including a typewriter, *Schreibmappe* (writing paper), two fountain pens, two wrist watches, an alarm clock, one bike, rugs, towels, underwear, bed linens, an electric stove, two casks (for hard cider), and firewood.[42]

Ruth Lang did not return to Süssen from Bromberg until September 1, 1945. Apparently the February 25 letter from Ruth to her Uncle Max in the United States had gone unanswered; perhaps it had gotten lost during the final turbulent months of World War II when there was no functional postal service. On August 14 she again wrote to Uncle Max, this time in transit from Hannover.

> You will be surprised to hear from me. I am, thank God, well and in good spirits. I am now on my way home to Stuttgart and Süssen and am curious what I will find. Together with my dear parents I was deported and I return alone. Dear Uncle, where are my brothers, and how are they? I am trying everything to get news of and help from them. I will stay in Stuttgart or Süssen. If you write, please write to the Stuttgart *Hilfsverein* [*der Juden in Deutschland*]. When we have established contact and I am settled, I will write in detail. I also want to travel to Odenkirchen [her mother's hometown] to see what's going on there. Dear Aunt Alice, how are you and how is Kurtchen?[43] I really want to see you and will then tell you everything. I am hoping that I will hear from Manfred and Hugo, they are my last hope. Dear Uncle, my dear friend will enclose a letter, please send it on for her.
>
> Hoping to hear from you soon, I remain with best wishes and a thousand kisses,
>
> Your solely surviving Ruth
>
> PS: This letter will be sent to you by an American soldier. I hope that we will be lucky enough to be able to establish contact with you.[44]

Of course Ruth was not sure that both of her brothers were American soldiers, and she did not know that Hugo was still a German prisoner of war in great personal danger when she was already liberated in January 1945. Hugo did not know that his sister Ruth had survived, and when he was discharged he returned to the United States.[45] This was the sensible thing to do, as the war was still raging on.

Even after the war ended, communications were extremely haphazard and tentative. Transmittal of information between survivors and the American population back in the United States was difficult, as the military exercised strict control over correspondence and access to DP camps. The Jewish voluntary organizations were not allowed to fully function in military zones until the fall of 1945. Much of the correspondence was transmitted to US recipients by American soldiers or chaplains stationed with the military in Europe.[46]

Ruth found Hugo and Fred with the help of a fellow Jew, Leo Kram, with whom she had worked in Riga and who now worked as a translator in Frankfurt. "In Frankfurt he was the first to greet me with Shalom. . . . He was in the concentration camp with me; we worked on the same work detail. He is an enthusiastic Zionist."[47] Even before arriving in Süssen, she wrote to her dear brothers from Stuttgart on August 26, 1945. One has to admire her calm demeanor in a time of extreme uncertainty and turmoil and her serenity of spirit after the ordeal she had undergone. "It is Sunday afternoon and I would like to converse with you a bit. I am sitting here outside under a tree, the sun is shining and the birds are chirping. It is quiet all around me, only my girl friend is sitting at the table with me, no one else anywhere close by." After the madness and overcrowding in the concentration camp this tranquility must indeed have been a G-d-send [G'd in the original, Orthodox]. She continues,

I have had much joy in the past few days, for there are many young men here who emigrated in 1938 and are now with the Allied forces. They are from Oberdorf, Rexingen, Baisingen, and Ellwangen, and know our parents and Uncle Louis very well, also Aunt Fanny, Alma and Lina [Jakob Lang's family]. Those young men will write you about me. Are you in contact with them? Do you get together with Henny and Inge? What is your relationship with our relatives? I am interested in everything. . . . Dear Fred, today is your birthday, and I am thinking of you. I hope that we can celebrate your next one together. That which persists eventually becomes true. What kind of work are you doing, dear Hugo? Waiter or cook? Dear Fred, I am sure you are already a supervisor. Do you still get together for a Göppingen evening? Please send me some pictures of yourselves, of our parents and friends. I don't have any. Erich Banemann [from Göppingen] is no longer alive. I'll soon travel to Süssen and ask about all the Göppingen friends. A family by the name of Auerbacher from Jebenhausen has returned to Göppingen. How are Onkel Hugo and wife? I saw Uncle Hugo's name on a list. It contained the European Jews who emigrated to England. Now I'll eat supper and write more later.

Supper was delicious and in a minute we will all get together in the courtyard. Then we tell stories, and laugh, and tell jokes. Often we get company. The boys come in their cars and then we speak English. As soon as I have time I will learn English so that I can at least make myself understood. . . . Dear Fred, do you get together with Sikni and Fred Rosental from Göppingen? . . . Yesterday I wrote to Grete Leven in Mönchen-Gladbach and I hope that she can write me more about our dear grandparents. [They are dead, which she doesn't know yet.] Uncle Max and Aunt Selma from Beckrath and Herta with family were in the ghetto and they were all deported with a transport. It is a miracle of G-d that we are alive, we had little strength and courage left. Many died from typhoid fever. In all the years [of incarceration] I was never seriously ill. Once in the ghetto I had strep throat, was excused from work for two weeks, once I sprained my foot and also was excused for two weeks, but otherwise I was always well.[48]

In a letter to her brothers and sister-in-law, Miriam, dated September 13, 1945, she recounted the joy of her cousins Kurt and Siegfried when she returned. Apparently someone had told them that she was dead. "Both were speechless when I showed up, tall, healthy, and good-looking."[49]

On September 3, 1945, Kurt Lang submitted requisitions to the Landrat in the name of his cousin Ruth. The request included items "which were stolen from my murdered parents in 1941," including a complete kitchen set (electric stove, dishes, eating and serving utensils).[50] An additional list detailed these items as well as a radio, bicycle, wristwatch, alarm clock, electric heater and firewood, vacuum cleaner, fountain pen, and pocketbook. Item no. 7 listed a request for replacing Ruth's dowry, "in the same condition as the one which was stored with Barr & Moering in Stuttgart and which was confiscated by the state." In addition, the list detailed personal items such as clothing, underwear, and outerwear. Kurt again reiterated that they wished to receive the items in the same first-rate condition as those that were stolen from them by the state in 1941.[51]

On September 6, 1945, these requisitions lists resulted in an order from the Landrat to the Requisitionsamt *"bei der Militär-Regierung"* (Allied Expeditionary Force with the Military Government Office) for the "requisition of clothing, furniture, etc. for Ms. Ruth Lang in Süssen," with two attachments. "Ms. Ruth Lang in Süssen demands the items listed in the attachments. She has spent years in a concentration camp and her parents, who were Jews (of the Jewish religion), were murdered in 1941. I ask that you requisition the items and put them at the disposal of Ms. Lang. I ask that you inform me upon completion."[52] Requisitions bill no. 6079 asked for one new living room set and one *Herrenzimmer* (parlor) set from manufacturer G. Schmid & Co. in Donzdorf-Hagenbuch, a neighboring town, "on order of Herrn Landrat Göppingen." There was a notation at the bottom that stated "disapproved," and the signature of C. R. Wilson, 1st Lt. Infantry.[53] Other requisitions from the time were bill no. 2703 for ten 60-watt bulbs and one electric stove, dated September 14, 1945.[54] Requisitions bill no. 2712, dated September 19, 1945, was for "one library of approximately 220 books" requested from R. H. in Gingen.[55] The Landrat took the requests from the survivors seriously, and inquired on October 17 "whether and to what extent the items that Ruth Lang requested were delivered." A respondent noted on a handwritten letter that "most of the items were acquired, and we are busy procuring the rest."[56]

On September 21, Kurt Lang put in a claim for "items that were confiscated from my sisters, Inge and Henny Lang, by the Zollfahndungsstelle (Customs Investigation Office) in February 1939, shortly before their emigration, although these items had been approved [for the emigrants to take with them] by the Foreign Currency Office."[57]

Once the Langs moved into their house, they had only one complaint—it took too long till they could emigrate. Ruth wrote to Hugo on September 28, 1945, "Kurt, Siegfried, and I are living in our old home in Süssen and I will take care of the household until I can get to you and Fred, which is my only wish."[58] On October 2, she reported to Hugo, "We have a full apartment— Uncle Louis's. Soon we will have furniture and a kitchen, also wood and coal, then I will play at keeping house. The military government takes care of everything and this year we do not have to freeze or go hungry."[59] This was good news indeed. Ruth reported on September 28, "I can withdraw money from Mayor Heinzmann's account. They take good care of us."[60] On October 10, 1945, Kurt wrote, "I think that we will be able to move into our old home next week. *I am ordering all new furniture and other items, at the state's expense. Only the two new bedrooms of your and my late parents*

*I found again and I immediately had them repossessed.*"[61] This was most important to Ruth, who reported simultaneously, "*I got my own bedroom set back. All other furniture is being newly built. . . .* Our wardrobes again fill up with underwear and clothes. It's important to get a good tailor."[62] In addition, Kurt was organizing their stockpiles for the coming winter. "Dear Hugo, you do not have to worry how we manage through the winter. We already have twelve *Zentner* [about 1,320 lbs.][63] potatoes, four *Zentner* fruit, one *Zentner* carrots, one cask of hard cider (350 liter) [1 liter is 0.908 quart], one small cask of wine (120 liter), thirty *Zentner* coal, five cubic meters of firewood. In addition we have an electric stove, electric heater. . . . No reason for concern."[64] On October 24 Ruth completed the inventory, "Today we got new mattresses and beds. We will also get curtains."[65]

Between the letters to his family in the United States and correspondence with the authorities, one can ascertain that Kurt was the organizer and the enforcer for the surviving Langs. He had little patience with the pace at which restitution progressed and exerted vigilante justice, getting personally involved in trying to recover family possessions, a practice that put his person in some danger and apparently caused some anxiety to the authorities. On January 24, 1946, he signed a statement that he would not make any claims against the US Army or the German authorities if he should get injured "during my travels with employees of the Office of Requisitions."[66]

The cousins commented several times on the local population. Ruth wrote on October 2, "Our neighbors are well and they are sweet as can be. We'll get everything we need for the winter."[67] And again on January 7, 1946, "Our neighbors are very friendly and we can't complain."[68] A former servant, Klaus Egentenmeyer, also came by to visit, although Ruth was not home. She commented that she wanted to go to Donzdorf and visit Maria, presumably another former maid of theirs.[69] Apparently Kurt Lang asked Klaus Egetenmaier to send Ruth a goose. He didn't forget, and when the requested treasure arrived, Ruth was overjoyed. "You can imagine my joy. Friday evening [Shabbat] is very pleasant here. We eat goose with side dishes, snow-white challah and wine. It is as it should be."[70] There were also American soldiers stationed in Süssen, apparently among them Jewish soldiers whom the Langs did not know from before the war.[71] However, Ruth commented several times that they did not come around and visit because, she thought, they were afraid that the Langs might want favors from them, such as mailing letters or help with emigration.[72]

While the survivors may have settled into a comfortable material life, mixed with their relief at being free was a deep sadness at the loss of their relatives and friends. Ruth was haunted by the memory, especially of her parents. Immediately after her return, the pain of her loss was deep and mingled with survivors' guilt. On September 28 she wrote to her brothers, "Unfortunately our dear parents can no longer enjoy life and that will always be a minus in my future." In the same letter she lamented, "Unfortunately our dear grandparents [Liffmann] also did not return."[73] In reference to a recent photo which she had taken of herself and an unidentified fellow survivor, she commented, "My hair was shaved on July 6, 1944, so we were all bald; all women who were in the concentration camp. Now that it has grown again, it is naturally curly, just like our dear mother's hair, only mine is somewhat darker. Father laughs contentedly in the picture. How wonderful everything could be if so many things had not happened. How terrible to be an orphan."[74] As it got closer to Hanukkah 1945, again her murdered family was on her mind. She admonished her brothers and Miriam to hallow the memory of their loved ones with a serious celebration. "Soon it will be Chanukkah and I hope that you light candles as we used to do. Our dear mother sat at the piano and played "Mao Zur Ishuati" [in Ashkenazi pronunciation] and we sang together.[75] Dear Hugo, do you remember when you received a candelabra from Herbert Himmelrick? I, too, will sing, only with slightly different words. For Chanukkah I will be in Stuttgart. There will be entertainment and one can get a bit distracted."[76] Kurt added on November 21, "Happy Chanukkah! Unfortunately we are lacking the candles."[77] Hugo, Fred, and Miriam, and even Jakob and Fanny's daughters, Alma and Lina, and all the other relatives did their best to quell the pain, with letters and packages. In a letter to Fred, Kurt thanked everyone for the gifts. "Many thanks for the greetings and the fine presents which arrived in three packages from Alma and Lina on Erev Chanukkah [eve of Hanukkah]. The table buckled under all the good things. You can imagine my joy, since for many years we have not celebrated a holiday in such a way."[78] About Chanukkah Ruth wrote, "The first days of Hanukkah we celebrated in Süssen. It was very comfortable. There were eight of us around the table. The Auerbachers were here and also Frau [Lina] Munz."[79] She wrote again from Stuttgart to thank her family for the package. "The package arrived on Erev Chanukkah and our joy was twice as great. . . . At the moment I am writing in Stuttgart, there is much going on around me. People speak German, Yiddish and Polish, so it is hard to write, but there is no other space."[80] But the respite was only temporary. On January 10, 1946, Ruth wrote, "Four years ago today I was separated from our dear parents and I never saw them again. On March 26, 1942 (13 Nissan 5702) [Hebrew date], they were murdered in one of the largest campaigns."[81]

All survivors felt the great void created by the murder of their loved ones. As a result a strong support network of distant relatives and old family friends who survived developed, including Jewish soldiers who, like Ruth's brothers, had managed to emigrate and who served as soldiers for the Allies. There were Sig and Fred Rosental from Göppingen, Kurt Einstein from Stuttgart, Max Gideon from Rexingen, Meta Meyer from Oberdorf; Rolf Dörzbacher, Erwin Ullmann, Richard Fleischer, Leo Guggenheim, Joseo Walz, Max Krämer, Karl Hirsch, and Kurt Oppenheimer from Göppingen, and others. Between all of them, an instant community of emotional support developed that was even more important than material comfort. Ruth wrote that "Frau Munz is very sweet. She wants to be a substitute for our dear mother." Also, "Only the Auerbacher family is still here, no one else is left. Where the synagogue once stood, there is now a storage place."[82] For their first High Holy Days [Rosh Hashanah and Yom Kippur] in freedom, the Langs went to Stuttgart.[83] Ruth was overjoyed, "Not everyone is as lucky as I am, everywhere I find relatives and good friends who are very nice to me. Everyone wants to help and is happy to meet a familiar face."[84] On January 7 Ruth tried to explain her *joie de vivre*, perhaps also to herself. "You'll be surprised that I travel around so much, but I am so happy when someone invites me. I have to get to know the world. We spent some very comfortable days, which is always nice. . . . Harry Kahn lives in Baisingen and has a large cattle business.[85] He is Sali's best friend and has already invited us often. Harry has a real cattle dealer personality and it reminds me of former times. He knew our late parents very well."[86]

A summary of what has transpired since their arrival back home can be found in a letter by Kurt Lang to Landrat Metz, confirming a telephone conversation that they had had. It appears that this may be a new official, as Kurt refers to Landrat Krauss in the letter.

March 7, 1946

Herrn Landrat Metz Göppingen

Dear Herr Landrat,

Respectfully referring to our conversation of a few minutes ago, I take the liberty to present the issue to you in writing. In November 1941, our family as well as some other related families were deported to a concentration camp in Lithuania because we are of the Jewish faith. Simultaneously all of our possessions, including our property as well as movable inventory were confiscated and expropriated by the Nazi government. After four years of incarceration my brother and I, sole survivors, were liberated and returned to Süssen. Upon our return Herr Landrat Krauss from the Office of Requisitions ordered the refurbishing of our residence. In part, our own furniture was located and returned, missing items were replaced from other sources. As only one of our three bedroom sets could be located, we were given the bedroom set of my uncle [Metzger], as it was [correctly] assumed that he and his wife had perished. This week I received the happy news from the U.S. that their daughter succeeded in fleeing to Sweden. She is now married and living in Mölndal. It goes without saying that I will send her parents' property to her as soon as possible. However, I urgently need a second bedroom set, as I took in two Jewish survivors who are homeless. I therefore ask you, Herr Landrat, to give the appropriate orders to the Office of Requisitions. Herr Wieland, director of the Office of Requisitions, knows about this business and is awaiting your response. Should it be difficult for the district [of Göppingen] or the state [of Baden-Württemberg] to cover the expenses, *I would be happy to cover the cost myself.*[87]

One of these homeless Jewish survivors to whom Kurt refers was Seppel Mann, a relative whom Ruth mentioned. Ruth writes, "Seppel Mann is now also in Süssen, and I now have a big family and also much work. I have a woman who helps me with the cleaning. I mostly cook."[88] The other may have been Sally Lemberger, Ruth's future husband, for on February 7, 1958, his lawyers wrote to the mayor in Süssen, asking whether he could confirm that Sally lived at 45 Hauptstrasse in Süssen after his liberation.[89] Although the response from the mayor was negative, it merely states that "Herr Sally Lemberger was not registered with the city hall,"[90] not that he didn't live there, perhaps only intermittently. In her letters Ruth mentioned that Sally came to visit, and on March 26, 1946, she even noted, "My Sali comes to visit me for a few days every week."[91] Was Ruth engaged in December 1945? We don't know, but in a letter dated December 3, 1945, she wrote, "I am enclosing a picture from the engagement [party]." Whose engagement we do not know. She also wrote about the papers for emigration from her sponsor.[92]

Ruth craved family. On January 7, 1946, she wrote to Miriam and her brothers, "Dear Brothers, I often think about our reunion. My mind can hardly handle it. I am full of joy, like a small child that receives a fabulous present. [How wonderful] to be together with one's family, to be in touch with people who have the same blood. We are only brother and sister, but this is something completely different for me today than five years ago. Family remains family."[93]

There was correspondence in the spring of 1946 indicating that the Langs' departure from Süssen was moving closer. In a postcard from February 19, 1946, via UNRRA, Ruth wrote to her brothers that she received the "affe-davit."[94] Another letter, dated February 1946, from Kurt, confirmed that Sgt. Danzig "brought . . . our Affi-davits [sic] from Henny and Eric, as well as from Alma and Fred, and from Lina and Sally."[95] He was pleased that they would make it if they all worked together. On March 26, 1946, Kurt inquired on behalf of Ruth, "What shall we do with Ruth's furniture? Shall we pack it in a crate and store it here or shall we sell it for jewelry and other valuables? There are two bedroom sets, one living room set, one kitchen, and more. Please respond quickly."[96] There is considerable uncertainty in the restitution papers as to their actual decision on the furniture, but it appears that shipping it to the United States proved to be impractical after all.

In a letter from Stuttgart-Degerloch dated April 24, Ruth wrote that this would be the last letter from Germany, as they would leave for the collection camp in Fellbach on April 25; the ship was to sail from Bremen on May 7, 1946.[97] "We are pretty much done with everything and are in Degerloch. Everyone is crazy and has traveling fever. . . . If you have received my most recent letters you know that I broke my right foot. I will have to go on board with a cast. The cast will come off on May 6."[98] The excitement is mirrored in the flurry of correspondence between all concerned. A telegram to Iska (Leo?) Kram, dated April 25, confirmed that "All is well with emigration. Embarkation end of April 1946."[99] On May 2, 1946, Leo Kram confirmed to Hugo that "the US visa was already granted to her [Ruth] and . . . she is probably leaving Germany with the first DP transport. . . . Between April 28 and May 3 the prospective emigrants from several areas will be brought by train to Bremerhaven to the Emigrants Assembly Staging Area. The first ship to leave Bremerhaven is scheduled for May 9, so the first transport may be expected in the States something about the 20th of May."[100] This all happened as planned. In spite of Ruth's broken foot, Kurt, Siegi, and Ruth Lang were able to leave Süssen for their future home in the United States on April 25, 1946.

There is also a letter from the National Refuge Service (NRS) to Fred's wife, Miriam, concerning Ruth Lang in Frankfurt, Germany, case number B9619. The money orders in the amount of $162 for "seven transportation receipt forms" were sent on May 11, 1946, and receipt was acknowledged on May 16.[101] This had to do with transportation within Germany. In a special delivery letter (dated May 17, 1946), the NRS in New York wrote to Herr Lang (Fred or Hugo, no first name given in letter) concerning "case number B9619, case name Lang, Ruth," notifying him that "the above name appeared on the passenger list of the SS *Marine Flasher*. . . . the *Flasher* will arrive on May 20, Pier 64 on West 23rd Street."[102] A Western Union telegram from Ruth to Fred, dated May 18, 1946, states finally, "Arrival Monday. Ruth."[103] And indeed, the Langs arrived in New York on Monday, May 20, 1946, as scheduled.

### Whose Restitution?

Following the Langs' departure, a most bizarre wrangling ensued over the previously requisitioned items. In the chaotic postwar days, there apparently was a less than adequate accounting procedure for items that were either reclaimed, bought for survivors such as the Langs, or even paid for by the survivors themselves. As a result, all sorts of outlandish claims were now being made.

The question that was most troublesome for the authorities was whether the movable goods that had been requisitioned for the Langs were only for their use or whether they owned them outright. Various offices got involved in the definition, with the result that they could not agree. There seem to have been three separate questions that were, however, painfully intertwined in reality.

1.  The first one had to do with whether personal belongings requisitioned "for the compensation of racially, religiously, or politically persecuted persons" were for *Besitz und Benutzung* (use only) or *Eigentumsübertragung* (constituted ownership).
2.  If for *Besitz und Benutzung*, the survivor needed to return them to the Office of Requisitions, presumably upon acquiring their own, or upon emigration.[104] If for *Eigentumsübertragung*, it is determined that they need to compensate the Office of Requisitions.
3.  The third point evolved as a result of actual acts of requisition by the District Council, the Military Government, or both. Those German citi-

zens who had acquired the Langs' and others' possessions at auction, or whose property was repossessed for survivors, now wanted to be reimbursed for "their" property which had been reclaimed for the heirs of the original owners or survivors in general. Who was responsible for compensating the perpetrators? The question of whether they should be compensated never came up; the answer was automatically yes, they should; the question was only by which office.

As this was a totally new situation, none of these questions had answers, and an effort to reach consensus on what the answers should be dragged on for twenty years.

Immediately after Ruth's, Siegi's and Kurt's departures, Hugo wrote to the military authorities in Göppingen about Ruth's belongings. Hugo's English still left something to be desired.

Gentlemen,

I am writing to you in behalf of my sister Ruth Lang which recently arrived here from Germany. The above mentioned person has been in various concentration camps for over four years and has seen our loved ones being killed by Nazi hangmen. When she returned after her liberation to our former residence, which happened to be in the U.S. Occupation Zone near Stuttgart, Germany, she found various possessions including furniture in homes of Nazis which belonged to our loved ones. With help of the U.S. Military Government she got most of our former belongings back and stored same before her departure to the U.S. in one of our rooms in our former home in Süssen, Württemberg, Germany. We three are having the intention to bring our property as soon as possible to the U.S.A. Before her departure she left all furniture in hands of a very good friend of ours, which has been taken care of same. Last week we received a letter from this friend of ours in which he stated that the U.S. Military Government will give away our property to other people, probably former Nazis. I gave him instructions not to sign any statements until I have further information about our case from your office. What I like to know is, has the Military Government the right to do with our belongings whatever they please? I also like to point out that this is American property since my brother Fred Lang and I, Hugo Lang, are citizens of the U.S.A.

Furthermore, I like to mention that we both are veterans of World War II and that I, Hugo Lang, have been captured during the Battle of the Bulge and have been a prisoner of war in Germany. I would appreciate if you could give us information how to proceed in this case.

Thanking you in advance for your kind assistance I remain

Respectfully yours,

Hugo Lang, Ex Prisoner of War.[105]

Within the three-month time limit from her departure date, on July 3, 1946, Ruth Lang wrote to Lt. Bennett of the Military Government in Göppingen, concerned about her family furniture.

Dear Sir:

Please excuse me for not saying good-bye to you, my broken foot prevented me from doing so. I hope Mr. Schlecht gave you my best regards. We had a splendid voyage, but unfortunately I was seasick for quite a time. I can hardly stop to look at everything in the U.S.A.

What a country! You are very fortunate to be an American, and I am very much looking forward to become an American citizen myself, my first papers are filed already.

May I ask you today for another favour, it concerns mine and my brothers' belongings, which are at present in Süssen. As you know, most of the furniture was recently bought. *I paid for it myself*, partly it was the property of my parents. Very few things have been reinstated by the order of the Military Government and District President, because of the loss of everything during the war. You know yourself what the Nazis have done with our property.

I would like to point out that both my brothers are American citizens and fought for this war. My young brother Hugo was even a prisoner of war in Germany. They also would appreciate your kindness of taking care of our affairs. Mr. Schlecht wrote us that Lt. Weinstein ordered that all our belongings have to be turned over to the District President. However, Mr. Schlecht did not agree to it and asked for a three months extension, which has been granted. We would appreciate very much if you could help us in this situation.

If Lt. Weinstein would not respect my and my brothers' wishes, we are forced to ask the War Department for aid.

Thanking you in advance for your kindness, I remain,

Cordially yours, Ruth Lang[106]

**The Process of Requisitions**

By December 1946, and following the passing of a Statute for the Care of Politically Persecuted Persons on November 13, 1946, an Office of Restitution for the state of Baden-Württemberg was established in Stuttgart. The Office of Occupation Disbursement in Göppingen, part of the Landratsamt, documented on December 13, 1946, that they disbursed RM 8,420.14 for three requisitions cases before the announcement of the statute and RM 808.10 afterwards, for a total of RM 9,228.24.[107] An even more detailed list for survivors dated August 5, 1947, is also extant. According to this compilation, eight separate types of items were provided for the Lang siblings. The list also details who provided the goods and how much they cost. These items were bought from a business and paid for, and not taken from civilians. The assumption is that the Landratsamt Göppingen paid for them. The legitimacy of the request was vouched for by the Amt für Besatzungsleistungen, Göppingen, signed by Breuling; the Landratsamt Göppingen was responsible for payment of the charges via the Kreispflege (District Welfare Office) Göppingen with money that the Landratsamt provided for that purpose. The official who signed the order was Brendle.

For the Lang brothers, Süssen:

. . .

| | | | |
|---|---|---|---|
| 8. Karl Laible, Salach[108] | 5 chairs, 1 couch frame, 2 armchair frames | RM | 137.00 |
| 9. Olympia-Büromaschinen, Stuttgart | 1 Olympia typewriter | RM | 290.00 |
| 10. Fa. G. Schmid & Co. Donzdorf | 1 dining room set, 1 *Herrenzimmer* | RM | 2,435.00 |
| 11. Ideal Steppdecken-fabrik | 5 fillers for quilts | RM | 110.00 |
| 12. Faber, Göppingen | 5 kg feathers | RM | 212.50 |
| 13. Bürgermeisteramt Göppingen | furniture transport | RM | 53.00 |
| 14. Helber Brothers, Göppingen | *Wäsche,** invoice 10/22/45 | RM | 82.33 |
| 15. Helber Brothers, Göppingen | *Wäsche,*** invoice 11/29/45 | RM | 15.70 |

* According to yet another table, *Wäsche* consisted of 30 meters of fabric, 6 pairs of pants, 3 pairs of pants, and 30 napkins.[109]
** According to yet another table, 6 pairs of pants. . . .[110] For a total of RM 3,335.53.

According to another table, the expense for the Langs for fiscal years 1945 and 1946 breaks down as follows:[111]

| Fire wood and coal | RM | 187.34 |
|---|---|---|
| Clothing | RM | 1,232.00 |
| Shoes | RM | 132.85 |
| *Wäsche* | RM | 344. 77 |
| Furniture | RM | 2,754.30 |
| Kitchen | RM | 700.87 |
| Bedding and feathers | RM | 1,973.11 |
| Transportation (of goods) | RM | 787.15 |
| Miscellaneous | RM | 819.42 |

News of the Langs' emigration to the United States traveled slowly. On August 28, 1947, the Landratsamt, Amt für Besatzungsleistungen, Göppingen, wrote to the mayor's office in Süssen asking whether the Langs had emigrated to the United States, or still lived in Süssen. If they had emigrated, then "When was their official date of departure? Where did they store their furniture? Who administers their property?" Gemeindepfleger Häfele, reinstated after returning from the prisoner-of-war camp [and before denazification], responded that Ruth, Kurt, and Siegfried Lang emigrated to Jackson Heights, New York, on April 23, 1946. The furniture was stored in a room in building no. 45 Hauptstrasse and the property was administered by Mr. Karl Schlecht, Ebersbach/Fils.[112]

The storm over the Langs' rightful ownership of any material possessions after their liberation continued until 1966. Schlecht's first letter to the Landratsamt Göppingen after his appointment, however, reveals something about the reality of their situation.

In response to your letter of December 3, 1947, I would like to inform you that I was appointed trustee of the Lang estate by the Finanzamt Geislingen on July 1, 1947. I am fully aware that the erstwhile Office of Requisitions in Göppingen requisitioned various items for the Lang brothers who were returning from the concentration camp. I do not know the nature of these items. The Lang brothers sold most of the movable property before their emigration to the United States in order to finance their emigration, as they had no other means. As far as I know the furniture that remains, and which is stored in a room in their house in Süssen, belonged to their parents. At the time, and with the support of the Office of Requisitions, this furniture was requisitioned from the families who had acquired it at an auction of Jewish property [in 1942]. If I may note, the entire Lang family was at that time [1941] deported to Riga concentration camp and had to leave behind all of their belongings. When the children came back, there was nothing left. One may judge this as one will, but the children received, upon their return and after their parents had been murdered, the emergency support of the state through the Office of Requisitions in Göppingen, so that they could live a normal life in their parental home. The Langs considered the requisitioned items as their property and treated them accordingly. The [requisition] measures were taken by the authorities and the authorities should therefore be held accountable. The requisitions were definitely not only for use, but for ownership, as this was ordered by the military government in cases such as this. Except for the furniture that was stored in Süssen and was the property of their parents, I do not know of any other furnishings.[113]

The specific question of the Langs' movable possessions was vigorously pursued by trustee Karl Schlecht and came before the Office of Property Control in Ulm on March 22, 1950,[114] the Landratsamt in Göppingen on April 1, 1950,[115] the Interior Ministry in Stuttgart on November 13, 1951,[116] and again on June 30, 1955.[117] The issue that would become important was, who authorized the requisitions for the survivors. By September 1947 the Justice Ministry in Stuttgart got involved. In a letter to the ministry, the Office for Compensation of Occupation Forces in Göppingen explained that from May 1945 to the middle of 1946 "in the process of reparations for politically, racially, and religiously persecuted individuals," the military government in addition to their personal care also ordered requisitions from private persons on the basis of so-called requisitions bills. Those individuals who were primary targets for confiscation were former Nazis, or *Belastete.*

On June 9, 1948, the Landratsamt Göppingen sent a circular to all of the mayors in the district admonishing them that "all natural and judicial persons who have in their possession items [looted by the Germans or requisitioned by the survivors] need to return them to their rightful owners." Noncompliance would result in a fine.[118] But since many original owners had been murdered and many perpetrators saw nothing wrong with having acquired the looted items from the state at auction, the above order could hardly be carried out voluntarily. Similarly, since many survivors considered the requisitioned items as their families' belongings, they also saw nothing wrong with considering these items as their property.

The Langs were fifth among ten recipients of requisitioned items. Theirs was the most extensive list, collected from a wide variety of individuals in places as far away as Böhmenkirch. In two cases, "bedroom sets that had been bought legally at the time of the auction [of the Lang property] by the Finanzamt [in 1942] were repossessed." There follows a list of items that the Office of Requisitions in Göppingen requisitioned on order of the Landrat. Listed are the requisitioned items as well as the owners of the items. The Ludwigsburg files contain letters, all dated July 1948, from a medical doctor,[119] a teacher,[120] and a dentist,[121] whose furnishings were repossessed, all from Böhmenkirch. The reason these claims were made at this time was because Kurt, Siegfried, and Ruth Lang had emigrated to America. Karl Schlecht, their trustee, informed the claimants that their furniture was not stored in the Lang apartment in Süssen, as Schlecht stated earlier that the Langs sold what didn't belong to their family to raise the money for emigration. The perpetrators now turned to the Landesbezirksstelle für Wiedergutmachung (State District Office for Reparations) to redress their claims.

Mr. S., a teacher, stated, "At the end of January 1946 the Lang siblings from Süssen requisitioned from my apartment in Böhmenkirch, district of Göppingen, two arm chairs of new value, one Junghans wall clock . . . , and one handmade couch pillow." Mr. K., the dentist, likewise requested that his "bedroom set requisitioned by Herr Lang and Herr Storer," consisting of "a four-door wardrobe, two bed frames, two night tables with glass plates, a dressing table with three-part mirror" which were taken in exchange for a lesser bedroom set, be replaced.

There are two letters from Dr. med. Z., one also from July 1948, and an earlier one, dated August 5, 1947. In 1948 Dr. Z. wrote, "In February of 1946 one of the Langs from Süssen and a companion with a requisitions bill from the Requisitionsamt in Göppingen confiscated from my apartment one couch and two arm chairs, for which I was given an inferior couch in exchange." He previously reported to the Landrat in Göppingen that in 1947 Messrs. Stohrer and Lang had undertaken requisitions in his office. According to requisitions bill no. 5093 the two gentlemen were authorized to claim a couch and two armchairs for the use of Mr. Lang. Since he was under scrutiny for being a Nazi, Dr. Z. was unable to pursue his complaint until after his own proceedings were completed in 1948. He had been found guilty of being a *Mitläufer* (bystander), a mild slap on the wrist, and now wanted to be compensated for his loss of furniture.[122] The Landrat Göppingen forwarded the letter to the Office for Payment of Occupation Forces with the request to ascertain where the confiscated furniture was located. A response from them to the Landrat noted that the furniture was requisitioned for the Langs in Süssen. And yes, the Langs emigrated to the United States, and the furniture was stored in a room [in their former house] in Süssen. The conclusion was that Dr. Z. would have to get in touch with the recently established Legal Counsel for Restitution who would have a representative in every district capital [such as Göppingen] throughout Germany.[123] Obviously this did not work, hence the 1948 request by Dr. Z. and others for "restitution."

Although "the circle of Geschädigten [victims]" contained primarily former members of the Nazi party, there were also a few innocent individuals who merely had their furniture stored in the area to get it out of harm's way and lost all of their belongings through the requisitions process.[124] For example, Frau P. H., who had sent her furniture for safekeeping from Stuttgart to Jebenhausen, lost a considerable part of her furnishings to requisition.[125] Similarly the furniture of Frau A. E. in Zuffenhausen, who was from Basel, was likewise wrongfully requisitioned. A letter from the Amt für Besatzungsleistungen, dated February 22, 1950, to her attorney noted that since the legal situation had not been finally resolved and the statutes and ordinances did not yet exist, they were not able to make a decision or give instructions, but simply had to wait for further orders.[126] And so the status quo continued, into the 1960s. In the opinion of the Justice Ministry, however, the requisitioned property should be returned to the previous owners and the survivors should acquire their own furniture.[127]

In the midst of this wrangling over personal property, more substantive issues surfaced as well. For a long time—much longer than the Nazi period—it had been a habit to designate persons of Jewish origin or religion as Jews first, and only secondly as Germans (German Jews). On June 4, 1948, a circular was issued by the Interior Ministry for Württemberg-Baden (later Baden-Württemberg) to the state police director which forbade the use of Jew as a designation of identification. "If the designation Jew is of importance for the juridical matter, if the individual was for example an inmate of a Jewish concentration camp, this can be noted in the body of the document. The term Jew may in no case be used as a professional or class designation on file covers or documents."[128] This was important in the reparations process, as German citizens could use this designation in their restitution efforts to unfair advantage in their dealings with a sympathetic judiciary.

In a grotesque turn of events, eventually a process of restitution for victims and perpetrators alike evolved that became known as *Entschädigung*. The Wiedergutmachungsamt (Office for Reparations) would deal with the property of the victims and their claims as well as the property of the perpetrators and their claims simultaneously. All items confiscated from non-Jewish Germans in District Göppingen at this point were valued at RM 35,000. Some of these individuals had put in a claim for compensation. There were about thirty such cases amounting to approximately RM 12,000.[129] Five claimants had repeatedly asked for settlement.[130] Their total claims amounted to DM 6,000.[131] On September 17, 1958, the Landrat wrote to the State Finance Ministry in Stuttgart that there were others, who "for understandable reasons" did not file a claim for damages.[132] These understandable reasons no doubt had to do with their Nazi past.

In the case of the Langs, there were claims from two perpetrators in the local reparations files. One of them was an invoice from R. H. in Gingen, dated September 1, 1946, and addressed to the Office of Requisitions in Göppingen, concerning the "220 books in good condition" that were requisitioned for the Langs in Süssen (requisitions bill no. 2712). At a cost of RM 5 per book, the restitution demanded by H. amounted to RM 1,100.[133]

On June 7, 1949 another claimant came forward—J. H., widow of *Bauer* E. H., from Süssen. Hers was the most extensive and protracted correspondence concerning restitution. She wrote to the Interior Ministry of Württemberg-Baden in Stuttgart that "on August 18, 1945, based on requisitions bill no. 1480 of the Office of Requisitions in Göppingen, the following items were requisitioned from me: two bed frames, two night tables, two wardrobes, one dresser, and one chest with washbasin and mirror. The requisition was authorized by the military government in Göppingen, for the Jewish brothers Siegfried and Kurt Lang in Süssen." She continued to explain that the furniture had been acquired by her late husband in 1942 from the Finanzamt in Geislingen, and that they used to belong to the Baer family. Someone annotated the letter to say that this was the brother-in-law of Louis Lang, which is correct. "I as well as my late husband were exonerated [from all wrongdoing] via the *Weihnachtsamnestie*."[134] That didn't exactly make them innocent, just pardoned. She further noted that this was a new bedroom set and wanted to know who would compensate her for her loss.[135] There was considerable correspondence concerning this claim, involving the Interior Ministry, the Finance Ministry, and the Justice

Ministry over a twenty-year period, "as this does not concern a requisition for the American military but for the purpose of restitution."[136]

On November 25, 1949, the Justice Ministry in Stuttgart, Department VI Wiedergutmachung (Reparations) wrote to the Landratsamt in Göppingen, Office for Payment of Occupation Forces, that the ministry was only now responding to the Landratsamt's letter of September 1, 1949, because they were hoping a law concerning the resolution of the legal status of residences and interior furnishings would be passed.[137] However, since passage of this law would be further delayed, they laid out the situation as it then stood.

> There can be no doubt that the persecuted [survivors] for whose benefit furniture and other household items were requisitioned need to pay a suitable restitution. . . . In as far as the requisition did not occur for the benefit of the military forces, but merely was ordered by the military, these are not occupation-related expenses. It is the consideration of the Justice Ministry that the statutes of the *Reichsleistungsgesetz* are to be applied meaningfully. Therefore the person who benefited from the requisition has to compensate the owner. Whether the survivor, who is responsible for the payment, receives the funds partially or in their entirety from the *Wiedergutmachungsfond* is a separate question which does not influence his financial obligation. There are no direct claims extant from the owners of the requisitioned items to be paid from the *Wiedergutmachungsfond*.[138]

Frau H. met with the mayor's office in Süssen on November 30, 1950, to plead her case. Of interest here are some of the details of Frau H.'s statement.

> In December 1941 [or spring 1942] numerous pieces of furniture belonging to the deported Jewish families Lang and Baer were auctioned off by the Finanzamt Geislingen. At my request my fiancé acquired a new, unused birch wood bedroom set that used to belong to the Baer family. . . . After the end of the war in 1945, Kurt Lang came to my home together with an official of the Office of Requisitions in Göppingen and told us that we had to return the bedroom set, that it did not belong to us, that it was being requisitioned by the Office of Requisitions, because it was the property of Kurt Lang. Although my husband was already sick, he immediately replied that that wasn't true, that it belonged to the Baer family. [Alfred Baer was Kurt's mother's brother]. They [Kurt and the official] wouldn't listen. The official

really helped the Jew and behaved rather arrogantly. We had no choice but to give up the bedroom set, which consisted of two smaller wardrobes, two bed frames without springs and mattresses, two nightstands, one dressing table, and one small cabinet. Kurt and Siegfried Lang came and picked it up and took it to their home, 45 Hauptstrasse. The Langs emigrated to the United States on April 23, 1946. As I was told, they didn't take along the bedroom set. It is supposedly still in the building at 45 Hauptstrasse. This past summer I met with Herrn Regierungs Rat Nagel at the Landratsamt Göppingen and gave him the receipt from the Office of Requisitions with the request to follow up on it. He promised, but I never got a response from him. I am asking you to assist me in regaining the previously legally obtained bedroom set from the Baer family estate.[139]

The letter was forwarded to the Landratsamt in Göppingen again with the suggestion to contact Herr Schlecht who might be able to provide additional information.

Apparently the matter was not resolved to Frau J. H.'s satisfaction, for on April 13, 1951, the Landratsamt in Göppingen once again wrote to the Office for Payment of Occupation Forces concerning the matter. Frau H. then asked for a return of the Requisitions Bill as she planned to file a civil suit for her money.[140] On April 19, the Requisitions Bill was returned to her by the Landratsamt Göppingen.[141]

A letter dated September 14, 1955, from the Landratsamt in Göppingen to the Regierungspräsidium (Administrative Authority) Nordwürttemberg in Stuttgart stated that in Göppingen there were at least 130 cases of reparations for damage to and loss of interior furnishings that had been requisitioned for racially, religiously and politically persecuted citizens.[142] The difficulty that would haunt all of these restitution cases for years was the lack of a "regulated legal basis" for the requisitions, hence clear directives for how to proceed. For that reason the processing of these claims had not yet been undertaken in 1955. Repeated inquires to the former Interior Ministry of the State Nordwürttemberg-Nordbaden as well as recent ones to the Regierungspräsidium Nordwürttemberg for the Interior Ministry did not receive a response. Only a ruling by the Interior Ministry for Baden-Württemberg dated May 11, 1956, and based on statute no. 386 of October 16, 1950 (Reg.Bl.S.117) for requisitioned apartments addressed this issue.

The Interior Ministry asserted that the responsible party for the Office of Requisitions during 1945 and 1946 was the district of Göppingen.

Hence, "the district is responsible for the compensation [of the local population/businesses]." Although the Office of Requisitions was housed in the Kreisverbandgebäude (District Organization Building) where the American military was also located and sometimes took orders from the American occupation forces, "it was nevertheless an office of the Landratsamt Göppingen. The employees of the Office of Requisitions were employed and paid by the district of Göppingen." Furthermore, the Requisitions Bills stated clearly that the confiscations occurred on order of the Landrat. For this reason, the *Geschädigten* [injured persons] need to contact the *Landkreis* Göppingen with their claims." According to statute no. 386, all claims were to be filed by February 23, 1951. This the claimants had successfully accomplished. A second question of who was ultimately responsible for providing the moneys for these claims was also being discussed in a preliminary way.[143]

In an effort to recreate how the requisitions process had worked, one of the officials interviewed the erstwhile director of the Office of Requisitions, Herr Wieland, on September 24, 1956, and the secretary, Fräulein Amalie Kessler, on September 29, 1956. Their testimonies in this *Aktennotiz* (note for the files) tell different stories. Wieland explained that "the Office of Requisitions was an office of the Landratsamt, which paid the employees. However, the Office of Requisitions was not housed in the building of the Landratsamt, but in the district building 5 Gerberstrasse which was confiscated [by the Allies]. . . . The offices of the Office of Requisitions were located next to the offices of the American military government and received its orders for requisition of personal property from them unless they carried out instructions from the Landratsamt." This is indeed highly confusing; however, it appears that the military had many needs for furniture and other items written on the Requisitions Bills already mentioned. "Whoever needed something either approached the military government, the Landratsamt, or the Office of Requisitions and put in their claims." Landrat Krauss determined the process of requisitions, being especially careful "that requisitions were carried out by Germans and not by Americans." Wieland further stated that they first tried to acquire items from industry and business. Only when this did not work out to their satisfaction did they carry out requisitions from private individuals. Wieland could not explain why the Requisitions Bills were in English and carried the designation "Allied Expeditionary Force Military Government Office."[144]

Amelia Kessler stated that she only began to work for the Office of Requisitions later and was not present when requisitions took place. By that time requisitions from private individuals had nearly ended. She claimed she only tended to office and translation work. However, in contrast to Wieland she did note that, as far as she knew, requisitions were first undertaken from private individuals, and only if unsuccessful, from businesses. This seems to be more in line with experiences in the Lang case as well. Surely, in trying to recover their own family's property, it made no sense to go to a business and buy a new set. However, required light bulbs, for example, were requisitioned against payment from a business.[145] Kessler noted that requisitions were carried out based on existing lists by seven individuals who were called upon as the need arose. She pointed out that Wieland did not speak English and thus could not exert much influence on the Americans. A postscript to this statement notes that requisitions did not end with the dissolution of the Office of Requisitions, but that the Occupation Forces continued to carry out regular and irregular requisitions on their own. However, the American Military Government compensated the owners for items that they took for their use.[146]

In anticipation of a bureaucratic avalanche that had not yet materialized and for which there were as yet no funds appropriated, Schuster noted that "Requisitions fall within the framework of Reparations," and were so far meant to cover urgent acquisitions for immediate needs of the survivors. Items above and beyond the most urgent needs were expected to be paid for by the Holocaust victims themselves, with the anticipation that they would later be reimbursed from a special fund. "The Kreis [Göppingen] is advised to request from the survivors a transfer of restitution claims which the Kreis in turn can submit to the Landesbezirksstelle [State District Office] Stuttgart for compensation." Schuster again stated that these cases had not been presented to the court "because of the completely murky legal situation," referring once more to the Württemberg-Baden statute no. 386. On December 13, 1956, Schuster wrote a letter to the Baden-Württemberg Justice Ministry, Abt. VIII Wiedergutmachung in Stuttgart, relating the history of requisitions, and asking the court to help determine how the district of Göppingen could get reimbursed for their expenses of DM 6,000 in connection with cases of restitution, among them also the Geschwister Lang, formerly from Süssen, in the amount of DM 5,300.[147] On March 20, 1957, Amtsgerichtsrat Bitzer from the Landgericht in Stuttgart wrote to the Landratsamt in Göppingen concerning Lang vs. the German Reich, asking primarily for the Lang files, as they have filed a claim for restitution for their furniture. The question the court wished to clarify was what the Langs received via the path of requisitions.[148]

In an effort to conclude the matter, the Landgericht in Stuttgart, Rück-erstattungskammer (Württemberg State Court of Restitution), attempted to effect a settlement on June 3, 1957. They made the following recommendations:

1. For loss of household furnishings,[149] the defendant pays DM 500 each to the heirs of Louis and Leopold Lang.
2. Court and other costs are to be settled based on Nos. 4 and 5 [$4,280.40] of the decision from March 19, 1956 in matters 'Rest U 1218 a (762)' [*Umzugsgut* (household items) stored with Bahr, Moering & Co.] and Nos. 3 and 4 [$5,035.40] of the decree of the same day in matters 'Rest U 242 (763)' [*Edelmetall* (precious metals) confiscated by the Städtische Pfandleihanstalt Stuttgart].[150]
3. Costs of the court case will even each other out.
4. This settlement concludes all claims for restitution of household items of the Lang family.

What was the reasoning by which the Landgerichtsdirektor arrived at a settlement of DM 500 each for the heirs of Louis and Leopold Lang? His calculations stated that according to the testimony of the Lang trustee, Carl Schlecht, "Kurt, and Siegfried paid for all the furniture themselves with the exception of two rooms."[151] He reasoned that even in this case, "they were only able to acquire the furniture in 1945 and 1946 because they were designated persecuted persons and were able to invest their money in items which they could sell after the currency reform from RM to DM in 1948," presumably while the general German population could do no such thing. "If one considers," continued the official, "that their auctioned-off belongings consisted of old, if usable items, that the Lang families took along voluminous luggage into deportation, that the applicants Ruth, Kurt, and Siegfried Lang upon return from the concentration camp were amply equipped by the Office of Requisitions for their circumstances, and that these items were sold for their benefit after their emigration, the court considers a restitution amount of DM 1,000 as necessary, but also adequate." He reiterated that the amount of DM 500 each "includes household items that the Louis and Leopold Lang families took with them into deportation."[152] By 1957 the official surely knew that deportees were not allowed to keep the possessions they took with them upon deportation. Their possessions were taken from the deportees before they were shipped "east," the victims arrived there with only their bare essentials.

The court noted that this settlement for loss of household furnishings was separate from the items in the crate deposited with Bahr, Moering & Co. and the watches, silver, and other valuables that were confiscated by the Städtische Pfandleihanstalt Stuttgart. This claim had been settled on March 19, 1956.[153] For these confiscated objects the Oberfinanzdirektion (State Treasury) Stuttgart allowed DM 4,280.40 for Leopold Lang's heirs and DM 5,035.40 for Louis Lang's heirs.[154] Although that matter had been concluded in 1956, the beneficiaries—ten years later—were not Leopold Lang's heirs, whose records are extant, but the State of Baden-Württemberg. On April 4, 1966, DM 4,462 was paid by the Oberfinanzdirektion Stuttgart to the Regierungsoberkasse für Nord-Württemberg in Stuttgart,[155] and not to the Langs.

What followed then was a discussion of the quality of the Lang property—Which items were they? What condition were they in? To which of the Lang families did they belong? And to what degree were the survivors compensated by the Office of Requisitions in Göppingen? The point of reference was the amount which the Finanzamt in Geislingen reported to have received for the auction of the Lang belongings [in 1942], namely RM 3,000. In addition, the *Gemeinde* Süssen paid RM 58 for some household items. However, the Landgericht Stuttgart was bothered by the fact that the auction receipts of RM 3,000 also included the bedrooms which did not belong to the Langs. According to witnesses Schlecht and Häfele, one of the bedroom sets belonged to the Metzgers, the other one, Schlecht and Häfele deduced, must have belonged to Louis's second wife, Fanny, whom he married in February 1941. "That the children of Louis Lang also became heirs of their father's second wife has not been established." These transactions say something about the mentality of the German authorities. The state just murdered twelve members of one extended family, and they worry about two indigent children inheriting their murdered stepmother's bedroom set!

The price paid for these two bedroom sets had also not been determined, even if the heirs of the murdered relatives were eligible. Perpetrator testimony revealed the divergent opinions as to the price paid by the local population. Häfele stated that his cousin E. H. paid "more than RM 1,000 for one of the bedroom sets," and the wife of policeman Holl "certainly" paid RM 1,300.[156] Another witness, Georg Niess, employee of the Finanzamt in Geislingen, only remembered one bedroom set which, he thought, netted the state RM 580 or RM 680. Another witness, K., stated in his testimony of March 4, 1954, that the two new bedroom sets were auctioned off for RM 950 and RM 1,100 respectively. Landgerichtsdirektor Marx noted that, based on these calculations, the rest of their belongings netted only RM 1,000. This, he concluded, was too low, based on the fact that "the objects were also confiscated which the Louis and Leopold Lang families took along when they were deported from Süssen. That this did not only deal with items which they wore can be assumed because they were then still allowed to take along luggage and because there were no linens and no bedding in the apartment after they left." Marx now added insult to injury, by declaring, "On the other hand, since the applicants Ruth, Kurt, and Siegfried Lang, after their return, were supplied by the Office of Requisitions in Göppingen with household items of all kinds, part of the damage caused by the deportation was again squared by these assignments."

An addendum from the Landratsamt to the Justice Ministry in Stuttgart followed on June 13, 1957. It referred to a visit from Mayor Schuster, Landratsamt Göppingen, to the caseworker of the Justice Ministry on June 5, 1957, two days after the letter from the Rückerstattungskammer of June 3. The letter writer (Schuster?) stated that "on the occasion of the return of survivors from concentration camps, especially the Lang siblings in Süssen, the military government and the German authorities fulfilled all wishes they presented concerning *Wiedergutmachung*." He reiterated that, based on requisitions bills, some of the desired items were confiscated from former party members. Others were bought in stores. Again it is noted that some of those whose personal belongings were confiscated were innocent, but two families are very clearly implicated in the purchase of the Lang bedroom furniture at auction. "In 1942 or 1943 the former household help of the Lang family, Frau K., in Weissenstein, on the occasion of the auctioning off of the Lang property legally acquired a bedroom set. This bedroom set was requisitioned for the benefit of the Lang siblings, as the owner was known. The H. family, Süssen, experienced the same, as they likewise had acquired one of the Lang bedroom sets at auction." It was the purpose of this letter to argue in favor of German families who demanded financial "restitution" for requisitioned items for the Holocaust victims, the Langs.[157]

Another letter from the Landgericht in Stuttgart, Landgerichtsdirektor Marx to the Landratsamt in Göppingen, dated June 19, 1957, concerned restitution for the Lang *Hausrat* that the family lost due to Aryanization and deportation. "One of the bedroom sets is said to have belonged to the Metzger family, who was evacuated from Palatine to Süssen in 1939, where they lived with the Lang family."[158] The letter contained additional information about the items for which Kurt paid, confirming that two bedroom sets and a living room set on the list of the Office of Requisitions were manufactured for the Langs by businesses, namely Adolf Wahl and Georg Schmid & Co. in Donzdorf and Christian Schöllkopf in Albershausen. "Two of the bills are in the name of Curt Lang and one in the name of Ruth Lang. *Two of them are marked paid.*"[159] This coincides with both Ruth's and Kurt's statements to their relatives that they paid for most of the furniture themselves.[160] This letter also corrects the record, as one of the two families who acquired the Lang bedroom sets at auction was not the Holl family, but the aforementioned former Lang household help K. in Weissenstein.[161] The concern here is that the Langs might not accept the proposed settlement (of DM 1,000, see letter dated June 3, 1957),[162] in which case the court would have to determine "exactly what the Lang siblings received from the Office of Requisitions in Göppingen as *Wiedergutmachung* upon their return from the concentration camp and what items they kept," suggesting that questioning of the employees of the Office of Requisitions might become necessary.[163]

A strongly worded letter from the Landratsamt Göppingen, hostile to the Langs' demands for restitution, went to the Landgericht Rückerstattungskammer (State Court of Restitution) in Stuttgart on August 2, 1957.[164] What is most notable in this letter as well as in the previous one is the fixation of the officials on whose bedroom sets in the extended Lang family Kurt, Siegfried, and Ruth actually received. "From the files one can see that the bedroom set that Frau H. acquired originally belonged to the Baer family who moved in with the Jews Lang."[165] This is also the information that Frau H. gave in her statement of November 30, 1950. While the officials went to a lot of trouble to demonstrate that the bedroom sets did not belong to the Leopold and Louis Lang families, they refrained from stating that they belonged to close relatives who lived with the Langs and were also deported and murdered. It is also amazing that after all these years of legal dealings with Kurt, Siegfried, and Ruth, the authorities continued to refer to them as "Geschwister Lang" (Lang siblings), instead of cousins. Only Kurt and Siegi are brothers, Ruth is their cousin.

A court date for the Lang case was set for September 3, 1957, in Stuttgart. The former director of the Office of Requisitions (Wieland) was called as a witness. The court was concerned with four questions:

What items did the plaintiffs Kurt, Siegfried, and Ruth Lang receive through
the Office of Requisitions upon their return from the concentration camp?
Did they receive all of the items on the list provided by the Landratsamt Göp-
pingen?
Were some of the items returned to the Office of Requisitions or the Landrat-
samt Göppingen upon the plaintiffs' emigration?
Did the Office of Requisitions or the Landratsamt Göppingen confirm to Carl
Schlecht, the trustee, which items did not actually reach the plaintiffs.[166]

Subsequently, new federal legislation was passed in matters of restitution, and on October 19, 1957, Landgerichtsdirektor Marx responded to
the Landratsamt Göppingen concerning matters of financial responsibility in the Lang case discussed in the August 2 correspondence. The main
question now was who was ultimately responsible for what in matters of
reparations, as there now was a *Bundesrückerstattungsgesetz* (Federal Restitution Law).[167] On October 28, 1957, the Landrat made another attempt
to clarify the murky legal situation concerning requisitions and limit the
damage to the *Landkreis* Göppingen. He made the strong statement that
"in connection with reparations the district of Göppingen practically completely refurbished the Langs' house upon their return from the concentration camp," and recorded that the Interior Ministry, Department Wiedergutmachung, on July 20, 1947, refused compensation for the costs [for the
Langs] with the explanation that these high costs, of DM 19,750, were not
an emergency measure for their daily life, but "complete reparations."[168]
And, that the Langs in fact should repay the state for restitution beyond
what was termed "emergency." This invited a response from the Oberfinanzdirektion (State Treasury) Stuttgart on November 26, 1957. "It is true
that the German *Reich* . . . was sentenced on March 19, 1956, to pay damages to the heirs of Leopold and Eva Lang as well as to the heirs of Louis
Lang for the confiscation of movable goods and valuables in the amount
of DM 4,280.40 and DM 5,035.40."[169] However, damages had not yet been
paid. Thus the State Treasury Stuttgart recommended to the District Göppingen to transfer their claims to the district to bring about "a confiscation
or transfer decree."[170] In other words, rather than for the Langs to receive
the above amount for the "Umzugsgut" that was stored in a crate by Bahr,
Moering & Co. and the valuables confiscated by the Städtische Pfandleih-
stelle, all of which was auctioned off by the Nazis, the district of Göppingen
should receive this amount in exchange for monies expended on behalf
of the Lang survivors during the requisitions period. The Bundesrepub-

lik Deutschland, which is the third defendant, after the District Göppingen and the Land Württemberg-Baden, and the republic's representative, the State Treasury Stuttgart, would support such a move.[171] This in fact happened.

A note in the files from an unnamed government official (*Oberregierungsrat*), dated December 19, 1957, recounted his testimony of December 16, 1957, in the Lang case. The case dealt primarily with whether the Langs received the items that were requisitioned for them, as their trustee apparently claimed otherwise. The conclusion reached was that only a civil suit could resolve this issue.[172] In 1958 the Landrat in Göppingen wrote to the Finance Ministry Stuttgart once more concerning reimbursement for restitution by the district of Göppingen for the racially persecuted children of the Lang brothers, Süssen. Dated September 17, 1958, it recounted the entire history of the requisitions and the course of the restitution efforts in order to register the claims of the district of Göppingen for reimbursement of expenses in connection with the monies paid to Germans for the confiscation of "their" property for the benefit of the survivors.[173]

Finally, on June 5, 1959, an official (*Regierungsassessor*) from the Landratsamt in Göppingen wrote to the State Treasury in Stuttgart that "the claim of reimbursement of the district [of Göppingen] should not be against the Lang heirs, but against the Federal Republic as the legal successor to the German *Reich*."[174] In other words, there was no reason to prosecute the Langs, they were not the perpetrators. It appears that the authorities finally figured out who the real victims were.

An inquiry from April 1, 1964, asked about the amount of DM 8,384.[175] A note in the files dated April 7, 1964, stated that they did not know how this amount came to be, but affirmed DM 4,462 and DM 5,035.40 expended for Lang emergency requisitions.[176] There is no paper trail for DM 5,035.40 as this was DM 4,462 plus fees, but we do have evidence that DM 4,462 was paid to the Regierungsoberkasse (Main Government Bursar) for Nordwürttemberg in Stuttgart by the State Treasury on April 4, 1966. This payment was in compensation for money paid by the State Baden-Württemberg for property disbursements in the form of household items that the Langs received in the course of *Naturalrestitution* (normal replacement) when they requisitioned furniture upon their return from the concentration camp.[177] Another letter from the State Treasury Stuttgart, dated April 13, 1966, and signed by Dr. Kling, to the Landratsamt Göppingen, and referring to a letter of February 2, 1966,[178] stated that in the matter of Restitution Lang Brothers, Süssen, both the Landgericht (State Court) and the Oberlandesgericht (State Supreme Court) Stuttgart decided in favor of the state [of Württemberg-Baden, not the district of Göppingen] and would award the state damages in the amount of DM 4,462 from the Federal Government within three months. The decision had gone into effect.[179]

The Leopold Lang heirs did not receive compensation for their confiscated *Umzugsgut* and valuables. Rather, the state claimed this amount in compensation for the necessary furnishing the Lang cousins (children of Leopold and Louis) received upon their return from the concentration camps. Compensation for the state theft of the Langs' movable property during the Nazi period was denied.

# 9                      Lang Reparations

*The applicants apply as heirs to their mother, Eva Lang, née Liffmann, born on November 11, 1896, in Odenkirchen for reparations for loss of liberty for the period from September 19, 1941, to May 8, 1945. . . . The testator was Jewish. She was legally obligated to wear the Star of David starting September 19, 1941, and wore it until her deportation on November 21, 1941, to Riga. From concentration camp Riga she was further deported to an unknown destination in March 1942 and has been missing since then. There is no declaration of death. By decision of the lower court Geislingen, dated March 29, 1951, the testator was declared deceased effective December 31, 1945. . . . According to paragraph 45, 48 BEG [Bundesentschädigungsgesetz], the reparations per each full month of loss of liberty or restriction are DM 150. These reparations for the entire applicable time period from September 19, 1941, to May 8, 1945—a full forty-three months—amount to DM 6,450.*

—Ludwigsburg State Archive[1]

The matter of the Lang real estate is dealt with separately from requisitions (immediate need) and restitution (replacement of movable and personal property) under the heading of reparations. This category also includes intangibles, such as loss of liberty, loss of health, emigration costs, loss of goodwill (assets = *Vermögen*), and loss of economic advancement. After the Lang's emigration, the Süssen property was assigned to the Finanzamt Geislingen for administration. This is the very institution that defrauded the Langs of their money from the house sale in 1939. One hopes that the Nazi officials had at least been replaced by individuals who were less tainted.

It appears that the Landrat in Göppingen sent queries to the mayors in the district inquiring about businesses that were Aryanized during the Third Reich. In Süssen they listed two, the Ottenheimers and the Langs. Concerning the Langs, it is clearly stated that Louis was the sole owner of the property, but also that he and Leopold ran the cattle dealing business together. According to the sales contract the property consisted of four distinct units: Hindenburgstrasse 45 family residence, 45a barn, 45b wash house, and 45c yard (with garage). They list the sales price as RM 30,000, the owner is the municipality of Süssen, and the sale occurred following a special circular of the District Office for Communal Politics dated November 25, 1938. The Ottenheimer brothers, Max and Alfred, sold their business, the Mechanische Weberei, to Eugen Weidmann, *Kaufmann* (businessman) in Süssen, and Johannes Abt, *Güterbeförderer* (moving company) in Süssen, on December 6, 1937, for RM 250,000 and an additional RM 150,000 for equipment and other movable property. The document is signed by the mayor, Friedrich Heinzmann, one of two post-1945 mayors before August Eisele.[2]

A matter that has not come up so far in the investigations is the difference between *einfache Entziehung* (coercively acquired property) and so-called *schwere* or *erschwerte Entziehung*, loosely translated as severe or aggravated confiscation. *Einfache Entziehung* or straightforward appropriation through coercion for racial reasons would presumably mean that property owners were "encouraged" coercively to sell their real estate to either an individual acceptable to the Nazis or a municipality, but would receive the sales amount for their use (as in the case of the Ottenheimers). *Erschwerte Entziehung* or severe or aggravated confiscation is based on the same tactics as straightforward coercive appropriation of Jewish property, with the added injustice that either the money for the property would never reach the owner or, as in the case of the Langs, the money was deposited into their accounts and then it was immediately frozen by the state and therefore never available to the sellers for their free use. Nowhere does the document concerning the Lang property make the distinction between merely coercive acquisition and *erschwerte Entziehung*.

The earliest correspondence available to help clarify the situation concerning the Lang property is from the mayor of Süssen to the Interior Ministry, Office for Reparations of the Consequences of Nazi Terror. It is dated November 1945,[3] referring to the Interior Ministry's letter of October 23 (not extant). The text states that "the municipality of Süssen acquired, via sales contract dated December 15, 1938, the properties listed in the contract from Louis Lang for RM 30,000." The municipality cannot accept Herr Lang's assertion that the properties were sold below a fair market price. The sales contract of September 27, 1929, states that seller Louis Lang purchased these properties from Fanny Lang and her children in Süssen for RM 25,000. That is not correct, it was 25,000 goldmarks which, depending on the economy, may have been more than the reichsmarks. It is alleged that while in his possession, Louis Lang made practically no improvement to the structures, so that the property did not increase in value. The proof for this is supposedly that others who were interested in the property offered the seller only RM 20,000. In order to avoid any financial shortfall to Louis Lang, the municipality of Süssen claims to have been willing to pay the unusually high price of RM 30,000 in 1938. The municipality of Süssen further claimed that they did not force the seller Lang into the sale. Therefore, they argue, the forced aspect of the sale can only be based on the directive to buy Jewish property for the Reich dated December 3, 1938 (*Verordnung über den Einsatz jüdischen Vermögens vom 3. Dezember 1938 [RGBl. I Seite 1709]*). Thus, in spite of an existing coercive sale, "the sales contract dated December 15, 1938, is in force and valid," meaning that they considered the Lang property paid for once and for all. What follows is some legalese for the purpose of discouraging the Langs from pursuing any claims and the conclusion that "the Office of Reparations has not passed any binding statutes yet, so that the Süssen municipality cannot yet enter into a formal debate with the Lang brothers. However, the municipality would not be adverse to entering into negotiations with the Langs without, however, acknowledging any of their claims."[4]

This was immediately followed, on January 2, 1946, by a circular from the Office of the Military Government, district of Göppingen, concerning the custodianship of former Jewish property. The particular circular to the mayor of Süssen (ser. no. XF 1903–51) notified the municipality, in English,

> 1. You are hereby informed that the building 45, [45]a, and [45]b Hindenburgstrasse, Süssen: dwelling-house, barn, washhouse with shed, kitchen-garden [including garage], orchard, meadow, according to contract of sale dated December 15, 1938, registered Grundbuch Süssen, Heft 435a Abt. I, Nr. 17 and 18, has been taken into custody by this Detachment, effective as of this date.
>
> 2. The State Revenue Office in Geislingen has been appointed custodian.
>
> 3. All transactions, except as provided in Law No. 52, or specially licensed, authorized or directed by this Detachment, are prohibited. Only the State Revenue Office in Göppingen may dispose of the property.[5]

The note was signed, for the Commanding Officer, by Marion B. Findley F.A., 1st Lt., Property Control Officer. Notices of custody for affected properties were posted throughout the town.[6]

The State Revenue Office in Geislingen lost no time in taking on its new responsibilities of custodian for the Lang property, which was still owned by the municipality of Süssen. On February 4, 1946, they wrote to the mayor of Süssen, informing him that the military government in Göppingen "has charged us with the property administration of former Jewish real estate in our financial district. In your community that would be the Lang property and real estate: 45, [45]a, and [45]b Hindenburgstrasse (Grundbuch Süssen 435 a I no. 17 and 18) and 'In den Sieben Jaucherten' (Grundbuch Heft 470, VIII/1639 and 1639/1). I ask that you send an excerpt of the Grundbuch record and a copy of the sales, rent, and lease contracts. You will no longer be allowed to collect the current rent and lease receipts; they have to be deposited into an as yet to be announced restricted account with the Kreissparkasse Geislingen."[7] The order was signed by Dr. Goller. Although this was a new day, the language of the order had not changed at all from the Nazi period. Then, too, in 1938, the municipality had been advised that they would no longer be allowed to pay Louis Lang for the house, as it was a coercive transaction. Rather, the monies had to be deposited into account no. 254 at the Süssen branch of the Kreissparkasse Göppingen, as per letter dated April 1, 1946.[8] A second circular to the *Oberbürgermeister* (mayors) in Göppingen and Geislingen and mayors in the district of Göppingen, dated February 8, 1946, and marked "*Eilt sehr!* [Urgent!]" concerned the supervision of property. The text noted that "on the order of the military government all communities are to determine which properties, buildings and similar assets have been acquired by the *Reich*, the state [of Württemberg], the municipalities or private individuals since 1933, properties that a) were owned by Jews, b) belonged to public religious organizations, such as *Caritas* or similar organizations, c) were illegally taken from their former owners or residents directly or indirectly through coercion or through other illegal means as stated in law no. 52, *Wiedergutmachung.*"[9] Landrat Metz then instructed the mayors "to provide copies of the sales contracts as well as other receipts which showed former as well as present owners and the reasons for the sale of the property as well as Grundbuch excerpts that determined *Einheitswerte.*" He held the municipalities responsible for the most exact accounting. Necessary investigations were to be undertaken forthwith and reports were to be submitted promptly. Those municipalities where no such transactions occurred also needed to acknowledge that.

On February 25, 1946, Mayor Heinzmann forwarded the requested information to the Finanzamt in Geislingen—Grundbuch excerpt and copy of sales contract from Louis Lang to the municipality as well as documentation of rental income to the municipality from a) ground floor (two rents at RM 25 each, for a total of RM 50 a month; b) first floor (no rental income as floor is occupied by the Lang siblings; c) stable and barn space used by the municipality for storage purposes at RM 50 annually; d) property no. 1580 meadow in Kappendobel at RM 6 annually; e) property *in den Sieben Jaucherten* rental at RM 1 per are.[10]

After the Langs' emigration to the United States in April 1946, Häfele wrote to the State Revenue Office asking what their custodianship entailed. "The Lang brothers emigrated to the United States end of April and have left no return address. We need to assign the apartment to new residents. Several building repairs also have to be undertaken. Can the rental income be used for the most urgent maintenance repairs?"[11] To this Dr. Goller of the State Revenue Office responded that the municipality could rent the first floor of the Lang house, and that they were to send a copy of the rental agreement to the account previously given. Urgent repairs were to be made and the bills were to be sent to the State Revenue Office for payment.[12] The *Hintergebäude* (45b washhouse) previously used as a prisoner-of-war camp now housed two refugee families and required some repairs. These were undertaken and the State Revenue Office advised the Kreissparkasse to transfer RM 165 to the municipality.[13] Although the Süssen municipality still owned the Lang property, the state took responsibility for all transactions concerning the real estate. This was a considerable burden to the state agency, as there were a number of such properties to be administered.

On January 21, 1947, Baumeister K., the municipal architect, was asked to go to the *Judenhaus* at Hauptstrasse because the toilet in one of the apartments was damaged and the floor needed to be replaced. K. was to prepare an estimate, and if necessary, order the materials through the regular monthly list of supplies for minor repairs.[14] But K.'s report to the municipal council on April 1, 1947, was grim.

Municipal building expert Baumeister K. notified us that the Lang house at 45 Hauptstrasse is very run down and that the foundation threatens to give way. Repairs are needed not only to save the house but also as a safety measure for the residents. The yard, too, needs to have a better sewage system. Costs are estimated at between RM 2,000 and RM 6,000. On March 27, 1947, the Finanzamt in Geislingen notified us that the Office for Property Control will give permission for the extraordinary expense for the repairs and suggested that the state revenue office ask the Süssen municipality to advance them the money in the form of a loan.[15]

The city council voted unanimously,

1. To charge the local building expert, *Baumeister* K., to begin negotiations for the repair work, especially the acquisition of the necessary building materials, to supervise the work, and to employ local laborers.
2. The Süssen municipality is willing to advance the moneys to the State Revenue Office for the repairs.[16]

But that was not all. Upon closer examination, *Baumeister* K. noticed, and the building committee of the municipality confirmed, that the building was unstable because all ground-joists (*Schwellen*) of the building were rotten. "The entire situation is threatening." The *Gemeindepflege* (municipal treasury) was encouraged to make the repairs quickly. Because at this time houses were not connected to actual sewage lines, sewage could be a major issue for a municipality. "We decided to thoroughly clean the main pipe at the southwest corner of the house and to dig a hole so we can determine how and where the existing sewage runs off. Only then will we decide on the general sewage of the house as well as the *Nebengebäude* which are not connected to a sewer."[17] It is likely that the water needs of the prisoners-of-war in the back of the house on the property contributed to the overuse of the available minimal water run-off. This, in turn, may have contributed to the rotting of the doorsteps and the weakening of the foundation. On May 16, 1947, carpenter Z. was charged with carrying out the wood repairs on the ground joists. A handwritten note by Häfele notes that the work was not carried out.[18] Likewise, mason B. was also charged with carrying out the work on the sewage system of the property. Again, a note by Häfele states that the repairs were not made.[19] In March of 1949 Schlecht notified the lower court in Ulm that the municipality had agreed to carry out the necessary sewage work on the Lang house as well as the necessary repairs so that living in it would no longer pose a safety hazard for the tenants.[20] Another transaction in connection with the Lang house documented that a tenant in the Lang house wished to rent a strip of the orchard that had so far been rented by carpenter Z. The rent of RM 20 was to be deposited to the Lang account no. 254 with the Kreissparkasse in Süssen.

As of July 1, 1947, the State Revenue Office in Geislingen was ready to divest itself of the Lang trusteeship. All such agencies designated suitable private citizens to become property administrators. The successor designate to the State Revenue Office was Mr. A. S. in Ebersbach.[21] Apparently this did not happen, for, on August 3, 1947, Karl Schlecht, the father-in-law of Mr. S., notified the municipality of Süssen that he was the new trustee of the Lang property. Schlecht stated that "the buildings at 45, a, b, c Hindenburgstrasse, as well as the meadow in Kappendobel and the properties of Alma Lang in den Sieben Jaucherten" would henceforth be administered by him. This made sense, as he had also been the executor for Siegfried, Kurt, and Ruth Lang since their emigration. Having gone over the file, he was aware that the building needed repairs and that the estimate would run from RM 2,000 to RM 6,000. He did not agree with the Office for Property Control that the municipality should incur debt to finance the repairs. "Every house that is regularly rented ought to pay for itself." He criticized the municipality for merely collecting the rent during the years they had owned the building and carrying out no repairs, so that now there were significant repairs with concurrent high costs. Schlecht absolutely rejected the notion that the municipality should take out a loan, and added that there might be even more problems than were known, and that the roof should be replaced as well. He asked for a meeting and inspection of the house with the mayor and the building inspector, date and time to be determined by the mayor's office. A handwritten note stated that the inspection was set for August 12 at 10 A.M.[22] The meeting did apparently not take place because Mr. Schlecht became ill.

Schlecht again wrote to the mayor on September 8, informing him that he had been discharged from the hospital in Geislingen the previous Saturday, and on the occasion of driving through the town, inspected the Lang house. "The house is in bad repair and it poses a physical danger for its residents, for which I will not take responsibility. I therefore ask you to find other living space for the tenants, so that a tragedy can be avoided." He again suggested a meeting on location.[23] This meeting seems to have taken place, on September 16, at 2:30 P.M. Those present included Schlecht, Häfele, Ortsbauverständiger K., director of the housing bureau R. The note for the file states:

1. Herr Schlecht is trustee for the entire property. He administers the house. The municipality is no longer responsible.

2. The house is in poor shape. The ground floor threatens to buckle. It will probably be necessary to replace an entire wall. . . .

3. Requests of the tenants are to be no longer addressed to the *Rathaus* (municipal administration) but to the building administrator . . . who will then pass them on to Herr Schlecht.[24]

Tenants seem to have continued to live in the house. In another communiqué Häfele noted that "the basement in the *Judenhaus* should be partitioned for the refugees."[25] The World War II refugees living in the house at the time of Kurt, Siegi, and Ruth's return were further cause for disagreement between Schlecht and the municipality because they, too, had small needs and Schlecht complained that those expenses should be borne by the town.[26] However, Häfele sharply retorted that Schlecht collected the monthly rent of RM 25 and therefore also ought to pay for any expenses in relation to minor repairs.[27] The Lang house was again a topic for discussion in the city council meeting of November 11, 1947, this at the suggestion of Schlecht because it would confirm the urgency of the repairs. The city council seemed to concur and approved unanimously to support the repairs on the Lang house.[28]

Apparently Hugo Lang wrote to Schlecht about their affairs, though which "Herr Lang" is never stated [letter is in Hugo's files]. On December 16, 1947, Schlecht responded to *"Herr* Lang" concerning a letter of December 8 with questions regarding the reparations process. Schlecht confirmed that the Reparations law was passed, but the statutes to go forward with claims had not yet been made public. A public prosecutor by the name of Eugen Nagel had been appointed for the lower court in Göppingen. It appears that "Herr Lang" was of the opinion that they might fare better if they applied for reparations as American citizens. Schlecht disagreed, and reminded him of the powers of attorney he was holding for Kurt, Ruth, Siegi, and Frau Fanny, Jakob's widow. One of the questions raised by the reparations negotiations was about ownership of the real estate, a thorn in the sides of Hugo, Fred, and Ruth, because their father Leopold was only "a silent partner" in Louis's business, but didn't own any real estate. Schlecht wrote, "The building in Süssen belonged to Louis Lang. Your father Leopold did not own any property. It is my opinion that reparations proceedings can be undertaken only by the former owners or their heirs."[29] In other words, only Kurt, Siegi, Henny, and Inge could apply for reparations based on what their parents possessed and lost. This would require Louis's and Leopold's heirs to be in agreement on their expectations. "Herr Lang" apparently responded to Schlecht's letter on January 12, 1948 (letter not extant), and Schlecht wrote on January 21, counseling that the surviving children of the two brothers Louis and Leopold should not quarrel over reparations, because they were "enormously sensitive matters." Schlecht counseled that "nobody should be angry. It is not important [now] what relationship the two brothers had, that's for later. The reparations process can only be initiated by the person whose name is in the Grundbuch as owner. I am sorry that you and Kurt had a disagreement." He tried to soothe "Herr Lang's" feelings by relating a conversation he had with Häfele about the situation. In Häfele's view, "the property was in Louis Lang's name, but the two brothers always got along well, and Louis allowed Leopold to participate as best he could." Schlecht then added that he knew this from his own experience. "At the time when they had to leave Süssen Louis gave me RM 9,000 in cash; RM 3,000 belonged to Leopold. [I agree that] the two brothers got along very well and worked together. Let's first get through the reparations process, then we can discuss the rest as well." Schlecht tried his best to be transparent, sending copies of his letters to the brothers, and asking Hugo to communicate with Ruth, so that everyone would be equally informed.[30]

Slowly, the reparations process seems to have gotten underway, as is evidenced by a letter from the lower court in Ulm, dated July 12, 1948, to the Grundbuchamt in Süssen, requesting copies of the property records for Lazarus Louis Lang.[31] On July 21 they requested an excerpt from the family register for Lazarus Louis Lang.[32] The new mayor, August Eisele, former city clerk during the Nazi years, responded to the request on July 22, 1948.[33] Eisele would remain mayor for more than twenty-five years, keeping a tight lid on Jewish matters. Apparently the lower court in Geislingen was also in touch with Schlecht. On October 8, 1948, Schlecht in turn got in touch with the mayor's office in Süssen, also requesting an excerpt from the family register for Louis Lang and Leopold Lang, and requesting death certificates.[34] However, it appears that at the time of this request no death certificates had yet been issued for any of the victims, for the mayor confirmed the deportation of the victims, but stressed that "from the day of their departure no one in the municipal administration has had any news about the well-being or place of residence of the Lang families. No news has been received by the mayor's office."[35] We know that there eventually were death certificates because they were discovered in the District Archive in Göppingen in 2002.[36]

The process for obtaining death certificates was complicated and lengthy and had to be initiated by a surviving family member. In the case of the Baer family, the only surviving family member, Herbert Baer of Brooklyn, N.Y., had to apply through the lower court in Geislingen to have his three brothers declared dead. In a letter dated August 12, 1960, "concerning the certification of the deaths of Hans Kurt, Werner Joseph, and Siegfried Baer," based on an affidavit from Siegfried and Kurt Lang, the lower court in Geislingen requested information on the Baers. "The parents and the children are said to have been deported from Süssen at the end of 1941 to the concentration camp Jungfernhof near Riga. Please advise us whether this is correct and other information on the address and fate of these individuals whose death we are to certify."[37] A representative for Mayor Eisele replied on August 17, 1960, that Hans Baer and his parents were "registered" as moving to the East together. Siegfried Baer is said to have moved to Frankfurt on December 8, 1940, and Werner Baer to Gross-Breesen, Silesia, on January 2, 1940."[38] On January 21, 1961, the lower court in Geislingen asked the mayor's office in Süssen to post the application for death notices on the city hall bulletin board for a three-month period.[39] When there were no objections, the notices were returned and an announcement of the decree was issued on July 18, 1961, and again posted on the city hall bulletin board.[40] On August 7, 1961, the decision of the lower court in Geislingen/Steige to declare Hans Kurt Baer dead took effect. "Born on April 12, 1917, in Pforzheim, resident in Süssen/Fils, district of Göppingen, he was deported in November [28] 1941 to concentration camp Jungfernhof near Riga, in fall 1944 to concentration camp Stutthof." Time of death is set as "December 31, 1945, 12 midnight." The court then stated the reasons why one can make this assumption, again not entirely forthrightly. "Based on the partly proven, partly credible testimony of the applicant and the investigations of the court it has been determined that the brother of the applicant (see details above) was missing before July 1, 1948, in connection with events or circumstances of the most recent World War and has been lost since then, raising serious doubts that he is still alive." The application was then registered in the official list of missing persons, in this case no. 599, List A, no. 8, on February 3, 1961, and was publicly posted on the bulletin board of the court house from January 21, 1961, to April 26, 1961. The missing person did not appear nor did the court receive any legally relevant information about him. After expiration of the required posting period, the papers were returned to the lower court for execution and the decree became legally binding on October 10, 1961.

On August 7, the mayor of Süssen, Eisele, wrote, "We certify that all three notices were posted on the bulletin board at the city hall from July 19, 1961 to August 3, 1961."[41] The other two were of course Herbert's brothers "Siegfried Baer—born October 4, 1930, in Rodalben, student, resident of Süssen/Fils, district of Göppingen, deported [on] November [28,] 1941, to concentration camp Jungfernhof near Riga," missing persons list A no. 9—and "Werner Josef Baer—born August 13, 1923, in Rodalben, resident of Süssen/Fils, deported to concentration camp Jungfernhof near Riga [on] November [28,] 1941, to concentration camp Stutthof" in fall 1944. Both were declared dead on December 24 (24 is crossed out and replaced by a handwritten 31), 1945. List A no. 10.[42]

There is a second set of official communications for the certification of the death of Alfred, Eugenie, and Rudolf Metzger dated April 2, 1951.[43] The process and language are eery, reminiscent of public postings for weddings. The notice is called an *Aufgebot*, and the posting on the city hall bulletin board is similar to that for a marriage. Again, Mayor Eisele confirmed to the lower court in Geislingen on September 19, 1951, that the posting had been completed.[44] In a further letter, dated July 18, 1951, the lower court asked the mayor's office to again post the death decree for a six-week period and return the document with a confirmation of the posting. This was confirmed on September 19, 1951, by the mayor.[45]

The Lang reparations proceedings continued on October 15, 1948, with a letter from the lower court in Ulm to the mayor's office in Süssen, sent by registered mail. The prosecutor Schnitzer vetoed the application of certain statutes.[46] The file name was "A[kten]z[eichen] Rest[itution] U 14." Thereafter the mayor's office objected to a return of the property to the original owners.[47] This issue was discussed in a city council meeting of January 11, 1949, and demonstrates the cavalier way in which loss of livelihood was treated. The minutes reflect that Karl Schlecht, who represented the Langs in all legal matters, had applied for reparations for the property, which was bought by the municipality of Süssen in 1938, with the justification that the then sales price of RM 30,000 did not reflect the value of the business and that the negotiations at the time occurred by the coercive measures of Nazi persecution.

The minutes continue that a suitable sales price for the property as well as the value of the cattle dealership together could be estimated at RM 250,000. These assertions are supported by statements from Karl Köhle, businessman; Karl Geyer, farmer, butcher and innkeeper; Karl Häfele, farmer; and Georg Bausch, farmer, all upstanding citizens of Süssen.[48] One should note that RM 250,000 is the total value for Louis and Leopold Lang, who were business partners.

Many years and many ugly accusations later the Landgericht in Stuttgart, Department of Reparations, ruled more conservatively, but nevertheless acknowledged that the heirs of Louis Lang had a business valued at DM 110,670. Given that the rate of conversion usually was 10 to 2, RM 250,000 would have amounted to only DM 50,000, and the above amount is more than double that.[49] The heirs of Leopold Lang, who could not claim reparations for real estate because it was all in Louis's name, had their transaction value set at DM 35,650. This was in addition to the DM 110,670 for Louis.[50]

Back in 1945 Kurt had asked his cousins Fred and Hugo to provide an affidavit that would detail their family's loss in Germany. Eventually Hugo and Fred sent such a letter, dated January 6, 1946:

I, Fred Lang, and I, Hugo Lang, having sworn before me [notary] on this date state, that we were both members of the United States Army and received an honorable discharge. At present, we are residing at 1025 North Broad Street, Elizabeth, N.J.

I, Fred Lang, left Germany in April, 1939.

I, Hugo Lang, left Germany in August, 1941.

While in Germany, we both resided with our parents, Leopold and Eva Lang, in the town of Süssen, District Göppingen (Germany), until the time of our departure. Shortly after our arrival in the United States, our parents wrote us that their assets including all other documents which they possessed in their home had been confiscated by the Nazis and that they were ordered to a concentration camp in Poland. Such a notification is confirmed by testimony that they requested warm clothing for the trip.

Prior to our departure for the United States, our parents told us that their assets amounted to RM 210,000, consisting of stocks, bonds and cash. Our parents were killed through Nazi oppression and the whereabouts of these assets are not known to us. We believe the cash assets were partly deposited in banks and we know positively that the amount of RM 183,000 was in a safe at our residence. As our father was taken to the concentration camp in Dachau in the year 1938, the Gestapo Stuttgart confiscated the amount of RM 183,000 from our safe. This money was intended to be exchanged and transferred to the United States. Our father was in touch with the Foreign Currency Exchange, Stuttgart (Germany) about this matter, but evidently he did not complete the transaction. It is our request to have our family's capital fully restored to our sister, Ruth Lang, at present residing at 45 Hindenburgstrasse, Süssen (Göppingen District), Württemberg, Germany.

Signed:

Hugo Lang

Fred Lang[51]

While this letter was written by the heirs of Leopold Lang, the business value they referred to was the total value, not only that of Leopold Lang's family. Kurt wrote a similar statement for the heirs of Louis Lang in the hope of getting "a few thousand dollars,"[52] though not expecting to get anything like the 1.7 to 5 million reichsmarks claimed by the Lang lawyers in 1950.

The municipality of Süssen wrote to Mayor Saalmüller, who was serving a life sentence for a war crime in Landsberg prison, asking him to help them put together a case against the Langs. Häfele must have asked him about the DM 200,000 (although he talked about reichsmarks which is closer to what Hugo and Fred wrote), for Saalmüller wrote, "I have to almost laugh about the RM 200,000 which [Louis] Lang is supposed to have had in papers. How on earth would anyone know that! Are we supposed to be able to prove that too!"[53]

After some additional discussions of the Lang house, the city council voted unanimously to reject the restitution claim and to hire their own attorney to pursue their interests. They additionally declared that the property was acquired so that a road could be built on that piece of land.[54] The municipality also put together a summary of expenses and receipts from the Lang house, claiming a loss of RM 7,092 for the period that the municipality owned the Lang house.[55]

Between January 27, 1949, and July 27, 1964, much correspondence accumulated concerning the Lang real estate. The municipality tried desperately to keep the property, but without putting large amounts into repairs, while the trustee for the Langs tried to get as much out of the municipality as he could. The mayor—stating that "the municipality bought the property for public purposes and for an absolutely appropriate amount"—tried to make Louis Lang look bad. He nevertheless indicated that the town was still interested in the property.[56] On January 27, 1949, he wrote to the lower court in Ulm that "the seller, Louis Lazarus Lang, personally offered the property to the municipality for RM 30,000 in December 1938."[57] This statement is not true. As the city council minutes show, it was Mayor Saalmüller who approached Louis Lang about selling the house following receipt of a circular instructing him to buy suitable Jewish property.

As the Ottenheimer factory had already been Aryanized, only the Lang property was still in Jewish hands. Mayor Eisele further insinuated that "everyone knew that building no. 45 suffered from dry rot so that no one really wanted to buy the house even though Lang tried again and again to sell the house and white-washed it nicely"[58] to hide the flaws.

Mayor Eisele also tried to mitigate the potentially damaging statements by fellow citizens that the Lang business deserved compensation. He wrote, not truthfully, "Lang closed down his [cattle] business on August 31, 1938 [sic]."[59] There was nothing voluntary about the shutdown of Louis's business. It was none other than Mayor Saalmüller who in 1938 informed Louis Lang that they were going to revoke his cattle dealing license as of July 1, 1938. Eisele further stated, "At the time of the house sale and the transfer which only occurred in March 1939, no cattle business was conducted on the property, so that the demands [for restitution] for the business have nothing to do with the municipality."[60] This likewise did not correspond to the truth. Four years later, on November 19, 1953, in response to a request for information concerning the fact that Leopold Lang was still allowed to work following the cessation of his business,[61] Mayor Eisele wrote that "according to the water tax records for building 45 Hauptstrasse (Lang property) from 1934 to 1947, in 1938, 1939, 1940, and 1941 each, two pieces of livestock aged one year or older were kept." This was close to the facts; the Langs each kept two pieces of cattle in 1941, including a bull. Even the dairy company was consulted, affirming that "cattle dealers Leopold and Louis Lang during the aforementioned period delivered milk to the Molkereigenossenschaft (dairy farmer's association)."[62] Still, the municipality declined responsibility for the loss of the business.

Mayor Eisele also detailed the "payments" at the time of the house sale. He stated correctly that RM 4,235.35 were deposited into a blocked account at Bankhaus Gebrüder Martin as well as the second rate of the Jewish property tax of RM 1,750, but it is not true that "about RM 24,000 went to the seller for his free use."[63] As has been shown previously these moneys, while apparently deposited into Louis Lang's bank account with Gebrüder Martin, were immediately frozen by the financial authority in Geislingen. Louis never got to use any of the money from the house. The mayor further recorded RM 3,500 which the municipality gave to Kurt and Siegfried Lang after their return from the concentration camp, asking that it be added to what was owed to the municipality.[64]

Trustee Schlecht was noncommittal about the house, saying simply that Kurt was not ready to make a final decision.[65] And then Schlecht was taken ill, spending some time in the hospital in Geislingen, which may have caused some delay in concluding the process.[66] While participating in negotiations for another client with Herr A. G. [Amtsgerichts] Director Heiss, the judge in Ulm, Schlecht had occasion to discuss the Lang reparations case with him. Schlecht indicated that Judge Heiss "expects this matter to be settled." He indicated in the letter that he was enclosing a *Vergleich* (settlement) for the municipality's perusal.[67]

Paragraph 104 of the city council minutes of May 31, 1949, deals with the Lang reparations, referring to paragraph 20 of January 11, 1949. At that time the municipality had decided to veto the *Rückerstattungsanspruch* (claim for restitution) of the Lang's general counsel, Karl Schlecht. In this meeting they were willing to discuss the offer from Herr Schlecht, dated May 17, 1949, which proposed:

1. The Süssen municipality returns buildings and land (to the Langs).
2. In return for usage since 1938 the municipality takes responsibility for the sewage and foundation repairs on the Lang house.
3. The new roof of the house and the painting will be paid from the rental income.
4. The paid sales amount will be refunded 1:10 in case of *Rückerstattung* (restitution). The municipality is awarded *Vorkaufsrecht* (first purchase option).[68]

The municipality again noted that they were RM 7,092 in the red on the house. They also reiterated their assertion that the poor condition of the house was not the town's fault. "A renewed inspection of the outer walls of the foundation of building 45 Hauptstrasse and the apartment occupied by B in this house confirmed the earlier impression that the necessary repairs on this building have not been caused by neglect by the municipality, but that the former owner hid the poor structural condition of the building by painting over it. This opinion is shared by *Zimmermeister* Z., who stated that he once before pushed back the foundation on the western side of the house, at which time the wooden beams were partly reinforced with cement. A partial exposure of the exterior paint confirmed this procedure."[69]

The municipality pretended that they did not know that Louis Lang did not get the sales amount of RM 30,000 minus state levies for his free use in 1938, something that would come back to haunt them. The *Bauausschuss* (building committee) nevertheless recommended that the city council "lift the veto and return the real estate and land to the Langs; carry out and pay for the sewage work; request *Vorkaufsrecht* in case of a sale [by the Langs]; prop up the building for safety reasons; not forego return of the sales amount; ask the trustee and authorities to resolve this matter as soon as possible." The city council accepted the recommendations of the building committee unanimously.[70]

The decision of the city council was conveyed to Karl Schlecht on June 20, 1949, focusing on three points. "1. The property is returned forthwith and the Grundbuch corrected. 2. The Lang siblings [Louis' heirs Kurt, Siegfried, Inge, and Henny] return to the municipality the amount 'which their parents received for their free disposal at a ratio of 10:1; *should they not have been granted the free disposal of the sales price, they will transfer their reparations claims concerning the sales amount to the municipality.* 3. Süssen will be granted the first purchase option."[71]

The date with the judge in Ulm was set for June 27, 1949. A note for the files by Mayor Eisele following the meeting confirmed that representative Schlecht stuck to his guns, and found the conditions of the city council conveyed to him on June 20, 1949, unacceptable. Schlecht demanded "that the building be returned to the Lang children in the same condition in which the municipality bought it from Louis Lang." He further reiterated his accusation that "the municipality neglected the building during their ownership period," rejecting the municipality's assertion that Louis deceived buyers by cosmetically covering over structural problems. Repairs would run from DM 10,000–15,000. Schlecht recommended a trial, suggesting that he would engage Herrn Dr. Jur. Ostertag, an attorney from Stuttgart, to represent the Langs' interests. Eisele noted in parentheses that "Ostertag is a Jew and will supposedly represent the Langs' interests free of charge."[72] Eisele further observed that Schlecht came back to the difference between *einfache* (simple) and *erschwerte Entziehung* (aggravated confiscation) repeatedly, rightfully so. While it would be another four years before the point of aggravated confiscation was accepted by the municipality, now it had at least been raised. It was a huge victory for Schlecht to be able to claim aggravated confiscation, if only for its effect on the court. Eisele was also impressed, though not intimidated, and noted Schlecht's comment that "Even if the case will not be decided in this sense by the Court of Restitution he would be willing to take the case to the [Allied] Board of Review in Nuremberg." Schlecht also rejected the arbiter's suggestions: to return the building to the Lang brothers and to correct the Grundbuch; and for the municipality to advance the moneys for the repairs of the house until the legal questions had been resolved. Herr Schlecht decided to bring retired Kreisbaumeister *a.D.* Stegmaier into the consultations. The mediation attempts ended at this point.[73] The ball seemed to be in Schlecht's court.

Indeed, on June 30, 1949, an inspection of the Lang property took place; Schlecht was also present. The experts were Kreisbaumeister i.R. Stegmaier and Architekt Kreisobmann d.B.D. Cziossek. On July 1 they issued a surprising report on the structural condition of the former Lang property at Hauptstrasse in Süssen:

> The *Fachwerkgebäude* (exposed wooden beam structure) [no. 45] which is about a hundred years old, shows strong damage on the outer walls. *The former owner Lang tried, as can still be seen, to take good care of the building and especially the outer walls* [emphasis added]. About twenty years ago [1929][74] he ordered the *Entlüftung* and *Isolierung* of the outer walls on the ground floor. However, no additional improvements have been made on the outer walls in the past ten years [since 1939 when Louis was forced to sell the house to the municipality]. The consequence is that the oak ground joists of the foundations of the outer wall completely disintegrated because the pelting rain penetrated under the plaster, so that the wall of the ground floor and first floor which are located above the ground joists settled and dislocated. With this settlement of the walls, cracks occurred both on the inside and outside of the building. The floors on the ground floor and first floor rotted along the outer walls. . . . The apartments on the ground floor and first floor are poorly maintained. Because of the cracks and indentations and curving of the walls, the paint has to be renewed and the wallpaper in the rooms has to be replaced. Although the wooden structure of the roof is good—there are no problems—the roof itself is in very poor condition. A completely new roof is recommended. Also outer maintenance work such as painting of windows, window shutters, gutters are to be undertaken, as the old paint has peeled off.

Buildings 45a (*Stallgebäude*) and 45b (*Nebengebäude*) have also been inspected, and found wanting in the report.[75]

An additional meeting between the Lang representative and the municipality with the lower court in Ulm took place on June 27, 1949, but with no new results.[76] Apparently Schlecht expected the municipality to pay the fee for architect Cziossek, who represented the municipality, while he would pay the fee for Mr. Stegmaier, who represented the Langs. The language in his letter of July 30 indicated that the municipality was put out with him. He stated that it was also his wish that this matter not become personal, for he, too, did not want an unfair outcome. But Häfele—who had survived the denazification process—was unhappy with Schlecht's letter, especially Schlecht's assertion that the inspection took place to determine "in how far the municipality is to blame for the current poor condition of the building." Häfele wrote in the margin, "For that we didn't have to engage an expert. That was not the purpose, but [rather] to determine its current condition and how to remedy that. A *Kreisbaurat* [district officer of public works] should know why it was impossible for the municipality to undertake these general repairs which went way beyond normal repairs. That should be blamed on the general conditions, which goes beyond our responsibility."[77] He referred here to the time of war when no materials could be obtained to carry out repairs, a true statement as we saw in 1939, when the municipality wanted to renovate the Lang house but had to desist because no building materials could be obtained for the renovation.

Between November 19, 1949, and May 20, 1952, enough progress was made that the property was returned on paper to the heirs of Louis Lang— Inge, Henny, Kurt, and Siegfried, all living in New York.[78] But the reparation proceedings continued. The heirs were given a court date of June 14, 1951, in Ulm.[79] There was additional correspondence between different offices, some of it concerning the Lang files. A letter dated August 3, 1951, to the Landgericht Wiedergutmachungskammer in Ulm stated that "the main files were sent some time ago to the Süssen municipality for inspection and were then sent on to another office of the district of Göppingen."[80] To make a long story short, the files were lost.

The final step in the very drawn-out proceedings was taken on September 9, 1952, when the city council met because Schlecht, with the assistance of attorney Dr. Ostertag, had indeed pushed the matter all the way to the Court of Restitution Appeals (CORA) in Nuremberg. The application made was for verification of *schwere Entziehung*. It seemed that the city council was tired of the matter, as the minutes merely reflect that "the city council takes note of the CORA decree."[81] Another excerpt from city council minutes, dated October 6, 1952, again dealt with CORA, noting that a court date had been set for October 8, at 11 AM. Mayor Eisele needed the approval of the city council members to engage attorneys Dr. Häberlen and Dr. Klenk, the latter of whom spoke fluent English, to represent the municipality. Mayor Eisele as the representative of the municipality would act as the defendant. The city council approved the retention of the two lawyers in the case.[82]

A communication from the Landgerichtsrat in Stuttgart to the attorneys Häberlen and Scherz, dated December 20, 1952, set the stage for the final scene.

> In matters of restitution *Lang et al. vs. Gemeinde Süssen*, CORA has verified the question of aggravated confiscation, in this case by a ruling of November 26, 1952. Whether or not the property was already in poor condition before the sale or whether and to what extent the municipality of Süssen is responsible would need additional clarification. In order to avoid additional testimony and new expenses we urge the parties, prior to such a move, to bring this restitution case which has been dragging on for five years to a close and to come to a settlement. Basis for such a consideration is that the return of the property has already been ordered. The only issue that still has to be settled is that of aggravated confiscation.

It had already been determined that Kurt and siblings would now get DM 30,000 for the house. Following the November 26, 1952, ruling of CORA in this matter it will hardly be possible for the municipality to deny aggravated confiscation. "We therefore suggest that the Süssen municipality pay an additional amount [in addition to the DM 30,000] as settlement." The amount stated is approximately DM 16,000. However, not even the court is willing to state that the municipality acted negligently, arguing, "Since it is not totally certain that the municipality of Süssen is solely responsible for the poor condition of the property, it is suggested that an additional settlement of DM 8,000 [50 percent of DM 16,000] be paid to satisfy all claims. This would seem to be an acceptable material and legal solution."

The parties had one month to respond to the offer.[83] The municipality's lawyer, Dr. Häberlen, recommended to the mayor additional expert opinion before deciding whether to pursue this matter in the courts or via a private settlement.[84] This again required a closed city council discussion on February 10, 1953. After hearing about the issues, the members of the city council expressed the opinion that the municipality should oppose the efforts of the claimant in principle, even if CORA determined aggravated confiscation. They thus decided to have the Lang house inspected once more by an expert whom Dr. Häberlen suggested, Wilhelm Aichmüller, an engineer and governmental construction supervisor from Ulm.[85]

It seems that the case was resolved through legal channels, based on a March 13, 1953, document from a regular session of the State Court of Restitution in Stuttgart over which Landgerichtsrat Dr. Kuttner presided. The case *Lang vs. Gemeinde Süssen* was tried by Dr. Ostertag. Karl Schlecht (plaintiff) and Mayor Eisele (defendant) represented the parties. After stating that the four Lang siblings were the owners of record of the properties under discussion in the Grundbuch in Süssen, it was further stated that the properties under discussion were sold by the plaintiff to the defendant on December 15, 1938. During the process of restitution they were returned by the defendant to the plaintiff; on May 20, 1952, the plaintiff (heirs Louis Lang) was recorded as the owner of record in the Grundbuch. Important is what follows: "Since the Court of Restitution Appeals in Decision no. 287 found the defendant guilty of '*schwere Entziehung*' [aggravated confiscation], the plaintiff sues the defendant for an additional payment of about DM 16,000."[86] The following settlement was suggested:

1. The plaintiffs [Langs] return the property to the defendant [municipality of Süssen] as of immediately. 2. All costs connected to these properties are to be borne by the defendant as of April 1, 1953. 3. The defendant will pay DM 38,000 [30,000 for house + 8,000, half of 16,000, for aggravated confiscation] into the account of the plaintiff with the Bank Gebrüder Martin in Göppingen. 4. The return of the property will not be subject to property acquisitions tax. Entry into the Grundbuch will likewise be free of charge. 5. The participants declare their agreement that the property shall return to the defendant. The parties are in favor of the ownership change in the Grundbuch. No public notice is requested. 6. Defendant bears court costs and other costs. 7. This settlement completes all legal claims between the parties. The plaintiff transfers all [further] reparations claims to the Süssen municipality. The parties have veto power which they must exercise by March 17, 1953. The transaction value is DM 16,000.[87]

The city council was informed of the proceedings on March 13, 1953. The mayor stressed that he did his best to keep the settlement within limits that the municipality could handle. There was no objection to the completed settlement; the approval was unanimous. The city council determined to instruct the municipal treasury in Süssen "to deposit the settlement of DM 38,000 for the [Louis] Lang siblings into their foreigner account with the Bank Gebrüder Martin in Göppingen, and to transmit the opponent's nonlegal costs of DM 2,405 to Herrn Karl Schlecht, Ebersbach."[88] Indeed, the municipal treasury was so instructed on April 1, 1953.[89] These moneys would be debited to the revised budget for fiscal year 1952.[90] No veto of this settlement occurred as of August 1, 1953. The transfer became legal on November 5, 1953.[91]

The reparations files only discuss the new amount of DM 16,000 in additional reparations for aggravated confiscation, plus Dr. Ostertag's and other lawyers' fees of DM 1,900 for a total of DM 17,900.[92] Whether the DM 30,000 for the house were paid, is not known. According to the Finanzamt's calculations, one fourth of DM 17,900 is DM 4,475, rounded off to DM 4,400. In a note to the Mayor's office, dated February 18, 1953, the State Revenue Office in Geislingen documented that 50 percent of the amount would be subtracted up front as tax at DM 2,200 each for the four Louis Lang heirs, leaving DM 8,800 (which adds up to only DM 17,600). Assuming that the case would be closed by February 28, 1953, they charged quarterly interest of 1.4 percent, it is not known for what period, leaving each of the four Louis Lang heirs only DM 1,168.31.[93] At an exchange rate of 4:1, $242.07 each was very little to show for the property Louis had owned in Süssen. Not to mention Leopold, whose real estate value was and is zero.

Every type of claim by Holocaust survivors required a separate application process. As I demonstrated with regard to the reparations proceedings for the Lang house, the process was lengthy, detailed, and often unsuccessful. There were a variety of attempts at restitution and reparations by both Lang families, the heirs of Leopold as well as the heirs of Louis, for the suffering and loss of their parents as well as for themselves. A number of these efforts failed. As early as February 22, 1950, the law firm of Ostertag, Ulmer, Werner, and Mangold in Stuttgart (perhaps engaged by Karl Schlecht) filed a claim with the Landesbezirksstelle für die *Wiedergutmachung* (State District Office for Reparations) in Stuttgart for Fred, Hugo, and Ruth. The claim was based on *Schaden am Vermögen* and *Sonderabgaben*, which included the confiscation of cash on November 27, 1941, in the amount of RM 201,000; boycott of their cattle business from 1938 on in the amount of 4 million RM, and confiscation of valuables in the amount of RM 11,600 and the contents of their crate (which was auctioned off by the Nazis) at RM 25,000, as well as the *Judenvermögensabgabe* (Jewish assets tax) of RM 5,000.[94] This application was unsuccessful as it was submitted, but was pursued in steps, some of which were successful, such as the previously mentioned restitution for the contents of the lift packed by Bahr, Moering & Co. and the valuables, which were confiscated by the Städtische Pfandleihanstalt Stuttgart.

On March 10, 1958, the descendants of Leopold Lang as well as Eva Lang did file a claim for *Schaden an Freiheit* (loss of liberty) for their father[95] and their mother[96]—separately—and apparently successfully. The wording and outcome was identical. In a later effort, Hugo unsuccessfully tried to claim damages for the poor health of his father, Leopold.[97] On December 8, 1964, attorney Reissmüller notified Hugo that his claim was denied by the court.[98] The lawyers likewise tried to file a claim for emigration costs for Eva and Leopold, but the only thing they had to show as evidence was the crate, and that had already been dealt with, hence their claim was not accepted.[99]

The path of reparations was full of land mines and confusing for those who chose to pursue it, as demonstrated by the Lang family efforts. As early as January 16, 1953, the Wiedergutmachungsamt (Office of Reparations) asked that the Langs' lawyers submit a specific application for damages concerning the *wirtschaftliche Fortkommen* [economic advancement] or, as they call it in the documents, *Goodwill*. The letter asked specifically for information concerning the fact that Leopold Lang was still allowed to work following the cessation of his business.[100] This information had come to the Office of Reparations through Karl Schlecht, in a letter dated November 10, 1953, after Schlecht asked Mayor Eisele to confirm what type of work the Langs were allowed to do after their business was dissolved.

On February 27, 1958, the seven surviving Lang children together filed a claim with the Landesamt für die Wiedergutmachung in Stuttgart through their lawyer. The documents filed on behalf of Hugo, Fred, and Ruth Lang are extant. "We are claiming aggravated loss of assets due to loss of 'Goodwill.'"[101]

On September 26, 1958, a formal judgment for *Schaden im beruflichen Fortkommen* [professional advancement, same as economic advancement] for Leopold Lang is rendered, with the following justification.

Testator Leopold Lang, born in Ernsbach near Heilbronn on February 11, 1895, was Jewish. Together with his brother Louis Lang he operated a cattle business in Süssen. On August 31, 1938 [*sic*],[102] the business was terminated. After that the testator had no income to speak of any more. On December 1, 1941, he was deported to Riga and did not return from there. According to a ruling of March 10, 1958, the heirs of Leopold Lang received reparations for loss of liberty. We refer to this ruling. Now they request reparations for loss of professional advancement . . . for the reparations period from September 1, 1938, to September 30, 1943 = 5 years, one full month. . . . It is assumed that the testator at the end time of the reparations period would surely have been drafted into the German Army, had he not been persecuted, and therefore would no longer have been able to use his labor for success in business. . . . According to his professional standing and according to his economic position, the testator is equal to a civil servant of intermediate rank, he was 43 at the beginning of the reparations period. Accordingly, the financial reparations amount to RM 3,600 annually or RM 300 monthly. This amounts to RM 18,300 for the five-year period and is converted at a rate of 10:2 and rounded off to DM 3,660.[103]

The state's hypothetical loopholes to get out of paying compensation to the surviving heirs are amazing, and offensive to the memory of the murdered Leopold! What happened to the amount of DM 3,660 is unclear, there is no further mention of it. There is no other communication by the Lang lawyers with the Landesamt für die Wiedergutmachung (State Office for Reparations) in Stuttgart on this matter until July 27, 1965.[104] In that letter, the Office of Reparations must have asked for details which the lawyers could not provide. In response, the Lang lawyers stated lamely that "our clients understandably cannot provide estimates."[105]

Hugo and his siblings' claim for *Schaden an Vermögen: Goodwill* was nevertheless settled on January 26, 1966, when Hugo, Fred, and Ruth were awarded together DM 2,080 for "loss of property due to cessation of business in 1938."[106] The justification stated,

> The applicants are the heirs of Leopold Lang, who was Jewish, and was deported to Riga in 1941, and died there. . . . The applicants, according to the *Bundesentschädigungsgesetz* (BEG) request reparations for loss of Goodwill due to the loss of their business and state that Leopold Lang operated a cattle dealing business in Süssen together with his brother Louis Lang. This business was dissolved in 1938 due to Nazi persecution. Through this measure the owner suffered loss of Goodwill. . . . Leopold Lang was declared dead on December 31, 1945. . . . Testator Leopold Lang operated a cattle dealership together with his brother Louis Lang in Süssen, which was not registered with the commercial register. The business was founded in 1922

and had to be dissolved in 1938 due to Nazi persecution. Please refer to the statutes concerning loss of professional advancement.

The document also contains some figures that differ significantly from another claim filed in 1950. The amount given is for the total business. "The investigations of the *Entschädigungsbehörde zum Anspruch auf Entschädigung wegen Schadens im beruflichen Fortkommen* [Office of Reparations for Claims Concerning Occupational Advancement] determined that the total annual prepersecution income of the business owners amounted to RM 12,000. Based on duration, size and sales of the business, we are giving a business value which, according to paragraph 56 of the *BEG* is to be compensated as loss of livelihood." The court classified the business as "a well-established business of average size." They estimated the profit at RM 5,200 times four, for a total of RM 20,800. At a conversion rate of 10 to 2 this amounts to DM 4,160 total, or DM 2,080 for the heirs of Leopold Lang and DM 2,080 for the heirs of Louis Lang.[107] To conclude the case, the lawyers needed new powers of attorney, as trustee Schlecht had died.[108] On January 28, 1966, Hugo sent two new powers of attorney, apparently for him and Fred. Missing was a power of attorney from Ruth, which Hugo then sent and which Reissmüller acknowledged on July 8, 1966.[109] The lawyers were ready to transmit the amount, but needed permission from Ruth and Fred if Hugo was going to divide the money. Hugo provided the necessary permission on July 12, 1966, and the lawyers were ready to order the transmittal of DM 1,799.20 (DM 2,080 minus fees of DM 280.80) to the First State Bank of Union, New Jersey.[110]

Apparently the above transaction did not happen as Kurt had somehow become involved in the matter, probably for the heirs of Louis Lang, completely confusing Hugo. A. S., son-in-law of the late Karl Schlecht of Göppingen, wrote to Kurt on April 14, 1966, acknowledging Kurt's letter of April 3. Kurt must have asked him to speed up the transfer of the money, for S. indicated that he "did what was necessary with the Bank Gebrüder Martin."[111] Indeed, on April 19, 1966, the amount of DM 4,148.20 was transferred by the Deutsche Bank Frankfurt to National Newark & Essex Bank in Newark, New Jersey, for Kurt Lang. This amount was DM 4,160 (2 x 2,080) less a fee of DM 11.80 charged by one of the banks. A notation stated "50% [DM 2,080] Leopold Lang Erben [heirs] = $514.38:3 = $171.46; 50% [DM 2,080] Louis Lang Erben = $514.38:4 = $128.60."[112] Indeed a payment order from the Oberjustizkasse (Highest Judicial Bursar) Stuttgart for two times DM 2,080 (DM 4,160 less DM 11.80 in fees) was paid by the Württembergische Girozentrale Stuttgart to the *Ausländer* DM Konto Bank Ge-brüder Martin Göppingen via the Kreissparkasse Göppingen, payable to Louis Lang heirs and Leopold Lang heirs.[113] On April 21, 1966, Fred, Hugo, and Ruth each received $171.46 from Kurt, deposited into their accounts with the Marine Midland Grace Trust Company of New York—checks nos. 952, 953, 954 respectively. Hugo has copies to prove it.[114]

# 10  Jews in Jebenhausen and Göppingen

*The story of the Jews of Göppingen does not begin with the modern founding of a Jewish community. Rather, it goes back to the dark Middle Ages, to that time of blind persecutions that are best remembered in the Jewish community. It was the horrible time of the great death, the years 1348 and 1349, when the Black Death raged in Europe and caused countless deaths. . . . The population believed willingly what conversion zeal and greed promised. And they murdered, murdered without pity, thousands of Jews, completely destroyed many hundreds of Jewish communities. Among these was also the Jewish community of Göppingen. . . . Thus, Göppingen already in the Middle Ages had a Jewish community. Exactly 500 years passed before Jews once again settled in Göppingen and formed the beginnings of a new Jewish community.*
—Aron Tänzer, *The Jews of Jebenhausen and Göppingen*, 1983.[1]

The beautiful Adirondack community of Saranac Lake, New York, is home to Lilo Guggenheim Levine and her husband Mel.[2] A serene community of year-round residents and numerous summer as well as winter tourists, Saranac Lake offers a well-rounded feast for the eyes, body, and spirit, an environment in which Lilo thrives. Lilo was the only child of Julius and Pauline Guggenheim, the owners of Einstein & Guggenheim at 20 Grabenstrasse in Göppingen as well as Wohlwert (Staufia) at the far end of Marktstrasse.[3] Lilo's two older half-brothers, Emil (1913) and Poldi (1915), were born to Julius's first wife, who fell victim to the 1918 flu epidemic. Before World War I, Julius also owned a store, Einstein & Guggenheim, directly at the Marktplatz. All stores sold linens and household items. Although now far from the town of her birth, which she was fortunately able to leave in 1939, Lilo has written about her life and work and returned to Göppingen a number of times.

During a visit to the Levines' home in August of 2007, the lost Jewish community of Göppingen came to life as Lilo reminisced about her childhood. We all received a special treat as her childhood friend Isolde Lilli Netter Vandermeulen joined us, along with her daughter Debbie, for some of the time.[4] The basis for our initial email correspondence was a photo that Hugo Lang had contributed to my research for this book in early 2000, a picture of a Hanukkah play that the children of the Göppingen Jewish community wrote, produced, and performed during a community Hanukkah celebration at the Hotel Dettelbacher in 1929. Hugo is in this photo, as is Lilo. With their help we were able to identify every child in that one picture. In 1984, Lilo Guggenheim Levine traveled to Göppingen for a reunion, which gave me the idea to use this chapter for an attempt at such a reunion of the Jewish children of Göppingen who are in this picture as well as the other children in the 1929 Hanukkah program with their families.

Although there had been a Jewish presence in Göppingen until the Black Death in 1348 and 1349, with few exceptions, the bulk of information available to us about the two Jewish communities of Jebenhausen and Göppingen is contained in a history of the two communities that Rabbi Aron Tänzer compiled during his tenure as *Landesrabbiner* from 1907–37. Rabbi Tänzer was an avid historian. *Die Geschichte der Juden in Jebenhausen und Göppingen* was published on the sixtieth anniversary of the founding of the Göppingen Jewish community. All of the Jewish community records were destroyed by the fire that gutted the Göppingen synagogue during Kristallnacht November 9–10, 1938. There is an indication that the Nazis were under the impression that Rabbi Tänzer's widow, Berta, had managed to remove the records in time, as there is one communication from the *Geheime Staatspolizei* in Stuttgart to the Landrat in Göppingen in which they are looking for the hiding place.[5] Unfortunately that was not the case, and the information in Rabbi Tänzer's book is all the documentation that we have on both communities.

In 1983 Dr. Karl-Heinz Ruess, Director of the Göppingen City Archive and champion of the Jewish Museum in Jebenhausen, expanded Rabbi Tänzer's history by adding a section on the fate of the Göppingen community during the Holocaust. He has also continued his efforts to work with survivors such as Inge Auerbacher,[6] Lilo Guggenheim Levine, Sig Fleischer and Erwin Tänzer z"l, as well as others who are willing to correspond or return to Göppingen in an attempt to preserve some of the family histories and artifacts. He made it possible to add a memorial plaque for Rabbi Tänzer in the Göppingen Public Library, an institution that Rabbi Tänzer created in 1910 in an effort to counter the rise of trashy literature. Dr. Ruess also initiated the process to have the plaza where the synagogue once stood named Synagogenplatz. Göppingen has a Holocaust memorial in the Jewish section of the Göppingen municipal cemetery and a city memorial in the municipal park. In 2010 there was one Jewish man still living in Göppingen, Rafael Mizrachi; he had fled to Israel as a child but chose to return and live out his life in Göppingen.

There is no dearth of literature on Rabbi Tänzer and on the Göppingen Jewish community, albeit all in German. This chapter introduces readers who may not have access to this literature to Rabbi Tänzer and to the communities of Jebenhausen and Göppingen. The chapter also sheds some light on the contribution of the two Jewish communities to the overall economy and the social well-being of the Jebenhausen and Göppingen municipalities, and explores the nature of the "Jewishness" of these two successive rural Jewish communities. What was it like to be Jewish in the Jebenhausen of the eighteenth and nineteenth centuries? And subsequently, what Jewish life was there in the city of Göppingen in the nineteenth and twentieth centuries?

### Jebenhausen

In 1777 Elias Gutmann, from Illereichen near Memmingen, beseeched Philipp Friedrich, Baron of Liebenstein, owner of the imperial estate of Jebenhausen, to allow him residence in the imperial territory. The Jews of Illereichen made their livelihood by doing business in Memmingen. When this became impossible for Gutmann—perhaps because he was too successful at his trade in Memmingen—he was forced to leave Illereichen.[7] The Baron thereupon invited twenty Jewish families to reside within the Liebenstein borders. He issued a *Schutzbrief* to them, a contract that stated in great detail the rights and duties of the group. Jews were not only allowed to stay for a fixed period of time but "as long as they are tolerated in the Holy Roman Empire" (Article 1). Although they were not allowed to buy houses owned by Christians (Article 6), the baron provided cheap land so that they could build their own houses (Article 4).[8] The land was located along the road to Göppingen (Aichgasse and Poststrasse), in the valley of the Fulbach.[9] The main street through Jebenhausen has changed very little to this day, except that it is now paved. Exceptions are the two synagogues, built in 1779 and 1804 respectively. Both buildings have been torn down.

The Jews of Jebenhausen were also allowed to build along the Hintere Berg and the Vordere Berg. Here the kosher inn Zum König David was built in 1799. A family was taxed twelve Gulden annually to live in Jebenhausen (Article 5). The community was allowed free practice of all of their laws, ceremonies, and customs (Article 7), including the construction of a synagogue and a cemetery. All trade was open to them with the exception of salt (Article 8). The nobility provided a well for use as a *mikvah* for the women and constructed a little house for it (Article 13). The community could themselves choose their rabbi, cantor, or teacher, as well as the communal administration (Article 14). In addition to the Liebenstein nobility who signed the contract, nine Jewish heads of household signed for the Jewish community of thirty-one individuals,[10] among them Salomo Ottenheimer,[11] the patriarch of the Ottenheimer clan, who would build a factory in Süssen in 1905. The community even had its own official seal, a Magen David with the word *kahal* (community) on the top point and the words *jeben* and *haisen* (Jebenhausen) to the right and left of the top point. In the center is written "1777 nach der kleinen Zählung," or 1777 CE.[12]

Why would this baron and others in imperial territories be so generous to a group of individuals who were otherwise shunned by society? It was not only pure kindness but also economic necessity. Much of the income for the *Rittergut* (nobleman's estate) had come from the mineral water spa; however, the well's production had declined and therewith the financial gain. Jews were known to be enterprising and resourceful, and the barons von Liebenstein expected their new residents to raise Jebenhausen's economic base. The nobility would not be disappointed. Already by 1800 the Jewish population had reached two hundred. By 1850, nearly half the population of Jebenhausen (555) was Jewish. The Jebenhausen Jews also were ahead of their brethren in other communities, as they voluntarily decided to take on surnames in 1818, ten years before this was required by the *Israelitengesetz*.[13]

The structure of the community was traditional, with the rabbi responsible to the *Vorsteher* (president) and the *Beisitzer* (board of trustees), who were in charge of administering all of the community organizations, such as the poorhouse, collections for Palestine, *Chevrah Kadisha* (to minister to the dead as well as the sick), *Talmud Torah* (for study), *Chevrat Nearim* (for young men), *Chevrah D'var Torah* (good deeds, as in paying for the education of poor children), *Chevrah Hachnassat Kallah* (for poor brides) and many others.[14] As caring for the poor is one of the 613 commandments Jews live by, Jebenhausen, like other Jewish communities, had its share of *Betteljuden*, indigent foreign Jews who were in need of assistance. Especially on Shabbat it would have been shameful to sit down to a festive meal—often the only adequate one all week—without remembering those not so fortunate. The Jebenhausen Jews had their own to take care of as well. In 1782 a few better-off Jews loaned eight poor families 200 florin each so they could build a home together. The loan had not been repaid as late as 1791, so that the families were put on a payment plan of 4 kreuzer per week.[15] This *Judenhaus* still exists today. In spite of its own poverty, Jebenhausen had a good reputation as a community that helped its less fortunate brothers and sisters by providing lodging and meals to strangers, either in their own home or in the local kosher inn, Zum König David.[16] "The system of Jewish communal self-organization continued to exist until the early 1830s, primarily autonomously. Among its characteristics was a strong 'democratic' trend in the sense that there was a consensus concerning the taxable heads of household. Only then did the Württemberg laws and the efforts of the Jewish Religious Authority in Stuttgart directly interfere with this system."[17]

As a traditional *kehillah*, Jebenhausen valued its religious life. Few rural Jewish communities could afford to build a house of worship on their own. Initially, the Jews of Jebenhausen held services in a room in someone's home.[18] With the arrival of additional Jews, the need for a synagogue became urgent. Rabbi Tänzer writes, "As the Jebenhausen Jews in those days were without means, they were unable to pay for the synagogue themselves. The construction of a synagogue was possible only with the aid of fellow Jews in other communities. In 1779, the two community leaders, Abraham Sandel Lauchheimer and Beerle Weil, set out with two collection books," a recommendation from the governmental representative, and a character reference from the rabbi of Illereichen, to *schnorr* on behalf of the Jebenhausen Jewish community.[19] No less than fifty-eight Jewish communities in Schwaben contributed to the building fund.[20] Archival sources reveal that the synagogue was built in the Aichgasse, although there is no information about its dedication date. Rabbi Tänzer comments that two decades later the synagogue had become too small.[21] Starting in 1798 there was a new effort to raise money for a larger synagogue, this time to be located at Poststrasse. The two ambassadors carried with them a letter in Hebrew which stated their case. "From 1779 until now we had a small house of worship which was built when the *kehilla* was founded, with only a few members. We built a small building based on our needs and ability then. But since then our community has grown. We have about forty families, about one hundred and fifty individuals frequenting the synagogue for prayer. . . . It is therefore necessary to build a new synagogue, a need that is no doubt looked upon favorably by God and humanity. . . . Every sponsor can be assured of God's most abundant blessings."[22] On June 13, 1800, the community bought a lot at Poststrasse for 148 florin.[23] In 1803, the *Oberamtmann* (district administrator) of Göppingen loaned the Jebenhausen *kehilla* 1,200 florin to build a synagogue and a school, and others lent money as well.[24] The new synagogue and school were dedicated right before Rosh Hashanah 1804.[25] In spite of the poverty of the community, the aforementioned loan to the Göppingen district administrator was completely repaid by 1835.[26]

The maintenance of communal worship, which was solely the burden of Jewish men, was strictly followed. If a man was not able to attend services due to illness, he was obliged to provide a substitute.[27] Illness was the only excuse, and every other absence was punished with a fine.[28] Active participation in the service was also expected, preferably in a loud voice, with *shakel* (body movement) if possible. This strong physical expression of participation, if not pious, was audible and disruptive, so that the *Ständer*, or reading desks, were bolted to the synagogue floor.[29] Every family member bought a seat in the synagogue, and honors for Shabbat and holidays were auctioned off to the highest bidder.[30] Stefan Rohrbacher points out how closely intertwined the religious and the social spheres were. It was not possible to be a one-day-a-week Jew, as Jewish law guided all aspects of life, from business to pleasure, from food to clothing. There was also a good bit of folk mysticism, from amulets to protect mothers in childbed and children after birth to the kabbalistic practice of welcoming the Sabbath bride dressed in white in the fields of Jebenhausen.[31] One of the colorful sons of the Jebenhausen Jewish community was Heinrich Sontheim (1820–1912), who had a gift for music. As he was born into a time of opportunity for Jews, he did not become a cantor, but an opera singer. Sontheim achieved quite a reputation at the Württemberg Opera House in Stuttgart, the virulent anti-Semitism of the "first city" notwithstanding.[32]

The Jews of Jebenhausen initially earned their living as peddlers, money lenders, butchers, inn keepers, and cattle dealers. They were very poor. "The Jebenhausen Jews peddled ribbons, trinkets (*Bijouterie*), and everyday items; cattle dealers often operated at the expense of others and with only small profit margins. Most, however, pursued *Nothandel*, any business whatsoever. Out of need they tried to turn a profit from any and all items, or they negotiated business deals as 'Schmuser' (brokers) for a tiny commission."[33] Sixty percent of Jewish children died within the first two years of life because of poor living conditions and malnourishment.[34] When factories and wholesale businesses were exempted from regulation by the guilds, the Jebenhausen Jews recognized the opportunity to participate in the industrialization of the region, specializing in the textile industry, which was also not restricted by guild membership.[35] Although a law was passed in 1809 that allowed Jews to join guilds, this was not a very realistic proposition. An effort to manufacture men's clothing failed because of the objection of the tailors' guild that wanted the men's haberdashery business within Germany limited to Christian tailors, in spite of the new law. Still nearly ten years later, in 1819, Pastor Payor and Mayor Menning of Jebenhausen complained to the Oberamt in Göppingen that "so far no local Jews have taken advantage of the offer to pursue a '*bürgerlich*' [bourgeois] occupation." Although two Jews were butchers, Payor and Menning noted that this was not the result of the 1809 statute and that they therefore could not be counted as an increase in the number of Jews pursuing a bourgeois occupation. "For them being a butcher is their sideline, while their main occupation is peddling."[36]

Full civil rights were granted to Jews in Württemberg in 1864.[37] Yet even before the *Israelitengesetz* of 1828, at a time when there were no Jews living in Göppingen, the merchants of Göppingen complained—in anticipation—to the Württembergische Ständeversammlung (Württemberg Assembly of Trades and Guilds) that the Jews of Jebenhausen, if they received civil rights, would enter the city and take over all branches of mercantilism with the most dishonorable means. They would plunge the local linen and wool weavers into economic misfortune,[38] for "Jews simultaneously peddle and barter all imaginable items, such as cloth, silk, linen, wool, cotton, ribbons, beds, leather, watches, tobacco products, even cattle and real estate, while Christian merchants . . . deal only in one item at a time."[39] So Christian businessmen specialized, and Jews did not. In addition, Jews were accused of buying, "in the inland and abroad, sizeable quantities of cloth and other textiles, for very low prices, and of poor quality, and then reselling the items quickly to burghers, farmers, and vintners with a profit," to the disadvantage of Christian merchants, who would sit on their merchandise because of the competition.[40] The Jewish community countered this assault on their honor head on. "We would like to note that it is not true that our closeness to the city of Göppingen is a disadvantage for the residents. Our business with the residents of Göppingen runs to more than 100,000 gulden annually. As we do not have many artisans among us, we are forced to buy many of our necessities in Göppingen, and we sell many of the wool products created by the workers in the city. We provide employment as well as income to these workers. If our opponents are upset at this relationship, it is because of ill will, because of pure envy, and because they would rather suppress us than enter into a competition."[41]

The *Schutz* of the Liebenstein nobility ended in 1805.[42] Rabbi Tänzer commented that "in the period of the statutes," between 1805 and 1828, the relationship of the Jebenhausen Jews to the civic administration was odd, because they were still *Schutzjuden*, as they had been under the Liebenstein administration, except now of the state. Thus, in relation to the municipality of Jebenhausen they were foreigners, who were entitled neither to the status of burgher nor resident, because that was dependent on Württemberg citizenship, which Jews did not receive until 1828. In reality, however, they were accorded *Heimatrecht* (same rights as a local person) in Jebenhausen, which was equal to that of resident.[43] Rabbi Tänzer thought that with this step they were tacitly acknowledged as equal, even though the law had not yet caught up with this progressive attitude of the Jebenhausen citizens.

In 1823 the Swabian poet Gustav Schwab traveled through his homeland and penned the most quoted description of the Jewish community of Jebenhausen.

Coming from the village of Bezgenriet one arrives at Jebenhausen, a village surrounded by orchards. Here, among the stooped farmers, one finds pleasant individuals, dressed in French fashions, well nourished women and girls. In the center of the village, in the vicinity of the church, there stands an elegant little synagogue. The side streets are dotted with small modern homes, and through the clear glass windowpanes one sees urban interiors—in short, the traveler has arrived in a shtetl, one of the many and one of the wealthiest in the country. Sixty families, or about 300 persons, live side by side with 500 Christian residents. Their synagogue was built in 1804. It is furnished with benches, *bimah*, balcony and chandeliers, and with its arched windows and Hebrew inscription on the outside, it blends in well.[44]

The Swabian poet perhaps saw things a bit too rosily. In spite of the governmental push for "reform," and trade accommodations with other states, there were not enough jobs for Jews or non-Jews in Jebenhausen before the Revolution of 1848, so that many of the most promising young people went in search of new opportunities elsewhere.[45] For the period of 1830–70, Rabbi Tänzer gives a figure of 329 Jewish individuals who left Jebenhausen, among them 317 who went to the *goldene medine* of America.[46] This loss hit the small community particularly hard.

According to Rabbi Tänzer, most Jewish manufacturers did not come from a merchant background, but learned the business from the bottom up.[47] This was to their advantage, as they understood the process of production, not just the sales side of the business. Rabbi Tänzer credits Simon Schimmele Raff (b. 1809), son of the Hohenems cantor Moses Raff, with being "the first Jewish youth in Jebenhausen who learned the weaving business, under the tutelage of a Christian *Meister* in Göppingen. Early every morning he had to walk there from Jebenhausen, even in the coldest of winters without an overcoat, because his father could not afford one."[48] Schimmele apparently did not yet earn the coveted certification as a master weaver of later Jewish weavers. Rabbi Tänzer noted that he was a well-known and popular person.[49] His uncle, David Raff, who was the president of the Jebenhausen Jewish community, founded his business, Raff & Söhne, as early as 1830. Another relative, Joseph Raff, born to poor parents in Altenstadt (Illereichen) in 1818, came to live with his uncle, David Raff, in 1832. He, too, learned manual weaving, and completed the prescribed apprenticeship, which included a three-year journey that took him all the way to northern Germany. Upon his return to Jebenhausen he worked in the weaving business for eight years before moving on to Ulm. He returned to Jebenhausen in 1847 to become a successful manufacturer and was one of the first to move his company to Göppingen in 1852. Joseph Raff became a founding member of the Göppingen Jewish community in 1867.[50] The younger Raffs joined the newly founded company, A. Gutmann & Co., described below.

The grandson of the Jebenhausen Jewish community's founder Elias Gutmann, Abraham, born in 1810 to Salomo Gutmann, was the first Jew to learn manual weaving and successfully pass his exam as *Meister*, a certification of proficiency in the craft of weaving. Since there was no Jewish *Meister* before him, it is virtually certain that he also served his apprenticeship with a Christian teacher in Göppingen. This was even before the *Israelitengesetz* of 1828. As there were no Jews living in Göppingen until 1849, one imagines that Abraham, too, returned every day from Göppingen to Jebenhausen, as he was in need of kosher food. Gutmann is credited with founding the first Jewish industrial enterprise in Jebenhausen, in 1840, under the name A. Gutmann & Co.[51] In Rabbi Tänzer's words, "The new firm prospered quickly. Together with the significant business talent of Isak Raff, the two industrious weaving masters, Abraham Gutmann and Schimmele Raff, made the business flourish and established a market, credit, and trust."[52]

Hand weaving was a simple process, carried out by individual weavers in their homes; it did not require a factory and looms, nor did it spawn any of the labor headaches that the later factories brought with them. All an entrepreneur needed was a modest starting capital. Beginning in 1835, hand weaving was superseded by a new approach to weaving, known as the *Verlagssystem*.[53] This process was of a transitory nature, facilitating production in the transition period from manual to mechanical manufacture. A consortium of Jewish merchants in Jebenhausen, the A. Rosenheim Handelskompanie, "ordered the yarn themselves and then allowed the weavers and helpers in the Oberamt Göppingen, who had become dependent on them, to process the yarn into fabric, paying them as home workers."[54] Most of the home workers still lived in villages of the Oberamt Göppingen, but there were also connections to other districts, such as Kirchheim, Ulm Münsingen, Nürtingen, and Böblingen. In 1844 A. Rosenheim and Co. employed twelve workers in the Jebenhausen factory, and at least two hundred individuals who worked at six hundred to seven hundred manual looms in the region.[55] This meant faster production and greater capacity for production—two million ells annually.[56] The method caught on quickly, and by 1852 eleven Jewish industrialists in Jebenhausen employed more than three thousand workers who used the *Verlagssystem*.[57] Among these, the Gebrüder Ottenheimer Company in Jebenhausen employed five hundred home workers.[58] The variety of products that the Jebenhausen textile manufacturers turned out at the height of their success included textiles, yarn, corsets, strong fabric for beds made of cotton and linen,[59] soft cotton fabric for beds,[60] felt, and cloth for book bindings, as well as all of the various materials needed to manufacture finished products.

Textiles were not the only type of business in rural Jebenhausen. Dealing in cattle was equally as important in this agrarian environment. In 1836 there were seventy-one cattle dealers; however, by 1863 the number had fallen to twenty-five.[61] It is not difficult to see what happened. As the cattle trade was often connected to peddling, which was outlawed after 1828, and as residency laws became less restrictive after the Frankfurt Assembly of 1848, cattle dealers either relocated to cities such as Göppingen, Stuttgart, or Ulm, where they had easier access to markets, or they emigrated to the United States. Education and transportation opportunities were some of the other reasons for the flight from the countryside that plagued many rural communities in the mid to late nineteenth century. As a result of the *Grundrechte* (basic rights) in 1849, Jewish citizens of Jebenhausen such as Joseph Leopold Einstein, Isak Raff, and Isai Ottenheimer eagerly served in the city council.[62]

After a steady decline in population at the end of the nineteenth century, the Jewish Religious Authority in Göppingen organized a final service in the Jebenhausen synagogue. It was simultaneously a celebration of the once vibrant life of the Jebenhausen Jewish community and the funeral of the defunct *kehillah*. On Sunday, December 31, 1899, at 10:30 A.M. many invited guests and former congregants participated in a festive and solemn *Schlussgottesdienst* (final service), led by Rabbi J. Strassburger. Thereafter the Torah scrolls were removed from the Holy Ark and the synagogue was officially closed.[63] The community disbanded that same year, and the synagogue building was torn down in 1905. The benches and chandeliers were installed in the Lutheran church that today is the Jewish Museum of Göppingen, located in the suburb of Jebenhausen.

In 1933 there was just one Jewish family still living in Jebenhausen, Max and Bella Lauchheimer. Max was a cattle dealer. His granddaughter, Inge Auerbacher, who was only five years old in 1939, remembers moving to the home of her maternal grandparents in Jebenhausen. After being incarcerated in Dachau following Kristallnacht, her father had sold their house in Kippenheim. While trying to find a refuge, they moved in with her mother's family. Inge remembers,

> Even though there was little anti-Jewish feeling in Jebenhausen, my grandparents had always practiced religion with caution. According to the Jewish religion, the forty-year period during which Moses and his flock wandered in the desert is commemorated through the Feast of the Tabernacles, or Succos. This festival calls for a symbolic hut (a succo) to be built of reeds, tree branches, and grass. The interior is decorated with colorful ornaments and fruits, vegetables, and flowers of autumn. The roof of the attic room in my grandparents' house was lifted off and the room converted into a succo. Although the room could not be seen, after my grandpa died we did not dare to celebrate even in this secret way.[64]

After Jewish children were excluded from German schools, Inge tells the harrowing story of her exclusion from the local elementary school. "[In 1940] Jewish children were no longer permitted to attend regular schools. I had to walk two miles to Göppingen, a larger neighboring town, and then travel one hour by train to attend classes in Stuttgart. This was the only Jewish school in the province. I needed special travel permission papers for this trip, since Jews were no longer allowed to move freely. The trip became even more hazardous when, on September 1, 1941, Jews were made to sew the yellow Star of David on their clothes as a distinguishing mark."[65] Imagine a six-year-old girl walking by herself from Jebenhausen to Göppingen in all kinds of weather, then taking the train, again by herself, for a one-hour train ride to Stuttgart, and then walking from the train station to the Jewish Community Center which was a good distance from the train station. In the afternoon, after hours of school, she would endure the reverse of the trip in the morning. Inge's grandfather, Max Wertheimer, was the last Jew to be buried in the Jebenhausen Jewish cemetery before deportations began.

## Göppingen

The Jewish community of Göppingen was formally established in 1867 with thirty-three families.[66] As early as 1849, Jewish businessmen from Jebenhausen started to transfer their factories to Göppingen. In this they were practical as well as *chutzpahdig* (bold), locating themselves in places that made sense for their business regardless of the local population's attitude towards them. While Jebenhausen suffered economically from the relocation of the Jewish businesses to Göppingen, the Staufer city benefited greatly, not only economically but also socially.

Joseph Raff and Salomon Einstein were the first to relocate in 1849, the Gutmann brothers following in 1850.[67] Another early company to relocate was Kaufmann & Söhne, which switched to mechanical looms in 1862. Rabbi Tänzer quoted from a brochure that "with the aid of the *Stadtbach* [creek] the first four mechanical looms were instituted by Kaufmann & Söhne. This early modernization by the Kaufmann firm was just as important for the development of our city's industry as was the introduction of the corset industry and the migration of the Jebenhausen businesses."[68] Here one should note that the manufacture of corsets in Germany was such a big business at that time that it had markets in the United States. Corset manufacturing had its beginnings in Württemberg and took hold especially in Göppingen in 1851.[69]

Large amounts of water were required for fabric dyeing, so that many of these factories located along the creek in the "Little Venice" section of Göppingen (vicinity of Marktstrasse and Geislinger Strasse) with the bleaching fields where the textile merchants could lay out their yarn in the sun. Others located near the railroad tracks for ease of transportation (Bahnhofstrasse and Gartenstrasse). After the synagogue was built, many

Göppingen Jews moved into buildings or built houses on Burgstrasse, Pfarrstrasse, and Hauptstrasse—in close proximity to the synagogue at Freihofstrasse. A good number of these Jewish houses are still standing today and one could walk to the synagogue from any one of them with relative ease. Even from the houses in outlying areas, such as the Leopold Gutmann residence at Poststrasse,[70] or the Villa Fleischer at Nördliche Ringstrasse, or Max Ottenheimer's villa at 14 Wolfstrasse, it probably was no more than the permissible distance on Shabbat to walk to the *shul* at Freihofstrasse.

A number of the houses around the market square and in the streets radiating out from there are former Jewish businesses and homes. Some of the structures have only changed owners and not appearance, while other buildings have been razed and new ones erected. These structures included a ladies' wear store at 2 Hauptstrasse (Marktplatz), owned by Adolf Heimann, southwest of the city hall; and the firm of Einstein and Guggenheim, a textile store, owned by Julius Guggenheim[71] at Obere Markstrasse at the corner of Kirchstrasse, right on the Marktplatz and east of the city hall.[72] This store closed during World War I, when Julius was a soldier. In the 1920s the Guggenheim family moved to 20 Grabenstrasse, closer to the railroad station, where Julius opened an *Aussteuergeschäft* (linen store). Next door to them, at 18 Grabenstrasse, resided kosher butcher Simon Oppenheimer. In 1930 enterprising Julius Guggenheim and his wife Lini opened yet another store, Wohlwert (later called Staufia), at 40 Hauptstrasse. As a marketing device, he engaged a blimp to drop chocolate bars on the population.[73] Moritz Neuburger owned an apothecary business at 34 Hauptstrasse. The shoe store which was owned by Peter Gold still exists at 11 Hauptstrasse; the department store Kaufhaus Lendt, owned by Georg Lendt, was located at 8 Marktstrasse until it gave way in the post-war period to a large department store; the clothing store of Freudenberger and Co., begun by Frieda Freudenberger and Ferdinand Oppenheimer and later managed by Willy Böhm, was located at 11 Lange Strasse; and a men's haberdashery at 20/22 Lange Strasse was owned by Josef Ostertag.

At 33 Freihofstrasse there also was the *Strickwarenfabrik* (knitting goods factory) of Josef Walz; the business Kaliko Kunstlederwerke (artificial leather works) owned by Netter and Eisig was located at 27 Bahnhofstrasse, the mechanical weaving business of Frankfurter Brothers at 34 Bahnhofstrasse as well as the textile wholesale business of Hugo Heiman at 20 Ziegelstrasse. The tobacco wholesale and *Brantweinbrennerei* (brandy manufacturing business) owned by Eugen Bernheimer was located at 3 Geislinger Strasse. The *Schutzdeckenfabrik* (quilt factory) owned by Emil Hilb was at 8 Schützenstrasse, and a company manufacturing mineral oils and chemical products, owned by Viktor Schwab, was located at 13 Bleichstrasse.

Other Jewish businesses were located in the outlying parts of Göppingen. The felt factory of Karl Veit, who donated part of his property for a *Sportplatz* (sports field) for the Jewish community, was located in the east, at Ulmerstrasse. In the north were found the corset factory owned by Daniel Rosenthal at the Nördliche Ringstrasse and the bandage manufacturing business, Paul Mitter K.G., at 40 Marstallstrasse, owned by Salomon (and Sana) Ottenheimer. In the west, at 16 Metzgerstrasse was located the Württembergische Filztuchfabrik owned by David Geschmay[74] as well as Kinessa Chemical Company, owned by Siegfried Rohrbacher, at 52 Filsstrasse.

Since the Sunday laws mandated the closing of all businesses on the Christian day of rest, Jewish stores were as a rule open for business on Saturday, the Jewish Sabbath. However, Jewish stores were closed for the High Holy Days, Rosh Hashanah and Yom Kippur, and other major Jewish festivals. The local businessmen prominently announced this in the local newspapers; the time for worship services at the synagogue was likewise published in the press.

Manufacturing had changed significantly since the early days of Jebenhausen. Factories were located almost exclusively in urban centers. According to the employment statistics of the Oberamt Göppingen for 1895, the textile industry employed the largest number of individuals in the city as well as in the district—2,208 for Göppingen and 2,130 for the district, for a total 4,338 workers, more than half of whom lived in the city.[75] The clothing and dry cleaning industry, which included the manufacture of corsets, was second with 1,531 in Göppingen and 655 in the district.[76] The textile businesses, Jewish and Christian, also boosted other industrial branches, such as the metal works industry, the machine industry, and construction. Metal works production drastically increased between 1882, when there were 522 workers in the city and 1895, when three times as many workers were registered in Göppingen, namely 1,581, and only an additional 206 in the whole district.[77] Predictably, construction, machine, and instrument production, and trade also rose significantly between 1882 and 1895.[78] In 1886, the corporate tax paid by Jewish businesses in Göppingen was 246,458 Mark, or 20.3 percent of the total *Gewerbesteuerkapital* (taxable corporate income). Thus, 1,990 Christian businesses made up approximately 80 percent of the local tax base, while 50 Jewish businesses—or 2.5 percent of commerce—brought in 20 percent of the tax.[79]

"Little Venice" has long since given way to impressive business complexes and department stores. The creek was covered in 1979.[80] Some former Jewish buildings in Göppingen were bombed during World War II and had to be rebuilt, while others simply fell victim to changing times and new demands. The Schillerschule from which the Göppingen Jews were deported on November 28, 1941, still stands at Schillerstrasse and Burgstrasse, on the same block as the erstwhile second prayer room of the Jewish community at 33 Pfarrstrasse.[81] How ironic, for their final journey into death, the Jews of Göppingen were taken to a building on the same street where they had found an early welcome to the city.

### Rabbi Dr. Aron Tänzer (1871–1937)

One yearns to get a sense of what life was like in the Göppingen Jewish community before the Nazis came to power in 1933. No one public figure is more important to this understanding than the spiritual leader of Jewish Göppingen from 1907–37, Rabbi Aron Tänzer, one of four rabbis in the history of the Göppingen Jewish community. Dr. Karl-Heinz Ruess has diligently collected most of Rabbi Aron Tänzer's historical writings, sermons, and speeches.[82] It is interesting, informative, and fascinating to analyze them, although they tell us more about Rabbi Tänzer's patriotism than about his Jewishness. Rabbi Tänzer's writings served two purposes—to provide guidance in Jewish matters to his respective communities and beyond and to document their histories, and to prove to his detractors that he was a good German. He did not have to prove to anyone that he was a good Jew as that was self-evident from his position.

Born on January 30, 1871, in Pressburg, Hungary, Aron's circumstances were modest. His mother worked as a seamstress for the Jewish community. A single parent, she raised Aron with the help of her mother who watched the child while the mother worked. His father, Heinrich, was a rabbi and divorced from his mother when Aron was a small child. After studying for the rabbinate in Pressburg, the young student in 1892 made his way to Berlin where he studied with the greats of his day, including Wilhelm Dilthey and Moritz Lazarus.[83] The humanistic direction of his studies—Goethe, basics of morality, history of ethics, psychology, and philosophy—complemented the Talmudic education he had received at the *yeshivah* in Pressburg. Jewish and German values were to guide his life.

After transferring to the University of Bern in 1894, Dr. Tänzer wrote a scientific treatise on the religious philosophy of Josef Albo (1381–1445) for his dissertation.[84] Following graduation from university, Tänzer found his future in a small Jewish community in Poznan, Obornik. Here he was issued the diploma he needed to become a rabbi, met and married his wife, Leonora Rosa Handler, and assisted his father-in-law who was a rabbi.[85] In 1896, twenty-five years after Jewish Emancipation, Tänzer assumed the office of rabbi in Hohenems, Vorarlberg, a community that, along with Tirol, also has a rich and detailed written history thanks to Rabbi Tänzer's zeal to document. His appointment occurred the year when Theodor Herzl wrote *Der Judenstaat*, a manifesto that led to a very important event the next year in Basel, Switzerland—the first Zionist Congress. However, that may not have held great significance for Rabbi Tänzer at that time; his concerns in 1897 were for the Jewish community that he now shepherded. After nine years he left Vorarlberg and spent two brief years (1905–7) in Meran, Südtirol.[86] Things did not work out and in 1907 he applied for the position of rabbi in Göppingen. This appointment was preceded by the second theological civil service exam, which he took in Stuttgart on July 11, 1907. His appointment to the rabbinate became official on July 19, 1907.[87] Rabbi Tänzer served the Göppingen Jewish community for thirty years with distinction.

Aron Tänzer, who in 1924 officially changed his name to the more German-sounding Arnold,[88] was the quintessence of a German Jew. Highly acculturated, his love for things German was legend. Yet, along with many of his congregants, acculturation did not mean assimilation. Rabbi Tänzer was both—a Jew and a German. There was room for Jewishness and Germanness in his life. All activities connected to his Jewishness were bound up in his family life and his rabbinic position. He wrote and gave sermons, ministered to the sick, buried the dead and welcomed the newborn. He conducted services with great enthusiasm and performed *b'nai mitzvah* and confirmations. According to Erwin, every week the family invited guests to Shabbat dinner at the Tänzer home. Rabbi Tänzer was deeply involved in the organizational life of the Jewish community, from the mundane, such as board meetings, to reorganizing the Israelitische Frauenverein in 1926.[89] Every Jewish organization enjoyed his attention and benefited from his counsel. He was a profuse author of sermons, eulogies, and speeches for many occasions. Rabbi Tänzer was a scholar. He loved to write and, with his scientific bent, he enjoyed the gathering of data. Due to his diligence and stamina, there are histories of the Jews in

Tirol and Vorarlberg, Part I, and in Hohenems, Meran, Part II (1905); a history of the Jews of Brest-Litovsk (1918), and of course, of the Jews of Jebenhausen and Göppingen (1927).[90] Additionally, Rabbi Tänzer published many essays, and between 1910–14 he served as the editor of the *Israelitische Wochenschrift* for Württemberg. He likewise taught a number of courses for the continuing education programs in Göppingen.[91]

And it was not only the Göppingen Jewish community that benefited from his wisdom and kindness, but also all of the Jews in the vicinity as well as Gentile Göppingen citizens. He was equally as dedicated to the city in which he lived as to his Jewish community, and all appreciated his hands-on approach to problem solving. He was a man of deed, as Zecha notes,[92] and served by example. His most lasting work was the creation of a public library to further the reading of good literature. A stubborn patriot, he volunteered to serve as a soldier in World War I. As it happened, the day of mobilization was August 1, which was a Shabbat as well as Erev Tisha B'Av, a day of mourning in the Jewish calendar, to commemorate the destruction of the First and Second Temples in Jerusalem. Within the first few hours of mobilization, he wrote a letter to his superiors volunteering to serve as an army chaplain. "After the conclusion of the worship service, around 10 P.M., I wrote my first application to the Israelitische Oberkirchenbehörde in Stuttgart and asked them for an assignment as an army chaplain. At midnight I hand carried the letter to the post office. I didn't need to hurry, as it took a whole year until my wish was granted."[93] Throughout this year, Rabbi Tänzer pestered the authorities until they assigned him to the German Command in the East. His provisions included a horse and buggy and a pistol for self-defense.[94] Leaving behind a wife and two young children, Erwin and Ilse, he and two of his grown sons served the fatherland with distinction. Fritz and Paul, two of his surviving four children from his first marriage (the other two were Hugo and Irene) served as *Gefreite* (lance corporals) in the Great War, they were wounded and decorated with the Eiserne Kreuz II. Klasse (Iron Cross Second Class),[95] but thankfully returned home in the end. Dr. Tänzer served with the Bug Army, primarily in Brest-Litovsk and Pinsk. Also wounded, he was honored with no less than four German and Austrian decorations—the Eiserne Kreuz II. Klasse, the F.O.I. (Ritterkreuz I. Klasse des württembergischen Friedrichs-Ordens mit Schwertern), the H.H. Kreuz (Hamburgisches Hanseatenkreuz), and the Österreichische F.J.O. (Österreichische Ritterkreuz des Franz-Josephs-Ordens).[96] He was one of ninety-three Jewish Göppingen citizens who participated in World War I; fifty-nine served at the front, seven lost their lives.⁹⁷ One of Rabbi Tänzer's proudest achievements while an army chaplain was the establishment of a soup kitchen to help the poor—and mostly Jewish—population.⁹⁸ Upon returning from the front, Rabbi Tänzer was at first lauded by his countrymen; later he suffered humiliation from Nazi sympathizers. But his spirit was not easily defeated. Even after his exclusion from German society, he still had one outlet, his congregation. Rabbi Tänzer's sermons were legendary. Lilo Guggenheim Levine remembers how moved she was by the Rabbi's words and ideas. "Rabbi Tänzer's sermons held our attention. Often he preached, 'Be glad you belong to the persecuted and not the persecutors.'"⁹⁹ Had he known that only two Göppingen citizens would follow his coffin to his final resting place in 1937, he would have been disappointed, but not surprised.¹⁰⁰ It was, as Hugo Lang says, *der Dank des Vaterlandes* (the gratitude of the fatherland) in depreciated currency.

### Göppingen Synagogue Life

It was considered one's civic as well as social and religious duty to support and participate in the local Jewish community, including the synagogue as well as the numerous Jewish organizations. But one's faith was an individual and private matter. Rabbi Tänzer's often laudatory characterizations of his upstanding and business-savvy congregants rarely included the adjectives *pious* or *religious*. That does not mean that they were not pious, only that religion was just one part of their lives; they were indeed Germans of the Mosaic persuasion. All the institutions needed to support Jewish life were available in Göppingen, except for a *mikvah*. Presumably not too many Göppingen Jews availed themselves of this traditional institution and those in need of ritual immersion had to travel to other Jewish communities for this service.

The Göppingen synagogue was built on a parcel of land at Freihofstrasse bought by the Jewish Religious Authority for 9,500 marks on September 16, 1878.¹⁰¹ The plan chosen for the edifice was designed in 1879 by *Oberbaurat* (state architect) Dr. Christian Friedrich von Leins, a non-Jew, who had also built the Stuttgart synagogue ¹⁰² He was considered one of the most significant architects of the nineteenth century. The synagogue had a total of 278 seats, 136 for adults and 40 for school-age youth in the main sanctuary as well as 102 in the gallery.¹⁰³ The building plans for the synagogue also included plans for an organ, which was constructed by *Orgelbauer* Johann Georg Schäfer from Göppingen in 1881 at a cost of 3,300 marks.¹⁰⁴ The synagogue, which cost 50,919.83 marks to build,¹⁰⁵ was dedicated "with great solemnity" on Friday, September 16, and Saturday, September 17, 1881.[106] The interior was renovated in 1925, primarily to replace the gas lamps with electric lights. The forty seats for students were also added at that time.[107]

What was it like to attend services in the Göppingen synagogue? We have both eyewitness reports as well as the very formal synagogue order to give us a sense of local practices. Erwin Tänzer remembered that there were no weekday services.[108] Services were held on Friday evening to usher in the Sabbath and on Saturday morning. Seating in the Göppingen synagogue was traditional, men and women sat on either side of the center aisle, separated by gender; boys and girls who had had their bar/bat mitzvah were seated separately upstairs in the balcony, and pre–bar/bat mitzvah boys and girls were seated up front downstairs, in front of the Ark, also separated by gender.[109] The congregation owned eleven Torah scrolls, one of which was loaned to the Jews in Kirchheim unter Teck.[110] Men wore hats rather than *kippot* to services, following the German custom rather than the Jewish one. Women also wore hats to services, as wearing hats for religious services and other occasions was also the fashion among German women.

Liturgical music included compositions by Rabbi Maier of Stuttgart. While the *Maiersche Gesangbuch* was mandatory, compositions by Louis Lewandowski (1821–94) as well as traditional melodies for taking out the Torah, *Aleinu*, and the hymn *Adon Olam* were also popular.[111] Lilo remembers, "Mr. Levi was the cantor. He sang the prayers accompanied by the organ. . . . On holidays Mr. Warscher . . . was the cantor. We had a fine choir, and I especially remember heart-warming solos sung by Trude Lendt."[112] Rabbi Tänzer proudly noted that it was "the joy of singing in the community that adds much to the worship service and deserves the credit for the Göppingen synagogue's well-trained choir and capable prayer leaders, who also lead services on the High Holy Days."[113]

After services, members of the congregation were fond of lingering outside in conversation—until the Nazis came to power, when it stopped. Lilo remembers those Friday nights fondly. "After the Friday service most people stood outside and visited together. Our family then walked home to Sabbath dinner. The table was set formally with a white newly laundered starched tablecloth. There was *challah* (Jewish Sabbath bread, which we called *berches*), followed by several courses starting with soup. There was much conversation, and often we had guests."[114] Erwin Tänzer remembered his mother's *berches*, and that she had many different recipes. On

Friday night they had out-of-town guests.[115] Hugo Lang of Süssen likewise remembers having *berches* for Friday night dinner.

The synagogue leadership produced a written synagogue order that regulated what was to happen during services. The purpose of this ordinance was decorum—a quiet and a peaceful atmosphere conducive to contemplation. Several aspects of the worship service were seen as problematic, and hence had to be regulated, such as the starting time of the service and the congregants' promptness (paragraph 1), restricting the use of a purchased seat to only one person in a family (paragraph 2), limiting the Shabbat Shacharit (morning) service to half an hour's duration (paragraph 3) without reciting the Shacharit Kedushah (Adoration). This may sound strange to American ears, as one would not think of having a Shacharit service on Shabbat without a Kedushah, but this holiest of holy sections of the Amidah prayer lent itself to cantorial orations, hence lengthening the Shacharit service considerably. At the time of the first recitation of the hymn Ashrei during *Psukei d'Zimra* (early morning service), the gate to the synagogue courtyard was to be closed and no one admitted after that. Exceptions were to be made on Rosh Hashanah (New Year) and Yom Kippur (Day of Atonement), when congregants were restricted from coming and going only during the Torah service. Congregants were to be dressed appropriately and modestly with an appropriate head covering, such as a top hat for men.[116] Appropriate shoes were to be worn. *Tefillin* (during the weekday morning service) were to be laid only at home, the removal of same was permitted in the synagogue courtyard or back home. However, this was not an issue in the Göppingen community since there were no weekday services. Those who were called up for an *aliyah* (honor) were to use a *tallit* (prayer shawl) provided near the *bimah* (platform) (paragraph 4). Entrance into the synagogue was to occur silently; conversation in the hallway or in the cloakroom was prohibited. Those entering were to sit down in their seats immediately and remain quiet, facing the Holy Ark. There was to be no conversation with new neighbors, no loud prayer or singing, or other noises (paragraph 5). There were provisions for sitting and standing during certain prayers (paragraph 6). Boys had to be at least seven and girls nine to be in the sanctuary, and they were to be supervised at all times by a parent or designated adult (paragraph 7). It was the duty of the *Kirchenvorsteher* (beadle) to enforce these rules. Those in violation were to receive a warning through the presentation of a white card and those who continued to cause a disturbance received a red penalty card which resulted in a fine.[117]

Life-cycle events such as circumcisions, *b'nai mitzvah* and confirmations, weddings, and sitting shivah for those in mourning were important
to Göppingen Jews, albeit adjusted according to a particular family's degree of observance. Göppingen Jews still sat shivah in Lilo Guggenheim's
youth. She writes, "The first time I heard about *Schiffe sitze* [shivah sitting, the mourning period in Jewish practice] was when Grandfather Sinn
died. Grandmother Sinn was an orthodox Jew, but most of the family had
come away from being orthodox. Father's sisters and parents continued to
be orthodox. Mother and grandmother Hammel went to synagogue every
Sabbath and every Jewish holiday. Grandmother Sinn prayed daily: she
was the first to arrive in synagogue on Friday evenings. I often walked to
synagogue with her."[118]

The ritual of bar mitzvah for boys at age thirteen was practiced un-
changed in Göppingen, but the equivalent ritual for girls was done dif-
ferently. Traditional Judaism has no coming-of-age ritual for girls. In the
mid-nineteenth century, a coming-of-age ceremony for girls was also introduced by progressive German rabbis. In Göppingen—as well as other communities—for girls the traditional age for coming-of-age ceremonies was
changed from twelve to fourteen and instead of calling it a bat mitzvah,
as is done today again, the ceremony was called *Konfirmation*, following
the German Lutheran tradition of confirmation.[119] The confirmands for
1931–32 included Rabbi Tänzer's daughter Ilse, along with Frieda Piotrkowsky, Selma Zitter, Elsa Srodek, Hanna Fleischer, Erna Oppenheimer,
Liese Rohrbacher, and Margot Krämer. That the Göppingen Jews were individualists can be seen from the strong will of Werner Ottenheimer, who
told me that he was not religious and therefore requested his father's permission to abstain from attending synagogue services after his bar mitzvah. His father acquiesced.[120]

Christian burghers joined their Jewish friends for concerts in the synagogue, such as the popular Sunday *Morgenfeier* (morning concert) of clas-
sical music. A photo shows the orchestra set up on the floor in front of the
Ark. There are two baby grand pianos, and the soloists were positioned
up on the bimah in front of the Ark.[121] One newspaper ad advertised a
mixed repertoire for September 22, 1929, at 10:45 A.M.—with compositions by George Friedrich Händel, Louis Lewandowsky, Felix Mendelssohn
[Bartholdy], Salomon Sulzer, Samuel Naumbourg, Yossele Rosenblatt, and
Heinrich Schalit. The performers were Oberkantor H. J. Fleischmann from
the Cologne Synagogue; Ilse Rosenthal, Göppingen, soprano; Otto Tröster,
organ, and the Göppingen synagogue choir, conducted by Siegfried Löwen-

stein. Admission was open to everyone, at 1 and 2 marks, and tickets could be obtained in the Dictler book store.[122] An article in the *Israelitisches Wochenblatt zu Göppingen* previewed the program. "Two choral compositions by Sulzer and the *Yigdal* by [Louis] Lewandowski [Rabbi Tänzer's favorite hymn] with bariton solo, as well as several Hebrew-language solos by Oberkantor Fleischmann.[123] He will also sing the aria 'Manoah' from Händel's 'Samson.' Ilse Rosenthal, whose beautiful voice we have previously recognized, will sing the aria, 'Hear oh Israel,' from the 'Elijah' oratorio by Mendelssohn."[124] The article praised the talents of *Oberkantor* Fleischmann "who has long been known in our circles through his wonderful Hebrew-language records." Cantor Fleischmann had toured in the United States the previous year and the article cited some of the American press. "We got to know a tenor of outstanding quality in Cantor Fleischmann. His well-chosen program proves that he also has excellent abilities in musical areas other than liturgical. We will not soon forget his Kaddish and his Jewish folksongs." The article concluded with the prediction that "the entire Göppingen community will attend this outstanding artistic event in order to demonstrate to the synagogue choir the community's great appreciation of your achievements." They further expected "great interest and numerous visitors from among local music friends." The concert was to be broadcast via the Süddeutsche Rundfunk to Stuttgart and Freiburg im Breisgau, the first time that the Südfunk broadcast from a synagogue.[125]

## Organizational Life

Jewish businessmen and women were deeply involved with the well-being of the Jewish community, having created a wealth of charitable and other service organizations, such as Merkuria (1868), an organization for young businessmen; Israelitische Wohltätigkeitsverein (Jewish Welfare Organization) (1875), Israelitische Lese- und Familienverein (Jewish Reading Club and Family Organization) (1876), Israelitische Frauenverein (Jewish Women's Organization) (1881), Israelitische Jungfrauenverein (Jewish Single Women's Organization) (1895), *Israelitische Männer-(Unterstützungs)-Verein* (Jewish Men's Support Club) (1901), Ortsgruppe des Central-Vereins deutscher Staatsbürger jüdischen Glaubens (local chapter of the Central Organization of German Citizens of the Jewish Faith) (1908), Israelitische Jugendverein (Jewish Youth Group) (1920), Israelitische Wohlfahrtszentrale (Jewish Welfare Center) (1921), Ortsgruppe des Reichsbundes jüdischer Frontsoldaten (local branch of the Reich Organization of Jewish Combat Soldiers) (1921).[126]

Göppingen Jews were equally as generous with their time and money in the community at large, led by Rabbi Tänzer. Daniel Rosenthal established a scholarship fund of 1,000 florin, the interest from which annually supported three elementary school pupils to attend a secondary school. In 1871 he also contributed 2,260 florin towards the construction of a municipal hospital. Jebenhausen and Göppingen Jews were also involved in local civics and politics. Among the Jewish *Bürger* who served on the city council were Josef Raff (1868–71), Daniel Rosenthal (1864–70), Samuel Fleischer (1910–19), Bernard Gutmann (1899–1904), Leopold A. Gutmann (1902–8), and Hermann Schottländer (1888–94). A number of these same individuals also served on the citizens' council. Among these were Josef Raff, 1866, Benno Kaufmann, 1901–4, Daniel Rosenthal, 1862, Bernard Gutmann, 1894–1904, and Leopold Gutmann, 1888–91.[127] Max Levi served as the German-Austrian consul in Stuttgart. Politically, Jews belonged to the Volkspartei as well as the Deutsche Partei.

A number of the Göppingen Jews were active in non-Jewish organizations beyond Göppingen, thereby demonstrating their German patriotism. During the Franco-Prussian War of 1870–71 Simon Raff served on the Verpflegungs Committee am Göppinger Bahnhof (soup kitchen at the Göppingen railroad station). As a result of his service in World War I, Rabbi Tänzer was an honorary member of the Veteranen- und Militärverein "Kampfgenossenschaft," a veteran's organization for those who fought in the Franco-Prussian War of 1870–71 and in World War I. In honor of the Kampfgenossenschaft's fiftieth anniversary, Rabbi Tänzer wrote their history.[128] In the 1930s, this organization ousted him rather unceremoniously because he was not Aryan. Another Jewish member of the Franco-Prussian War was twenty-one-year-old Samuel Fleischer, one of the founders of the Jewish organization Merkuria in 1868.[129] Membership in trade organizations was valued greatly. Leopold A. Gutmann of A. Gutmann & Co. was the president of the Göppingen Handels- und Gewerbeverein (Commerce and Merchants' Association) from 1888–94 and served as a board member of many organizations, including the municipal gas company. He also served as a member of the Reutlinger Handelskammer (chamber of commerce), and in 1898 was even granted the title of *Kommerzienrat* (minister of commerce) by the King of Württemberg. Max Gutmann likewise served as a member of the Reutlinger Handelskammer in 1925. Samuel Fleischer served as *Vertrauensmann* (representative) of the Bekleidungs-Industry-Berufsgenossenschaft des Donau-Kreises (Donau district union of the clothing industry), as well as a board member of the Verein deutscher Korsett-Industrieller. He further served on the board of directors of the Württembergische Exportmusterlager (state repository for samples for export) as well as the Göppingen Handels- und Gewerbeverein.

### Jewish Social Life before 1933

Jews in rural communities had much closer relations with their Christian neighbors than Jews in an urban environment. In small communities, Christian and Jewish *Bürger* (citizens) focused on what they shared and relied on each other for products and services. This frequent interaction created a desire to be on friendly terms with one's neighbors, rather than to alienate.

The practice of Judaism in Göppingen was, as I gathered from my contacts with some of the old-timers, diverse. The culture of Göppingen's Jews included things German and things Jewish. Göppingen Jews were individualists whose highest good was to belong—to Göppingen. Lilo Guggenheim Levine proclaims in her book, *This Too Shall Pass*, "We were Göppinger."[130] Werner Ottenheimer stated, "We were *lokaltreu* [loyal to Göppingen]"[131] That was most important. They were residents of Göppingen, Swabians, Jews, Germans—probably in that order. As such, they participated in the life of their town in the same ways as those who were not Jewish. Göppingen Jews socialized at the Café Heidle enjoying a *Mohraköpfle* (chocolate trifle) or at the Pio *Eisdiehle* (ice cream parlor). Children rode bikes, jumped rope, and played *Indianerles* (cowboys and Indians)[132] Many participated in sports such as handball, soccer, swimming, ice skating, and skiing; outdoor activities included hiking to Wasserberg, Hornberg, or the Teck; primary cultural events were concerts, plays, *Fasching* (Mardi Gras) celebrations, and parades. Of special interest were birthday celebrations. Lilo recalls, "On birthdays, presents were displayed on a table in the living room. The table was covered with a tablecloth used only for birthdays. We had marble cake for every birthday. I had parties with friends."[133] They also loved the local culinary specialties. While *berches* like other traditional Jewish food was served regularly, Swabian dishes were just as popular. Göppingen residents cooked and baked according to local recipes; many Jews took care to make them kosher, even permitting a double standard. Some Jewish families in Göppingen bought kosher meat from butcher Simon Oppenheimer at 18 Grabenstrasse for one occasion and *traif* (non-kosher) *Wurscht* (cold cuts) from butcher Kümmerle, located practically across the street, for others. Keeping kosher was not a priority for every family, as Werner Ottenheimer noted when I interviewed him. However, no matter whom one asks, be it Hugo Lang from Süssen or Werner Ottenheimer or Lilo Guggenheim Levine from Göppingen, lentils and *Spätzle* (homemade noodles) with *Saitenwürstle* (hot dogs) were everyone's favorite weekday staple.

The primary address for specifically Jewish cultural events in Göppingen, including weddings and dinners connected to other religious *simchahs* (celebrations) such as *b'nai mitzvah*, confirmations, and religious holidays was the kosher Hotel Dettelbacher, founded by the Dettelbacher family in 1862 and later owned by Max Krämer.[134] Lilo remembers that "the Dettelbacher" had "a beautiful stage upstairs where my love for performing and dance was born."[135] One of the few surviving texts from a community event is quite humorous, poking fun at conventions practiced in Jewish Göppingen, such as card games at the Hotel Dettelbacher, which were for men only. Lilo remembers that her father went to "the Dettelbacher" to play cards after lunch every day. "Every afternoon Father went there after our mid-day meal to play cards before going back to the store."[136] One of the parodies dealing with the "D" was sung to melodies from Johann Strauss's "Die Fledermaus."

How fortunate we are
to have the D[ettelbacher].
If that would disappear some day
may God help us.
We do not need dance and cinema
nor automobile excursions.
We only know one ideal
we play cards every day.

What do we care about the EFK
[or] the Kulturbund Zionisten [Cultural Zionists].
whether it is Sukkot or Purim,
whether we are in the choir or soloists,
whether there is a handball competition,
whether the track-and-field team competes.
None of that interests us,
we play cards every day.

. . .

We hardly have a minyan for the service,
the Rav may have to wait forever.
There are more than ten in the Dettelbacher,
that's because of the cards.
We don't need Hebrew here,
that is for the Utopians.
We don't go to Erez [Israel],
That's for the Zionists.[137]

Another example of the young people's attitude, about school, can be found in a *Singspiel*, entitled *"Ein Schulerlebnis,"* or a school adventure. The play was written by Trude Rohrbacher for six little girls. Those participating in the performance were Anne Bernheimer, Erika Veit, Henny Lang (Süssen), Helga Freudenberger, Lilo Guggenheim, and Doris Fleischer.[138] The sampling of one verse will give us an idea of the story line.

Today we are coming home from school much too early
that's because we skipped school
secretly, after the break.
The teacher taught
difficult subjects
arithmetic, handwriting, geography
oh, it is so funny. . . .[139]

Being a serious student was not necessarily seen as a virtue!

Of great interest to the entire Jewish community were two minor festivals—Hanukkah and Purim. From the little information that exists one can say that these minor Jewish holidays were celebrated with great enthusiasm by the entire community. One cannot but wonder whether the dedication to Purim was a response to the hostile environment after World War I. German Jews were stung by the accusation that they stabbed the fatherland in the back by not serving in the World War I. This was a lie, of course, and must have made the Göppingen Jews somewhat weary of the sincerity of German Christians. Perhaps they were not as far removed from evil Haman in ancient Persia, even in the Weimar Republic, as one would have wished. A picture of a 1927 Purim celebration with Lilo Guggenheim and friends, taken in the garden of the Villa Fleischer in the Nördliche Ringstrasse, has survived.[140] Lilo writes that they performed for "Her Highness," aunt Emilie Fleischer, who commanded great respect.

Traditional Jewish elements were an intrinsic part of events in the Göppingen Jewish community, although they are intermingled with German, if not Christian, customs and conventions as well. As Lilo describes in her book, *This Too Shall Pass*, Hanukkah was kept separate from Christmas. Christmas was for the Christian employees who worked for a Jewish family or business, Hanukkah for the family. Writes Lilo, "Mother made a fuss over Christmas. Baking started six weeks beforehand. Many kinds of Christmas cookies went into jars which were hidden from us children, but Poldi and I managed to find them. . . . Christmas Eve Mother had the big table filled with presents for our cook. We children got our presents mostly for Hanukah."[141]

It was not uncommon for a Jewish family to have a tree for Hanukkah, though not in Lilo Guggenheim's home.[142] After all, her father was the president of the Jewish community. Jewish children received the same types of presents their Christian friends were given, typically a toy railroad for boys and a grocery store for girls, to be replenished year after year. Lilo remembers, "Emil and Poldi had a fancy train. I had a store with a cash register and drawers for my merchandise (food-shaped candy). I sold the candy in tiny paper bags and collected the money in my cash register. The store and the trains were put away after New Years and brought out again the next Christmas."[143] Erwin Tänzer, son of Rabbi Aron and Berta Tänzer, did not remember many specifics when I visited with him in 2004, but he did remember that Richard Ottenheimer, Werner's older brother, had a Märklin train set.[144] This was confirmed by Werner Ottenheimer in Cuba with equal nostalgia in 2007. His eyes lit up when he reminisced about the Märklin railroad that he and his older brother Richard played with to their hearts' content. If there is one common denominator for Jewish as well as non-Jewish boys for this time period, it is their love for their Märklin *Eisenbahn*.[145]

Today in America Hanukkah celebrations, at home and in the community, are common. Many public holiday displays also include a *hanukkiah*, so that the general public is familiar with at least the symbols of Hanukkah. It was not a custom to celebrate Hanukkah extensively among German Jews before 1895, as they wanted to integrate into German society, not separate from it. In Göppingen, the Hanukkah celebration started in 1895 as a charitable event by the Israelitische Jungfrauenverein (Jewish Spinster Group).

The popularity of Hanukkah in the Jewish community of Göppingen seems to have been at its height in the 1920s. Jews during the Weimar

Republic felt that they had achieved the ultimate experience—integration into German society and perhaps also the freedom to flaunt their Jewish identity. As all social events, the festival of Hanukkah was celebrated at the Hotel Dettelbacher.

By 1929 the holiday had become very popular in the entire community. As Rabbi Tänzer tells us, a very generous group of young women, led by Miss Fanny Gutmann, intended it to be "a modest celebration for poor children, who were to be gifted and cared for." He continues, "It soon became a very popular institution for the entire community and its youth. Theater performances, dramatic readings, gift giving, and so on were enjoyed by old and young and gained the organization's recognition."[146] Rabbi Tänzer's son, Erwin, remembered participating in a Hanukkah play when he was six or seven in 1920 or '21.[147] Several pictures of Hanukkah celebrations have survived, one from from 1920/21,[148] which may be the one Erwin remembered; another from 1922/23,[149] and an announcement of the 1936 celebration in the *Israelitisches Wochenblatt zu Göppingen*.[150] I chose a picture of one event in the 1929 celebration, "Prinzes[s]-Forget-Me-Not's Wedding,"[151] as the focus for a "reunion" of the Göppingen Jewish community post facto.

### A Hanukkah Reunion

The idea of a "reunion" was inspired by Lilo G. Levine who traveled to Göppingen for such an event in 1984. The nature of the reunion in this study is multivalent—Lilo and Hugo, as representatives of Göppingen and Süssen; Hugo and his brother and cousins, as the representatives of one family; the children of the 1929 Hanukkah celebration as Jewish Göppingen's future, and the Göppingen Jewish children in the Hanukkah program and their families. From the young people participating in the 1929 Hanukkah celebration we get a good sense of the Jewish children in grades one to six [the age of bar mitzvah] and who their families were between World War I and the end of the Weimar Republic.[152] The list reads like a "Who's Who" of Göppingen Jewry. It appears that the entire youth of the Jewish community including the satellite communities of Süssen and Kirchheim was involved, truly a communal celebration.

Erev Hanukkah 5690 fell on December 26, 1929—a Thursday. Lilo recalls that "a talented musical family in Göppingen wrote plays and musical skits for us. Every year Jewish children rehearsed for six weeks for a Hanukkah show. I see those rehearsals in front of me when I rehearse my own dance students."[153] The skits were written by the Rohrbacher family, and the dedication was indeed wholehearted. What commitment—to practice for one production for six weeks! Indeed, the *Israelitisches Wochenblatt* of December 1, 1929 announced that "practice was well underway," noting that there will be the premiere of a fairytale "which has been written by one of the youngest girls in our community."[154] At 5 P.M. the Jüdische Jugendbund (Jewish Youth Group) Göppingen led the community in the celebration of Hanukkah with a lively program of traditional rituals as well as original pieces created by the participants at the Hotel Dettelbacher.[155]

Several types of activities made up the program—theatrical performances, singing, and dancing. Many parts of plays were sung to well-known operatic or light-opera melodies by Johann Strauss and other popular composers. The evening began with a greeting by Elisabeth Wertheimer.[156] Four boys, Rolf Heimann,[157] Hugo Lang, age six,[158] Erich Rosenthal,[159] and Kurt Wassermann,[160] lit the Hanukkah candles. This ritual was followed by the singing of the Hanukkah hymn, "Mao Zur" (Rock of Ages), which presumably was sung by all present. One play, focusing on the traditional Hanukkah *dreidl* (spinning top) game, followed the candle lighting. Participants included older children—Alfred Srodek[161] who played the father; Ilse Tänzer, age twelve,[162] as the mother; the children Jacob and Rachel were played by Rolf Gutmann[163] and by Erna Oppenheimer, age twelve.[164] Richard Dörzbacher[165] was a magician. Four other children represented the different aspects of the game: the loser in the game was played by Manfred Lang, age eight;[166] Sidney Rosenthal was the winner of the pot,[167] Rolf Heimann was awarded half the pot; and Erich Banemann[168] replenished the stakes.

Several more plays, written by participants, followed. One play focused on the Hanukkah lights and the *shammes* (the helper candle used to light the other eight candles). Participants included Poldi Guggenheim, z"l, Lilo's brother; Rolf Gutmann, David Kuttner,[169] Erich Levi,[170] Lothar Oppenheimer, brother of Selma and Erna; and Erich Ottenheimer, cousin of Werner.[171] The theme of another skit was a day in court. Here the participants included Erich Levi, Walter Böhm,[172] and Arnold Fleischer.[173] A puppet dance was performed by Erika Ries,[174] Elfriede Salinger,[175] Elsa Srodek, age twelve,[176] and Selma Zitter, age twelve.[177] A play about wicked boys included Poldi Guggenheim, Erich Levi, Lothar Oppenheimer, brother of Erna; Erich Ottenheimer, and Sidney Rosenthal; the dancing girls included Ilse Böhm,[178] Margot Krämer,[179] Ella Petrikowsky (Piotrkowsky),[180] Liese Rohrbacher,[181] Ilse Tänzer, and Frida Zitter.[182]

The high point of the evening was a play, entitled, "Prinzes[s] Vergissmeinnichts Hochzeit" (the Wedding of Princess Forget-me-not). The picture that has survived is of this production.[183] The play, whose text is lost, was written by one of the older girls, Liese Rohrbacher (age fifteen), and directed by her sister-in-law, Trude Lendt Rohrbacher. In the play, Lilo Guggenheim[184] plays a flower along with her friends Anne Bernheimer;[185] Doris Fleischer, sister of Arnold; Erika Veit,[186] and Inge and Henny Lang,[187] both from Süssen. Presiding over the event is the queen, Elfriede Salinger. And the happy couple, Princess Forget-me-not and Prince Butterfly, is played by Beate Bernheimer, sister of Anne, and Manfred Rosenthal, younger brother of Sidney, respectively. The pages at court are Helga Freudenberger[188] and Lore Ottenheimer.[189] Dwarfs are played by Erich Banemann; Hugo Lang, age six, from Süssen; Kurt Oppenheimer,[190] and Kurt Wassermann. Erika Ries plays a lady-in-waiting. Important officials are Minister Schneck, a court official played by Erich Rosenthal, and Pastor Engerling,[191] played by Walter Böhm.

While the 1929 Hanukkah program concludes with a universal custom, gift giving, traditionally this would be in the form of Hanukkah *gelt* (money). As the date for Hanukkah is close to Christmas, in this play, a *Glücksack* (sack of goodies) for the children is reminiscent of Santa Claus or, in the German tradition, his helper *Knecht Ruprecht*. A review in the *Israelitisches Wochenblatt zu Göppingen* of January 16, 1930, praised the harmonious flow of the evening. Frau Dr. Steiner received kudos for her work with the children, as did Frau Trude Rohrbacher. Ilse Rohrbacher, "a fifteen-year-old girl from our community," who wrote the play "Prinzes[s] Vergissmeinnichts Hochzeit," a play in three acts written in verse form, received highest praise for her masterpiece.[192]

This Hanukkah program and the pictures and texts of other events that have survived reveal a lot about the Göppingen Jewish community. After studying the different elements, one can come to the conclusion that the German-Jewish symbiosis, so celebrated by Martin Buber, worked quite well in Göppingen. Although the Germanization of the Göppingen Jews was near complete in some instances, there were also clear markers that this was acculturation and not assimilation—a celebration of Germanness, though not of Christianity, and continuing pride in the Jewish heritage. Just as the Göppingen Jews drew the line with Christianity, so the Christians welcomed Jewish integration only to a point.

The 1929 Hanukkah celebration included the usual conventions—lighting of the candles, the traditional hymn of "Mao Zur," and a version of the *dreidl* game. Yet the wedding play showcases royalty, an unattainable status for Jews in Germany, and the representation of flowers and gnomes introduces favorite German children's motifs. *Latkes* (potato pancakes), eaten widely in American Jewish families for Hanukkah, were not part of the German Hanukkah celebration in Lilo Guggenheim Levine's youth.[193] Magicians were a favorite component of Jewish children's events, as they still are, but the *Kasperles Theater* (puppet theatre) was more at home in the German tradition. Similarly, the "Dancing Girls" and "Wicked Boys" echo German children's characters, such as Max und Moritz, who are called *böse Buben* (bad boys) in Wilhelm Busch's book of the same name.[194] Although the wedding play is mixed by gender, several of the program numbers are for either boys or girls. Gender separation was not only a traditional Jewish convention, but a German one as well. Even after 1945, German elementary school classes were still separated by gender.

With Jews and Christians meeting in their everyday activities, some intermarriage followed. Although the statistics seem inconsequential to us today, as the American intermarriage rate has exceeded 50 percent, Rabbi Tänzer was nevertheless concerned that intermarriage was not good for the Jews. According to the statistics he cites in his article on mixed marriage, the number of mixed marriages in Württemberg between 1901–9 never exceeded twelve per year, compared to eighty-three Jewish marriages in 1908.[195] Until after 1933, these families often chose not to be part of the Jewish community, they stressed their Germanness. When they were increasingly excluded from German society by the Nazis, they rejoined their fellow Jews for social activities.

At the height of the Göppingen Jewish community's existence in 1900, there were 324 Jewish residents, or 1.7 percent, of a population of 19,384.[196] Some happened to migrate to larger cities or abroad before the Nazis came to power, but the majority of Göppingen Jews did not leave quickly enough to escape persecution. They felt relatively secure in this city.

Few Göppingen Jews were Zionists, as were few German Jews in general. It was only relatively late that there was some enthusiasm on the part of a few individuals, such as the Siegfried Rohrbachers, for the ancient homeland Eretz Israel. In spite of Rabbi Tänzer's support for Zionist activities late in his life, he hung on to his love for things German, even when his attachment was trampled with Nazi boots.

### Göppingen under the Nazis

Although the region was rich in factories that produced everything from textiles to fertilizer, Göppingen was not a mecca for workers. The 1920s were characterized by labor strikes and a rise in organized hooliganism. Nazism was embraced early and easily in Göppingen as well as Geislingen, and with Süssen not lagging behind. The sense of security that most Göppingen Jews had enjoyed quickly dissipated with the rise of Nazism. In 1932 voter figures in the area came in at over 40 percent for the NSDAP.[197] Dr. Ruess wrote about the Nazi boycott of Jewish businesses on Saturday, April 1, 1933.[198] "The Jewish businesses were marked with a black sign with a yellow dot; and flyers with the slogan, 'The Jews are our misfortune,' were pasted on shop windows, calling shoppers to observe the boycott. Armed SA [Brown Shirts] and SS [Black Shirts] men stood in front of store entrances, so that the storeowners had no choice but to keep their businesses closed. There [also] were isolated protests [against the closures]."[199] Nazis guarded the entrance to Eugen Bernheimer's tobacco store at 4 Markstrasse, so that no customers could enter.[200] From this time forward the Nazis again and again physically attacked and verbally abused members of the Göppingen Jewish community, so that the message became abundantly clear. Of the 352 Jews who lived in Göppingen in 1933, 207 emigrated to other countries, mostly the United States.[201] At that time they were still able to sell their property for a fair price and take their belongings with them.

In 1934 most of the Jewish businesses mentioned previously were still intact, but by the end of 1938 all of these businesses as well as additional ones were Aryanized. Newspaper articles boldly broadcast the takeover and new ownership. Julius Guggenheim's textile store, Einstein & Guggenheim, came under new ownership as early as May 1937, when the family decided that life would be safer in Stuttgart. The headline in the Göppingen newspaper reads, "One Jewish Business Less."[202] Julius Guggenheim's other store, Wohlwert, was Aryanized after Kristallnacht in December 1938. The new owner, Helmut Degenkolb, advertised just in time to get all the Christmas business.[203] The best-known department store in Göppingen, Kaufhaus Lendt, was also Aryanized after Kristallnacht. An article in the *Hohenstaufen* (*Göppinger Zeitung*) trumpets the news, "The Last Large Jewish Business Has Disappeared," and tells the population that "they now can breathe easier [because] the Jewish names have completely disappeared from the business area of our city."[204] An advertisement dated December 7, 1938, announces the reopening of the store under the name Krayl & Theile, assuring the customers that "the path is open" to "German" shopping. "With the transfer of the department store Georg Lendt into

German hands the population has once more access to a large and good store."[205]

Kristallnacht, the night of broken glass, which occurred on November 9–10, 1938, was one of unspeakable terror in Göppingen. The synagogue was set on fire and burned to the ground by an organized pogrom carried out by members of the Geislingen Brown Shirts. Writes Dr. Ruess, "In the meantime the Geislingen SA group had carried out their orders. Around 2 A.M. the arsonists had forced entry into the synagogue, deposited the straw that they had brought along, and then poured gasoline on it as well as on the rolled-up carpets. The synagogue burned completely to the ground, the copper-coated cupola crashed into the synagogue interior, [only] the blackened brick walls remained standing."[206] The fire engine, housed next door to the synagogue on Freihofstrasse, was allowed to protect only the neighboring buildings, but not assist with the synagogue. Hugo Lang's former classmate [Walter Sauter], who went to school in Göppingen, remembered that he and his "brothers, sisters, and cousins were late for school the next morning," November 10, 1938, because on their way to school they stopped and watched the synagogue building burn.[207] The group of Brown Shirts also damaged Jewish businesses. After burning the synagogue, "they smashed the windows and destroyed the displays in the department store Georg Lendt in the Untere Marktstrasse, at the Hotel Dettelbacher near the railroad station they demolished the entrance and sections of the dining room."[208] Jewish citizens were likewise harassed and abused. An eyewitness recounted,

On November 9, 1938, about 4:00 A.M. [November 10] I was walking to the railroad station via Gartenstrasse. When I reached the inn "Zum Bock" I heard someone calling for help. I wanted to continue along Betzstrasse, but a man came towards me holding a pistol and yelling at me, "Go back!" Thereupon I went again via Gartenstrasse to Schützenstrasse and entered Geislinger Strasse from there. There I met the former owner of the inn "Kohlesbeck," Mr. Straub. We both watched as that man wildly fired into the property of the Jew Dörzbacher. Dörzbacher, barefoot and in his nightshirt, crawled out of his garden and ran along the street in the direction of the railroad station, screaming the entire time. The man [with the pistol] again came towards us and told us to leave. . . .[209]

The perpetrators were not prosecuted until 1948, when it was discovered that one perpetrator had already been tried and sentenced for his participation in the arson of the Buchau synagogue. This information helped to get the prosecution of fifteen individuals in the fire of the Göppingen synagogue under way.[210]

During and after Kristallnacht the Göppingen police arrested all male Jews between the ages of sixteen and sixty-five,[211] thirty-four total, twenty-seven of whom were sent to Dachau.[212] Some were first taken to the *Bahnhof*, where they were detained, while others were held at the Hotel Dettelbacher.[213] From there they were shipped to the Dachau concentration camp for about four weeks, as was the case with Louis and Leopold Lang from Süssen. The Jewish community had to pay the city RM 3,858 for the clean-up of the synagogue ruins.[214] Needless to say, these actions sent a clear message to the Jewish population. However, as in other places, emigration options were limited. With no country except the Dominican Republic taking in European Jews in sizeable numbers, there was no place to go. One hundred and forty three Göppingen Jews managed to emigrate between Kristallnacht and the beginning of World War II on September 1, 1939. Yet even if there was a chance to get out—because the victims had applied for visas—as was the case with Berta Tänzer,[215] or Luise Ottenheimer,[216] the wheels of the bureaucracy turned too slowly to be of use to all but a few. Most, in the end, shared the fate of Luise and Berta—deportation and death.

Fortunately, Rabbi Tänzer died a natural death before the Nazi harassment affected him directly. His second wife, Berta, was not so fortunate. After vacating her home in Göppingen so that the new rabbi could move in, Berta moved to the Jewish old-age home Wilhelmsruhe in Heilbronn-Sontheim where her sister Emilie also lived. Wilhelmsruhe had been built in 1907,[217] with financial support also from the Jebenhausen Jews. In a letter dated Göppingen, December 10, 1937 she writes to her son Erwin, "It is accomplished! . . . Here I am in my home in Sontheim. . . ."[218] In a poem, dated January 31, 1938, so just a month after she arrived, she describes her new life in a Jewish old-age home to Erwin. ". . . How would it be if I told you what my days are like." Her description shows the comfort, even elegance of her new home, which is enhanced by the presence of her sister. Her account also reveals that the home is religious, as meals are concluded with the traditional prayer after meals (*mesumen benschen*, in Hebrew *Birkat HaMazon*). She describes the beginning of Shabbat. "Shabbat is welcomed with the hymn L'cha Dodi and kiddush wine. The table is set festively. As is customary, only the best is served." Their pastime is spent listening to the radio, knitting and crocheting, and playing bridge.

For diversion, Berta and her sister take the bus to town to go shopping.[219] When the home was confiscated by the Nazis in 1940 and had to be vacated, Berta Tänzer and her sister found refuge with her brother Max, a former Heilbronn businessman. Still in 1940 she writes to her son Erwin, "So that you don't worry I want to let you know that Aunt Emilie and I are with Uncle Max in Heilbronn since Monday, November 18 [1940], together we have a room upstairs. . . . The other 160 people have been privately housed, with different people, in different places."[220]

But the "peace and quiet" Berta yearned for in 1940 was not to be.[221] In 1942 all three were sent to a collection camp in Haigerloch. This was very late in the process, as the major deportations occurred in November 1941 and April 1942. On August 3, 1942, Berta Tänzer wrote a cryptic message to her daughter Ilse through the International Red Cross. "Moved to Haigerloch 234 in March [1942]. We are well and together. Congratulations to August, 18. With much love, Mother, Emilie, Max, Hermine. Kisses, Mutter."[222] From Haigerloch they were deported to Theresienstadt, probably with the last German transport, in August of 1942. On June 17, 1943, Berta Tänzer wrote to Frau Witwe Kozak in Vienna that her address was Theresienstadt 808. This was her last communication. The message reads, "Dear Family, I am happy to be able to write to you and hope that you are well. I have been sick, but am, thank God, better. I hope to soon receive good news from you. Give my best regards to the brothers and sisters, and best wishes to you. Berta." As a postscript she wrote, "Letters and packages arrive in a timely manner." On the face of the postcard, whose post office stamp announces, "The homeland gives assistance," she wrote in the bottom left corner, "Baking goods, beans, sugar, flour, marmelade, . . . , coffee."[223] This either tells them what arrived or what she needs. On September 25, 1943, Berta Tänzer succumbed to the harsh conditions in the camp. Her brother Max wrote to Frau Trude Zohrab in Vienna on December 19, 1943. "Dear Emmy, We received your cards from August 31 on September 28 and were very happy to receive them. Unfortunately my sister was no longer able to read them, but she did receive the three packages and was overjoyed. Unfortunately I can only now let you know that my sister Berta Tänzer died on September 25." He asked the recipient to pass on the information as well as his address in Theresienstadt, and signed the card with "Aunt and Uncle Max and Hermine Strauss."[224] We have about three hundred pages of letters that Berta Tänzer wrote to her children Erwin and Ilse and Rabbi Tänzer's children by his first wife. In some of them

Mrs. Tänzer shares her concern for the survival of Jews and Judaism in Germany, a concern that was certainly justified.

As of September 1, 1941, the yellow star had to be worn by all the Württemberg Jews, in Göppingen, Kirchheim, and Süssen. The terrible end began on December 1, 1941, when forty-one Jews in Göppingen were rounded up and taken to the Schillerschule, just north of the community's second *Betsaal*. From there they were sent by train to a camp in Stuttgart, on the Killesberg fair site, where they joined many others from Württemberg, including thirteen Jews from Süssen, for a total of one thousand persons. They were loaded onto trains and sent on a days-long journey to Riga. Fourteen-year-old Richard Fleischer remembered,

> At 4 A.M. we were loaded onto railroad cars at the *Nordbahnhof* and rode three days and four nights in unheated railroad cars to Riga. We received water only twice. We were dehydrated when we arrived. When we disembarked we were treated like cattle, with beatings and yelling. Many fell on the ice and were shot. In ten minutes, twenty-eight were dead. That gave us an accurate impression. To quench our thirst we ate ice and snow. We were herded to a few old barns and sheep pens, where we remained, in ice and snow, until the end of March. Every day between eighteen and twenty-five men died in our barrack; they froze to death or died from typhoid fever, diarrhea, and frost bite.[225]

There were two more transports from Göppingen, in April and August 1942. Inge Auerbacher, whose family was forced to move from Jebenhausen into a *Judenhaus* in Göppingen, remembers,

> Finally, our turn to be deported came on August 22, 1942. There was no longer any way to avoid a transport. I was now number XIII-1–408, a person without any citizenship. We packed our meager belongings according to the very specific instructions we were given. All our money was taken from us. The police came to our apartment. Mama was told to place our keys on the dining room table. The official then said, "Now you can go!" We were herded into a school gymnasium in Göppingen and searched. . . . From Göppingen we were taken to Stuttgart, which was the main gathering place for Jews who were being transported. I was the youngest of almost twelve hundred people in the group. We were housed in a large hall at Killesberg that was usually used for flower shows. We bedded down for two days on the bare floor.[226]

Thereafter not only the city, but the entire District of Göppingen, was "free of Jews." Two Jews under special circumstances were able to remain in the city until 1945, among them Lina Munz, who became a maternal substitute to Ruth Lang when they both returned from the concentration camp in 1945. Then they, too, were sent on a pointless journey east while some concentration camps were already being liberated.

Today Göppingen is a strapping, bustling, multicultural city. One can see people from many backgrounds, with one exception. Only one elderly Jew again settled in Göppingen a number of years ago to live out his life in the city of his birth. He still lives there, and no others have joined him. Jews are absent from the tapestry of nations represented in the Staufer city, they are present only through forty recently placed *Stolpersteine* (stumbling stones), who memorialize Nazi victims including Berta Tänzer, Betty Heimann, Louis Heimann, Erich Banemann, Hedwig Banemann, Inge Banemann, Stephan Banemann, Helene Simon, Sofie Simon, Frida Oppenheimer, Simon Oppenheimer, and most recently, Lilo's mother, Pauline Guggenheim.[227]

# 11 Kirchheim unter Teck

*Kirchheim unter Teck is a fortunate combination of city and country with a special atmosphere. [Kirchheim] is a city to which one likes to return and which offers quality living.*
—Kirchheim unter Teck website[1]

On a clear day, one can see the Teck, remnants of a castle that belonged to the Duke von Teck in the Middle Ages, from anywhere within a hundred kilometers. Sticking up into the sky like a single finger, situated on a lonely butte, it is a famous and popular excursion spot in the summer and equally popular in the winter. When one goes on a hike in the Filstal, and climbs to the top of a mountain, the popular question is, "Can you see the Teck?" Although only about 12.5 miles from Göppingen and 18.6 miles from Süssen, Kirchheim feels different. The windswept hills, some of which used to be bare of vegetation except for thistles and juniper berry bushes, have filled in with lush trees. Once a landscape of solitude, of natural beauty, and of sheep, the lonely shepherds, gruff and monosyllabic, have given way to a multicultural population. Today Kirchheim is a bustling multinational town.

Unlike Süssen, Kirchheim had a Jewish presence as early as 1329, or even earlier.[2] When the fortunes of the Duke of Teck experienced a downturn, they were forced to sell off their possessions piecemeal. The city of Kirchheim was sold to the dukes of Württemberg in 1381, who soon ended Jewish life in Kirchheim, as in the rest of Württemberg, until 1898, with two minor exceptions. First, when Duke Friedrich I of Württemberg, who was less anti-Jewish than other lords, engaged the services of a court Jew in 1598, the guilds caused such an uproar over the Jewish presence in Stuttgart that the duke decided to domicile his court Jews and entourage in the town of Neidlingen, which, although located in the Kirchheim unter Teck district, did not yet belong to Württemberg.[3] Second, Rabbi Tänzer remarks in connection with the finances of Jebenhausen that "the

Jebenhausen *kehillah* only infrequently received supplemental income from new members to the congregation or contributions from 'Israelites' in other places." Two exceptions were Friedrich Rödelsheimer from Würzburg (Bavaria) and Nathan Barbier from Hürben (Württemberg), both of whom had settled in Kirchheim in 1857 and regularly sent donations to the Jebenhausen Jewish community which they considered their synagogue.[4]

In 1898 two Jewish families moved to Kirchheim, not the first since 1381, as Kneher notes, but the first since 1857. Louis Kahn from Lowenbrücke/Saar (Prussia) established a cattle business at 12 Dettinger Strasse[5] and Albert Salmon from Merzig/Saar (Prussia) launched a men's clothing store at 3 Dettinger Strasse.[6] Soon others arrived from far and near, like the Emanuel Reutlinger family from nearby Haigerloch/Hohenzollern (Prussia), who moved to 18 Jesinger Strasse in 1899. There were new residents from Schwetz, Kulm, Graudenz, Cannstatt, Stuttgart, Haigerloch, Karlsruhe, Berwangen, Rossdorf, Trier, Heilbronn, Bodersweier bei Kehl, Kitzingen, Seeheim, Feuchtwangen, Frankfurt/Main, Buchau, Miehlen, Mönchsrot, Merzig, Colomea, Heddesheim, Freudenstadt, Tübingen, Berlin-Weissensee, and Kochendorf.[7] By 1933, about fifty-nine Jews had settled in or traveled through Kirchheim.[8] Some were born and died there, others stayed for a short time and then moved on. Like those in Göppingen and Süssen, they were horse and cattle dealers, storeowners, manufacturers, real estate agents, and insurance and advertising salesmen. Although Stuttgart was an equal distance away and Esslingen was even closer (less than 10 miles), the Jewish families of Kirchheim became part of the Jebenhausen and Göppingen Jewish communities, along with those in Süssen. Two publications on Kirchheim unter Teck, published in 1985 and 2006, include details on the local Jewish population. This chapter summarizes the relevant information on the local Jewish population since the original publications are not readily available.[9]

Jews moved to Kirchheim for the same reason they moved to Göppingen—good rail and road access, and they were generally well received in the villages and small towns of rural areas. In the twentieth century, Jewish and Christian children attended the same village elementary schools, and it was understood that Jewish children were instructed in the Jewish religion while Christian children learned the Christian catechism. Neighbors helped each other and Jews and Christians alike belonged to the same community organizations. "The Christian population was not unfriendly towards the new residents. They got used to each other, and lived in economic and social communion. The children grew up together and attended the same schools."[10] Just as there were not enough jobs in Jebenhausen and Göppingen, there were not enough jobs in Kirchheim. As a result, many sons or daughters—Jewish and non-Jewish—were forced to emigrate if they wanted to improve themselves.

Religiously, the Kirchheim Jews spanned the spectrum from traditional to liberal, as in Göppingen and other towns. The Emanuel Reutlinger family was Orthodox, according to Brigitte Kneher, the chronicler of Jewish life in Kirchheim.[11] Even the more liberal Jewish families continued to adhere to some of the religious laws such as keeping the Sabbath, keeping kosher, and observing the major holy days such as Rosh Hashanah and Yom Kippur. Christian servants and neighbors served as *shabbes goys*, as they did in all Jewish habitations. One unlikely anecdote can be found in the *Stadt Kirchheim* publication. "Frau Berta K., who in former times worked as a tailor, also in Jewish households, remembers witnessing an incident at the lunch table. The two-year-old daughter, in an unsupervised moment, took the ladle from the broth and lowered it onto the butter nearby."[12] If true, this way of "separating" meat and milk may have served as just a faint remembrance of traditional observance. A family who kept kosher would not have had butter on the same table with meat, as there is a strict temporal separation between the two.[13]

With so few Jews in Kirchheim, religious practice had to be cobbled together. According to Kurt Vollweiler, "Every second Wednesday, Rabbi Tänzer came to Kirchheim. He instructed four to six children in their religion. For this purpose we used a classroom in the *Oberrealschule* [nonacademic track high school]."[14] Like the Langs of Süssen, the Kahns and the Salmons attended synagogue in Göppingen for the High Holy Days—Rosh Hashanah and Yom Kippur.[15] Kneher concludes, "One may assume that Louis Kahn of Kirchheim [who was] of the priestly cast [cohen—Kohn—Kahn] pronounced the priestly blessing [*Birkat Cohanim*] during services in Göppingen."[16] This traditional ritual was usually not continued in progressive synagogues and the Göppingen synagogue with its organ and German sermon could be considered progressive. The Kirchheim Jews' mode of transportation to Göppingen early on is not known as there is no mention of an automobile for any of the families in contrast to the Langs in Süssen or the Ottenheimers in Göppingen, who owned an automobile in the 1920s. It is conceivable that businessmen in these remote locations did own an automobile in addition to the horse-drawn wagons in use then.

One interesting detail specifically concerns services for a loved one's *yahrzeit* (anniversary of death).[17] Ordinarily, a Jewish community holds services at the synagogue every morning and afternoon or evening so that the Mourner's Kaddish (prayer for the dead) is said as part of the service. It sounds like Kirchheim did not have daily services—for lack of a *minyan*, no doubt. When someone required a minyan for a *yahrzeit*, they gathered together for a special service in the home of the affected family, provided that they could get together the required minyan (a quorum of ten men is mentioned specifically, so that is an Orthodox practice). Services in one's home are customary for shivah, at the time of death, so this custom of having a service on the anniversary of a death in someone's home is based on the custom of sitting shivah. Communities who could not afford a house of worship held services in a private home, so the Kirchheim custom for observing *yahrzeit* was based on the older custom of having regular services in someone's home in the absence of a house of worship. We also have evidence from other Swabian towns of such a *Betsaal*—Bad Buchau and Unterlimpurg (Schwäbisch Hall) are just two. Kilian, in the publication *Kirchheim unter Teck*, notes that "later"—until 1933—"the High Holy Days were celebrated in a room of the Salmon clothes factory at 7b Schlierbacher Strasse; the attic room was equipped as a *shtiebl* [prayer room]."[18] The worshippers used a Torah scroll that the Göppingen congregation had loaned to them, as Rabbi Tänzer noted already in 1927. Burials took place in the Jewish section of the Göppingen municipal cemetery, dedicated May 4, 1903,[19] where the Jews from Süssen were also buried. The funeral procession must have been lengthy, as with horse and carriage it is a long way from Kirchheim to Göppingen, especially during the forbidding winter weather. Cemetery records document at least ten adults from Kirchheim who were buried in Göppingen before deportation in 1941.[20]

Since there were not enough Jews in Kirchheim to form separate Jewish organizations, those who were interested in a *Vereinsleben* (organizational life) needed either to travel to Göppingen (or Esslingen or Stuttgart) for Jewish activities or join the local organizations, which were populated by Christians. Kneher lists Albert Salmon, who, upon arrival in Kirchheim in 1898, joined the local Red Cross unit as well as the volunteer fire company. Son Manfred Salmon remembers, "When there was a fire, I still remember the trumpeter running through town in the middle of the night sounding the call to the hoses. Everyone in our family jumped out of bed—father, mother, sons, and even the maid, in order to dress the impatient man. [In good Swabian he called out] Bring me my pants, my fire brigade jacket, my belt, my axe, my rope, and my helmet.'" Manfred continues, "My mother held his face in both of her hands and admonished him to take good care, asking God to send him back home in good health."[21]

Sports were beloved by all. The *Turnverein* Kirchheim-Teck counted several Jewish members.[22] Manfred Salmon writes, "My father loved 'his' *Turnverein*, especially on Thursday nights, in the circle of his friends, who completely accepted him. When he became an honorary member, he was in seventh heaven."[23] Becoming a regular member, however, was beyond reach. This love for sports was shared by Kurt Vollweiler, who remembers, "From a very early age I loved sports, especially handball and soccer. From the time I was twelve years old, I belonged to the VfB Kirchheim [soccer association]."[24] Hugo Lang, who likewise loved soccer and handball, mentioned that he knew Kurt Vollweiler and his family, who also were cattle dealers. Kurt was ten years older than Hugo.

Although Rabbi Tänzer does not have a chapter on Kirchheim (and Süssen) in his book on Jebenhausen and Göppingen, he specifically lists the businesses in Kirchheim. Among them were Mechanische Kleiderfabrik GmbH Albert Salmon (clothing manufacture); Warenhaus Gebrüder Stern (department store); Warenhandlung Bernhard Bernstein (textile store); Gustav Reutlinger (parts business and travel agency); Viehhandlung (cattle dealer) Louis Kahn, Gebrüder Reutlinger (Emanuel and Jakob Reutlinger), and Moritz Vollweiler.[25]

The Kirchheim Jews, like many other Jews in Württemberg, were loyal Germans who willingly served the fatherland in World War I. Emil Salmon, Gustav Reutlinger, Sally Reutlinger, Salie (Siegbert) Reutlinger, and Moritz Vollweiler all fought for Germany and were wounded and decorated. Fortunately all returned home.[26]

According to Kneher and Kilian, at the end of 1933, twenty-nine Jewish individuals lived in Kirchheim unter Teck.[27] These were the Kahn, Salmon, Reutlinger, Bernstein, Hirsch, Vollweiler, Stern, and Schächter families.[28] As in other locales, a local Nazi chapter formed quickly. On March 31, 1933, the local Nazis made it known that they would join the war against the Jews with a boycott of Jewish businesses on April 1. "At 10 A.M. sharp on Saturday the Jews will understand on whom they [the Jews] have declared war." This notice was signed by the NSDAP Ortsgruppe Kirchheim-Teck.[29] From here to total disenfranchisement was only a short step. Kilian details the harassment of the Kirchheim Jews in some detail.[30] Ruth Vollweiler, who was two years younger than Ruth Lang in Süssen, started school in 1934. "I went to school in Kirchheim. It was difficult during the Nazi period, because I did not make any friends. Some of my classmates wrote in my *Poesiealbum* [poetry book], which I still have and which I peruse every so often."[31] In 1938 the Jewish pupils of Kirchheim were forced to leave the local elementary school and, if too young to travel by themselves to schools elsewhere, had to live in the Jewish orphanage in Esslingen. Those old enough to travel by bus attended a Jewish school in Göppingen which must have taken more than an hour each way and surely was a traumatic experience for the children involved.[32]

By 1938 the exclusion of Jews from Kirchheim was nearly complete. Businesses were Aryanized and the permits of cattle dealers were revoked. Margit Bernstein, who visited Kirchheim while on a hike in the area, remembers, "At the entrance to town there was a sign that read, 'Juden ist der Zutritt verboten' [No Jews allowed]."[33] Thereafter, those unable to emigrate were sent to Jewish old-age homes, such as the one in Haigerloch, from where they were soon deported "to the East." According to Kneher, ten Kirchheim Jews were deported. Only one of them survived the concentration camps: Julius Mayer, who subsequently lived in Stuttgart, where he died in 1954.[34] As in other rural areas with a formerly Jewish population, there are no Jews living in Kirchheim unter Teck today. But the town has researched the Nazi past and memorialized their Jewish citizens as well as three forced laborers. In front of the former Bernstein department store at 12 Max-Eyth-Strasse, two *Stolpersteine* have been embedded in the sidewalk to memorialize Hulda Bernstein, née Jutkowsky (born September 4, 1883 in Kulm)[35] and her daughter Jeanne (born July 27, 1924) and their life in Kirchheim before the Nazis brought it to a forcible end.

# 12

*Lonely and abandoned*
*You stand high up on your perch*
*Above the mountain forest,*
*Desolate tower,*
*A monument to ancient times!*
*Centuries passed you by,*
*Countless storms,*
*Powerful thunderstorms*
*And wildly gushing cloudbursts,*
*They all pounded your body:—*
*[But] you stand there on your rocky pinnacle,*
*Staunch, unperturbed,*
*A giant protruding from the past.*
—Gustav Häcker (1822–96), *Der Ödenturm* 1853[1]

The city of Geislingen, some 5.6 miles east of Süssen, is situated in a geographic cauldron surrounded by impressively high mountains that are dotted with castles. Most famous among them are the Ödenturm, a medieval watchtower, and the Helfenstein, the ruins of a castle belonging to the Counts of Helfenstein who were allied with the Imperial City of Ulm during their reign.

From 1806 until 1938, Geislingen was the capital of the Oberamt Geislingen. The district was comprised of a number of smaller entities, from former possessions of the Imperial City of Ulm such as Gross-Süssen to the local possessions of noblemen such as Donzdorf (Graf von Rechberg) and Klein-Süssen (Bubenhofen). The landscape is varied, from wildly romantic mountainous crevasses to a fertile and gently picturesque valley surrounded by rolling hills and traversed by the river Fils. In 1841 the Oberamt consisted of three cities, thirty-four villages, and numerous estates.[2] The 26,148 residents were split almost evenly along gender as well as religious lines: 11,537 residents were Lutheran, while 12,872 were Catholic.[3] There were no Jews. Most of the residents worked as businessmen, farmers, and in government service; 387 were on welfare.[4]

Geislingen, like many of these remote locales, became accessible due to the construction of the railroad in the mid-nineteenth century. The Stuttgart-Ulm line reached Geislingen in 1849. Its continuation east up the steep mountain towards Ulm was considered an engineering marvel and became known as the Geislinger Steige. The railroad enabled industrial development. Today, the most important factory in the area is the Württembergische Metallwaren Fabrik (WMF), which manufactures quality stainless steel and glass tableware that is sold worldwide. Geislingen also was the center of a regional ivory carving business, and mining was an important branch of the local economy. The last producing iron ore mine in the region, Grube Karl, was located in Geislingen.

Unfortunately, during World War II, Geislingen's zeal to participate in the war industry plunged it into the abyss of slave labor and forced labor. Early in the war, more than two thousand forced laborers from many countries, housed in ten barracks in the *Barackenstadt* at Heidenheimer Strasse in Geislingen as well as other locations in town, were conscripted to work in the various businesses in Geislingen.[5] This forced labor camp for foreign workers was established to increase production for the war effort and make up for the loss of labor from German men and women who served as soldiers in the war.[6]

In 1944 a new camp was established within the foreign labor camp "which was secured with special safety devices, barbed wire, ditches, etc."[7] A subcamp of concentration camp Natzweiler (in the Elsass) at Robert-Bosch-Strasse and Heidenheimer Strasse, for 699 Hungarian Jewish, German, and Czech women and children, the camp was in operation from July 28, 1944, to April 10, 1945.[8] Every day the prisoners marched in closed columns to twelve-hour shifts at the factory, through the deserted Talgraben to Werkstrasse, and from there past German homes on Eberhardstrasse to Gate 1 of the factory. I retraced the inmates' steps on May 1, 2007, a labor holiday in Germany, and a fitting day to remember those who were murdered through excessive work and insufficient nourishment and hygiene. There is no way the local population could not have noticed the work detail of women and girls who trudged through their streets daily for several months. Twelve inmates died of their ordeal in Geislingen; eight of them were Jewish women. Their bodies were originally dumped in a mass grave at the edge of the municipal cemetery, but were later exhumed and properly buried in the Jewish section of the Göppingen municipal cemetery.[9]

These women were supervised by German and Czech female inmates who were sent to Geislingen from Ravensbrück. Women prisoners who themselves expected to be killed often were the worst types of *kapos*—cruel and heartless. Gertrud Müller, a victim of Nazi persecution because of her anti-Fascist, pro-Communist activities, was a *kapo* in Geislingen. Arrested in 1942, she was sent to Ravensbrück with the comment "Rückkehr unerwünscht [return undesirable]." To be sent to Geislingen was her last chance to live.[10] As the Allies approached, the camp population was transferred to Allach camp near Dachau. There Mrs. Müller and the other prisoners were liberated on April 30, 1945.[11]

In 1935 the district of Geislingen had a population of 42,902, while the city of Geislingen's population was at 14,349.[12] Although Rabbi Tänzer noted a Jewish presence in Geislingen for the Middle Ages,[13] there is no landmark or even record of any kind that would support this. Neither is Geislingen known for many Jewish residents in the modern period. Renate Kümmel, in her study, located a couple, Max Weil and Helena Tannhauser, who lived in Geislingen from 1910 until 1925, when they left Germany for Barcelona, Spain.[14] From a Jewish point of view, Geislingen is seen as inconsequential by author Dorothea Abt. "Geislingen was far from the center of action concerning Jews."[15] One Jewish woman, Else Burger, was married to a Catholic man and lived in Geislingen during the Holocaust.[16] The mayor of Geislingen wrote to the Landrat in Göppingen on January 24, 1939, "According to our inquiries there lives in Geislingen a *Volljüdin* (full-blooded Jewess), namely Else Burger née Bellson, born on December 20, 1878, in Kassel. She is the wife of *Kaufmann* Willy [Willi] Burger, 66 Bahnhofstrasse. Burger and his three children are Catholic, his wife is Jewish."[17] After the Nazis began to take all radios owned by Jews, on October 2, 1939, Willi Burger wrote to the Göppingen district office concerning the confiscation of his radio. "I refer to the meeting here with police inspector D. My wife, Else née Bellson, from Kassel, is not Aryan, but I am Aryan and we have been married since 1906 (for 33 years). My wife is ill, she cannot leave the house and the radio is her only entertainment, as she loves music. The radio belongs to me, I worked hard for it and paid for it. I therefore ask the Oberamt Göppingen to let me, the owner, keep my radio." The letter is signed, "Heil Hitler! Willi Burger, Bahnhofstrasse 66 III." He also enclosed an invoice from Ernst Bickel, Altenstadt, the store where he bought the radio.[18] The response was prompt. The next day the police inspector in Geislingen wrote to the head of the district administrator in Göppingen concerning the confiscation of radios from Jews. "The husband of the Jewess Elsa Sara Burger, Aryan Willi Burger, testified upon inquiry about ownership of his radio that he bought it in 1930 from the Bickel Company. The Bickel Company confirmed this upon request. Burger was asked to document that he is the owner of the radio. He submitted the enclosed bill from the Bickel Company, and attached a request to let him keep his radio."[19] Contrary to what one might expect, the assistant judge of the district office responded on October 10 in a surprising way. "I would like to inform the husband of the Jewess Elsa Sara Burger, Willi Burger, in response to his letter of October 2, 1939, that he can keep the radio he bought until further notice. Please return the enclosed invoice to Burger."[20] It appears that Elsa and Willi survived the Holocaust, suffering some harassment but no loss of life. Renate Kümmel, in a 1994 MA thesis (published in 1995), also mentioned Else Burger. She noted that Else lived in Geislingen from 1909–56 and moved to Zurich at age 68.[21] She survived the Holocaust in Geislingen, apparently not even hiding.

The mayor's office also listed "two *Mischlinge* first degree." One was Erna Burger, single, sales person, born October 4, 1919, in Geislingen, and the daughter of Else Burger. The other was "Johanna Mathilde Bosler, née Löwi, born July 24, 1908, in Zurich. She is the wife of financial employee Isak Bosler, 5 Notzentalweg. They are both Catholic."[22] What happened to them is not known, and other researchers do not mention them at all. Kümmel also mentions a Henryk Schiffmann.[23]

Abt notes optimistically that "in spite of it all, the attitude of the citizens of this small town for this time period is to be admired. They continued to live their lives without paying much attention to the promises of National Socialism; for them their [small] personal circle was more important than big politics. They functioned within their small circle and tried to stretch this as far as possible without getting involved in grand negotiations . . . not even the party functionaries managed to turn them into more than *Volksgenossen* [comrades]."[24] In spite of this positive assessment and the author's assurance that "the Nürnberg Laws met with little understanding by most people,"[25] these were precisely the individuals who sent a group of comrades to Göppingen during Kristallnacht to terrorize Jewish citizens there, to destroy Jewish property, and to burn down the synagogue, even though Ms. Abt notes that the leader of the SS "refused to participate."[26] These would also be the good Germans who later, during the denazification process, were classified as bystanders.

In part 2 of her study, Ms. Abt conducted interviews with ordinary Geislingen citizens. Question no. 3 of the interview, "On the Jews," underscores her own attitude, which resembles *Vergangenheitsverdrängung* (repressing the past) more than *Vergangenheitsbewältigung* (dealing with the past). While several interviewees had no opinion about the Jews, others stated that "the Reichskristallnacht did not affect them directly" (Prot. no. 1, p. 41), "for members of the S.A. 'orders were orders'" (Prot. no. 2, p. 43), "about the Reichskristallnacht we only knew what we read in the newspapers," (Prot. no. 4, p. 46). Some Geislingen residents were troubled. "The Reichskristallnacht and euthanasia were upsetting" (Prot. no. 5, p. 48), "before the war there were no Jews in Geislingen. It was only during the war that a camp was established for those Jewish women who worked in the WMF. Most people felt that the Reichskristallnacht was unjust" (Prot. no. 6, p. 50), "most people felt that Jews should emigrate as they were unpopular, but they didn't condone murdering them. We did not know anything about the exterminations" (Prot. no. 7, p. 53). Some citizens indicated to Ms. Abt that an occasional Nazi objected to the Kristallnacht plan. "During the night of November 9, 1938 Herr A. was awakened by the S.A. and ordered to gather his S.S. men and travel to Göppingen with them. Herr A. resisted because 1) an S.S. leader does not take orders from a leader of the S.A., and 2) because he had nothing to do with the Jews in Göppingen, and 3) because he was responsible for his S.S. men and didn't want to involve them in something that they found unconscionable" (Prot. no. 8, p. 55). In another response, "many thought that the Reichskristallnacht was unjust. Geislingen citizens respected the S.S. leader who did not go along to Göppingen [to set the synagogue on fire]" (Prot. no. 11, p. 62).[27] As previously noted in chapter 10, after World War II ended, there was a search for and trial of some of the guilty in the case.

In 1984 the city council, "after a contentious debate," concurred that a monument in memory of the forced laborers should be established. Designed by artist Heinz Knödler from Ellwangen, the memorial is named "*Geschundener Kopf.*" The name conjures up a variety of images, but perhaps primarily the humiliation that the women had to tolerate when their hair was shorn, like that of sheep. The inscription on the memorial in Heiligenäcker Cemetery, Geislingen reads,

. . . es schwinden, es fallen, die leidenden menschen . . .
gedenke der frauen des kz-aussenlagers geislingen
28. juli 1944—10. april 1945
und aller opfer der gewalt.
Willkür und wahn nahmen ihnen würde und leben.

[The suffering persons disappear, fall . . .
remember the women of the concentration subcamp Geislingen
July 28, 1944, to April 10, 1945,
and all the victims of force.
Wantonness and madness robbed them of dignity and life.][28]

On April 10, 1995, a memorial service for the victims of Nazi terror was held in Geislingen.[29] Two hundred and fifty persons attended. The locale is an out-of-the-way cemetery in [Geislingen] Altenstadt named Friedhof Heiligenäcker. This memorial service was initiated by Martin Bauch, former mayor of Süssen. In 1989 in Süssen, he had initiated a visit by the Lang family to their former home. Interestingly, the memorial services in both Süssen and Geislingen were held towards the end of Mr. Bauch's mayoral terms. He left Süssen to become mayor in Geislingen; in Geislingen he was not reelected.

As previously noted, administratively Geislingen remained important for the citizens of Süssen such as the Lang family beyond 1933, because the state's financial control center for Süssen remained in Geislingen even as the administrative center shifted to Göppingen in 1938.

# Conclusion

*The dignity of the individual is inviolable. To value and protect the dignity of the individual is the duty of all state powers.*
*—Grundgesetz für die Bundesrepublik Deutschland,*
I. Die Grundrechte, Artikel 1.[1]

April 4, 2008—A copy of a letter from Germany to Hugo Lang arrives in the mail, accompanied by a slightly exasperated note from Hugo that someone in Germany "after sixty-seven years . . . would like to return some items [to the Lang family]." Contrary to the well-intentioned gesture, Hugo is not pleased. What is this all about? The messenger from Süssen writes to Hugo, "When the Jewish families in Süssen received the deportation order to the 'East' in November 1941, your Aunt Fanny [second wife of Louis Lang] asked the owner of the business located at . . . Bachstrasse . . . to give her some warm underwear. Since your aunt had no more money, she offered the above-mentioned vases and the carpet in exchange. These items still exist, and Mr. M. would like to return them to their former owners."[2]

An email query from Germany suggests that my working title for the book, "Suezza—No Grazing Land for Jews," might be unduly harsh. "Es war doch nicht alles schlecht [it wasn't all bad]" is the justification. "Doch, es war [Yes, it was]," is my reply. The murder of twelve members of one family forever overshadows whatever was good prior to the Holocaust.

March 4, 2008—Dr. William Berez, psychologist and child of Polish Jewish survivors, is visiting my RS/JS 386 "Voices of the Holocaust" class at the University of Tennessee to tell the students about his own family's experiences in Poland during the Holocaust and to help the students make sense of what we are studying. His story contains the account of his parents' separation when his father joins the Soviet army and his mother decides to find the partisans so they can all join up with them while her two daughters stay with the grandparents in her hometown. It is an *Aktion* that separates her forever from her beloved children, as most of the village is rounded up and murdered by the Nazis, including her two small daughters. The students are well acquainted with the *Einsatzgruppen* (special service detail) and their bloody work, and stunned by this personal encounter with a witness once removed.

March 4, 2008—At the end of a long day I open my personal mail at home. Among the envelopes is one I have been waiting for, from Germany, with newspaper clippings from an event that will remind any future visitors to Süssen of Jewish life in that village and the atrocities committed by the Nazis. I open the sweet card that accompanies the clippings, and read, *"Am Tag vor Süssen war in Göppingen ebenfalls eine Aktion.* [On the day prior to the *Aktion* in Süssen, there likewise was an *Aktion* in Göppingen.]" The word *Aktion*, used innocently by the writer in connection with the *Stolpersteine* initiative, jumps out at me, momentarily disorienting me, so that I have an image of Nazi atrocities rather than of a well-intentioned memorial event by twenty-first-century Germans for the twentieth-century victims of these atrocities.

One word, two settings—one leading to death, the other, if not to life, at least to remembrance.

As I am concluding this study, on February 16, 2008, artist Gunter Demnig placed thirteen *Stolpersteine* (stumbling blocks) into the sidewalk in front of 45 Hauptstrasse in Süssen, the *Judenhaus*, as it is still called by the local population. This number includes the Langs' *Knecht*, Falk Sahm, who was like a member of the family. The decision to commit this act of remembrance was hard wrought, as the vote in the second city council meeting on the matter was eight for, six against, with four abstentions—not exactly a vote of confidence. Long gone were the memories of Jakob, Louis, and Leopold Lang and their families when, in the late 1980s, Mayor Martin Bauch brought the memory back with an invitation to the once unwelcome survivors of the Lang family. The pejorative *Judenhaus* has become a term of endearment, and the physical evidence of the stumbling stones in front of the Lang house will forever remind those who see them of the crime that was committed here against a Jewish family. It is the mark of Cain for the city of Süssen, a distinction that is shared with many other German municipalities. But it is also a victory, a victory of morality and of humanity, which allows us to realize that "never again" is taken seriously in Süssen and other German towns; and that the dignity of the individual, any individual who passes through here, be they Muslim, Jew or Christian, or indigenous African, is indeed inviolable.

But the price for this teaching is high, because numerous families who once called this town and this area home are dispersed to all four corners of the earth. Lest one fall into the old anti-Semitic trap that Jews are meant to wander to the ends of the earth until the end of time for being complicit in the crucifixion of Jesus, there is nothing to be learned from this reality. Families were torn apart in the cruelest way by the Nazis, and rarely reunited at the end of World War II. It is a crime to brutally force individuals to give up what they have labored for, what they treasure, what they hope to bequeath to their descendants. The right to "life, liberty, and the pursuit of happiness" for Jews, Roma and Sinti, gays, Jehovah's Witnesses, and mentally and physically challenged Germans, as well as Polish civilians and Russian POWs was cruelly trampled by the Nazis. Yet, this was the least severe offense German Jews and the families in this study had to suffer. Losing hearth and home and material possessions is one thing, bad enough to be sure, but to lose one's parents, brothers, sisters, grandparents, and aunts and uncles because of a criminal regime is quite another. The familial fabric can never be restored. And as if this were not far-reaching enough, to murder individuals so that there will be no future, no new generation, is an even greater crime. Yet this is precisely what the Nazis planned. Jews were to be looked at in a museum, eradicated from among the living peoples. And the Nazis almost succeeded. With the help of millions of silent or complicit neighbors, six of the nine million Jews in Europe perished. The remaining three million will never again together inhabit the same space that had been home to them before 1933.

The full force of the tragedy of this dispersion became clear to me during the course of this study. If I wanted to spend the rest of my life chasing after descendants of the Langs and the Ottenheimers and the Tänzers and the Guggenheims who fled from Nazi Germany or survived the concentration and death camps, I could do so. There are Ottenheimers in Los Angeles, in Latin America, in Florida and many other places, and there are Langs in Israel and the United States. But one has to stop somewhere. The two visits in 2007 to Lilo Guggenheim Levine in Saranac Lake, New York, and to Werner Ottenheimer in Havana, Cuba, made me realize that it is time to stop, even though I understand that I will never be finished. Many a day the postman or an email brings a new connection and a new story, and the realities behind the stories are always absolutely grim. There is no silver lining; there is no redemption for the perpetrators. Murder is murder.

I knew little about Lilo Guggenheim Levine until the summer of 2007, even though Lilo had returned to Göppingen as early as the 1950s. After a very generous newspaper article about this study appeared in the *Stuttgarter Zeitung*, I was contacted by Lilo Levine and plans were made for a meeting. Meeting Lilo made me comprehend that the tragedy of the Holocaust is much greater than one-time displacement and loss. Survivors from Nazi Germany are forever haunted, they are forever "wandering Jews," not because of any guilt of theirs, but because of the crimes of others. Lilo lost her mother to suicide, her father to a broken heart; her way of life and culture were ruthlessly destroyed by the ideas of a madman and his accomplices. Did she ever get over her losses? It appears that way, but when I saw Lilo together with her childhood friend "Solde," picking up their respective accordions and hesitatingly pressing down the individual keys to recreate childhood melodies, I knew that the pain was only right beneath the surface, and while they both smiled, bravely, I could feel their pain and their longing for something that has been dead for seventy years, their entire adult life. The Holocaust is never over for those who were affected by the atrocities.

In Cuba there was an old man in a walk-up apartment, near yet so far from the beautiful beaches of Playas del Este. He knew nothing of the frolicking of European tourists, although one tourist from Stuttgart came to visit him every year. He could only deal with one day at a time, because of his poverty, caused by the political isolation between Cuba and the United States. He was lonely, and with nothing but time on his hands, he was tempted to wallow in the losses and horrors of the past. He remembered a princely childhood, with everything a child could wish for, a doting mother and a successful father, an older brother for a companion, a solid education, university in Switzerland, with ambitious plans to follow in his father's footsteps in the textile business. But that was then. The reality of his entire adult life bore no resemblance to his upper-class childhood. After emigrating to Cuba, he remained there, working in Cuban factories, even becoming a supervisor, and after nationalization, he participated in trade negotiations for the Cuban government with Chiang-Kai-shek's Chinese government. He married a beautiful local woman, Isabel, who preceded him in death. Looking at her picture, he whispered, "She was too good for me." His longing and loneliness were palpable, in spite of the two children and several grandchildren who live on.

And what about Werner's father? At the end of 1937 Alfred Otten-heimer sold his hard-earned business to two German Christian business-men, under the threat of Aryanization, in the hope that he could at least save himself and his family. But the relief was short-lived, and the cruel experience of giving up everything he had toiled for broke his heart. After becoming ill, he died within six months of the sale. Werner's mother, now alone, was resettled to Stuttgart, moved from family to family, until she was deported from Stuttgart to Riga in 1941, along with a thousand other Swabian Jews. It was a journey she did not survive. Werner's brother, Richard, also managed to escape, to the United States, where he died at a relatively young age. Now Werner Ottenheimer has joined his loved ones in the hereafter and his soul is finally at peace (he died on December 19, 2008).

And then there is the central person in this book, the man who so bravely handed me every single document and picture he could come up with from his family, Hugo Lang. He and his wife Inge and their daughter Evelyn and her husband Tony have been the strongest possible supporters of this project from the beginning, because Hugo realized that it would give his family life once more, something the Nazis made every attempt to snuff out. But his satisfaction at seeing his family's story in print cannot still the lasting pain over the loss of his parents, grandparents, aunts and uncles. No book and no memorials will bring them back. A heavy pall of uncertainty hangs over the account of his sister Ruth about the day their parents were taken away "to the beyond." How did his mother and father die? Did they suffer? What about the grandparents Liffmann? What was their fate in Theresienstadt? Though never spoken, these questions hang over any conversations to do with the past. The satisfaction at having the wrong put right by having the facts documented for posterity is small con-solation in the face of the loss of thirteen members of his family [includ-ing Falk Sahm, their *Knecht*]. Hugo bravely carries on, yet when I arrive with more questions, one sees how difficult it is for him to face the past once more. Seventy years after escaping from the Nazis, he still finds the memory of the Holocaust to be a nightmare.

In spring 2002, I made plans to explore a village in northern Israel, Shavei Zion, near Naharia, in order to find a link to the founders of the moshav who included some of Hugo's relatives by marriage. But terrorists blew up the train station at Naharia and 2002 was not the time to travel the country. I did not have another chance to pursue this thread until 2010. A fortunate coincidence sent an Israeli scholar from Haifa to Knoxville. Dr. Rivka Ribak and her husband Yair Gil with their three children spent the 2008–9 academic year at the University of Tennessee. When completing the manuscript in spring 2010, I contacted Rivka, asking if they had any connections in Shavei Zion. Israel is a small country, and before I departed for Israel for Passover, Rivka sent me contact information for the archive director at Shavei Zion. I called, and was told that there was a daughter of Alfred Pressburger's living in Shavei Zion, and I was given a phone number to contact Alisa. Hugo and Alisa did not know of each other. I showed her pictures of Hugo and Inge, and of the rest of the family who were murdered by the Nazis. In return, Alisa shared pictures and information of her family, including pictures of her father and mother, aunts, uncles and grandparents. Hugo is related by marriage to Alisa several times over. Alisa's given name had been Frieda in Germany. Hugo's father's half brother Jakob Lang married Fanny, Alisa's father's (Alfred Pressburger's) sister, and one of Jakob's sisters married one of Fanny's other brothers. In addition, Jakob's sister Hermine married Alfred Baer, the brother of Pauline, who married Hugo's uncle, Louis Lang (Hugo's father's brother). Hugo and Alisa were very excited to learn of each others' existence after so many years and have been in contact by telephone.

One gets a sense of the immensity of the Nazis' crimes against humanity, above and beyond the murder of twelve million human beings, when one traverses the web of displaced persons—even from just one family—who can be found on all continents. They had to find a way to somehow survive this sudden rupture in their lives, the desperate measures they had to take to escape, and the humiliation they had to endure in trying to start a new life. I agree with Martin Dean when he writes that "No amount of restitution or compensation, which in any case would be quite modest, could make up for the wrenching effects of uprooting oneself and having to make a fresh start, usually with only a fraction of the capital that had been built up over years, decades, or even generations."[3]

Although I have been teaching the Holocaust for nearly twenty years and have close friends who are survivors, nothing prepared me for the excruciating details of the Lang and Ottenheimer families' suffering during nazification, denaturalization, dispossession, emigration, deportation and murder, and then the long and unsatisfactory road of reparations. When

I began this work I was told that there were no files to research, but every year for the past decade new and more troubling records surfaced, so that the ghosts of Hugo Lang's and Werner Ottenheimer's families continued to haunt the survivors, the recorder, and all those associated with this project. To be sure, the documents are only scattered fragments, held together with the spittle of time, but a living record of a once beautiful garden nevertheless.

One gets an even better sense of the long shadow that the Nazis cast into these people's lives to this day, through the second, and now third generation of survivors. Can it ever end? Actually, it must not end. For, if we do forget, history is doomed to repeat itself. We have vowed to never forget the atrocities that the Nazis perpetrated against innocent human beings only because of their identity.

Though not related to either the Langs or the Ottenheimers, I began this study as the recorder who wanted to ensure that two Jewish families in the village of Süssen would be included in what Kugelmass and Boyarin call the "giant paper cemetery" of yizkor books.[4] Since the Langs were deported the year that I was born in Bad Cannstatt, I wanted to understand what life might have been like in this wooded grazing land that was shared by all for a few months.

My quest has taken me on many adventures, to a number of excellent archives, to wonderful collaborations and lifelong friendships, to exciting discoveries that have not yet ended, and on true treasure hunts. I found ample, at times surprising, answers to my questions about Jewish identity in rural Southern Germany. Although I shouldn't have been surprised, having read Rabbi Tänzer's writings, I was nevertheless taken aback by the strength of these families' attachment to these locales. When Werner Ottenheimer told me, "we were *lokaltreu*," I finally understood what Hugo had shown me in so many ways without verbalizing it. The rural Jews in Süssen, Göppingen, and Kirchheim had close bonds with neighbors and customers and local organizations. With some adjustments, they adopted local eating habits. They also tenaciously adhered to things Jewish, though perhaps not in the Orthodox sense, and treasured this tradition alongside the Swabian way. It was evident that these families were deeply rooted in their communities, Jewish and German. On the one hand, they contributed through traditional activities in the Jewish community, holding office and establishing endowments, celebrating holidays, especially Hanukkah and Purim, proudly observing Rosh Hashanah and Yom Kippur, and by participating in the good and welfare of the Jewish community. At the same time they proudly shared in the larger communal life of their German hometown, participating in organizations, holding elected office, contributing to the good and welfare, and in every way enhancing the quality of life wherever possible, whether through the creation of a municipal public library or a local swim club. Religion was an individual and private matter for these Swabian Jews that informed their ethical dealings in business and life, but they did not carry it on their sleeves. Christian employees were treated with utmost respect and consideration, their religious holidays were acknowledged, and German customs such as formal gift-giving on Christmas Eve were followed meticulously. This was civilized, this was cultured; it was not an abrogation of their Judaism.

No words will ever be able to express my gratitude to every single person who contributed to the success of this project. A small piece of each of their lives is woven into the fabric of this study, holding it together as an eternal testimony to humanity's inhumanity to each other, but also as an affirmation of the goodness of humanity and of the resiliency of the human spirit.

# Notes

## Acknowledgments

1. Walter Strauss, ed., *Signs of Life: Jews from Württemberg* (New York: Ktav Publishing House, Inc., 1982). In German: Walter Strauss, ed., *Lebenszeichen: Juden aus Württemberg nach 1933* (Gerlingen: Bleicher Verlag, 1982).

2. Süssen. *Ehemalige jüdische Mitbürger in Süssen. Dokumentation des Besuches vom 2.–9. Oktober 1989 in Süssen*, 1989.

3. The number of extended Lang family members who were deported from Süssen is not even clear today. We do know for sure who was murdered, so that there is a final count, but the number of individuals who were actually deported from Süssen varies according to the sources. The town chronicle lists thirteen Lang family members for November 28, 1941, while the memorial plaque in the cemetery lists fourteen individuals, twelve of them Langs. In addition, it lists Falk Sahm, the Lang's servant, who was deported earlier, and Walter Zeimann, a Jewish businessman, who also was deported earlier. A total of twelve Lang family members were murdered, plus Sahm and Zeimann, for a total of fourteen victims. If one adds Luise Ottenheimer, the total number of Jews from Süssen who were murdered by the Nazis is fifteen. Three deportees, Kurt, Siegfried, and Ruth Lang returned to Süssen in 1945.

4. Süssen, Lang *Dokumentation*, 97.

5. See "Lebendiges Bild von der Zeit vor unserer Zeit," *Süssen: Ortsportrait. Sonderveröffentlichung der NWZ*, February 18, 1995, 4.

6. "Ehrung: Bürgermedaille für Werner Runschke: Süssener Geschichte lebendig gemacht," *Neue Württembergische Zeitung*, November 25, 2006, and "Personen: Archivar Werner Runschke erhält Bürgermedaille der Stadt Süssen: Ein Fundus, den kaum jemand sieht," *Neue Württembergische Zeitung*, November 23, 2006. See Suessen website, http://www.suessen.de.

7. See "The 'Jewish Museum' in Jebenhausen," http://www.edjewnet.de/jewmuseum/jmus_en.htm.

8. See "The Veterans' Oral History Project: Interviews: Hugo Lang," http://web.utk.edu/~csws/interview.html.

**Introduction**

1. "Hohenstaufen. Ich sah ihn fern, / Er glich dem Sarge; / Ich kam ihm nah, / Rings Grabesstille; / Ich stieg hinauf, / Zwei Genien flattern / Am Abhang nieder / Ein Totenkopf, / Ein Trauermantel." Quoted in Walter Ziegler, *Von Siezun bis Süssen. Ein Streifzug durch 900 Jahre* (Süssen: Buchdruckerei Beck and Hecker, 1971), 214.

2. The region has been a virtual treasure chest of relics from ancient times. The many finds include imprints of skeletons and actual skeletons of dinosaurs, among them *Plesiosaurus brachypterygius*, see "Eislinger Saurier," *Neue Württembergische Zeitung*, July 9, 2006, sec. "Zwischen Alb und Filstal." In the fall of 2006 an exhibition was created in the town of Eislingen, just west of Süssen, by the regional archaeologist, Dr. Reinhard Rademacher, entitled "In An Ocean Before Our Time." This exhibition displayed several different types of fossils from the region and reconstructed the dinosaurs of 181 million years ago in their entirety. Exhibition brochure, "In einem Meer vor unserer Zeit: Das Jurameer vor 181 Millionen Jahren." Stadthalle Eislingen, *Südwest Presse/NWZ*, September 2–October 29, 2006.

3. K. Eisele, M. Köhle, Chr. Schöllkopf, eds., *Geschichtliche Heimatkunde des Filsgaus, mit einem geologischen Anhang* (Göppingen: Verlag von Johannes Illig, 1926), 170. See also Walter Ziegler, ed., *Der Kreis Göppingen* (Stuttgart: Konrad Theiss Verlag, GmbH, 1985), 20.

4. Ziegler, *Kreis Göppingen*, 20.

5. Ibid., 32.

6. Ibid., 43. Süssen, too, had a mineral water well for some time in the 1950s. Jebenhausen has had a continuous mineral water well since the time of the Barons of Liebenstein in the 1700s. Today only locals are allowed to harvest the water on a daily basis. Göppingen likewise owned several mineral water wells. Thermal spas abound as well, as in Bad Überkingen. The area also claims one sulphur spring, in Bad Boll, which contains many different healing properties. The source was already appreciated by Herzog Friedrich I of Württemberg (1593–1608), who had a fountain built that is still in use today. See also Paul Groschopf and Winfred Reiff, "Landschaft und Geologie," in ibid., 17–47.

7. Ziegler, *Kreis Göppingen*, 46.

8. The process of *Verkarstung* began during the Tertiary period and continued into the Quaternary period. The precondition for *Verkarstung* is the existence of appropriate natural resources such as carbon dioxide gases and water-soluble stone in the form of white Jura. While white chalkstone is not soluble in pure water alone, the situation changes when there is carbonic acid in the water. Carbon dioxide seeps into the soil with drip water which can help to widen the crevices in chalkstone. These processes are most obvious in the water flow through caves. The surface above is flat and dry as all of the water seeps through the porous rock and settles on an impenetrable surface. From there it is chan-

neled along to a flowing body of water, such as a creek, which it then helps to feed. Ziegler, *Kreis Göppingen*, 34–35.

9. Ziegler, *Kreis Göppingen*, 67–68.

10. Ibid., 68.

11. Ibid., 70.

12. Johannes Illig, *Geschichte von Göppingen und Umgebung* (Göppingen: Druck Johannes Illig, 1984), 256–57.

13. Finanzrath Moser, *Beschreibung des Oberamts Göppingen* (Stuttgart and Tübingen: Verlag der J. G. Cotta'schen Buchhandlung, 1844), 1–3.

14. Ziegler, *Kreis Göppingen*, 17. See also Kurt Wehrberger, "Das Rätsel der Steinzeit, Knöpfe," in *Südwest Magazin, Neue Württembergische Zeitung*, Saturday, July 22, 2006.

15. Aron Tänzer, *Die Geschichte der Juden in Jebenhausen und Göppingen*, ed. Karl-Heinz Ruess (Weissenhorn: Anton H. Konrad Verlag, 1988), 392.

16. Uri Kaufmann, "Jüdisches Leben auf dem Land," in *Schwäbisch Hall, In Baden-Württemberg*, vol. 48 (Karlsruhe: G. Braun Buchverlag, n.d.). See also Utz Jeggle, *Judendörfer in Württemberg* (Tübingen: Tübinger Vereinigung für Volkskunde, e.V., 1999).

17. Georg Munz and Walter Lang, *Geschichte regional*, Heft 2 (1982): 135, cited in Paul Tänzer, *Die Rechtsgeschichte der Juden in Württemberg* (Stuttgart, 1922), 2.

18. *Juden in Buttenhausen*, Münsingen Stadtarchiv (Wannweil: B. Kemmler GmbH, 1994), 15–16.

19. Karl-Heinz Ruess, *Spuren schreiben Vergangenheit* (Ebersbach an der Fils: Stadtarchiv Göppingen and Bechtel Druck GmbH, 2001), 11.

20. Gernot Römer, *Schwäbische Juden. Leben und Leistungen aus zwei Jahrhunderten in Selbstzeugnissen, Berichten und Bildern* (Augsburg: Presse-Druck-und Verlag-GmbH, 1990), 115. See also "'Der Viehjud'—Berater und Vertrauensperson" in ibid., 136–56.

21. Paul Sauer und Sonja Hosseinzadeh, *Jüdisches Leben im Wandel der Zeit* (Gerlingen: Bleicher Verlag GmbH, 2002), 23.

22. Karl Heinz Burmeister, *Der Schwarze Tod: Die Judenverfolgungen anlässlich der Pest von 1348/49*, ed. Karl-Heinz Ruess (Ebersbach an der Fils: Jüdisches Museum Göppingen, Stadt Göppingen, Bechtel Druck GmbH, 1999), 15.

23. Burmeister, *Der Schwarze Tod*, 12–13. "Medinat Schwaben" is the first one at the top of p. 13.

24. Ibid., 12.

25. Helmut Walser Smith, *The Continuities of German History: Nation, Religion, and Race across the Long Nineteenth Century* (Cambridge: Cambridge University Press, 2008), 74–77.

26. Anna-Ruth Löwenbrück, "Ein langer Kampf um die Emanzipation: Die rechtliche Gleichstellung der württembergischen Juden im 19. Jahrhundert." *Momente* 1 (2003): 26–31.

27. Aron Tänzer, *Die Geschichte der Juden in Württemberg* (Frankfurt a. M.: Verlag Weidlich, 1937/1983), 2.

28. Ibid., 2.

29. Ibid.

30. Sauer and Hosseinzadeh, *Jüdisches Leben*, 23.

31. Ibid., 23.

32. Tänzer, *Geschichte der Juden in Württemberg*, 4.

33. Sauer and Hosseinzadeh, *Jüdisches Leben*, 24.

34. Munz and Lang, *Geschichte regional*, 2:135.

35. Ibid.

36. Sauer and Hosseinzadeh, *Jüdisches Leben*, 25.

37. Ibid.

38. Ibid., 26. Thanks to Michael Booker for his help with the term "gibbet."

39. Munz and Lang, *Geschichte regional*, 2:136.

40. In Eppingen in 1765, the annual protective tariff varied from thirty gulden per person to zero. Ralph Bischoff and Reinhard Hauke, eds., *Der jüdische Friedhof in Eppingen: Eine Dokumentation*. Rund um den Ottilienberg, vol. 5 (Eppingen: Pentadruck, 1996), 11. In Jebenhausen the annual *Schutz* tariff was twelve florin. Tänzer, *Juden in Jebenhausen und Göppingen*, 18. In Buttenhausen for adults twelve gulden per year. *Juden in Buttenhausen*, 30. In 1805 in Haigerloch sixteen gulden annually. Karl Werner Steim, *Juden in Haigerloch* (Haigerloch: Druckerei ST Elser, n.d.), 13. In Baisingen fifteen gulden per person. Karlheinz Geppert, *Jüdisches Baisingen* (Haigerloch: Verlag Medien und Dialog Klaus Schubert, 2000), 8. And in Bad Buchau twelve florin *Schutzgeld*. Joseph Mohn, *Der Leidensweg unter dem Hakenkreuz* (Bad Buchau: Vereinigte Buchdruckereien A. Sandmaier & Sohn, 1970), 37.

41. Munz and Lang, *Geschichte regional*, 2:135–36. One gulden or florin equaled sixty kreuzer. A kreuzer bought a pound of bread, and a gulden a pound of butter. A bricklayer in 1750 earned about thirty kreuzer a day. A *meile* is 7.4 kilometers or 4.6 miles.

42. F. F. Mayer, *Sammlung der württembergischen Gesetze in Betreff der Israeliten* (Tübingen: Verlag und Druck von Ludwig Friedrich Fues, 1847), 4.

43. Mayer, *Sammlung der württembergischen Gesetze*, 4.

44. Theobald Nebel, *Die Geschichte der Freudentaler Juden* (Ludwigsburg: Historische Verein für Stadt und Kreis Ludwigsburg e.V. and Kreis Ludwigsburg e.V. and Süddeutsche Verlagsanstalt and Druckerei GmbH, 1985), 13.

45. Sylvester Lechner, ed., *Synagoge Ichenhausen* (Günzburg: Appel-Druck Donau-Verlag GmbH, 1987), 18.

46. Susanne Wetterich, *Davids Stern an Rhein und Neckar* (Stuttgart: Silberburg Verlag, 1990), 85 (Rexingen); and Geppert, *Jüdisches Baisingen*, 8.

47. See Munz and Lang, *Geschichte regional*, 2:135.

48. Baisingen was a *reichsritterschaftliches Dorf* and belonged to the *Schenken* (cup-bearer) of Stauffenberg; Laupheim to the *Reichsfreiherren* of Welden; Ichenhausen belonged to the *Markgrafschaft* Buchau and was *reichsunmittelbar*; Hechingen belonged to the Hechingen *Fürsten von Hohenzollern*, and so forth.

49. Sylvester, *Synagoge Ichenhausen*, 18.

50. Tänzer, *Juden in Württemberg*, 8–9. See also Sauer and Hosseinzadeh, *Jüdisches Leben*, 29.

51. Tänzer, *Juden in Württemberg*, 10.

52. Sauer and Hosseinzadeh, *Jüdisches Leben*, 30

53. Tänzer, *Juden in Württemberg*, 10.

54. Stefan Rohrbacher, Die *jüdische Landgemeinde im Umbruch der Zeit*. Traditionelle Lebensform, Wandel und Kontinuität im 19. Jahrhundert. Stadt Göppingen. (Ebersbach an der Fils: Bechtel Druck GmbH), 5.

55. Tänzer, *Juden in Württemberg*, 15.

56. Ibid., 10–11.

57. Ibid., 11–12.

58. Sauer and Hosseinzadeh, *Jüdisches Leben*, 30.

59. Tänzer, *Juden in Württemberg*, 13.

60. Ibid.

61. Dieter Kauss, *Juden in Jebenhausen und Göppingen 1777–1945*. Exhibition Catalog, 1981. Veröffentlichungen des Stadtarchivs Göppingen, vol. 16 (Stadtarchiv Göppingen, 1981), 8.

62. Tänzer, *Juden in Württemberg*, 13–14.

63. Munz and Lang, *Geschichte regional*, 139. The dates for changes in individual statutes differ slightly from source to source. See also Sauer and Hosseinzadeh, *Jüdisches Leben*, 30.

64. Tänzer, *Juden in Württemberg*, 21.

65. Sauer and Hosseinzadeh, *Jüdisches Leben*, 31. See also Smith, *Continuities of German History*, 109–14, on the difficulties of Jewish integration.

66. Sauer and Hosseinzadeh, *Jüdisches Leben*, 31.

67. Ibid., 32.

68. Ibid., 33.

69. Kauss, *Juden in Jebenhausen und Göppingen*, 8.

70. Tänzer, *Juden in Württemberg*, 31–37.

71. See Jacob Katz, *Out of the Ghetto. The Social Background of Jewish Emancipation, 1770–1870* (Syracuse: Syracuse University Press, 1973), 197; and Isaac Marcus Jost, *Neuere Geschichte I*, 78–93 and 158–177 (cited in Katz, *Ghetto*, 256). See also Jacob Katz, *Jewish Emancipation and Self-Emancipation* (New York/Philadelphia/Jerusalem: The Jewish Publication Society, 1986).

72. Sauer and Hosseinzadeh, *Jüdisches Leben*, 34. Also Tänzer, *Juden in Württemberg*, 37.

73. Ibid.

74. Tänzer, *Juden in Württemberg*, 37.

75. Rohrbacher, *Die jüdische Landgemeinde*, 4.

76. Munz and Lang, *Geschichte regional*, 2:139. Also Tänzer, *Juden in Württemberg*, 33.

77. Tänzer, *Juden in Württemberg*, 35.

78. "Erlass des Ministeriums des Innern an die Regierung des N[eckar].-Kreises, betreff den Viehhandel der Israeliten," January 4, 1936, in Mayer, *Sammlung der württembergischen Gesetze*, 111–12.

79. Sauer and Hosseinzadeh, *Jüdisches Leben*, 32.

80. Tänzer, *Juden in Württemberg*, 38.

81. Ibid., 60.

82. It was no longer possible for a village Jew to gain favor with a ruler as he no longer had direct access.

83. Tänzer, *Juden in Württemberg*, 38.

84. Ibid., 54.

85. Ibid.

86. Ibid., 56.

87. Ibid., 60.

88. Ibid. There is a list of all thirteen Rabbinic Districts and their communities, 61–62. These again shifted and changed almost immediately.

89. Ibid., 62.

90. Ibid., 78.

91. Ibid., 76.

92. Ibid., 78.

93. Ibid., 79.

94. The eleven schools were in Mühringen, Nordstetten, Esslingen, Pflaumloch, Laupheim, Jebenhausen (1824), Buttenhausen, Baisingen, Oberdorf, Buchau and Hochberg. A. Tänzer, *Geschichte der Juden in Württemberg*, 82. David Sorkin, *The Transformation of German Jewry 1780–1840* (Oxford: Oxford University Press, 1987), 130. For comparison, see also Reinhard Rürup, "Die Emanzipation der Juden in Baden," in *Emanzipation und Antisemitismus: Studie zur "Judenfrage" der bürgerlichen Gesellschaft* (Göttingen: Vandernhoeck & Ruprecht, 1975), 54.

95. Tänzer, *Juden in Württemberg*, 83.

96. Ibid.

97. Tänzer, *Juden in Jebenhausen und Göppingen*, 180.

98. Ibid.

99. Tänzer, *Juden in Württemberg*, 83.

100. Ibid., 84.

101. Ibid., 57.

102. Casimir Bumiller, *Juden in Hechingen* (Hechingen: Initiative Hechinger Synagoge e.V. and Verein Alte Synagoge e.V. and Verlag Glückler, n.d.), 41.

103. Nachum T. Gidal, *Jews in Germany from Roman Times to the Weimar Republic* (Cologne: Könemann Verlagsgesellschaft mbH, 1988), 168–70.

104. See Jack Kugelmass and Jonathan Boyarin, eds. and trans., *From a Ruined Garden. The Memorial Books of Polish Jewry*. 2nd expanded edition (Bloomington: Indiana University Press, 1998); and Omer Bartov, *Erased: Vanishing Traces of Jewish Galicia in Present-day Ukraine* (Princeton: Princeton University Press, 2007).

105. The scholar who is credited with creating the category of *Landjudentum* is Monika Richarz. See "Die Entdeckung der Landjuden. Stand und Problem ihrer Erforschung am Beispiel Südwestdeutschlands," in *Landjuden im süddeutschen- und Bodenseeraum* (Dornbirn: Vorarlberger Verlagsanstalt, 1992).

106. Laura Levitt, *American Jewish Loss After the Holocaust* (New York/London: New York University Press, 2007), 38–84.

## 1. Post-Nazi Süssen: An Attempt at Reconciliation

1. See "Der historische Marktbrunnen zu Süssen," *Stadt Süssen Information*, new edition, 2001, 2–4; also in Gemeinde Süssen, "Der neue Marktbrunnen auf dem neugestalteten Rathausvorplatz, eingeweiht am 12. September 1981." In the brochure for the dedication of the fountain fifteen scenes are depicted. The new edition of the *Stadt Süssen Information* (2001) only depicts thirteen. The fifteen scenes depicted reflect events in 1071 (1), 1267 (2), 1493 (3), 1531 (4), 1552 (5), 1596–1648 (2) (6 and 7), 1806 (8), 1847 (2) (9 and 10), 1933 (11), 1933–45 (12), 1945–58 (13), 1981 (14), and current Süssen emblem (15). The 1981 description of a new beginning with the erection of the fountain corresponds to Scene 14.

2. Süssen, *Ehemalige jüdische Mitbürger in Süssen. Dokumentation des Besuches vom 2.–9. Oktober 1989 in Süssen*, 66. Hereafter cited as Lang *Dokumentation*.

3. Süssen, Volkshochschule, *50 Jahre Süssen. Süssen in der Anfangszeit von 1933 bis 1945* (Süssen, 1983). For more details on the history of Süssen see chapter 2 in this book.

4. "50 Jahre Gemeinde Süssen," *Neue Württembergische Zeitung*, July 1, 1983.

5. Collection Hugo Lang. Bauch correspondence with Ruth Lang.

6. Bauch speech on the occasion of the *Volkstrauertag* (National Day of Mourning), November 13, 1988. Lang *Dokumentation*, 54.

7. Ibid., 57. In his speech, the mayor didn't have all of the historical facts. He wrongly claimed that Eva Lang, Hugo's mother, is not on the memorial plaque for the war dead in the Stiegelwiesen cemetery; he correctly noted that Hugo's cousins Hans and Siegfried Baer are not on the plaque, but failed mention their brother, Werner, who is also memorialized on the plaque; and he claimed that Falk Sahm was killed in the concentration camp of Minsk, when he was in fact brutally murdered in Maly-Trostinec, near Minsk. While he mentioned Ruth and Siegfried Lang as survivors, he omitted Kurt Lang, Hugo's cousin, who was the

terror of the post-Holocaust period for Süssen Nazis, traveling the region with an American Army escort to reclaim his family's property. None of these inaccuracies are surprising, as the research at that time was incomplete—the information concerning reparations was considered "lost" at the time because Süssen's mayor of twenty-five years, August Eisele, had the reparations file locked away. During my first research trip in 1999—four years after Eisele's death—the reparations file miraculously appeared. Also mentioned in Mayor Bauch's speech, though not by name, are two euthanasia victims from Süssen whose names are not known publicly and who are not memorialized anywhere. According to local rumors, there were three victims. It will be up to the city administration of Süssen to also document and memorialize the fate of these unfortunate individuals.

8. Some time after the visit the regional newspaper noted that Mayor Bauch at the end of his tenure as mayor of Süssen contacted the former Jewish citizens of Süssen. This is not correct, for Ruth took the first step. One could imagine, though, in light of his comments in the speech for the Volkstrauertrag in 1988, that this would not have been a step he would have undertaken before 1989, for as he stated in his speech, the citizens of Süssen simply weren't ready to face their victims. And, conceivably, it might have hurt his political career. Collection Hugo Lang. "Begegnung dokumentiert." No name or date on newspaper clipping.

9. Süssen, Lang *Dokumentation*, 4.

10. Häfele was *Gemeindepfleger* (municipal treasurer).

11. Göppingen District Archive, A 2163, List of Holocaust and World War II dead. Courtesy of Frau Hofacker.

12. In a letter in which she thanked Herr Bauch for the invitation, Ruth Lang Lemberger wrote, "Dear Mr. Bauch, I received your kind invitation and thank you very much. Unfortunately I must decline as we have a business and cannot leave it. My brother [Hugo] and his family will represent us. Many thanks for your efforts. With best wishes, Ruth Lemberger." Süssen City Archive, Martin Bauch File.

13. Siegfried Lang, son of Louis, was the first to respond to Mayor Bauch's invitation. On May 24, 1989, he wrote from Florida, "Please forgive me for writing to you in English. I have not spoken German for 42 years. . . . My overall health is very, very poor. . . . Dear Mr. Bauch, please permit me to speak from the heart (the only way I know). My cardiologist advised me strongly not to return to Germany. I cannot forget the past even after 43 years. . . . My heart is in no way strong enough to take the emotional strain. I have very limited ability to walk (crutches). . . . I would like to thank you so very much for your thoughtfulness. Your letter, the things you have done in regard to 'Familie Lang Weg' and many other things. . . . Dear Martin, if I may be so frank to call you by your first name, I would like to invite you to come to the States and be my honored guest. . . ." Collection Hugo Lang.

14. It is a Jewish custom to curtail all normal activities completely for seven days, somewhat less thereafter for the remaining days of the first month, and to abstain from major celebrations for a total of eleven months. Kurt Lang, Siegfried's brother, Food Broker in Englewood Cliffs, New Jersey, responded to Mayor Bauch's invitation on May 28, 1989. "Dr. Mr. Mayor, I would like to thank you as well as the city council very much for your invitation to visit Süssen during the week of October 2–9. Unfortunately I must decline for the following reason. My son Michael died last month at age 27 after suffering from cancer for one year. I am sure you will understand that we cannot think of traveling this year as we are in deepest mourning. . . . Allow me to thank you, dear Mayor Bauch, very much for your efforts so that the persecution of the Jewish citizens of Süssen is not forgotten. I was very moved by the speech you gave on the occasion of the Volkstrauertag, a copy of which was sent with the letter of invitation." Collection Hugo Lang.

15. Süssen, Lang *Dokumentation*, 26. Henny Lang Gutenstein, Kurt and Siegfried's sister, responded with regrets, "I am sorry that I cannot participate. Thank you very much for the invitation." See Süssen City Archive, Martin Bauch File.

16. Süssen, Lang *Dokumentation*, 9.

17. Ibid., 32. For an account of the long-term effects the Holocaust has had on survivors and their children, the second generation, and the possibilities for *rapprochement*, see Lev Raphael, *My Germany* (Madison: Terrace Books/University of Wisconsin Press, 2009).

18. Süssen, Lang *Dokumentation*, 31.

19. Hugo Lang speech in Lang *Dokumentation*, 33.

20. Collection Hugo Lang, "Jahrgang 1922/23."

21. Hugo Lang speech in Lang *Dokumentation*, 32.

22. Süssen City Archive, Martin Bauch File.

23. Ibid.

24. *Süssener Mitteilungen*, October 12, 1989, in Süssen, Lang *Dokumentation, 40.*

25. Süssen City Archive, Martin Bauch File.

26. Ibid.

27. During a research stay in Süssen in 2006, a little notebook was shown to the author that had the name "Ruth Lang" on the cover, in Ruth's handwriting. It was being used as a recipe book. When I asked how it had come into the possession of the current owner, I was told that the owner had gotten it from her grandmother.

28. *Süssener Informationen*, no. 41, October 15, 1989, front page. Courtesy of Hugo Lang.

29. Müller, *1896–1996: Sozialdemokraten in Süssen*, 186.

30. Collection Hugo Lang, dated January 23, 1991. In 1999 Mayor Karrer strongly supported my plan to document the story of the Süssen Jews.

31. For example, Werner Baer is missing from the original list, though not from the plaque. They were asking whether Fanny Lang died a natural death. It may have been confusing because Louis's second wife, who was deported, was also named Fanny, like Jakob's wife, who emigrated to the United States. The municipality asked Hugo to confirm that Fanny was deported.

32. See announcements in *Süssener Mitteilungen* 36, no. 29, July 25, 1991, front page; also *Süssener Informationen*, no. 30, July 26, 1991, front page. Courtesy of Hugo Lang.

33. Collection Hugo Lang. Walter Lang letter dated November 16, 1992. Inge Auerbacher, *I am a Star: Child of the Holocaust* (New York: Puffin Books, 1993).

34. *Süssener Mitteilungen* 36, no. 30, August 15, 1991, front page. Courtesy of Hugo Lang. Alas, even this report contains a factual error. Louis Lang was not Hugo Lang's brother, but his father's brother, hence Hugo's uncle.

35. Süssen City Archive, Martin Bauch File. Card from Hugo to Mayor Karrer dated August 8, 1991.

36. Collection Hugo Lang. Rolf Karrer letter dated July 4, 1995. City status was achieved on July 1, 1996.

37. Süssen City Archive, Martin Bauch File. Letter from Hugo Lang to Mayor Karrer dated July 10, 1991.

## 2. A Village Called Süssen

1. Johann Georg Fischer cited in "Ein historischer Rundgang durch Süssen," in *100 Jahre Süssener Bank 1886–1986* (Süssen: Beck-Druck, 1986), 39. The full poem reads: Farewell Once More // I wish to rush from my home / For it is no longer such! / Alien and oppressed I feel here / Never again will I return. // Unrecognized I reach the last house / And here I stand before the vast valley; / Oh yes, here I sang for the first time / At a funeral. // And then I encounter the mill / (Is the roof already covered with gray moss?) / Which my father erected, / Where he spoke the blessing. // Dear mill, if only the farmer who owned you, / Would have lasted as long as you did! / But look!—There is the cemetery, / There he rests among the deceased. // If only the gate would not be locked! / (Mother dear, you, too, are resting here!) / Dearest loved ones! Your son must take leave, / Dear souls, don't forget him! // I want to stop and see the garden once more, / (There we can still see evidence of your diligence) / Dear parents! A stranger / Harshly forbids entry to your son. ("Der Wiederabschied // Aus der Heimat will ich eilen, / Ist sie es doch nimmermehr! / Fremd und drückend ist mir's drinnen, / Niemals wieder komm' ich her. // Unerkannt vor'm letzten Hause / Steh' ich schon, am off'nen Tal;- / Ach! Hier war's!—bei einer Leiche / Sang ich da zum erstenmal. // Da begegn' ich noch der Mühle- / [Schon ein grau bemoostes Dach!] / Die mein Vater aufgerichtet, / Wo den Zimmerspruch er sprach. // Liebe Mühle, hätt' dein Bauer, / Auch so lang gedau'rt, wie du! / Aber sieh!—dort liegt der Kirchhof, / Dort hat er bei Toten Ruh'. // Wäre nicht das Tor verschlossen! — /

[Mutter, du auch ruhst wohl da!] / Teure! Euer Sohn muss scheiden, / Teure Seelen, bleibt ihm nah'! // Noch zum Garten will ich wandern, / [Dort lebt euer Fleiss noch fort] / Gute Eltern! Euerm Sohne / Wehrt's des Fremden raues Wort").

2. The castle was built around 1070 by Friedrich of Büren, who became Duke of Schwaben in 1079. The name is derived from a clan of knights who called themselves "von Staufen," first mentioned in 1171. See Bernardin Schellenberger, *Zwischen Rechberg und Staufen: Ottenbach und das Tal der Höfe*, ed. Walter Ziegler (Weissenhorn: Anton H. Konrad Verlag, 1996), 18.

3. On Siezun, Siaza, Sioza, see Ziegler, *Siezun*, 8; on Siezon and Siezzen, ibid., 14; on Siessen, ibid., 15. Also "Syesen" in Manfred Akermann, *Ein Grenzstreit im Filstal*. Stadtarchiv Göppingen, vol. 1 (Geislingen/Steige: Industrie-Druck GmbH, 1960), 10.

4. In 2006 there were about three million Muslims living in Germany. Until 1933 the Jewish population never exceeded 600,000 (in 1910), or one percent of the population. In other words, in 2006 there are five times as many Muslims living in Germany as Jews at the height of German Jewish existence. Approximately 2,000 "foreigners" live in Süssen; no figures are available on how many are Muslim.

5. For a detailed account, see Werner Runschke, "Fünfzig Jahre Heimatvertriebene in Süssen," in *Süssen: Vom Dorf zur Stadt*, eds. Walter Ziegler and Werner Runschke. Herausgegeben von der Stadt Süssen und dem Verein zur Förderung von Kunst und Kultur in Süssen (Weissenhorn: Anton H. Konrad Verlag, 1996), 125–84.

6. See "Baden-Württemberg soll 'Muslimtest' beenden," accessed January 13, 2012, http://aufenthaltstitel.de/zuwg/1155.html.

7. "Ein historischer Rundgang durch Süssen," 36.

8. "Der neue Marktbrunnen zu Süssen," The 1071 description of first mention of Süssen corresponds to scene 1.

9. Ziegler, *Siezun*, 9.

10. Ibid., 14.

11. Ibid.

12. Ibid.

13. Schellenberger, *Ottenbach und das Tal der Höfe*, 23.

14. Ziegler, *Siezun*, 16. Also "Der neue Marktbrunnen zu Süssen." The 1267 description of a Gross-Süssen church gifted to Cloister Adelberg corresponds to scene 2.

15. Ziegler, *Siezun*, 15.

16. "Der neue Marktbrunnen zu Süssen," The description of the new Süssen emblem corresponds to scene 15.

17. Ziegler, *Siezun*, 21.

18. Ibid. For an excellent explanation of the medieval property system see Schellenberger, *Ottenbach und das Tal der Höfe*, 11.

19. Ziegler, *Siezun*, 23.

20. Schellenberger in *Ottenbach und das Tal der Höfe* notes that it is not possible to translate old currencies and measures into contemporary values because the economic conditions were totally different. One can at best get a sense of the value of items by comparing goods. So, for instance, in 1634 a horse was worth 40 gulden or florin. So 40 horses would have been worth 1,600 florin, or conversely, the stolen amount would have bought 125 horses. Schellenberger, 25.

21. Ziegler, *Siezun*, 29.

22. "Der neue Marktbrunnen zu Süssen." The 1493 description of a Klein-Süssen church receiving the right to hold mass corresponds to scene 3.

23. "Der neue Marktbrunnen zu Süssen." The 1531 description of Reformation corresponds to scene 4.

24. "Der neue Marktbrunnen zu Süssen." The 1552 description of pleading wives of indentured subjects corresponds to scene 5.

25. For an explanation of the Schmalkaldische Krieg see "Schmalkaldic War," accessed January 13, 2012, http://en.wikipedia.org/wiki/Schmalkaldic_War.

26. Ziegler, *Siezun*, 94.

27. "Der neue Marktbrunnen zu Süssen." 1596–1648 description of devastation from plague and military invasion corresponds to scene 6.

28. Ziegler, *Siezun*, 95.

29. Schellenberger, *Ottenbach und das Tal der Höfe*, 175.

30. See Alfred Haverkamp. ed., *Geschichte der Juden im Mittelalter von der Nordsee bis zu den Südalpen*. Kommentiertes Kartenwerk (Hannover: Verlag Hahnsche Buchhandlung, 2002). Courtesy of Dr. Ruess, Göppingen City Archive.

31. Schellenberger, *Ottenbach und das Tal der Höfe*, 176.

32. Ziegler, *Siezun*, 97.

33. See K. Eisele, M. Köhle, and Chr. Schöllkopf, eds., *Geschichtliche Heimatkunde des Filsgaus*, 94. These authors wrote in 1926 that Gross-Süssen had to come up with 500 marks.

34. Ziegler, *Siezun*, 104.

35. Ibid., 105.

36. Ibid., 114.

37. Ludwig Wilhelm earned his nickname Türkenlouis "as imperial field marshal and through his successes in the war against the Ottomans in the great Turkish war of 1683–99. Because of his red collar, which was visible across the battlefields, the Turks named him the Red King." "Louis William, Margrave of Baden-Baden," accessed January 13, 2012, http://tinyurl.com/margrave-of-baden. A red poppy is also called Papaver Türkenlouis, no doubt because of the connection between the red color of the flower and Ludwig Wilhelm's symbolic red jacket. See "Poppy 'Türkenlouis,'" accessed January 13, 2012, http://tinyurl.com/poppy-turk.

38. Ziegler, *Siezun*, 115.

39. Ibid., 126.

40. "Süssen: Stadterhebung July 13–14, 1996," *NWZ/Geislinger Zeitung,* July 10, 1996. Courtesy of Hugo Lang.

41. "Der neue Marktbrunnen zu Süssen." The 1596–1648 description of French troops who burn down two thirds of Gross-Süssen in 1707 corresponds to scene 7.

42. Ziegler, *Siezun,* 131. This curious statement has been of much interest to me, as are other statements referring to the "*Judengasse,*" identified as the *Hauptstrasse* (main street) in 1832, as there is no evidence of any kind that any Jews lived in Süssen prior to 1902. There is an even earlier reference to a "*Judenzoller,*" in 1730 on page 153 in *Siezun,* also without any further identification.

43. Ziegler, *Siezun,* 133.

44. Ibid., 158.

45. Ibid., 184.

46. *Geschichte regional,* Heft 2, 1982, 138; Ziegler, *Siezun,* 186.

47. "Der neue Marktbrunnen zu Süssen." The 1806 description of Napoleon's triumphant return through the Filstal corresponds to scene 8.

48. Stälin, *Oberamt Geislingen,* 203–4. My thanks to Werner Runschke for the information on the type of tree used to accomplish this goal.

49. Ibid., 212–13; "Ein historischer Rundgang durch Süssen," 34.

50. See Ziegler, *Siezun,* 414.

51. *Vom Gasthaus Krone zur Volksbank Süssen: 300 Jahre Geschichte eines Hauses* (n.p., n.d.). See also Ziegler, *Siezun,* 277.

52. Ziegler, *Siezun,* 259.

53. Ibid., 275 and 368.

54. "Ein historischer Rundgang durch Süssen," 40.

55. Ibid., 41; and Ziegler, *Siezun,* 403.

56. "Ein historischer Rundgang durch Süssen," 42.

57. Ziegler, *Siezun,* 194.

58. Helmut Keller, ed., *Johann Georg Fischer, Person und Werk* (Hamburg: Verlag Dr. Kovac, 1997), 11, 20–22.

59. Ibid., 12 and 24.

60. "Ein historischer Rundgang durch Süssen," 38–39.

61. "The Bausch + Lomb Story," accessed January 13, 2012, http://tinyurl.com/bauschstory.

62. Ziegler, *Siezun,* 232–48.

63. "Ein historischer Rundgang durch Süssen," 51–2.

64. "The Bausch + Lomb Story," accessed January 13, 2012, http://tinyurl.com/bauschstory.

65. "Ein historischer Rundgang durch Süssen," 48; also Gemeinde Süssen, "Übergabe des J.J. Bausch Bürgerhauses an die Süssener Vereine," September 3–4, 1982, 13–4.

66. Various Süssen calendars of *Sozialdemokraten.*

67. "900 Jahre Süssen." *Sonderbeilage* of the *NWZ*, n.p.

68. Ziegler, *Siezun*, 158–9.

69. "Der neue Marktbrunnen zu Süssen." The 1847 description of industrialization corresponds to scene 10.

70. Stälin, *Oberamt Geislingen*, 204.

71. Ziegler, *Siezun*, 230.

72. Schellenberger points out that "until 1849 no farmer owned his farm, rather it was merely 'on loan' to him for a high fee. . . . All farmers depended for their livelihood on a lord." In *Ottenbach und das Tal der Höfe*, 157. Note also that the *Kirchenbauer* was the farmer who supplied food to the church and the pastor. The title follows the farm, not the family who owns it.

73. "Der neue Marktbrunnen zu Süssen." The 1847 description of railroad tracks corresponds to scene 9.

74. "900 Jahre Süssen," *Sonderbeilage* of the *NWZ*, n.p.; also *1071–1971: 900 Jahre Süssen*. Festprogramm. (Süssen: Beck-Druck, 1971).

75. Ibid.

76. *1071–1971: 900 Jahre Süssen.*

77. Süssen Gemeindechronik, (loose sheet) n.d. (after 1945).

78. *1071–1971: 900 Jahre Süssen.*

79. Fifty years later, in 1989, the Strassacker firm created the historical fountain for the city of Süssen, and two years later the Holocaust memorial that Hugo Lang desired for his family. See chapter 1.

80. *1071–1971: 900 Jahre Süssen.*

81. Ibid. Also Süssen Gemeindechronik, *Geislinger Zeitung* (*Amtsblatt*), no. 215, September 16, 1933, 2–3.

82. Süssen Gemeinderats-Protokoll, 24 January 1936, para. 281, 370; also in *Hohenstaufen*, January 30, 1936, no. 24.

83. "Der neue Marktbrunnen zu Süssen." The 1933 description of the unification of the two villages corresponds to scene 11.

84. Süssen City Archive: K/B 22, Klein-Süssen Gemeinderats-Protokoll, Band 14, 1931–33, June 9, 1933, 462.

85. Ibid., 466.

86. Müller, *1896–1996 Sozialdemokraten in Süssen*, 140.

87. Süssen Gemeindechronik, *Hohenstaufen*, no. 254, October 31, 1933.

88. Süssen Gemeindechronik, *Geislinger Zeitung*, no. 299, December 23, 1933, reprinted in *50 Jahre Süssen*, 32.

89. "Der neue Marktbrunnen zu Süssen." The 1933–45 description of the Holocaust corresponds to scene 12.

90. Süssen Gemeindechronik, *Hohenstaufen*, no. 57, March 9, 1934.

91. Süssen Volkshochschule. *50 Jahre Süssen*, 1983, pages not numbered.

## 3. Klein-Süssen: The Ottenheimer Family

1. Ziegler, *Siezun*, 159.
2. Sadly, Werner Ottenheimer died on December 19, 2008, just a year after I visited him. May his memory be for a blessing.
3. Graves of Ottenheimer family members are in Jebenhausen Jewish Cemetery: Madel née Dreifuss, grave no. 320 F; Salomo Ottenheimer, grave no. 281 D. No known gravesites for Jettle and Zettlin Ottenheimer.
4. Tänzer, *Juden in Jebenhausen und Göppingen*, 403.
5. Göppingen District Archive, Sammlung Walter Ziegler, Max Ottenheimer 1929 speech.
6. Göppingen District Archive, Sammlung Walter Ziegler, newspaper article, "Mechanische Weberei Süssen, Gebrüder Ottenheimer A.G., gegründet 1854," no name or date.
7. Göppingen District Archive, Sammlung Walter Ziegler, Max Ottenheimer 1929 speech. The German word *Zettel* has a double meaning in German: warp and slip of paper. In Yiddish, the slip of paper given by a Jewish community to a transient Jew for a free meal in a specific community, i.e. Jebenhausen, is also called a *Zettel*, literally a scrap (of paper and of food as well). See Werner J. Cahnman, "Village and Small-Town Jews in Germany. A Typological Study," in *Leo Baeck Institute Year Book 19* (1974): 111.
8. Göppingen District Archive, Sammlung Walter Ziegler. Max Ottenheimer 1929 speech.
9. Werner Ottenheimer, interview with the author, December 24 and 25, 2007.
10. Tänzer, *Juden in Jebenhausen und Göppingen*, ed. Ruess, 442.
11. District Archive Göppingen: Göppingen Address Books 1912, 1930, 1934, 1937.
12. Tänzer, *Juden in Jebenhausen und Göppingen*, 443.
13. Ibid.
14. Ibid., 424.
15. Ibid., 532.
16. Ibid., 526.
17. Ibid., 523.
18. Ibid., 536.
19. Ibid., 538.
20. One are is 100 square meters or 119.60 square yards.
21. Göppingen District Archive, Sammlung Walter Ziegler, Max Ottenheimer 1929 speech. Also Müller, *1896–1996: Sozialdemokraten in Süssen*, 127.
22. Ibid.
23. City of Süssen: Grundbuch Heft 164, no. 18 Handelsregister Abschrift Abt. 2, Band 1, Blatt 132.
24. Ibid.

25. All three pictures and identification, Göppingen City Archive. Courtesy of Dr. Ruess.

26. Süssen publication, *1071–1971: 900 Jahre Süssen*. Festprogramm (Süssen: Buch- und Offsetdruckerei Beck, 1971), n.p.

27. Süssen City Archive, Ottenheimer company letterhead, August 2, 1906.

28. Süssen City Archive, letter on company letterhead, June 2, 1905.

29. Süssen City Archive, K/B 16, Klein-Süssen Gemeinderats-Protokoll, Band 8 1907–11, November 16, 1910, no para., 206 (wrong in the index, says 287). Courtesy of Werner Runschke.

30. GP KRA: A 145.19. Göppingen District Archive, Ottenheimer letterhead dated December 1, 1908. Courtesy of Rolf Jente.

31. Müller, *1896–1996: Sozialdemokraten in Süssen*, 57.

32. Süssen City Archive: G/A 57/1743 Ott Akten.

33. Loose sheet with gold currency and grocery prices 1914–25, courtesy of Werner Runschke.

34. Süssen City Archive, K/B 145, Verzeichnis über Gewerbeanzeigen *(1906–23)*, 10.

35. Süssen City Archive, K/B 17, Klein-Süssen Gemeinderats-Protokoll, Band 9, 1911–14, December 4, 1913, para. 1, 273.

36. Süssen City Archive, K/B 18, Klein-Süssen Gemeinderats-Protokoll, Band 10, 1914–21, January 20, 1915, para. 2, 56.

37. Ibid., January 10, 1917, para. 6, 113–14.

38. Ibid., December 18, 1918, para. 6, 202–4. Tänzer in Ruess, *Juden in Jebenhausen und Göppingen*, 443.

39. Süssen City Archive, K/B 18, Klein-Süssen Gemeinderats-Protokoll, Band 10, 1914–21, July 25, 1918, para. 2, 188.

40. Süssen City Archive, K/B 145, Verzeichnis über Gewerbeanzeigen *(1906–23)*, 24.

41. Süssen City Archive, K/B 18, Klein-Süssen Gemeinderats-Protokoll, Band 10, 1914–21, March 15, 1921, para. 1, 459–60.

42. Süssen City Archive, K/B 19, Klein-Süssen Gemeinderats-Protokoll, Band 11, 192–25, June 23, 1921, para. 7, 5.

43. Ibid., November 2, 1921, para. 5, 67–68.

44. Ibid., November 17, 1921, para. 3, 72–75.

45. Ibid., 1921–25, November 17, 1921, meeting in minutes of June 30, 1922 201. This does not make sense; above he says construction is saturated with the third house, should it be lot no. 189? If it is a mistake, it is in the documents.

46. Ibid., November 17, 1921, para. 3, 73–74.

47. Ibid.

48. Tänzer, *Juden in Jebenhausen und Göppingen*, 442.

49. Göppingen District Archive, Sammlung Walter Ziegler, Max Ottenheimer 1929 speech.

50. City of Süssen Grundbuch Heft 164, December 4, 1922.

51. Süssen City Archive, K/B 145, Verzeichnis über Gewerbeanzeigen (*1906–23*), 39.

52. Süssen City Archive, K/B 19, Klein-Süssen Gemeinderats-Protokoll, Band 11, 1921–25, June 30, 1922, para. 5, 201.

53. Ibid.

54. Ibid.

55. Jürgen Klotz, *Der Geldschein Sammler* 13, no. 8, (November 1999): 6–7. Courtesy of Werner Runschke.

56. Süssen City Archive, K/B 19, Klein-Süssen Gemeinderats-Protokoll, Band 11, 1921–25, February 1, 1924, para. 14, 456–57.

57. Ibid., May 23, 1924, para. 8, 514–16.

58. Ibid., June 25, 1924, para. 7, 548–49.

59. Süssen City Archive, K/B 20, Klein-Süssen Gemeinderats-Protokoll, Band 12, 1925–28, August 6, 1926, para. 314, 316–17.

60. Ibid., December 21, 1927, para. 620, 629.

61. Müller, *1896–1996: Sozialdemokraten*, 127.

62. Ibid., 127–28.

63. *FVZ* of July 2, 1927, in Müller, *1896–1996: Sozialdemokraten*, 128.

64. "Göppingen-Süssen, 9. Mai," in Müller, *1896–1996: Sozialdemokraten*, 73.

65. Süssen City Archive, K/B 21, Klein-Süssen Gemeinderats-Protokoll, Band 13, 1928–31, July 23, 1929, para. 341, 290.

66. Ibid., July 24, 1930, para. 564, 461–2.

67. Süssen City Archive, K/B 22, Klein-Süssen Gemeinderats-Protokoll, Band 14, 1931–33, September 4, 1931, para. 99, 89–90.

68. Ibid., October 23, 1931, para. 128, 111–12, and December 30, 1931, para. 171, 147.

69. Ibid., October 23, 1931, para. 128, 111–13.

70. *Geislinger Zeitung* in Müller, *1986–1996: Sozialdemokraten*, 127.

71. Göppingen District Archive, Sammlung Walter Ziegler, Max Ottenheimer 1929 speech.

72. Süssen City Archive. Letter from mayor to Mechanische Weberei Süssen, Gebrüder Ottenheimer A.G. regarding Ottenheimer anniversary.

73. Göppingen District Archive, 9895, regarding Ottenheimer taxes, October 24, 1958.

74. Süssen City Archive, K/B 19, Klein-Süssen Gemeinderats-Protokoll, Band 11, 1921–25, November 7, 1924, para. 15, 596–7.

75. Ibid., February 6, 1925, para. 2, 621–22.

76. Ibid., February 21, 1925, para. 5, 635.

77. See Göppingen District Archive, A 865, regarding Ottenheimer sewage.

78. See ibid.

79. Süssen City Archive, K/B 20, Klein-Süssen Gemeinderats-Protokoll, Band 12, 1925–28, January 29, 1926, para. 169, 152.

80. Ibid., August 6, 1926, para. 306, 310–11. See also K/B 19, Klein-Süssen Gemeinderats-Protokoll Band 11, 1921–25, November 2, 1921, para. 5, 67–8.

81. Süssen City Archive, K/B 21, Klein-Süssen Gemeinderats-Protokoll, Band 13, 1928–31, December 21, 1928, para. 151, 131.

82. Ibid., December 21, 1928, para. 151, 131.

83. Süssen City Archive, K/B 22, Klein-Süssen Gemeinderats-Protokoll, Band 14, 1931–33, July 23, 1931, para. 87, 76–77.

84. Süssen City Archive, Gemeinderats-Protokoll, Band 1 and 2 1933–38, Band 1, May 18, 1934, para. 116, 151.

85. Ibid., Band 2, July 30, 1937, para. 17.3, 32.

86. Süssen City Archive, K/B 21, Klein-Süssen Gemeinderats-Protokoll, Band 13 1928–31, May 27, 1930, para. 515, 425–6.

87. Gross-Süssen Gemeindechronik, Sonderbeilage des *Hohenstaufens. Zur Feier der Vereinigung von Gross- und Klein-Süssen*, September 16, 1933, 11 (pocket on p. 43). Also Sonderbeilage der *Geislinger Zeitung zur Vereinigung von Gross- und Klein-Süssen am 16. und 17. September*, September 16, 1933, no. 215, 2–3 (pocket on p. 42) (emphasis added).

88. Heinrich Landes, July 1947. "Mechanische Weberei Süssen," typescript, in Göppingen District Archive, Sammlung Walter Ziegler (emphasis added).

89. Süssen City Archive, A734/3225 high voltage cable. Courtesy of Frau Hofacker.

90. Ibid.

91. Süssen City Archive, Gemeinderats-Protokoll Band 1 and 2 1933–38, Band 2, July 8, 1938, para. 103.3, 172.

92. Süssen City Archive, *Geislinger Zeitung* of July 1935 regarding *Handelsregister* entry, July 18, 1935. Courtesy of Werner Runschke.

93. Süssen City Archive, Handelsregister entry of December 2, 1937. See also cover sheet, Grundbuch Heft (G.B.H.) 1105 excerpt Ottenheimer/Weidmann, Ludwigsburg State Archive FL 300/33II, Bü 255.

94. Göppingen District Archive, Sammlung Walter Ziegler, *Geislinger Zeitung*, August 12, 1950.

95. Süssen Grundbuch Heft 1105, sect. 1.

96. In a 1948 reparations document from Ludwig Ottenheimer the amount of 670,000 RM is listed as the amount on the sales contract, with "additional subsequent negotiations" that were said to be "not substantial." Ludwigsburg State Archive, FL 300/33II. Bü 255 Ottenheimer, 4. See also "Schlussbericht," in ibid, 102, in the amount of DM 650,000.

97. This entry is found in the Süssen Grundbuch Heft 1105, sect. 1, 151.

98. See Göppingen District Archive, A 442, 12 about first purchase option for Ottenheimer property.

99. Ludwigsburg State Archive, FL 300/33 II, Bü 255,102, Ottenheimer, 1.

100. See ibid. about Sana Ottenheimer reparations.

101. I would like to thank the archive librarians at the Ludwigsburg State Archive for their extraordinary helpfulness during this research, especially Frau Michaela Mingoia and Herr Wolfgang Schneider, whose kindness, efficiency, and timely assistance was much appreciated.

102. Ludwigsburg State Archive, FL 300/33 II, Bü 335, 0005761 on Alfred and Luise Ottenheimer house in Göppingen.

103. The *Israelitische Wochenblatt zu Göppingen* reported on July 1, 1938, that "our community member Alfred Ottenheimer died in Baden-Baden after a long and serious illness on June 14, at age 60. . . . In spite of his heavy responsibilities as partner in the company Gebrüder Ottenheimer in Süssen, the deceased put his considerable capabilities also at the service of the Jewish community," 64. Courtesy of Dr. Ruess, Göppingen City Archive.

104. I owe this more detailed information to Dr. K.-H. Ruess, director of the Göppingen City Archive. According to his information, the questionnaire that communities filled out to document the fate of Jews in Göppingen stated that Luise was moved to Stuttgart on October 12, 1938.

105. Ludwigsburg State Archive, FL 300/33 II, Bü 335, 100695/12–15/3, 1, on Alfred Ottenheimer house sale, Luise's Stuttgart residence.

106. Ibid., 0005761/6, 1.

107. Ibid., 0005761/6, copy of reparations document Ottenheimer/R.

108. Ibid., 100695/12, 1.

109. Ibid., 0005761/6, 2, on Alfred and Luise Ottenheimer house in Göppingen.

110. Ibid., 0005761/4, 2. "On January 29, 1940, the amount of 44,000 RM was deposited to the restricted account of Alfred Ottenheimer's widow, Mrs. Luise Ottenheimer, with the Deutsche Bank Stuttgart, in Stuttgart."

111. Ludwigsburg State Archive, FL 300/33 II, Bü 335, 100695/12, 1, on Alfred Ottenheimer house sale and Luise's Stuttgart residence.

112. During a 1999 visit to Süssen I was told by a local resident that after the war one of the Ottenheimer sons, who had emigrated to the United States, came back to see about reclaiming the business. However, because of the Cold War, he felt that there was the possibility of a Soviet invasion which was not a far-fetched idea then. This son therefore decided against reclaiming his property, as he would then again lose it to the state if Germany would become Communist, and he remained in the United States. The son was Werner's brother Richard who was an American soldier in World War II, stationed in Germany. When I told Werner Ottenheimer this anecdote, he dismissed it.

113. Ludwigsburg State Archive, FL 300/33 II, Bü 335, 1006951/12–15, on Alfred Ottenheimer house sale and Luise's Stuttgart residence.

114. Ludwigsburg State Archive, FL 300/33 II, Bü 335, 1006951/39, on Alfred Ottenheimer house sale and Luise's Stuttgart residence.

115. Ludwigsburg State Archive, FL 300/33 II, Bü 255, on Richard Ottenheimer.

116. Ludwigsburg State Archive, FL 300/33 II, Bü 335, 1006951/28–29, 1, on Alfred Ottenheimer house sale and Luise's Stuttgart residence.

117. Göppingen District Archive: Ausbürgerungsverzeichnisse 1040, AR 3491 Max Ottenheimer.

118. Ludwigsburg State Archive, FL 300/33 II, Bü 432 Max and Hedwig Ottenheimer, also FL 300133II, Bü 255, 067228, 5.

119. Ibid.

120. Ludwigsburg State Archive, FL 300/33 II, Bü 217 on sale of Max Ottenheimer home, 041618/2. See also actual *Kaufvertrag* (bill of sale), same file, 041618/7. "As soon as the approval of this sales contract is received from the responsible authorities, the buyer must agree to the transfer of the stipulated amount to the restricted account of the seller."

121. Ludwigsburg State Archive, FL 300/33 II, Bü 217/17, 4, on sale of Max Ottenheimer home.

122. Ludwigsburg State Archive, FL 300/33 II, Bü 217/44, on sale of Max Ottenheimer home.

123. Ludwigsburg State Archive, FL 300/33 II, Bü 217, 2, on sale of Max Ottenheimer home.

124. Ludwigsburg State Archive, FL 300/33 II, Bü 432, 97601, 2/4 on Max and Hedwig Ottenheimer.

125. Götz Aly, *Hitler's Beneficiaries. Plunder, Racial War, and the Nazi Welfare State* (New York: Metropolitan Books, Henry Holt & Co., 2006).

126. Aly, *Hitler's Beneficiaries*, 51 and 200.

127. Ludwigsburg State Archive, FL 300/33 II, Bü 432, 97601, 2/4, on Max and Hedwig Ottenheimer. See also Aly, *Hitler's Beneficiaries*, 200, on emigration tax.

128. Ludwigsburg State Archive, FL 300/33 II, Bü 432, 10/17, on Max and Hedwig Ottenheimer.

129. Ibid., 45/48, on Max and Hedwig Ottenheimer.

130. Ibid., 51/53, on Max and Hedwig Ottenheimer.

131. Ibid., 58/60, on Max and Hedwig Ottenheimer.

132. Ludwigsburg State Archive, FL 300/33 II, Bü 432/62, on Max and Hedwig Ottenheimer.

133. *1071–1971: 900 Jahre Süssen*. Festprogramm (Süssen: Buch- und Offsetdruckerei Beck, 1971).

134. I am not aware of any contact between the city of Süssen and any of the Ottenheimer descendents or survivors.

## 4. Gross-Süssen: The Lang Families, 1902–37

1. Müller, *1896–1996 Sozialdemokraten in Süssen*, 19.

2. Tänzer, *Geschichte der Juden in Jebenhausen und Göppingen*, ed. Ruess, 392.

3. "The citizens of Gross-Eislingen, who belonged to the Count of Rechberg, paid obeisance to the Count [of Württemberg, who did not allow Jews in his territory], as they were feuding with their lord because of the Jews who were forced on them. . . . The feud was ended in a settlement which obligated Rechberg, among other things, not to accept any more Jews into their territories." Eisele, Köhle, and Schöllkopf, eds., *Geschichtliche Heimatkunde*, 67–68.

4. G/B 240 Gross-Süssen, Saalbuch 1735 (2), fol. 210 v. Courtesy of Werner Runschke

5. Ibid.

6. Ziegler, *Siezun*, 63 and 82.

7. "Hier geht das Hochfürstlich Württembergisch Glait auf und an." G/B 240 Gross-Süssen, Saalbuch 1735 (2), fol. 210 v.

8. Eisele, Köhle, and Schöllkopf, eds., *Geschichtliche Heimatkunde*, 110.

9. *The Memoirs of Glückel of Hameln*, trans. Marvin Lowenthal (New York: Schocken Books, 1977).

10. Eisele, Köhle, and Schöllkopf, eds., *Geschichtliche Heimatkunde*, 110.

11. Daughter of *Zimmermeister* (carpenter) Z., who wanted to rent the "Judengarten" to store his wood and who later manufactured the crate used to pack and ship the Langs' belongings.

12. Jürgen Hermann Rauser, Forchtenberger Heimatbuch. Stadtverwaltung Forchtenberg (1983), n.p. Courtesy of Hugo Lang.

13. Rauser, n.p.

14. Ibid.

15. Ibid.

16. Sauer, *Die jüdischen Gemeinden in Württemberg und Hohenzollern* (Stuttgart: W. Kohlhammer Verlag, 1966), 72. See also *Beschreibung des Oberamts Öhringen* (Stuttgart: H. Lindemann, 1865), 201–5. Also Naftali Bar-Giora Bamberger, "Die jüdische Gemeinde Ernsbach," in *Memor-Buch. Die jüdischen Friedhöfe im Hohenlohekreis*, vol. 1 (Künzelsau: Swiridoff Verlag, 2002), 17.

17. Rauser, n.p.

18. Sauer, *Die jüdischen Gemeinden*, 72.

19. Rauser, n.p. The two Jews left were Moses Stern, who died a natural death on July 12, 1933, and his housekeeper, Fanny Lehrberger. After his death, she was sent to the Jewish Old Age Home in Heilbronn-Sontheim, from which she was deported to Delmersdingen. She died there and is buried in the Jewish cemetery of Laupheim (author's visit to cemetery).

20. Sauer, *Die jüdischen Gemeinden*, 72.

21. Beysass is the same as the modern *Beisitzer*. It is an honorific for a community member who has been appointed to the election commission, for example. The *Beisitzer*'s function is to observe and advise on communal matters.

22. Graves of Lang family members are in Berlichingen Verbandfriedhof: Falk (Felkle) Feis [Lang], grave no. 679; Madel Krautheim, grave no. 685; Bela

Feis, grave no. 560; Frummet Isak, grave no. 413; Isak Falk Lang, grave no. 309; Zipora Bauer, grave no. 542; Adelheid Victor, grave no. 474; Fanny Hirsch, grave no. 1243; Regine (Rachele) Heilbronner, grave no. 1066.

23. Göppingen District Archive, Jakob Lang engagement announcement. *Göppinger Zeitung*, no. 34, February 11, 1902.

24. Göppingen District Archive, Jakob Lang marriage announcement. *Göppinger Zeitung*, 1902.

25. Collection Hugo Lang; also Süssen City Archive, G/B 309 Gross-Süssen Steuerbuch 1900–38, 321; and G/B 322 Gross-Süssen Gebäudesteuerkataster 1903–63, beginning 1 April 1909, 14.

26. Süssen City Archive, 9897/14, "Judenhaus."

27. See *Wiedergutmachung* document 9897/68 in chapter 9 in this book.

28. Picture in SPD Kalender 1998, December. The picture caption reads, "Older brother of the Jewish families Louis and Leopold Lang: Jacob Lang married a woman from Göppingen, his wife Sally [sic] with children. Older girl Lena (right) [sic] completed an apprenticeship in Grau's mill. The younger girl Alma and brother Otto died young." This account is flawed. Jakob's wife was from Rexingen and her name was Fanny. All three children were alive in 1929, when Fanny sold the property to Louis. Lina (Lena) was the youngest, not the oldest. There is no indication that any of the children had died when Louis, on the death of his wife Pauline in 1935, had the property reassessed and reassigned. Fanny's three children are mentioned in present tense.

29. Süssen City Archive, G/B 5 Gross-Süssen Schultheissenamts-Protokoll, August 4, 1906, 48.

30. A *Kalbel* is a cow that is pregnant for the first time.

31. See Süssen City Archive, Nachlass Otto and Eugen Eisele, regarding the purchase of pregnant cow.

32. Göppingen City Archive, Jakob Lang horse advertisement in *Göppinger Zeitung*, August 1911.

33. Süssen City Archive, A1062/4340, Bezirks-Pferde-Versicherungs-Verein, Geislingen-Stg.

34. Süssen City Archive, G/B 79, Verzeichnis über ausgestellte Prädikatsvermögenszeugnisse 1889–1912, Vorstrafen, no. 785 (1908) and no. 1052 (1912). Courtesy of Werner Runschke.

35. Süssen City Archive, G/B 80, Verzeichnis über ausgestellte Prädikatsvermögenszeugnisse, no. 42 (1913) and no. 202 (1917). There is also one for Louis Lang, G/B 80, no. 435 (1925). Courtesy of Werner Runschke.

36. Süssen City Archive, G/B 83, Bauschauprotokoll und Gemeinderatsprotokoll in Bausachen 1906–33, November 11, 1908, 126. "Jakob Lang hat in seinem Haus no. 15 zwei Heizöfen ohne Genehmigung aufgestellt. Es gibt keine Einwände." Courtesy of Werner Runschke.

37. Süssen City Archive, G/B 30 Gross-Süssen, Gemeinderats-Protokoll Band 17, 1912–15, December 6, 1912, para. 1.3, 124, "Jakob Lang, Viehhändler [cattle dealer] hier, geboren 23 November 1873 in Ernsbach, bittet um Aufnahme in das hiesige Bürgerrecht."

38. The following tables list the employees who worked for Jakob Lang.

### 1914 Register

| Name, Residence | DOB | Occupation | Period |
|---|---|---|---|
| 1. Lang, Leopold, Ernsbach | February 11, 1895 | Handlungsgehilfe (clerk) | May 3, 1913–? |
| 2. Zehnder, Johann, Unterurbach | December 11, 1882 | Knecht (servant) | December 29, 1913–March 30, 1914 |
| 3. Fuchs, Euphrosine, Böhmenkirch | July 2, 1900 | Magd (maid) | April 18, 1911–? |
| 4. Weber, Karl, Gmünd | December 26, 1876 | Servant | March 29, 1914–April 19, 1914 |
| 5. Stütz, Josef, Donzdorf | July 19, 1896 | Servant | April 3, 1914–May 16, 1914 |
| 6. Stoss, August, Buttenhausen | August 2, 1885 | Servant | May 17, 1914–August 22, 1914 |
| 7. Eckert, Karl, Niederstotzingen | November 23, 1880 | Servant | September 5, 1914–Sept. 14, 1914 |
| 8. Schneider, Karl, Kaiserslautern | April 7, 1876 | Servant | September 17, 1914–September 21, 1914 |
| 8a. Weissinger, Wilhelm, Schlierbach | November 16, 1895 | Servant | |
| 9. Schmid, Joh. Georg, Biberach | February 1, 1994 | Servant | September 23, 1914–September 29, 1914 |
| 10. Humm, Karl, Deisslingen | December 31, 1888 | Servant | September 27, 1914–? |
| 11. Reich, Gotthilf, Renningen | September 18, 1876 | Servant | October 11, 1914–November 7, 1914 |

### 1915 Register

| Name, Residence | DOB | Occupation | Period |
|---|---|---|---|
| 1. Lang, Leopold, Ernsbach | February 11, 1895 | Clerk | May 3, 1913–February 1, 1915 |
| 2. Weissinger, Wilhelm, Schlierbach | November 16, 1895 | Servant | November 19, 1914–May 19, 1915 |
| 3. Gideon, Samuel, Rexingen | August 22, 1897 | Gehilfe (Assistant) | March 16, 1915–April 1, 1905 |
| 4. Kemmer, Wilhelm, Ebnat, Oberamt Neresheim | October 20, 1896 | Servant | May 20, 1915–? |
| 5. Fischer, Hermann, Treffelhausen | Jan. 27, 1901 | Servant | June 15, 1915–July 9, 1915 |

| | | | |
|---|---|---|---|
| 6. Werner, Ludwig. [No birthplace] | March 29, 1873 | Servant | June 30, 1915– July 6, 1915 |
| 7. Fischer, Hermann, Treffelhausen | Jan. 21, 1901 | Servant | August 6, 1915– August 8, 1915 |
| 8. Hieber, Eugen, Gmünd | September 7, 1882. | | August 30, 1915–September 12, 1915 |
| 9. Walter, Max. (No birthplace) | May 3, 1872. | | September 22, 1915–? |
| 10. Haigis, Friedrich, Sulz | March 23, 1895. | | ?–Nov. 26, 1915 |

**1916 Register**

| Name, Residence | DOB | Occupation | Period |
|---|---|---|---|
| 1. Landauer, Martin, Rexingen, OA Horb | May 28, 1900 | Clerk | October 20, 1915– January 6, 1916 |
| 2. Mainz, Johann, Schwend | February 8, 1890 | Servant | January 10, 1916– January 30, 1916 |
| 3. Dangel, Alois, Stafflangen, OA Biberach | September 9, 1874 | Servant | February 2, 1916–? |
| 4. Klein, Hermann, ? | ? | Servant | July 23, 1916–?. |
| 5. Schmid, Josef, ? | ? | ? | August 16, 1916–? |
| 6. Hähsle, Johannes, Westerstetten | July 13, 1859. | ? | September 26, 1916–? |
| 7. Seybold, Jakob, Stubersheim | February 16, 1873 | Servant | October 12, 1916–? |
| 8. Hirneisen, Emanuel, Unterscheindorf, OA Nagold | March 13, 1863 | Servant | November 6, 1916–? |
| 9. Landauer, Martin, Rexingen, OA Horb | May 28, 1900 | Clerk | October 20, 1915– January 6, 1916 |
| 10. Fuchs, Euphrosine, Böhmenkirch | July 2, 1890 | Maid servant | April 18, 1911–? |

*Source:* Süssen City Archive, list of insured by Allgemeine Ortskrankenkasse Geislingen an der Steige. Mitglieder-Verzeichnis der allgemein versicherungspflichtigen Mitglieder für das Geschäftsjahr 1914, 1915, 1916.

39. Süssen City Archive, G/B 385 Verzeichnis der Dienstboten, Lehrlinge, Gehilfen und Arbeiter von Gross-Süssen.

40. See Jürgen Hagel, *Das Filstal—Natur, Kultur, Geschichte, Orte* (Tübingen: Silberburg-Verlag Titus Häussermann GmbH, 2003), 61.

41. Süssen City Archive, G/A 195 Kundenliste der Metzger, Kolonialwaren- und Milchhändler, 1918.

42. Göppingen District Archive, 9895, June 26, 1959.

43. Göppingen District Archive, 9895/9880 Eisele correspondence, letter 26 June 1959.

44. *Jüdische Frontsoldaten aus Württemberg und Hohenzollern. Württembergischer Landesverband des Zentralvereins deutscher Staatsbürger jüdischen Glaubens* (Stuttgart: J. Fink, 1926), 7. See also Sauer and Hosseinzedeh, *Jüdisches Leben*, 86; for Württemberg they mention 1610 men.

45. *Jüdische Frontsoldaten*, 33.

46. Ibid. See also John Keegan, *The First World War* (New York: Vintage Books, 2000), 149–50.

47. City of Süssen, Lang *Dokumentation*, 73.

48. Picture of Louis and Leopold as World War I soldiers, courtesy Hugo Lang.

49. Hugo Lang interview with Professor Piehler, 3; see also Süssen, Lang *Dokumentation*.

50. "Battle of Tannenberg," accessed January 13, 2012, http://tinyurl.com/battle-of-t.

51. Keegan, *The First World War*, 149.

52. Süssen City Archive, G/B 212, *Eisernes Buch der Gefallenen des I. Weltkriegs*.

53. Storr was mayor from 1911–22.

54. Süssen City Archive, (no G/B or K/B number) Süssen Gemeinderats-Protokoll, Band 1 and 2, 1937–38, Band 2, December 14, 1937, para. 49, 85–87.

55. Süssen Gemeindechronik, loose-leaf advertisement.

56. *Jüdische Frontsoldaten aus Württemberg und Hohenzollern*, 33.

57. Süssen City Archive, Gemeinderats-Protokoll, Band 1 and 2, 1933–38, Band 2, July 8, 1938, para. 106c, 177.

58. Süssen City Archive, Gemeinderats-Protokoll, Band 1 and 2, 1933–38, Band 2, July 8, 1938, para. 103.3, 172. Also in Klein-Süssen Gemeindechronik, *Geislinger Zeitung*, August 30, 1938, no. 201, 6.

59. Süssen City Archive, 9897/50. Poem in Collection Hugo Lang.

60. Collection Hugo Lang. "Nachruf für unsern, am 4. Mai ds. Js. verstorbenen Bruder Jakob Lang, Süssen. Nur zu sehr sind wir in Gefahr, / Hier tief in Feindesland. / Wir geben unser Leben dar, / Das steht in Gottes Hand. // Doch nicht uns traf des Todes Pein; / Dem Bruder galt's dem Braven. / Die Seinen stehen jetzt allein, / Er ist in Gottes Hafen. // Nicht in dem Schlachtenlärm starb er, / Zu Hause wohl in Pflichten; / Drum traf die Kunde doppelt schwer / Uns Brüder zwei mitnichten. // Aus Deines Lebens Blütezeit / Hat Dich der Tod gerissen, / Der Zeit, wo Dir kein Weg zu weit, / Kein' Arbeit Dich wollt missen. // Nun stehn die Deinen an dem Grab / Beweinen den Ernährer / Und senden Liebe nur hinab, / Ein Trost, ein grosser, hehrer. // Die Arbeit, die der Krieg gemacht, / Die mehr verlangt von Allen, / Hat Dir den Stachel 'Tod' gebracht; / Gott hat es so gefallen. // Trotz Deiner Krankheit Meister stets / In allen Lebenslagen; / 'Vor's brechen will, ich wett', da geht's,' / Konntest Du immer sagen. // Im Haushalt warst Du auch ein Muster, / Ein Beispiel weit und breit, / War da der Himmel dunkel, duster, / Aufheiternd jederzeit. // Doch auch die Prüfung blieb nicht fort, / Die Gott uns allen sendet; / Die Krankheit, dieses schlimme Wort, / Hat sich an Dich gewendet. // Sie raffte Dich mit Allgewalt / Aus Deinem Glückesgang. / Nur allzufrüh und allzubald; / Dein Bleiben war nicht lang. // Gott tröst' die Deinen allzumal, / Die liebvoll an Dir hingen. / Das ist der Trost im Erdental; / Nur Gott kann ihn Euch bringen. // Denn Menschentrost, so klein, so schwach / Ist selten ganz hin-

länglich; / Nur Gottes Trost wirkt lange nach, / Der menschliche ist vergänglich. // Nun ruhe sanft in Deinem Grab / Vor dem wir traurig stehen, / Wir schau'n zu lang nicht dort hinab, / Auch uns heisst man noch gehen! // Heisst gehen uns aus dieser Welt / Der Mühen und der Sorgen. / Was nützt uns da alles Geld, / Wenn man uns ruft schon morgen? // Drum warte still in Deiner Gruft, / Bis wir uns wiedersehn, / Bis Gott uns einstens zu sich ruft / Und seinen Weg wir gehen. // Nun lasst die Tränen, / lasst den Schmerz. / Wir hoffen alle drauf, / Dass Gott jed' gutes Menschenherz / Zu sich nimmt freudig auf. // Gewidmet von seinen im Feld stehenden Brüdern Leopold und Louis."

61. Collection Hugo Lang; also City of Süssen Grundbuch Heft 470, "Sieben Jauchert."

62. Collection Hugo Lang. Fanny Lang re *Sieben Jauchert.*

63. Ibid.

64. Collection Hugo Lang.

65. Collection Hugo Lang. "Alma Lang ist Jüdin und erhielt durch Erlass des Württembergischen Wirtschaftsministeriums, Abteilung für Landwirtschaft, in Stuttgart (28 March 1941, no. D 1484) die Auflage die Grundstücke zu veräussern."

66. Collection Hugo Lang.

67. Süssen City Archive, 9897/5.

68. Collection Hugo Lang, sale of "Sieben Jauchert" for DM 2,800.

69. Göppingen District Archive, Louis Lang Engagement Announcement. *Göppinger Zeitung* 93, no. 64, March 3, 1920.

70. Süssen City Archive, A1887, Horse Census of 1919.

71. Süssen City Archive, 9897/12. Also Collection Hugo Lang.

72. Collection Hugo Lang.

73. Collection Hugo Lang, also City of Süssen, Grundbuch Heft 435a, sect. 1.

74. City of Süssen, Grundbuch Heft 435a, vol. 449, sect. 1, 16 February 1925.

75. Süssen City Archive, G/B 33, Gemeinderats-Protokoll 20 1924–25, 32.

76. Collection Hugo Lang; also City of Süssen, Grundbuch Heft 435a, vol. 449, sect. 1.

77. Collection Hugo Lang. City of Süssen, Grundakte to Grundbuch Heft 435a, vol. 449, sec. 1.

78. Collection Hugo Lang, re Louis & Pauline Lang Will.

79. Süssen City Archive, 9897 6/50, 3.

80. Süssen City Archive, Gemeinderats-Protokoll, July 11, 1924, 59.

81. Süssen City Archive, "Lang Gross-Süssen," Flattich-Plan 3221.

82. Süssen City Archive, A1883/8512.

83. Süssen City Archive, A1883/8512.

84. Collection Hugo Lang, picture of Leopold and Eva.

85. Collection Hugo Lang.

86. Collection Hugo Lang.

87. Collection Hugo Lang, 1923 picture of Leopold, Eva, Fred and Hugo.

88. Sauer, *Die jüdischen Gemeinden in Württemberg und Hohenzollern*, 72. The Jewish community was dissolved on March 24, 1925.

89. Source for "Regina" is Ludwigsburg State Archive, EL 350 I, ES 25334/20, 1.

90. See Levitt, "Looking at the Pictures," in *American Jewish Loss After the Holocaust*, 111–16; and Marianne Hirsch, *Family Frames: Photography, Narrative, and Postmemory* (Cambridge: Harvard University Press, 1996), 25–28.

91. Collection Hugo Lang, 1930 picture of Leopold, Eva, Ruth, Hugo and Fred.

92. Süssen City Archive, G/B 34, Gemeinderats-Protokoll Band 21, 1925–27, December 10, 1925, para. 36.6, 21–22.

93. Ibid.

94. Süssen City Archive, Allgemeine Ortskrankenkasse Geislingen/St., Mitgliederverzeichnis 1925.

95. For a brief bio on Falk Sahm, see Ulrich Seemüller, *Das jüdische Altersheim Herrlingen und die Schicksale seiner Bewohner*. Gemeinde Blaustein (Alb-Donau-Kreis), (Ulm: Rudi Rampf GmbH, n.d.), 177–78. Sahm was sent to the retirement home in Herrlingen after several displacements. Courtesy of Werner Runschke.

96. The Jewish community of Jebenhausen had helped to fund this old-age home. See J. Hahn, *Erinnerungen & Zeugnisse jüdischer Geschichte in Baden-Württemberg* (Stuttgart: Konrad Teiss Verlag, 1988), 211 and 214. "In 1907 the Jewish old-age home "Wilhelmsruhe" was built in Sontheim. At first, it had room for 32 senior citizens, then it was expanded several time (in 1939, 160 people were housed there). End of November 1940 the home was forcibly vacated; the residents were sent to other old-age homes at other locations."

97. Süssen City Archive, Gemeinderats-Protokoll, Band 1 and 2, 1933–38, Band 2, 28 May 1937, para. 9.3, 12. " . . . einen laufenden Zuschuss von 13 Mark 10 Pfg. monatlich verwilligt."

98. Hugo Lang interview with Professor Kurt Piehler, 1.

99. Göppingen District Archive and Göppingen City Archive, newspaper ads, *Göppinger Zeitung*, January 17, 1925, and no. 21, January 27, 1925; also *Göppinger Zeitung*, no. 236, 9 October 1929; and *Geislinger Zeitung*, no. 43, February 21, 1925.

100. Hugo Lang interview with Professor Kurt Piehler, 18. Picture property of Hugo Lang.

101. Ibid., 19.

102. Hugo Lang Collection, letter from Ruth, August 31, 1941.

103. Süssen City Archive, G/B 35, Gross-Süssen Gemeinderats-Protokoll Band 22 1927–30, February 26, 1929, para. 3, 320–21. "Louis Lang, Viehhändler hier, hat sein Anwesen in der Heidenheimerstrasse der Gemeinde zum Preise von ca. 30,000 RM zum Kauf angeboten." The town later mistakenly claims that he offered the property at Hauptstrasse for sale for RM 30,000.

104. Collection Hugo Lang. Also Süssen City Archive, 9897 8/50, and Grundbuch Heft 435a, vol. 449, sect. 1. One goldmark is specified in the sales contract, and in 1929 is worth 1/2790 kg of refined gold according to the London gold standard. See Grundbuch Heft 729.

105. Collection Hugo Lang. Also Süssen City Archive, 9897 8/50, 3.

106. Ibid., 4.

107. City of Süssen, Bauakte Louis Lang, Grundbuchamt.

108. Collection Hugo Lang, Heidenheimer Strasse gasoline storage shed building request, Flattich-Plan 3221.

109. Collection Hugo Lang, Lang building permit for garage at Hauptstrasse.

110. Süssen City Archive, Lang gasoline storage shed permit at Hauptstrasse.

111. Göppingen District Archive, A 692c, d Lang-Rothschild house sale.

112. City of Süssen, Grundbuch Heft Gross-Süssen, vol. 105a, sect. 1, no. 2, 3, 4, Properties of Markung Gross-Süssen, Buildings no. 89, etc.

113. Collection Hugo Lang, General-Vollmacht (power of attorney) for Fanny Lang.

114. Collection Hugo Lang, Alma Lang.

115. Until January 28, 2007, the birth date for Otto, whose given name was Adolf, was unknown. I assumed that he must have been born in Süssen, yet the information eluded me. Thanks to Werner Runschke, we now know it.

116. Göppingen City Archive, Hanukkah 5682, picture courtesy of Dr. Ruess.

117. Strauss, Signs of Life: Jews from Württemberg, 253.

118. In conversation with Hugo Lang, August 2005, Newton, New Jersey.

119. Strauss, Signs of Life: Jews from Württemberg, 252.

120. Ibid.

121. Süssen, Lang Dokumentation, 31.

122. Ibid.

123. Collection Hugo Lang, Hugo Lang curriculum vitae, 1. See also Göppingen District Archive, 9892 2/1 and 9892 1/1, 15 December 1938.

124. Collection Hugo Lang, Hugo Lang curriculum vitae, 1.

125. Ibid. See picture with all seven cousins.

126. Collection Hugo Lang, Hugo Lang curriculum vitae, 2–3.

127. Collection Hugo Lang, 1933 picture with Fred, Ruth, Hugo and kitten.

128. Collection Hugo Lang, 1930s picture with Eva and boys at Sarenwang.

129. Collection Hugo Lang, 1930 picture of Hugo, Fred and Ruth.

130. "Wir haben nun auch eine Deutsche Schule in Süssen, nachdem sich alle evangelischen Eltern und die Hälfte der katholischen Eltern über konfessionelle Bedenken und kleinliche Tagesfragen hinweg für die Deutsche Schule entschieden haben." In Geislinger Zeitung, 8 June 1936. Also Gemeinderats-Protokoll Band 1 and 2, 1933–38, June 5, 1936, para. 340.

131. Süssen City Archive, File Manfred Lang.

132. Collection Hugo Lang. Both of these teachers, Schnitzler and Reick, continued in their posts beyond 1945.

133. Collection Hugo Lang, 1936 Hugo class picture.

134. Collection Hugo Lang, Hugo Lang curriculum vitae, 3.

135. Collection Hugo Lang, 1933 picture of Hugo, Fred and Ruth in gym suits.

136. Süssen City Archive, Manfred Lang file.

137. Collection Hugo Lang, 1936 picture of outing to Wasserberg.

138. Collection Hugo Lang, Hugo Lang curriculum vitae, 3.

139. Collection Hugo Lang, Hugo Lang report card is dated February 15, 1937.

140. Süssen City Archive, Martin Bauch file. Hugo writes 1938 in his *vitae*, 3.

141. *Progressive* in the European sense of today might be a better term.

142. Hugo Lang interview with Professor Kurt Piehler, 2–3.

143. Collection Hugo Lang. 1929 picture of "Prinzes[s] Forget-me-Not's Wedding" Hanukkah play.

144. Süssen City Archive. Letter from Erwin Tänzer to Walter Lang, November 20, 1990. When I showed Erwin a picture of Hugo, he identified him as the "Lang brother" at Ft. Dix. Also, KP means *Küchenpflicht* or kitchen duty.

145. Hugo Lang interview with Professor Kurt Piehler, 3.

146. Collection Hugo Lang. Also Süssen City Archive 9897 6/50.

147. Ibid.

148. Göppingen District Archive, 9895 5/50.

149. For more on the Nazi "furniture operation," see Aly, *Hitler's Beneficiaries*, 119, 183–84.

150. Süssen City Archive, 9897 6/50.

## 5. Süssen under the Nazis: The Lang Families, 1937–41

1. Ludwigsburg State Archive, E 352 Bü 3782, Mayer, October 6, 1948, 2 (emphasis added). See also Uri Robert Kaufmann und Carsten Kohlmann, eds. *Jüdische Viehhandler zwischen Schwarzwald und Schwäbischer Alb.* "Horb-Rexingen: Barbara Staudacher Verlag, 2008).

2. Renate Welsch and Sinja Dillenkofer, *Begegnungen* (Horb am Neckar: Geiger-Verlag, n.d.), 45.

3. Monika Richarz and Uri Kaufmann have written about cattle dealers in southern Germany and Switzerland. See Monika Richarz, "Die soziale Stellung der jüdischen Viehhändler auf dem Lande am Beispiel Südwestdeutschlands," in *Jüdische Unternehmer in Deutschland im 19. und 20. Jahrhundert*, eds. Werner Mosse and Hans Pohl (Stuttgart, 1992), 271–83; Robert Uri Kaufmann, *Jüdische und christliche Viehhändler in der Schweiz 1780–1930* (Zürich: Chronos Verlag, 1988). See also Uri Kaufmann and Carsten Kohlmann, eds., *Jüdische Viehhändler zwischen Schwarzwald und Schwäbischer Alb* (Horb-Rexingen: Barbara Staudacher Verlag, 2008).

4. See "Als die Kuh am Berg noch besser aussah," in Rottenburg newspaper on conference, October 5, 2006, 32.

5. Ibid.

6. Süssen City Archive, Gemeinderats-Protokoll, Band 1 and 2, 1933–38, Band 2, October 20, 1938, para. 118, 190–92.

7. Göppingen District Archive, A142.10/4160, May 28, 1925. One flaw in these documents is that they are all from the Oberamt Göppingen, not from Oberamt Geislingen to which Süssen belonged.

8. Göppingen District Archive, A142.10/4160, September 19, 1925.

9. Ibid., August 30, 1926.

10. Ibid., December 2, 1925.

11. Ibid.

12. Ziegler, *Siezun*, 411.

13. Ibid.

14. Walter Ziegler and Martin Bauch, *Süssen: Eine Dorfmitte erzählt* (Salach: Kaisser Verlag, 1989), 37.

15. Süssen City Archive, G/B 35, Gemeinderats-Protokoll, Band 22, 1927–30, January 22, 1929, para. 3, 293. *Kirchweih* means "dedication of the church," and is a popular folk holiday, today less associated with the dedication of the [Lutheran] church than with a good time at the fair.

16. Süssen City Archive, A1009a/4182, fair date moved to October.

17. Süssen City Archive, A1009a/4182. Württembergisches Landesgewerbeamt, June 4, 1929.

18. Süssen City Archive, G/B 35, Gross-Süssen Gemeinderats-Protokoll, 1927–30, June 11, 1929, para. 2, 393–94.

19. Süssen City Archive, A1009a/4182, re trial period with new fair date.

20. Süssen City Archive, G/B 36, Gross-Süssen Gemeinderats-Protokoll, Band 23, 1930–32, November 3, 1931, para. 9, 279.

21. Süssen City Archive, A1009a/4182.

22. Süssen Gemeindechronik, notice about Easter fair in *Geislinger Zeitung*, March 31, 1934, no. 75.

23. Süssen Gemeindechronik, *Hohenstaufen*, April 3, 1934, no. 76. There is even a poem, unattributed, in Ziegler, *Siezun*, 413. "On Easter Monday there is life / on the left and right banks of the river Fils / it's super busy during the spring festival / they prepared for many guests! / You should know / that visitors happily go to Süssen / for the Easter fair." (Am Ostermontag, auf, da gilt's! / In Süssen links und rechts der Fils / herrscht Hochbetrieb beim Frühlingsfest, / gerüstet ist's für viele Gäst'! // . . . Am Ostermarkt, des müsst'r wisse, / do goht mer emmer gern nach Süsse!)

24. Süssen Gemeindechronik, *Nationale Rundschau*, April 4, 1934, 56.

25. Süssen City Archive, Gemeinderats-Protokoll, Band 1 and 2, 1933–38, Band 1, October 6, 1934, para. 172, 212.

26. Ibid.

27. Süssen City Archive, A1009a/4182, about discontinuation of fair.

28. Süssen City Archive, Gemeinderats-Protokoll, Band 1 and 2, 1933–38, Band 1, March 6, 1935, para. 219, 277.

29. Ibid.

30. Süssen Gemeindechronik, *Geislinger Zeitung*, April 25, 1935, no. 96.

31. Süssen Gemeindechronik, *Hohenstaufen*, April 14, 1936, no. 86, 139.

32. Süssen Gemeindechronik, *Geislinger Zeitung*, April 15, 1936, no. 87.

33. Süssen City Archive, Süssen Gemeinderats-Protokoll, Band 1 and 2, 1933–38, Band 1, May 7, 1936, para. 323, 418. ". . . Kitsch und Juden vom Markt fernzuhalten."

34. Süssen Gemeindechronik, *Geislinger Zeitung*, April 28, 1936, no. 98, "Jungviehprämierung in Geislingen."

35. Süssen City Archive, Süssen Gemeinderats-Protokoll, Band 1 and 2, 1933–38, Band 1, January 7, 1937, para. 389, 510.

36. The comparison here would be with the Cannstatter Volksfest, an annual statewide fair in a suburb of Stuttgart.

37. Süssen Gemeindechronik, *Geislinger Zeitung*, April 1, 1937, no. 75.

38. Süssen Gemeindechronik, *Geislinger Zeitung*, April 1938, no. 91.

39. Ibid., April 13, 1939, no. 86.

40. Ibid., April 11, 1939, no. 84.

41. Süssen City Archive, Süssen Gemeinderats-Protokoll, Band 1 and 2, 1933–38, Band 1, January 7, 1937, para. 389, 511.

42. Süssen City Archive, Süssen Gemeinderats-Protokoll, Band 1 and 2, 1933–38, Band 2, December 14, 1937, para. 48.4, 81.

43. Süssen City Archive, 9897/13", to "Süssen, Lang *Dokumentation*, 80.

44. Ibid.

45. There is an entire file of police interrogations concerning Sally Sommer, dated February 20, 1937. Göppingen District Archive, 4160/A142.10

46. Göppingen District Archive, 4160/A142.10, February 20, 1937.

47. Ibid., March 3, 1937.

48. Göppingen District Archive, *Göppinger Zeitung*, May 15, 1937.

49. Süssen City Archive, 9897/13.

50. Süssen, Lang *Dokumentation*, 29.

51. Collection Hugo Lang. Also Süssen City Archive: File 9897/48. But see Ludwigsburg reparations files. The amount of the business stated here is between RM 1 and 2 million.

52. Hugo Lang interview with Professor Kurt Piehler, 8. Note also, it was the Gestapo, not the SS.

53. Ludwigsburg State Archive, E352 Bü 3782, Ö., September 27, 1948, front page.

54. "I have been working as *Gemeindepfleger* for the mayor's office in Süssen since 1933. Already then there were two Jewish families in town named Lang."

Ludwigsburg State Archive, E352 Bü 3782, Häfele, September 27, 1948, front page.

55. Ludwigsburg State Archive, E352 Bü 3782, Häfele, September 27, 1948, 1.

56. Martin Dean, *Robbing the Jews: The Confiscation of Jewish Property in the Holocaust, 1933–45* (Cambridge: Cambridge University Press in association with the United States Holocaust Memorial Museum, 2008), 73–75.

57. Göppingen District Archive, 4165 in GPAR 3862, courtesy of Rolf Jente.

58. On Kristallnacht see Dean, *Robbing the Jews*, 111–27.

59. Government questionnaire (not mentioned by municipality in Lang *Dokumentation*). Collection Hugo Lang.

60. Ludwigsburg State Archive, EL 350 I, ES 12116/41.

61. Ibid.

62. Collection Hugo Lang. See also 1946 letter from Kurt to Hugo on this matter.

63. Collection Hugo Lang, Fred and Hugo Lang statement, January 6, 1946, for reparations.

64. Hugo Lang interview with Professor Kurt Piehler, 7.

65. Süssen City Archive, KAG A 003.66 AR 236, 3.

66. Ibid., 5.

67. For one story of a Jewish family in Ulm, see Amalie Fried, *Schuhhaus Pallas: Wie meine Familie sich gegen die Nazis wehrte* (Munich: Carl Hauser Verlag, 2008).

68. Süssen City Archive, 9897/14, KAG A 003.66 AR 236, 14.

69. Collection Hugo Lang. The designation "Bader Eislingen" raised eyebrows in Süssen when the information was first discovered, because the main company was located in Süssen on the way to Salach. But Hugo remembers right. On Metzger residence card, see addition in pencil "bei Bader Eisl.," where the company had a *Sägewerk* (sawmill). Collection Hugo Lang. See also *1071–1971: 900 Jahre Süssen*, Festprogramm, on Bader company.

70. Hugo Lang interview with Professor Kurt Piehler, 12. In my 2005 conversation with Hugo, he seemed to think that Uncle Louis and Mr. Metzger received train passes.

71. Collection Hugo Lang, letter to Fred and Hugo, October 6, 1941.

72. Ludwigsburg State Archive, E 352 Bü 3782, Schlecht testimony, October 2, 1948.

73. Ludwigsburg State Archive, E 352 Bü 3782, Ö., September 27, 1948, front page.

74. Ibid.

75. Ludwigsburg State Archive, E 352 Bü 3782, Schlecht testimony, October 2, 1948.

76. Collection Hugo Lang, Kurt letter to family in United States. N.d., probably November 1945.

77. Hugo Lang interview with Professor Kurt Piehler, 6. See also Kaplan, *Between Dignity and Despair*, 32–46.

78. Kaplan, *Between Dignity and Despair*, 39.

79. Dean, *Robbing the Jews*, 2.

80. See Aly, *Hitler's Beneficiaries*, 51.

81. Süssen City Archive, 9897/5. In the National Archives in College Park, Maryland, there is correspondence between the Landgericht Wiedergutmachungskammer in Ulm and the WCP 1 in Landsberg, dated February 21 and 23, 1951, respectively, about the court interviewing former Mayor Saalmüller who is imprisoned in War Criminal Prison 1 in Landsberg. The statement the court wishes to interrogate him on deals with a threat Saalmüller allegedly made to Louis Lang concerning the sale of the property. Louis Lang's heirs allege that "the former mayor of the *Gemeinde* Süssen, named Saalmüller, in December 1938 ordered their father, after his return from Dachau concentration camp, to come to the *Rathaus*, where Saalmüller told him that he would make sure that Louis Lang would be sent back to Dachau if Louis did not sell his property to the municipality." Landgericht Wiedergutmachungskammer letter dated February 21, 1951 in matters Rest U 14 (62) to the director of the WCP 1 in Landsberg. Saalmüller, Fritz U Aug 54, box 104, record group 549, National Archives Building, Washington, DC, no p.n.

82. Süssen City Archive, Süssen Gemeinderats-Protokoll, Band 1 and 2, 1933–38, Band 2, December 13, 1938, para. 132, 206–8.

83. Ibid.

84. "A 'Beigeordneter' is a communal elected official. The city council elects the *Beigeordnete* for an eight-year term. The *I. Beigeordnete* is also the deputy of the mayor. *Beigeordnete* are responsible for a certain area of administration." Quoted from http://de.wikipedia.org/wiki/Beigeordneter, 1 (accessed July 11, 2006). Courtesy Werner Runschke.

85. Süssen City Archive, Süssen Gemeinderats-Protokoll, Band 1 and 2, 1933–38, Band 2, December 13, 1938, para. 132, 208.

86. Dean, *Robbing the Jews*, 118. Süssen City Archive, 9897/9.

87. Süssen City Archive, 9897/16.

88. Ibid.

89. Collection Hugo Lang. Sales contract to Louis Lang.

90. Süssen City Archive, 9897/6.

91. Ibid.

92. Ibid, 1.

93. Ibid, 2.

94. Süssen City Archive, 9897, Lang sales contract 12/15/38, 6. Also Hugo Lang Documents.

95. Süssen City Archive, 9897, Lang sales contract 12/15/38, 3. Also Hugo Lang Documents.

96. Collection Hugo Lang, district notary public Stohrer, December 19, 1938. For levy on Jewish wealth, see Aly, *Hitler's Beneficiaries*, 200.

97. Dean defines Aryanization as "the transfer of Jewish property to non-Jewish hands in a broad sense," see *Robbing the Jews*, 15.

98. Collection Hugo Lang, attachment order, December 21, 1938.

99. Aly, *Hitler's Beneficiaries*, 200.

100. For more about frozen accounts, see also Aly, *Hitler's Beneficiaries*, 41–51, and On blocked accounts, see Dean, *Robbing the Jews*, 132–71 and Kaplan, *Between Dignity and Despair*, 71. Kaplan wrote about the plunder of the Jews during the Holocaust a full decade before Aly and Dean.

101. This is correct. See sales contract, para. 5, 3.

102. Süssen City Archive, 9897/7.

103. Collection Hugo Lang, letter dated April 12, 1939.

104. Ibid.

105. Helmut Walser Smith, ed. *The Holocaust and Other Genocides: History, Representation, Ethics* (Nashville: Vanderbilt University Press, 2002), 23.

106. Süssen City Archive, 9897/10.

107. Süssen City Archive, 9897/12.

108. Süssen City Archive, Süssen Gemeinderats-Protokoll, Band 1 and 2, 1933–38, Band 2, December 13, 1938, para. 132, 106–8.

109. Süssen City Archive, File 9897/13.

110. Süssen City Archive, 9897/13. This is the only prewar source by Louis Lang himself about the business arrangement he had with his brother. This document, not available to the heirs of Leopold in the restitution process, could have served as evidence of their financial loss, and hence their eligibility to file a claim. Also, there are statements by various officials that the brothers ran the business together. In the health insurance lists, Leopold is listed as an employer independent of Louis.

111. It is difficult to ascertain who the six family members may have been. Surely Louis, Eva, and Leopold, but the rest of the family came and went in an effort to find a way out.

112. There is only one prewar source for the date when Louis and Leopold's business was closed down, this letter by Mayor Saalmüller, dated January 28, 1939. See Süssen City Archive, 9897/13.

113. Dean, *Robbing the Jews*, 3.

114. Süssen City Archive, 9897/14.

115. Süssen City Archive, KAG A 003.66 9398 AR 243 (110); KAG A 003.66 9398 AR 239 86 (125).

116. Ludwigsburg State Archive, EL 350 I, Bü 1925/1, 1.

117. Ibid.

118. For more on Nazi plunder, see Aly, *Hitler's Beneficiaries*, 125.

119. Süssen City Archive, 9897/17.

120. Süssen City Archive, 9897/23.

121. Süssen City Archive, 9897/20; also Collection Hugo Lang.

122. Süssen City Archive, 9897/20.

123. Collection Hugo Lang. "Zur Erklärung der Auflassung bin ich jederzeit bereit." See Saalmüller note to March 4, 1939, letter from Württembergische Wirtschaftsminister to Landrat in Göppingen.

124. Süssen City Archive, File 9897/21, March 9, 1939.

125. Süssen City Archive, File 9897/22, March 14, 1939.

126. Collection Hugo Lang, "Auflassung," March 17, 1939.

127. Süssen City Archive, 9897/24.

128. Süssen City Archive, 9897/25, March 17, 1939.

129. An account from which the owner cannot withdraw funds because the assets are blocked.

130. Süssen City Archive, 9897/1.

131. Ludwigsburg State Archive, Finckh, E 352 Bü 3782, October 2, 1948, 1. Emphasis added.

132. Süssen City Archive, 9897/26.

133. Collection Hugo Lang, Lang lease in sales contract.

134. Süssen City Archive, 9897 2/1.

135. Ibid.

136. Süssen City Archive, 9897 3/1. "Vom Rathaus Süssen," in *Geislinger Zeitung*, June 10, 1939. See Süssen, Lang *Dokumentation*, 95.

137. Süssen City Archive, 9897 4/1, Aktennotiz, dated June 2, 1939.

138. Süssen City Archive, request to extend stay until July 1, 1940.

139. Süssen City Archive, KAG A 003.66 AR 236, 10.

140. Süssen City Archive, KAG A 003.66 AR 236, 17.

141. Süssen City Archive, KAG A 003.66 9398 AR 243 (101).

142. Süssen City Archive, KAG A 003.66 AR 236, 24. Fred and Kurt are reported on same memo, dated May 5, 1939.

143. Hugo Lang Interview with Professor Kurt Piehler, 8.

144. Ludwigsburg State Archive, EL 350 I, ES 25333/4, Fred Lang.

145. Ludwigsburg State Archive, EL 350 I, ES 25333/8, Fred Lang.

146. Ludwigsburg State Archive, EL 350 I, ES 25333/7, 1. Fred lost his citizenship when he left Germany.

147. Süssen City Archive, Manfred Lang File. Two Fleischer letters (original source in English).

148. Ludwigsburg State Archive, EL 350 I, ES 25333/7, Fred Lang.

149. Hugo Lang, conversation with the author in 2002.

150. Ludwigsburg State Archive, EL 350 I, ES 25333/8, Fred Lang.

151. Ludwigsburg State Archive, EL 350 I, ES 25333/19, Fred Lang.

152. Ludwigsburg State Archive, EL 350 I, ES 25333/22, Fred Lang.

153. Ludwigsburg State Archive, EL 350 I, ES 25333/25, Fred Lang.

154. Ludwigsburg State Archive, EL 350 I, ES 25333/25, Fred Lang.

155. Ludwigsburg State Archive, EL 350 I, ES 25333/27, Fred Lang.

156. Ludwigsburg State Archive, EL 350 I, ES 25333/46, Fred Lang.

157. Süssen City Archive, Manfred Lang File.

158. Collection Hugo Lang. Fred Lang death notice.

159. Süssen City Archive, KAG A003.66 AR 236, 24.

160. Süssen City Archive, KAG A003.66 AR 236, 48; also Lang *Dokumentation*.

161. Süssen City Archive, KAG A003.66 AR 236, 52.

162. Süssen City Archive, KAG A003.66 AR 236, 51, dated May 24, 1940. Name should be listed as Siegfried Israel Lang.

163. Courtesy of Mr. P. C. from Rodalben, who got in touch with the Süssen City Archive when he found correspondence between the mayors of Rodalben and Süssen concerning the Baer and Metzger families. All of the Plaut family information was also provided by Mr. C. to Hugo Lang. I am including this information, as only Mrs. Plaut's name and that she came to Süssen in 1939 was known. What happened to her or her children remains unknown. For March 27 as an alternate date of birth for Mrs. Plaut, see P. C. document in Süssen City Archive.

164. Süssen City Archive, KAG A003.66 AR 236, 28. Spelling in document is "Eleonore."

165. Süssen City Archive. P. C. notes in a letter, dated December 3, 2007, that the Samuel family from Rodalben emigrated via Göppingen in 1939, and suggests that Frau Plaut may have emigrated with them. However, Mr. Fred Samuel in Florida, in a letter to Hugo Lang, dated January 7, 2008, stated that he does not know an Eleonore Plaut, that his mother was the only Plaut and that her name was Johanna. One would think that he would remember Eleonore Plaut if she emigrated with them in 1939, so it is more than likely that she did not. Courtesy of Hugo Lang.

166. Collection Hugo Lang. Also Göppingen District Archive, 9895, June 26, 1959. Hans was born on April 12, 1917, Hermine Lang and Alfred Baer were married on July 2, 1920.

167. Collection Hugo Lang. P. C. letter to Hugo Lang, November 6, 2007.

168. Süssen City Archive, KAG A 003.66 AR 236, 53 (24), Siegfried Baer.

169. Süssen City Archive, KAG A 003.66 AR 236, 46 (28), Werner Joseph Baer.

170. See Avraham Shapira, ed., *Martin Buber: Pfade in Utopia. Über Gemeinschaft und deren Verwirklichung* (Heidelberg: Verlag Lambert Schneider, 1985).

171. Unidentified newspaper article, and "A Teen Holocaust Story," accessed on January 19, 2012, http://tinyurl.com/uufaithworks.

172. Süssen, Lang *Dokumentation*, 72.

173. Süssen City Archive, KAG A 003.66 6104 AR 235, 1.

174. Süssen City Archive, 9897, Letter from lawyer for Henriette Mary Schloss, neé Metzger, to Mayor Eisele, July 15, 1958, in A2090, courtesy Frau Hofacker.

175. Süssen City Archive. Information in the Saalmüller-Willenbacher correspondence courtesy of P. C., Rodalben, via the Süssen City Archive.

176. Süssen City Archive, courtesy of P. C., Rodalben City Archive, *Massnahmen gegen Juden*, 1939–42, 31.131.

177. Ibid.

178. Süssen City Archive, courtesy of P. C., Rodalben City Archive.

179. Ibid.

180. This apparently was the case, as P. C. mentions that Hugo's parents helped the Metzgers to move some of their furniture. In the reparations documents there is mention of the Baers' bedroom set.

181. Thanks to Werner Runschke for clarification of *HK*.

182. Courtesy of Süssen City Archive and P. C., Rodalben.

183. Ibid.

184. Saalmüller then posed seven questions to the mayor, including no. 6, "Who gave the orders for the seizure of the homes belonging to the Jewish families Baer and Metzger? And whether these orders were in writing.

185. A newspaper article, "Förderer von Sport und Kultur," in the *Saarbrücker Zeitung* on the death of Willenbacher, dated March 10, 1974, states that "Eugen Willenbacher was also a politician. He was appointed as mayor of Rodalben before the war; after the war, and after overcoming certain difficulties, he worked at the Homburg *Katasteramt*, where he served for forty years." Courtesy Süssen City Archive and P. C., Rodalben.

186. Ludwigsburg State Archive, E 352 Bü 3782, Häfele, September 27, 1948, 1.

187. Ludwigsburg State Archive, E 352 Bü 3782, Finckh, October 2, 1948, front page.

188. Ludwigsburg State Archive, E 352 Bü 3782, Schlecht, October 2, 1948, front page.

189. See *Gräfensteinbote* and *Mitteilungen*, courtesy of Süssen City Archive and P. C., Rodalben.

190. Advertisements maligning Eugenie Metzger in *Gräfensteinbote*, April 24, 1933, and *Mitteilungen*, April 26, 1933. See also Edmund Heringer, "Stationen auf dem Weg zur Vernichtung jüdischer Mitbürger," in *Rheinpfalz*, November 7, 1988. Courtesy of Süssen City Archive and P. C., Rodalben.

191. Süssen City Archive, KAG A 003.66 AR 236, 39.

192. Süssen City Archive, KAG A 003.66 AR 236, 53; also 9895.

193. Süssen City Archive, KAG A 003.66 AR 136, 53. The file reference is Reg. no. 6104 (*Überwachung der Juden*). See File no. KAG A 003.66 AR 136, 53 re Siegfried Baer.

194. Süssen Gemeindechronik. A notice in the *Hohenstaufen* of April 21, 1937, no. 91, states, "On the Führer's birthday, and upon consultation with the city council members, the mayor promoted administrative assistant August Eisele from Eislingen, who has been working for the Rathaus since September 1, 1935, to *Obersekretär*." See also Gemeinderats-Protokoll, April 6, 1937, 558.

195. Süssen Gemeindechronik. Postcard from August Eisele, dated 22 September 1939.

196. Robert P. Ericksen and Susannah Heschel, eds., *Betrayal: German Churches and the Holocaust* (Minneapolis: Fortress Press, 1999), and Helmut Walser Smith, *The Continuities of German History: Nation, Religion, and Race across the Long Nineteenth Century* (Cambridge: Cambridge University Press, 2008).

197. Collection Hugo Lang. Also *Geislinger Zeitung*, March 7, 1941, no. 56.

198. Süssen City Archive, A 404f, Fanny Landau Lang.

199. Süssen City Archive, KAG A 003.66 AR 236, 56.

200. Ludwigsburg State Archive, E 352 Bü 3782, Ö., September 27, 1948, 1.

201. Schmidt interview with Frau W. in 1999.

202. Süssen City Archive, KAG A 003.66 AR 236, 62.

203. Süssen City Archive, KAG A 003.66 AR 236, 63.

204. Süssen City Archive, KAG A 003.66 6104 AR 235, 4. The curfew affects Stephan Israel Banemann of Göppingen.

205. See the case of Willi and Elsa Burger, Geislingen, who really gave the designated officials a run for their money. They ultimately win and get to keep their radio. See Süssen City Archive, KAG A 003.66 6104 AR 235, 13 (59).

206. Süssen City Archive, KAG A 003.66 6104 AR 235, 2.

207. Ibid.

208. Süssen City Archive, KAG A 003.66 6104 AR 235, 8/7.

209. Ibid., 5.

210. Ibid., 17 (56). Max Neuburger had acquired the textile firm *Tuchfabrik August Borst* from Borst's heirs on July 7, 1869. They modernized the factory, replacing old water wheels with turbines and replacing the mechanical looms with new ones from England and Switzerland. See *700 Jahre Salach 1275–1975*. Gemeinde Salach (Salach: E. Kaisser, 1975), 39–40.

211. *700 Jahre Salach 1275–1975*, 39–40.

212. Süssen City Archive, KAG A 003.66 6104 AR 235, 6.

213. Ibid., 7.

214. Ibid., 14.

215. Ibid., 17.

216. Ibid., 21. "Erledigt mit Bericht vom 11. November 1939."

217. See "Synagogues by Country: Germany," accessed August 3, 2011, http://www.edwardvictor.com/Germany.htm.

218. Süssen City Archive, 9887/74, Saalmüller letter.

219. Süssen City Archive, Süssen Gemeinderats-Protokoll, April 25, 1939, para. 17, 40; also 9897/3.

220. Süssen City Archive, Süssen Gemeinderats-Protokoll, April 25, 1939, para. 17, 40; also 9897/26.

221. Süssen City Archive, 9897/15, E. K. request.

222. Göppingen District Archive, 9895 1 K. Courtesy of Frau Hofacker.

223. Ibid.

224. Ibid.

225. Ibid. "War nur kurze Zeit vermietet." Süssen Gemeinderats-Protokoll, 1939–46, April 25, 1939, para. 17 b, 40.

226. Göppingen District Archive, 9895 2.

227. Göppingen District Archive, 9895 1.

228. Süssen City Archive, 9897 3/1, Spar- und Darlehenskasse, as well as Göppingen District Archive, Sammlung Walter Ziegler, *Geislinger Zeitung*, June 10, 1939.

229. Süssen City Archive, 9897 4/1, Spar- und Darlehenskasse.

230. Göppingen District Archive, 9895 3, Spar- und Darlehenskasse.

231. Göppingen District Archive, 9895 4, Spar- und Darlehenskasse.

232. Ibid.

233. Süssen City Archive, 9897 3/1, Spar- und Darlehenskasse.

234. Göppingen District Archive, 9895 4, Z. request.

235. Göppingen District Archive, 9895, A 253. Also Collection Hugo Lang.

236. Göppingen District Archive, 9895 1, B. request.

237. Ibid., Finck to Lang re B. request.

238. Göppingen District Archive, 9895 2, B. request.

239. Göppingen District Archive, 9895 3, Z. request.

240. Süssen City Archive, Süssen Gemeinderats Protokoll 1939–46, December 5, 1941, para. 173, 232–31.

241. Göppingen District Archive, 9895 3, Z. request.

242. Ibid.

243. Göppingen District Archive, 9895 4, Z. request.

244. Göppingen District Archive, 9895 5, Z. request.

245. Göppingen District Archive, 9895 6, Z. request.

246. Süssen City Archive, Süssen Gemeinderats-Protokoll, 1942, May 8, 1942, para. 187, 254.

247. Ibid.

248. Süssen City Archive, Süssen Gemeinderats-Protokoll, 1939–46, April 25, 1939, para. 17 c, 40.

249. Süssen City Archive, 9897 3/1, renovation plan for Lang house.

250. Göppingen District Archive, 9895, renovations. See also Gemeinderats-Protokoll 1939–46, 12 March 1940, para. 80, 110.

251. A *Freibank* is a slaughtering facility for second-rate meat, animals that have been damaged, and so on. It was pointed out to the author that one happily ate such meat when no other meat was available.

252. Süssen City Archive, Süssen Gemeinderats-Protokoll, 1939–46, March 12, 1940, para. 80, 110.

253. Süssen City Archive, 9897 3/1. "Was not carried out. From August 1940 on prisoner of war camp."

254. Müller, *1896–1996: Sozialdemokraten in Süssen*, 142.

255. Ibid.

256. Ibid., 142–49, see map on p. 146.

257. Handwritten note from Hugo Lang, 2007. The miller's wife, Mrs. Schuler, remembered that in 1944 they received four prisoners of war as laborers. She thought they were Flemish. In archival documents and invoices from the Gasthaus Hirsch that fed the forced laborers they are throughout listed as French prisoners of war. The miller's wife tells that at first her husband was aghast because the prisoners were white-collar workers—one of them was deputy mayor at home. But Maurice, Jacques, Leo, and Gaston turned out to be really good helpers. Indeed, according to the invoices there were four such prisoners of war assigned to Schuler. Maurice, Gaston and Leon worked as *Lagerarbeiter* (warehouse workers), and "Jean" was a miller. The miller's wife may not remember the name right. According to the records, they received breakfast, lunch, and dinner for 30 days in the month of June 1944 at RM 2 per meal, amounting to a total of RM 240. According to Mrs. Schuler's memory, they lived in the former *Judenhaus*, together with the other prisoners of war. In the Schulers' garden the prisoners of war built a rabbit cage and raised some rabbits. "This way they occasionally had a good roast." However, these records are only for the years 1944 and 1945; there are no such records for earlier years. Süssen City Archive, R/G 4 Beilagen zur Gemeindepflegerechnung 1944/45, 637–92. Correspondence is with the Kgf.-Manusch.-Stammlager VA Ludwigsburg, Abrechnungsliste (Lohnkarte) für die in der Zeit v. 1. Juli–31. Juli 1944 beschäftigten französischen Kriegsgefangenen." See also Welsh and Dillenkofer, *Begegnungen*, 85–86.
258. Göppingen District Archive, 9895, March 13, 1941.
259. Ibid., June 13, 1941.
260. It has been suggested that this might be a typo.
261. Göppingen District Archive, 9895, June 3, 1941.
262. Göppingen District Archive, 9895 5, July 30, 1941.
263. Göppingen District Archive, 9895 6, August 28, 1942.
264. Göppingen District Archive, 9895 4, October 13, 1942.
265. Müller, *1896–1996: Sozialdemokraten in Süssen*, 148.

## 6. Hugo Lang's Escape and Life in the United States

1. Collection Hugo Lang. This notification of August 29, 1938 was sent to Ulm (an der Donau), 3 Weinhof . Hugo was apprentice in the restaurant Moos at that address. Another one was sent to 45 Hindenburgstrasse in Süssen.
2. Collection Hugo Lang, Häfele memo.
3. Ibid.
4. Per Hugo Lang, August 3, 2010.
5. Collection Hugo Lang, Hugo Lang cable to Max Liffmann, April 23, 1941.
6. Ibid., May 12, 1941.
7. Ibid., May 30, 1941.
8. Ibid., June 24, 1941.

9. Ibid., July 17, 1941.

10. Collection Hugo Lang, August 23, 1941, communication from "Joint" to Fred Lang. This is the date on which Hugo's visa expired!

11. Collection Hugo Lang. There is a second earlier affidavit, dated March 24, 1939, which lists both Fred and Hugo. Hugo says that is a mistake. According to Hugo's curriculum vitae, however, they both went to Long Island to thank their uncle.

12. Hugo Lang curriculum vitae, 4.

13. Süssen City Archive, Martin Bauch File.

14. See Gerda Hofreiter, *Allein in die Fremde: Kindertransporte von Österreich nach Frankreich, Grossbritannien und in die USA 1938–1941* (Innsbruck, Vienna, Bozen: StudienVerlag, 2010), 92.

15. Collection Hugo Lang, letter from Eva Lang, August 14, 1941.

16. When I asked Hugo about this, he merely said that it had to do with affidavits for the entire family. Isidor only wanted to sponsor the young ones who were healthy and could work and wouldn't be a burden on him. This explanation does not answer the question of the two names, Fred and Hugo, on one version of the affidavit, when Isidor then only sponsored Hugo. Fred was young and able to work, so why did he only sponsor Hugo? Perhaps it had something to do with Fred's arrest in England.

17. It was not Fred's wedding, his was on June 3, 1945. See Ludwigsburg State Archive EL 350 I, ES 25333/4.

18. Collection Hugo Lang. Postcard from Eva Lang, dated August 27, 1941.

19. Hugo did not recall who Cantor Hohenemser was but, while in Jerusalem perusing compositions for a project on Jewish music in April 2007, I came across a composition by Cantor Joseph Hohenemser. He had been the cantor in Haigerloch and succeeded in emigrating to the United States. His name reappears in connection with the Cantor's Assembly of the Jewish Theological Seminary in New York.

20. Collection Hugo Lang. Eva Lang letter, August 31, 1941.

21. Collection Hugo Lang. Postcard from Eva Lang, dated September 11, 1941.

22. Süssen, Lang *Dokumentation*, 23. Speech by Hugo Lang in Süssen, 1989. In conversation with the author on August 7, 2005, he confirmed that his arrival date was September 2.

23. Collection Hugo Lang. Hugo Lang curriculum vitae, 4–5.

24. Süssen, Lang *Dokumentation*, 25. This was the *Freigrenzbetrag* that was given to Hugo on June 6, 1941, in anticipation of his impending departure. When this didn't happen, he had to return the $4 on July 10. They were once more issued to him on August 1 in anticipation of his August 3 departure, which did happen. See Hugo's passport, Hugo Lang Documents.

25. Hugo Lang curriculum vitae, 4.; also Süssen *Dokumentation*, 23.

26. Collection Hugo Lang. Letter from Ruth, undated, but 1941.

27. Alice Liffman, wife of Max, and sister-in-law of Eva, was a concert pianist. She had a studio at 160 Irving Avenue in Providence, R.I. where she gave piano lessons. Her biography from 1941 states, "Alice Liffman is a graduate of Dr. Hoch's Conservatory in Frankfort on Main, where she received her degree of Bachelor of Music. Here she also specialized in the study of chamber music, and prepared for concert performance." Collection Hugo Lang.

28. Collection Hugo Lang, letter from Eva Lang, dated September 24, 1941.

29. Collection Hugo Lang, letter from Kurt Lang, dated October 5, 1941.

30. Collection Hugo Lang, letter from Eva and Leopold Lang, dated October 6, 1941.

31. Feed for cows and pigs.

32. Collection Hugo Lang, letter from Eva Lang, dated October 19, 1941.

33. Collection Hugo Lang, postcard from Eva Lang, dated November 16, 1941.

34. In fact, the Reparations documents, dated November 19, 1953, reveal that "cattle dealers Leopold and Louis Lang during the aforementioned period [1938–41] delivered milk to the *Molkereigenossenschaft* (Dairy Farmer's Association)." Ludwigsburg State Archive, EL 350 I, ES 12116, 26.

35. Collection Hugo Lang, postcard from Eva Lang, n.d. (after October 15, 1941).

36. Collection Hugo Lang, Max Liffmann letter, n.d. (1941).

37. Collection Hugo Lang, Hugo Liffmann letter, November 17, 1941.

38. Collection Hugo Lang, letter from Resi Gideon, dated November 25, 1943.

39. Hugo is not sure of the relationship to Bertha. In records, Sofie's last name is also spelled Behr, perhaps her sister?

40. Courtesy of Kurt Piehler. Letter from Manhattan Screw Co. Inc., dated October 12, 1942.

41. Ibid. Letter from Stuart Machine & Tool Co., dated April 22, 1946.

42. Süssen, Lang *Dokumentation*, 23; also Professor Piehler interview with Hugo Lang, 35. This is corroborated in Stanley Weintraub's account in *11 Days in December: Christmas at the Bulge, 1944*, with insightful glimpses into the attack on St. Vith and the transportation of the prisoners-of-war to Bad Orb on December 25, 1944 (New York: NAL Caliber, 2007), 48–53. In the Piehler interview Hugo says it was in December around Christmas.

43. Charles Guggenheim, producer, *Berga: Soldiers of Another War* (New York: Thirteen WNET New York, Educational Broadcasting Corporation, 2003).

44. Guggenheim, *Berga: Soldiers of Another War.*

45. Roger Cohen, "The Lost Soldiers of Stalag IX-B," *New York Times Magazine*, February 27, 2005, 46–112. Courtesy Hugo Lang.

46. Ibid., 50.

47. Hugo Lang speech 1989, see Süssen, Lang *Dokumentation*, 23–24.

48. Guggenheim. *Berga: Soldiers of Another War.*

49. Howard Byrne, "Geneva Convention is Joke to Yanks in Bad Orb." Courtesy Hugo Lang.

50. Hugo Lang documents. Also Süssen, Lang *Dokumentation*, 23.

51. Cohen, "The Lost Soldiers," 50.

52. PBS Preview 2003. *Berga: Soldiers of Another War*, accessed July 10, 2003, http://www.pbs.org/previews/Berga. Courtesy Hugo Lang. Click on 'Programs,' then 'B.'

53. Ibid.

54. Cohen, "The Lost Soldiers," 49.

55. Professor Piehler interview, 28.

56. Ibid., 42.

57. Ibid.

58. Collection Hugo Lang. Also Süssen, Lang *Dokumentation*, 24.

59. According to a conversation with Hugo Lang on August 3, 2010, his brother-in-law Sally Lemberger died in 2009.

60. Poem for Ruth, courtesy Hugo Lang.

61. Collection Hugo Lang, Persky letter.

62. Collection Hugo Lang, Silverman letter.

63. Collection Hugo Lang, letter Charms Candy Co., February 15, 1950. Courtesy of Kurt Piehler.

64. Bristol-Myers letter, July 28, 1952.

65. Collection Hugo Lang, letter Bristol-Myers, February 27, 1985. Courtesy of Kurt Piehler.

66. Collection Hugo Lang, letter Bristol-Myers, March 6, 1985. Courtesy of Kurt Piehler.

67. Collection Hugo Lang, Article, "Service Anniversaries," re Hugo's thirty-fifth anniversary with Bristol-Myers. Courtesy of Kurt Piehler.

68. Süssen, Lang *Dokumentation*, 23.

69. Lang Ketubah, Collection Hugo Lang.

70. Inge Lang autobiography, November 16, 2000, 1–2.

71. According to Jewish law, a child born of a Jewish mother is Jewish. Inge's mother was Jewish and had not converted to any other religion, therefore Inge is Jewish. The term *Mischling* was a Nazi term for any child born of a Jewish/non-Jewish union, regardless of the ethnicity of the mother, similar to other terminology such as halfbreed, mixed breed, and so on.

72. Süssen, Lang *Dokumentation*, 27–28.

73. Inge Lang autobiography, 3–4.

74. Süssen, Lang *Dokumentation*, 28.

75. Inge Lang autobiography, 5.

76. Collection Hugo Lang. Süssen City Archive, 9897/85.

77. Collection Hugo Lang. Süssen City Archive, 9897/85. This law has the number BGBl. I S. 1387 in Eisele's letter, and BGBl. S1387 in Hugo's letter.

78. Collection Hugo Lang, postcard dated March 23, 1954.

79. Collection Hugo Lang, Hugo Lang affidavit, June 17, 1957.

80. Collection Hugo Lang, Bader ledger excerpts.

81. Collection Hugo Lang, Reismüller letter, September 18, 1964.

82. Collection Hugo Lang, Reismüller letter from June 1967.

83. Collection Hugo Lang, Reismüller letter re compensation.

84. Collection Hugo Lang, ship's voyage.

85. Collection Hugo Lang, Reismüller letter re transportation costs, July 17, 1964.

86. Collection Hugo Lang, Reismüller letter to Hugo, July 29, 1964.

87. Collection Hugo Lang, Reismüller letter re transportation costs, August 27, 1964.

88. Collection Hugo Lang, Reismüller letter re transfer of money, September 9, 1964.

89. Collection Hugo Lang, compensation of DM 1,478.45.

90. Collection Hugo Lang, receipt for transfer of $369.60.

91. Collection Hugo Lang.

## 7. Deportation of the Lang Families

1. Ludwigsburg State Archive, Häfele testimony, E 352 Bü 3782, September 27, 1948, 1.

2. Ibid., 2.

3. Ludwigsburg State Archive, Finckh testimony, E 352 Bü 3782, October 2, 1948, front page.

4. Mrs. M. W. in an interview with the author, spring 1999.

5. Süssen City Archive, Süssen Gemeinderats-Protokoll, 1939–46, December 5, 1941, para. 173, 230–31.

6. Göppingen District Archive, 9895 5; 9895 2, Süssen Gemeinderats-Protokoll, 1939–46, December 5, 1941, para. 173, 230–31.

7. Although no physical violence took place in Süssen, one is nevertheless reminded of Jan Gross's disturbing recreation of the murders of Jedwabne. Jan Gross, *Neighbors: The Destruction of the Jewish Community in Jedwabne, Poland* (Princeton: Princeton University Press, 2001).

8. Süssen, Lang *Dokumentation*, 97.

9. Süssen City Archive, Gemeindechronik, "Süssen ist nun judenfrei." Also Lang *Dokumentation*, 97.

10. Collection Hugo Lang, Lang lease.

11. Süssen, Lang *Dokumentation*, Fred "Israel" Lang.

12. Ludwigsburg State Archive, E 352 Bü 3782, Häfele, September 27, 1948, front page.

13. Süssen, Lang *Dokumentation*, 75.

14. Or possibly, had been ordered to give.

15. Ulrich Seemüller, *Das jüdische Altersheim Herrlingen und die Schicksale seiner Bewohner* (Blaustein: Gemeinde Blaustein, n.d.), 177–78. Many thanks to Werner Runschke for finding this book.

16. Göppingen District Archive, 9895, Zeimann, April 13 and 15, 1959.

17. Süssen, Lang *Dokumentation*, 72.

18. Göppingen District Archive, 9895, April 13, 1959.

19. Mayor Bauch mentions "at least two euthanasia victims" in his speech on the occasion of the *Volkstrauertrag* 1988. In Süssen, Lang *Dokumentation*, 70.

20. Ludwigsburg State Archive, Finckh testimony, E 352 Bü 3782, October 2, 1948, 1.

21. Ludwigsburg State Archive, Häfele testimony, E 352 Bü 3782, September 27, 1948, front page.

22. Ibid.

23. Ludwigsburg State Archive, Schlecht testimony, E 352 Bü 3782, October 2, 1948, front page–1.

24. Ibid, 1.

25. Ibid.

26. Ludwigsburg State Archive, Häfele testimony, E 352 Bü 3782, September 27, 1948, 2.

27. Collection Hugo Lang. Eva Lang's last postcard before deportation, n.d.

28. Collection Hugo Lang. Schlecht letter, January 21, 1948, "als mir Louis seinerzeit, bevor sie in Süssen weg mussten, die 9,000 RM in bar gegeben hat."

29. Collection Hugo Lang. Letter from Kurt to Miriam, Fred and Hugo, no date, probably November 1945. "You knew Herr Schlecht from Ebersbach (cigar factory). He was well acquainted with my late father and helped us much in the most difficult of times."

30. Ludwigsburg State Archive, Häfele testimony, E 352 Bü 3782, September 27, 1948, 1.

31. Ludwigsburg State Archive, Häfele and Finckh testimonies, E 352 Bü 3782, September 27, 1948, 1, and October 2, 1948, front page.

32. Ludwigsburg State Archive, Häfele testimony, E 352 Bü 3782, September 27, 1948, front page.

33. Ibid., 2.

34. Ludwigsburg State Archive, Finckh testimony, E 352 Bü 3782, October 2, 1948, 1.

35. Ludwigsburg State Archive, Häfele testimony, E 352 Bü 3782, September 27, 1948, 3.

36. Ibid., 1.

37. Ludwigsburg State Archive, Schlecht testimony, E 352 Bü 3782, October 2, 1948, front page.

38. Ludwigsburg State Archive, Ö. testimony, E 352 Bü 3782, September 27, 1948, front page.

39. Ludwigsburg State Archive, Finckh testimony, E 352 Bü 3782, October 2, 1948, front page.

40. Ludwigsburg State Archive, Schlecht testimony, E 352 Bü 3782, October 2, 1948, 2.

41. Ludwigsburg State Archive, Häfele and Finckh testimonies, E 352 Bü 3782, September 27, 1948, and October 2, 1948.

42. Ludwigsburg State Archive, Häfele testimony, E 352 Bü 3782, September 27, 1948, 1.

43. Ibid., 2.

44. Ibid., 1.

45. Ibid.

46. Ludwigsburg State Archive, Finckh testimony, E 352 Bü 3782, October 2, 1948, front page.

47. Ludwigsburg State Archive, Schlecht testimony, E 352 Bü 3782, October 2, 1948, 1.

48. Ludwigsburg State Archive, Ö. testimony, E 352 Bü 3782, September 27, 1948, front page.

49. Ludwigsburg State Archive, Häfele testimony, E 352, Bü 3782, September 27, 1948, 3.

50. Hugo Lang Interview with Professor Kurt Piehler, 7.

51. Ludwigsburg State Archive, Häfele testimony, E 352, Bü 3782, September 27, 1948, 2.

52. Ludwigsburg State Archive, Rall testimony, E 352 Bü 3782, October 26, 1948, 2.

53. Ludwigsburg State Archive, Moll testimony, E 352 Bü 3782, October 12, 1948, front page–1. April 1942 was the second deportation from Weissenstein. The Jewish community in Stuttgart, of course, had been completely ravaged as a result of the Holocaust and of World War II. By 1949 the Israelitische Kultusvereinigung Württemberg (Württemberg Jewish Community Organization) was reaching out to various government offices, among them the Landratsamt Göppingen, to try and get a sense of the fate of their members. On May 2, 1949, they asked, "Do you know what happened to the resettlement files of the Jews who were taken to Schloss Weissenstein? At the beginning of 1942 Jews from Stuttgart were resettled to Schloss Weissenstein and deported from there at various times. It is of great importance to us to obtain documents concerning the deportation (personal data and date of deportation), as the files of the Jewish community were destroyed during the bombardment of Stuttgart in 1944." Süssen City Archive, KAG A 003.66 250/7 (15), Israelitische Kultusgemeinde Württemberg. An answer went out to the Jewish community in Stuttgart on July 18, 1949, with some attachments concerning the surveillance of Jews, but it was not very helpful in clearing up what happened to the Stuttgart Jews in Weissenstein. "When and where the Jews who were housed in Schloss Weissenstein

were deported cannot be ascertained from the files." The writer mused that the deportations were carried out directly by the Gestapo. Süssen City Archive, KAG A 003.66 250/7 (14), Israelitische Kultusgemeinde Württembergs. Additional files only surfaced after 2000, so that a history of the Stuttgart Jews who were taken to the old-age home in Schloss Weissenstein and deported from there could finally be written by Dr. Ruess. See Karl-Heinz Ruess, *Die Deportation der Göppinger Juden* (Ebersbach: Bechtel Druck GmbH, 2001), 29–33.

54. Ruess, *Deportation*, 30.

55. Ibid., 31.

56. Ibid., 33.

57. Ibid.

58. Ludwigsburg State Archive, Moll testimony, E 352 Bü 3782, October 12, 1948, 1.

59. Ludwigsburg State Archive, Häfele testimony, E 352, Bü 3782, September 27, 1948, 2.

60. Ibid.

61. Sauer, *Die jüdischen Gemeinden in Württemberg und Hohenzollern: Denkmale, Geschichte, Schicksale*. Archivdirektion Stuttgart (Stuttgart: W. Kohlhammer Verlag, 1966), 22.

62. Alfred Winter, *The Ghetto of Riga and Continuance. A Survivor's Memoir* (Self-published, 1998), 33.

63. Sauer, *Die Jüdischen Gemeinden in Württemberg und Hohenzollern*, 22.

64. Winter, *Ghetto of Riga*, 33.

65. Ibid.

66. Sauer, *Die Jüdischen Gemeinden in Württemberg und Hohenzollern*, 22.

67. See http://www.yadvashem.org/.

68. Ibid.

69. Göppingen District Archive, 9895 3.

70. Collection Hugo Lang, Ruth Lang letter of February 25, 1945.

71. Süssen City Archive, KAG A 003.66 AR 236, 65.

72. Ludwigsburg State Archive, Häfele testimony, E 352 Bü 3782, September 27, 1948, 1.

73. Ludwigsburg State Archive, Petzold testimony, E 352 Bü 3782, October 14, 1948, front page.

74. Ibid.

75. Ludwigsburg State Archive, Häfele testimony, E 352 Bü 3782, September 27, 1948, 2.

76. Ibid., 2.

77. Ludwigsburg State Archive, Finckh testimony, E 352 Bü 3782, October 2, 1948, 2.

78. Ludwigsburg State Archive, Niess testimony, E 352 Bü 3782, October 18, 1948, front page.

79. See Aly's discussion of the German war chest, in *Hitler's Beneficiaries*, 184.

80. Ludwigsburg State Archive, Finckh testimony, E 352 Bü 3782, October 2, 1948, 2.

81. Ibid., 2.

82. Süssen City Archive, KAG A 003.66, 9398 AR 239, 62, 9. "The Court accepts the existing flyer from the mayor, dated 12/9/41, page 32, enclosure 10 in the files as evidence that the Finanzamt only auctioned off furniture in Süssen. The town crier announced two older living room sets and four bedroom sets, some wardrobes and kitchen equipment. This list only shows furniture for six rooms, while the apartments of the two Lang families consisted of at least four rooms each of which, according to reliable testimony by witnesses Häfele and K., were completely furnished before deportation. Bed frames, tables, and chairs must also have been part of the rooms in which the children slept. Since the flyer only served as the basis for the town crier's announcement, it is possible that it did not contain all, but only the most important, items." There also was a kitchen cabinet with the cookbooks mentioned in chapter 1.

83. See Lang restitution in chapter 8.

84. Ludwigsburg State Archive, Petzold testimony, E 352 Bü 3782, October 14, 1948, front page.

85. Oberregierungsrat Muschgai, Württembergisches Innenministerium; see Niess testimony in Ludwigsburg State Archive, E 352 Bü 3782, October 18, 1948, 1.

86. Ludwigsburg State Archive, Petzold testimony, E 352 Bü 3782, October 14, 1948, front page.

87. Ibid. There are two (conflicting) dates for the auction. Document KAG A 003.66 9398 AR 239, 62, p. 12, from Landgericht Stuttgart Rückerstattungskammer says auction took place on December 10, 1941.

88. On the role of the *Preussische Seehandlung*, see Aly, *Hitler's Beneficiaries*, 41–68.

89. Ludwigsburg State Archive, Petzold testimony, E 352 Bü 3782, October 14, 1948, front page and p. 1. See also Dean on Patzer files, in *Robbing the Jews*, 230.

90. Dean, *Robbing the Jews*, 231.

91. Ludwigsburg State Archive, Petzold testimony, E 352 Bü 3782, October 14, 1948, 1.

92. Ludwigsburg State Archive, Ö. testimony, E 352 Bü 3782, September 27, 1948, 1. See also Kaplan, *Between Dignity and Despair*, 234.

93. Collection Hugo Lang, Ruth Lang letter of November 17, 1945. See also Kaplan, *Between Dignity and Despair*, 186.

94. Photo of Lang clock in Süssen City Hall, courtesy of Werner Runschke in 2002. See also Süssen City Archive, A 003.66 9398 AR 239, 62.

95. Ludwigsburg State Archive, Petzold testimony, E 352 Bü 3782, October 14, 1948, 1.

96. Süssen City Archive, KAG A 003.66 9398 AR 239, 44 (167) Reparations document re auction receipts.

97. Dean, *Robbing the Jews*, 374.

98. Göppingen District Archive, 9895 9, December 5, 1941.

99. Göppingen District Archive, 9895 2, December 5, 1941 and 9895 6, April 14, 1942.

100. Ibid.

101. Göppingen District Archive, 9895 3/12. Süssen Gemeinderats-Protokoll, 1939–46, May 8, 1942, para. 187, 254–55. "The soldier and the day laborer are drafted as of May 1, 1942. The miller would also soon be drafted, but had been renting the apartment since February 1, 1942." See also notification to *Gemeindekasse* April 14, 1942, about rental of two apartments to day laborer and soldier signed by Finckh. Süssen City Archive 9897/6.

102. An informant from the time states that immediately upon his return, Kurt moved in with the Schlechts.

## 8. Lang Family Liberation, Requisitions, and Restitution

1. "Hallowed and enhanced may God be throughout the world of God's own creation. May God cause God's sovereignty soon to be accepted, during our life and the life of all Israel. And let us say: Amen." Quoted from *Siddur Sim Shalom. A Prayerbook for Shabbat, Festivals, and Weekdays*, ed. with trans. Rabbi Jules Harlow (New York: The Rabbinic Assembly/The United Synagogue of America, 1985), 195.

2. There is no record that Louis and Fanny were ever declared dead as were the other family members.

3. Göppingen District Archive, Süssen City Archive A 2090. Courtesy Frau Hofacker. Only in 2002 was a folder found that contains death certificates for the Baers (1961), the Metzgers (1951), and some of the Langs (1951). KRA GP A 2090, now Süssen City Archive, courtesy of Frau Hofacker. The folder includes individual death notices for Siegfried, Hans Kurt, and Werner Josef Baer as well as the Metzgers. In addition, Falk Sahm, Walter Zeimann, and Luise Ottenheimer were murdered, for a total of fifteen.

4. Göppingen District Archive, Süssen City Archive A 2090.

5. Ibid.

6. Ibid.

7. Ibid.

8. Ibid.

9. Different sources give different dates for Baers. "Time of death was determined to be December 31, 1945, 12 midnight."

10. Göppingen District Archive, Süssen City Archive A 2090.

11. Ibid.

12. Ibid.

13. Collection Hugo Lang. Letter from Ruth Lang to Hugo, Fred, and Miriam, January 21, 1946.

14. Ibid., October 2, 1945.

15. Bromberg, in Poland, was a satellite camp of Stutthof. According to Alfred Winter, "In Bromberg the women worked under worse conditions than on the railroad trucks [tracks?] and their living conditions were inhuman." See Winter, *Ghetto of Riga*, 215.

16. Collection Hugo Lang. Ruth Lang letter dated February 25, 1945.

17. Ibid.

18. Collection Hugo Lang. Ruth Lang letter dated September 13, 1945.

19. Müller, *1896–1996: Sozialdemokraten in Süssen*, 150.

20. Christopher Ziedler, "'Ganget hoim zu eire Weiber': Das Kriegsende auf dem Land am Beispiel Süssen," *Stuttgarter Zeitung*, April 20, 2005.

21. Süssen Gemeindechronik, *Neue Württembergische Zeitung*, no. 10, February 4, 1947, n.p.

22. Memorandum for the file, case 12–45 Konstanz, dated February 4, 1946, box 89 (1), record group 549, National Archives and Records Administration (NARA), Washington, DC. See http://www.jewishvirtuallibrary.org/jsource/Holocaust/dachautrial/fs30.pdf.

23. AG 383 JAG, Headquarters European Command, October 29, 1948, "Execution of Sentence" in the case of the *United States vs. Albert Heim, et al.* (case no. 12–45), Box 89 (2), record group 549, NARA, Washington, DC.

24. Information in Military Court document, *United States vs. Albert Heim et al.*, case no. 12–45, Deputy Judge Advocate's Office, 77–8 War Crimes Group, European Command, APO 407, dated November 19, 1947. Document courtesy of Landsberg City Archive. My profound gratitude to Ms. Elke Kiefer, Diplom-Archivarin (FH) of the Landsberg City Archive, for this document as well as other valuable sources. I am further indebted to Dr. Jürgen Klöckler, Konstanz City Archive Director, and to Mr. Robert Bierschneider, *Archivamtmann* of the Munich State Archive, Bavarian State Archive, for their prompt assistance with this matter. And most importantly, my deepest gratitude to Mrs. Michaela Mingoia of the Ludwigsburg State Archive, Baden-Württemberg State Archive, for her invaluable guidance in this matter as well as throughout the course of the research for this project. The Ludwigsburg State Archive contained the information that "Mayor [Saalmüller] was arrested, he was a party member since 1933, and sentenced to lifelong imprisonment." Ludwigsburg State Archive, EL 402/9 Bü 658, March 11, 1947. The document from the Vermögenskontrolle Amt (Property Control Office) did not give the reason for the judicial proceedings, but did note that the property of Mayor Fritz Saalmüller had been confiscated on January 16, 1947. A similar document, dated August 28, 1947 states that Saalmüller was sentenced to life imprisonment "for political reasons." Ludwigsburg State Archive, EL 402/9 Bü 658.

25. Mayor Saalmüller's wife, Hedwig Saalmüller, was not implicated in any way during the Nazi period. While all of their property was confiscated initially, she was able to prove that she had been neither a party member nor a member of the Nazi *Frauenschaft*, or women's organization, nor any other Nazi organization. Ludwigsburg State Archive EL 402/9 Bü 658. To get some clarity about her financial situation, Frau Saalmüller wrote to the Office for Property Control, telling them that her husband was sentenced to lifelong imprisonment already in December 1946 "because of a military matter." Ludwigsburg State Archive EL 402/9 Bü 658. On March 5, 1947, the Public Prosecutor wrote that "based on the information in your questionnaire you are not affected by the Denazification Law of March 5, 1946." Ludwigsburg State Archive EL 402/9 Bü 658. Hence she was able to get her share of their property back, although not her husband's share.

26. Landeskirchliches Archiv Stuttgart. Martin Pfleiderer, Pfarrbericht 1948 for Pfarrei Süssen, August 3, 1948, 12. The document from the Konstanz City Archive, *United States vs. Albert Heim, et al.*, and dated November 19, 1947 is the "Review and Recommendations" document for the three prisoners. The court recommends in Saalmüller's instance "that the findings and sentence be approved." Kurt Lang in a letter to his cousins in the United States, dated November 21, 1945, also remarks that Saalmüller is serving a life sentence. Collection Hugo Lang.

27. Office of the United States Parole Officer, January 28, 1955, "Change of Parole Area and Plan." Case 12–45, box 89 (3), record group 549, NARA, Washington, DC. Also American Embassy in Germany, Office of the US Parole Officer. Case file for Saalmüller, Fritz, con. 5, box 104, record group 549, National Archives Building, Washington, DC.

28. Müller, *1896–1996: Sozialdemokraten in Süssen*, 150.

29. From "Wir haben uns die Hände gereicht," *Süssener Mitteilungen*, No. 28, July 14, 1983. Courtesy of Werner Runschke.

30. Ludwigsburg State Archive: E 352 Bü 3782, Schlecht testimony, October 2, 1948, 2.

31. Süssen, Lang *Dokumentation*, 29.

32. Collection Hugo Lang, Ruth Lang letter dated September 13, 1945.

33. Collection Hugo Lang, Siegfried Lang letter dated September 1, 1946.

34. Collection Hugo Lang, Ruth Lang letter dated November 17, 1945.

35. Collection Hugo Lang, Siegfried Lang letter dated September 22, 1945.

36. Collection Hugo Lang, Kurt Lang letter dated November 21, 1945.

37. This is a known fact because the miller had made some permanent improvements in the apartment for which he was to be compensated. The *Finanzamt* approved the request on November 7, 1946, and RM 329.80 was deposited into his savings account. Süssen City Archive, 9897/16.

38. Heinzmann also made a statement about Aryanized businesses, dated October 20, 1945 (Süssen, KAG AR 7 2272), courtesy Frau Hofacker, Göppingen District Archive.

39. In a much later document we learn that it was not police chief Holl who acquired the second bedroom, but a Frau K. in Weissenstein, former help to the Langs. See Süssen City Archive, KAG A 003 66 9398 AR 239, 45 (165, 166).

40. Süssen City Archive, KAG A 003.66 9398 AR 243 (98).

41. Süssen City Archive, KAG A 003.66 9398 AR 243 (99).

42. Süssen City Archive, KAG A 003.66 9398 AR 243 (102).

43. Kurtchen is Kenneth in Providence, Max and Alice Liffmann's son, who becomes bar mitzvah during WWII.

44. Collection of Hugo Lang, Ruth letter dated August 14, 1945.

45. Kurt Piehler, interview with Hugo Lang, 26.

46. For more on the post–World War II complications for survivors and refugees in Europe, see introduction to *Life beyond the Holocaust: Memories and Realities* by Mira Ryczke Kimmelman, ed. Gilya Gerda Schmidt (Knoxville: University of Tennessee Press, 2005).

47. Collection Hugo Lang. Leo Kram letter dated September 24, 1945, and Ruth Lang letter dated October 24, 1945.

48. Collection Hugo Lang, Ruth Lang letter, August 26, 1945.

49. Collection Hugo Lang, Ruth Lang letter, September 13, 1945.

50. Süssen City Archive, KAG A 003.66 9398 AR 243 (118).

51. Süssen City Archive, KAG A 003.66 9398 AR 243 (119).

52. Süssen City Archive, KAG A 003.66 9398 AR 243 (114).

53. Süssen City Archive, KAG A 003.66 9398 AR 243 (115).

54. Süssen City Archive, KAG A 003.66 9398 AR 243 (109). On March 13, 1946, there is a letter from the *Amt für Besatzungsleistungen* Stadt Stuttgart to the Landratsamt in Göppingen asking that this bill be paid. A handwritten note dated March 8 [1948?] states that this invoice was referred for payment on May 5, 1947, and was paid as no. 505.

55. Süssen City Archive, KAG A 003.66 9398 AR 243 (107).

56. Süssen City Archive, KAG A 003.66 9398 AR 243 (117).

57. Süssen City Archive, KAG A 003.66 9398 AR 243 (101). See also Dean, *Robbing the Jews*, 135n14, re this order.

58. Collection Hugo Lang, Letter from Ruth Lang to Hugo, September 28, 1945.

59. Collection Hugo Lang, Ruth Lang letter of October 2, 1945 to Hugo.

60. Collection Hugo Lang, Ruth Lang letter dated September 28, 1945.

61. Collection Hugo Lang, Kurt Lang letter dated October 10, 1945 (emphasis added).

62. Collection Hugo Lang, Ruth Lang letter dated October 10, 1945 (emphasis added).

63. One *Zentner* is 100 German lbs. or 50 kg.

64. Collection Hugo Lang, Kurt Lang letter to Hugo, no date, but late 1945. See same information in Ruth Lang letter of October 10, 1945.

65. Collection Hugo Lang, Ruth Lang letter of October 24, 1945.

66. Süssen City Archive, KAG A 003.66 9398 AR 243 (104).

67. Collection Hugo Lang, Ruth Lang letter dated October 2, 1945.

68. Collection Hugo Lang, Ruth Lang letter dated January 7, 1946.

69. Collection Hugo Lang, Ruth Lang letter dated October 2, 1945.

70. Collection Hugo Lang, Ruth Lang letter dated December 19, 1945.

71. Collection Hugo Lang, Siegfried Lang letter dated January 9, 1946.

72. Collection Hugo Lang, Ruth Lang letter dated November 21, 1945.

73. Collection Hugo Lang, Ruth Lang letter of September 28, 1945.

74. Collection Hugo Lang, Ruth Lang letter of October 10, 1945.

75. "Mao Zur," often called "Rock of Ages," is a traditional Hanukkah hymn.

76. Collection Hugo Lang, Ruth Lang letter dated November 17, 1945.

77. Collection Hugo Lang, Kurt Lang letter dated November 21, 1945.

78. Collection Hugo Lang, Kurt Lang letter dated December 3, 1945.

79. Collection Hugo Lang, Ruth Lang letter dated December 3, 1945. Auerbachers and Munz were from the Göppingen Jewish community.

80. Collection Hugo Lang, Ruth Lang letter to Miriam, et al., dated December 3, 1945.

81. Collection Hugo Lang, Ruth Lang letter dated January 10, 1946.

82. Collection Hugo Lang, Ruth Lang letter dated September 2, 1945.

83. Collection Hugo Lang, Siegfried Lang letter dated September 22, 1945. September 8 and 9, Rosh Hashanah, and September 17, 1945, Yom Kippur.

84. Collection Hugo Lang, Ruth Lang letter of September 13, 1945.

85. He remained there until his death in 1978. See account of son, Dr. Fredy Kahn of Nagold, in Uri R. Kaufmann and Carsten Kohlmann, eds., *Jüdische Viehhändler zwischen Schwarzwald und Schwäbischer Alb* (Horb-Rexingen: Barbara Staudacher Verlag, 2008), 170–88. See also Kaplan, *Between Dignity and Despair*, 186.

86. Collection Hugo Lang, Ruth Lang letter to brothers and Miriam, dated January 7, 1946.

87. Süssen City Archive, include KAG A 003.66 9398 AR 243 (105), dated by the Office of Requisition and Housing [Refugees] March 13, 1946. Additional correspondence concerning requisitions include 116, 120, 110, 111, 112, 108, 103, 90, 91, 95, 96. Emphasis added.

88. Collection Hugo Lang, Ruth letter with no date, but after November 21, 1945.

89. Göppingen District Archive KRA GP 9895 1, Sally Lemberger letter. Courtesy of Frau Hofacker. Name spellings vary in sources.

90. Ibid.

91. Collection Hugo Lang. Ruth Lang letter dated March 26, 1946. Sali Lemberger was one of only two survivors from Rexingen. See also chapter 13 in Mimi Schwartz, *Good Neighbors, Bad Times: Echoes of my Father's Village* (Lincoln and London: University of Nebraska Press, 2008). This is a slightly

disguised retrospective by an aged Sali Lemberger whom Mimi interviewed for her book. Ruth mentions in her letter of September 2, 1945 that "Sali Lemberger and a Mrs. Schwartz are the only ones who survived from Rexingen." The other survivor, Hedwig Schwarz, had bad legs and had difficulty walking. She was deported to Theresienstadt and fell off a wagon before getting to the camp. She was taken to a hospital where she spent the war years. At the end of the war she asked to return to Stuttgart, where she spent the rest of her life, cared for by nuns. She is buried in the Rexingen Jewish cemetery. Hedwig Schwartz was a relative of Marilyn Kallet's in Knoxville, Tennessee. Source my visit to Rexingen and conversation with keeper of local Jewish archives, *Herr* Sayer, in 2002.

92. Collection Hugo Lang, Ruth Lang letter dated December 3, 1945.

93. Collection Hugo Lang, Ruth Lang letter dated January 7, 1946.

94. Collection Hugo Lang.

95. Collection Hugo Lang, Kurt Lang letter dated February 2 (?), 1946.

96. Collection Hugo Lang, Kurt Lang letter dated March 26, 1946.

97. Collection Hugo Lang, Ruth Lang letter dated April 24, 1946.

98. Ibid.

99. Collection Hugo Lang, Ruth Lang telegram via Deutsche Reichspost to Iska Kram (?). "Auswanderung in Ordnung. Überfahrt Ende April 1946."

100. Collection Hugo Lang, letter by Leo Kram to Hugo Lang, dated May 2, 1946. Original text in English.

101. Collection Hugo Lang, NRS letter dated May 16, 1946. Hugo does not know who the seven people were. We know that there were six affidavits.

102. Collection Hugo Lang, NRS letter dated May 17, 1946.

103. Collection Hugo Lang, Ruth Lang telegram to Fred Lang, dated May 18, 1946.

104. A conversation between a government official and Lt. Weinstein on May 16, 1946, at 9:30 A.M., yielded the following directions, "When Jewish families and individuals emigrate to the U.S. and the Office of Requisitions had requisitioned and bought furniture and clothing for them, all bought and requisitioned items of the emigrants are to be returned to the Office of Requisitions within three months. Cost for the removal and transport are to be absorbed by the persons who are emigrating or by the persons who have been charged with the administration of their possessions. Vacated apartments may again be rented out after one month, even in the case of houses owned by the emigrants." Süssen City Archive, KAG A 003.66 9398 AR 243 (97).

105. Collection Hugo Lang, letter from Hugo Lang to the US Military (?), only addressed to "Gentlemen."

106. Collection Hugo Lang, letter from Ruth Lang to Lt. Bennett in Göppingen, dated July 3, 1946. Emphasis added.

107. Süssen City Archive, KAG A 003.66 AR 241 (11). Office of Occupation Disbursement. A document dated April 14, 1947, detailed the expenses for the Lang siblings in Süssen, for furniture, beds, quilts, shoes (RM 8,420.14) and diverse furniture and kitchen equipment according to the attached bill (RM 808.10). Süssen City Archive, KAG A 003.66 AR 241 (10), Office of Occupation Disbursement.

108. On June 23, 1947, Karl Laible K.G. in Salach wrote to the Landratsamt in Göppingen because their invoice to the Landratsamt for the armchair and couch frames was returned unpaid. Karl Laible writes, "The Lang brothers at that time ordered the frames specifically on your orders and accompanied by one of your gentlemen, that had to be enough [authorization]. For this reason I have tried repeatedly to get my money from you." Süssen City Archive, KAG A 003.66 9398 AR 243 (113).

109. Süssen City Archive, KAG A 003.66 AR 241 (9).

110. Süssen City Archive, KAG A 003.66 AR 241 (4).

111. Süssen City Archive, KAG A 003.66 AR 241 (5), "Zusammenstellung."

112. Süssen City Archive, KAG A 003.66 9398 AR 243 (93).

113. Süssen City Archive, KAG A 003.66 9398 AR 239 12 (186).

114. Süssen City Archive, KAG A 003.66 9398 AR 239 21 (183).

115. Süssen City Archive, KAG A 003.66 9398 AR 239 22 (182).

116. Süssen City Archive, KAG A 003.66 9398 AR 239 25 (179).

117. Süssen City Archive, KAG A 003.66 9398 AR 239 33 (178).

118. Süssen City Archive, 9897 40.

119. Ludwigsburg State Archive, EL 350 I, Bü 1925/6.

120. Ludwigsburg State Archive, EL 350 I, Bü 1925/7.

121. Ludwigsburg State Archive, EL 350 I, Bü 1925/5.

122. In the correspondence, Dr. Z. was confused about the reason the two gentlemen were confiscating his furniture. He thought that they were looking for furniture that had been in the Jewish old-age home in Schloss Weissenstein. It is more than likely that they were searching for the Lang family furniture that had been bought at auction also by individuals who lived far from Süssen, such as the former Lang maid, Frau K., in Weissenstein and that they got carried away in their zeal.

123. Süssen City Archive, KAG A 003.66 9398 AR 243, August 5, 1947.

124. Süssen City Archive, KAG A 003.66 9398 AR 243, 4 (86), 8.

125. Süssen City Archive, KAG A 003.66 9398 AR 239 40c (174), 1; also Süssen City Archive, KAG A 003.66 9398 AR 239, 49, 2.

126. Süssen City Archive, KAG A 003.66 9398 AR 243 (80).

127. Süssen City Archive, KAG A 003.66 9398 AR 243 (85).

128. Süssen City Archive, KAG A 003.66 7613 AR 250, about using the term *Jew* on files.

129. See also Süssen City Archive, KAG 003.66 9398 AR 239, 49 (160, 161).

130. These were Frau H., Stuttgart, and Frl. E., Zuffenhausen/Basel, previously mentioned, as well as Herr H., Süssen; Herr K, Weissenstein, and Frau M., Salach. Süssen City Archive, KAG 003.66 9398 AR 239, 63 (133).

131. Süssen City Archive, KAG A 003.66 9398 AR 239 40c (174).

132. Süssen City Archive, KAG 003.66 9398 AR 239, 63 (133).

133. Süssen City Archive, KAG A 003.66 9398 AR 243 (106).

134. *Weihnachtsamnestie* is a legal concept of pardoning criminals some time before Christmas so that they are not only free for Christmas, but have time to reintegrate themselves into society before the holiday. In addition, Nazis were also exonerated and pardoned via a variety of amnesties by the German government as well as the Allies. See Norbert Frei, *Adenauer's Germany and the Nazi Past: The Politics of Amnesty and Integration*, trans. Joel Golb (New York: Columbia University Press, 2002).

135. Süssen City Archive, KAG A 003.66 9398 AR 243 (84).

136. Frau H.'s letter dated June 7, 1949, was first forwarded by the Interior Ministry to the Finance Ministry in Stuttgart. The Finance Ministry, in turn, sent the letter to the Justice Ministry. The Finance Ministry also responded to the Landratsamt in Göppingen, noting that "the requisition based on requisitions bill no. 1480 occurred in the name of the U.S. Occupation Forces and one would assume that a timely presentation of the bill would have resulted in payment by the Office of Requisitions." On September 22, 1949, the Interior Ministry in Stuttgart wrote to the Landratsamt in Göppingen, Office for Payment of Occupation Forces, concerning the matter. They included a copy of Frau H.'s letter verbatim, and then asked for clarification on several points: "1) Which authority did the Office of Requisitions in Göppingen belong to? 2) What was the basis of the requisition of the bedroom set from Frau H. for the Lang brothers? Did it occur on the basis of a general or a specific statute of the military government? There is a request for appropriate documentation. 3) Does widow H. have any documents? If yes, they are to be provided to the Landratsamt. 4) Did Frau H. receive any kind of compensation so far?" Süssen City Archive, KAG A 003.66 9398 AR 243 (83). A response from the Landratsamt to the Interior Ministry's letter of September 22, 1949, concerning the H. matter followed on November 26, 1949. Their investigations confirmed that the information given by the complainant was correct. "The furniture which the couple H. bought was indeed a new bedroom set that belonged to the former Jewish Süssen residents Baer. The furniture was confiscated for the benefit of the German Reich and was auctioned off by the Finanzamt Geislingen/Steige. The [subsequent] requisition of the bedroom set occurred via the Office of Requisitions in Göppingen on order of the military government (requisitions bill no. 1480)."

The questions the Interior Ministry had posed were answered by the Landratsamt in the following way:

The legal character of the Office of Requisitions in Göppingen cannot be ascertained. This was an office that had been created by the military government that was charged with requisitions for the benefit of the occupation forces. This can be seen from the designation "Allied Expeditionary Force Military Government Office" and the use of the English language. The Office of Requisitions was in the same building as the military government. The payroll for the employees of the Office of Requisitions was only later transferred to the *Kreisverband* (district organization) on orders of the military government.

The question, on the basis of which legal statutes the bedroom set was requisitioned, does not have to be answered separately, as the enclosed Requisitions Bill shows clearly that the requisition was ordered by the military government in Göppingen. Additional documents do not exist.

Widow H. is only in possession of the enclosed Requisitions Bill no. 1480, dated August 18, 1945.

She has no other documents.

"Frau H. did so far not receive any compensation from any office." Süssen City Archive, KAG A 003.66 9398 AR 243 (81).

137. Not extant.

138. Süssen City Archive, KAG A 003.66 9398 AR 243 (82).

139. Süssen City Archive, 9893/1.

140. Süssen City Archive, KAG A 003.66 9398 AR 243 (79).

141. Süssen City Archive, KAG A 003.66 9398 AR 243 (78).

142. Süssen City Archive, KAG A 003.66 9398 AR 239 36 (176).

143. Süssen City Archive, KAG A 003.66 9398 AR 239 40c (174, 175). Entschädigung für zu Gunsten von rassisch, religiös, oder politisch Verfolgten beschlagnahmte Wohnungsgegenstände, 2–3.

144. Süssen City Archive, KAG A 003.66 9398 AR 239 40a–c (173).

145. See bill for lightbulbs, KAG A 003.66 9398 AR 243 (108), and KAG A 003.66 9398 AR 243 (109).

146. Süssen City Archive, KAG A 003.66 9398 AR 239 40a–c (173). A letter by official Schuster, Wiedergutmachungsamt in the Landratsamt in Göppingen, dated October 6, 1956, and an undated document with similar contents reveals more about the complexity of the compensation issue for the German population. Süssen City Archive, KAG A 003.66 9398 AR 239 49 (160, 161). The letter interprets directives of the Interior Ministry for the *Kreisrat* (district council) and reiterates the social welfare measures taken by the American Military Government during the first few months after occupation to requisition needed furniture and personal items for racially, religiously, and politically persecuted persons via the Office of Requisitions. Most of the confiscations occurred for the benefit of the Lang cousins (falsely identified as "siblings"), who were Jewish, upon their return from the concentration camp. The total amounted to about DM 20,000. When the Lang "siblings" emigrated to the United States on April 23, 1946, the items were first stored in Süssen by their trustee, Karl Schlecht from Ebersbach, and later sold for the benefit of the Langs, including their own bedroom sets. According to the letter, acquisition of the items occurred via the Office

of Requisitions, which, on order of the U.S. Occupation Forces, issued so-called Requisition Bills. When acquisitions based on these bills occurred in businesses, the Kreispflege paid for the purchases. "Based on Decree 'Az.: 201 a' which the Interior Ministry, Department VI Wiedergutmachung (reparations) passed on July 20, 1947, the Bezirksfürsorgeverbände received compensation for the expenses they incurred from May 1945 until July 31, 1947, from the *Wiedergutmachungsstock* (reparations fund)."

Schuster then discusses at some length the question of "ultimate financial responsibility," which had only recently begun to be debated. At the end of the letter he returned, "regardless of the ultimate financial responsibility," to the assertion that "individuals who experienced damage due to requisitions" for the benefit of the survivors have a claim for restitution from the district of Göppingen. He thus recommended to the *Kreistag* that the five individuals [H., E., H., K., and M.] who are requesting specific amounts for a total of DM 6,000 be paid; others who registered their claims before the deadline in 1945 need to explain why they waited until now to pursue these claims further; and ultimate financial responsibility needs to be determined and reported to the *Kreisrat*. Süssen City Archive, KAG A 003.66 9398 AR 239, 49 (160, 161); Süssen City Archive, KAG A 003.66 9398 AR 239, 40c (174, 175).

147. Süssen City Archive, KAG A 003.66 9398 AR 239 (171).

148. Süssen City Archive, KAG A 003.66 9398 AR 239 41 (172).

149. "The opponent of the [restitution] petition will pay DM 500 each to the Louis and Leopold Lang heirs for confiscation of furnishings (including bed linens, table linens, and clothing, carpets, bedding and shoes) belonging to the Louis and Leopold Lang families, formerly from Süssen, at the time of deportation." Süssen City Archive, KAG A 003.66 9398 AR 239, 44 (167).

150. This dealt with the household items stored with Bahr, Moering & Co. and precious metals confiscated by the Städtische Pfandleihanstalt Stuttgart.

151. These are the two family bedrooms.

152. Süssen City Archive, KAG A 003.66 9398 AR 239 44 (167, 168).

153. Rest U 1218 1 (762), sometimes listed as Rest U 1218 1a (762), and Rest U 242 (763).

154. Süssen City Archive, KAG A 003.66 9398 AR 239 71 (127). This is echoed by lawyer Reissmüller on October 29, 1958. See also Ludwigsburg State Archive, EL 350 I, ES 25334, 26, Lang.

155. Ludwigsburg State Archive, EL 350 I, ES 25334, 26, Lang.

156. Frau Holl did not acquire one of the Langs' bedroom sets, it was Frau K. in Weissenstein. See Süssen City Archive, KAG A 003.66 9398 AR 239, 45 (165).

157. Süssen City Archive, KAG A 003.66 9398 AR 239 45 (165).

158. Süssen City Archive, KAG A 003.66 9398 AR 239 43 (169). An interested researcher from Rodalben notes a night-and-fog operation in which Hugo's parents helped the Metzgers get their furniture out of Rodalben. See P. C. correspon-

dence with Süssen City Archive and documents from Stadtarchiv Rodalbern, *Massnahmen gegen die Juden 1939–1942*, 31. Bl.

159. Süssen City Archive, KAG A 003.66 9398 AR 239 43 (169). Emphasis added.

160. Collection Hugo Lang, Ruth Lang letter dated July 3, 1946.

161. Süssen City Archive, KAG A 003.66 9398 AR 239 43 (169).

162. See Süssen City Archive, KAG A 003.66. 9398 AR 239 44 (167, 168).

163. Süssen City Archive, KAG A 003.66 9398 AR 239 43 (169–170). Wieland and Kessler had already been interrogated on September 24 and September 29, 1956, respectively.

164. Süssen City Archive, KAG A 003.66 9398 AR 239 47 (163).

165. Ibid.

166. Süssen City Archive, KAG A 003.66 9398 AR 239 48 (162).

167. Süssen City Archive, KAG A 003.66 9398 AR 239 52 (159).

168. Süssen City Archive, KAG A 003.66 9398 AR 239 53 (158).

169. Süssen City Archive, KAG A 003.66 9398 AR 239 54 (157).

170. Süssen City Archive, KAG A 003.66 9398 AR 239 54 (157).

171. Ibid.

172. Süssen City Archive, KAG A 003.66 9398 AR 239 56 (156).

173. Süssen City Archive, KAG A 003.66 9398 AR 239 63 (133–134).

174. Süssen City Archive, KAG A 003.66 9398 AR 239 70 (128).

175. Süssen City Archive, KAG A 003.66 9398 AR 239 85 (126).

176. Süssen City Archive, KAG A 003.66 9398 AR 239 86 (125). See also Süssen City Archive, KAG A 003.66 9398 AR 239 (121, 122).

177. Ludwigsburg State Archive, EL 350 I, ES 25334, 26, Lang.

178. Not extant.

179. Süssen City Archive, KAG A 003.66 9398 AR 239 (121, 122). See also Süssen City Archive, KAG A 003.66 9398 AR 239 86 (125).

## 9. Lang Reparations

1. Ludwigsburg State Archive EL 350 I, ES 25334, 20.

2. Göppingen District Archive, AR 7 2272, 12.

3. Süssen City Archive, 9897/3.

4. Süssen City Archive, 9897/3.

5. Süssen City Archive, 9897/4.

6. Göppingen District Archive, 9895 9, notice of Custody for Alma Lang-Friesner.

7. Göppingen District Archive, 9895 457.

8. Göppingen District Archive, 9897/7, Finanzamt letter April 1, 1946.

9. Göppingen District Archive, 9895 5.

10. Süssen City Archive, 9897/6.

11. Süssen City Archive, 9897/8.

12. Süssen City Archive, 9897/15.

13. Süssen City Archive, 9897/11, 12.

14. Süssen City Archive, 9897/14.

15. Süssen City Archive, 9897/21.

16. Süssen City Archive, 9897/21.

17. Süssen City Archive, 9897/22.

18. Süssen City Archive, 9897/23.

19. Süssen City Archive, 9897/24.

20. Süssen City Archive, 9897/58.

21. Süssen City Archive, 9897/25.

22. Süssen City Archive: 9897/26. In an email dated August 12, 2006, a correspondent wrote to me offering to introduce me to L. S., the wife of Herr A. S. above, who was the daughter of Karl Schlecht. Mr. K. reported that Kurt Lang, upon his return from the concentration camp, first stayed with the Schlecht family before moving into his family home in Süssen. As stated in previous chapters, the Schlechts were helpful to the Langs before deportation. Likewise, the director of the Göppingen District Archive pointed out that Frau S. frequented the archives, but I never met her because I didn't understand the connection to Herr Schlecht. Reading between the lines is a skill.

23. Süssen City Archive, 9897/28.

24. Süssen City Archive, 9897/30.

25. Süssen City Archive, 9897/31.

26. Süssen City Archive, 9897/33.

27. Süssen City Archive, 9897/33.

28. Süssen City Archive, 9897/35.

29. Collection Hugo Lang, Schlecht letter dated December 16, 1947.

30. Collection Hugo Lang, Schlecht letter dated January 21, 1948.

31. Süssen City Archive, 9897/41.

32. Süssen City Archive, 9897/42.

33. Süssen City Archive, 9897, dated July 22, 1948.

34. Süssen City Archive, 9897/43.

35. Ibid.

36. Göppingen District Archive, A 2090 Süssen City Archive. Courtesy of Frau Hofacker.

37. Göppingen District Archive, 9895, letter dated August 12, 1960.

38. Göppingen District Archive, 9895, letter dated August 17, 1960.

39. Göppingen District Archive, A 2090 Süssen City Archive, letter dated August 7, 1961.

40. Göppingen District Archive, A 2090 Süssen City Archive, decree dated July 18, 1961.

41. Göppingen District Archive, A 2090 Süssen City Archive, Eisele letter, August 7, 1961.

42. Ibid.

43. Ibid.

44. Ibid.

45. Ibid.

46. Süssen City Archive, 9897/44.

47. Süssen City Archive: 9897/47.

48. Süssen City Archive: 9897/48, city council minutes, January 11, 1949.

49. Süssen City Archive, KAG A 003.66 9398 AR 239 60 (154).

50. Süssen City Archive, KAG A 003.66 9398 AR 239 59 (155).

51. Collection Hugo Lang. Hugo and Fred Lang affidavit.

52. Collection Hugo Lang. Kurt Lang letter, December 3, 1945.

53. Süssen City Archive: 9897/74, Saalmüller letter.

54. Süssen City Archive: 9897/48.

55. Süssen City Archive: 9897 51/3.

56. Süssen City Archive, 9897/49.

57. Süssen City Archive, 9897/52.

58. Ibid.

59. The correct date was July 1, 1938.

60. Süssen City Archive, 9897/52.

61. Ludwigsburg State Archive, EL 350 I, ES 12116, Lang.

62. Ludwigsburg State Archive, EL 350 I, ES 12116, 26.

63. Süssen City Archive, 9897/52.

64. Süssen City Archive, 9897/54, see also 9897//5.

65. Süssen City Archive, 9897/53.

66. Süssen City Archive, 9897/56.

67. Süssen City Archive, 9897/62.

68. Süssen City Archive, 9897/63.

69. Ibid.

70. Ibid.

71. Süssen City Archive, 9897/65. Emphasis added.

72. Süssen City Archive, 9897/66.

73. Ibid. The abbreviation a.D. stands for *ausser Dienst*, or retired.

74. Year when Louis purchased the property from Fanny Lang.

75. Süssen City Archive, 9897/68.

76. Süssen City Archive, 9897/67.

77. Süssen City Archive, 9897/73.

78. Collection Hugo Lang. Also Süssen City Archive, 9897/76.

79. Süssen City Archive, KAG A 003.66 9398 AR 239 23.

80. Süssen City Archive, KAG A 003.66 9398 AR 243 (75).

81. Süssen City Archive, 9897/78.

82. Süssen City Archive, 9897/77.

83. Süssen City Archive, 9897/80.

84. Göppingen District Archive, 9895/2.

85. Süssen City Archive, 9897/82.

86. Süssen City Archive, 9897/83.

87. Ibid.

88. Ibid.

89. Göppingen District Archive, 9895 3.

90. Süssen City Archive, 9897/84.

91. Süssen City Archive, 9897/83.

92. Göppingen District Archive, 9895 1.

93. Göppingen District Archive, 9895 5.

94. Ludwigsburg State Archive, EL 350 I, ES 12116, 2.

95. Ludwigsburg State Archive, EL 350 I, ES 12116, 47.

96. Ludwigsburg State Archive, EL 350 I, ES 25334, 20, 2.

97. Collection Hugo Lang. Claim for Leopold's poor health.

98. Ibid.

99. Ludwigsburg State Archive, EL 350 I, ES 12116, 99.

100. Ludwigsburg State Archive, EL 350 I, ES 12116, 10.

101. Ludwigsburg State Archive, EL 350 I, ES 25335, 1.

102. The business was terminated on July 1.

103. Ludwigsburg State Archive, EL 350 I, ES 12116, 54–56.

104. Not extant.

105. Ludwigsburg State Archive, EL 350 I, ES 25335, 5. Süssen City Archive, KAG A 003.66 9398 AR 239 90 (124), dated February 2, 1965, and Süssen City Archive, KAG A 003.66 9398 AR 239 91 (123), dated February 11, 1965, split hairs on whether requisitions were carried out based on an oral or written order.

106. Collection Hugo Lang. See also Ludwigsburg State Archive, EL 350 I, ES 12116, 103.

107. Ludwigsburg State Archive, EL 350 I, ES 12116, 105.

108. Collection Hugo Lang, letter dated December 22, 1965.

109. Collection Hugo Lang, letter dated July 8, 1966.

110. Collection Hugo Lang, letter dated August 8, 1966.

111. Collection Hugo Lang, letter dated April 14, 1966.

112. Collection Hugo Lang, letter dated April 19, 1966.

113. Collection Hugo Lang, reparations transfer order dated January 26, 1966.

114. Collection Hugo Lang. Hugo was subsequently confused. Not realizing that the amount of DM 1,799.20 was indeed the DM 2,080 minus expenses awarded to them on January 26, 1966, in matters *Schaden an Vermögen: Good-will,*" and received through Kurt on April 21, 1966, he wrote to lawyer Reissmül-ler on January 12, 1967, expecting an additional amount. Reissmüller wrote him on January 23, 1967, explaining that the lawyers never had the money and that it was directly transferred to the Bank Gebrüder Martin. Inquiry with the bank yielded the correct information, namely that "on April 12, 1966, on order of Herrn Fabrikant A. S.," they transmitted the amount of DM 4,154 [DM 4,160 less

DM 6 fees, not reflected in the DM 1,799.20 amount quoted by Reissmüller] to the account of Kurt Lang in New Jersey. From this DM 5.80 are subtracted for fees for a net gain of DM 4,148.20. This is accurate, and the amount—split in half and converted into dollars—was deposited by Kurt into the accounts of all seven surviving heirs as stated previously. The Bank Gebrüder Martin in Göppingen once more corresponded with Hugo on the same matter on February 7, 1967, when they stated that "DM 4,154 [DM 4,160 less DM 6 fees] minus our bank fees of DM 5.80, so DM 4,148.20 were transmitted to Mr. Kurt Lang, 83 Robert Road, 07632 Englewood Cliffs, New Jersey, on the instructions of Herr Fabrikant A. S., Göppingen. You should have received your share from Herr Kurt Lang." Indeed Hugo had. With the exception of DM 280.80 owed to the lawyers Reissmüller et al., "the reparations proceedings . . . Lang, Leopold-Erben ES/A 12116" is "completely finished." Fred's wife, Miriam Lang, transmitted a money order for this amount on March 17, 1967. All information in Collection Hugo Lang.

## 10. Jews in Jebenhausen and Göppingen

1. Tänzer, *Juden in Jebenhausen und Göppingen*, 391–92.

2. See Lilo Guggenheim Levine, *This Too Shall Pass* (Self-published, n.d.). Also, Claudia Liebenau-Meyer, *Lebenswege jüdischer Frauen: Lilo Guggenheim, Betty Heimann, Bertha Tänzer*; "Lilo Guggenheim verh. Levine (geb. 1921): Sonnige Kinderjahre in Göppingen"; Karl-Heinz Ruess, ed. *Jüdisches Museum Göppingen* (Birenbach: Mediendesign Späth GmbH, 2007), 4–21. My gratitude to Lilo and Mel for their kindness in seeing me and their patience during the interviews. I would also like to thank Mel for copying materials, digitizing photographs and burning CDs of additional interviews for this project. Poldi Guggenheim, z"l, answered several questions by telephone.

3. See Lilo Guggenheim Levine and Julius and Lini Guggenheim, *Auch das geht vorüber* (Frankfurt a. M.: Haag and Herchen, 1991). Also Lilo G. Levine, *Dancing Girl* (Self-published, n.d.).

4. It was a fortunate coincidence that Lilli Netter Vandermeulen and her daughter Debbie happened to be leaving Maine at this time and were able to stop in Saranac Lake. What a treat to have Lilo and Lilli together. My gratitude to Lilli and Debbie for bringing pictures and family history and for answering my questions. Ruth and Kurt Lang, in their post-Holocaust letters, several times mention Poldi Guggenheim. Ruth also writes that she saw Isolde Netter in Degerloch after many years.

5. Süssen City Archive, KAG A 003.66 6104 AR 235, 1, dated August 11, 1939. "It is reported that the Jewess Tänzer, widow of the rabbi, moved from Göppingen to Stuttgart a few years ago, taking along some crates (which probably contain documents of the Jewish community of Göppingen). Please ascertain the exact whereabouts of the Tänzer woman. Where does she live or a family member?"

6. See Auerbacher, *I Am A Star*.

7. Walter Lang, "Juden in Göppingen und Jebenhausen," in *Der Kreis Göppingen*, 284. Also Munz and Lang, *Geschichte regional*, 2:136–37; and Tänzer, *Juden in Jebenhausen und Göppingen*, 4.

8. If a Jew came in the possession of a Christian house he had to resell it to a Christian citizen within six years. See Tänzer, *Geschichte der Juden in Jebenhausen und Göppingen*, 109.

9. Akermann and Schmolz, *Fusstapfen der Geschichte im Landkreis Göppingen*, 94.

10. *Göppinger Geschichten*, 93. Tänzer, *Geschichte der Juden in Jebenhausen und Göppingen*, 15, 24.

11. Rabbi Tänzer traces the Ottenheimer name to Odenheim near Eppingen in Baden. Tänzer, *Juden in Jebenhausen und Göppingen*, 40.

12. *Göppinger Geschichten*, 93.

13. Tänzer, *Juden in Jebenhausen und Göppingen*, 28, 38.

14. Rohrbacher, *Die jüdische Landgemeinde im Umbruch der Zeit*, 23.

15. Tänzer, *Juden in Jebenhausen und Göppingen*, 111.

16. Karl-Heinz Ruess, *Jüdisches Museum Göppingen in der alten Kirche Jebenhausen*, vol. 29. Stadt Göppingen. (Weissenhorn: Anton H. Konrad Verlag, 1999), 11. Also Rohrbacher, *Die jüdische Landgemeinde im Umbruch der Zeit*, 24.

17. Rohrbacher, *Die jüdische Landgemeinde im Umbruch der Zeit*, 15.

18. Tänzer, *Juden in Jebenhausen und Göppingen*, 190.

19. Ibid., 190–91.

20. Ibid., 192.

21. Ibid.

22. Ibid., 194.

23. Ibid., 192.

24. Ibid., 194.

25. Ibid., 194–95.

26. Ibid., 28.

27. Rohrbacher, *Die jüdische Landgemeinde im Umbruch der Zeit*, 18.

28. Ibid.

29. Ibid.

30. Ibid.

31. Ibid., 29.

32. Daniel Jütte, *Der jüdische Tenor Heinrich Sontheim*, ed. Karl-Heinz Ruess. Stadt Göppingen (Birenbach: Mediendesign Späth GmbH, 2006).

33. Rohrbacher, *Die jüdische Landgemeinde im Umbruch der Zeit*, 25.

34. Tänzer, *Juden in Jebenhausen und Göppingen*, 110.

35. See *Heimatbuch des Landkreises Göppingen*, 449. See Tänzer, *Geschichte der Juden in Jebenhausen und Göppingen*, 431. Also Munz and Lang, *Geschichte regional*, 2:141.

36. Munz and Lang, *Geschichte regional*, 2:140.

37. Tänzer, *Juden in Württemberg*, 96.

38. Munz and Lang, *Geschichte regional*, 2:140. Also Kauss, *Juden in Jebenhausen und Göppingen 1777 bis 1945*. Exhibition catalogue. September 16–November 81981, 8. See later Nazi slogans such as "The Jews are our misfortune."

39. Munz and Lang, *Geschichte regional*, 2:140. Also Kauss, *Juden in Jebenhausen und Göppingen 1777 bis 1945*, 8.

40. Munz and Lang, *Geschichte regional*, 2:140.

41. Ibid.

42. Ibid., 2:138. See also Tänzer, *Juden in Jebenhausen und Göppingen*, 29. Tänzer writes that this occurred by order of Kurfürst Friedrich II before the Peace of Pressburg, not after, as is the case with other imperial properties or local territories of the nobility.

43. Tänzer, *Juden in Jebenhausen und Göppingen*, 43–44.

44. Gustav Schwab, *Die Neckarseite der Schwäbischen Alb*, 1823, cited in *Geschichte regional*, 2:139–40.

45. Munz and Lang, *Geschichte regional*, 2:141.

46. Tänzer, *Geschichte der Juden in Jebenhausen und Göppingen*, 89. See also Stefan Rohrbacher, "From Württemberg to America: A Nineteenth-Century German-Jewish Village on Its Way to the New World." *American Jewish Archives 41* (Fall/Winter 1989).

47. Tänzer, *Juden in Jebenhausen und Göppingen*, 432.

48. Ibid., 445–46.

49. Ibid., 445.

50. Ibid., 438–39.

51. Ibid., 435.

52. Ibid., 444.

53. Munz and Lang, *Geschichte regional*, 2:141.

54. Ibid.

55. Ibid.

56. Ibid. An *Elle* is a measure from elbow to fingertips.

57. Ibid.

58. Ibid. See chapter 3 in this book on the Ottenheimers.

59. On *Bettdrelle*, see *Geschichte regional*, 2:141.

60. On *Bettbarchente*, see *Geschichte regional*, 2:141.

61. See Kauss, *Juden in Jebenhausen und Göppingen*, 10. See also Auerbacher, *I am a Star*.

62. Tänzer, *Juden in Jebenhausen und Göppingen*, 53.

63. Ibid., 279.

64. Auerbacher, *I am a Star*, 26.

65. Ibid., 27–28.

66. Munz and Lang, *Geschichte regional*, 2:142.

67. Ibid.

68. Tänzer, *Juden in Jebenhausen und Göppingen*, 441. Corset manufacture was introduced to Germany by a French officer who settled in Stuttgart in 1848. However, he failed in his attempt. The Göppingen undertaking was the second such effort in the country (ibid., 453).

69. F. C. Huber, *Festschrift zur Feier des Bestehens der Württembergischen Handelskammern. II. Teil: Grossindustrie und Grosshandel in Württemberg* (Druck der Hoffmannschen Buchdruckerei, 1910), 218–20.

70. *Göppinger Geschichten*, 185. A picturesque *Jugendstil* house at the Galgenberg which is still standing, was built by banker Leopold Gutmann for the newly regrouped *Schützengesellschaft*, an organization for marksmen, in 1902. It is located across the street from the Gutman home at 2 Poststrasse.

71. Markus Zecha, "Ich fürchte mich vor den Gefängnismauern," in *Juden in Göppingen: Geduldet-entrechtet-deportiert*, Sonderveröffentlichung der *NWZ*, Göppingen, December 1999, 20. See also Peter Herwig, "Julius Guggenheim 1882–1960," in *Göppinger Portraits* (Göppingen: Peter Herwig Verlag, 2002), 37–42. Courtesy of Lilo Guggenheim Levine.

72. See *Göppingen in Alten Ansichtskarten*, 25.

73. See Levine, *This Too Shall Pass*, 23.

74. Anna Laura Geschmay Mevorach, *Von der Schwäbischen Alb zur Venezianischen Lagune. Ein Füllhorn von Erinnerungen.* Anton Hegele, Karl-Heinz Ruess, eds., *City of Göppingen*. Translated from Italian by Leopoldo Bibbo. (Birenbach: Mediendesign Späth GmbH, 2011). Courtesy of Dr. K. H. Ruess.

75. Munz and Lang, *Geschichte regional*, 2:143.

76. Ibid.

77. Ibid.

78. Ibid. See also Lang, "Juden in Göppingen und Jebenhausen," in *Kreis Göppingen*, 288.

79. Munz and Lang, *Geschichte regional*, 2:148.

80. *Göppinger Geschichten*, 300.

81. Location of the first *Betsaal* was in the home of *Sattler* (tanner) Hangleiter at Schützenstrasse 2. See Tänzer, *Geschichte der Juden in Jebenhausen und Göppingen*, 487.

82. Ruess, *Geschichte der Juden in Jebenhausen und Göppingen*, 620–51.

83. Marcus Zecha, "Heller Geist und williger Untertan, deutscher Patriot und Zionist," in *Geduldet-entrechtet-deportiert: Juden in Göppingen*, 12. See also Karl-Heinz Ruess, "Dr. Aron Tänzer—Leben und Werk des Rabbiners," in Ruess, *Geschichte der Juden in Jebenhausen und Göppingen*, 620–51.

84. Ruess, *Geschichte der Juden in Jebenhausen und Göppingen*, 624.

85. Ibid.

86. Tänzer, *Juden in Jebenhausen und Göppingen*, 479.

87. Ibid.

88. Ruess, *Geschichte der Juden in Jebenhausen und Göppingen*, 633.

89. *Satzung des Israelitischen Frauenvereins in Göppingen, entworfen von Rabbiner Dr. A. Tänzer.* Göppingen (Buckdruckerei Johannes Illig, 1926).

90. See Tänzer's own curriculum vitae, *Juden in Jebenhausen und Göppingen*, 479–80.

91. Ibid.

92. Zecha, "Heller Geist und williger Untertan, deutscher Patriot und Zionist," 12.

93. A. Tänzer. A fragment of experiences as army chaplain with the Bug Army, typescript, 3. Courtesy of Dr. K. H. Ruess and the Göppingen City Archive and the Leo Baeck Insitute, New York (C407). See also "Aron Tänzer" in *Jewish Life in Germany: Memoirs from Three Centuries*, ed. Monika Richarz. (Bloomington: Indiana University Press, 1991), 270–79.

94. See the essay on Rabbi Tänzer by Dr. Ruess, 629–30; also Tänzer's essay, "A fragment of experiences as army chaplain with the Bug Army," typescript, 12–13. See also Vejas Liulevicius, *War Land on the Eastern Front: Culture, National Identity, and German Occupation in World War I* (Cambridge: Cambridge University Press, 2000).

95. *Jüdische Frontsoldaten aus Württemberg und Hohenzollern. Württembergischer Landesverband des Centralvereins deutscher Staatsbürger jüdischen Glaubens* (Stuttgart: J. Fink, 1926), 36.

96. *Jüdische Frontsoldaten aus Württemberg und Hohenzollern*, 36.

97. See *Jüdisches Museum Jebenhausen*, on *Kampfgenossenschaft* and exclusion, 78.

98. About soup kitchen, see Tänzer, *Juden in Jebenhausen und Göppingen*, 629.

99. Levine, *This Too Shall Pass*, 34.

100. Tänzer, *Juden in Jebenhausen und Göppingen*, 645.

101. Ibid., 488.

102. Ibid., 489.

103. Ibid., 504.

104. Ibid., 503.

105. Ibid., 497. The community was tremendously helped by a favorable loan of 40,000 marks from Ernst Ezechiel Pfeiffer, *Hofrat* in Stuttgart (Tänzer, 498). *Hofrat* Pfeiffer employed Rabbi Max Herz of Jebenhausen and Göppingen as a *Hofmeister* (tutor) while he was studying to be a rabbi with Stuttgart Kirchenrat Dr. von Maier (Tänzer, 471).

106. Ibid., 492.

107. Ibid., 503.

108. Erwin Tänzer interview with author, July 27, 2004.

109. See also Levine, *This Too Shall Pass*, 34–35.

110. Tänzer, *Juden in Jebenhausen und Göppingen*, 504.

111. Lilo Guggenheim Levine and I sat down and sang through some of the hymns for Friday night, to see which we both remembered and knew. There was a mix, some were traditional, some were Lewandowski, and some that she remembered but I did not know.

112. Levine, *This Too Shall Pass*, 35.

113. Tänzer, *Juden in Jebenhausen und Göppingen*, 501. Tänzer mentions Samuel Dörzbacher, Max Hirsch, Simon Krämer, and Siegfried Rohrbacher for Göppingen, and Maier Lindauer for Jebenhausen, all of whom were capable of leading services.

114. Levine, *This Too Shall Pass*, 35.

115. Erwin Tänzer interview with the author, July 27, 2004.

116. There is no evidence that top hats were worn during services in Göppingen, only regular hats.

117. Synagogue order, Leo Baeck Institute, New York, BM 318 G 64 A4, 3–6. Copy in Göppingen City Archive. Courtesy of Dr. Ruess, Göppingen City Archive.

118. Levine, *This Too Shall Pass*, 13.

119. Ruess, *Jüdisches Museum Göppingen*, 50. Ilse is in fact 16 in 1931.

120. Werner Ottenheimer, interview with the author, December 24 and 25, 2007.

121. *Jüdisches Museum Jebenhausen*, 66.

122. Advertisement in the *Göppinger Zeitung* no. 221, September 20, 1929. Also *Israelitisches Wochenblatt zu Göppingen*, September 16, 1929, no. 12, 160, and Ruess, *Jüdisches Museum*, 66. Courtesy of Dr. Ruess and Göppingen City Archive.

123. *Israelitisches Wochenblatt zu Göppingen*, March 1, 1938, no. 23, 212. Courtesy of Dr. Ruess and Göppingen City Archive. September 16, 1929, no. 12, 165.

124. Ibid.

125. Ibid.

126. Tänzer, *Juden in Jebenhausen und Göppingen*, 515.

127. Ibid., 469.

128. A. Tänzer, "Die Geschichte des Veteranen- und Militärvereins 'Kampfgenossenschaft' in Göppingen 1871–1921." Courtesy of Dr. Ruess and the Göppingen City Archive. See also Ruess, *Jüdisches Museum Göppingen*, 78–79.

129. Tänzer, *Juden in Jebenhausen und Göppingen*, 518, 516.

130. Levine, *This Too Shall Pass*, 43.

131. Werner Ottenheimer, interview with the author, December 24, 2007.

132. Levine, *This Too Shall Pass*, 27. Being American Indian "braves and squaws" was inspired by the German books of author Karl May.

133. Ibid., 18.

134. Date of founding of hotel in *Israelitisches Wochenblatt zu Göppingen*, February 16, 1936. Courtesy of Dr. Ruess and Göppingen City Archive. Frieda

Dettelbacher was murdered by the Nazis. She is buried in the Jewish cemetery in Laupheim.

135. Levine, *This Too Shall Pass*, 33.

136. Ibid.

137. No title. Text courtesy of Lilo Guggenheim Levine.

138. Last names were identified by Lilo G. Levine. Many thanks to Lilo for her help.

139. "Ein Schulerlebnis," courtesy of Lilo G. Levine. No date.

140. Purim picture also in Liebenau-Meyer, *Lebenswege jüdischer Frauen*, 11, and Levine, *This Too Shall Pass*, 30. In the picture are front row left to right: Susan, Beate, Erwin [Tänzer], Friedericke; second row: Arnold, Lilo, Eva, Doris; third row: Erika and Hannah.

141. Levine, *This Too Shall Pass*, 17.

142. Ibid.

143. Ibid.

144. Erwin and Ruth Tänzer, interview with the author, July 27, 2004.

145. Göppingen is the headquarters of the now world-famous Märklin company, which has a reputation for its high-quality toy railroad products.

146. Tänzer, *Juden in Jebenhausen und Göppingen*, 533–34.

147. Erwin Tänzer, interview with the author, July 27, 2004.

148. In *Jüdisches Museum Göppingen*, 42. Names of children are not included.

149. Gift to Göppingen City Archive from Sig Rosenthal. Names are from left to right: Margot Gutmann, Helene Gutmann (?), Elisabeth Ries, Liese Heimann, Regina Lauchheimer, Alice Berta Ottenheimer (married Arthur Rothschild), Hede Rosenthal, Irene Krämer. Kneeling: Ilse Rosenthal, Trude Lendt, Lina Lang (Süssen). Courtesy of Dr. Ruess. See also chapter 4 in this book.

150. *Israelitisches Wochenblatt zu Göppingen*, January 16, 1936, 160. Courtesy of Dr. Ruess and Göppingen City Archive.

151. Picture of participants in the play, "Prinzes[s] Vergissmeinnichts Hochzeit," was originally given to the author by Hugo Lang. It is also included in the book, *This Too Shall Pass*, 33. My thanks to Hugo and Lilo for identifying all the children in the picture.

152. In his history of Jebenhausen and Göppingen, Rabbi Tänzer added a very valuable section containing family trees of the Jebenhausen families. While many of these families moved to Göppingen and joined that community in the second half of the nineteenth century, these family trees have never been updated and the families who were not included in Rabbi Tänzer's collection have not been added. This is a task beyond this study. But this chapter—with Lilo Guggenheim Levine's much appreciated and invaluable help—at least connects—reunites—the children in the 1929 Hanukkah program, and the children with their families, giving a sense of what happened to the children

through the ordeal of the Holocaust. In this way one can somewhat resurrect the Göppingen Jewish community in its golden age. 1929 seems a good year to choose because the program for the Hanukkah celebration provides evidence of a normal and full community life. Neither the program nor the texts for the skits or the posturing of the children from the religious school are yet affected by the panic of the Nazi period.

153. Levine, *This Too Shall Pass*, 33.

154. *Israelitisches Wochenblatt zu Göppingen*, December 1, 1929, no. 17, 258. Courtesy of Dr. Ruess and the Göppingen District Archive.

155. The following section would not have been possible without the help of Lilo Guggenheim Levine. I am deeply indebted to Lilo for uniting the young people mentioned in the 1929 Hanukkah program with their siblings and parents and for confirming the accuracy of the information the author was able to figure out. The connections are not complete, but at least it is a beginning. For every child, we added as much information about that child and their family as Lilo knew. In 1984 there was a reunion of many of the Göppingen émigrés at the invitation of the city. Lilo had a chance to visit with the participants. Thank you very much for your generosity and help with this chapter, Lilo!

156. Elisabeth Wertheimer was the daughter of cattle dealer Berthold Wertheimer and Klara, née Fellheimer. Lilo thinks that Elisabeth emigrated to Chicago.

157. Rolf Heimann is the son of Louis (Ludwig) and Betty Heimann. Both parents were murdered by the Nazis. See *Lebenswege jüdischer Frauen*, 22–37. Rolf emigrated to the United States and is now deceased.

158. Chapters 4 and 5 deal with the history of the Lang family. Chapter 6 deals specifically with Hugo's life from 1941 on. He was the son of cattle dealer Leopold Lang and his wife Eva, née Liffmann, in Süssen. Both parents were murdered.

159. Erich Rosenthal was the son of Moritz and Rosa (Rosel) Rosenthal, née Wolffenstein. He had a younger brother, Walter; both emigrated to the United States.

160. Kurt Wassermann was the son of Nathan and Therese Wassermann. His mother was murdered; Kurt emigrated to the United States.

161. There is no information on Alfred Srodek, although Elsa may have been his sister.

162. Ilse was the daughter of Rabbi Aron and Berta Tänzer. Her mother was murdered; Ilse emigrated to England.

163. Rolf Gutmann was the son of Sigmund and Marie Gutmann. He had two brothers, Alfred and Otto. Otto and Rolf survived, no information is known on Alfred. Otto is now deceased.

164. Erna Oppenheimer was the daughter of Simon and Frida Oppenheimer, the kosher butcher who lived next door to Lilo at 18 Grabenstrasse. Both parents

were murdered. She had a sister, Selma, who emigrated to Israel and her brother Lothar lives in New York City. Her brother Kurt, whom Lilo calls "Kurtle" in her book, died during World War II on his way to Canada when the boat was torpedoed. Erna Oppenheimer, who was confirmed in 1931/32, is now deceased. See Levine, *This Too Shall Pass*, 9.

165. Richard Dörzbacher was the son of Julius and Hermina Dörzbacher.

166. Manfred was Hugo Lang's older brother from Süssen. He emigrated to England in 1939, and to the United States from there in 1940.

167. Sidney Rosenthal was the son of Leopold and Gerta Rosenthal; he had an older brother Manfred. Lilo thinks both boys came to the United States.

168. Erich Banemann was the son of Stefan and Hedwig Banemann, née Wortsmann. He had a sister, Inge. The entire family was murdered by the Nazis. See Inge's story in the Jebenhausen exhibition, *Jüdisches Museum Göppingen*, 110. Also Ruess, *Die Deportation der Göppinger Juden*, 21. There is also a document which grants Stefan Banemann permission to stay away from home after curfew. Süssen City Archive, KAG A 003.66, 6104, AR 235,4, April 18, 1940 (50).

169. No information is known about David Kuttner other than that he emigrated to France. Is he the son of Esther Kuttner née Zitter?

170. The identity of this boy is not clear. If it is Erich Levi, he was the son of Cantor and teacher Berthold Levi and his wife Paula née Gummersheimer (*Israelitisches Wochenblatt zu Göppingen*, December 1, 1929, 258) and had a bar mitzvah on November 30, 1929. Courtesy of Dr. Ruess and the Göppingen City Archive.

171. Erich Ottenheimer is the son of Max and Hedwig Ottenheimer, and Werner's cousin. In 1939 he emigrated with his father Max to England and from there Erich continued to Caracas.

172. Walter Böhm is the son of Willy and Ida Böhm. He had a brother, Werner, who emigrated to Palestine around 1933 and a sister, Ilse, who came to the 1984 reunion. Walter is now deceased.

173. Arnold Fleischer is the son of Julius and Irma Fleischer, née May. Both were murdered by the Nazis. He had three siblings, two sisters, Doris Sylvia and Susan, and a brother, Richard. Arnold lived in Canada, Susan married a GI and is deceased. Doris lives in England, and Richard in Canada.

174. Erika Ries is the daughter of Eugen and Paula Ries. She has a sister, Rita Elisabeth, and a brother, Herbert. Erika emigrated to Israel, Rita Elisabeth, Herbert, and mother Paula to England.

175. Elfriede Salinger was the daughter of Dr. med. dent. Albert Salinger, who was murdered by the Nazis, as was his wife, Milda. Lilo thinks that Elfriede emigrated to England.

176. Elsa Srodek is the daughter of Mr. and Mrs. Samuel Srodek. She was confirmed in 1931/32. She perhaps has a brother, Alfred.

177. Selma Zitter was the daughter of Mr. and Mrs. Samuel Zitter. She was confirmed in 1931/32. Did she have a sister named Esther who married a Kuttner?

178. Ilse Böhm is the sister of Walter, who is deceased, and of Werner. Their parents are Willy and Ida Böhm. Ilse came to the 1984 reunion.

179. Margot Krämer is the daughter of Dr. S. Krämer and his wife (Marie?) who had his practice at Marktplatz and emigrated to the United States. Margot was confirmed in 1931/32 and married Jos Sommer. She emigrated to Atlanta and is deceased.

180. The correct spelling of the name is Piotrkowsky. Are Isaak and Rebekka Piotrkowska related, perhaps parents? They were both murdered. There is a Frieda Piotrkowsky who was confirmed in 1931/32.

181. Liese Rohrbacher is the sister of Siegfried, who married Trude Lendt. Parents are Milton and Berta Rohrbacher. Trude's parents are Georg and Mathilde Lendt. Georg was murdered by the Nazis.

182. No information is known about Frida Zitter. Lilo thinks she worked at Wohlwert as a sales person. Is she related to Selma Zitter, daughter of Mr. and Mrs. Samuel Zitter? And to Esther?

183. The picture was given to me by Hugo Lang. Lilo G. Levine also reproduced it in her book, *This Too Shall Pass*, 33, but without identifying the individuals in the picture. They are back row left to right: Doris Fleischer, Erika Veidt, Erich Rosenthal, Erika Ries, Walter Böhm, Lore Ottenheimer, Elfriede Salinger, Helga Freudenberger, Beate Bernheimer, Manfred Rosenthal. Front row left to right: Anne Bernheimer, Lilo Guggenheim, Kurt Oppenheimer, Inge Lang, Kurt Wassermann, Erich Banemann, Henny Lang, and lying on the floor, Hugo Lang.

184. Lilo Guggenheim lives in Saranac Lake and very generously helped with this Göppingen chapter. Her father Julius emigrated to the United States. Unfortunately, her mother Pauline committed suicide because she feared being arrested by the Nazis. Lilo escaped to England and in 1945 moved to the United States. Her half-brother, "Poldi," went to England, then to the Unites States, where he recently died. Her half-brother, Emil, moved to South Africa.

185. Anne Bernheimer was the daughter of Eugen and Selma Bernheimer. She had an older sister, Beate, and a younger sister, Margot. Her parents had a tobacco store in the Gartenstrasse. They all came to the United States.

186. Erika Veit is the daughter of Carl and Grete Veit, who gave land for the *Sportplatz*. Erika emigrated to South America and has an older sister, Liese, who lives in Germany.

187. Inge and Henny Lang were the daughters of Pauline and Louis Lang and sisters of Siegi and Kurt in Süssen. Pauline died in 1935, Louis was deported and murdered. Inge and Henny emigrated to the United States and are deceased.

188. Helga Freudenberger was the daughter of Hermann Freudenberger. She is the older sister of Inge. Mother's name is not known. They emigrated to the United States.

189. Lore Ottenheimer is the daughter of Salomon and Sana Ottenheimer.
190. Lilo's neighbor and childhood friend Kurtle Oppenheimer.
191. An *Engerling* is a larva, and the word has an unpleasant connotation.
192. *Israelitisches Wochenblatt zu Göppingen,* January 16, 1930, 278. Courtesy of Dr. Ruess and Göppingen City Archive.
193. Lilo, interview with the author, August 2007.
194. Wilhelm Busch, *Max und Moritz: eine Bubengeschichte in sieben Streichen.*
195. A. Tänzer, *Die Mischehe in Religion, Geschichte und Statistik der Juden* (Berlin: Verlag Louis Lamm, 1913). Courtesy of Dr. Ruess, Göppingen City Archive.
196. Munz and Lang, *Geschichte regional,* 2:149.
197. Jürgen Hagel, *Das Filstal—Natur, Kultur, Geschichte, Orte* (Tübingen: Silberburg-Verlag Titus Häussermann GmbH, 2003), 77.
198. There is a plethora of information of life under the Nazis, starting with a postscript by Dr. Ruess in the Tänzer edition, "Die Israelitische Gemeinde Göppingen 1927–1945," 575–651.
199. Tänzer, *Juden in Jebenhausen und Göppingen,* 579.
200. Ruess, *Jüdische Museum Jebenhausen,* 90.
201. Walter Lang in Ziegler, ed., *Kreis Göppingen,* 289.
202. *Jüdisches Museum Göppingen,* 100, quoted from *Göppinger Zeitung,* May 19, 1937.
203. *Jüdisches Museum Göppingen,* 101, quoted from *Hohenstaufen* (*Göppinger Zeitung*), November 30, 1938.
204. *Jüdisches Museum Göppingen,* 94, quoted from *Hohenstaufen* (*Göppinger Zeitung*), December 6, 1938.
205. *Jüdisches Museum Göppingen,* 100, quoted from *Hohenstaufen* (*Göppinger Zeitung*), December 3, 1938.
206. Ruess, *Was in Paris geschah,* 9–10.
207. Süssen, Lang *Dokumentation,* 30.
208. Ruess, *Die Deportation der Göppinger Juden,* 14.
209. Ruess, *Was in Paris geschah,* 17–18.
210. For information on the trial, see Ibid., 25–28.
211. Ibid., 17.
212. Ibid., 21.
213. Ibid., 17.
214. See Marcus Zecha, *Geduldet-entrechtet-deportiert: Juden in Göppingen,* 17; also Lang in *Kreis Göppingen,* 289.
215. In Liebenau-Meyers, *Lebenswege jüdischer Frauen,* 51.
216. Interview with Werner Ottenheimer, December 24, 2007.
217. See Joachim Hahn, *Erinnerungen & Zeugnisse jüdischer Geschichte in Baden-Württemberg* (Stuttgart: Konrad Teiss Verlag, 1988), 211, 212, and 214.
218. Berta Tänzer letter to her son Erwin, dated December 10, 1937. Acc. 1997.A. 0201, Archive, United States Holocaust Memorial Museum, Washington, D.C.

219. Berta Tänzer letter dated January 31, 1938. Acc. 1997.A.0201, Archive, United States Holocaust Memorial Museum, Washington, D.C.

220. Berta Tänzer letter dated 1940. Acc. 1997.A.0201, Archive, United States Holocaust Memorial Museum, Washington, D.C.

221. Ibid.

222. Tänzer postcard, dated August 3, 1942 in Acc. 1997.A.0201, Archive, United States Holocaust Memorial Museum, Washington, D.C.

223. Tänzer postcard, dated June 17, 1943 in Acc. 1997.A.0201, Archive, United States Holocaust Memorial Museum, Washington, D.C.

224. Max Strauss postcard, dated December 19, 1943, regarding Berta Tänzer in Acc. 1997.A.0201, Archive, United States Holocaust Memorial Museum, Washington, D.C. See also Liebenau-Meyer, *Lebenswege jüdischer Frauen*, 55–63.

225. Richard Fleischer, in Karl-Heinz Ruess, *Die Deportation der Göppinger Juden*, 25.

226. Auerbacher, *I am a Star*, 33–34.

227. See the Stolpersteine Initiative Göppingen website, accessed January 17, 2012, http://www.stolpersteine-gp.de/.

## 11. Kirchheim unter Teck

1. Kirchheim unter Teck website, accessed December 6, 2011, http://www.kirchheim-teck.de.

2. Tänzer, *Juden in Württemberg*, 1n5. Tänzer cites a work by Moser, *Beschreibung des Oberamtes Kirchheim* (Stuttgart, 1842), 153.

3. Tänzer, *Juden in Württemberg*, 5.

4. Tänzer, *Juden in Jebenhausen und Göppingen*, 93. These two families are not listed in Brigitte Kneher's or Rainer Kilian's studies. Presumably they moved away again.

5. Brigitte Kneher, "Chronik der jüdischen Bürger Kirchheims seit 1896," *Stadt Kirchheim unter Teck*, Schriftenreihe des Stadtarchivs, Band 3, Kirchheim, 1985, 73 and 75. Also Rainer Kilian, ed., *Kirchheim unter Teck: Marktort, Amtsstadt, Mittelzentrum. Stadt Kirchheim unter Teck*, 2006, 718. According to Kilian, Louis Kahn emigrated to Paris on May 15, 1936, where he died on August 11, 1936. He is buried in the Jewish section of the Göppingen municipal cemetery.

6. Kneher, *Stadt Kirchheim*, 73 and 75. According to Kilian, Albert Salmon emigrated to the United States on August 25, 1938, where he died in 1942, 719.

7. Kilian, *Kirchheim unter Teck*, 717–20.

8. For a list of Kirchheim Jews, see Kneher, *Stadt Kirchheim*, 111–12; and Kilian, *Kirchheim unter Teck*, 717–20.

9. For those who can read German, Kirchheim unter Teck has an excellent website with a detailed history, also of the Kirchheim Jews. It can also be accessed in English. See http://www.kirchheim-teck.de.

10. Kneher, *Stadt Kirchheim*, 75–76.

11. Ibid., 76.

12. Ibid., 77.

13. The traditional proscription is a six-hour waiting period between milk and meat dishes.

14. Kneher, *Stadt Kirchheim*, 79–80.

15. Ibid., 77.

16. Ibid., 80.

17. Ibid., 77–78; and Kilian, *Kirchheim unter Teck*, 714.

18. Kilian, *Kirchheim unter Teck*, 714.

19. Kneher, *Stadt Kirchheim*, 78.

20. These are Jakob Reutlinger, Friedericke Kennedy, née Merklinger; Helene Salmon, née Merklinger; Bernhard Bernstein; Ida Reutlinger, née Schmal; Helene Kahn, née Sinn; Louis Kahn; Mathilde Gutmann, Ilse Martha Vollweiler (infant), and Flora Vollweiler (infant). See Kneher, *Stadt Kirchheim*, 79 and 106. See also Göppingen Cemetery book by Naftali Bar-Giora Bamberger, *Die jüdischen Friedhöfe Jebenhausen und Göppingen*. Stadtarchiv Göppingen, vol. 24, Karl-Heinz Ruess, ed. (Göppingen: Rung-Druck GmbH and Co., 1990).

21. Kneher, *Stadt Kirchheim*, 83.

22. Ibid., 83.

23. Ibid., 84.

24. Cited in Kneher, *Stadt Kirchheim*, 84. Kurt Vollweiler, born on October 30, 1913 in Kirchheim, emigrated to the United States on February 21, 1940, where he settled in Silver Springs, Maryland. Kilian, *Kirchheim unter Teck*, 720.

25. Tänzer, *Juden in Jebenhausen und Göppingen*, 467, and Arnold Kuppler, "Juden in Kirchheim," in *Beiträge zur Heimatkunde des Bezirks Kirchheim unter Teck*. Heft 34, new series, 1981.

26. Kneher, *Stadt Kirchheim*, 85.

27. Ibid., 73; Kilian, *Kirchheim unter Teck*, 714.

28. Kilian, *Kirchheim unter Teck*, 714.

29. Ibid., 715.

30. Ibid.

31. Kneher, *Stadt Kirchheim*, 82.

32. Ibid.

33. Ibid., 92.

34. Ibid., 96. See also Kilian, *Kirchheim unter Teck*, 718.

35. Kneher, *Stadt Kirchheim*, 97. See also http://www.kirchheim-teck.de.

## 12. Oberamt Geislingen

1. "Einsam und verlassen / Hoch oben auf deiner Felsenwarte / Stehst du über dem Bergwald, / Öder Turm, / Ein Denkmal alter Zeiten! / Jahrhunderte gingen an dir vorüber, / Wetterstürme ohne Zahl, / Feuersprühende Ungewitter / Und

Wolkengüsse, wilderbrausend, / Sie alle haben dir an den Leib geschlagen: / Unerschüttert, unbekümmert/Stehst du auf deinem Felsengipfel, / Ein Riese, ragend aus der Vorzeit." Gustav Häcker, "Der Ödenturm," in Wolfram Haderthauer/Paul Thierer, *Geislinger Impressionen. Stadt und Umgebung in Schilderungen aus 5 Jahrhunderten* (Geislingen [St.]: Verlag Carl Maurer, 1982), 99. Courtesy of Göppingen District Archive [2230]. The term *öde* also refers to a vast, uninhabited area, a wasteland.

2. Professor Stälin, *Oberamt Geislingen* (Stuttgart und Tübingen: Verlag der Cotta'schen Buchhandlung, 1842), 50.

3. Stälin, *Oberamt Geislingen*, 42.

4. Ibid.

5. *Gedenkstunde für Häftlinge des ehemaligen KZ-Aussenlagers 1944–45 in Geislingen an der Steige*, 1995, 2–3. Courtesy of Göppingen District Archive [7655].

6. Richard Wagner, "Das K.Z.-Aussenlager in Geislingen," in Walter Ziegler, ed., *Geschichte regional: Quellen und Texte aus dem Kreis Göppingen*, Heft 2 (Göppingen: Geschichts- und Altertumsverein Göppingen, 1982), 98–111.

7. Martin Bauch, in *Gedenkstunde für Häftlinge*, 6.

8. Wagner, "Das K.Z.-Aussenlager in Geislingen," in Ziegler, ed., *Geschichte regional*, 1982, 98–111. A very interesting and historically significant sequel to the suffering of these poor women can be found in the United States Holocaust Memorial Museum (USHMM). A full discussion of my new findings is beyond the pale of this study, but it should at least be noted that, as a result of the USHMM's acquisition of the Arolsen Search Files, information about some of the female victim survivors from Geislingen is available. In a place search of Geislingen an der Steige on December 17, 2008, I found a list of "82 survivors associated with Geislingen an der Steige, Germany before and during the war." Zero were listed in the category "Before War," so all of these individuals are during the war. All eighty-two survivors were women. Just as an example, we searched further for one of the women, Molly Ash, from Lodz, Poland. The ITC files revealed a registration card for Molly, giving her Polish name as Mala Maroko, born October 19, 1923, deported to Bergen-Belsen as inmate number 3843 in October 1944 and from there to Geislingen in December 1944. Molly was one of the women who was relocated to Allach, a subcamp of Dachau, in March 1945. Whether all of these eighty-two women belonged to the batch of women brought to the newly created 1944 camp was not determined, but could be, and the museum affords the possibility to contact the still living survivors.

9. See Naftali Bar-Giora, *Die jüdischen Friedhöfe Jebenhausen und Göppingen*; also Renate Kümmel, *Erfahrungen des Nationalsozialismus einer Kleinstadt—Verarbeitung oder Verdrängung? Vom Umgang mit der Stadtgeschichte in Geislingen/Steige*. Diplomarbeit zur Erlangung des Grades einer Diplom-Sozialarbeiterin/Sozialpädagogin (Berlin: Alice-Salomon-Fachhochschule für

Sozialarbeit und Sozialpädagogik, 1995). Courtesy of Göppingen District Archive [7843]. Also Martin Bauch in *Gedenkstunde für Häftlinge*, 9.

10. *Gedenkstunde für Häftlinge*, 11.

11. Gertrud Müller in "Ansprache" in *Gedenkstunde für Häftlinge*, 5.

12. Dorothea Abt, *Der Nationalsozialismus in Geislingen an der Steige 1938–9* (Reutlingen: Pädagogische Hochschule, 1980), 8.

13. Tänzer, *Juden in Jebenhausen und Göppingen*, ed. Ruess, 392.

14. Kümmel, *Erfahrungen des Nationalsozialismus einer Kleinstadt*, 18.

15. Abt, *Nationalsozialismus in Geislingen/Steige*, 41.

16. Süssen City Archive, KAG A 003.66 AR 236, 14, 13. Some documents list Elsa, others Else.

17. Süssen City Archive, KAG A 003.66 AR 236, 14, 13.

18. Süssen City Archive, KAG A 003.66 6104 AR 235, 11 (61).

19. Süssen City Archive, KAG A 003.66 6104 AR 235, 12 (60).

20. Süssen City Archive, KAG A 003.66 6104 AR 235, 13 (59).

21. Kümmel, *Erfahrung des Nationalsozialismus einer Kleinstadt*, 19.

22. Süssen City Archive, KAG A 003.66 AR 236, 14, 13.

23. Kümmel, *Erfahrung des Nationalsozialismus einer Kleinstadt*, 19.

24. Abt, *Der Nationalsozialismus in Geislingen/Steige*, 29.

25. Ibid., 34.

26. Ibid.

27. Ibid., 40–63.

28. Bauch in *Gedenkstunde für Häftlinge*, 2.

29. See *Gedenkstunde*. There was tremendous press coverage, both advance notification and coverage of the event in the town press. See Roderich Schmauz, "Die Würde des Menschen ist unantastbar," *Geislinger Zeitung*, April 11, 1995. Courtesy Göppingen District Archive.

## Conclusion

1. For the text of the German Constitution, accessed January 13, 2012, http://tinyurl.com/german-constitution.

2. Courtesy Hugo Lang.

3. Dean, *Robbing the Jews*, 83.

4. Kugelmass and Boyarin, *From a Ruined Garden*, 38.

# Bibliography

This bibliography is divided into the following sections:
   Archival Sources
   Pamphlets
   Newspapers
   Books and Articles
   Personal Interviews
   Videos

## Archival Sources

*City of Süssen*

Grundbuch Gross-Süssen, Heft 105a, sect. 1, no. 2, 3, 4. Properties of Markung Gross-Süssen, building no. 89, etc.

Grundbuch Heft 164, no. 18. Handelsregister Abschrift Abt. 2, Band 1, Blatt 21, February 23, 1866.

Grundbuch Heft 164, no. 18. Handelsregister Abschrift Abt. 2, Band 1, Blatt 132.

Grundbuch Heft 435a, sect. 1, vol. 449, February 16, 1925.

Grundbuch Heft 470. Fanny Lang purchase of property "Sieben Jauchert."

Grundbuch Heft 1105, sect. 1. On sale of Ottenheimer business to Weidmann.

Grundbuchamt: Bauakte Louis Lang.

Grundbuchamt: Information on Ottenheimer business.


*Stadtarchiv (City Archive) Süssen*

"Massnahmen gegen Juden" (Rodalben), 1/31/31 (Stadtarchiv Rodalben).

9893 11 Häfele meeting regarding bedroom set.

9897 1, 2/1, 3, 3/1, 4/1, 5, 6, 6/50, 7, 8/50, 10, 11, 12, 13, 14, 15, 16, 17, 20, 21, 22, 23, 24, 25, 26, 28, 30, 31, 33, 35, 40, 41, 42, 43, 44, 47, 48, 49, 50, 51, 52, 53, 54, 56, 58, 59, 60, 62, 63, 65, 66, 67, 68, 73, 74, 75, 76, 77, 78, 80, 81, 82, 83, 84.

9897 Lang sales contract December 15, 1938.

9897 Saalmüller letter.

A 1009a/4182. Date for cattle fair.

A 1062/4340. Bezirks-Pferde-Versicherungs-Verein.

A 1883/8512. About Louis and hoof and mouth disease.

A 1887. Horse census of March 1919.

A 404f. Fanny Landau Lang.

A 734/3225. Hochspannungskabel.

Allgemeine Ortskrankenkasse Geislingen/Steige. Mitglieder-Verzeichnis 1925.

Allgemeine Ortskrankenkasse Geislingen an der Steige. Mitglieder-Verzeichnis der allgemein versicherungspflichtigen Mitglieder für das Geschäftsjahr 1914, 1915, 1916.

File Manfred Lang.

File Martin Bauch.

Flattich-Plan 322, "Lang Gross-Süssen."

G.B. Gross-Süssen, Saalbuch 1735 (2), fol. 210 v.

G/A 195 Kundenliste der Metzger, Kolonialwaren- und Milchhändler 1918.

G/A 57/1743 Ott Akten.

G/B 212 *Eisernes Buch der Gefallenen des I. Weltkriegs.*

G/B 30 Gross-Süssen, Gemeinderats-Protokoll vol. 17, 1912–15.

G/B 309 Gross-Süssen Steuerbuch from 1900–38.

G/B 322 Gross-Süssen Gebäudesteuerkataster, 1903–63, April 1, 1909.

G/B 33 Gemeinderats-Protokoll, vol. 20, 1924–25.

G/B 34 Gemeinderats-Protokoll, vol. 21, 1925–27.

G/B 35 Gemeinderats-Protokoll, vol. 22, 1927–30.

G/B 36 Gemeinderats-Protokoll, vol. 23, 1930–32.

G/B 385 Verzeichnis der Dienstboten, Lehrlinge, Gehilfen und Arbeiter von Gross-Süssen.

G/B 5 Gross-Süssen, Schultheissenamts-Protokoll April 4, 1906.

G/B 79 Verzeichnis über ausgestellte Prädikatsvermögenszeugnisse, 1889–1912.

G/B 80 Verzeichnis über ausgestellte Prädikatsvermögenszeugnisse.

G/B 83 Bauschauprotokoll und Gemeinderatsprotokoll in Bausachen, 1906–33.

Gemeinderats-Protokoll (79).

Gemeinderats-Protokoll (80).

Gemeinderats-Protokoll (83).

Gemeinderats-Protokoll, February 26, 1929.

Gemeinderats-Protokoll, July 11, 1924.

Gemeinderats-Protokoll, March 6, 1935.

Gemeinderats-Protokoll, May 28, 1937.

Gemeinderats-Protokoll, October 6, 1934.

Gemeinderats-Protokoll, April 25, 1939.

Gemeinderats-Protokoll, December 13, 1938.

Gemeinderats-Protokoll, December 14, 1937.

Gemeinderats-Protokoll, December 5, 1941.

Gemeinderats-Protokoll, January 7, 1937.

Gemeinderats-Protokoll, July 8, 1938.

Gemeinderats-Protokoll, March 12, 1940.

Gemeinderats-Protokoll, May 7, 1936.

Gemeinderats-Protokoll, October 20, 1938.

Gemeinderats-Protokoll, Band 1 and 2, 1933–38.

K/B 145 Klein-Süssen Verzeichnis über Gewerbeverzeichnis (1906–23).

K/B 16 Klein-Süssen Gemeinderats-Protokoll, Band 8, 1907–11.

K/B 17 Klein-Süssen Gemeinderats-Protokoll, Band 9, 1911–14.

K/B 18 Klein-Süssen Gemeinderats-Protokoll, Band 10, 1914–21.

K/B 19 Klein-Süssen Gemeinderats-Protokoll, Band 11, 1921–25.

K/B 20 Klein-Süssen Gemeinderats-Protokoll, vol. 12, 1925–28.

K/B 21 Klein-Süssen Gemeinderats-Protokoll, vol. 13, 1928–31.

K/B 22 Klein-Süssen Gemeinderats-Protokoll, vol. 14, 1931–33.

KAG A 003.66 250 7, 15. Letter Israelitische Kultusvereinigung Württemberg to Landratsamt Göppingen.

KAG A 003.66 6104 AR 235 1, 2, 4, 7, 8/7, 11, 12, 13, 14, 17, 21.

KAG A 003.66 6104 AR 236, 1, 3, 5, 10, 13, 14, 17, 24, 28, 35, 39, 48, 51, 52, 53, 54, 56, 62, 63, 65.

KAG A 003.66 6104.

KAG A 003.66 7613 AR 250.

KAG A 003.66 8/11/39.

KAG A 003.66 9398 AR 239, 12, 21, 22, 23, 25, 33, 36, 40a, 40b, 40c, 41, 43, 44, 45, 47, 48, 49, 52, 53, 54, 56, 59, 60, 62, 63, 70, 71, 85, 86, 90, 91.

KAG A 003.66 9398 AR 243, (75), (78), (79), (80), (81), (82), (83), (85), (86), (90), (91), (93), (95), (96), (97), (98), (99), (102), (103), (104), (107), (108), (109), (110), (111), (112), (113), (114), (115), (116), (117), (118), (119), (120).

KAG A 003.66 A 1887.

KAG A 003.66 AR 241, (4), (9), (10), (11).

Letter from Erwin Tänzer to Walter Lang, November 20, 1990.

Nachlass Otto und Eugen Eisele.

R/G 4 Beilagen zur Gemeindpflegerechnung 1944/45.

Rodalben documents courtesy P. C.

Süssen Gemeindechronik.


*Stadtarchiv (City Archive) Göppingen*

Jakob Lang horse advertisement in *Göppinger Zeitung*, 1911.

Louis Lang newspaper advertisement in *Göppinger Zeitung* no. 236, October 9, 1929.

Louis Lang newspaper advertisement in *Geislinger Zeitung* no. 43, February 21, 1925.

Materialiensammlung, *Israelitisches Wochenblatt zu Göppingen*.

Synagogue order. Leo Baeck Institute, New York. BM 318 G 64 A4. Courtesy Dr. Ruess and Göppingen City Archive.

*Kreisarchiv (District Archive) Göppingen*
4160/A142.10. Cattle dealing licensure.
4165 in GP AR 3862. About Jewish cattle dealers in District Göppingen.
985 457. Letter to mayor from Finanzamt Geislingen.
9892 1/1 and 2/1, dated 12/15/38. Layout of Lang house.
9895 1, 2, 3, 3/12, 4, 5, 5/50, 6, 9.
9895 6/26/1959.
9895 A 253. Z. to Gemeinde Süssen.
9895. Letter regarding Ottenheimer taxes dated 10/24/58.
9895/9880. Eisele correspondence.
A 142. 10/4160. *Hauptkontrollbücher* for cattle dealers.
A 145.19. On Ottenheimer business.
A 2090. Death certificate for Langs, Baers, and Metzgers.
A 2163. About Jewish victims and soldiers on same list.
A 442, 12. About right of first refusal for Ottenheimer business.
A 692c, d. Lang-Rothschild house sale.
A 734/3225. Ottenheimer high voltage cable.
AR 349.
AR 3491. Ottenheimer *Ausbürgerungsverzeichnisse* 1040.
AR 3862–4165.
AR 7 2272, 12. Heinzmann re aryanized businesses.
File 865. Regarding Ottenheimer sewage.
G/B 212. *Eiserne Buch* Gross-Süssen.
Göppingen Address Books 1912, 1930, 1934, 1937.
Jakob Lang engagement announcement.
Jakob Lang marriage announcement.
Louis Lang engagement announcement.
Louis Lang newspaper advertisement in *Göppinger Zeitung*, January 17, 1925.
Louis Lang newspaper advertisement in *Göppinger Zeitung*, January 27, 1925.
Max Ottenheimer 75th anniversary speech 1929, in Sammlung Walter Ziegler.
Sammlung Walter Ziegler.
"A Chapter in the Jewish Question – Jews Participate in the Göppingen Fair – Is that Necessary?" in *Göppinger Zeitung*, May 15, 1937.

*Landeskirchliches Archiv (State Church Archive) Stuttgart*
Martin Pfleiderer 1948 Pfarrbericht for Pfarrei Süssen, August 3, 1948.

*Staatsarchiv (State Archive) Ludwigsburg*
E 352 Bü 3782. Mayer 10/6/48, Ö. 9/27/48, Häfele 9/27/48, Schlecht 10/2/48, Finckh 10/2/48, Niess 10/18/48, H. 9/27/48, Petzold 10/14/48, Moll, 10/12/48, Rall 10/26/48.

EL 350 I, ES 25333. Fred Lang, 4, 7, 8, 19, 22, 25, 27, 46.

EL 350 I, ES 25334 20. Source for "Regina."

EL 350 I, ES 12116. Leopold Lang heirs, 2, 12, 26, 41, 47, 54, 55, 56, 61, 99, 103, 105.

EL 250 I, Bü 1925 1, 5, 6, 7. Nazi "victims."

EL 350 I, ES 24334 26. Concerning *Naturalrestitution*.

EL 350 I, ES 25335, 1, 5. Loss of Goodwill.

EL 402/9, Bü 658. Property Control Fritz Saalmüller.

FL 300/33 II, Bü 217. Sale of Max Ottenheimer home.

FL 300/33 II, Bü 255. Ottenheimer.

FL 300/33 II, Bü 335. Alfred Ottenheimer house sale; Luise's Stuttgart residence.

FL 300/33 II, Bü 432. Max and Hedwig Ottenheimer.

FL 300/33 II, Bü 335 0065761. Alfred and Luise Ottenheimer house in Göppingen.

FL 300/33 II, Bü 335 100695/12. Alfred and Luise Ottenheimer house in Göppingen.

*The US National Archives and Records Administration (NARA) Washington, D.C.*

AG 383 JAG, Headquarters European Command, October 29, 1948, "Execution of Sentence in the Case of the *US vs. Albert Heim, et al.*" Case 12–45, box 89 (2), record group 549.

American Embassy in Germany, Office of the United States Parole Officer. Case file for Saalmüeller, Fritz, con. 5, box 104, record group 549.

Memorandum. Case 12–45 Konstanz, dated February 4, 1946, box 89 (1), general records 549.

Office of the United States Parole Officer, January 28, 1955, "Change of Parole Area and Plan." Case 12–45, box 89 (3), record group 549.

*United States Holocaust Memorial Museum*

Acc. 1997.A.0201. Berta Tänzer letters.

*Collection Hugo Lang*

Alma Lang power of attorney for Fanny Lang.

Byrne, Howard. "Geneva Convention is Joke to Yanks in Bad Orb," Newspaper article.

Fred Samuel letter dated January 7, 2008.

Government questionnaire re Holocaust.

Hugo Lang curriculum vitae.

Inge Feldtmann Lang curriculum vitae.

Lang correspondence.

Lang reparations documents.

P. C. letter dated November 6, 2007.

## Pamphlets

*100 Jahre Süssener Bank 1886–1986: Ein historischer Rundgang durch Süssen.* Süssen: Beck-Druck, 1986.

*1071–1971: 900 Jahre Süssen.* Festprogramm. Süssen: Buch- und Offsetdruckerei Beck, 1971.

*Gedenkstunde für Häftlinge des ehemaligen KZ-Aussenlagers 1944–45 in Geislingen a.d. Steige.* Geislingen, 1995.

Gemeinde Süssen, "Der neue Marktbrunnen auf dem neugestalteten Rathausvorplatz, eingeweiht am 12. September 1981."

Kauss, Dieter. *Juden in Jebenhausen und Göppingen 1777–1945.* Exhibition catalogue. Veröffentlichungen des Stadtarchivs Göppingen, vol. 16. Göppingen: Stadtarchiv, 1981.

*SPD Calendar.* Süssen, December 1998.

*Stadt Süssen Informationen.* "Der Historische Marktbrunnen zu Süssen." New edition, 2001.

*Südwest-Presse/NWZ.* "In einem Meer vor unserer Zeit. Das Jurameer vor 181 Millionen Jahren". Exhibition brochure. Eislingen/Fils, 2006.

Süssen: *Ehemalige jüdische Mitbürger in Süssen. Dokumentation des Besuches vom 2.–9. Oktober 1989 in Süssen.*

Süssen: *Stadterhebung, Stadtfest, July 13–4, 1996. Neue Württembergische Zeitung/Geislinger Zeitung,* July 10, 1996.

"Übergabe des J. J. Bausch Bürgerhauses an die Süssener Vereine." Süssen, n.d.

Volkshochschule Süssen. *50 Jahre Süssen. Süssen in der Anfangszeit von 1933 bis 1945.* Gemeinde Süssen, 1983.

*Vom Gasthaus Krone zur Volksbank Süssen: 300 Jahre Geschichte eines Hauses.* Süssen, n.d.

WNET. "Berga: Soldiers of Another War," THC program insert. Based on *Berga: Soldiers of Another War.* New York: Thirteen WNET, Educational Broadcasting Corporation, 2003.

## Newspapers

*Geislinger Zeitung,* "Zur Vereinigung von Gross- und Klein-Süssen am 16. und 17. September." Sonderbeilage, September 16, 1933.

*Göppinger Zeitung,* May 15, 1937.

*Göppinger Zeitung.* "Israelitische Morgenfeier." September 20, 1929.

*Gräfensteinbote.* Advertisement maligning Eugenie Metzger, April 24, 1933.

*Hohenstaufen,* September 16, 1933–April 21, 1937.

*Hohenstaufen,* "Zur Feier der Vereinigung von Gross- und Klein-Süssen." Sonderbeilage, September 16, 1933.

*Nationale Rundschau,* April 4, 1934.

*Neue Württembergische Zeitung,* "50 Jahre Gemeinde Süssen," July 1, 1983.

*Neue Württembergische Zeitung.* "900 Jahre Süssen." Sonderbeilage. July 9, 1971.

*Neue Württembergische Zeitung.* "Ehrung: Bürgermedaille für Werner Runschke: Süssener Geschichte lebendig gemacht." November 25, 2006.

*Neue Württembergische Zeitung.* "Eislinger Saurier." July 9, 2006

*Neue Württembergische Zeitung.* "Lebendiges Bild von der Zeit vor unserer Zeit." In *Süssen: Ortsportrait.* Sonderausgabe. February 18, 1995.

*Neue Württembergische Zeitung.* "Personen: Archivar Werner Runschke erhält Bürgermedaille der Stadt Süssen: Ein Fundus, den kaum jemand sieht." November 23, 2006.

*Neue Württembergische Zeitung/Geislinger Zeitung,* "Süssen: Stadterhebung July 13–14, 1996," July 10, 1996.

*Mitteilungen (Rodalben),* on Eugenie Metzger, April 26, 1933.

*Rheinpfalz.* Edmund Heringer, "Stationen auf dem Weg zur Vernichtung jüdischer Mitbürger," November 7, 1988.

*Rotenburger Zeitung.* "Als die Kuh am Berg noch besser aussah," October 5, 2006.

*Saarbrücker Zeitung,* "Förderer von Sport und Kultur," March 10, 1974.

*Süssener Gemeindechronik.*

*Süssener Informationen,* 1989–1991.

*Süssener Mitteilungen,* 1983–1991.

Wehrberger, Kurt. "Das Rätsel der Steinzeit, Knöpfe," *Südwest Magazin, NWZ,* July 22, 2006.

Ziedler, Christopher, "'Ganget hoim zu eire Weiber.' Das Kriegsende auf dem Land am Beispiel Süssen," *Stuttgarter Zeitung,* no. 90, April 20, 2005.

**Books and Articles**

*700 Jahre Salach 1275–1975.* Gemeinde Salach. Salach: E. Kaisser, 1975.

Abt, Dorothea. *Der Nationalsozialismus in Geislingen/Steige 1938–9.* Reutlingen: Pädagogische Hochschule, 1980.

Adams, Myrah and Benigna Schönhagen. *Jüdisches Laupheim.* Haigerloch: ST Elser, n.d.

Akermann, Manfred. *Grenzstreit im Filstal.* Geislingen/Steige: Industrie-Druck GmbH, 1961.

Akermann, Manfred and Helmut Schmolz. *Fusstapfen der Geschichte im Landkreis Göppingen.* Weissenhorn: Anton H. Konrad Verlag, 1988.

Aly, Götz. *Hitler's Beneficiaries: Plunder, Racial War, and the Nazi Welfare State.* New York: Metropolitan Books, Henry Holt & Co., 2006.

———. *Hitlers Volksstaat: Raub, Rassenkrieg, und Nationaler Sozialismus.* Frankfurt am Main: S Fischer Verlag GmbH, 2005.

Auerbacher, Inge. *I am a Star: Child of the Holocaust.* New York: Puffin Books, 1993.

Bamberger, Naftali Bar-Giora. *Die jüdischen Friedhöfe Jebenhausen und Göppingen.* Edited by Karl-Heinz Ruess. Göppingen und Jerusalem: Stadtarchiv Göppingen and Rung-Druck GmbH, 1990.

————. *Memor-Buch. Die jüdischen Friedhöfe im Hohenlohekreis.* Herausgegeben vom Landratsamt Hohenlohekreis. Vol. 1. Künzelsau: Swiridoff Verlag, 2002.

Bartov, Omer. *Erased: Vanishing Traces of Jewish Galicia in Present-day Ukraine.* Princeton: Princeton University Press, 2007.

Bischoff, Ralph and Reinhard Hanke, eds. *Der jüdische Friedhof in Eppingen: Eine Dokumentation.* Rund um den Ottilienberg, vol. 5. Eppingen: Pentadruck, 1996.

Bumiller, Casimir. *Juden in Hechingen.* Hechingen: Initiative Hechinger Synagoge e. V. and Verein Alte Synagoge e. V. and Verlag Glückler, n.d.

Burmeister, Karl Heinz. *Medinat Bodase[e].* Konstanz: Universitäts-Verlag Konstanz, 1994.

————. *Der schwarze Tod: Die Judenverfolgungen anlässlich der Pest von 1348/49.* Edited by Karl-Heinz Ruess. Jüdisches Museum Göppingen/Stadt Göppingen. Ebersbach an der Fils: Bechtel Druck GmbH, 1999.

Cahnmann, Werner. "Village and Small-Town Jews in Germany. A Typological Study." In *Leo Baeck Institute Year Book XIX*, 1974.

Cohen, Roger. "The Lost Soldiers of Stalag IX-B," *New York Times Magazine*, February 27, 2005.

Eisele, K., M. Köhle, Chr. Schöllkopf, eds. *Geschichtliche Heimatkunde des Filsgaus, mit einem geologischen Anhang.* Göppingen: Verlag von Johannes Illig, 1926.

Fischer, Johann Georg. "Der Wiederabschied." In *100 Jahre Süssener Bank 1886–1986: Ein historischer Rundgang durch Süssen.* Süssen: Beck-Druck, 1986.

Frei, Norbert. *Adenauer's Germany and the Nazi Past: The Politics of Amnesty and Integration.* Translated by Joel Golb. New York: Columbia University Press, 2002.

Fried, Amelie. *Schuhhaus Pallas. Wie meine Familie sich gegen die Nazis wehrte.* Unter Mitarbeit von Peter Probst. Munich: Carl Hauser Verlag, 2008.

Geppert, Karlheinz, *Jüdisches Baisingen.* Haigerloch: Verlag Medien und Dialog Klaus Schubert, 2000.

Gidal, Nachum T. *Jews in Germany from Roman Times to the Weimar Republic.* Cologne: Könemann Verlagsgesellschaft mbH, 1998.

Gmähle, Albrecht. *Durch den Landkreis Göppingen. Kunstwerke, Land und Leute um den Hohenstaufen.* Horb am Neckar: Geiger-Verlag, 1995.

*Göppingen in alten Ansichtskarten.* Würzburg: Weidlich Verlag, 2002.

*Göppinger Geschichten. Von Menschen, Ereignissen und Bauwerken.* Neue Württembergische Zeitung Series, Stadtarchiv Göppingen, vol. 44. Göppingen: Rung-Druck GmbH & Co., 2005.

Groschopf, Paul and Winfred Reiff, "Landschaft und Geologie." In *Der Kreis Göppingen*. Edited by Walter Ziegler. Stuttgart: Konrad Theiss Verlag, GmbH, 1985.

Gross, Jan. *Neighbors: The Destruction of the Jewish Community in Jedwabne, Poland*. Princeton: Princeton University Press, 2001.

Haderthauer, Wolfram and Paul Thierer. *Geislinger Impressionen. Stadt und Umgebung in Schilderungen aus 5 Jahrhunderten*. Geislingen: Verlag Carl Maurer, 1982.

Häcker, Gustav. "Der Ödenturm." In *Geislinger Impressionen. Stadt und Umgebung in Schilderungen aus 5 Jahrhunderten*, by Wolfram Haderthauer and Paul Thierer.

Hagel, Jürgen. *Das Filstal—Natur, Kultur, Geschichte, Orte*. Tübingen: Silberburg-Verlag Titus Häussermann GmbH, 2003.

Hahn, Joachim. *Erinnerungen & Zeugnisse jüdischer Geschichte in Baden-Württemberg*. Stuttgart: Konrad Teiss Verlag, 1988.

Haverkamp, Alfred, ed. *Geschichte der Juden im Mittelalter von der Nordsee bis zu den Südalpen. Kommentiertes Kartenwerk*. Hannover: Verlag Hahnsche Buchhandlung, 2002.

Herwig, Peter. "Julius Guggenheim 1880–1960." In *Göppinger Portraits*. Göppingen: Peter Herwig Verlag, 2002.

Hirsch, Marianne. *Family Frames: Photography, Narrative and Postmemory*. Cambridge: Harvard University Press, 1996.

Hofreiter, Gerda. *Allein in die Fremde: Kindertransporte von Österreich nach Frankreich, Grossbritannien, und in die USA 1938–1941*. Innsbruck/Vienna/Bozen: StudienVerlag, 2010.

Huber, F. C. *Festschrift zur Feier des Bestehens der Württembergischen Handelskammern. II. Teil: Grossindustrie und Grosshandel in Württemberg*. Druck der Hoffmannschen Buchdruckerei, 1910.

*Hundert Jahre Süssener Bank 1886–1986: Ein historischer Rundgang durch Süssen*. Süssen: Beckdruck 1986.

Illig, Johannes. *Geschichte von Göppingen und Umgebung*. Göppingen: Druck Johannes Illig, 1984.

Jeggle, Utz. *Judendörfer in Württemberg*. Tübingen: Tübinger Vereinigung für Volkskunde e. V., 1999.

*Juden in Buttenhausen*. Münsingen Stadtarchiv. Wannweil: B. Kemmler GmbH, 1994.

*Jüdische Frontsoldaten aus Württemberg und Hohenzollern*. Württembergischer Landesverband des Centralvereins deutscher Staatsbürger jüdischen Glaubens. Stuttgart: J. Fink, 1926.

Jütte, Daniel. *Der jüdische Tenor Heinrich Sontheim*. Edited by Karl-Heinz Ruess. Stadt Göppingen. Birenbach: Mediendesign Späth GmbH, 2006.

Kaplan, Marion A. *Between Dignity and Despair: Jewish Life in Nazi Germany*. New York/Oxford: Oxford University Press, 1998.

Katz, Jacob. *Jewish Emancipation and Self-Emancipation*. New York/Philadelphia/Jerusalem: The Jewish Publication Society, 1986.

———. *Out of the Ghetto: The Social Background of Jewish Emancipation, 1770–1870*. Syracuse: Syracuse University Press, 1973.

Kaufmann, Robert Uri. "Jüdisches Leben auf dem Land." In *Schwäbisch Hall*. Series "In Baden-Württemberg," Vol. 48. Karlsruhe: G. Braun Buchverlag, n.d.

———. *Jüdische und christliche Viehhändler in der Schweiz 1780–1930*. Zurich: Chronos Verlag, 1988.

Kaufmann, Robert Uri and Carsten Kohlmann, eds. *Jüdische Viehhändler zwischen Schwarzwald und Schwäbischer Alb*. Horb-Rexingen: Barbara Staudacher Verlag, 2008.

Keegan, John. *The First World War*. New York: Vintage Books, 2000.

Keller, Helmut, ed. *Johann Georg Fischer, Person und Werk*. Hamburg: Verlag Dr. Kovac, 1997.

Kilian, Reiner, ed. *Kirchheim unter Teck: Marktort, Amtsstadt, Mittelzentrum*. Kirchheim: Stadt Kirchheim unter Teck, 2006.

Kimmelman, Mira and Gilya G. Schmidt, ed. *Life Beyond the Holocaust: Memories and Realities*. Knoxville: The University of Tennessee Press, 2005.

Klotz, Jürgen. *Der Geldschein Sammler* 13, no 8 (November 1999).

Kneher, Brigitte. "Chronik der jüdischen Bürger Kirchheims seit 1896." In *Stadt Kirchheim unter Teck*. Schriftenreihe des Stadtarchivs, Band 3. Kirchheim: Stadt Kirchheim, 1985.

Kugelmass, Jack and Jonathan Boyarin, eds. and trans., *From a Ruined Garden. The Memorial Books of Polish Jewry*. 2nd expanded edition. Bloomington: Indiana University Press, 1998.

Kümmel, Renate. *Erfahrungen des Nationalsozialismus einer Kleinstadt— Verarbeitung oder Verdrängung? Zum Umgang mit der Stadtgeschichte in Geislingen/Steige*. Diplomarbeit zur Erlangung des Grades einer Diplom-Sozialarbeiterin/Sozialpädagogin. Berlin: Alice-Salomon-Fachhochschule für Sozialarbeit und Sozialpädagogik, 1995.

Lang, Walter. "Juden in Göppingen und Jebenhausen." In *Der Kreis Göppingen*. Edited by Walter Ziegler. Stuttgart: Konrad Theiss Verlag, GmbH, 1985.

Lechner, Sylvester, ed. *Synagoge Ichenhausen*. Günzburg: Appel-Druck Donau-Verlag GmbH, 1987.

Levine, Lilo Guggenheim, ed. *Auch das geht vorüber*. Frankfurt a. M.: Haag und Herchen, 1991.

———. *Dancing Girl*. Self-published, n.d.

———. *This Too Shall Pass*. Self-published, n.d.

Levitt, Laura. *American Jewish Loss After the Holocaust*. New York/London: New York University Press, 2007.

Liebenau-Meyer, Claudia. *Lebenswege jüdischer Frauen: Lilo Guggenheim, Betty Heimann, Bertha Tänzer.* Edited by Karl-Heinz Ruess. Stadt Göppingen. Birenbach: Mediendesign Späth GmbH, 2007.

Liulevicius, Vejas. *War Land on the Eastern Front: Culture, National Identity, and German Occupation in World War I.* Cambridge: Cambridge University Press, 2000.

Löwenbrück, Anna-Ruth. "Ein langer Kampf um die Emanzipation: Die rechtliche Gleichstellung der württembergischen Juden im 19. Jahrhundert." *Momente* 1 (2003).

Mayer, F. F. *Sammlung der württembergischen Gesetze in Betreff der Israeliten.* Tübingen: Verlag und Druck von Ludwig Friedrich Feres, 1847.

*The Memoirs of Glückel of Hameln.* Translated with Notes by Marvin Lowenthal. New York: Schocken Books Inc., 1977.

Mevorach, Anna Laura Geschmay. *Von der Schwäbischen Alb zur Venezianischen Lagune. Ein Füllhorn von Erinnerungen.* Edited by Anton Hegele and Karl-Heinz Ruess. Translated from Italian by Leopoldo Bibbo. City of Göppingen. Birenbach: Mediendesign Späth GmbH, 2011.

Mohn, Joseph. *Der Leidensweg unter dem Hakenkreuz.* Bad Buchau: Vereinigte Buchdruckereien A. Sandmaier & Sohn, 1970.

Moser, Finanzrath. *Beschreibung des Oberamts Göppingen.* Stuttgart und Tübingen: Verlag der J. G. Cotta'schen Buchhandlung, 1844.

Müller, Karl, jun. *1896–1996: Sozialdemokraten in Süssen, Ein historisches Lesebuch.* Herausgeber: SPD-Ortsverein Süssen. Ebersbach: Bechtel Druck, 1996.

Munz, Georg and Walter Lang, "Die Jebenhäuser Judengemeinde und ihre Bedeutung für die wirtschaftliche Entwicklung der Stadt Göppingen." In *Geschichte regional*, Heft 2, 1982.

Nebel, Theobald. *Die Geschichte der Freudentaler Juden.* Ludwigsburg: Historische Verein für Stadt und Kreis Ludwigsburg e. V. und Süddeutsche Verlagsanstalt und Druckerei GmbH, 1984.

Raphael, Lev. *My Germany.* Madison: Terrace Books, University of Wisconsin Press, 2009.

Rauser, Jürgen Hermann. *Forchtenberger Heimatbuch.* Forchtenberg: Stadtverwaltung, 1983.

Richarz, Monika. "Die Entdeckung der Landjuden. Stand und Problem ihrer Erforschung am Beispiel Südwestdeutschlands." In *Landjudentum im süddeutschen- und Bodenseeraum.* Dornbirn: Vorarlberger Verlagsanstalt, 1992.

———. "Die soziale Stellung der jüdischen Viehhändler auf dem Lande am Beispiel Südwestdeutschlands." In *Jüdische Unternehmer in Deutschland im 19. und 20. Jahrhundert.* Edited by Werner Mosse and Hans Pohl. Stuttgart: 1992.

———, ed. *Jewish Life in Germany: Memoirs from Three Centuries.* Translated by Stella P. Rosenfeld and Sidney Rosenfeld. Sponsored by the Leo Baeck Institute. The Modern Jewish Experience, edited by Paula Hyman and Deborah Dash Moore. Bloomington: Indiana University Press, 1991.

Rohrbacher, S. *Die jüdische Landgemeinde im Umbruch der Zeit. Traditionelle Lebensform, Wandel und Kontinuität im 19. Jahrhundert.* Edited by Karl-Heinz Ruess. Ebersbach an der Fils: Bechtel-Druck GmbH, 2000.

———. "From Württemberg to America: A Nineteenth-Century German-Jewish Village on Its Way to the New World." *American Jewish Archives* 41 (Fall/Winter 1989).

———. "Medinat Schwaben. Jüdisches Leben in einer süddeutschen Landschaft in der Frühzeit," *Judengemeinden in Schwaben im Kontext des Alten Reiches.* Edited by Rolf Kiessling. Berlin: Akademie Verlag GmbH, 1995.

Römer, Gernot. *Schwäbische Juden. Leben und Leistungen aus zwei Jahrhunderten in Selbstzeugnissen, Berichten und Bildern.* Augsburg: Presse-Druck-und Verlags-GmbH, 1990.

Ruess, Karl-Heinz. *Jüdisches Museum Göppingen in der alten Kirche Jebenhausen.* Vol. 29. Stadt Göppingen. Weissenhorn: Anton H. Konrad Verlag, 1999.

———. *Die Deportation der Göppinger Juden.* Stadt Göppingen. Ebersbach: Bechtel Druck GmbH, 2001.

———. *Spuren schreiben Vergangenheit.* Göppingen: Stadtarchiv und Bechtel Druck GmbH, Ebersbach an der Fils, 2001.

———. *Was in Paris geschah, das habt ihr zu büssen. Die Reichspogromnacht in Göppingen.* Stadt Göppingen. Ebersbach an der Fils: Bechtel Druck GmbH, 2001.

Rührup, Reinhard. "Die Emanzipation der Juden in Baden." In *Emanzipation und Antisemitismus: Studien zur "Judenfrage" der bürgerlichen Gesellschaft.* Göttingen: Vandenhoeck & Ruprecht, 1975.

Sauer, Paul. *Die jüdischen Gemeinden in Württemberg und Hohenzollern: Denkmale, Geschichte, Schicksale.* Archivkirektion Stuttgart: W. Kohlhammer Verlag, 1966.

Sauer, Paul and Sonja Hosseinzadeh. *Jüdisches Leben im Wandel der Zeit: 170 Jahre Israelitische Religionsgemeinschaft, 50 Jahre neue Synagoge Stuttgart.* Israelitische Religionsgemeinschaft Württembergs. Gerlingen: Bleicher Verlag GmbH, 2002.

Schellenberger, Bernardin. *Zwischen Rechberg und Staufen. Ottenbach und das Tal der Höfe.* Edited by Walter Ziegler. Weissenhorn: Anton H. Konrad Verlag, 1996.

Schmidt, Gilya Gerda. "Die anderen Süssener," *Hohenstaufen/Helfenstein* 13 (2003): 157–96.

Schubert, Klaus. *Jüdisches Baisingen.* Haigerloch: ST Elser, n.d.

———. *Jüdisches Haigerloch.* Haigerloch: ST Elser, n.d.

Schwab, Gustav. *Die Neckarseite der Schwäbischen Alb, 1823.* In *Geschichte regional,* Heft 2, 1982.

Schwartz, Mimi. *Good Neighbors, Bad Times. Echoes of My Father's German Village.* Lincoln & London: University of Nebraska Press, 2008.

Seemüller, Ulrich. *Das jüdische Altersheim Herrlingen und die Schicksale seiner Bewohner.* Gemeinde Blaustein (Alb-Donau-Kreis). Ulm: Rudi Rampf GmbH, n.d.

Shapira, Avraham, ed. *Martin Buber: Pfade in Utopia. Über Gemeinschaft und deren Verwirklichung.* Heidelberg: Verlag Lambert Schneider, 1985.

*Siddur Sim Shalom. A Prayerbook for Shabbat, Festivals, and Weekdays.* Edited, with translations, by Rabbi Jules Harlow. New York: The Rabbinic Assembly/ The United Synagogue of America, 1985.

Smith, Helmut Walser. *The Butcher's Tale: Murder and Anti-semitism in a German Town.* New York and London: W. W. Norton & Co., 2002.

——. *The Continuities of German History: Nation, Religion, and Race across the Long Nineteenth Century.* Cambridge: Cambridge University Press, 2008.

——, ed. *The Holocaust and Other Genocides: History, Representation, Ethics.* Nashville: Vanderbilt University Press, 2002.

Sorkin, David. *The Transformation of German Jewry 1780–1840.* New York/Oxford: Oxford University Press, 1987.

*SPD Calendar.* Süssen, December 1998.

Stälin, Professor. *Oberamt Geislingen.* Stuttgart und Tübingen: Verlag der Cotta'schen Buchhandlung, 1842.

Steim, Karl Werner. *Juden in Haigerloch.* Haigerloch: Druckerei ST Elser, n.d.

Strauss, Walter, ed. *Lebenszeichen: Juden aus Württemberg nach 1933.* Gerlingen: Bleicher Verlag, 1982.

——. *Signs of Life: Jews from Württemberg.* New York: Ktav Publishing House, Inc., 1982.

Tänzer, Aron. *Die Geschichte der Juden in Jebenhausen und Göppingen.* Edited by Karl-Heinz Ruess. Stadt Göppingen. Weissenhorn: Anton H. Konrad Verlag, 1988.

——. *Die Geschichte der Juden in Württemberg.* Frankfurt a. M.: Verlag Weidlich, 1937/1983.

——. *Die Geschichte des Veteranen- u. Militärvereins 'Kampfgenossenschaft' in Göppingen 1871–1921.* Eine Festschrift zur Feier seines 50 jährigen Bestehens. Göppingen: Buchdruckerei der *Göppinger Zeitung,* Inh. J. Kirchner, 1921.

——. *Die Mischehe in Religion, Geschichte und Statistik der Juden.* Berlin: Verlag Louis Lamm, 1913.

Tänzer, Paul. *Die Rechtsgeschichte der Juden in Württemberg.* Stuttgart, 1922.

Wagner, Richard. "Das KZ Aussenlager in Geislingen." In *Geschichte regional. Quellen und Texte aus dem Kreis Göppingen.* Edited by Walter Ziegler. Heft 2. Göppingen: Geschichts- und Altertumsverein Göppingen, 1982.

Weber, Franz and Albrecht Gmähle. *Der Fils entlang. Eine Reise durch den Stauferkreis Göppingen.* Weissenhorn: Anton H. Konrad Verlag, 1992.

Weintraub, Stanley. *11 Days in December. Christmas at the Bulge, 1944.* London: Penguin Books, Ltd. Via NAL Caliber, 2007.

Welsch, Renate and Sinja Dillenkofer. *Begegnungen.* Horb am Neckar: Geiger-Verlag, n.d.

Werner, Otto. *Jüdisches Hechingen.* Verein Alte Synagoge Hechingen e. V. Haigerloch: ST Elser, n.d.

Wetterich, Susanne. *Davids Stern an Rhein und Neckar.* Stuttgart: Silberbuch Verlag, 1990.

Winter, Alfred. *The Ghetto of Riga and Continuance. A Survivor's Memoir.* Self-published, 1998.

Zecha, Markus. *Geduldet-entrechtet-deportiert: Juden in Göppingen. Sonderveröffentlichung der Neuen Württembergischen Zeitung.* Göppingen. Dornstadt: Zipperlen Druck, 1999.

Ziegler, Walter. *Von Siezun bis Süssen, Ein Streifzug durch 900 Jahre.* Süssen: Buchdruckerei Beck und Hecker, 1971.

———, ed. *Der Kreis Göppingen.* Stuttgart: Konrad Theiss Verlag, GmbH, 1985.

———, ed. *Romantische Filstalreise.* Weissenhorn: Anton H. Konrad Verlag, 1983.

Ziegler, Walter and Martin Bauch. *Süssen: Eine Dorfmitte erzählt.* Salach: Kaisser Verlag, 1989.

Ziegler, Walter and Werner Runschke, eds. *Süssen: Vom Dorf zur Stadt.* Weissenhorn: Anton H. Konrad Verlag, 1996.

**Personal Interviews**

M. W. Interview by Gilya G. Schmidt. Süssen, Germany. Spring 1999.

Hugo Lang. Interview by Kurt Piehler. Newton, NJ. 2000.

Hugo Lang. Interview by Gilya G. Schmidt. Newton, NJ. 1999, 2000, 2001, 2002, 2003, 2004, 2005, 2006, 2007, 2008.

Werner Ottenheimer. Interview by Gilya G. Schmidt. Havana, Cuba. December 24–25, 2007.

Erwin and Ruth Tänzer. Interview by Gilya G. Schmidt. Newtowne, PA. July 27, 2004.

Lilo Guggenheim Levine. Interview by Gilya G. Schmidt. Saranac Lake, NY. August 2007.

Alisa Klapfer. Interview by Gilya G. Schmidt. Shavei Zion, Israel. April 2010.

**Video**

Guggenheim, Charles. "Berga: Soldiers of Another War." New York: Thirteen WNET. Educational Broadcasting Corporation, 2003.

# Glossary

*I. Beigeordneter*  elected official
*abmelden*  notify of departure
*abschreckend*  horrible
*Abschub, Abschiebung, Abtransport*  deportation
*Akkord arbeiten*  to do piecework
*Aktennotiz*  memo
*Aktie*  share
*Aktiengesellschaft*  publicly traded company
*Aktion*  action, Nazi raids on Jewish population
*Aliyah*  emigration to Palestine (Israel), synagogue honor
*Allgemeine Ortskrankenkasse*  local health insurance company
*Allgemeine Ortsschule*  local public elementary school
*Altbulle*  senior bull
*Altwürttemberg*  Württemberg territory before 1805
*Amt*  office
*Amt für Besatzungsleistungen*  Office for Allied Occupation Payments
*Amt für Vermögenskontrolle*  Office for Property Control
*Amt für Wiedergutmachung des Naziterrors*  Office for Reparations for
    Nazi Acts of Terror
*Amtmann*  official
*Amtsgericht*  lower court
*Amtsgerichtsrat*  official of lower court
*Amtsversammlung*  official meeting
*Anerkennungszinsen*  user fees
*Anfechtung*  challenge
*Angestellter*  employee
*anmassend*  arrogant
*Anmeldeamt*  registration office
*Anspruch*  claim
*Arbeitsdienst*  labor service

*arisieren*   to Aryanize
*Armenpflege*   welfare organization
*Arondierung*   alignment
*Assessor*   assistant judge
*Asylrecht*   right to asylum
*Aufgebot*   public notice
*aus dem Gefüge kommen*   dislocate
*Ausbildungsschaden*   loss of professional training
*Ausbuchtung*   curving
*ausfaulen*   decay
*Ausländer*   foreigner
*Ausschliessungsgesetz der Juden*   exclusionary law for Jews
*Aussenstelle*   branch office
*Aussteuergeschäft*   dowry store
*auswandern*   emigrate
*Bach*   creek
*Badeofen*   furnace for heating bath water
*Bandfabrik*   ribbon factory
*bar mitzvah*   coming of age ritual for boy
*bat mitzvah*   coming of age ritual for girl
*Bauhof*   municipal lumber yard
*Bauingenieur*   construction engineer
*Baumeister*   master builder
*Bedenken*   objections, concerns
*bedrohlich*   threatening
*Beisitzer*   elected official; member of board of directors; resident
*beit chaim*   House of the Living, cemetery
*Bekleidung*   clothing
*Belasteter*   a Nazi, someone who is implicated
*Beratungsstelle*   application office
*berches*   challah
*Berufsgenossenschaft*   union
*Beschluss*   resolution, decision, decree
*Beschlussausfertigung*   decree
*Besitz und Benutzung*   ownership for the purpose of use
*Betriebsfaktotum*   soul of the company, caretaker
*Bezirkskrankenkasse*   district health insurance company
*Bezirkskrankenpflegeversicherung*   district health care

*Bezirksnotariat*   district notary
*bimah*   platform
*b'nai mitzvah*   plural of bar mitzvah
*Brandschatzung*   arson and robber
*Branntweinbrennerei*   brandy manufacture
*Brause*   shower
*Bundesrückerstattungsgesetz*   Federal Restitution Law
*Bundesverfassung*   German constitution
*Bürger*   citizen of a town, burgher
*Bürgerausschuss*   citizens council
*Bürgerhaus*   communal meeting house
*bürgerlich*   bourgeois
*Bürgermeister*   mayor
*Bürgermeisteramt*   mayor's office
*Bürgerrecht*   status as citizen
*Centralverein der Juden in Deutschland*   Central Organization of Jews in
   Germany
*challah*   braided white bread, berches
*Chevrah D'var Torah*   Society for Good Deeds
*Chevrah Hachnassat Kallah*   Group for Poor Brides
*Chevrah Kadisha*   Burial Society
*Chevrat Nearim*   Youth Group
*Chronik*   chronicle, history
*chutzpahdig*   bold
*Damenaussteuer*   lady's dowry
*Dekanat*   District Church Council
*Devisenstelle*   Foreign Currency Exchange
*Dienstknecht*   male servant
*Dienstmädchen*   female servant (girl)
*Dienstmagd*   female servant (woman)
*Direktrice*   office manager
*Dokumentation*   a collection of documents
*Donauschwaben*   Hungarians of Swabian descent
*Doppelwohnhaus*   two-family house
*Dorfjuden*   village Jews
*Drehmaschine*   lathe
*dreidl*   spinning top
*Edelmetall*   precious metal

*Eigentumsübertragung*   transfer of ownership
*einfache Entziehung*   coercively acquired property
*einheitlich*   uniform
*einmütig*   unanimously
*Einsatzgruppen*   special service detail
*Einstellvieh*   boarding cattle
*Einwohnermeldeamt*   resident registration office
*Einzelverordnungen*   individual statutes
*einziehen*   confiscate
*Einziehungsverfügung*   order for seizure
*Eisenwarenhandlung*   hardware store
*Eisernes Buch*   honor roll of World War I soldiers
*Eisernes Kreuz*   Iron Cross
*Elle*   ell, a unit of measurement
*endgültige Kostentragung*   ultimate financial responsibility
*Entlüftung*   aeration
*Entschädigung*   compensation or restitution
*Entschädigungsbehörde zum Anspruch auf Entschädigung wegen Schadens*
    *im beruflichen Fortkommen*   Reparations Office for Claims Concern-
    ing Loss of Occupational Advancement
*Entschädigungsbehörden*   Reparations Office
*Entschädigungsverfahren*   reparations proceedings
*Entscheidung*   decision
*Entziehung*   confiscation
*Erbe*   heir
*eretz*   land
*erev*   evening
*Erziehungsgesetz*   Education Law
*eshet chayil*   woman of valor
*evangelisch*   Lutheran
*Fabrikant*   businessman
*Fachwerk*   exposed wooden beams
*Fahrnis*   goods
*Fahrzeug*   vehicle
*Fasching*   carnival, Mardi Gras
*Faulgrube*   cesspool
*Feiertage*   holidays, festivals
*Feldweg*   rural pathway
*Festkonto*   restricted account

*Filztuch*   felt
*Finanzamt*   financial authority, state revenue office
*Finanzkasse*   treasurer, cashier
*fleischig*   meat and meat products
*Florin*   old German currency
*Freibank*   slaughtering facility for second-rate meat
*Freiheit*   freedom
*Freiherr*   baron
*freiwillige jüdische Konfessionsschule*   voluntary Jewish religious school
*Fremder*   foreigner
*für tot erklären*   to declare dead
*Fürsorgemassnahmen*   social welfare measures
*Fürsorgeverband*   welfare agency
*Fürst; Kurfürst*   prince
*Gastarbeiter*   guest worker
*Gatter*   wood cutting machine
*Gau, Landgau*   province
*Gauamt für Kommunalpolitik*   province office for communal politics
*Gaujugendtreffen*   regional youth meet
*Gauleitung*   province leadership
*Gauwirtschaftsberater*   province economic advisor
*gediegen*   decent, solid
*Gefreiter*   lance corporal
*Gehilfe*   helper
*Geleit*   guard detail
*Geleitgeld*   safe passage fee
*Gelt*   money
*Gemeinde*   community, municipality
*Gemeinde Kataster*   municipal land registry
*Gemeindeamtmann*   municipal employee
*Gemeindebezirk*   municipal district
*Gemeindegrundbesitz*   municipal real estate
*Gemeindekasse*   municipal cashier, treasury
*Gemeindepfleger*   municipal treasurer
*Gemeinderatsprotokoll*   minutes of city council meeting
*Gendarmerie*   police
*Gendarmeriekreisführer*   district police chief
*Gerichtstafel*   bulletin board at court
*Geschädigter*   injured person

*geschäftsfähig*   of sound mind

*Gesinnung*   disposition

*Gewerbe*   business, commerce

*Gewerbeamt*   Office of Commerce

*Gewerbelegitimationskarte*   business permit

*Gewerbeschule*   trade school

*Gewerbesteuerkapital*   taxable business income

*Gewerbeverzeichnis*   trade registry

*Gipsmühle*   gypsum mill

*Glückssack*   bag of goodies

*goldene medine*   golden state

*Graf*   count

*Grundbuch*   real estate registry

*Grundbuchamt*   Real Estate Registry Office

*Grunderwerbsteuer*   real estate acquisitions tax

*Grundrechte*   basic rights

*Grundstücksverwertungsgesellschaft für das jüdische Vermögen*
    *GmbH*   Real Estate Distribution Agency for Jewish Property, Inc.

*Gruppenpostenfüher*   chief of police station

*Gulden*   old German currency

*Gut*   estate

*Güter*   real estate

*Güterbeförderer*   moving company, moving consultant

*Hab und Gut*   belongings

*Handelsjude*   Jew in commerce

*Handelskammer*   Chamber of Commerce

*Handelsmann*   business man, merchant

*Handelsregister*   trade registry

*Handelsverein*   business association

*Handelsverzeichnis*   transaction ledger

*Handlungsgehilfe*   sales helper

*Hanukkah*   Jewish Festival of Lights

*Hauptkontrollbuch*   main ledger

*Hausierhandel*   peddling

*Hausrat*   household goods, belongings

*Hebung*   [cultural] amelioration

*Heft*   issue

*Heim*   house, home

*Heimat*   home, birthplace

*Heimatrecht*   right of domicile
*Herbeischaffung*   procurement
*Herrenzimmer*   sitting room
*Herrschaft*   nobility
*Herzog*   duke
*Hilfsarbeiter*   day laborer
*Hilfsverein der Juden in Deutschland*   Self-help Organization of Jews in
   Germany
*Hinterhaus*   rear house
*Hoffaktor*   court Jew
*Industrie- und Handels-Beratungs- und Vermittlungszentrale*   Consul-
   tation and Referral Center for Industry and Commerce for Jewish
   emigrants
*Inventierer*   inventory taker
*Israelitengesetz*   Law for Jews
*israelitisch*   Jewish
*Israelitische Frauenverein*   Jewish Women's Organizaton
*Israelitische Jugendverein*   Jewish Youth Organization
*Israelitische Jungfrauenverein*   Jewish Single Women's Group
*Israelitische Lese- und Familienverein*   Jewish Reading and Family
   Organization
*Israelitische Männer-Unterstützungsverein*   Jewish Men's Support Club
*Israelitische Oberkirchenbehörde*   Jewish Religious Authority
*Israelitische Wohlfahrtszentrale*   Jewish Welfare Center
*Israelitische Wohltätigkeitsverein*   Jewish Welfare Organization
*Israelitische Zentralkirchenkasse*   Central Treasury of Jewish Religious
   Community
*Jude*   Jew
*Judenanwesen*   Jewish property
*judenfrei*   free of Jews
*Judengarten*   Jewish garden
*Judenhaus*   Jewish house
*Judenhetze*   hep hep, Jew-baiting
*Judenkind*   Jewish child
*Judenrat*   Jewish council
*Judensache*   Jewish matters
*Judenvermögensabgabe*   Jewish assets tax
*Judenzoller*   Jewish tax collector
*Jüdischer Jugendbund*   Jewith Youth Organization

*Jüdischer Kulturbund*   Jewish Cultural Organization
*Jugendstil*   Art Nouveau
*Jungviehprämierung*   prize competition for young cattle
*Justizpraktikant*   legal assistant
*Kachelofen*   tile stove
*Kaderschaft*   cadre work
*Kammer*   court, small room
*Kammerknecht*   valet
*Kampfgenossenschaft*   name of veterans organization
*Kasperles Theater*   puppet theater
*Kassierer*   treasurer, cashier
*Kaufmann*   businessman, merchant
*Kaufvertrag*   sales contract
*Kedushah*   Adoration part of Jewish religious service
*kehillah*   community
*Kindermädchen*   nanny
*kippah*   head covering
*kippot*   plural of kippah
*Kirchengemeinde*   religious community
*Kirchenvorsteher*   warden, shames
*Kirchweih*   celebratory dedication of a church; today: fair
*Knabenschule*   boys school
*Knecht*   servant
*Kommerzienrat*   Minister of Commerce
*Konfirmation*   confirmation
*konstitutionelle Monarchie*   constitutional monarchy
*Kontrollblock*   block register
*Kontrollbuch*   ledger
*Korsett Industrie*   corset industry
*Kreis*   district, more recent term than *Oberamt*
*Kreisamtsleiter*   district administrator
*Kreisbaumeiser*   district architect
*Kreisleitung*   district leadership
*Kreispflege*   district welfare office
*Kreisrat*   district council
*Kreisverbandgebäude*   building of district offices
*Kreutzer*   old German currency
*Kriegsgefangenenlager*   prisoner-of-war camp
*Kristallnacht*   Night of Broken Glass, November 9–10, 1938

*Kulturbund Zionisten*   Cultural Zionists
*Kultusvereinigung*   (Jewish) community
*Kundenliste*   customer list
*Kunstlederwerke*   artificial leather works
*Lagerarbeiter*   warehouse worker
*Land*   state
*Landesamt für Wiedergutmachung*   State Office for Reparations
*Landesbezirkstelle für Wiedergutmachung*   State District Office for Reparations
*Landesgewerbeamt*   State Labor Authority
*Landeskirche*   state church
*Landespolizeiamt*   state police authority
*Landesrabbiner*   district rabbi
*Landesunterthanen*   subjects
*Landflucht*   flight from the countryside
*Landgau, Gau*   province
*Landgericht*   state court
*Landgericht Wiedergutmachungskammer*   State Court Office of Reparations
*Landgerichtsdirektor*   director of the state court
*Landgerichtsrat*   state court official
*Landjäger*   policeman
*Landrat*   district councilor, head of district administration
*Landratsamt*   district council
*Landstrasse*   main road
*latkes*   potato pancakes
*Lederhosen*   leather pants
*Lehen*   loan
*Lehrling*   apprentice
*Leibzoll*   tax for person
*leichtatlethische Meisterschaften*   track and field competition
*Leiterwägele*   pull cart
*Leitstelle*   headquarters
*Liftvan*   crate
*lokaltreu*   loyal to one's hometown
*Mädchenschule*   girls school
*Magd*   female servant
*Mahnmal*   monument
*Markgrafschaft*   margravedom

*Markt*  fair
*medinah*  state
*Meile*  (old geographical unit of measurement) 7.4 kilometers
*Meister*  master
*Meldeamt*  registration office
*Memorbuch*  memorial book
*Merkuria*  young businessman's organization
*Messungsamt*  surveyor's office
*mikvah*  ritual bath
*milchig*  dairy and dairy products
*Militär*  military
*minyan*  quorum
*Mischling*  Nazi-coined term for a person who was part Jewish
*Missgunst*  ill will
*Mitarbeiter*  partner, colleague
*Mitglied*  member
*Mitläufer*  bystander
*Mobilar*  furniture
*Morgenfeier*  morning concert
*moshav*  communal settlement (not a kibbutz)
*Mostkeller*  cellar for cider storage
*mourner's kaddish*  prayer for the dead
*Muster*  sample
*Nachlassgericht*  inheritance court
*Nachprüfung*  verification
*Nachsicht*  leniency
*Naturalrestitution*  natural restitution
*Nebenkontrollbuch*  subledger
*Nennwert*  face value
*Nestkönig*  nest king
*Neugestaltung*  reorganization
*Neuwürttemberg*  territory after 1805
*Notar*  Notary public
*Nutzungsrecht*  usage right
*Oberamt*  administrative district
*Oberamtmann*  Administrator
*Oberbaurat*  chief architect
*Oberbürgermeister*  Lord Mayor

*Oberfinanzdirektion*   State Treasury
*Oberfinanzpräsident*   president of the State Treasury
*Oberjustizkasse*   Highest Judicial Bursar
*Oberlandesgericht*   Highest State Court
*Oberlandesregierung*   highest state government
*Obermeister*   Supervisor
*Oberost*   German-administered section of Poland during World War I
*Oberrealschule*   commercial high school
*Oberschulbehörde*   state school board
*Obersekretär*   chief clerk
*Obmann*   chairman
*offene Handelsgesellschaft*   trade partnership
*Ohmd*   hey
*ordentlich*   normal
*Ordnung für die Juden in den königlichen Staaten*   Ordinance for Jews in
   the Royal States
*Ordonanzen*   orderlies
*Orgelbauer*   organ builder
*Ortsbauernführer*   leader of local farmers
*Ortsbauernschaft*   local farmers organization
*Ortsbaulinie*   local building zoning line
*Ortsbauplanberatungsstelle*   local zoning office
*Ortsbausachverständiger*   municipal building expert
*Ortsgruppenleiter*   local Nazi group leader
*Ortspolizeibehörde*   local police station
*Ortsvorsteher*   administrator
*Ortsweg*   local pathway
*Page*   page
*Papierfabrik*   paper mill
*Partei*   party
*Patronatsrecht*   right to appoint the priest
*Pfandleihanstalt*   pawn shop
*Pfändungsverfügung*   attachment order
*Pfarrer*   pastor
*Pfarrhaus*   parsonage
*Pferd*   horse
*Pflegerin*   nurse
*Poesiealbum*   album of personal poetry

*Polizeihauptwachtmeister*   police supervisor
*Polizeirat*   police official
*Polizeiwachtmeister*   police officer
*Praktikant*   intern
*Preisstoppverordnung*   ordinance capping real estate prices
*Privatmann*   independently wealthy individual
*Prokurist*   business manager
*P'sukei d'zimra*   preliminary service
*Purim*   Feast of Esther
*Rabbinat*   rabbinic district
*Rat*   counsel, official, council
*Realschule*   non-academic track secondary school
*Rechtsanspruch*   claim
*rechtserheblich*   legal
*rechtskräftig werden*   to go into effect
*Regierungsassessor*   assistant judge
*Regierungsoberkasse*   main government bursar
*Regierungspräsidium*   top government office
*Regierungsrat*   government official
*Reich*   empire
*Reichsbund jüdischer Frontsoldaten*   National Organization of Jewish Combat Soldiers
*Reichsbürgergesetz*   national citizenship law
*Reichsfluchtsteuer*   tax to prevent escape from Germany
*Reichsfreiherren*   imperial baron
*Reichsfürsorgeverordnung*   imperial welfare ordinance
*Reichsgartenschaugelände Killesberg*   a large exhibition area outside of Stuttgart
*Reichsgut*   imperial estate
*Reichsjugendwettkämpfe*   national youth competitions
*Reichskommissariat Ostland*   Nazi-administered Poland
*Reichsleistungsgesetz*   national disbursement law
*Reichsmeldeordnung*   national registration ordinance
*Reichsritter*   imperial knight(s)
*Reichsrittertum, Reichsritterschaft*   imperial nobility
*reichsunmittelbar*   directly under the jurisdiction of the emperor
*Reichsvereinigung*   national organization
*Reichswirtschaftsministerium*   National Commerce Ministry
*Religionsgemeinschaft*   religious community

*Requisitionsamt*   Office for Requisitions
*Rittergut*   nobleman's estate
*Rosh Hashanah*   Jewish New Year
*Ross-stall*   horse stable
*Rüben*   turnips or beets
*Rückerstattung*   restitution
*Rückerstattungsanspruch*   claim for restitution
*Rückerstattungskammer*   court of restitution
*SA*   Brown Shirts
*Sack und Pack*   all belongings
*Saitenwürstle*   hot dogs
*Sammellager*   collection camp
*Schacherjud*   peddler
*Schaden*   damage, loss
*Schaden am Vermögen*   loss of property
*Schaden an Freiheit*   loss of liberty
*Schadenersatz*   damages
*Schatzkammer*   treasure chest
*Schenk*   butler, cup-bearer
*Schinderei*   drudgery
*Schirmherr*   lord
*Schlagbaum*   gate
*Schlepperführer*   tractor operator
*Schlosser*   tool and die maker
*Schlussbericht*   final report
*Schlussgottesdienst*   final service
*Schmuser*   broker
*Schreibgehilfin*   secretary
*Schreibmappe*   portfolio
*Schund*   trash
*Schuppen*   shed
*Schussmaterial*   yarn for weaving
*Schutz*   protection
*Schutzbrief*   letter of protection
*Schutzdeckenfabrik*   quilt factory
*Schutzgeld*   protective tariff
*Schutzjuden*   special status Jews, protected Jews
*Schwaben*   Swabia, Swabians
*Schwamm haben, den*   to suffer from dry rot

*Schwelle*   ground joist
*schwere Entziehung*   aggravated confiscation
*Schwimmverein*   swim club
*Shabbat*   Sabbath
*Shabbes goy*   Gentile helper on Shabbat
*Shaharit service*   morning worship service
*shames (shamash)*   helper
*shivah*   seven-day mourning period
*shochet*   kosher butcher
*shtiebl*   prayer room, Betsaal
*simcha*   celebration
*Singspiel*   musical play (operetta)
*Sonderabgaben*   special taxes
*Spätzle*   homemade noodles
*Sozialdemokratische Partei Deutschlands (SPD)*   Social Democratic Party
*Sperrkonto*   restricted account
*spionagepolizeilich*   on suspicion of espionage
*Sportplatz*   sports field
*Springfedern*   coils, springs
*SS*   Black Shirts
*Stadtarchivar*   director of city archive
*Stadtbach*   local creek
*Stadtfriedhof*   municipal cemetery
*Städtische Pfandleihanstalt*   municipal loan office (pawn shop)
*Ständer*   reading desk
*Standesamt*   office of vital statistics
*Ständeversammlung*   assembly of professions
*steigen*   climb
*Steuer*   tax
*Steueramtmann*   tax official
*Stolpersteine*   stumbling blocks, stones
*Strickwarenfabrik*   knitting goods factory
*Sukkot*   Festival of Booths
*tallit*   prayer shawl
*Talmud Torah*   study group
*Technische Hochschule*   technical college
*tefillin*   phylacteries
*Teilhaber*   partner
*Teuerung*   economic downturn

*Thomasfeier*   Christian religious holiday
*Torah*   Five Books of Moses
*Träger*   party, carrier
*traif*   nonkosher
*Treppenhaus*   staircase
*Treuhänder*   trustee
*turnen*   calisthenics
*Turnhalle*   sports hall
*Turnverein*   sports club
*übertünchen*   to whitewash
*Umsicht*   wisdom, discernment
*Umzugsgut*   household items being moved
*unselig*   unfortunate
*unter der Hand*   privately
*Untertan*   subject
*unvollständig*   incomplete
*Verbandsfriedhof*   regional cemetery
*verdrängt*   repressed
*Verein*   club, organization
*Vereinsleben*   organizational life
*Vergangenheitsbewältigung*   dealing with the past
*Vergangenheitsverdrängung*   repression of the past
*Vergleich*   settlement
*Verlagssystem*   production system for yarn in the nineteenth century
*Vermögenskontrolle*   property control
*Vermögensverwertung*   property distribution
*Vermögensverzeichnis*   property inventory
*Verordnung*   statute
*Verpflegung*   care
*Versammlung*   meeting
*verscharren*   dump
*Vertragspartner*   treaty partner
*Vertrauensmann*   representative
*Verwertung*   distribution
*verziehen*   relocate
*Vesper*   snack
*Veteran*   veteran
*Viehhandelsverein*   cattle dealers association
*Viehhandelsverordnung*   cattle trade ordinance

*Viehhändler*   cattle dealer
*Viehmarktplatz*   cattle fair plaza
*Viehmästerei*   cattle fattening business
*Viehpfleger*   cattle helper
*Viehverstellen*   boarding cattle
*Vierkampf*   tetrathlon
*Volk*   people
*Volksfest*   popular festival, fair
*Volksgenossen*   comrades
*Volkshochschule*   adult education program
*Volksschule*   elementary school
*Volkstrauertrag*   national day of mourning
*Volljude*   full-blooded Jew
*Vollstreckungsbeamter*   executory official
*Vollstreckungsschuldner*   debtor
*Vorderhaus*   front house
*Vorkaufsrecht*   right of first refusal
*Vorsteher*   president, community leader, top person
*Vorstrafe*   warning
*Wachtmeister*   policeman
*Wandergewerbeschein*   peddler's license
*Waschanlage*   washing machine
*Waschhaus*   wash house, laundry room
*Waschkessel*   cauldron
*Waschschleuder*   laundry wringer
*Wasen*   grassy area
*Webschule*   weaving institute
*Webstuhl*   loom
*Weihnachtsamnestie*   amnesty for prisoners at Christmastime
*Werkschlosser*   tool and die maker
*Wertsachen*   Valuables
*Wiedergutmachung*   reparations
*Wiedergutmachung der Folgen des Naziterrors*   Reparations of the conse-
   quences of Nazi terror
*Wiedergutmachungsamt*   Reparations Office
*Wiedergutmachungsstock*   reparations fond
*Winterhilfe*   poor people's assistance program
*Wirtschaftsminister*   Interior Minister
*Wirtschaftsministerium*   Interior Ministry

*Wurst*   sausage, cold cuts

*Würstchen*   hot dog

*Württembergisches Wirtschaftsministerium*   State Interior Ministry

*Yad Vashem*   Holocaust Memorial Museum in Jerusalem

*yahrzeit*   anniversary of a loved one's death

*Yom Kippur*   Day of Atonement

*Zählung*   census

*Zentner*   German weight

*Zentral*   central

*Zentralkirchenkasse*   central treasury of (Jewish) religious authority

*Zentralmeldeamt*   central registration office

*Zettel*   warp

*Z"l (zichronoh livrachah)*   may his/her memory be for a blessing

*Zimmermeister*   master carpenter

*Zollfahndungsstelle*   customs search office

*Zollhaus*   customs house

*Zusammenbruch*   collapse (of Nazi Germany)

*Zwang*   coercion

*zwangsverkauft*   Aryanized

# Index